lonely planet

D0728366

THE CAREER
BREAK BOOK

Charlotte Hindle, Joe Bindloss, Clare Hargreaves,
Jill Kirby, Andrew Dean Nystrom

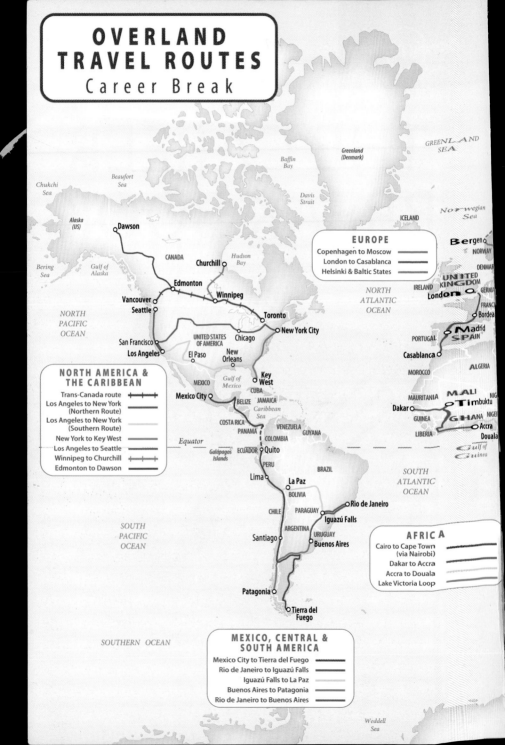

TAKE GREAT PICTURES

...and remember your career break forever

Your career break **will be a once-in-a-lifetime experience** that you will treasure forever. With **Travel Photography** in your hand luggage, you can use your break to become an expert photographer, or simply to capture your adventures on the road.

The second edition of this best-selling guide to travel photography has been thoroughly updated and revised to include a special new section on digital photography.

- **Great for beginners** and a handy reference for more **experienced photographers**
- **Technical know-how** in succinct, **easy-to-understand** text
- **Packed with tips** and invaluable suggestions from a professional travel photographer
- Amply illustrated with **examples of what to do and how to do it**, and how to rectify photographic disasters
- **Sized to fit** neatly into **all photo bags**

Available from all good bookshops or **www.lonelyplanet.com**

Contents

The Authors

CHARLOTTE HINDLE
Post-university, Charlotte travelled overland to Australia. After temping in Melbourne for a couple of months, she got a job with Lonely Planet (LP) and worked at their head office for three years. In 1991 she returned to England to set up LP's UK office, which she ran until June 2002. She then took a mini–career break to spend the summer with her growing family and to consider more-flexible, child-friendly working options. Over the next four months, she and her family took extended holidays in the Outer Hebrides, Sweden, Slovenia, Austria and Greece. In the end, Charlotte decided to set herself up as a freelance travel writer, photographer and gap-year consultant. Over the years Charlotte has written for the following LP guides: *The Gap Year Book, Travel Writing, Australia, Mediterranean Europe, England, Britain* and *Walking in Britain*.

JOE BINDLOSS
Joe was born in Cyprus, grew up in the UK and has since lived and worked all over the world on a succession of career breaks. His favourite career-break experiences include volunteering on a turtle-conservation project in Cyprus, learning to cook Thai food in Thailand, diving with sharks in the Philippines and working at a rock-climbing centre in Chicago. He has previously written for more than 20 Lonely Planet titles, including guidebooks to Asia, Africa, Europe and Australasia.

CLARE HARGREAVES
Clare took her first career break at the age of nine months to live in East Africa and only just survived, following a close encounter with a python. Her love of things foreign later led her to study French and Spanish at Cambridge, after which she trained as a journalist with Reuters and worked for them in Paris for 16 months. After five years working as a foreign-affairs writer on the *Daily Telegraph*, she took a one-year career break to write a book on the cocaine trade. She subsequently worked in TV documentaries for five years, then took another career break to train in antiques restoration. Since then she has led a portfolio career that includes writing books, freelancing for newspapers, teaching and lecturing on Mediterranean cookery, and leading gourmet walking tours in Europe. Her previous books include *Snowfields* and the *Cadogan Guide to Normandy*.

JILL KIRBY

Jill departed England and an established career in current affairs TV in 1993. She left behind her family, friends and an empty savings account to travel the world in pursuit of adventures and a little freedom. After meeting fellow career-renegade John Allen, they travelled for two years before happily making Australia their home. As a freelance journalist and TV producer Jill has worked for national current affairs TV in Sydney and stateside TV in Adelaide, where she now lives. Sidelines have included researching and writing for an Internet travel guide, a TV travel program and the British media. A three-month break in 2002 to explore South America was organised between freelance writing projects. Jill has previously written for Lonely Planet's *Australia* guide.

ANDREW DEAN NYSTROM

In between several sabbaticals funded by travel writing, Andrew earned a BA in Geography and Education from the University of California, Berkeley. He's since taken time away from the freelance writing life to try his hand at editing, bicycle messengering, hot-springs researching, Web monkeying and organic farming. His Lonely Planet author credits include *Bolivia, Las Vegas Condensed, Mexico, Out to Eat – San Francisco, Rocky Mountains, South America on a shoestring* and *Yellowstone & Grand Teton National Parks.* He has also written for Fodor's and Flyguides.com. Current experimental projects include creating an interactive travel blog documenting his search for the Real America online via audio and visual postings from a mobile phonecam. When not out rambling, he hangs his hats in a garden cottage straddling a major earthquake fault in Alta California.

Career Breaks Explained

Up, begin it!
What's left today, tomorrow's still to do.
Lose not a day, but straight prepare,
And grasp your chance with resolute trust,
And take occasion by the hair

Goethe's Faust: Part One

WHAT IS A CAREER BREAK?

A gap year for grown-ups, a chance to take life by the scruff of the neck and give it a shake, a pause for breath, an opportunity to fulfil a lifelong dream – whatever you call it, the career break has become a firm fixture in many people's lives, even a rite of passage. Young professionals to baby-boomers in their fifties are taking time out to expand their horizons for anything from three months to two years. Even celebs are taking them: in 2004 the Scottish-born Hollywood actor Ewan McGregor stepped off the set to embark on a 32,000km (20,000-mile) round-the-world motorbike expedition. Whether your dream is to row across the Atlantic, cycle around New Zealand, study Spanish in Central America or work in an African orphanage, this book is for you. Its pages will give you inspiration and help turn what may at present be a hazy half-formed dream into a reality. Career-breakers are, by definition, part way through a career, so, unlike people taking a gap year before or after university, the stakes are higher. But a major plus is that with more maturity you'll get more out of it.

A career break doesn't have to take you abroad, of course. Some take time out to write a book, build a house or, in the case of academics, to undertake in-depth research. Some of the organisations listed in this book will help if you're in this category. Predominantly, though, it's aimed at career-breakers who want to travel. Starting with how to hatch your escape plan and tie up your affairs before you go, this guide suggests where you might go, how to get there and what you can do once you've arrived. Some career-breakers will choose to take a paid break – like teaching English in Japan – but most career breaks mean stumping up the money yourself either for a good time, a voluntary placement or an inspiring course or two. A career break can be life changing, with the result that settling back into your old life may be more of a challenge than you anticipate, so we look too at how to cope with coming home.

If you look for obstacles to taking a break, you'll find them. Put off taking the plunge, though, and you will miss out on the experience of a lifetime. To paraphrase the words of American management guru Peter Drucker, the challenge in life is not the absence of knowing what to do, but the absence of doing it. As Clare Montserrat, who took a year out of a high-flying journalistic career on a national newspaper to go travelling, puts it:

I was terrified before I took my break but I decided to feel the fear and do it anyway. It transformed my life. It taught me that I, not my company or other people's expectations, am in charge of my life. It also made me realise how unhappy I'd been in my old job and I changed my career as a result. People kept saying 'You're so lucky,' but I've learnt that you make your own luck. I say 'Live your dream'.

GROWTH IN CAREER BREAKS

Ten years ago, a request to take time out from a job would have been seen as frivolous and eccentric at best, downright foolhardy at worst. If you left your seat in your job-for-life when the music stopped in the corporate musical chairs someone else would, likely as not, grab it and you'd be out of the game. Or at least, that was the fear. There were exceptions: a few career breaks were seen as respectable, such as sabbaticals which allowed university lecturers to recharge their batteries and undertake new research. (The word 'sabbatical' derives from the word 'sabbath', and a sabbatical year – every seventh year – was traditionally the year when the land was left fallow). Women, of course, through necessity have taken breaks from their careers to have children, although in the past those were more often tolerated by employers rather than supported and accepted as part of life's course.

Happily, things are changing. Most of us know people who have dipped out of the rat race to go travelling or do voluntary work for a while. Statistics are scarce, but the Confederation of British Industry's (CBI) 2003 Employment Trends Survey showed that around a quarter of all firms asked offered a career break as part of flexible working arrangements. A report by Lloyds TSB found that among Britain's high earners over a third had taken a career break or had considered taking one (among those under 34 the percentage was nearly half).

Now, having a career break on your CV can be a plus rather than a minus: far from showing you are irresponsible, it proves you have get-up-and-go. This reflects changes in the way we see jobs and what we expect out of them. The job-for-life is gone, and successions of jobs (the average now lasting six years) or short-term contracts are becoming the norm. Caroline Waters, Director of People Networks for British Telecommunications (BT), says:

Once we had linear careers; now they move in zigzags. We're continually moving in and out of various forms of paid and unpaid employment.

In addition many of us are working until far older, so there's a growing need to sandwich career breaks between jobs as a breather, rather than waiting until retirement to have our fun. We want to be in the driving seat rather than cogs in a vast company machine. Increasingly we're working at home, choosing flexitime or becoming self-employed. We, not the company, are in charge of our lives.

Expectations of life are higher too. The Victorian grin-and-bear-it work ethic is increasingly seen as a mug's game. We no longer live to work; we want to work to live, and to live in the now. Spurred on by the media, we want stimulation and variety. Many of us expect to travel regularly, either on extended long-haul trips or on numerous short holidays. And more of us are single than ever before, allowing us to up and off when we want. Career breaks are here to stay.

CAREER BREAK–FRIENDLY COMPANIES

Most companies have now heard of career breaks. Whether they actively promote them, or merely pay lip service to them, depends on the company. Many blue-chip companies realise that to attract and retain high-calibre staff they need to offer flexible working conditions, and that includes career breaks. Happy employees mean well-run, profitable companies. Caroline Waters, from BT, says:

Offering career breaks is a critical attraction and retention tool in the highly competitive people market. It gives us a competitive edge over other companies and improves our employer brand.

Sasha Hardman, Senior Human Resource Manager at accounting firm Pricewaterhouse-Coopers (PwC), agrees:

If we don't accommodate what people want, they'll go elsewhere and we'd be in the recruitment market. So it makes good business sense to offer time out. Our people come back invigorated. It's a win-win scenario.

Employees in such companies can now expect to take at least one or two sabbaticals at some point in their career.

The UK government is waking up to the change, too, realising that hideously long working hours – the longest in Europe (with 14-hour days not uncommon in the City of London) –

may be counterproductive. In 2000, it introduced its Work–Life Balance campaign, which, although not specifically mentioning career breaks, encourages employers to allow more flexible working patterns. More recently it poured around £6 million into a Work–Life Balance Fund to help companies walk their walk. This has been done by offering consultancy, advertising in the business press and directly mailing companies to raise their awareness.

Not surprisingly, conditions for career breaks, if allowed, vary from company to company (and within a single company can vary from line manager to line manager). Most expect you to have worked a minimum of one or two years before you are eligible. The majority offer unpaid leave, though a few pay you a percentage of your salary while you are away, or pay your fixed home costs, such as a mortgage, if you are doing voluntary work overseas. The maximum amount of time you can spend on sabbatical varies widely: many companies have a limit of two years. Most companies are relaxed about what you do with your time, while others are more specific. Some tailor their conditions to the type of break you intend to take; BT, for instance, might pay your full salary if you are on a secondment to a nongovernmental organisation (NGO), whereas if you are simply travelling you might get unpaid leave. Often companies stipulate that employees must not do paid work while on a career break unless it's in the charity sector.

Perhaps the thorniest issue in negotiating time off is whether your job will be kept open. This is generally only possible if you take just a few months off; if you take longer, career-break friendly employers tend to guarantee only a job and salary at the same level as when you left (normally the salary increases in line with inflation and across-the-board pay increases).

An interesting sign of the times is that many high-profile companies and organisations, including Shell, the management consultants Accenture and McKinsey, and PwC, now have business partnerships with Voluntary Service Overseas (VSO; www.vso.org.uk). Employees are offered placements of between six to nine months in the developing world. Since 1999 around 90 management secondees from UK-based companies have taken part in the scheme (for more on VSO see the Volunteering & Conservation chapter). Local education authorities and the National Health Service (NHS) are also being encouraged to set up similar partnerships with VSO, allowing teachers and health professionals to work abroad. Sharon Leverett, a pharmacist in a UK teaching hospital, worked in a large referral hospital in Namibia sponsored by VSO:

Although I was the first person in the pharmacy department to have requested such leave, my boss was very supportive. With six years' experience under my belt, I had useful skills to offer. It was a truly worthwhile experience and gave me a totally new perspective.

The day when career breaks become legally compulsory may still be some way off in the UK, but maybe some day we'll follow countries like Australia that have already taken the plunge. For more information on career-break friendly companies in Australia and the US see the Appendices.

TAKING A BREAK: THE USA

The United States may have invented workaholics, but there's much evidence of a growing acceptance of career breaks (aka 'leaves of personal absence'). The good news is that sabbaticals are institutionalized in academia, and the concept of retirement leave spread throughout a career is gaining traction in corporate circles, where it's seen as both an antidote to burnout and as a cost-cutting measure. The governmental, ecumenical and new-economy sectors are also increasingly jumping on the bandwagon: A third of American employers now offer sabbatical programs. For younger workers, it's not a question of *if* they will change jobs, but rather how and when. Labor experts forecast that recent college graduates will change *careers* five times, whereas their parents worked an average of five *jobs* during their lifetime.

TAKING A BREAK: AUSTRALIA

An upsurge in long-term international departures began in the 1990s. Since 62% of Australians are now entitled to three months' long-service leave (following 10 to 15 years' employment within an organisation) a career break of some kind is a reality for many. With Australia's colonial and migrant connections to Europe and Asia, it is widely accepted within industry that many Australians will take a pilgrimage to explore their ethnic heritage and the wider world. In fact, government departments actively encourage sabbaticals by guaranteeing employees a job upon their return.

Research suggests that many career-breakers are also driven by the need to improve their professional prospects by heading overseas. Since the 1990s, long-term departures have increased by 41%, two-thirds of which are highly educated and skilled professionals. So, although many Australians will return home, the government has indicated concerns about a possible brain drain in some areas.

WHY TAKE A CAREER BREAK?

For Ann Selby it was simple:

After I heard a woman tell a friend of mine how excited she was to find someone who steam cleans curtains, I knew it was time. I went home that afternoon and suggested to my husband, David, and two sons, aged seven and nine, that we put our things in storage, buy a camper trailer and hit the road.

Boredom with the trivialities and routines of everyday life, or burnout from long working hours and continuous stress, are common reasons for people to take career breaks. Your gut tells you there must be more to life than self-checkouts at supermarkets, ready-made meals, or commuting to work on the 6.32am train and returning home at 8.30pm. A career break is a search for meaning in your life, a chance to face challenges that your life doesn't normally provide.

You may feel your career has reached an impasse and that studying, working or travelling in a new environment will help you find a new direction – or at least offer the chance to test the water doing something else. Sarah Woolf quit her job as the deputy director of a large national charity to go travelling for a few months:

I'd been in my job for four years but I knew in my heart of hearts that becoming a director of the charity I was working for wasn't what I wanted to do. What to do next? I felt I was banging my head against a brick wall and was coming up with no answers. Then a friend who was travelling in Africa asked if I'd like to join him. It felt pretty scary leaving my job and letting my flat out: I felt I was jumping off a cliff and wondered where I would crash-land. But after travelling across East Africa and meeting the mountain gorillas in Zaïre I was able to look at life afresh. Instead of banging my head against a wall, I realised that what I needed was to take a sideways step. I came back to England and built up a successful life as a freelance fundraising consultant. Instead of landing with a crash, I feel my life has been floating ever since. I love it!

A career break also opened new doors for Emma McMahon, who left a career as a bookseller in the UK to travel and work in Australia. It was while in Melbourne that Emma finally managed to land her dream job in publishing:

You only get one life. Life's too short to restrict yourself to just one career. You may have undiscovered talents and your life can take exciting turns if you have the guts to get yourself out there.

There are plenty of projects you can take part in and courses you can undertake. You may decide you want to give something back by doing voluntary work. In our 'me-first' society,

---

FAMILY & MEDICAL LEAVE: THE USA

Officially speaking, the US Family and Medical Leave Act of 1993 entitles eligible employees (both women and men) to take up to 12 work weeks of unpaid leave for the birth or adoption of a child, and for the care of a child, spouse, or parent who has a serious health condition. Only employers with over 50 employees are bound by these regulations, but most progressive smaller firms follow suit.

Fully paid leave under any of these circumstances, however, is rare. Most employers offer continued insurance coverage and allow the use of sick and annual leave to extend maternity leave. These same conditions apply to paternity leave at the majority of US firms. Wannabe stay-at-home parents beware: Recent US case studies have found that maternity leave, in particular, often leads to a desire for a more profound career change.

---

helping others often takes a back seat to personal achievement, and countless volunteers report that the rewards are huge (see the following Pros & Cons section). Michael Shann, Marketing Manager for VSO, says:

When you're young, the expected thing is to travel. But that can be quite passive. People now want more; they want to contribute to alleviating the poverty that they've seen when visiting other countries.

Itchy feet, pure and simple, may be your driving force. Maybe your friends took gap years before or after university, or you see younger people taking them now and you missed out. Maybe you took a gap year but feel that with more maturity you could make far more of it now.

Others are catapulted into career breaks by life-changing events such as redundancy, bereavement, a long illness or the breakdown of a relationship. Agonising as they are at the time, these happenings can often prove to be the wake-up call that we've needed. Time away somewhere different can be the first stepping stone back to normality, and mark a separation between past and future. Michelle Hawkins packed her bags and threw in a publishing job after spending three months off work while seriously ill with pneumonia:

My 36th birthday was spent at the GP's surgery then back in bed with a respirator to ease my breathing. I was as miserable as hell. I vowed that if I ever got better, I'd do something radical. I decided life was too short to return to the same office, so I willed myself back to good health by focusing on travelling and working abroad.

An unexpected windfall – perhaps the result of an inheritance or a big win in the lottery – may also create the perfect opportunity for a career break. Finally, you may take time off work to have a baby. In 2003, the statutory length of maternity leave in the UK was upped to 26 paid weeks, with an option to take another 26 weeks unpaid. Although this is not technically a career break, some families are taking advantage of the time to turn it into one by travelling and living abroad for this period. Sleepless nights and dirty nappies are diluted by exotic experiences and, in some cases, affordable childcare.

PROS & CONS
Pros

What you bring back from a career break will depend on you: it may simply be a suntan and a scrapbook of adventures, or it may be a new direction in life or an injection of self-confidence. But career-breakers never return empty-handed and overwhelmingly say the experience enriched their lives. Following are some of the benefits you may reap.

PERSONAL DEVELOPMENT & SELF-CONFIDENCE

Your outlook may change; you may find the poise you've always sought. You may not reach complete Buddhahood, but things that stressed you out before may bug you less after your break. With more maturity and experience, the gains are likely to be even greater than for people taking gap years before or after university. They can be huge, according to life coach Pam Richardson:

You learn to believe in yourself and understand who you are. By choosing to go beyond your known life experiences you can gain crucial life skills such as self-reliance, survival and how to cope with stress and fear. You learn how to get on with people who are different from you.

PROFESSIONAL SKILLS
These may include communication, negotiation and organisational skills and well as practical skills such as new languages (for more on these, and their benefits to your career, see p10).

CLOSER RELATIONSHIPS
With more time together, your relationships will grow in directions you never dreamed of (see the section on partners and children, p12).

NEW INTERESTS, SKILLS & PASSIONS
With more money in your wallet than a gapper (those taking a gap year), you have the opportunity to try some mind-blowing experiences or unearth skills that inspire a change in direction. Who knows, your course in Thai cooking may lead to a new career as a chef. Or you may discover you have a passion for Mexican orchids that will last for the rest of your life.

A NEW PERSPECTIVE ON LIFE
Lisa Borg's year off from her job as a project manager in publishing gave her the chance to stand back from her own life:

It was the first time I felt like I sat back and thought about myself and who I was and what I wanted out of life. It gave me the opportunity to digest a lot that had gone on in my life, to assess what I wanted and really think about things rather than just make do to get all the things done that need doing.

Cons
THE COST
Career breaks can be expensive: a year on the road can cost anything from £5000 to £15,000. Don't let this put you off – read the Budget section on p37 for loads of ideas on how to save and raise money.

RESPONSIBILITIES
Unlike people taking a gap year who have never heard of the 'R' word, you may well have a mortgage, children, pets and partners to worry about (not necessarily in that order). None of these, however, need stop you from considering a break, and the next chapter (Tying up Loose Ends, p17) offers practical solutions on how to deal with such issues.

FAMILY & MEDICAL LEAVE: AUSTRALIA

Most working parents in Australia have access to 12 months unpaid parental leave following the birth of a child. This break is only for those with a minimum one-year tenure at the workplace prior to the birth (around 75% of all Australians) and the leave is a joint award. In other words the mother and father will share access to the 12 months' unpaid sabbatical. A few industrial award agreements have given some professions access to longer entitlements; for instance, some employees within the retail sector can apply for an unpaid two-year break.

Paid maternity and paternity leave is a different matter, and the patchy provisions for this are currently under debate inside and outside government circles. Only 38% of Australian women receive an average of four to six weeks' maternity pay, with some men receiving wages for one to two weeks. Many couples use their paid annual holidays and long-service leave to finance leave from work.

YOUR TRIP DOESN'T WORK OUT AS EXPECTED

Once you reach your destination, your travel plans may turn pear-shaped or you may find voluntary work in the African bush just isn't for you. Yes, shit happens, but it's not a reason not to take the risk. Unlike a gapper, you have the skills to negotiate a successful exit and, who knows, what looked like a disaster may turn out not half so bad.

COMING HOME

Having to find another job and look for accommodation (unless you have a house) can be tough. So can the personal aspects of coming home, such as finding your once single friends married off with babies. We look at ways to soften the impact of all of these in the final chapter, Coming Home (p246).

YOUR FEARS

These are probably the biggest obstacle to your taking time out. But ask yourself if your doubts are excuses rather than reasons. Life coach Ralph Peters says:

People are prevented from taking the leap by their limiting beliefs – things like 'My employer would never let me go' or 'I might be lonely'. These need to be challenged, and that can be scary. To effect change, you have to identify what your true values and passions are.

You may find it useful to write down your list of dreams and, next to them, your limiting beliefs. Look at the latter closely as they may turn out to be less substantial than you thought.

TEST THE WATER

Weighing up the pros and cons can be hard. How do you know if you'll actually enjoy learning Spanish in Guatemala, backpacking in Asia or learning t'ai chi in Beijing? The key is to do your research. Speak to other people who have taken career breaks already, consult a life or career coach (see p12), and read the literature and websites of organisations you're interested in working for. If you're thinking about learning a language abroad, do some classes at home beforehand to find out if you enjoy it. If you're considering conservation work, look at doing a weekend or two in the UK with the National Trust (www.nationaltrust.org.uk/volunteering/workinghols.asp) or the British Trust for Conservation Volunteers (www.btcv.org). If you're tempted to work for VSO, test the water by attending one of its regular *Meet VSO* video presentations. Other volunteering and conservation organisations run similar introductory days or talks.

YOUR CAREER: MAKE OR BREAK?

The effect a break will have on your career will be one of your biggest concerns. Will it bring years in the corporate wilderness, while your colleagues glide effortlessly up the promotion and pay ladder? Will it look flaky on your CV? (For more on the latter see p249.) Or could it, on the other hand, enhance your career? All of this will depend on you and how you spend your break, as well as on a modicum of luck – or do we make our own?

   If you return to your old job after your break, you may stand still rather than get a promotion, as you've not been around to prove you have the skills to take you to the next level. However, many career-breakers who quit their jobs to go travelling find jobs at a higher level and salary when they get back. Graham Williams and his partner Louise quit their jobs in publishing and the law to take their career break and found employment easily on their return. Graham says:

If you have built a decent reputation in your profession, you will be able to come back to it. We both did, with no problems. Louise actually got a better job. You'd have to have put in five or six years' spadework first, but if you're good you will work again. I think people look at me with different eyes; I've done something that most people only dream of and there is a sort of implied respect associated with that.

Whether you keep your job or find a new one when you return, your career break may equip you with valuable professional skills. A survey by VSO reported that volunteers returned from placements with an average 15% gain in skills, particularly in areas such as communication, flexibility and collaboration. You may also have learned new languages. Employers endorse this. Sasha Hardman of PwC says:

People come back energised and with a new perspective on life, ready to take on new challenges. They bring back new skills and experiences which can be invaluable in the work environment. For example, working outside one's comfort zone, using initiative, an understanding of cultural differences and working with diverse groups of people.

Although it is very unlikely that a career break will damage your career, there's no denying there can be sticky moments along the way if you opt to keep your job. Attitudes towards those making a bolt for freedom can be frosty, especially in companies where there is no precedent. When Alison Rich announced she was interrupting her medical career to get married and go on honeymoon to Australia for six months, she found her employers and (envious) colleagues decidedly cool:

People seemed to think that taking time off to have children was okay. But they seemed to disapprove of taking a break simply to enjoy quality time together.

When you return, employers may be slow to recognise the new skills you have acquired. Superna Khosla, an audit senior manager for PwC who did a nine-month VSO placement as a management adviser to a health research centre in Tanzania, says:

It's very hard to get away from the view that you've just been on holiday! The current appraisal system didn't acknowledge the very genuine skills that I developed from my experience. It's great that employers are beginning to accommodate VSO placements but this needs to work its way all the way through the organisation to translate at every level.

Some career-breakers are downright unlucky and find that the job they were promised on their return doesn't materialise. Anne-Marie Harris, for example, was given a verbal assurance by her merchant-bank employers that her job would be kept open while she went to Zambia for six months to run a safari camp but returned to find her seat had been filled:

The timing was terrible. It was just after 9/11, and the company was making redundancies across the board. The manager who had promised me my job back was one of the casualties. They kept me hanging on for eight weeks, then I decided it was time to start job hunting. I eventually found a job with another investment bank after five months. I would say the experience set my career back by around two years. My advice to anyone wanting to take a career break would be make sure you get it all in writing. You have to expect to find your peers have advanced when you get back, but unless you have a disaster like I did, you should catch up before too long.

Such cases, though, are the exception. As Chris Allin, a senior commercial manager for British Airways who took six months off to travel in Asia and Central America, points out, the costs of recruiting new staff mean that companies are likely to be accommodating:

Constant recruitment costs, so it pays for companies to allow career breaks and recognise a need to work hard, play hard and look after employee personal needs as well.

Another plus of a career break is that it may propel you and your career in new directions. It may provide you with time to think or the chance to dip your toes in fresh waters. Michelle Hawkins, for example, was working in travel publishing then spent her career break volunteering for Raleigh International in Ghana, Costa Rica and Nicaragua. She says:

I realised I wanted to change direction. My experience with Raleigh and the references from my expedition leaders got me interviews for humanitarian jobs which I may not otherwise have obtained. I now have my dream job working for the international aid organisation, Médecins du Monde. It's as if a new fourth dimension has been added to my present and future.

Sarah Woolf, who threw in her job on a national newspaper to go on a round-the-world trip in her mid-twenties (the first of two career breaks), also found new pastures:

When I told my friends I was going they thought I was mad. What about my career prospects? During my two years away I felt more alive than at any time in my life so far. I got back to find my friends in the same old jobs. My travels made me want to find a career with more meaning. I started working in charity fundraising – at the same level of seniority and salary as if I'd never had a break.

The issues raised here require careful thought. In the end, though, a career break is very unlikely to dump you in the employment doldrums. In many cases, it could positively help your career. Even if you think it won't, is your career break important enough to you to take the risk?

LIFE COACHES

If you're still dithering, a life or career coach may be of some help (for contact details see the Coming Home chapter, p253). A good coach will support you in exploring major life changes and realising your potential. Check a coach's qualifications and experience before taking them on. Prices vary, but expect to pay around £250 for four 40-minute sessions. Some coaches offer coaching by email and/or phone as well as face to face.

PARTNER & CHILDREN

Okay, so you're itching to fulfil your lifelong dream, but what about your partner and your children? Is canoeing down the Zambezi or tagging leatherback turtles in Costa Rica their idea of fun as well or are they routine-addicted home-lovers whose notion of bliss is watching *Neighbours* on TV?

If you are part of a couple you'll need to find out if your partner wants or is able to join you. If you go alone, work out how long it is acceptable for you to be separated before you risk growing apart. Thanks to modern communications, keeping in touch is a lot easier than it once was; work out the practicalities of how you will keep the flame burning and whether you'll try to meet up. Bear in mind, however, that distance can be quite emotionally disruptive. If you're worried about growing apart, you may opt to take a career break at home.

If you persuade your loved one to accompany you, it's important their consent is heartfelt and they genuinely want to share your adventure; otherwise there's room for resentment if there are problems or it all goes down the gurgler. Travel can put strains on relationships which don't occur when both of you are working and living at home. Are you sure you and your partner will be compatible on the road? Should you build in some time apart during your trip? On a positive note, shared experiences can bring a couple far closer. Later, when you're both tottering around on your Zimmer frames, your joint career break may be one of your fondest memories!

COPING ON A ROCKY ROAD

Planning and sharing travel with your partner is an experience that can bring you closer. But it can test your relationship, too. Relate, the UK's relationship expert, offers a few tips on how to cope on the road:

Expectations Discuss your mutual expectations before you set off. Don't assume that just because you want to hike off the beaten track that your partner will too. Ask each other what you want to get out of the trip as a couple and as individuals.

Finances Agree in advance how much money you'll need and plan a budget together. If you're using a joint account for travel, consider whether you want to have your own funds to get home separately, just in case things go wrong. Or, if you think you won't always agree on how much to spend, plan to have some cash that is yours to use as you like.

Spending 24/7 together Instead of seeing each other for a couple of hours morning and evening you're suddenly together all day, every day. Such a big change can take getting used to. Factor in some time to yourself. This will give you time to reflect on what you and your partner are getting from the trip and give you something new to talk about when you meet up.

Sex The thought of not having to get up for work in the morning may sound like bliss for your sex life, but don't put too much pressure on yourself if things don't always live up to your expectations of nonstop passion. Dicky tummies, an outbreak of thrush or lost-luggage stress can dampen anyone's ardour. Be understanding if you can't always meet each other's desires.

Arguments It can be really easy for an argument to escalate quickly, especially when you're out of familiar surroundings. Talk about how you will handle any bust-ups before they happen. Agreeing on some rules will help: set aside time to talk when you will not be interrupted; take it in turns to have air time – some people find setting a timer for five minutes, one speaking while the other listens, then reversing the process, can create a space for each to talk without interruption; tell your partner how you feel about something without blaming them. This can be tricky, but it's more important that you get an understanding of each other's feelings so you can work out a compromise. Sometimes you might have to agree to disagree, and sometimes you might need to apologise, but don't let it fester.

Support RelateOnline offers relationship support via email while you're travelling; check out their website, www.relate.org.uk

If you have children, they'll obviously have an impact on the shape your career break takes. The experience can be enriching and bring a family closer, as Ralph Peters, who went walking in Austria with his children, found:

They say a family who eats together, grows together. I would say that a family who travels together, grows together far more. Many of us live as islands in our everyday lives. Doing an activity together certainly made us a better family.

Give careful thought to the practicalities of taking the children. If they're of school age you'll need to consider their education (for more on this see p31). Check that the country you're going to is safe healthwise and ask yourself if the activities you're planning are child-friendly. How much of the trip is *for* the kids and how much is *with* them? How are you going to transport them from A to B? Will they find train travel more exciting than motoring? (Probably yes.) Will they be happy eating the local food? Once you've answered these questions, and have decided to take your children, involve them in the planning. Read stories about the places you are going to before you leave, or learn a few words of the language.

The educational benefits for your children may, with luck, be huge. Countless parents report returning from career breaks with children who have grown far more confident.

Ann Selby, who travelled around Australia with boys aged seven and nine, and taught them herself, says:

We had plenty of negative reactions to us taking the boys out of school but we feel our trip enriched their lives immensely. They are far more open as a result and have a 'give anything a go' attitude. They are doing really well at school and their teachers say they've developed excellent communication skills with both children and adults. We would recommend a family travelling trip to anyone.

WHEN TO TAKE A CAREER BREAK

Around 60% of those who take a career break are aged in the 25 to 35 bracket. At this age you may have saved up enough money to do something really spectacular and you may still be free of responsibilities such as children and mortgages. The average age of people applying to VSO is now 38. Having said that, though, there's no one right time to take a break. There are plenty of baby-boomers in their fifties itching to explore the world before they are too doddery to enjoy it, who then return for another decade or so in their careers. Various factors, such as those listed here, might decide when you take a break.

STAGE IN YOUR CAREER

Taking a break in the middle of training is not recommended but taking one at the end could be ideal. For doctors, the end of pre-registration training makes a natural break. Some companies don't allow you to take leave of absence unless you've worked in the company for at least two years. Graham Williams found his mid-thirties an ideal time to go travelling in Asia with his partner:

An advantage was that we had built up contacts within our professions that allowed us to get jobs in Hong Kong. We also had few commitments, a manageable mortgage and no kids, which allowed us to save cash to travel. We had built up a reputation in our respective professions which allowed us to feel more relaxed about finding another job when we got home.

As you climb the seniority ladder, it may become harder for someone else to fill your shoes. On the other hand, if you've had a chance to prove yourself in your career you may feel more secure about taking time out, and keener to try something else. Sarah Anderson, for example, decided it was time to take a career break at the age of 56 after running the Travel Bookshop in London for 25 years:

Twenty-five years feels exactly the right time. I feel I've finished that job and it's time to move on and think about my next career. It's both terrifying and exciting. I feel full of energy for something new. In our parents' generation you were past it at my age, but we post-war babies are forging in new directions.

FAMILY/PERSONAL COMMITMENTS

If you're single and fancy-free, taking off will be far easier than if you have a partner or children to take into account. If you have children you may decide to time your break when they are preschool age – or when they've left home. If you're an older career-breaker you may need to wait until children or parents no longer need looking after. Or you may be free of ties, as was the case for Sarah Anderson:

I don't have children, there's no man at the moment and my parents are dead. So I'm free of ties. It's the perfect time to go travelling. When I was 22 I travelled for 10 months. I'd like to do the same kind of things, but with an older perspective.

WHERE TO GO & WHAT TO DO

The options of what to do while on a career break are limitless, and may include a combination of work, study and travel, as shown in the following suggested itineraries.

Buy an RV in British Columbia, spend a couple of months snaking down the USA's glorious West Coast, taking in the famous Redwood National Park and San Francisco's Golden Gate National Recreation Area along the way. Spend a month in San Diego to study Spanish, then wind through Mexico and Central America for two or three months. Stop off to join a week-long field survey of rare orchids in the El Petén jungle that straddles Mexico and Guatemala or join a conservation project tagging and monitoring green and leatherback turtles in Costa Rica (from one week upwards). In the final month, hitch a ride home as crew on a yacht sailing out of the Caribbean.

Travel the classic overland route from Istanbul and Cairo, taking in the Turkish coast, Syria, Jordan (take a day out to float on the Dead Sea and another to visit the hidden rock city of Petra), Sinai and Egypt (three months). In Egypt take a felucca up the Nile from Aswan then do an archaeological dig for a month before flying to Nairobi. Train to be a ranger on a game reserve in Kenya or Tanzania, tagging animals and escorting guests in 4WDs (two to four weeks). Then do a six-month stint teaching English in Tanzania or assisting on a social-development project in Uganda with one of the organisations listed in the Volunteering & Conservation chapter (see p121). Round off your trip with a trek up Kilimanjaro (three to five days) or a week or two of well-earned R&R on the white sands of Zanzibar.

Take the *Trans-Mongolian Express* from Moscow to Beijing, via Ulaan Baatar, the capital of Mongolia (one week to 10 days). In Beijing flex your muscles with a course in kung fu or t'ai chi at a martial arts institute (one to 12 weeks). Then zig-zag your way to Hong Kong via Xi'an and Chengdu, taking in the Great Wall of China, the Terracotta Warriors, baby pandas at the Giant Panda Breeding Research Base, and a cruise through the Three Gorges (six to seven weeks). Fly from Hong Kong to New Zealand and cycle or trek across the South Island before flying to Los Angeles, travelling overland to New York and flying home from there.

Fly to Bangkok and learn Thai massage at a monastery (five to 10 days), or nip up north to Chiang Mai to do a cookery course and perfect the art of making red-hot curries (five days). Trek among the hill tribes, then spend a good three months touring Vietnam, Laos and Cambodia. Push south through Malaysia and take a ferry to Sabah to learn scuba diving (five days) and join a project to help preserve the coral reefs (from two weeks upwards). If you've got any energy left, shin up Mt Kinabalu. Then, fly from Bali to Darwin in Australia and take the newly completed *Ghan* railway all the way south to Adelaide. Indulge yourself with a tour of the wine estates and then roll up your sleeves for a month's grape harvesting. Stop off on your way home in the Pacific islands of Tonga and Samoa for a final and well-deserved chill-out.

Fly to Toronto, take a peek at Niagara Falls and spend a week or two canoeing in Algonguin Provincial Park. Take the train to Vancouver, enjoying the lake lands of northern Ontario, the Canadian Prairies and the Canadian Rockies en route (allow one to three weeks). Walk the Rockies' fabulous hiking trails or if you're there between November and March learn to ski in Banff National Park or on Whistler Mountain (courses last three to nine weeks). Encounter bears and enjoy wilderness around Vancouver Island, then head north to the spectacular Mackenzie Mountains and explore the canyons forged by the South Nahanni River. Make your way back eastwards through the Northwest Territories, ending up in Churchill on Hudson Bay. Arrive before the end of August to spot glossy white beluga whales, then in October or November spend a week watching polar bears congregating while waiting for the ice to freeze and get out on the ice in a tundra buggy. Catch a sighting of the winter aurora borealis (northern lights – at their clearest from December to March) before flying home from Toronto or winding south down the West Coast of the US and flying back from there.

Walk the pilgrimage route to Santiago de Compostela in Spain – either all 750km of it, or just the last bit. The classic route enters Spain just north of Roncesvalles in the Navarran Pyrenees. The best time to go is Easter to October. Prepare or recover by doing a Spanish-language course in Salamanca, Spain's answer to Oxbridge (from one week, but most people give it at least a month).

FINANCIAL SITUATION

Your twenties or thirties may be a good time to take a break, before you have major financial commitments like a mortgage. But then, you may have more money in your wallet after a decade or three in your career.

PERSONAL SITUATION

You may have been made redundant or recently split up with a partner. Perhaps illness or bereavement has led you to reassess your life. Sometimes a change in your personal life can be the impetus for you to take time out from the nine to five.

FOLLOW YOUR INSTINCT

Ultimately, your instinct will tell you when it's the right time. The timing may have been thrust on you by life events or you may spend years planning. Don't take a career break just because everyone else is doing so. Make sure it's your decision, at the right time for you.

Tying Up Loose Ends

Whether it's sorting your moggie or your mortgage, planning is the key to a successful career break. This may be a once-in-a-lifetime trip, so you don't want to spoil it by leaving loose ends trailing at home. Write yourself a checklist of what needs tying up. This chapter outlines some of the details that need finalising before you go.

JOB

Negotiating time out from work is the most important and potentially hardest loose end to tie up. Bungle your approach to the boss and you could blow your dream out of the water – unless you've decided that you'll resign anyway. Planning your conversation carefully is crucial, especially if you work for a company that doesn't have a policy on career breaks or where no precedent has been set.

Before anything else, do your homework. If you work for a large organisation, consult your company's staff handbook, staff intranet and personnel department to get yourself up to speed on its policy. Find out if anyone else has taken a career break and, if so, discreetly sound them out. It's important to equip yourself with all this information so that you can ask for something that's realistic (even if you push the boundaries a little further). Find out the company's general attitude to time out: is it openly supportive of career breaks, does it tolerate them, or is it hostile? Armed with this information, you can plan your negotiation strategy accordingly.

Work out exactly what you're going to ask for and what you can offer in return. Do you want the same job when you get back? Smaller companies may be able to accommodate this, but larger ones are unlikely to unless you're only going for a short time. Instead they will normally promise employment at the same level and salary. If your company won't give you what you want, are you willing to quit? If so, are you going to be upfront about it, or will this be a secret weapon that will give power to your elbow? If you opt to keep your job, are you asking for unpaid or paid leave, or a mixture? If the company doesn't agree to the period of time you are requesting, will you settle for less and, if so, how much less? Evaluate your worth to the company as this will determine how accommodating they will be. Have you worked there for enough time to prove your value? (Many companies set two years as a

---

TAKING EXTENDED LEAVE: THE USA

The US is the only industrialized country without a minimum paid-leave law. If your employer doesn't already offer an extended leave plan (many do), poke around the HR department a bit. You may be pleasantly surprised to find that your employer is considering implementing such a plan, pending employees expressing interest. Be careful, however, about bandying about the word 'sabbatical,' which is loaded with a sense of entitlement – instead, ask about extended personal leave policies. Some companies offer unpaid leave programs, while others may allow valuable employees to work overtime in exchange for future vacation credits.

Many companies will offer key employees time off and tuition grants to encourage a return to graduate school. Of course, these offers come with strings attached: You must study something relevant to your job and return to work for your employer. Whichever route you select, start saving ahead of time.

If you're forced to push the leave issue, negotiate. Pitch your potential time off as (warning: cliché alert) a win-win situation. Surprise your boss by asking for 'time on,' rather than down time. Emphasize the potential benefits for the company – ie, how you will build job skills via broadened horizons. If it's true, emphasize that competitors are offering employees similar opportunities. If worst comes to worst, valuable employees who cite burnout as a reason for quitting during exit interviews are often presented with the option of taking a sabbatical instead.

minimum requirement.) Assess how much of a blow your absence will be (this will probably depend on your seniority) and how best you can soften it. Draw up ways in which you can be replaced temporarily so that continuity is ensured and minimum expense incurred. Make life as easy as possible for your boss by doing the thinking and forward planning for them. Finally, work out your case for how a career break is going to benefit both your company and you: will it make you a better leader and equip you with useful new skills (such as a language) and experiences? Present your career break as a win-win situation.

How long in advance should you pop the question? Antonia Stokes, a conference organiser who took a four-month break to work for Raleigh International in Namibia, found her employers wanted over a year's notice. She says:

I would advise giving as much notice as possible about your plans, even up to a year in advance, so they can arrange proper cover for you. Be as honest and accommodating as possible, especially if you want your old job back.

The danger of giving plenty of notice is, of course, that you might be left out of any forward-planning meetings and effectively replaced long before you go. To avoid this scenario, other career-breakers suggest giving three to six months' notice. Think about the precise timing of your meeting. Is your boss in a good mood? Do they have time to hear you? Monday morning might be a stressful time and Friday afternoons are probably a complete no-no. Avoid company-results week if business is shaky. You know your boss best.

Chris Allin, a senior commercial manager who took a six-month break to travel around India, Australia and Central America, says:

I have a good, perceptive, empathetic boss and boss's boss and they understood my reasons for wanting a break. They wanted to keep me motivated as they want me to stay with the company.

Antonia Stokes found it harder:

I was terrified. Having chatted to the only other person in the company I knew who had taken time out, I went to see my line manager. She referred me up to the general manager. With him it got quite heated: he made me feel as if I was asking to go to the moon. The company openly encourages time out as part of their work–life policy, but they did not appear to have guidelines or a consistent approach to granting sabbaticals. When it came to the crunch, they made it quite difficult. First of all, they made me defer a year – I think they hoped the problem would go away. Then they refused to give me the time as all unpaid leave. I had to take five weeks of my four months' career break as holiday leave saved up from two separate years. I was going to be leading

---

TAKING EXTENDED LEAVE: AUSTRALIA

State governments in Australia encourage career breaks for all their public servants and government employees. The idea is that anything involving work in the private sector, travel or study will help shake up a moribund public-service culture by introducing a regular dose of reality.

The corporate sector, however, is very different. Although the personal growth achieved through a career break is seen as positive, most companies will greet the idea as happily as they welcome maternity leave. So, assess your company before you ask for a sabbatical. Do they have family-friendly policies? Have colleagues taken breaks? Is maternity leave perceived as a problem?

Also prepare your proposal carefully. A break must also be seen as being beneficial to your employers, as replacing you will cost the company money. A two- to three-month break is normally acceptable, but six months and over will require some fancy footwork. Management positions may need to be resigned. However, with the growing change in employment patterns, many employees are contractors, while others change companies every two or three years. Breaks can therefore be taken without disrupting long-term career prospects.

STEPS TO SUCCESSFUL NEGOTIATION

Prepare your case Know what you are asking for and evaluate your worth to the company.

Choose your timing When is the boss likely to give you a receptive ear?

Propose Present your case, being careful to put yourself in your employer's shoes. Be firmly but quietly persuasive. Make it look as easy as possible for your manager.

Benefits to the company Make sure your boss feels they are gaining almost as much as you are by your career break. Stress what you will be giving back to the company as a result.

Listen This shows your boss that you're willing to understand their point of view. Try to anticipate their objections so you're ready to persuade them otherwise.

Stay cool Even if it's looking tricky, don't get personal and don't get stuck on a single detail.

Build on a good relationship This is key. Even if you end up resigning, you mustn't leave on bad terms.

Get it in writing If you're successful in your bid for leave, ensure there's no scope for misunderstanding later on.

---

a team of 45 venturers so I tried to argue the case for one week of the break being seen as leadership training, but they didn't buy that. They were happy to talk the talk, but were less willing to walk the walk. Throughout, they made it look as if they were granting me a huge favour.

Whatever the company's attitude, stick to well-worn negotiating tactics such as listening, expressing your wishes without being aggressive, and showing that you can see things from your boss's point of view (see Steps to a Successful Negotiation, above). However tricky it gets, your goal should be to remain on friendly terms with your employer. Even if you've decided to quit if you don't get what you want, the benefits of leaving on good terms will pay dividends in the future.

Once you've got agreement in principle from your employers, get it in writing. Make sure this includes the dates of your leave of absence, how much of your time off is unpaid and paid (ie are you taking any holiday leave as part of your career break?), what position (or level of position) and salary you'll return to, whether you're being funded on your break (some company schemes pay your fixed costs at home, such as your mortgage, while you are away) and whether your pension and other company benefits are affected (see the Finances section below).

If you know your company is looking to cut costs and staff, offer to take voluntary redundancy – it's a great way of funding your trip. Not surprisingly, eight out of 10 career-breakers choose to resign because it gives them more freedom. This is what Graham Williams advises:

Most employers don't understand the concept of a career break or are jealous – you're off to that beach and they're stuck with the mortgage and kids. Make a clean break. Control your time.

FINANCES

Once you've decided you're taking a career break, it's crucial to sort your finances well in advance. Gone are your carefree student days when you could pretty much take off; as an adult, your financial ties are likely to be far more complicated. This may not be the most scintillating part of your preparations, but if your affairs aren't in order it could ruin your time away or give you a nasty shock when you return. In the long run, giving your finances a shake-up may be a good thing. You could get the ball rolling by discussing your affairs with a independent financial adviser. The following are some of the areas you may need to look at. (For information on institutions that can help you manage your finances in the USA or Australia, see the Appendices.)

PENSION

Whether or not you need to lose sleep over your pension depends on what type of scheme you are in. If you are part of a defined contribution scheme, which includes personal pensions, stakeholder or executive pensions, and some employers' occupational schemes, your pension prospects will be largely unaffected. If, however, you belong to a defined benefit or final salary pension scheme (so called because your pension is calculated on your final salary and years of service), to which your employer contributes, the picture is less rosy and you will need to think and negotiate hard to ensure that a break from employment doesn't damage your long-term finances.

Personal pension schemes, and other types of defined contribution set-ups, are ideal for career-breakers. The beauty of them is that they usually allow you to reduce your contributions to a level you are happy with, or even to freeze them, while you are away. Some older schemes, however, impose penalties if you choose to reduce your payments, so check the situation with your financial adviser. If your scheme does penalise you, this may be an opportunity to switch to a scheme with lower charges (you shouldn't be paying more than 1%). Note that you can only join a personal stakeholder plan while you are UK resident. A handy option is to use any of the five years before your departure abroad to create a 'basis year' to make ongoing contributions after your departure; the benefit is that you can simply carry on paying into your plan and get full tax relief on the contributions. If you become a nonresident you are legally entitled to make contributions to your scheme for up to five years.

If you are part of a final salary scheme, you should be aware that taking a career break, particularly late on in your career, could have financial consequences. This is because most companies who offer this type of pension require you to leave the scheme if you take a sabbatical. When you return you may or may not be allowed to rejoin; around 75% of companies are now closing their schemes to new members, which includes career-breakers. Even if you are allowed to rejoin, you will have to start a new period of scheme service, and you will lose earnings linkage for the first period of service (the link to earnings gets replaced by a link to prices, which usually rise less quickly). If you are in your forties or fifties, this could be bad news. There are other snags too: some companies insist on a six-month wait before you can join a scheme, or have set entry points during the year. If you belong to a final salary scheme and are planning a break, seek financial advice. You may have to negotiate hard to retain your pre–career-break pension rights after you return, and in many cases this will be impossible. Whatever you agree, get it in writing.

If you take leave of absence and belong to an occupational scheme but have worked for less than two years, your employer will normally refund your contributions and remove you from the scheme. If you're given the choice of leaving your money in the scheme, go for it, as you'll get much more in the long run than if your contributions are returned. This is especially true if your employer is also making hefty contributions on your behalf.

COMPANY-SHARE SAVE SCHEMES

If you work for a large company you may belong to a share save scheme. If you are going away but intend to return, you should check how this will be affected by a break in employment and ask for the advice to be put in writing. You will almost certainly have to opt out of the scheme while you are away, but your goal should be to re-enter it as soon as you return. Many companies require employees to have worked for two years before qualifying to join such schemes, so you may decide to wait until you've notched these up before going travelling. Some also have set entry points during the year so, again, this may affect your departure date.

MORTGAGE

See p24 for details on the best way to deal with your mortgage while you're away.

INVESTMENTS

Given the potentially volatile state of the stock market, some financial experts advise moving some of your assets out of stocks and shares and into secure investments before you go. Max Tennant, an independent financial adviser, warns:

It's unwise to view equity-based investments as a short-term reserve while you are away. The stock market may fall and then you're left short just when you need funds most.

You may decide to build up cash reserves in the currency of the country you are going to (provided it's a solid currency) as a hedge against currency fluctuations, which could affect the amount of money you have to dispose of while on the road. This could obviously go either way, but at least you won't suddenly have to curtail your trip if the currency plummets. Otherwise you should consider buying a mini-cash ISA, for a maximum of £3000 each year. You can buy one online from anywhere in the world. Legally you must be classified as UK resident or ordinarily resident to pay into an ISA, but an account can be frozen if you become nonresident and then reinstated on your return. (If you're unsure about your status, contact your tax office.) If you are going away for more than a complete tax year, and will qualify as nonresident, you could move your funds to an offshore bank or building society where no tax is deducted from your interest.

Lastly, do keep some savings for when you get back as that will make settling back in much easier.

LOANS

If you have outstanding loans, make sure you have direct debits in place for these while you are away and that you have left enough funds in your account to cover these payments. You can try to freeze them but lenders are unlikely to allow this.

BANK ACCOUNTS

If someone else has agreed to manage your finances while you are away, you may wish to set up a special bank account to which they have access. (However much you trust your best buddy, you may not want them to have access to your main account.) You can set up this special account by filling in a Third Party Mandate form, which is available at your bank and which you both need to sign. Your friend will need proof of address and photo ID. With online banking, you can keep an eye on this account from abroad and top it up with funds when it gets low.

TELEPHONE & ONLINE BANKING

Thanks to online banking, tracking your finances while on the road has never been easier. So, if you haven't already plugged yourself into the 21st century, now may just be the perfect time. Over 11 million Britons have online bank accounts that they can access at home or abroad, and from which they can check balances, pay bills, transfer money between accounts, set up direct debits and standing orders, and increase an overdraft. Smile (www.smile.co.uk) from the Cooperative Bank, First Direct (www.firstdirect.com) from HSBC, and Nationwide (www.nationwide.co.uk), came out on top in a recent online banking poll carried out by Virtual Surveys (www.virtualsurveys.com), but all high street banks now have online services. Most online banks also have a telephone backup service which you can ring 24 hours a day (check the number isn't premium rate); not all have a real live person on the other end, though First Direct makes this one of its selling points. First Direct is also one of the few banks that will text you your bank balance or send you a text when you are overdrawn. Smile notifies you if you've overshot your overdraft limit. Some banks, such as First Direct, offer a small cash bonus if you apply online, so if you don't have an online bank account already, here's an incentive to take the plunge.

Security, however, is still a major concern. There are email scams directed at banks' online operations and designed to trick users into disclosing their bank password. Internet cafés are notoriously insecure, so, unless you have your own laptop with Internet access, use telephone banking rather than logging on in a café if possible. (Note that ☎ 0800 numbers aren't accessible from abroad, so ask your bank for its international helpline numbers.)

If there's just no alternative to an Internet café in the middle of Mali, Madagascar or Massachusetts, be cautious. Don't, for instance, shout your PIN out to your friend sitting on the other side of the café; never write down your PIN or password; and be aware that the two guys having a chat behind you may also be keeping a watch on your monitor and taking note of your bank details. Even if your memory is the size of a pea, it's important to come up with different passwords for your bank account and your email account: using the same one increases the chances of fraud. If you receive an email from your bank that links you to a site asking for your full security information, treat it with extreme suspicion and contact your bank directly. Do *not* divulge any personal information.

PLAYING SAFE: INTERNET BANKING ON THE ROAD

The following are a few more precautions to take in Internet cafés. However, we cannot guarantee that they will make for risk-free banking on the road; your best bet is to ring your bank immediately afterwards and change your password. These guidelines are written for Internet Explorer in Windows but they broadly apply to any system:

- Check that the Internet browser you are using is safe. If it is Internét Explorer, it should be Version 6 with Service Pack 1 or Version 5.5 with Service Pack 2 and be using strong encryption. In Internet Explorer click on Help on the tool bar and select About Internet Explorer. It will tell you the version of the software and the cipher strength (how crackable it is). Anything less than 128-bit is risky and you should go elsewhere.

- Check that the browser software is not saving any username and password you type that others can then use. Click on Tools on the menu bar and click again on Internet Options. Click on the AutoComplete button and untick all the checkboxes, particularly the 'User names and passwords on forms' box. This will ensure that no traces are left behind.

- Ask whether the machine you are using has up-to-date antivirus software and whether it is working. There are viruses called backdoor programs or Trojan Horses that can record what you are typing at the keyboard and save it or send it on to others. To be absolutely sure, close all running programs and open a command window. Click Start, then Run, type 'command' and press OK. When the black window appears, type: netstat -a -n. This will list all network activity. You can compare the list of programs running with a list of known Trojans at the following web address: www.pestpatrol.com/WhitePapers/About_Ports_And_Trojans .asp#portlist. If you see anything suspicious or are at all uncertain, quit what you are doing and ask for help.

- It is possible for someone to plug a device into the computer that will physically record all the keys you press. Examine the cable coming out of the keyboard and make sure this goes directly into the computer and not via any suspicious-looking boxes. Again, if you are uncertain, ask.

- It is now reasonably secure to use the computer for online banking but, remember, there is always a risk. When you go to your bank online always type in the web address yourself rather than clicking on a preset link. That could possibly connect you to a spoof copy of the bank's website set up to trap the unwary. If at any time you are offered an option saying 'keep me logged in on this machine', click No.

- When you have finished your banking transactions, log off from the website following the bank's on-screen instructions. Next you should clear the history of what you have done from the machine's cache. To do this, click on the Tools menu, select Internet Options, then click on the Clear History button. On the same tab, select Delete Files in the Temporary Internet Files section, and tick the Delete All Offline box. Finally click OK. This should delete all copies of the pages you have visited from the machine.

- As a final check, type in the web address of the bank again to see if it automatically logs you in. It should take you to your bank's login screen but do nothing else. This confirms nothing has been left behind on the computer. Do not connect again. Simply delete the address before you leave.

BILLS

If you are keeping your house and car, think ahead and make advance payments for items such as insurance, tax and other ongoing bills. Alternatively, set up direct debits or ask a trustworthy friend to post cheques off at the appropriate time. For more details relevant to house and car owners, see p24 and p30.

CREDIT-CARD BILLS

Paying your credit-card bills while you are away is simple. There are three ways to do it. You can arrange for them to be paid by a friend who has access to one of your accounts; you can set up a direct debit which covers either the minimum payment or the full payment or a fixed amount (some banks, like National Westminster, allow you to pay a fixed amount each month but many don't); or you can pay the bills yourself online (see Telephone & Online Banking, p21). Make sure you alert your credit-card company before you go travelling or they may assume the card has been stolen and cancel it.

STANDING ORDERS & DIRECT DEBITS

Go through these and reassess them; cancel those that you don't need and set up new ones. Have you remembered to sort out your council tax, for example? Or do you have a tenant who will pay it?

INSURANCE POLICIES & INCOME PROTECTION

Check your life or private health insurance policy for any exclusions before you go, as certain insurance companies deny cover if you are going to various 'undesirable' areas such as South America or Africa. Be aware that getting insured after you've returned home from these areas can be difficult – but don't let this deter you from going! It's very unlikely that you'll be able to suspend payments while you are away, as most policies become void if you fail to make payments for two months or more. Some providers, such as Friends Provident (www.friends provident.co.uk), will cover your income even while you are away – ask if you're eligible.

MAINTENANCE PAYMENTS

Before you go abroad you should notify the Child Support Agency (CSA); otherwise you risk building up arrears. If you are giving up a job and won't have any income, your payments will be reassessed. You should contact the CSA again on your return.

SUBSCRIPTIONS

If you're going away for a long time remember to cancel subscriptions to newspapers and magazines. If you're going to be in one place abroad, you may consider taking out subscriptions to publications like the *Guardian Weekly*, the *Week* or the *Weekly Telegraph*.

TAXATION & NATIONAL INSURANCE

TAX

'In this world nothing can be said to be certain, except death and taxes,' wrote Benjamin Franklin in 1789. The first subject isn't our concern here (it's dealt with in the next chapter) but tax, like it or not, very much is. Most of us don't like it much and Franklin might have added another certainty to his list: completing a tax return is the last thing you want to be doing while you are living out your lifelong dream. If you can, deal with it before you go.

If you need to file a tax return while you are away, work out exactly how you're going to do this. If possible, pick up a form from your local tax office, fill it in and post it off before you go. For those planning a long absence, possibly covering two tax years, your local tax office can post a form to your foreign address. You can also file your return online via the Inland Revenue website (www.inlandrevenue.gov.uk). To do this you must first apply to your tax office for a secure password – again, do this before you go. A bonus of filing online is that your tax is calculated immediately.

Your tax status is unlikely to be changed by a career break if the break is for less than a complete tax year, but check this with a tax expert or your local tax office. If you meet certain criteria you may possibly be considered nonresident, in which case you will be exempt from paying UK tax on non-UK–related earnings. These criteria include going away for more than a complete tax year (April to April) and either working full time abroad under a contract of employment or going for a 'settled purpose'. But you mustn't return to the UK for more than 183 days in any tax year and your visits to the UK must average fewer than 91 days per tax year. If this applies to you, contact your tax office to get a rebate. Baffled already? Try seeking enlightenment on the Inland Revenue's website or ringing its nonresident tax helpline (☎ +44 (0)151 472 6196). Useful information leaflets (if you can fathom them), also on the website, are IR138 *Living or Retiring Abroad* and IR20 *Residents and Non-Residents – Liability to Tax in the United Kingdom*. The frequently asked questions page (www.inland revenue.gov.uk/cis/section4a.htm) may also be of some help.

You should also seek advice if you intend to earn money abroad, or if you intend to dispose of any assets (eg your home or shares) before leaving or while abroad. If you work abroad during your career break you may have to pay taxes on your earnings in that country even if you're not officially resident (see p157 for more details). Many countries, but by no means all, have double taxation agreements with the UK to provide relief from being stung for tax twice. If you're going abroad for a substantial period, check with the tax authority of your destination to find out if it has an agreement and how you can claim relief (details can also be found in the IR20 leaflet). Note that some relief is often available even if there is no treaty between the UK and the country you are visiting. A useful step may be to contact the consulate of the country you are going to before you leave.

If you are jacking in your job, your employer will give you a P45 (which shows your total taxable earnings and amount of tax paid for the current tax year). Hang onto this as you'll need it to claim any tax refund. Any future UK employer will also require it.

If you rent out your home while abroad, you will be taxed on any profit, minus expenses such as wear and tear, new decoration and repairs. If you are using an agent and are going away for more than six months, they will normally forward the rent to you after deducting UK income tax. This is on the basis that you are a nonresident landlord, which means that your 'usual' place of abode is outside the UK. The Inland Revenue's leaflet IR140 *Non-Resident Landlords and Their Agents and Tenants* may be useful. For more details on this, see the House section, below.

The Appendices list organisations that can advise about taxation in Australia and the US.

NATIONAL INSURANCE

It may sound boring, but sorting out your national insurance (NI) situation before going away for an extended period is vital. If you don't catch up on payments you have missed, you may not be entitled to full maternity or unemployment benefits, or to a full state pension when you retire. To qualify for full state benefits in the UK when you get back, you must have paid national insurance contributions for 90% of your working life. If you are taking a career break of less than a year, this is unlikely to affect your national insurance history. If you are going abroad for longer and are in danger of falling below the 90% mark, top up your national insurance by making voluntary Class 3 contributions while you are away. The rate of voluntary contributions at the time of writing was £6.95 per week. (If you work abroad for VSO they will pay your contributions for you.) Bear in mind that for any one financial year to qualify, you must have paid NI for the full 52 weeks. Voluntary contributions can be backpaid up to seven tax years after the year you missed. For more information, ring the helpline at the NI centre for nonresidents: ☎ 0845 915 4811 or if calling from outside the UK ☎ +44 191 225 4811.

HOUSE

Unlike people taking gap years after school or university, you may well own a house or flat that you'll be leaving behind. If you're renting, you'll simply give notice and put your stuff into storage. If you own a property you may choose to let it, get house sitters in, swap it, leave it empty, or even sell it. Your home is likely to be your most precious asset, so think carefully about what to do with it.

MORTGAGE

If your mortgage isn't going to be covered by rent from tenants while you are away, and keeping up regular payments is likely to be problem, speak to a financial adviser about switching to a flexible mortgage with online facilities. This is the perfect mortgage for career-breakers as you can pay bigger monthly payments before you leave or after you come back, and in return make smaller payments or even take a complete mortgage holiday while you are abroad. In addition, you can usually withdraw lump sums from your mortgage account to pay for, say, your travels without going through the formality of applying for a new loan. The latter may be conditional on your having built up a reserve of overpayments. If a flexible mortgage looks like a good option, shop around (as conditions vary) and try to arrange it at least six months before leaving. Ideally, do it a year in advance and make overpayments during that year so that the pressure is off while you travel. Most flexible mortgages have a current account linked to them, and you can check both your monthly mortgage payments and your current account online from an Internet café in Timbuktu or wherever you are. Ross Kelly, a partner with Kelly Mears financial advisers, says:

Flexible mortgages are the perfect solution for people wanting to take time out to travel. It's never been easier to have your cake and eat it at the same time.

SELLING

The beauty of selling your home (and maybe all your possessions too) is that you're free of worries; you have no truculent tenants to mar the tranquillity of your South Pacific beach and no boring bills to gnaw at you like mosquitoes. If you invest the money in a high-interest earning account, you may be able to keep your savings safe so that you are in a position to buy another home on your return. The downside, of course, is that if property prices rise faster than your savings, you may be forced to downsize when you buy. Don't underestimate the cost of buying again – stamp duty and real estate agency and legal fees all add up.

Clearing out your life in this way can be incredibly purging. You may decide to give your possessions away to friends or a charity shop. Otherwise, you could sell them to fund your travels.

LETTING

This can be a lucrative option. With luck your tenants will cover your mortgage, your bills and even give you a modest income while you are away. Bear in mind, though, that rental income is taxable. Here is a step-by-step guide to letting.

Telling Your Mortgage Lender

Look carefully at the small print in the terms and conditions of your mortgage and it will invariably stipulate that you need to notify the lender if you rent out your home. Provided you are away for less than two years, they are likely to give their consent. Your monthly payments will probably stay the same or rise insignificantly.

Finding Tenants & an Agent

You may decide to rent privately and to find your tenants by advertising in local papers, shops or websites (universities often have websites that are referred to by visiting teaching staff). Remember to obtain character and bank references and a watertight tenancy agreement. Although renting to friends might seem the easiest option, it can be disastrous: if something goes wrong with the rental arrangement, your friendship may be knocked on the head for ever. The other option is to rent through a reputable agent. Although this will cost you more (usually 10% of the rental income for just finding a tenant and setting up the tenancy agreement; 12% to 15% plus VAT for managing a property and collecting rent) it's probably the safest, but certainly not totally watertight, option. An agent may also be a better rent negotiator than you. When choosing an agent the best procedure is to invite at least three to your house to give you quotes and to check their professionalism. Jon Bryant, a branch manager for Andrews Letting and Management says:

Remember this is a two-way interview. You are putting your biggest bit of capital into the hands of this person. You need to really grill them and make sure that they are totally reliable.

Don't just go for the agent that quotes you the most rent: there's no guarantee they will achieve this. Check the agent is well established and affiliated with a respected body such as the Association of Residential Letting Agents (ARLA; www.arla.co.uk), which imposes certain standards. Whether you use an agent or go it alone, you should start looking for tenants around four to eight weeks before leaving.

Safety Issues
By law you must take a number of steps to ensure your house is safe. First you must have your gas appliances, such as boilers, tested and approved by a CORGI-registered engineer. (They will issue you with a Landlord's Gas Safety Certificate, which must be renewed annually). Second, all electrical appliances and fixed electrical installations in your house must be tested for safety. All electrical equipment manufactured after January 1995 should carry the CE symbol. Third, you must ensure all upholstered furniture is fire resistant; this includes beds, mattresses, sofas and other soft furniture. If you are renting through an agent they will normally arrange for these checks to be carried out for a fee.

Tax
If you are going away for more than six months, you will probably have tax deducted at source from your rental income. The 1995 nonresident landlord regulations require tax at a basic rate to be withheld by your letting agent (or by your tenant if there is no agent), unless they have authority from the Inland Revenue to pay you the rent gross. If you think you qualify for gross payments you can apply to the Inland Revenue; if you meet the criteria, they will send written authority to your agent or tenant. The Inland Revenue's leaflets IR87 and IR150 may guide you through the bureaucratic fog. If you rent out your home for an extended period, you may be liable for Capital Gains Tax (CGT) if you sell it later on. This will depend on your circumstances – whether you own another house, whether you rent it out, and whether you live in your home again on your return to the UK. Check out your status with a tax adviser. However, if you are away from your house for less than three years during your ownership, and you live in it on your return, you could be exempt from CGT altogether.

Redecorating
Sprucing up your property before renting it out will often ensure a better rent. The agent, if you are using one, will often suggest ways in which your property could be made more attractive, such as new carpets or a lick of paint. If you're after a corporate let, you'll need to furnish and decorate accordingly. Don't expect to get away with furnishing your property with items you nicked out of the skip when you were a student.

Removing Items of Value
You should take out items that are of sentimental value or that you could not replace, such as photos and antiques. Always assume the worst-case scenario, which is that the contents of your place get trashed. It probably won't happen, of course, but it's sod's law that the irreplaceable photo of your dead grandmother left on the mantelpiece is the one thing your tenant accidentally knocks over and spills coffee on. It's a good idea to remove items such as hi-fi systems, too. Another reason to remove items of value is that you may find your insurance doesn't cover you if a third party gets into your home and steals something (see the section on Buildings & Contents Insurance, opposite).

Furniture Storage

If you only need to remove a few items, you may get away with leaving them at a friend's or parent's house. However, you may decide to remove substantially more, or to let the house unfurnished, in which case you will need to put your furniture in storage. As with real-estate agents, shop around; get quotes and ask probing questions. For instance, find out how much notice is needed to return your stuff; what insurance cover is offered; if insurance is included in the price; if the price includes VAT; what the storage conditions are like and if you can see the place where it will be stored (look out for damp areas that could damage your antiques); and whether you can get access while your stuff is in storage and, if so, how much it costs. Prices for storage range from £7 to £18 per week per container (a container measures seven cubic feet), including VAT and insurance. It's normally cheaper if you book storage for a long period of time (rather than constantly renewing) and don't need access. If you're away for a while, though, bear in mind that the company's charges may rise, so you need to budget for this. Some companies can store individual items, such as a bed or piano. Never put precious items such as jewellery, money or documents into storage – put them in a safe-deposit instead. For extra peace of mind you should check whether the company is affiliated with the British Association of Removers (www.removers.org.uk).

Inventory

This is essential for avoiding potential conflict when you reclaim your home. You can draw up an inventory yourself or pay an agent to do it as part of their service. If you are doing it yourself be meticulous: for example, write down the exact make and model of cookers and fridges and make a note of every blemish so there's no dispute later. One landlord who merely noted 'fridge, cooker' and so on returned to find that the fridge and cooker in his kitchen were totally different from the ones he had left, but when he took the matter to court he lost, as he'd failed to note the exact makes. It's a good idea to take electronically dated photographs of your contents as a backup. But don't rely on them: they are no defence in court, as dates can be fabricated.

Building & Contents Insurance

If you tell your normal insurer that you're renting out your house, they will almost certainly not want to provide cover. However, do not despair: there are specialist insurers who will cover both buildings and contents. Premiums will probably be around 10% to 20% more. Ask an insurance broker to get quotes. It's hard, however, to get cover for a period of less than three months.

Tenancy Agreement

This agreement between you and the tenant is the key safeguard of your precious asset, so make sure it's done properly. If you are letting through an agent, they will issue their own version. If you are letting privately, you can buy off-the-shelf agreements from legal stationers such as Oyez (www.oyezformslink.co.uk), but make sure they are up to date, as the law changes. Far better, get a solicitor to draw up an agreement. Make sure you have agreed who is paying contentious rates like water, council tax and TV licence. There is no legal minimum period for letting a property, but the minimum notice period is two months, so in effect you can't let for a shorter period than this. The normal minimum is a six-month let. If you get a company let you are better protected legally, as company lets, unlike shorthold tenancy agreements with individuals, are considered contractual agreements and are not covered by housing law. If a company doesn't pay, you can sue. If an individual doesn't pay, it's far more complicated.

Rent

When the tenancy agreement is signed, you or the agent will probably ask for a month's rent in advance, plus one or possibly two months' rent as a deposit against damages or unpaid bills. Be sure to insist, or get your agent to insist, that the tenant sets up a standing order (or direct debit) for rent payment, which will give you far greater peace of mind than cheques, which may or may not arrive and may be forwarded to either you or your bank. If you are paying an agent to manage your property, they will collect rent monthly and forward it to your bank using BACS (Banks Automated Credit System).

What happens if the tenant cancels a standing order or does a runner? This is unlikely to happen if you've taken references, but we've all heard horror stories. Having your estate agent keep an eye on your rent should help prevent this, but there's no guarantee that a tenant will not leave early as a result of redundancy, marital break-up or illness. In short, if you are renting out a property there is always some element of risk involved. To keep this risk to a minimum, you can take out rent-protection insurance like Rentsure Gold Rent Protection, sold by **Letsure** (☎ 08700 770660; www.letsure.co.uk). Such policies, which you obtain through your managing agent, also cover legal expenses should you incur these as a result of the tenant breaking the tenancy agreement.

Utilities

If you are using an agent, they will transfer accounts for utilities such as gas, electricity and water into the tenant's name. Otherwise, you will need to do it yourself by contacting each company in turn, and the tenant will have to do the same. If you are only going for a short trip, you may prefer to leave accounts in your own name and get bills forwarded to the tenant to pay. The risk, though, is that the tenant won't cough up, in which case the responsibility is yours. The telephone is the biggest gamble; you may decide to stipulate that the tenant use their mobile and stop your line or switch it to incoming calls only (for more on this see Technology & Communications, p35).

Inspections & Repairs

If you rent privately, you would be wise to appoint a friend to be on stand-by should anything go wrong, such as the boiler breaking down. Ask them to inspect the property – every three months is the norm. If you are employing a managing agent, they will normally do this.

LEAVING YOUR HOUSE EMPTY

If you are away for a short period, it may not be feasible to rent out your house and you may decide to leave it empty. If so, be sure to appoint a friend to keep a regular eye on it. This particularly applies in winter when there's a danger of burst pipes (you'd be advised to leave the heating on low). But at any time of year a water tank can leak, potentially wreaking havoc on your house and its contents. One of the biggest problems with leaving a house empty is insurance. Most normal policies state that a house must not be left empty for more than 30 days (some say 60). Insurance broker Chris Howgate says:

Insurance companies loathe unoccupied properties. They're a target for thieves and malicious people. And if something does happen, you're not there to sort it. The majority of companies will not give full cover if a house is unoccupied.

There are specialist companies, however, that will give cover, but you are likely to pay more – perhaps as much as 40% above your normal premium. Make sure the insurer tells you what perils they are covering and what special restrictions apply. Some will throw in contents too but are unlikely to cover valuables such as jewellery, so you should lock this up in a safe-deposit. Full accidental damage cover will be virtually impossible to get. If you're not going far, one way around these problems is to continue with a normal policy and pop back home just before the legal limit for leaving it untended expires.

HOUSE SITTERS

Another option is to get a friend or relative to look after your house, pets and garden in return for rent-free accommodation. A number of companies provide a professional house-sitting service. The good thing about this is peace of mind – your home is occupied and disasters such as burst water pipes will be dealt with. It's especially attractive if you have pets, as house sitters will look after them too, saving the expense of putting them into a kennel or cattery.

Professional house sitters don't come cheap though: you're likely to pay around £300 per week if you've a house, dog and cat to mind, so it's probably not feasible if you're away for several months. House sitters do domestic chores, such as mowing lawns, weeding, watering plants, cleaning and fielding phone calls. Other tasks, such as checking emails, overseeing building work or keeping an eye on an aged relative in the attic, may cost extra. Sitters may be single or come as a couple (the fee is the same). On the whole, you can expect retired professionals – former police and army officers are popular – and nonsmokers. They are not allowed to entertain visitors in your house, so there's no danger of coming back to find a secret policeman's ball in full swing.

Agencies either employ staff directly as employees, or act as agents. Sitters should be fully insured by their agency (check that they are) and you may even get a discount on your home insurance if you let your insurers know that sitters are in residence. All sitters are rigorously vetted, and sitters and sat are matched so that the green-fingered, for example, get gardens to care for and canine lovers get dogs. The two parties usually meet beforehand to check compatibility. Here are a few house-sitting companies to check out:

- **Homesitters** (☎ +44 (0)1296 630730; www.homesitters.co.uk)
- **Absentia** (☎ +44 (0)1279 777412; www.home-and-pets.co.uk)
- **The Home Service** (☎ 0845 130 3100; www.housesitters.co.uk)
- **Animal Aunts** (☎ +44 (0)1730 821529; www.animalaunts.co.uk)

HOUSE SWAPS

In many ways this is a perfect option: your house is occupied and cared for, you have accommodation (and sometimes even a car) during your time away, and it doesn't cost you a penny. As this is a particularly good option for career-breakers wanting to live and work abroad, see p158 for more details.

SECOND HOMES

If you're away for more than a few months and you have a second home that you use as a bolt hole or rent out, you'll need to make arrangements. Probably the most secure and lucrative option is to get a full-time tenant (see Letting p25). You may decide to rent it out as a holiday let through an agent. In this case, you'll need to arrange for someone who lives relatively close to the property to keep an eye on it. If you've previously rented it out as a holiday let, you'll probably already have a local person who goes in to clean and to change the linen on changeover day, and the person may be willing to extend their duties to act as caretaker as well. Even if you are letting through an agency, it is unlikely to be able to perform these roles on your behalf and will need a contact it can get hold of when something goes wrong.

You will need to budget anything up to £1000 per year to pay someone to act as caretaker (the sum is up to you to negotiate). You also need to make arrangements for the payment of council tax, water rates and utility bills while you are away, unless the caretaker is dealing with these. Let the agency know whom to notify about bookings – your caretaker or you.

CLEANERS

If you have a cleaner, you will need to negotiate an arrangement that suits you both while you are away. If you are renting the house out, your tenants might wish to keep the cleaner on. If you are only going away for a few months, you may consider paying the cleaner a retainer or asking them to come and clean (and check) the house while you are away. If you're letting your cleaner go, don't forget to get the keys back.

For details of organisations that can help you deal with your house in the USA and Australia, see the Appendices.

VEHICLE

If you and your car/van/motorbike are inseparable, you may decide to take it with you on your travels. Talk to your insurance company about extending cover to the country or countries you are visiting. If you're going to Europe you might decide to arrange breakdown cover through a company like **Europ Assistance** (☎ +44 (0)1444 442211; www.europ-assistance.co.uk).

If you leave your vehicle behind, what you do with it depends on how long you intend to travel. If it's just a few months, your best option is to leave the car outside your house (or in the garage if you have one) and ask a friend or relative to drive it around the block once or twice. Note that they need to be named drivers on your insurance policy. If you park your vehicle on the road outside your home, it must be both taxed and insured.

Many career-breakers going away for a year or two decide to sell their car, adding welcome cash to the career-break fund. To find out what it's worth, *Parker's Car Price Guide* (www .parkers.co.uk) is useful. You might also check with a local garage what they would give you for it. You can also advertise in local papers or *Autotrader* magazine (www.autotrader.co.uk).

If you don't want to sell your car, you can take it off the road and put it into a locked garage. If you decide to do this you must fill in a *Statutory Off Road Notification* (SORN) form, which you can pick up from a post office and send to the Driver and Vehicle Licensing Agency (DVLA; www.dvla.gov.uk) in Swansea. Failure to submit a SORN form can lead to a maximum fine of £1000. The good news is that you won't have to pay road tax and you can even claim a rebate for tax you've already paid by filling in a V14 form; note that there must be more than a complete month left on your licence disc and you can only get refunds for full months. The V14 form can be used both to claim a rebate and to declare SORN. If your vehicle is in a garage but you want it covered for malicious damage you still need comprehensive insurance; insurance companies used to offer 'laid-up cover' for such situations but no longer do. If you own an old banger you'll probably be content with a wing and prayer, but if you've a new Jag you might prefer to pay up for peace of mind.

Another option is to lend the car to a friend while you are away. Again, there can be insurance snags but they are not insuperable. You can either add the friend as a named driver to your policy, or you can get your friend to insure the car in their name; they will have to give details of its ownership, but if the car is to be kept at their home that will count as the car's address rather than yours. If you add your friend to your policy and something happens to the car, your no-claims bonus will be affected. The best bet is to discuss the options in full with your insurance broker.

OTHER TRANSPORT

If you have an annual rail ticket and are leaving before it expires, you can apply for a refund by returning it to the ticket office where it was bought. If the season ticket is valid for a month or more, there must be at least seven days' validity left on it. For any other season ticket, there must be three days' validity left. Your refund is calculated from the day you show up at the issuing office.

To get a refund for a London Underground season ticket you must have at least a month left on it if it's an annual one and a week on it if it's a monthly one. You can claim by visiting any ticket office or by calling London Underground's Refund Department on ☎ 0845 330 9881. Both the rail and underground networks deduct a small administrative fee from your refund.

For information on organisations that can help you deal with your vehicle in Australia or the US, see the Appendices.

PARTNER & CHILDREN

If you have a partner and/or children, you may wish to time your break to fit in with their needs and wants. In the case of your partner, there may be an optimum time for both of you to

take a joint break from your jobs. Or you may decide to spend the time
who spent four months in Namibia, had just started a relationship wh

I'd been planning the trip for over a year so decided to go ahead with it a
behind. A break of three or four months can improve a relationship,
issues in it. It definitely pushes you to make decisions about your future

Alternatively, you may choose to take time out now because you have just split up from
a partner. Travel can be a great healer and spending time away is an ideal way to cement
the break.

In the case of children, age is an important factor. You may decide to whisk them off
while tiny to take advantage of reduced fares offered by airlines to children under two. You
may feel it's a good idea to take your children abroad before they are of school age to avoid
taking them out of school. If you do take them out of school, you need to get the head
teacher's permission, or risk paying a £100 fine. If you are going away for a long period,
you must officially deregister your child. Be aware that on your return your child's place
may not be guaranteed, so check with the school first.

Health and safety will also be issues: you may want to avoid war zones and highly malarious areas! Child benefit may be a concern too. If you leave the UK you're only entitled to
child benefit for the first eight weeks, and this money won't be paid until you return. For
details ring ☎ 0845 302 1454.

Lonely Planet's *Travel with Children* is a useful resource if you are taking kids with you.

SCHOOLING ON THE ROAD

If your children are of school age you might enrol them in a school abroad, educate them
yourself or try a combination of the two. If you're looking for schools abroad, language
is obviously the main issue. There may be an international school, where teaching is in
English, in the place you are going. Or you may opt for 'total immersion', whereby your
children attend a local school, pick up the local language (you hope) and interact with local
children. If you are travelling on a tourist visa outside of Europe you may find it difficult
to get your children into a state school abroad free of charge, but if one of you has a special
visa, such as a work permit or an academic visitor visa, you may be able to. In Europe you
should be able to get your children into a state school free of charge, provided you have a
permanent address. Be warned that international schools can cost an arm and a leg, so make
sure you budget for this. There are some cheaper options, such as the United World Colleges (www.uwc.org), where admittance is by scholarship only, and international sections
attached to state schools (there are several of these in France, for example). For information on schools, contact the UK embassy of the country you plan to be in or get in touch
with the **Council of International Schools** (☎ +44 (0)1730 263131; www.cois.org). Other useful websites
include http://privateschool.about.com/cs/schoolwebsites and www.international-schools
.com. Once you've selected a school, apply well in advance, as many fill up quickly. Your
child may have to take an entrance exam or attend an interview, which may be conducted
over the phone. A school may require your child to speak the language of that country
and may request detailed records from your child's current school so they can be placed
in the right class.

Oscar Wilde said that 'nothing that is worth knowing can be taught' and you may agree
that the experience of travelling is an education in itself. The educational benefits of seeing the world can be huge: visiting the real Taj Mahal rather than looking at a picture of
it, or tracking tigers in the flesh, is likely to stimulate children's imaginations far more
than school textbooks back home. Despite this, legally your children need to be educated
properly, either at a school or by you.

Single mum Linda Irene'schild took her two boys travelling through Spain for six months
when they were 11 and six. While in the parched region of Almería, they become involved in
projects to tackle desertification, and their 'science lesson' was learning about biodynamics
and irrigation. Their education extended to other areas too:

rded goats, milked them, then made cheese from the milk. They rode donkeys, learned to look after them and helped collect fresh water from a spring near the house where we were staying. The best thing was that they didn't even know that they were studying; they just absorbed it all. It's certainly enriched their lives and turned them into confident people.

Ann Selby, who quit her job as an administrator in the construction industry to travel around Australia with her chef husband and their two primary-school age boys for two years, is equally enthusiastic. They took a maths book the boys' teacher had recommended but soon found more interesting ways to learn the art of addition:

We would create sums by getting the boys to write down the price of each type of fuel at each petrol station. After we had passed several they were asked to work out the difference between fuel from one petrol station and the other – was it lower, higher etc. The boys also noted all the animals they saw on a driving day and totted up the numbers at the end of the day. They were always sad when the roadkill outweighed the live animals.

If your child has never been registered at a state school in the UK, you have no obligation to tell your local education authority that you are going abroad. Educating them at home in the UK or abroad is perfectly legal. With the Internet and online book-ordering services like Amazon, it's never been easier. Written materials, including coursework for the National Curriculum, can be obtained from organisations such as **Education Otherwise** (helpline ☎ 0870 730 0074; www.education-otherwise.org; PO Box 7420, London N9 9SG) and the **Home Education Advisory Service** (www.heas.org.uk; PO Box 98, Welwyn Garden City, Herts AL8 6AN). Both organisations prefer you to write. If you want your child to study for the General Certificate of Secondary Education (GCSE), AS or A levels, you can get the syllabuses and resource lists from the awarding body beforehand and take the relevant textbooks with you. One of these is Cambridge International Examinations (www.cie.org.uk), part of the University of Cambridge Local Examination Syndicate. Exams can be taken at an approved centre abroad. Many of these are administered by the British Council (www.britcoun.org).

If you're taking children with you, give some thought as to how they'll keep in touch with friends back home. Will they write letters, or will they have access to email or phones? These can be good educational tools too – even if what the little dears write isn't always what you expect. Ann Selby says:

It always amused us that whenever they communicated with their friends it was always about which new Pokémon card they had and if their friends had any new ones. They rarely mentioned the extinct volcano they'd just walked around or the outback trip sleeping among wild donkeys. This is when you understand that kids just take things in their stride.

MAKING A WILL

It may not be the cheeriest subject, but if you don't already have a will you should make one before you depart (the country, not this world). A will sets out what happens to your estate

---

HOMESCHOOLING: THE USA

Thanks to a renaissance in the 1970s and '80s, homeschooling (not to be confused with the unschooling or delight-driven education movements) is alive and well across North America, especially in rural and conservative religious communities. Today, compulsory school attendance is a thing of the past in most states, and two-thirds of them now have laws regulating homeschooling. In some states, laws even oblige public school districts to provide parents with textbooks and other materials to support long-distance learning. Adventurous parents looking to teach their kids while, say, sailing around the world, will discover many eager support groups and curriculum providers online. The website of the magazine *Practical Homeschooling* (www.home-school.com) is a good place to start your search.

DISTANCE & HOME EDUCATION: AUSTRALIA

The Australian state education laws generally agree: under certain circumstances children can be taken out of school to either be taught at home or become part of a distance-education network.

If they are taught at home, most children will need to be assessed annually to see if they are achieving approved educational standards. State education departments will normally supply information on where parents can find educational materials, Internet sites and support groups. Distance-education organisations follow the state's school curriculum and utilise regular telephone lessons for pupils. The parents pay similar amounts for this service as for government schooling.

---

when you die. If you don't make one, and you die intestate (ie, will-less), your family and loved ones could end up with little. Your partner is particularly vulnerable if you are cohabiting but not married, as the intestacy rules do not recognise unmarried partners. Failure to make a will can also mean an unnecessarily large portion of your estate disappears in the form of inheritance tax. Another very important reason for making a will if you have a young family is that it enables you to name who you want to look after your children if you die.

You can buy a DIY will from any high-street stationers. These appear simple to fill in, but often they're not: remember the case recorded in *The Guinness Book of Records* where the writer wrote 'All for mother'? Obvious? Well, no – he meant his wife, not his mother, and the matter ended up in court.

Solicitors claim they make more money out of unravelling DIY wills than they ever do drawing them up. So, for a fee of between £60 and £80, why not do it properly and get yourself a solicitor? Whatever you choose, give your friends and relatives copies of your will, or tell them where copies are kept – your will is of little use if it's never found. According to the Which? Guide *Be Your Own Financial Adviser* you should opt for a solicitor rather than a DIY will if you are in any of the following categories: you live outside England or Wales; you have young children by a former marriage; you run your own business or farm; you have been married more than once and your ex-partner is still alive. For a higher fee, a solicitor can give you advice on how to protect your estate from inheritance tax (for instance, by setting up trusts) and draft up a more in-depth will. This, however, requires time and thought. Be careful when choosing your executors: professional will-writing services can be overpriced and impersonal, while friends or beneficiaries may lack the time or technical expertise. The best is to appoint one beneficiary, friend or relative and one professional. Agree on the charges first. The professional can do the donkey work and the beneficiary can sort personal matters.

OTHER DEPENDENTS

You can take your partner and children on your dream trip, but dragging your elderly mum or disabled aunt along may not be so easy. If you are someone's main carer, sorting out care arrangements can be challenging and require careful planning; your obligations may determine if and when you take a career break, how long you go for and how far afield. If you are lucky, a sibling or close family friend may be willing to step into your shoes while you are away. If the person you care for needs a lot of support at home, call their local social services office. They will assess the needs of your relative and decide what services are required while you are away, such as domestic help, nursing or aid getting to a day centre. (This is means-tested, so the person you care for may have to pay.) Social services can also put you in touch with privately run organisations and voluntary bodies providing domestic help, nursing care, shopping, transport and help during the night. An excellent source of information on where to get support is **Carers UK** (helpline ☎ 0808 808 7777; www.carersonline.org.uk). If you are going away for just a few months, one option is to arrange a short stay in a residential-care home or nursing home or to get temporary live-in help. Social services can advise on this. If the person being cared for cannot afford to pay for care, they may be eligible for financial help.

PETS

Until recently, if you wanted to take a career break you'd have had to leave Fido or Felix at home, or subject them to six months of quarantine on your return from abroad. With the introduction of the Pet Travel Scheme (PETS) in 2000, your cats and dogs can accompany you on your career break and see the world too – provided you travel to the right countries and use approved sea, air and rail routes to get home. The list of countries taking part in the scheme is fairly limited, but does include most European countries, the USA and Canada, so check the government's Defra website (www.defra.gov.uk/animalh/quarantine/pets) or ring the PETS helpline on ☎ 0870 241 1710. If the country you are visiting is not on the government's approved list, you'll have to put your animals into quarantine for six months upon returning to the UK. Rules and regulations apart, though, it may not be feasible to take animals with you if you're going to an area such as rural Africa, where pets would simply not fit into the scene or would be at risk of parasite or tick-transmitted diseases. Consult your vet first. Similarly, if you're about to embark on a non–pet-friendly activity such as climbing K2 for three months, taking the pets along will be a complete no-no. Many airlines refuse to transport pets. In these cases you will need to find a friend who is willing to adopt your pets while you are away, find a pet-sitting agency or put them into a kennel or cattery.

TAKING PETS ABROAD

It's only worth taking your beloved beasts with you if you are going to a foreign country for more than six months. This is because your animals must be proven to be free of rabies for six months before being allowed back into the UK, and symptoms of the disease take six months to appear. The procedure is as follows: first your pet must be fitted with a microchip so it can be identified (this can be done in the UK before you go). It must then be vaccinated against rabies and later have blood tests to ensure the vaccinations have worked. Next you must obtain an official PETS certificate from a government-authorised vet. Then, 24 to 48 hours before you re-enter the UK, the animal must be treated against ticks and tapeworm by a qualified vet, who must issue a certificate to show this treatment has been carried out. You will have to sign a declaration to say that your animal has not been outside PETS-qualifying countries during the six months before it enters (or re-enters) the UK. You must return home on an authorised route, using an approved transport company. Check which companies do this by ringing the PETS helpline; they vary according to whether you are returning from Europe or outside Europe. Note that *Eurostar* does not accept pets. Animals going by air must travel in a container. If there is no approved route to the UK from the country you are coming from, you will have to put your pet into quarantine on arrival in England with a view to early release. If you're entering the UK from outside the EU, you will have to complete customs formalities, although many travel agencies will do this for you for a fee. Cats that have been travelling in Australia need an extra certificate before returning to the UK.

If that all sounds like too much hassle, there are agencies that will do the paperwork and organise transport on your behalf, such as Easipet (www.easipet.com). Dogs Away (www .dogsaway.co.uk) provides information and can arrange treatment against tapeworm and ticks before you return to the UK.

LEAVING PETS AT HOME

If you're leaving your darlings at home, the ideal option is to treat them to a career break too by sending them off to a relative while you're away. If, however, you don't have an animal-loving relative, friend or neighbour, there may be no escaping the cost of kennels, catteries or pet-sitting agencies. For more information on these, see www.dogsit.com, www .pets999.com and www.darwinvets.plus.com/topical/cattery.htm

If you are travelling from Canada, the USA or Australia, see the Appendices for information on what to do with your pets.

POWER OF ATTORNEY

In certain circumstances you may wish to grant someone power of attorney over your affairs while you are away. It's a drastic step and not one to take lightly, as it gives the person power to do anything from selling your house or taking out a mortgage in your name to skinning your dog. If, however, you are selling your house but have been let down at the last minute so can't complete the sale before you go abroad, this may be a situation where you'd give your solicitor a limited form of power of attorney. Likewise, if the stock market is looking dodgy, you might give your stockbroker limited power of attorney so that they can buy and sell on your behalf. If you are thinking of taking such a step the rule is, as ever, to seek professional advice first.

If you simply need to give someone the ability to pay bills or deal with contingencies on your behalf, rather than grant power of attorney the best option is to set up a special bank account that your contact is authorised to access (see Finances, p21). This is far more secure than granting power of attorney: even if your contact is trustworthy, there is always the possibility that their home could be burgled and the power of attorney documents stolen.

For advice on how to grant power of attorney in the USA and Australia, see the Appendices.

VOTING

If you're leaving the UK for a while but want a say in how the country's run, decide how you're going to vote. If you know an election is looming and you'll miss it, arrange a proxy vote by filling in a form obtained from your local council before you go. The form authorises someone else to vote in your polling station on your behalf, so don't forget to tell them who to vote for. Your proxy must be a British, Irish or Commonwealth citizen, old enough to vote, and living in the UK. If your proxy can't get to your polling station, they can apply to vote by post.

Postal voting is another option but not much use to most career-breakers as postal votes are only sent out between seven and 10 days before an election and need to be returned by polling day. If you're on an island in the South Pacific, the chances of your ballot being registered on time will be as slim as your bikini thong.

If you are staying abroad for a while you can register as an overseas elector. This entitles you to vote in UK and European Parliament elections, but not local ones. To register you need to contact the electoral registration office of your local authority at home. You must do this at least six weeks before an election. The registration lasts for 12 months and you'll receive a reminder two to three months before it runs out.

For further information, consult the Electoral Commission (www.electoralcommission. org.uk) or check www.upmystreet.com. If you are from the USA or Australia, see the Appendices for advice on voting.

TECHNOLOGY & COMMUNICATIONS

You may want a break from routine, but not necessarily from friends, colleagues and family. Think well ahead about how to stay in touch while on the road – see p62 for ideas. And don't forget to send out change-of-address cards or emails before you go.

While you are away, the Royal Mail can forward your post either to your address abroad (if you have a fixed one) or to a reliable friend or relative in the UK who is willing to sift through it for you. Mail can be redirected for anything from one month to two years. You can pick up a *Moving Home* redirection form from your post office, or ring ☎ 0845 774 0740 (if calling from abroad ☎ +44 (0)1752 387 116) to request that a form be sent to you. You must produce proof of ID when applying. Five days' notice is needed to set up the service. You can renew a redirection from abroad by post, over the phone or online. To renew online the Royal Mail will send you a renewal reference and PIN number two to four weeks before your redirection runs out.

If you have a phone or a broadband or mobile phone subscription, you'll need to sort these out before you go. If you're renting out your home, you need to come to an arrangement about the phone; you're strongly advised to transfer the account into the tenant's name, although this is only possible if they are renting for three months or more. Technically the tenants then have the power to change the number, so if you want to hang onto your old number make this clear to them and to your line provider. Make this clear again when you get the line transferred back into your name on your return or your friends could lose touch with you forever. If you keep the phone in your name but agree with the tenant that they won't use the phone, you can pay for an Outgoing Call Barred service. Or you can use the less secure calling feature known as Call Barring, which allows you to be selective in the type of call you want to bar (ring ☎ 150 to set this up). If the house is left empty, you must keep the line open and pay rental if you wish to retain the number. To view or pay your phone bill from abroad, go to www.bt.com and click At Home/Manage Your Account. Or set up a direct debit before you go. Many broadband and mobile phone subscriptions are unbreakable for a year, so you will not get a rebate if you wish to cease your subscription before that time. However, some companies, such as Orange, do allow you to suspend your contract for a maximum period of six months (ring customer service to arrange this). You may decide to take your mobile phone with you, but it'll cost an arm and a leg to stay with your UK network (see p63).

For information on technology and communications in the USA and Australia, see the Appendices.

Practical Plans & Travel Tips

BUDGET

Remember how the lyrics go for Abba's song 'Money, Money, Money'? Well, that is how it can sometimes feel when you're working out your career-break budget. Basically, your costs can be divided into three areas: predeparture, the trip and coming home.

Predeparture costs include flights, immunisations, travel insurance, visas, medical kit, equipment etc. A huge chunk of this cash will go on your flights: a RTW ticket costs in the range of £900 to £2200 including tax, depending on your itinerary. See the Tickets section (p40) for details. In terms of all other items, your visit to the travel clinic will set you back around £100 (vaccinations cost from £7 to £40); good worldwide (including the USA) travel insurance for 12 months will cost anywhere from £245 to £465; most visas cost between £11 (Jordan) and £60 (USA); a useful medical kit is £30; and equipment, well, that's between you and your savings account.

The main expenses you'll incur on your trip will be accommodation, food and drink, entertainment, shopping, laundry, adventure activities, sightseeing, transport, departure taxes and treating yourself. What you end up spending will depend on how you want to structure your break and the style in which you want to travel. For instance, do you want to supplement your savings by doing some work? Many career-breakers do this, although just as many figure they've spent too much of their lives working already and certainly don't plan on doing it now. Will you be travelling on your own or with someone? A lot of career-breakers go with a partner and this certainly defrays costs. Are you going to spend long periods of time in one place or will you be travelling quite swiftly from region to region? A rule of thumb is that every day on the road can cost twice as much as a day in one place. The most expensive element of your trip will be accommodation. Do you want to stay in mid-range hotels with the occasional night in a luxurious safari lodge or spa resort? At the other end of the spectrum, do you enjoy the camaraderie of staying in youth and backpacker hostels? Many youth hostels these days are pretty comfortable places with single rooms, double rooms and family rooms and are not overpopulated by the sock and open-toed sandal brigade.

Where you want to go will have a huge impact on what you're likely to spend. The cost of living in some regions is cheap, as is the case in many parts of Southeast Asia, the Indian subcontinent, China, Mexico and Latin America, while other places such as Australia, New Zealand, the Pacific, Europe, Russia, Japan, North America and much of the Caribbean are relatively expensive. Much of Africa is cheap but some countries, such as those using the West African CFA currency (Senegal, Mali etc), can be surprisingly costly. For an estimate of what you'll spend on accommodation and food in various countries, visit Lonely Planet's Worldguide at www.lonelyplanet.com/destinations.

When you know how you want to travel, where you want to go and how long you'll be away, you can start to do your sums. For instance, travelling comfortably in Australia will burn around £50 a day, whereas in India a budget of £20 a day will go a long way. In the Bahamas £80 a day will buy what you'd get in Mexico for only £30. To cut to the chase, career-breakers usually budget between £30 to £40 a day or between £11,000 to £15,000 a year. (To compare, most gap-year students travel for a year on between £5000 to £6000.) This sort of money will buy an experience of a lifetime and ensure you get to fulfil some of your wildest travel dreams.

Coming home is a costly business too, unless you want to arrive home broke (been there, done that). Ideally, you need enough money to cover several months of living expenses while you look for a job. Realistically, this will amount to at least £5000, and plenty of career-breakers wish they'd kept £10,000 aside. Of course, it all depends on your circumstances. Will you be able to stay with friends or family while you find work or will you straight back into your house and have to cover the mortgage? Will you need to find several months' rent plus a deposit? What did you do with your car when you went away? Will you have to fork out for its tax, insurance and a service when you return home? And, what about those clothes, particularly work ones, that fitted you perfectly before you left? Do you need a new wardrobe to reflect the new you? In addition, don't forget that when you do get a job, you'll get paid in arrears.

Wow, add all that up and it sounds like a heap of money. So, how do you go about raising these sorts of funds? Perhaps you'll get lucky and receive a windfall from an elderly relative or a building society demutualising. Some of you will turn misfortune into an opportunity and spend your redundancy money on a career break. Or perhaps you started your own business a number of years ago and now is the right time to sell. David Orkin did just that:

At 32, two friends who had recently started up a business offered me the chance to buy in. We worked day and night for the first five to six years and didn't slow down much after that. We paid ourselves very low salaries and ploughed all our profits back into the business. As the years went by, I guess we all began to burn out: we'd invested the hours and the effort and it was time to reap the harvest. We found a buyer and I found myself with a healthy sum in the bank and time on my hands. Rather than rushing into something else, I decided to use some of my modest new-found wealth to finance a two-year career break.

Otherwise, if you're getting married, consider doing what Richard and Sue Livingston did:

We wanted to combine a career break with an extended honeymoon, so we asked our guests to sponsor certain parts of our trip. We made a map of our route, highlighted the sections that needed funding and sent it out with our wedding invites (instead of a wedding list). We asked friends and relatives to pay for nights in certain hotels, meals in particular restaurants, special train trips etc. When we were away we'd write a postcard to thank whoever had given us the money to do whatever it was that we'd just experienced. In our opinion, we received the best wedding presents ever.

This idea is catching on. The travel agent Trailfinders has a wedding list service (www .trailfinders.com/wedding.htm) where guests can contribute towards the cost of your honeymoon. You can do this online by purchasing gift vouchers and accompanying messages.

If you're not one of these lucky few, then you're going to have to start saving and fundraising. If you can, give yourself at least a year to do this (although the urge for a career break can sometimes strike suddenly). If you've ever filled in one of those super-detailed confidential questionnaires that financial advisers insist you complete, then you'll have a good idea of all outgoings and incomings. If not, then set up your own spreadsheet to work out where you can make cuts and savings. Following are some pick 'n' mix tips to help you on your way, divided into four categories: your finances, your home and car, at work and luxuries:

YOUR FINANCES

- **Money-saving tips** Subscribe to Martin Lewis' free e-newsletter on money-saving tips at www.moneysavingexpert.com or buy his new book, *The Money Diet*.
- **Interest rates** Ensure your savings are attracting a good rate of interest. In particular, some of the older types of building-society accounts are paying pathetic rates of return by today's standards. Take a look at what some of the online banks such as ING Direct (www.ingdirect.co.uk) are offering.
- **Cash back** Use a credit, debit or charge card that offers you cash back. Some good ones at the time of writing were American Express Blue (which you can't use everywhere) and the Nationwide's cash-back card.

- **Loyalty programs** Watch where you shop – reward or loyalty cards can help you on your way. For instance, collect Air Miles with Tesco (particularly useful) or shop at Boots and spend your points on predeparture items.
- **Tax rebate** If your career break means not working for a full tax year, you may be eligible for a tax rebate to top up funds. See p23 for details.
- **ISAs** If you've got any ISAs, work out when they mature. Your original lump sum plus the tax-free interest can definitely boost a career-break fund.
- **Sponsorships** Consider sponsorship from friends or local businesses for any part of your career break that involves a stint of voluntary work (see p117 in the Volunteering & Conservation chapter for ideas).
- **Taking out a loan** As a last option, you can take out a loan to finance your trip. This isn't desirable, for obvious reasons, especially if you don't have a job to come back to. If you want to go down this route, apply for your loan before giving up your job, as your new unemployed status might affect your credit rating.
- **Selling up** Now is definitely a good time to get onto www.ebay.co.uk and sell that dusty collection of *Melody Makers* or anything else you've carted from house to house since you were 15. In a recent issue of *Wanderlust* magazine this plea appeared:

Once again I have the lust to wander, so my back issues I must squander. I am skint so need the cash, if before Christmas I am to make a dash. So please be generous with your bid, coz I really need a few quid!

YOUR HOME & CAR

- **Renting** If you own your home then renting it out can bring in very useful income while you're away (see pp25-8 for advice on letting your home).
- **Selling** Sell your car or motorbike – it is unlikely your vehicle will appreciate rusting away in the garage while you're off enjoying yourself (and could cost a lot to get back on the road when you return) See p30 for advice on selling vehicles.
- **Cable TV** Cancel your subscription to satellite or cable TV – watch the match at the pub or the movies at your friends' houses.
- **Phone bills** Check you're not wasting money on your home telephone calls by ensuring you're on the right telephone billing tariffs and with the cheapest telephone providers.
- **Utility bills** Switch your gas and electricity provider if they're not giving you the best deal.

More desperate than the above is what career-breaker Claire McKenzie did:

To raise the funds needed for my trip, I had to move back in with my parents and work part-time at the weekends...it felt like the longest summer ever.

AT WORK

- **Overtime** Sign up for any paid overtime, or, if you work on commission, put in the extra hours to boost your pay packet.
- **Second job** Take on a second job either at the weekend or in the evenings.
- **Frequent-flyer points** If you travel overseas for business then the chances are you've accumulated a fair few frequent-flyer points (FFPs). These are in your name (regardless of who paid for your air tickets) and cannot be used without your authority. As such, 99% of career-breakers leave a company with all their points intact, and use them to help fund their plane ticket out of the office.
- **Lunch** Make your own sandwiches to take to work – you will not believe how much you spend on buying lunch every day. This could save you around £700 a year.
- **Market research** Sign up for some market-research nights – at least you won't be out on the razzle spending the cash you're trying to save. You'll be paid for your time, too.
- **Voluntary redundancy** If your company is offering voluntary redundancy, grab it.

LUXURIES

- **Cancel your cleaner** That could amount to a saving of between £1000 to £1500 a year. Doing the housework burns up calories, too.
- **Cancel your gym membership** Instead of running on the spot, run around the local park or around your home with a vacuum cleaner. This could save £1000 or more a year.
- **Public transport** Take public transport instead of taxis.
- **Cut down on eating out** Eating at restaurants twice a month instead of once a week could save another £500 or so.
- **Visit your local library** Don't buy the latest bestselling book, get it out at your local library (what a terrible thing for an author to say).

TICKETS

Do you have any friends who are travel agents? If so, ignore what it says in the Budget section about not eating out and take them to a jolly good restaurant and pump them for information. In terms of time and money it could save you a fortune. Your flights will probably be your single largest expense and there are a bewildering amount of ticket options, fare structures, destination computations and pitfalls to negotiate. In this section all fares quoted are for departures in May 2004.

A few basics to begin with. Even if you're a seasoned traveller or have previously taken a gap year, a refresher course in ticket etiquette won't hurt:

SEASONAL LIMITS

The price of your ticket will depend on your departure date. Avoid leaving the UK during the school holidays as all airline fares are jacked up at this time. The cheapest months to leave for Australia or New Zealand tend to be May and June, followed by February and November.

WHEN TO PURCHASE

Start looking for special or bargain fares eight to 12 months in advance of your departure date. Note that many of the best deals will require you to pay in full soon after booking. Special or bargain fares often carry stricter and heavier change penalties (and these changes are rarely covered by your travel insurance). You may get cheap tickets at the last minute if you're super-flexible, but it is more likely that you'll end up delaying your departure date. Very rarely do long-haul airlines slash prices for imminent departures, even if all seats do not have bums on them.

CANCELLATION PENALTIES

These vary considerably but it is not unusual to lose the entire value of your ticket if you cancel it once booked. (Most travel-insurance policies will protect against unavoidable cancellation fees but only if the reason for cancelling is covered by the particular policy.)

CHILDREN'S FARES

Infants over the age of two years must occupy an airline seat and pay a child fare (you might want to pocket their in-flight alcohol allowance to offset this cost). Under the age of two they sit on your lap (or in a skycot) and pay between 10% and 20% of the adult fare. After a child's 12th birthday you'll have to pay a full adult fare for them.

REFUND POLICY

Despite what you might be told by the local airline office, if you don't use a certain sector or portion of your ticket it is unlikely that you'll get any money back. Airline staff in Bangkok, for example, don't know all the rules associated with a discounted ticket sold by an agent in London. If you are entitled to a refund then this can usually only be arranged through the travel agency where your ticket was purchased. This isn't terribly useful if you're in the middle of nowhere having the time of your life.

CHANGE PENALTIES

There are three main types of changes: name, dates and routes. In terms of the first, it is very rare that a name change will be permitted, so don't book a ticket, break up with your partner and hope to replace them with a new lover. Regarding dates, there are usually restrictions about changing your departure date from the UK. However, the dates of onward flights can often be changed, subject to seat availability. Although in many cases date changes are permitted free, quite hefty fees can be charged, depending on the rules of the ticket and the policy of the travel agency and the airline(s) concerned. In some cases, no date changes are allowed at all. Route changes may be possible but usually attract a fee and, where they are permitted, there is likely to be a stipulation as to how many route changes you're allowed (often only one).

TIME LIMITS

It is virtually impossible to find a ticket that allows you to be away for more than 12 months. If you want to travel for longer than a year you might decide not to use the last leg of your ticket. A round-the-world (RTW) ticket is still good value even if you only end up using three-quarters of it. Before you go down this route, do some research on the web to see how much it'll cost you to buy a ticket home from wherever you end up. Some tickets also state that you cannot return to the UK within a certain period of time.

STOPOVER LIMITS

Most fares restrict the number of stopovers permitted. See the Round-the-World chart (p44) for details.

TYPES OF TICKETS
Discount Return Tickets

If you plan to spend your career break exploring one country in depth and will not be flying to another country from there, all you need is a normal return ticket. The humble return can, however, be jazzed up with one or more stopovers, allowing you to explore other regions on the way to your main destination. This traveller-friendly system has mainly developed due to airline alliances or partnerships. It means you can disembark at any airport your carrier and their friends fly to, as long as it is roughly between your starting and finishing points. In other words, you don't have to buy a relatively expensive RTW ticket in order to see a large chunk of the world. OK, you won't be going around it, but you can get to see a heck of a lot of it on a return ticket to Australia or New Zealand that is routed through cities in Africa and Asia, for instance. Examples of possible itineraries include:

- London–Dubai–Maldives–Colombo–Bangkok overland to Singapore–Sydney overland to Melbourne–Singapore–Colombo–Delhi overland to Mumbai (Bombay)–London. This route flies with Emirates and Sri Lankan Airlines and costs £834, plus tax.
- London–Dubai–Kolkata (Calcutta)–Singapore overland to Bangkok–Brunei–Perth overland to Darwin–Brunei–Abu Dhabi–London. This Royal Brunei route costs £589 plus tax.

In addition, if you want to fly domestically within your destination then it will probably be cheaper for you to purchase a return ticket to one city with a stopover in the other. For instance, a ticket to Sydney with a stopover in Perth is likely to be much cheaper than getting to Perth and then doing a side trip to Sydney.

Open-Jaw Tickets

With these tickets you fly to one destination and out of another. This allows you some good old-fashioned overland travel between your two points. For instance, flying into Bangkok and out of Singapore (£430 to £650 plus taxes) means you can loop through Cambodia, Vietnam and Laos and travel down the southern gulf of Thailand into Malaysia, before flying out of Singapore. Open-jaw tickets are rarely more expensive than standard return fares. They are also an excellent way to see a lot of Europe, as the UK's no-frills airlines always sell single tickets. A return on a no-frills airline is simply two one-way tickets, which means you could fly into Nice and out of Barcelona.

One-Way Tickets

If you intend to be away for longer than a year or just don't know where you want to go next, you might purchase a one-way ticket to ride. Proportionally a one-way long-haul ticket is very expensive, almost always costing a lot more than half the price of a return. In fact, they are sometimes even more expensive than a return. If you only want a single ticket, check in case a return is cheaper; if it is then buy the return and don't use the homeward part.

One drawback with one-way tickets is that often you have to show how you're going to get out of a country before you can get in (immigration officials may want to see an onward ticket). Often, if you can prove that you've got sufficient funds for your stay and enough to purchase an exit ticket (whether by air, land or sea), you will be fine.

Round-the-World (RTW) Tickets

To begin at the beginning: you can't buy a ticket on a single airline that goes around the world. A RTW ticket is a series of coupons (in one or more tickets) that will take you around the globe on two or more airlines. Although these tickets have been around in one form or another for 25 years, they didn't really come into their own until the mid-1990s when British Airways and Qantas joined forces. BA flew between London and a wide variety of worldwide destinations, but only a few of their flights went on to Australia. Qantas flew between Australia and numerous cities across the globe, but had relatively few flights to the UK. However, with the two of them working together, over 20 cities that both airlines flew to could now be used as stopover destinations on tickets to Australia. These places were in both the eastern and western hemispheres and fares were introduced that allowed passengers to go out to Australia via one hemisphere and back via the other.

To compete, other airlines quickly followed suit and in the last decade there has been much alliance-building across the airline industry. Several more airlines joined with BA and Qantas to form Oneworld (www.oneworldalliance.com), and the Star Alliance (www.star-alliance.com) and SkyTeam (www.skyteam.com) also sprang up. (Members of these alliances tend to fall in and out of love with each other, so for up-to-date information on who's in and who's out it's best to check the alliance websites.) The upshot is that today almost anywhere you want to visit can be folded into your RTW ticket. If your destinations are on mainstream routes then your RTW ticket will be relatively cheap; if not, then flying to and from certain places may well have a nasty upwards effect on your overall ticket costs.

Other points to bear in mind include:

- **Maximum time limit** You usually have up to one year to get around the globe.
- **Mileage allowance** Most RTW tickets give you a mileage allowance, which means that your trip can't be longer than a certain amount of kilometres. This is typically between 40,000km to 46,400km (25,000 to 29,000 miles); for instance, London–Singapore–Sydney–Los Angeles–London is 37,600km (23,500 miles). You may be allowed to backtrack, as long as you can still meet this criterion. Some fares allow you to pay a surcharge to buy more kilometres (or, in the case of Oneworld Explorer, to visit more continents).
- **Stopover limit** Most deals restrict you to a set number of stopovers, though you can often pay higher fares that allow more. Many fares only let you stop in a particular city once; others allow you to change planes in that city but not break your journey there more than once.
- **Frequent-flyer points** Some RTW deals allow you to collect FFPs (particularly Oneworld Explorer, Global Explorer and Star Alliance). With many other deals, restrictions apply.

So, where to start? Make a list of everywhere you want to go and then prioritise under three headings: Must See, Would Like to See, and Nice to See but Could Drop if Too Expensive. Be aware that one or more of your chosen destinations might be better visited on a separate trip from the UK. Areas such as the Caribbean, some European cities, Russia or Central Asia might make your RTW fare too expensive. If, for instance, you're looking at Prague,

Hong Kong, Singapore, Australia, New Zealand, Tahiti and Los Angeles, you might have to drop Prague. This is because at certain times of the year all of these destinations except Prague can be visited for £843 (plus tax). Having Prague on your itinerary, however, would push the price of your RTW ticket up to £1249 plus tax. So, forget it – go there another time and take advantage of a low, no-frills fare (around £80 return).

In addition, though there are almost limitless possible RTW routes, wanting to visit certain places (or certain combinations of destinations) can prove very costly. For instance, going to South Africa instead of Southeast Asia might not push the price up much, but going to South Africa *and* Southeast Asia might. The same applies to South and North America. RTW tickets that don't include Australia or New Zealand are generally more expensive.

When you've decided where you want to go, think about the order in which to visit your destinations. Are you visiting friends or family and do you need to fit in with their dates? Do you want to be in a particular city for a festival or special event? You also need to work out how long you want to spend in each area. Think about what you want to see and do when you're there. Remember that you don't have to fly everywhere and that many parts of your itinerary will lend themselves perfectly to a 'surface sector'. For instance, you might want to do the odd road trip between Los Angeles and New York or San Francisco. You might want to rough it between Nairobi and Cape Town or Bangkok and Bali, and go by rail between Vancouver and Toronto or Adelaide and Darwin. Rather annoyingly, the kilometres you cover overland will still count as part of your total mileage package on most tickets (the main exception is Oneworld Explorer, which uses a different system based on the number of flights you take per continent rather than the total mileage flown.)

By the time you've got this far you probably feel like a well-seasoned traveller, even though you haven't gone anywhere yet. You are also ready to talk to a specialist travel agent. Your cheapest, most basic RTW ticket goes London–Bangkok (or Singapore)–Sydney–Los Angeles–London. The cost will depend on what fares are available at the time you want to go but will start from £843, plus tax. The main RTW deals are put out by members of the major airline alliances, and the more meat you put on the bones the more expensive your ticket becomes. See the table outlining the main RTW deals and criteria on the next page. All fares exclude prepayable taxes (usually between £70 to £125 depending on each routing).

When discussing your trip with a specialist travel agent, think about the following:

- If you live a long way from the capital, ask about flying out of your local airport as well a London one. Many fares allow provincial departures at little or no extra cost.
- Don't stopover in too many places – you won't be able to do them justice. Every travel agent will tell you that most travellers cram too much into their itinerary.
- If you're travelling through a lot of different regions, you might not fit them all in during the so-called 'best time to visit.' Don't spend too much time and effort trying to achieve the impossible.
- In general, the best RTW fares tend to be for departures just after Easter until mid-June. Next best is February until Easter, and then November. The fortnight before Christmas is the worst of all – don't even go there (so to speak).
- When booking a ticket your travel agent will ask you to give exact dates for all the flights on your ticket, even though you may be unsure of the timing on some. Don't worry, apart from your departure date from the UK, all other dates are usually 'provisional'. Before handing over any money, check the agency's policy on changing these dates before you depart. After you take off, date changes are often free but some airline offices will charge you a small administration fee. Again, be sure to check the rules before handing over any cash.
- Think about your visas when choosing dates. Touching down in Thailand with a 60-day visa and a ticket that says you'll be flying out in four months will not endear you to immigration officials.
- Don't bother asking your travel agent about paying for an upgrade on longer sectors because this will end up being so expensive that you might as well buy a business-class ticket.
- Remember, you don't have to go to Australia or New Zealand – if this is your second

(Continued on page 46)

RTW FARES & RESTRICTIONS

Fare	Major Airlines	Maximum Mileage	Mileage Surcharges
Great Escapade	• Air New Zealand • Singapore Airlines • Virgin Atlantic	46,400km (29,000 miles)	Up to 48,800km (30,500 miles) for £75; up to 51,200km (32,000 miles) for £145; up to 53,600km (33,500 miles) for £215
World Discovery	• Air Pacific • British Airways • Qantas	46,400km (29,000 miles)	Up to 51,200km (32,500 miles) for £275
Voyager	• American Airlines • British Airways • Cathay Pacific • Qantas	46,400km (29,000 miles)	None
Star Alliance	• Air New Zealand • Air Canada • Austrian Airlines • Lufthansa • SAS • Singapore Airlines • Thai • United Airlines	46,400km (29,000 miles)	Three fare levels based on mileage: 46,400km (29,000 miles) – £1249 54,400km (34,000 miles) – £1549 62,400km (39,000 miles) – £1749
Oneworld Explorer	• American Airlines • British Airways • Cathay Pacific • Lan Chile • Qantas	Unlimited; based on continents	NA, but extra sectors can be bought
Global Explorer	• American Airlines • British Airways • Cathay Pacific • Gulf Air • Iberia • LAN Airlines (formerly LanChile) • Qantas	46,400km (29,000 miles)	Based on two fare levels & the season; you can buy up to 54,400km (34,000 miles)
Worldwide Journey	• Continental • Emirates • KLM • Malaysia Airlines • Northwest Airlines • South African Airways • Plus lots of smaller airlines	40,000km (25,000 miles)	Four fare levels based on mileage: 40,000km (25,000 miles) – £1099 48,000km (30,000 miles) – £1239 56,000km (35,000 miles) – £1539 64,000km (40,000 miles) – £1739
SkyTeam	• Aeroméxico • Air France • Alitalia • Delta • Czech Airlines • Korean Air	41,600km (26,000 miles)	Four fare levels based on mileage: 41,600km (26,000 miles) – £1124 46,400km (29,000 miles) – £1249 54,400km (34,000 miles) – £1549 62,400km (39,000 miles) – £1749

Maximum Stops	Good For	Bad For	Reroute Fees	Cost Range
Unlimited – maximum of 3 stops in New Zealand	Asia, NZ & Pacific Islands	Australia (domestic flights), Africa, South America & US	£75 before departure £100 after departure from the UK	£843-1403
7 stops	Africa, Asia, Australia, South America & US	Only bad thing is the maximum number of stops	£50 before & after departure from the UK	£891-1625
7 stops	Africa, Asia, Central & South America & US	As for World Discovery, above	£50 before & after departure from the UK	£1003-1454
Maximum of 15 stops but restrictions in certain regions. No more than: 3 in Japan 5 in Australasia 5 in Europe 5 in US & Canada	Australia, Asia, NZ, Pacific Islands & US	Not great for Africa. If South America is your destination after Australia/NZ, then you'll be in the highest mileage bracket	£55 but not permitted to change the first intercontinental sector	£1249-1749
Unlimited but restrictions within continents. No more than: 4 flight sectors in each of Africa, Asia, Europe, America & 6 flight sectors in North America	Everywhere – if you want to see it all then this is the fare		£40	£1169-2119
10 stops with 46,400km (29,000 miles) & 15 stops with 54,400km (34,000 miles)	Everywhere – but limited by stop allowance		£40 en route but £55 before departure from the UK	£1319-1919
10 stops, plus extra stops for £55 each. Maximum of 5 in each region: Africa; Asia; Central, North & South America; Europe; Middle East; & southwest Pacific	Africa, Asia, Australia, NZ, Pacific Islands & US	South America	£80	£1099-1739
Five stops on 41,600km (26,000-mile) tickets but up to 15 on 46,400km (29,000 miles), plus a maximum of 5 stops in Australia, Europe & US & Canada	Asia, Central America, Europe & US	Africa & South America	Around £55	£1124-1749

(Continued from page 43)

or third big trip then you've probably already travelled around this part of the world. There are numerous routing possibilities across the north Pacific. For starters, try London–Delhi–Singapore–Beijing overland to Hong Kong–San Francisco overland to New York–London for £843 plus tax with the Great Escapade. However, as already mentioned, the least expensive routes do take in Australasia.

- Ask to be put on your travel agent's mailing list. Although you'll receive a lot of information you don't want, you'll also be first to hear about the fares that do interest you.
- To wrap up this section on RTW travel, if you want to go around the world then a RTW ticket is the way to go. Buying tickets as you travel according to whim and fancy may sound appealingly nonprescriptive but will cost a fortune. In addition, you'll always have the onward ticket problem when entering new countries.

Circle Fares

Some circle fares are a bit like RTW tickets that don't actually go around the world (ie they're subject to similar rules and regulations); others allow you to fly to a region and then do an itinerary with lots of stops (sometimes forming a rough circle) before returning to your point of departure. Though often promoted for those starting their long-haul trips in countries such as Australia or the US, circle fares are rarely used by travellers whose trips originate in the UK. In fact, perhaps the most popular circle fare is the Circle Pacific Fare offered by the Oneworld alliance (see their website, www.oneworldalliance.com). This, however, is only sold for travel commencing and terminating in Asia, Australasia or the Americas.

No-Frills Tickets

There are lots of no-frills carriers around the world and an increasing number in Europe (see www.attitudetravel.com/lowcostairlines/europe/bycountry.html for details). Virtually all the no-frills carriers operating in the UK only travel short-haul. If you know how to play the game they can offer great value for money. Simon Calder, author of *No Frills: The Truth Behind the Low-Cost Revolution in the Skies,* says:

A no-frills flight will carry some passengers who booked months ahead for, say, £50; others who bought in the few days before departure and paid as much as £150; and some crafty travellers who took advantage of special 'top-up' promotions aimed at filling substantial numbers of seats at barely more than marginal cost, typically £15. All kinds of variables affect the demand for a particular flight, and the more flexible you are about when you travel, the less you will pay. Tuesday and Wednesday are traditionally the days of lowest demand, though events such as big sporting fixtures and public holidays can distort this. The departure time is also critical: very early, very late or middle-of-the-day flights tend to be cheaper. Finally, you can save cash by being flexible about where you start and finish. A traveller from, say, Leicester is closest to Nottingham airport, but Birmingham, Coventry and Luton are also easily accessible. And anyone heading for Spain's Costa del Sol (and perhaps a ferry to Morocco) can choose from Murcia, Almeria, Málaga and Gibraltar airports. There are hundreds of options – but you could save hundreds of pounds.

TICKETS: THE USA

Online airline ticket consolidators (such as Hotwire, Priceline and Onetravel) offer much to choose from, but since they don't index every airline, they are not always the cheapest option. RTW tickets originating from East and West Coast hubs can be quite good deals, with prices starting around US$1250. Circle Pacific deals out of San Francisco – home to the USA's best RTW ticket brokers – start around US$1000, but can end up costing well over US$4000 depending on your desired number of stops. A popular RTW route is Los Angeles (or San Francisco)–New Zealand–Australia–Southeast Asia–London–New York, or vice versa.

TICKETS: AUSTRALIA

Many established Australian travel companies offer discounts for bus and plane tickets purchased online. There are also companies offering purely online facilities, but it is worth checking them out with consumer and travel associations before purchasing tickets.

RTW plane tickets are available from most travel agencies and are better value than long-haul tickets that normally only allow one or two stopovers. A typical RTW ticket will incorporate four to six stopovers, including the UK and the USA, and cost A$2400 to A$4000 (excluding taxes). Stopover choices include Auckland, Santiago, Miami, Los Angeles, New York, Frankfurt, London, Singapore and Bangkok.

e-tickets

An increasing number of companies are issuing electronic tickets instead of paper ones. You are given a computer reference number and issued with a paper receipt/itinerary in order to show immigration officials that you have onward travel booked. For complicated itineraries, especially those involving more than one airline, you may still receive a paper ticket. Some airlines allow you to choose between paper and e-tickets, but paper versions usually cost more.

Air Passes

To explore a large country in depth (eg Brazil, India or Malaysia), ask your travel agent about air passes. These offer you a certain quota of flights within a single country. The flights are worked out either using a points system, a total mileage limit or a number of flights within one region. They are usually valid for 30 days. Air passes are often very good value as long as journeys involving plane changes are not counted as two flights. You usually have to buy them in advance of your arrival in that country.

IT Fares

Give your travel agent the fright of their life by asking about these. IT (Inclusive Tour) fares were designed so that tour operators could put package holidays together, using especially low fares that are available only when 'bundled' with accommodation. Many airlines have relaxed their definition of inclusive tours. In many cases agents no longer have to book accommodation or other land arrangements for all (or the majority) of your time away to be able to use these fares. They may just need to be sold in conjunction with a few days' car hire or a couple of nights' accommodation but can be much cheaper than a return ticket (even when you include accommodation costs). Though some IT fares used to restrict you to a stay of a month or less, others may allow stays of six months or more.

WHICH AIRLINE?

Sad but true, the older you are the more interested you become in airline safety records. The age of a fleet becomes important and you start to wonder if the planes are nice and new or as old as you are. Some airlines, such as Emirates and Singapore Airlines, fly the equivalent of new-born babes or toddlers, while others are flying around in planes that have beer-bellies and middle-age spread. The age of a fleet also impacts on reliability. Log onto www.airsafe.com for more information.

Chances are, you'll be interested in an airline's frequent-flyer program. Go to the airline's website or call their reservations number to find out what is on offer. Although these programs are becoming less generous, the schemes are generally free to join and might end up benefiting you eventually. Unfortunately, most schemes won't register kilometres flown on discounted tickets towards your totals, and it's often far from easy to find out who allows what. Rules of frequent-flyer schemes often include phrases such as 'kilometres flown on all qualifying fares' and then don't define what is meant by 'qualifying fares'. If you ask your travel agent for clarification, they'll often refer you back to the airline. Some schemes require you to make dozens of return trips to accumulate enough 'kilometres' exchangeable for one return ticket from, say, London to Paris. Bearing in mind how little you have to pay to fly to Paris these days, that's hardly an attractive scheme.

In-flight entertainment might also be an important factor in your decision-making. If so, then fly with British Airways, Emirates, Singapore Airlines or Virgin Atlantic.

BUYING YOUR TICKETS
Buying from Airlines

For short-haul flights this is almost always the best plan. For long-haul flights this is almost always the worst plan. Firstly, airlines use travel agencies to sell tickets at less than you can buy direct. Secondly, airlines won't tell you about deals that their competitors are offering. An agent's job is to compare different to get the best deal for you.

Buying from Specialist Travel Agents

If you grew up wary of travel agencies because you never knew which were bona fide and which were dodgy, then rest assured. The industry has cleaned up its act. Of course, your airline might still go bust, but for the last few years most travel agencies have added a charge of £2 to £5 per person for Scheduled Airline Insurance. This will protect you if your airline goes belly up, as Ansett, Sabena and Swissair have done. If you hear that an airline you're flying with is in financial difficulties, check with your travel agent that you're covered.

There are high-street travel agencies and then there are specialist travel agencies. For a week in the sun you're better off visiting the former but to work out a career break itinerary it's best to go through a specialist travel agent. A good specialist travel agent will be familiar with all routes that airlines fly, will have up-to-the-minute information on discounted fares, and may well have visited many of the places you're considering. If you're booking a RTW fare they will tell you which destinations are pushing up the price of your ticket and if there's anywhere else you could include in your itinerary without increasing the price. They can suggest the most efficient order in which to visit your destinations to take advantage of the best-value fares. They'll also have a view on how long you'll need at each destination and can advise on any compulsory visas that you'll need to obtain in advance of travel.

On the whole, all the specialist travel agents have access to the same fares, so there isn't much to be gained by talking to a long list of them. Where there might be a difference is in how quickly they react to new fares on the market. Specialist travel agencies include:

- **Airline Network** (☎ 0870 241 0011, 0870 234 0729; www.airlinenetwork.co.uk)
- **Austravel** (☎ 0870 166 2020; www.austravel.com)
- **Bridge the World** (☎ 0870 443 2399; www.bridgetheworld.com)
- **ebookers** (☎ 0870 010 7000; www.ebookers.com)
- **Flight Centre** (☎ 0870 890 8099; www.flightcentre.co.uk)
- **Quest Travel** (☎ 0870 442 3542; www.questtravel.com)
- **Trailfinders** (☎ 020-7938 3939; www.trailfinders.com)
- **Travelbag** (☎ 0870 890 1456; www.travelbag.co.uk)
- **Travel Mood** (☎ 0870 660004; www.travelmood.com)

For travel agents in the US and Australia, see the Appendices.

For long-haul or RTW itineraries, by all means try out some possible itineraries using a RTW route planner. A good one is on the STA Travel website (www.statravel.co.uk) – there's a box to tick if you're over 26. However, for these more complicated fares there's nothing like talking it through with an experienced, real-life travel agent.

Buying Online

For point-to-point travel you can find some great bargains online. Have a look at any of these and you're sure to be jetting off this weekend, let alone on your career break:

- **ebookers** (www.ebookers.com)
- **Expedia** (www.expedia.co.uk)
- **Opodo** (www.opodo.co.uk)
- **Travelocity** (www.travelocity.com)

Or, for travel to/from airports you've never heard of in Europe, try the no-frills airlines:

- **Air-Berlin** (www.airberlin.com)
- **Airpolonia** (www.airpolonia.com)
- **Basiq Air** (www.basiqair.com)
- **Bmibaby** (www.bmibaby.com)
- **easyJet** (www.easyjet.com)
- **Flybe** (www.flybe.com)
- **Germanwings** (www.germanwings.com)
- **Hapag Lloyd Express** (www.hlx.com/en)
- **Jet2** (www.jet2.com)
- **MyTravelLite** (www.mytravellite.com)
- **Thomsonfly** (www.thomsonfly.com)
- **Ryanair** (www.ryanair.com)
- **Sky Europe** (www.skyeurope.com)
- **Snowflake** (www.flysnowflake.com)

SURFACE TRAVEL

Britain has some of the best ferry connections in the world. The more unusual ones include Newcastle to Stavanger or Bergen (Norway) on Fjord Line (www.fjordline.co.uk). From Bergen you can join the Hurtigruten (www.hurtigruten.com) coastal steamer on its six-day journey to Kirkenes, deep inside the Arctic Circle. DFDS Seaways (www.dfdsseaways.co.uk) has some interesting routes, including Newcastle to Kristiansand (Norway) and on to Göteborg (Sweden) or from Harwich to Esjberg (Denmark). If you went overland from there to Copenhagen you could pick up the DFDS ferry to Gdańsk. For something really remote, the Smyril Line (www.smyril-line.fo) runs ferries between Lerwick in Sheltland, the Faroe Islands and Iceland. For more-pedestrian destinations log onto www.ferrybooker.com or www.ferrysavers.co.uk.

Another way to see the world is by cargo ship. How does this 84-day RTW itinerary grab you: Tilbury (UK)–Hamburg–Rotterdam–Dunkirk–Le Havre–New York–Norfolk (Virginia, USA)–Savannah (Georgia, USA)–Manzanillo (Panama)–Panama Canal–Pape'ete (Tahiti)–Auckland–Noumea (New Caledonia)–Sydney–Melbourne–Adelaide–Fremantle (Australia)–Singapore–Jeddah (Saudi Arabia)–Suez Canal–Damietta (Egypt)–Malta–La Spezia (Italy)–Tilbury? Prices start from £6225 per person, based on two sharing a cabin. As you can imagine, there are freighters in almost every conceivable port around the globe, many of which take on a limited number of passengers. Passages can be booked departing from the UK or foreign ports and you can travel one way or return on these ships. This is not cruising. There is no entertainment or activities – most of the crew are working and won't be donning a red jacket to keep you amused. The stretches at sea are long and the ports of call are far from mainstream. You're not roughing it, though – cabins are much larger than on cruise ships and you get to eat the same meals as the officers. For further details contact Strand Voyages (www.strandtravel.co.uk) or the Cruise People (www.cruisepeople.co.uk).

If you want to cruise but also hanker after a slightly different experience, then why not think about taking a repositional cruise? Cruise liners have to change their cruising base when the seasons change and they like to do this with some fee-paying passengers on board. These cruises tend to be longer than normal and have more days at sea. They also tend to be cheaper and can accommodate the one-way traveller. Repositional cruises usually travel between the Mediterranean and the Caribbean, from the East to the West Coast of the USA via the Panama Canal, or between the Mediterranean and South Africa. For more information see the Repositional Cruising Factsheet at www.cruiseinformationservice.co.uk or ring ☎ +44 (0)20 7436 2449 to find your nearest PSARA (Passenger Shipping Association Retail Agents Scheme) cruise specialist.

If you commute to work by train then the last thing you'll want to do is travel by train on your career break. In fact, you've probably got 'train strain' and can't wait to leave this everyday battle far behind. But, guess what, other countries 'do' trains so much better than

Britain. You'll be amazed. They run on time, they're relatively cheap, you get a seat, there's room for the children's buggies, and not a single leaf dares fall on a single line. So, don't discount this form of transport. Eurostar (www.eurostar.com) travels to three Continental hubs that can all take you deeper into Europe: from Brussels there are frequent trains to Amsterdam or Vienna; from Lille the warm climate of the south of France beckons; and from Paris you can pick up trains to Italy or Spain. The cheapest way of booking French rail tickets is online at the SNCF (French railways) website (www.voyages-sncf.com; in French). You then need to get yourself to Paris, as the trains depart from there. Otherwise, in the UK try Trains Europe (www.trainseurope.co.uk); among others, they can sell you tickets for the *Trans-Siberian Express*, the *Blue Train* and the *Ghan* as well as a good range of rail passes.

These days coach travel seems to be the preserve of the very young or the very old. Eurolines (www.eurolines.com) operates Europe's largest coach network; serving over 500 destinations. Yes, it's cheap but, to be honest, who wouldn't pay a little more and go by no-frills airline?

ESSENTIAL TRAVEL INFO

Even if you took a gap year or have always been a frequent flyer, it is worth reminding yourself of a few travel essentials.

PASSPORTS, VISAS & TRAVEL INSURANCE
Passports
Just as we've all got used to our titchy, school-uniform maroon EU passports, changes at the UK Passport Service are back. And this time it's personal.

Identity theft is one of the world's fastest-growing crimes. To help combat this, from mid-2005 new UK passports will include a facial biometric identifier that will comply to standards established by the International Civil Aviation Organisation (ICAO). This will be stored on a paper-thin computer chip and inserted into new passports. And, hey presto, this is what is meant by biometric or 'smart' passports, as they are becoming known. Soon, a second biometric – either a fingerprint or an iris pattern – will be incorporated.

So, what does this mean for you? Well, at the time of writing, it was hard to ascertain exactly. However, it appears, not a lot. If you're applying for your first passport, no change is planned in the usual paperwork needed to prove your British nationality. Cunningly, your facial biometric is obtained by scanning the passport-sized photos you get from any old photo booth. However, it is likely that some first-time adult applicants will be called for an interview. If you're renewing a passport, the situation appears to be similar. Your new passport, though, could be shorter than 10 years (due to the computer chip conking out earlier). In addition, you don't have to apply for a 'smart' passport straight away (unless you intend to visit the USA – see the following Visas section); it is anticipated that they'll be phased in over a period of time. For up-to-date information check the UK Passport Service website (www.passport.gov.uk).

The following are various other things to bear in mind:

- **Passport expiry dates** Just like birthdays, expiry dates on passports have a habit of stealing up on you. It might only seem like yesterday that you got a brand new one but actually it was 10 years ago so, yikes, you'd better get a new one quickly. Even if your current passport isn't yet on its last legs, ensure that it's valid for at least six months after you get home from your trip.
- **Blank pages** If you do a lot of travelling for business, or your current passport is the one you used for your gap year or first career break, then you might be running out of blank pages. Unlike in travel guidebooks, blank pages in passports are good. Many immigration officials around the world refuse to issue visas, entry or exit stamps on anything but unsullied Spyrographed pages. You can apply for a new passport at any time (celebs renew their passports all the time because they want the photo to match their new image) – your old one doesn't have to be old.

- **Jumbo** Consider getting what is known in the trade as a 'jumbo'. This is a ?
  instead of the normal 32 pages. It will cost £54.50 instead of £42 but will
  life left in it when you come home.
- **Birth certificate** From 4 May 2004 people born after 1 January 1983 applying
  for the first time had to provide a 'long' birth certificate, ie one that include⸺ ⸺ names
  and place of birth of both parents. If you're about to register the birth of a baby who will
  be accompanying you on your career break, ensure you pay for the 'long' one and not
  the 'short' one.
- **Machine-readable passport** From 26 October 2004 anyone wishing to enter the US under
  the Visa Waiver Program (VWP) needed to have a machine-readable passport (MRP).
  Most UK passports are but some older ones, or passports issued by British Missions
  outside the UK, might not be. (Does your passport have two lines of print on the white
  strip below the personal data page? If so, you're readable.) Basically, what all this means
  is that if you have a MRP passport issued before 26 October 2004 you will be able to
  get into the US on the VWP until your passport expires. If you have a MRP passport
  issued after 26 October 2004 you'll need a visa to enter the US until such time as you
  can get hold of a British biometric passport. This requirement is likely to be postponed,
  so for up-to-date information on entry requirements to the USA check the US Embassy
  website at: www.usembassy.org.uk/cons_web/visa/niv/mrp.htm.

Visas

If you're British or have British residency, the best way to research visas is to log onto the
Thames Consular Services website (www.thamesconsular.com). Sorting out your visa requirements can take ages, especially if you've got quite a few to procure before departure.
So, if you're working up until the last minute it might be worth spending some of that
income on a visa agency. Trailfinders (www.trailfinders.com) has two visa and passport
agencies in London (Kensington High St and the City), and Thames Consular Services
(www.thamesconsular.com) is based in Chiswick, London. In most cases, Trailfinders is
slightly cheaper than Thames. Whether you're a visa-virgin or a visa-vamp, going DIY or
through an agency, keep in mind the following tips:

- **Validity** Nine out of 10 visas are valid from date of issue, which means that you'll be getting most of them on the road. For instance, if you're going to China, a tourist visa runs
  for three months from date of issue, so you'd only get one in advance if this was early in
  your itinerary. However, an Indian visa runs for six months from date of issue, so you
  might be alright if you weren't going there immediately.
- **Children** All visa regulations apply to children. Unfortunately, it's not like visiting your local
  aquarium where children under three go free and everyone else gets a family discount.
- **Transport & visas** Remember that visa requirements can sometimes be affected by the
  transport you've used to enter a country. For instance, if you fly into Cambodia or Laos
  you can get visas on arrival, but if you go overland you must arrange them in advance
  (usually in Bangkok).
- **When to apply** In some instances you can get a longer visa if you apply before you travel.
  For instance, Romania will give you six months if you apply in your home country but
  only 30 days if you rock up at the border.
- **Israeli stamp** If you have an Israeli stamp in your passport from earlier travels, it can cause
  problems when entering countries such as Syria and Lebanon (Jordan and Egypt are OK).
  If you're travelling around the Middle East on this trip and you have evidence of a visit
  to Israel in your passport, consider getting another passport.
- **Visa-Waiver Program** If you want to visit the US and don't qualify for the VWP, you'll have
  to travel to London or Belfast for a personal interview before you're given a visa. See the
  previous Passports section for reasons why you might need a visa.
- **Working holiday visa** Career-breakers under the age of 30 years 11 months can stay in Australia for 12 months on the Working Holiday Program. However, if you're not the right age
  or have already had one of these, you'll be travelling to Australia on an Electronic Travel

Authority. This allows stays of only three months. If you want to remain for up to six months then you'll need a Long Stay Visitor Visa (see www.australia.org.uk for details).

- **Extra photos** Take lots of passport-sized photographs with you. Many countries require two to four photos to process a visa and it's a hassle finding local photo booths abroad.
- **Border crossings** Some overland border crossings are open for a relatively short time during the day, so try to find out the 'opening hours' in advance. Also, they are often closed during religious holidays, so keep an eye on these. Connie Howton had this problem in Israel:

We'd so completely relaxed we didn't know what day it was, let alone what week, month or religious festival. We wanted to cross from Eilat in Israel to Aqaba in Jordan and arrived one hour after the border closed (it was only mid-afternoon). There was then a combination of Israeli and Arab holidays that meant it remained closed for the next five days.

Travel Insurance
Travel insurance might be the world's best cure for insomnia but don't go to sleep just yet. Prop your eyes open with paperclips and think about what you need. At the very least, buy a policy with medical cover up to £5,000,000. Make sure that it covers repatriation – you really don't want a policy that only covers evacuation to the nearest regional medical facility rather than back to your home country. In the words of career-breaker Graham Williams:

I regard travel insurance as essential for one thing only – medical. If I have an accident in a third-world country I want the best care I can get, including a plane to first-world care. I know people who have had to do this. Everything else, luggage, delays etc, is just the icing on the cake.

While you're at it, check how large your medical excess will be – good policies will only charge around £50, but some try to get away with up to £200. Next, make sure that you and your insurance company are talking the same language when it comes to geography. What do they understand by Europe, for instance? Are Turkey and Russia included? Thirdly, be afraid, be very afraid, of visiting a country that the Foreign & Commonwealth Office has advised against travelling to, as this will usually invalidate your travel insurance. Make sure you understand your insurance company's exact policy on this. Some insurance policies will still pay out if your visit is within seven days of your destination being named but others won't. This means that you need to check the Foreign & Commonwealth Office website (www.fco.gov.uk) regularly when you're away, as you might have to make alternative travel arrangements. And, get this, many insurance companies will not pick up the tab for any additional travel costs incurred as a result of your adhering to this condition.

Skipping the obvious travel insurance advice, here are some other points to think about:

- **Repatriation** Ensure this means you'll be flown home and not to the country where you bought the travel insurance.
- **Pre-existing medical conditions** If you've got high blood pressure, diabetes, asmtha etc, make sure you are covered. Usually you're OK if your condition is diagnosed and stable, but all policies vary.
- **Activities** Study the list of activities you're covered for. Often you'll be allowed one or two bungee jumps within a policy but have to pay twice as much if, for instance, you want to go gliding. If you want to try snowboarding or scuba diving then ask about these activities because often they're not included. Also, look at the list of sports you're allowed to play.
- **Children** Infants under two often travel for free under your policy as long as their name is included on the certificate. For families travelling together, sometimes a special premium applies for children aged 18 or less.
- **Geography** Cover for Europe, Australasia and worldwide excluding North America is not too expensive. Premiums go way up when you want to visit Canada and the US.
- **Extending cover** If you suddenly decide to stay away for longer, ensure that you can extend your policy while you're away and only pay for the difference between the two periods rather than taking out a fresh policy for your additional time away.

- **Baggage & personal effects** Keep receipts at home for anything you might lose on your travels.
- **Curtailment & cancellation** If you're travelling *en famille*, make sure that everyone's covered should you need to cancel or curtail your trip due to the sudden illness of one family member.
- **Acts of war & terrorism** No-one will give you cover for nuclear, chemical or biological warfare, but some policies do insure you against acts of terrorism.
- **Happy birthday** Many policies are unashamedly ageist – often the price will double if you're 65 or over and on some policies restrictions apply if you're younger. Some gap-year policies are available only to travellers under 35.
- **Zzzzzzzzzzzzzzzzzzzzz**

Some of you will have travel insurance at work. If you do and you've negotiated a sabbatical, don't assume that this cover will continue or be appropriate for your career break. Chances are you'll join the rest of us and will be wading through piles of policy small print from various insurance companies, tour operators and travel agents. A few places to start your reading include:

- **Columbus Direct** (☎ 0845 330 8518; www.columbus-direct.com) A Super Policy with an additional Adventure Pack costs £393.50 for 12 months' worldwide cover. (There's a 10% discount for YHA members.)
- **Direct Line** (☎ 0845 246 1637; www.directline.com) The Discoverer Policy is prescriptive and you can't buy any extra activities, but it does come as cheap as £245 for 12 months' worldwide cover.
- **Endsleigh** (☎ 0800 028 3571; www.endsleigh.co.uk) Its Backpacker cover is limited to those under 35 and comes in at £297 for 12 months, worldwide. The Globetrotter policy costs £464 and the Extreme Activity policy £929 for the same period of time.
- **STA Travel** (☎ 0870 160 6070; www.statravel.co.uk) The Premier policy has unlimited medical expenses and costs £379 for 12 months' worldwide cover. A good range of activities are automatically covered but repatriation is to the UK only.
- **Trailfinders** (☎ +44 (0)20 7938 3939; www.trailfinders.com) There's only the one policy and it covers all the points mentioned earlier. Twelve months' worldwide cover will cost you £447.

MONEY, MONEY, MONEY

Thanks to online banking, organising your money at home, while you're away, is a piece of cake. Meanwhile, organising your money abroad, while you're away, is like pinning jelly on a notice board. OK, that's a slight exaggeration but there isn't a good-value, one-stop shop solution to the basic problem of converting your money into cash while on the road. The best approach remains taking a mixture of credit or debit cards, travellers cheques and old-fashioned bank notes. Whichever combination works for you, do remember to keep your exchange receipts in case they're needed as proof either within a country or when leaving. Also, if you're travelling with a partner or friend, divide up your financial wealth just in case one of you is robbed or you're separated. And, to find out how much you've lost (to a mugger or a lousy exchange rate), log onto the Universal Currency Converter at www.xe.com/ucc.

Credit & Debit Cards

It's best to take several of these because it'll give you a better chance of finding an ATM that accepts your particular form of plastic. Nowadays, 'hunt the ATM' is a more popular game for the long-term traveller than juggling. The rules do allow you to log onto the ATM locator for the MasterCard family at www.mastercard.com/atmlocator/index.jsp and for Visa at http://visaatm.infonow.net/bin/findNow?CLIENT_ID=VISA. However, ATMs don't exist in all parts of the world, often break down and sometimes choose to eat your card. Check with your bank that your card is linked to a network that will give you access to ATMs abroad. You may also need a new PIN.

The rate of exchange for cash withdrawals from ATMs is often pretty good but that's offset by costly transaction charges. What you need is a card that doesn't charge you each time you get cash out. At present, the best option is a Nationwide FlexAccount Visa debit card (www.nationwide.co.uk). Nationwide will not charge you for cash withdrawals while you're abroad and you get to keep your savings in a relatively high-interest–bearing current account. The only problem with this card is that it cannot be replaced when you're abroad – so, don't lose it.

Other things to think about when taking plastic abroad include:

- **Expiry dates** Check when your cards are due to expire and make sure they're not going to die while you're on the road.
- **Demagnetisation** If the magnetic strip on the back of your card is scratched it might not work when swiped, so get a new card. Some travellers replace all their cards before they travel, just to be on the safe side. (With luck, this problem will be solved shortly by the new 'contactless' cards.)
- **PIN** Remember it.
- **Communication** Tell your credit-card company or bank that you're going travelling and that your user pattern will change. If you don't do this, your card might be blocked by a well-meaning employee who thinks it may have been stolen.
- **Protection** You might want to take out some sort of card protection plan, usually offered by your bank or credit-card company.

Travellers Cheques

For the money-wise traveller one of the issues with travellers cheques is that you're usually charged a commission when you buy them, a commission when you convert them and, to add insult to injury, you often get a rubbishy rate of exchange. Regardless, it's still a good idea to have a few of these in your money belt.

In the UK you can buy American Express travellers cheques free of charge from the post office (www.postoffice.co.uk), as long as you don't want them in UK pounds. This is fine, as you probably want them in US dollars anyway. You can exchange American Express travellers cheques commission-free at most American Express offices when you're abroad. You can also buy commission-free travellers cheques online from the Nationwide (www.nationwide.co.uk), though there is a £3.50 delivery charge and a cash-advance charge of 1% unless you pay with your FlexAccount debit card. These are Travelex travellers cheques and you can change them without commission at most Travelex offices worldwide.

Cash

There's nothing like a few low-denomination greenbacks stuffed away somewhere safe. These are very useful for tips, taxi rides, 'baksheesh', and hundreds of other times when they'll get you out of a spot of bother.

HEALTH

As you'll probably need an armful of jabs and a headful of current health advice, get along to a travel clinic six to eight weeks before you travel. You can visit your local GP but they are rarely experts in travel health. Which immunisations you need depends on where and when you're going and what you plan to do when you get there. Ensure that all your vaccinations are recorded on a vaccination certificate and take this with you, as proof of immunisation against certain diseases (yellow fever, for instance) might be needed at particular borders. Also, check that you're up to date with routine immunisations like tetanus, diphtheria and polio and any childhood ones such as MMR (measles, mumps and rubella).

Next, head to your doctor, dentist and optometrist for your predeparture checkups. Tooth trouble, in particular, can be a real pain in the jaw when you're on the road (especially if it could have been fixed before you left). At the optometrist, get a spare pair of glasses – you'll probably find yourself wearing glasses much more frequently than contact lenses on the road.

On your way home, stop by your local bookshop and get yourself a practical book on travellers' health. Lonely Planet publishes a range of pocket-sized Healthy Travel books or else try *Travellers' Health: How to Stay Healthy Abroad* edited by Dr Richard Dawood. If you're travelling with children, an excellent book to take with you is *Your Child's Health Abroad* by Dr Jane Wilson-Howarth and Dr Mathew Ellis. A new edition of this book was published in December 2004.

When you have a window in your diary, get online. There's some really informative international sites out there telling you everything you ever wanted to know about travel health but never dared to ask:

- **Centers for Disease Control & Prevention** (www.cdc.gov/travel)
- **Department of Health** (www.dh.gov.uk/PolicyAndGuidance/HealthAdviceForTravellers)
- **Diabetes Travel Information** (www.diabetes-travel.co.uk)
- **Diving Medicine Online** (www.scuba-doc.com)
- **fit for travel** (www.fitfortravel.scot.nhs.uk)
- **Hospital for Tropical Diseases** (www.uclh.org/services/htd/advice.shtml)
- **International Society of Travel Medicine** (www.istm.org)
- **Malaria Foundation International** (www.malaria.org)
- **Masta** (www.masta.org)
- **Nomad Travel Clinics** (www.nomadtravel.co.uk)
- **Shoreland** (www.tripprep.com)
- **The Travel Doctor TMVC** (www.tmvc.com.au)
- **World Health Organisation** (www.who.int/ith)

Advice for travellers can vary from country to country so remember to follow the advice given by your home country.

This health section was written with advice from Nomad Travel Clinics, UK.

First-Aid Courses

Even if you're the office first-aider, think seriously about some upskilling, especially if your career break will consist more of leeches than beaches. See the Studying chapter (p244) for details of courses. Some of the best are run by:

- **Lifesigns Group** (www.adventurelifesigns.co.uk)
- **Wilderness Expertise** (www.wilderness-expertise.co.uk)
- **Wilderness Medical Training** (www.wildernessmedicaltraining.co.uk)

Children's Health

As a parent, your primary concern when travelling with children will be their health. A whole book could be written about this subject – and, of course, it has been – see the recommendation above. According to the author, Dr Jane Wilson-Howarth:

The best age to travel with children is either while they are taking nothing but breast milk, or after the age of three years. At three they can tell you that they are unwell and so treatment of any serious disease is likely to be sorted promptly.

Talk through travelling with little ones at the travel clinic. You'll probably be surprised at how many countries you can travel to with children of a very young age. You might also be delighted to discover that they can take antimalarial medicines from a very young age. Whether you want to risk taking them to a malarious area when they are young is a completely different matter. A highly malarious area should certainly be avoided until they are much older. Many children suffer from asthma and eczema and travelling can either make these conditions better or worse. Ensuring that they are protected against the sun and making sure they don't become dehydrated will go a long way towards helping them stay happy and healthy.

It might also be wise to do a first-aid course specialising in babies and children. St John Ambulance (www.sja.org.uk) runs a four-hour Lifesaver Babies & Children course and a two-day Early Years First Aid course.

CHILDREN'S KITS

If you're a parent, you could happily fill the entire cargo hold of a jumbo jet with medical or first-aid equipment for your child. However, much of what you've packed for yourself can also be used for them. In addition, take the following basics for the kiddies, but get up-to-date advice from your travel clinic before you depart:

- antimalarials
- paracetamol syrup such as Calpol and an ibuprofen syrup such as Nurofen for Children
- high-factor (SPF 15-20) sunscreen
- travel-sickness syrup or tablets
- antiseptic wipes
- Bach Flower Rescue Remedy – yes, it can 'comfort and reassure' your little one
- decongestant drops like Karvol

Medical Kits

Many travel clinics sell a range of prepared medical kits to suit different types of travel – overland, expedition, independent etc. Nomad Travel (www.nomadtravel.co.uk), for instance, has a range of kits that cost between £25 and £45. Many companies or charities organising voluntary and conservation placements like you to make up a medical kit that they've recommended. Otherwise, what you pack will depend on where you're going and what you plan to do. The following is a list of your basic requirements:

- any prescription medicines, including antibiotics and antimalarials
- painkillers such as paracetamol and aspirin for pain and fever and an anti-inflammatory such as ibuprofen
- antidiarrhoeals – loperamide is probably the most effective or the preventative Pepto-Bismol
- indigestion remedies such as antacid tablets or liquids
- oral rehydration sachets and measuring spoon for making up your own solution
- antihistamine tablets for hay fever and other allergies or itching
- sting-relief spray or hydrocortisone cream for insect bites
- sunscreen and lip salve with sunblock
- insect repellent (DEET or plant-based) and permethrin (for treating mosquito nets and clothes)
- water-purifying tablets or water filter/purifier
- over-the-counter cystitis or thrush treatment (if you're prone to either of these)
- calamine cream or aloe vera for sunburn and other skin rashes
- antifungal cream
- cough and cold remedies, and sore-throat lozenges
- eye drops
- laxatives (particularly if you're headed to an area like Mongolia, where there's little fibre in the diet)

Remember, keep your medical kit in your day pack – it's going to be of limited use in an emergency if it's back at your hotel.

First-Aid Equipment

Remember to stow this in your luggage on flights because anything sharp in your hand-luggage will get confiscated:

- digital thermometer (not mercury – can you imagine if it broke?)
- scissors
- tweezers to remove splinters, cactus needles and ticks
- sticking plasters
- gauze swabs and adhesive tape

- bandages and safety pins
- non-adhesive dressings
- antiseptic powder or solution (eg povidone-iodine) and antiseptic wipes
- wound-closure strips
- syringes and needles – ask your doctor for a note explaining why you have them

If you're really going remote then you'll also need:

- antibiotic eye and ear drops
- antibiotic cream or powder
- emergency splints (eg Sam splints)
- an elasticated support bandage
- a triangular bandage for making an arm sling
- a dental first-aid kit (either a commercial kit, or make up your own – ask your dentist to advise you)

Natural Remedies

Some alternatives to conventional medicine that you might want to consider are:

- **Tiger balm** Use for muscular aches and pains, tension headaches, menstrual cramps and tired, aching feet. It's an excellent chest rub if you're coming down with a cold and can also bring speedy relief from insect bites.
- **Calendula tincture** This is a herbal antiseptic that helps heal cuts and grazes. It can be used neat on boils or pimples. Diluted with clean water it can treat blisters and yeast infections such as athelete's foot. You can also gargle with it to treat simple mouth and throat infections.
- **Arnica ointment** This is excellent for deep-tissue trauma such as pulled ligaments, bruising and sprains. Do not apply it to broken skin.
- **Bayberry tincture** This helps prevent and treat bacterial or parasitical gut infections. Seasoned herbal travellers like to take five drops of standard tincture each morning to protect their digestive tracts. It is not suitable in pregnancy.
- **Lavender oil** This can be used neat on bites and stings and rubbed into aches and pains. It aids relaxation and promotes good sleep. Mixed with carrier oil it's excellent for sunburn and is a soothing massage for an upset stomach.

For more information on herbal medical matters, contact the **National Institute of Medical Herbalists** (☎ +44 (0)1392 426 022; www.nimh.org.uk).

Health-Related Documents

When travelling, try to keep the following information in your day pack:

- vaccination certificate
- travel insurance emergency number and serial number of your policy
- contact details of the nearest embassy
- summary of any important medical conditions you have
- contact details of your doctor back home
- copy of prescription for any medication you take regularly
- details of any serious allergies
- blood group
- prescription for glasses or contact lenses
- letter from your doctor explaining why you're carrying syringes in a medical kit

Malaria

Malarial risks and antimalarial drug–resistance patterns change constantly. If you're going to a malarial area, you need to get expert advice from your travel clinic on how to prevent catching this potentially fatal mosquito-borne disease.

There are a number of antimalarial medicines on the market and they all have their pros and cons (see www.fitfortravel.scot.nhs.uk for a full list). Your friendly travel clinic will discuss these with you and come up with the best solution for you and the type of trip you're planning. Remember, if you need to take antimalarial pills, you generally have to start taking them at least one week before you leave and continue taking them for four weeks after you depart a malarial area. This means you could still be popping pills by the office water cooler weeks after you're back at work.

It is easy to forget that antimalarials do not stop you getting malaria – they just suppress it if you do. This means that you always need to combine antimalarials with proper precautions against being bitten in the first place. These should include:

- changing into permethrin-treated long-sleeved tops, long trousers and socks at dusk
- using a DEET-based inspect repellent on any exposed skin
- using electric insecticide vaporisers or burning mosquito coils in your room or under restaurant tables
- spraying your room, tent or campervan with a knock-down insect spray before you bed down for the night
- sleeping under a permethrin-treated mosquito net.
- travelling at the height of the dry season – the risk of being bitten and therefore catching malaria is far less at this time

How do you know if you've caught malaria? You'd think this was an easy question to answer. It isn't. What you need to remember is that any flu-like symptom could be malaria. If you're feeling off colour in a malarial area then go and get a test. In Thailand, for instance, most local hospitals will test you on the spot – it takes 20 minutes and costs 20 pence.

Staying Healthy

Even though you bought travel insurance with medical cover of up to £5,000,000, you don't really want to use it. If you've heard it all before, then read through this section quickly, but don't forget: it's better to be safe than sorry.

ACCLIMATISATION

This noun covers a multitude of conditions – heat, sun, cold and altitude. At the most basic level, you need to give yourself a break (and not just from your career) when you arrive in a new place. Whether you're moving between hot and cold or high and low, take your time. Don't hire mountain bikes the moment you land, and, most importantly, drink lots of fluids. Whether you're hot or cold, this can also be a good moment to use your rehydration salts, as the heat makes you sweat a lot and the cold makes you pee more.

Protection from the sun is pretty basic stuff but, if you do forget, try to remember the Aussie mantra of Slip, Slop, Slap – slip on a shirt, slop on some sunscreen and slap on a hat. Don't get it confused with Lick, Sip, Suck, which is all about drinking tequila.

Acute mountain sickness (AMS) caused by lack of oxygen at altitude (usually over 2400m or 7874ft) is potentially fatal. You might get the early signs of headache, nausea, loss of appetite, difficulty sleeping and lack of energy when you first arrive at altitude. The best way to prevent AMS is to rest. If you're trekking or climbing then you need to ascend slowly, and if symptoms persist you must descend. You must never continue to climb if you have symptoms of AMS.

FOOD, WATER & HYGIENE

Hepatitis A, typhoid, diarrhoea and dysentery (bloody diarrhoea) are all transmitted by poorly prepared food and water. As you never know what might be lurking in your lunch, or cowering in your cup, here are a few tips to digest:

- Always wash your hands prior to eating.
- Avoid food that is peeled, sliced or nicely arranged as this means it's been handled a lot – you might have washed your hands but did the head cook and bottle washer wash theirs?

- Remember that food can get contaminated from dirty dishes, cutlery, utensils and cups; blenders or pulpers used for fruit juices are often suspect.
- Raw fruit and vegetabes are hard to clean. Only eat them if you know they've been washed in clean water or if you can safely peel them yourself. Bananas and papayas are good to eat in the tropics.
- Only eat food that's freshly prepared and piping hot – avoid the hotel buffet like the plague.
- Be wary of ice cream and seafood – though for totally different reasons.
- Think twice before you drink water from the tap or brush your teeth with it.
- Drink bottled water or canned drinks where possible.
- Avoid ice cubes in drinks, as they may have been made from contaminated water.
- The simplest way of purifying water is to bring it to a 'roaring boil', otherwise use chlorine, iodine or a water purifier.

Despite all these precautions, it's likely you will get Delhi belly (wherever you are in the world). When you do, you must drink as much as you can to ensure you don't become dehydrated.

INSECT BITES
Those mozzies have a lot to answer for. It isn't only malaria that is transmitted by mosquitoes but also diseases such as yellow fever, Japanese encephalitis and dengue fever. The carrier of this last disease is a daytime biting mosquito and is especially prevalent in Central America, Malaysia and Queensland (Australia). In these parts of the world you'll have to practise bite avoidance – see the section on malaria (p57) – 24 hours a day. Ensure that you pack an effective DEET-based insect repellent – one application should last up to four hours. Otherwise, there are lemon eucalyptus–based natural products on the market that are pretty effective (DEET is still your best bet in high-risk areas). For clothes and mosquito nets you need permethrin, a pyrethrum-like compound that repels mosquitoes, fleas, ticks, mites, bedbugs, cockroaches and flies (sounds too good to be true, doesn't it?).

HEPATITIS B
Did you know that hepatitis B is spread by bodily fluids, including saliva? This means it's wise not only to practise safe sex but also safe snogging (ie it's not how you snog but whom).

RABIES
You don't have to be bitten by a rabid-seeming beast (it doesn't have to be a dog) to be at risk of rabies. For starters, the animal may seem as cute and placid as any puppy in *101 Dalmations*. In addition, you need only to be scratched or licked by an animal with rabies in order to be at risk of the disease and only Cruella De Vil deserves this fate.

STAYING SAFE
Road accidents are the single most common reason for injury or death when travelling abroad. This is closely followed by water-related traumas (eg jet-ski accidents or drowning) and hotel-related problems (eg falling from balconies, diving in at the shallow end of a swimming pool). So, keep off the roads, stay away from the beaches and pitch a tent for a safe but rather grim career break. If you haven't done a big trip in a while, why not consider taking a safety refresher course for independent travellers with a group like Planet Wise (www.planetwise.net)? They run a one-day course for career-breakers – see p242 for details.

Travel Hotspots
The UK Foreign & Commonwealth Office website (www.fco.gov.uk) has two grades of warnings. The 'amber' list advises against 'all but essential travel on business' and the 'red' list, or Premier League, is places where you should not visit at all. At any one time there

are usually over 40 countries considered unsafe enough to feature on this part of the site. The information is updated daily. If you travel to a place on either list it will invalidate your travel insurance; see the Travel Insurance section (p52) for full details.

The Bureau of Consular Affairs at the US Department of State (www.travel.state.gov) tends to be more specific in its advice – reading its information for Mexico City, for example, you wonder how anyone ever gets out alive. The information on the Australian Department of Foreign Affairs and Trade site (www.dfat.gov.au/travel) is worth reading through, too.

If things start to hot up when you're on the road, keep up to date with events by logging on or tuning in to the BBC World Service news (www.bbb.co.uk/worldservice) and, most importantly, by talking to local people and travellers.

Theft

The time to get cash out of your money belt and into your pockets is in your hotel room or in a restaurant loo. It isn't at the market, in the shop or at the bar, where everyone can see where you keep your valuables. As Michelle Hawkins found, it is also unwise to carry your money belt instead of wearing it:

I was in a market in Kinabalu, Borneo. My day pack was on my back. Classic scenario whereby it suddenly got crowded, I felt something, pulled the pack round, and it had been ransacked. Stupidly, it was so hot and sweaty that I'd put my money belt in the pack instead of wearing it. My entire ID had gone: passport, air ticket back to mainland Malaysia, money, credit cards and address book (aaargh!).

If you're travelling as a couple or with friends, have a system for looking after your belongings. Louise Jones set one up:

Apart from losing an old T-shirt and a pair of shorts off a washing line in the Philippines, we lost nothing to theft. Being alert helps. What always surprised me was the number of people who put everything of value in a bum bag then left it on the back of a chair, then wondered at their bad luck when it got nicked. All our valuables were concealed deep in money belts. We also had a formal system of handing over responsibility for watching kit, where the other person had to acknowledge responsibility verbally, so there was never a question of 'I thought you were watching that?'. We also used karabiners and thick para cord to clip bags to each other and to furniture. A snatch thief would find that instead of grabbing a small bag he would also be carrying another one weighing 30kg plus a couple of chairs, hampering that quick getaway. This never happened, fortunately.

Most ne'er-do-wells operate as a team (usually three, usually men) and want you to be stationary while they operate. However, this gender assumption is not always the case, as Michelle Hawkins (again) explains:

In Otavalo market in Ecuador I was suddenly surrounded by four little old Indian ladies. They started pushing in on me from all sides, with hands grabbing my waist for my money belt. I managed to break free of the ambush. Had I really been overrun by a bunch of grandmothers? I took my day pack off, and saw that it had been slashed with a knife – just centimetres from my ribs.

Beware also if you're stopped in the street for directions, a light, a chat etc. Try not to stop; keep going and if you twig to what's going on accelerate out of trouble.

There are lots of other basic, common-sense precautions you can take to avoid being robbed or mugged:

- **From the start** You're at your most vulnerable when you first set off on your trip. You haven't got into the rhythm of travelling, you haven't established all your safety routines and you're less worldly-wise now than you will be in a few months' time.

- **First night's accommodation** If you haven't already booked somewhere, this is not a time to be choosy about where you stay. Find the first half-decent place you can and hole up for the night. You can look for something better, classier or cheaper in the morning. At all costs avoid walking around at night with all your possessions while you look for your ideal hotel or hostel.
- **ATMs** Watch out when you use these, particularly when they're right on the street. It is very obvious that you're getting money out and if you're not careful it is obvious too where you're putting it for safe keeping. In cities with a reputation for street crime take extra precautions. If you are travelling with a partner, have one of you on the look out for trouble (cross the road to get a better view of the street scene) while the other does the banking. Be very cautious for the rest of the day – it is no coincidence that most travellers get mugged on the day they've got money out.
- **Hotel safe** Use it, and get a receipt for your goods.
- **Hotel lifts** Regardless of where you're staying, beware in hotel lifts, particularly if you're on your own. Never take a lift to the basement floor on your own.
- **Pack safe** Buy yourself a stainless-steel net that fits around the outside of a backpack or bag. These are almost impossible to slash through and most travel stores stock them.
- **Cooperate** OK, you've heard it a million times, but if it happens to you: cooperate. Give the thieves or the muggers everything but your life.

Scams

Who, at some time on their travels, hasn't fallen for the odd scam or two? Indeed, many of you will currently be looking for somewhere to store that carpet you bought on your gap year. You know, the one you were told you could sell at a massive profit in your home country to that carpet agent who never existed.

Many scams are the same old ones – it's just that each year a new crop of travellers fall for them. Even seasoned travellers who know they should know better can come a cropper when they encounter a masterful performance. James Ingham admitted:

I'm slightly embarrassed to say that I fell foul of one scam, changing money on the street in Dar es Salaam, Tanzania. My friend and I did it only as we desperately needed money that night and everywhere else had closed. When we were handed the wad of notes by the moneychanger (who was an accomplice) we counted it and found it a few dollars short. He then apologised, recounted it in front of us and then handed the bundle over, bound together with an elastic band. Fine we thought and off we went, but on checking later we discovered the bundle had somehow been swapped. I do not know to this day how they did it, but they did – I guess that's their livelihood so they're bloody good at it – but we felt sick. It was less then US$50 each but enough to hit us hard. Don't be tempted to deal with these crooks who seem so nice and chatty!

Many scams play on your good nature, your natural urge to help someone in distress or your willingness to receive help from others. These types of scams are the most destructive, as they often shake your belief or trust in a whole country or people. They are also the most difficult to avoid, because it isn't until afterwards that you realise you've been targeted.

Without becoming paranoid, the best course of action is to travel with a hip flask of healthy suspicion and a water bottle of trust.

Drugs

Drug offences in Algeria, Indonesia, Iran, Malaysia, Singapore and Thailand can incur the death penalty. In Cyprus, Greece, Jamaica, Spain, Tunisia or Venezuela you're looking either at a decade or so in prison or sometimes life. Log onto the Prisoners Abroad website (www.prisonersabroad.org.uk) to put you right off trying any sort of soft or hard drug while abroad, even if you don't inhale. Take care not to become an unwitting accomplice in South or Central America, India, Thailand or Jamaica.

Hitchhiking
You know the risks. You know the rewards. You decide.

If You Get into Trouble
You'll need a police report to claim on insurance, replace travellers cheques or get a new passport. There's a high likelihood that the local police won't be particularly interested in your case unless it's a serious assault, but them's the rules. If your passport gets stolen abroad, report it to the local police, then contact the nearest British consulate, embassy or high commission. They will help you report it to the UK Passport Service and provide you with replacement travel documents.

KEEPING IN TOUCH
When was the last time you received a picture postcard, let alone an airmail letter, from anyone other than your mum? Options for communicating with friends and family while away are now endless and increasingly sophisticated. Some are expensive but convenient, while others are cheap but a hassle; a few need to be organised before you travel, and many are easy to set up while you're on the road. This subject is endlessly discussed on the Computers, Cameras & Phones branch of Lonely Planet's Thorn Tree; the queries and questions posed make fascinating reading. Two indispensable resources when looking at how you'll choose to keep in touch are Lan's Technical Travel FAQ page (http://adrianwarren.com/faq) and Steve Kropla's Help for World Travelers (http://kropla.com/index.html).

Integrated Communications Package
'Beam me up, Scotty'! The service offered by communications company ekit does most things except transport you instantly back home. There's a global calling card, a voice-mail service, free email, text messaging, text message alerts, a faxmail service, 24-hour travel assistance, an online travel vault for storing details of your travel documents, and 24-hour customer service in six languages (English, German, Spanish, Italian, French and Portuguese). To find out more, log on to the travel services section of the Lonely Planet website (www.lonelyplanet.com/travel_services).

International Calling Cards
Using an international calling card can be one of the cheapest ways of calling home when you're abroad. These are not usually cards that you insert into a phone to make a call. They usually work by giving you a toll-free number which then connects you to another telecom provider who can offer you a better rate on your call than the local provider can. These cards are often sold in local newsagents and shops in well-touristed areas, but they are not available in all countries, so you may want to organise one before you leave (try looking at www.1st4phonecards.com). There isn't one card that works everywhere, although the ekit Global Phonecard comes close (see above).

Net to Phone
This is one of the cheapest ways of communicating with your loved ones. An increasing number of Internet cafés are offering Net phone technology, which allows you to place calls over the Internet. Techie career-breaker Peter Ritchie has this to say about them:

Ten years ago, I was paying US$6 a minute for a crackly phone link between Latin America and the UK. By 2004, I was paying $0.20 a minute for a mushy but acceptable phone link with home, and looking forward to a further decline in the rate. The difference is down to the Internet. Improvements in the World Wide Web mean that data connections between computers at opposite sides of the world are effectively free, once the fixed charge for broadband access to the service provider has been paid.

Around 2001, the first widespread 'Net to phone' services began to appear at Internet cafés on the backpacker trail. They were fairly primitive, and required the user to wear a headset and dial up a number on screen. Luckily, this was merely transitory technology.

By 2003, a much more user-friendly system became prevalent: the traveller originating the call simply goes into a booth and dials the number, often using the US international access code (001). The reason: many of these systems use a telecom company based in the USA. The Internet café pays the firm a set rate per minute to route the call to its final destination, and adds its profit margin. The impediment to call charges falling sharply is the far end of the call: the charge made by the local telecom company. This is often particularly high if you are calling a mobile phone, which is why the rates for land lines are lower.

Mobile Phones

For emergencies, it can be good to have your mobile phone with you. Using it regularly to make or receive calls will cost a fortune, though SMS can often be relatively inexpensive. If you're going to keep it turned off most of the time, don't forget to turn off voice mail too.

If you're going to Europe, Africa or Asia then a dual-band phone will work in most areas. For a RTW trip what you really need is a tri-band GSM handset, as it can be used in parts of North America as well. For more detailed information on where your phone will and won't work, check GSM World at www.gsmworld.com/roaming/gsminfo/roa_cucc.shtml. This will also tell you if the countries you're going to visit have a GSM roaming agreement with your service provider.

Before you set off, check with your provider that your 'international roaming' has been activated, otherwise your phone won't work in Calais, let alone Kolkata. At the same time, ask whether your phone is SIM locked. If it is then get the code to unlock it, because that means that you'll be able to buy local prepaid SIM cards when you're abroad, making phone calls much cheaper. You can buy local SIM cards almost everywhere in Asia and Africa and in most other places from telephone or service-provider shops.

Finally, have a think about the call plan you're currently on and whether it is the most appropriate for your trip (probably not). As your call pattern will change, it might be best to switch to pay-as-you-go.

Email

If your work email address has always doubled as your personal one then you'll need to sign up with one of the free email services. With Yahoo! (www.yahoo.co.uk) you get a whopping 100MB, with ekit (see opposite) 10MB (and 1MB for attachments) and with Hotmail (www.hotmail.co.uk) a minuscule 2MB. OK, you don't need to be a maths teacher to work out the best deal, if you're not keen on buying more space. If you're going to be away for a long time and plan check your email irregularly then your mail box will fill up quickly. With Hotmail, in particular, the spam (unsolicited advertising) you'll attract will fill up your 2MB in two minutes flat.

Of course, if you've already got an internet connection at home for personal use then many internet service providers (ISPs) will allow you check email via Webmail.

Internet cafes have spread faster than the most contagious computer virus. You can find one in virtually any part of the world. Log onto www.cybercafes.com for a database of 4208 cafes in 140 countries worldwide. You can also usually get online in libraries, hotel receptions and hotel business centres.

Blogs

An increasingly popular way of letting friends and family know what you're up to is by maintaining a 'weblog', or 'blog'. This is like having a website but with five main differences: it costs nothing to set up; it costs nothing to maintain; it's easy to update (no coding); your posts are published immediately; and your blog can be private or public. It's a great way of letting everyone know where you are, where you're headed and what you're thinking. You can even upload your travel photos. For more details see the websites of MyTripJournal (http://lonelyplanet.mytripjournal.com), Blogger (www.blogger.com/start) or TravelPod (www.travelpod.com), which all offer similar services. They'll also send an email to your friends and family telling them when you've added information to your travelogue.

Laptops

Although you're supposed to travel with them, they prefer going to a lunch-time meeting in Crawley than on a six-month dash through Asia. Having said that, some travellers do take them along for the ride, protecting them from the heat, the dust, the humidity and general wear and tear. Most laptop power supplies are designed to be used all over the world, but if you're unsure refer to Steve Kropla's World Electric Guide (http://kropla.com/electric.htm#computer).

Plugging in your laptop to do your email is really only an option if you stay in mid-range and top-end hotels, though some Internet cafés may let you plug in for a fee. If you're intending to communicate this way, then try using a prepaid Internet card, rather than your roaming Internet account. This will give you a list of dial-up numbers for towns around the country, a user name and password, plus a number of free hours. In busy travellers' hubs like Bangkok, cards can be bought in newsagents or IT centres. Check your guidebook for further details.

GUIDEBOOKS & USEFUL RESOURCES

Your first instinct will be to get online to do your research. And, perhaps you want an excuse to maximise your time with your computer now because it's likely you'll be leaving

---

DON'T FORGET YOUR TOOTHBRUSH...

See the Universal Packing List (http://upl.codeq.info), which can be tailored to your trip, for details of every conceivable item you may want to take with you. The following list suggests some useful items to pack:

- **medical kit** (see p56)
- **practical travel-health manual** – take your favourite
- **permethrin-treated mosquito net** – take one even if you don't think you'll be travelling in high-risk areas
- **money belt** – to be worn under your clothes at all times
- **driving licence** – get a photocard driving licence as you often need photo ID when you're on the road
- **padlocks** – for your backpack, bag or bedroom door
- **worldwide adapter** – for your mobile-phone charger or laptop
- **Swiss army knife** – get the model with the scissors and don't take it as hand-luggage or it will get confiscated; see how long you go before you use the corkscrew
- **safety whistle** – keep it around your neck for emergencies
- **Petzl head torch** – keep your hands free in the dark
- **ear plugs** – in case you get the room above the hotel disco
- **gaffer tape** – it'll save your life when you don't quite expect it
- **Teva sports sandals** – wear them white-water rafting or hostel showering
- **marriage certificate** – take a copy; it could be useful
- **glasses** – a spare pair is invaluable
- **compass** – old-fashioned but light, cheap and very handy when you're lost
- **fruit peeler** – essential when travelling with children
- **gravy granules** – good to pour over rice, pasta, potatoes etc when there's nothing on the menu that's bland or familiar enough for your children's tastes
- **traveller guitar** – fits easily into an overhead locker and has a performance-size fretboard, leg rest, and private listening stethophone (no batteries required). See Magellan's Travel Supplies (www.magellans.co.uk) for details.

it behind when you go. However, why not start cutting the apron strings and sample other ways of gathering travel information? If you're planning well ahead then a trawl through *Wanderlust* magazine (www.wanderlust.co.uk), which is published eight times a year, will give you both inspiration and practical information. Otherwise, travel porn can be found in *Condé Nast Traveller* (www.cntraveller.com) and the *Sunday Times Travel Magazine*. The weekend papers are full of travel, with many newspapers producing stand-alone travel sections like the *Independent Traveller*. For background information, current affairs magazines like the *Economist* (www.economist.co.uk), *Newsweek* (www.newsweek.com) and *Time* (www.time.com) are good to read (and not only on planes). TV channels such as *Discovery* and *National Geographic* can also give you some good ideas (that's if you haven't cancelled your subscription to save up for your trip).

Best of all is to get along to some travel events in the lead up to your career break. The Royal Geographical Society (www.rgs.org) and the Royal Scottish Geographical Society (www.geo.ed.ac.uk/~rsgs/menu.html) run a variety of travel lectures, films and events that are open to nonmembers. Local travel clubs (for your nearest, see www.wanderlust .co.uk/travclub/clubs01.html) are always good value. For instance, the Globetrotters Club (www.globetrotters.co.uk) meets on the first Saturday of every month in London and guest travellers speak about their adventures. They also have a bimonthly printed magazine called *Globe* and a monthly e-newsletter. In the spring and autumn of each year there are also a number of travel fairs for independent travellers, mostly held in London and Manchester. The main one is the Daily Telegraph Adventure Travel & Sports Show (www .adventureshow.co.uk). If you weren't planning a career break before going to one of these then you will be afterwards – they're full of inspiring talks, travel deals, travel companies and travel products. For a full list of forthcoming travel events there's a monthly round-up in *Wanderlust* magazine.

To work out the nuts and bolts of your trip, nothing beats poring over a guidebook. Lonely Planet has over 600 titles covering countries and regions, along with books on specialist areas such as language, food and walking. For maps, charts and to see what's available from almost every conceivable travel publisher, get to a branch of Stanfords (www .stanfords.co.uk), which has stores in London, Bristol and Manchester.

For information on planning and researching your trip in the USA and Australia, see the Appendices.

Oh, all right, go online then. Here are some useful sites for travel information and planning:

- **CIA World Factbook** (www.cia.gov/cia/publications/factbook) Here you'll find everything you ever wanted to know about individual countries but never dared to ask.
- **Embassy World** (www.embassyworld.com) There's lots more to this site than just the location of world embassies.
- **Festivals.Com** (www.festivals.com) Discover festivals around the world.
- **i-escape.com** (www.i-escape.com) Get some inspiring ideas about where to stay.
- **Lonely Planet's Worldguide** (http://www.lonelyplanet.com/destinations) This site has information on nearly every country in the world.
- **Museums around the World** (http://vlmp.museophile.com/world.html)
- **Time and date.com** (www.timeanddate.com) And also the times of sunrise, sunset, international country codes and city coordinates.
- **Tourist Office Worldwide Directory** (www.towd.com)
- **TravelNotes** (www.travelnotes.org/events) Plan your itinerary to fit in with some special or spectacular world events or seasons.
- **Whatsonwhen** (www.whatsonwhen.com) Don't miss out on what event is being held where.
- **World Heritage List** (http://whc.unesco.org) The 754 properties the World Heritage Committee has inscribed on the World Heritage List.
- **World Information** (www.worldinformation.com) Read up on business, economic and political information on every country in the world.

ETHICAL TRAVEL

Ecotourism, responsible travel, sustainable tourism, ethical travel, fair-trade tourism – so many terms, shades of meaning and sometimes bandwagons for travel companies to jump on. Don't be put off by these labels or the bad press that some of these terms have generated. Tourism is the world's largest industry with upwards of 700 million people travelling internationally each year. With these types of numbers, it is crucial that travel and tourism should strive to protect and conserve natural and social environments, rather than destroying them.

The world woke up to this idea in the late '80s. The recent travel boom had taken the industry by surprise and no-one was ready for its negative impact, particularly in the more remote regions of the world. Suddenly, Nepal hit the headlines because its forests were being cut down to build accommodation for trekkers. Goa became a hot issue due to local water shortages caused by the construction of new hotels for Western tourists on cheap charter holidays.

In the '90s, ecotourism became all the rage. Countries with delicate flora and fauna and a strong cultural heritage started promoting themselves as holiday destinations. Visitors had to travel in such a way that preserved what they'd come to see as well as contributing to the local economy. Costa Rica, with its fragile rainforests, became the world leader in this type of tourism. It was a successful combination. Eco-lodges and eco-tours sprang up in many parts of the world. Unfortunately, not all of them were genuine. Some operators saw it as a free meal ticket and bunged 'eco' in front of everything they did. Obviously, this started to give ecotourism an undeserved bad name. Thankfully, the industry has worked through this difficult phase, culminating in the year 2002 being designated International Year of Ecotourism. This was also the year that saw the first World Ecotourism Summit organised by the World Tourism Organization (www.world-tourism.org) and the United Nations Environment Programme (www.unep.org). It goes without saying that, done properly, ecotourism is one of the most sustainable forms of tourism. Done properly, though, ecotourism is low impact on the environment but often very high impact on your wallet.

It is, however, only one frame of the total tourism picture. Ultimately, sustainable tourism is what the world needs in the long term and what many travellers and travel companies are signing up for. There's no one definitive code of practice but its criteria encourage us all to travel responsibly and to:

- **Be informed** Read up on the countries you intend to visit so that you arrive with an understanding of their political, economic and cultural diversity.
- **Conserve resources & protect the environment** Be considerate when using water, electricity and fuel. Instead of hiring a car, think about walking, cycling or using public transport. Minimise your contribution to pollution – use biodegradable products and take your expendables home, especially used batteries. Ask your hotel or hostel if it has a green policy or recycles and minimises waste and pollution. Some international hotels and luxury lodges are members of the Green Hotels Association (www.greenhotels.com) so if you're planning on living it up you can make sure it doesn't cost the earth.
- **Respect local culture & traditions** Don't cause offence by gesture or dress, whether you're at the beach or in a place of worship. Learn a few words of the local language. Be sensitive when taking photos, particularly of people.
- **Benefit the local communities** Make sure that what you spend contributes to the local economy. Stay in locally run hotels, B&Bs or guesthouses; eat from street stalls and family-run restaurants; shop in markets; drink the local beer (not the imported stuff); use public transport; and hire local or indigenous guides. Also, be aware and be fair when bargaining.

Bear in mind that ethical travel is rarely black and white; often it will resemble the murky grey of your travelling underwear. For instance, which countries would you not visit due to their human rights record, if any? What is your position on travelling to Myanmar (Burma) and on boycotts of countries? (See http://shop.lonelyplanet.com/misc_images/burma.pdf for a discussion of some of these issues.) Should tourism be allowed in Antarctica or is this its main protection against being mined? There are no easy answers to any of these questions but part of being an ethical traveller is being ready to ask them.

ETHICAL TRAVEL RESOURCES

- **Amnesty International** (www.amnesty.org)
- **British Airways Tourism for Tomorrow Awards** (www.britishairways.com/travel/crt4t/public/en_gb) These are annual awards for sustainable tourism projects; a list of past winners makes interesting reading.
- **Climate Care** (www.co2.org) This organisation encourages people to become 'carbon neutral' by planting trees to counter the effects of carbon dioxide emissions. Enter the number of kilometres you intend to fly by plane into their Air Travel Calculator and get ready for a shock. There's also a list of companies, some of them tour operators, that have signed up to offset the emissions from clients' flights.
- **Earthscan** (www.earthscan.co.uk) This is the UK's main publisher of books about the environment and sustainable development.
- **Ethical Traveler** (www.ethicaltraveler.com) This US site has an interesting message board called Ethosphere.
- **Friends of the Earth** (www.foei.org)
- **Green Globe 21** (www.greenglobe21.com) Headquartered in Australia, this worldwide benchmarking and certification program promotes sustainable travel and tourism for consumers, companies and communities.
- **Green Map System** (www.greenmap.org/atlas) This organisation published an international *Green Map Atlas* in February 2004.
- **Greenpeace** (www.greenpeace.org)
- **Green Tourism Association** (www.greentourism.ca) This nonprofit organisation is trying to develop and cultivate a green tourism industry within the Toronto region.
- **Human Rights Watch** (www.hrw.org)
- **International Ecotourism Society** (www.ecotourism.org) To find out what's happening in the world of ecotourism, check out this is a useful US site.
- **Responsibletravel.com** (www.responsibletravel.com) This UK Internet site sells holidays from companies that fulfil strict responsible-travel criteria.
- **Tourism Concern** (www.tourismconcern.org.uk) This is the UK's leading organisation dealing with fair-trade tourism. Its book *The Good Alternative Travel Guide* by Mark Mann lists loads of 'ethical' holidays.

No Regrets

Plenty of people use a career break to do something extraordinary. If there is anything that you have always wanted to do but have never had the time, this could be your moment – you don't want to wake up 20 years down the line and suddenly realise that you missed the chance to live your dream.

We say it's better to live like Edith Piaf and say *'Je ne regrette rien'* – I regret nothing! Most dreams are perfectly achievable – the only thing holding you back is making the decision to do it.

The Studying, Volunteering & Conservation, Going Travelling and Living & Working Abroad chapters are for people who dream of doing those sorts of things. This chapter covers some of the quirkier things that you might consider doing on your career break – such as climbing a mountain or writing a novel – that will give you a lifelong sense of achievement.

PHYSICAL FEATS

After sitting behind a desk for years, many people are itching do something physical with their career break. This might be a once-in-a-lifetime opportunity to test your personal limits to the max.

It could be something fairly straightforward such as learning to scuba dive or something truly dramatic such as climbing a mountain or rowing across the Atlantic. Each person has their own threshold and the great thing about organising your own challenge is that you can set the bar at whatever level you like.

Achieving a physical feat can take a lot of planning and money and you may have to train for a long time before you can achieve your goal. However, you'll have something definite to work towards and you can often obtain commercial or private sponsorship if you agree to donate some of the money raised to charity.

The following are a few suggestions based on our conversations with past career-breakers, but the possibilities are endless – you might also consider learning to fly a plane, cycling across Australia, walking the Sahara, riding a horse across Mongolia…

DRIVE OVERLAND ACROSS AFRICA

Travelling overland across Africa is one of the great travel adventures and every year hundreds of people buy old trucks or jeeps and kit them out for the epic journey between the

---

Do It for Charity…

Quite a few people get sponsorship for physical feats by raising money for charity. Most charities will welcome your support and many can provide branded materials to help your fundraising efforts if you contact them ahead of time. The golden rule is that all the sponsor money must go to the charity, apart from the legitimate costs of arranging the event.

If you would rather have things arranged for you, many charities offer special programs where you can take a parachute jump or join an expedition for free if you raise a minimum amount of sponsorship. For listings of charities, contact the Charity Commission (www.charity-commission.gov.uk), Australian Charities (www.auscharity.org) or local state government departments in the USA. (To find state department websites, search for your state and type 'state department' into www.google.com.)

The organisation Charity Challenge (www.charitychallenge.com) arranges sponsored treks all over the world for charity fundraisers, including walks along the Great Wall of China and treks to Everest Base Camp and Mt Kilimanjaro – see the website for the latest challenges and charities that money is being raised for.

Mediterranean and South Africa. This is one of the last hard-core travel experiences and overlanders are a tough breed – equally at home with bribing officials, making tea in the bush, defusing dangerous situations with drunken mercenaries and taking afternoon tea with ordinary Africans and expats.

Understandably, there's more to overlanding than buying a Land Rover and a Primus stove. You need permits and insurance to get your vehicle across dozens of international borders, which can be slow and expensive. You must also be mechanically savvy to keep your vehicle going on some of the most unforgiving roads in the world.

The Overland Africa Network (www.africa-overland.net) has links to hundreds of websites with advice on driving across Africa, including weblogs from people currently on the road. Another good source of information is the Royal Geographic Society's Expedition Advisory Service (www.rgs.org/eac).

Ruth Thomsen drove overland from Cape Town in South Africa to London in a 1978 Land Rover as part of a career break from working as an audiologist for the NHS (National Health Service):

Me and my best mate decided to drive across Africa while very drunk at the hospital New Year's Eve party and we told everyone, so we couldn't back down. Before we left, we contacted the Commonwealth Society for the Deaf and asked how we could help out during our journey – they put us in touch with various missions in Africa and we delivered basic ear-treatment kits for primary health-care workers sponsored by various charities (eg the Lions Club) and taught about audiology at health centres and clinics along the way.

I know so many people since who have planned a trip like this and spent so long acquiring equipment, roof racks, tents, water filters and fitting out their vehicles. My advice is don't do it. All we had was an old tent and two big plastic boxes for stuff, plus a little meths burner for quick cups of tea. This meant we had very little that people could steal and we used less fuel. I have since visited Africa on a number of occasions and I always find myself teary-eyed the minute the smell hits my nostrils and the memories come flooding back.

If the full overland experience sounds a little tough on the suspension, see p96 for details of companies arranging overland trips in converted trucks and buses. However, you will miss out on the sense of total adventure and interaction with local people that comes from organising everything yourself.

DRIVE IN AN ENDURANCE RALLY

If driving across Africa in an old truck seems too mundane, why not enter an endurance rally? There are several historic cross-Africa motor races that will let you relive the devil-may-care attitude of the early motoring pioneers. You need to have mechanical know-how and you must have a car to race in, but the main requirements are a competitive spirit and the desire to give it a go.

The Endurance Rally Association (www.endurorally.com) can provide information on most of the famous rallies, including the World Cup Rally (France to Tunisia), the Classic Safari Challenge (Cape Town to Kenya) and the Peking to Paris Rally (www.pekingparis.com). Another epic race is the Telefonica Dakar Rally (www.dakar.com), which pits motorbikes, cars and trucks against each other on the gruelling 10,000km (6210-mile) route from Paris to Dakar.

Philip Young from the Endurance Rally Association has this advice for would-be rally drivers:

You totally lose yourself in a long-distance car rally – the pressure of time checkpoints, keeping it all going, the planning before hand, trying to beat your team mates. Even if you are not particularly competitive, you will still witness the remarkable scenery of places you would never normally get to visit – such as Peking to Paris via Tibet and Nepal (the next race is in 2007).

The World Cup series of long-distance events, including the Paris to Dakar and London to Athens races, is a great first step into rally racing. No past experience or special licences are required, just a sense of adventure and self-sufficiency. Everyone helps everyone else and the camaraderie is fantastic. Older the better seems to be the advice on cars – simplicity has its benefits, and distance is a great leveller. After a few days of being the tortoise, you should expect to grow horns and become more competitive than you ever imagined.

SAIL IN A ROUND-THE-WORLD YACHT RACE

The nautical equivalent of the great overland adventure is the round-the-world yacht race – a worthy challenge for any career-breaker. Most of the famous round-the-world races are reserved for professional crews, but the organisation Clipper Ventures (www.clipper -ventures.com) runs an annual yachting race for paying crew on the eastbound route around the world.

Ian Dickens, the great-great-grandson of Charles Dickens, wrote the book *Sea Change* about his experiences on the round-the-world race and says:

Like all the crew, I should not really have been there. The mortgage should have had my money, not a life-changing adventure. The year should have been spent bolstering the CV, rather than surfing the Pacific swells. But there we all were, careers cashed in, flats sold, savings plundered, united by the common goal of getting more out of life.

Some of the crew had never sailed. Others, like me, were at home on a yacht but had never experienced the intensity of serious competition for months at a time. Eleven months and 35,000 miles later, we stumbled ashore again and the spirit, tenacity and commitment that came from each crew member was incredible. While the mortgage demanded my return to a nine-to-five routine, the memories – fuelled by a true global perspective – will stay with me for the rest of my life.

The race leaves from Liverpool in the UK in September and heads to Brazil, South Africa, Australia, China, the West Coast of America and finally through the Panama Canal and back across the Atlantic to Britain, arriving mid-July. The £28,500 fee includes all training, meals and other on-board expenses, or you can join six- to eight-week sections of the route for £6000 to £6800. Clipper Ventures is also responsible for the Around Alone race (www.aroundalone.com), the solo round-the-world race.

If the world circuit seems too much, there are less ambitious races that accept amateur sailors. One of the more interesting options is to race in a traditional tall ship with the Jubilee Sailing Trust (www.jst.org.uk), which provides sailing experiences for able-bodied and disabled crews. Prices for able-bodied sailors range from £500 for a one-week experience on the English channel to £1200 for two weeks racing in America.

ROW ACROSS THE ATLANTIC

It might sound like a foolhardy venture, but rowing across the Atlantic is an increasingly achievable dream. Hundreds have now completed the crossing, either solo or in crews of two or four, and the epic journey can take anything from 36 to 110 days, depending on the size of the crew. Of course, you can't do it in a rubber dinghy – ocean rowing boats are highly specialised vessels, with cabins, cooking facilities, water makers and all sorts of emergency equipment.

The governing body for ocean rowing is the Ocean Rowing Society (www.oceanrowing .com). It runs an annual transatlantic rowing regatta from La Gomera in the Canary Islands to Port St Charles in Barbados for solo rowers, doubles and fours. Any fit adult with determination and previous sea experience can take part, but you must raise an entry fee of £8750 and cover the cost of the boat and safety equipment, travel expenses and insurance – most crews spend at least £28,000 in total.

Mark Mortimer told us, just before leaving to row the Atlantic solo:

I decided to do the row partly because I have a need to test myself, to know what I'm capable of. I don't want to get to 80 and regret never having found out. Right from the start, the head of the school where I work was very supportive, and argued that since we encourage the pupils to take opportunities we shouldn't deny the staff. The school sponsored me generously and, in return, I helped promote the school as part of the publicity.

I appreciate that I am lucky in not having a wife or children, in terms of being able to do something like this, and that does make a difference, but the rewards are huge. I defy anyone not to return to work a much stronger, more relaxed person, with an altered perspective. As one of my heroes – Mallory, who died on Everest in 1924 – said 'the danger in life is not taking the adventure'.

CLIMB A MOUNTAIN

What could be a bigger career-break achievement than climbing a mountain? Ascending one of the world's highest peaks is probably the ultimate test of human determination and endurance, and only a handful of people have managed to climb the famous Seven Summits – the tallest mountains in each of the seven continents.

There are companies that offer people with no climbing experience the chance to climb giant peaks like Everest, but there have been some tragic accidents on some of these expeditions. It is far better to train the old-fashioned way, moving slowly up from hill-walking to rock-climbing, then to ascents of smaller peaks before finally tackling the Himalaya. A climbing course is a logical starting point – see p242 for some recommendations.

English teacher Robert MacFarlane turned his experiences of mountaineering trips to the Himalaya, Central Asia, Canada and Europe into an award-winning book on what drives people to climb – *Mountains of the Mind*. This is what he has to say about organising a mountaineering trip:

I was an experienced mountain-goer when I began exploring the Alps and the Greater Ranges, but I am not – and still am not – an accomplished mountaineer, so there was some learning on the job, which isn't always the wisest way to learn mountaincraft. My advice to others is spend years in the smaller hills doing your apprenticeships. If you make mistakes there, the environment tends to be more forgiving.

I recall one moment, having crossed a steep and avalanche-prone slope deep in the Tian Shan range in Central Asia, and looking back to watch the two younger, inexperienced climbers I was with trying to make the same crossing. One of them slipped and almost pulled both of them off the slope.

That moment took root in my brain, and I generated an entire alternative world in which they had slipped, and had fallen, and I had to fly their bodies back to Britain, and tell their parents and...The nearness of that scenario made me think much more urgently than I had before about the dangers of what we were doing, and why we were doing it!

Popular starting peaks for beginners include Mt Kilimanjaro in Tanzania, Mt Kenya in Kenya, Mt Fuji in Japan and Mt Kinabalu in Borneo, though these are more like high-altitude treks. If you already have some climbing experience, you can improve your skills on Mont Blanc in France, or attempt Mt Elbrus in Russia, Mt McKinley in Alaska and Aconcagua in Argentina, which are the tallest mountains in Europe, North America and South America.

Several expedition companies run climbing trips to mountains around the world, including peaks in the Himalaya, for both new and experienced climbers. High & Wild (www.highandwild.co.uk), World Expeditions (www.worldexpeditions.com.au), the American Alpine Institute (www.mtnguide.com) and International Mountain Guides (www.mountainguides.com) are all reliable companies.

Be warned that climbing in the Himalaya comes with a hefty price tag. To climb Mt Everest (8848m; 29,028ft), expect to pay upwards of £25,000. Everest News (www.everest news.com) is the leading information source for people interested in attempting the world's highest peak.

RUN A MARATHON

Since ancient Greek times, the marathon has been seen as one of the great tests of human endurance. The standard marathon course covers 42km (26.2 miles) and most people manage the distance in four to six hours, though the record for the fastest marathon currently stands at two hours, four minutes and 55 seconds. Out of interest, the slowest ever marathon time was six days, 30 minutes and 56 seconds, clocked by a runner in a deep-sea diving suit!

James Tennant ran the Chicago Marathon as part of a career break in the USA:

There are specialist travel companies that run marathon holidays, but I was already travelling in the States so I just sent in an application a few months early and got accepted. I started my training running along the edge of Lake Michigan during the hottest summer in living memory – the humidity and heat were unbelievable and I had to plan a training route that passed a series of drinking fountains and lawn sprinklers to keep cool. By the time the marathon day approached, I was running seven miles every other night and 10 to 15 miles each weekend.

The night before the race, I stayed in and ate bowl after bowl of pasta to boost my carbo-hydrate levels. This kept me going quite comfortably for the first 15 miles but then the pain kicked in. I just had to keep reminding myself that if I stopped now, the weakness of my body would be greater than the strength of my will – that kept me going to the finish line. In the end, I made it into the top 3000 of 13,000 runners and even managed a sprint finish in front of a cheering crowd – I just wish I'd been wearing a Union Jack shirt!

The website www.marathonguide.com has listings of marathons around the world, but be sure to register early – the large international marathons often run out of numbers for runners months in advance. If there are no more spaces, you can sometimes get a sponsored place if you agree to raise money for charity.

Alternatively, some specialist travel agencies offer all-inclusive running tours, with a guaranteed running number, flights and hotel accommodation. The website www.marathon-training.net contains information on all aspects of marathon running, including suggested training schedules.

TREK THE HIMALAYA

The Himalayan mountain range stretches from Pakistan to Tibet and includes the world's 10 highest mountains, as well as providing some of the best high-altitude trekking in the world. Completing the Everest Base Camp Trek or one of the other famous trekking routes in Nepal is a fantastic career-break goal.

John Southgate took a break from a career in publishing and says:

I'd always dreamed of seeing the Himalaya with my own eyes, so I decided to walk the Anna-purna Circuit Trek, an epic 300km walk that winds around the mountains of Annapurna, Dhaulagiri and Machhupuchhare. The trek takes about four weeks and passes through an incredible variety of landscapes, from lush green hills to rhododendron forests and bleak areas with no vegetation at all – it's amazing to see the Nepalis making a life for themselves in this terribly harsh environment.

The hardest part of the walk was crossing the Torung La pass – the air at 5300m is ex-tremely thin, so you are gasping for breath the whole time and you have to keep checking yourself for symptoms of altitude sickness. Overall it was such an incredible experience, and I felt a sense of freedom then that I have never felt before or since. I dream of going back one day and doing the whole thing again!

Lonely Planet's *Trekking in the Nepal Himalaya* has all the information you need, and you can either join an organised trek or go it alone. The website www.trekinfo.com provides lots of useful trekking information. Other useful resources for would-be trekkers include the private tourist-information site www.visitnepal.com and the official site of the Nepal Tourism Board – www.welcomenepal.com.

International companies that arrange organised treks in Nepal include Explore World-wide (www.exploreworldwide.com) in the UK, Wilderness Travel (www.wildernesstravel .com) in the USA and Peregrine Adventures (www.peregrineadventures.com) in Australia. Himalayan treks are also possible in Tibet, Bhutan, Pakistan and the states of Himachal Pradesh, Uttaranchal and Sikkim in India.

WALK THE GREAT WALL OF CHINA

If you want a truly epic challenge, you could become one of the elite group of people who have walked the Great Wall of China. In fact, the wall is a series of walls and it covers over 7200km (4471 miles) in total, but the main wall section stretches 4000km (2484 miles) from the desert province of Xinjiang all the way to Shanhaiguan on the coast northeast of Beijing.

You can't see the Great Wall from space – that was just a bit of Cold War propaganda – but you can still walk the route of the wall. Karen Churches decided to walk the length of the Great Wall in 2003 and turned the expedition into a fundraiser for a breast-cancer charity:

In April 2003 I set out on an epic journey in a bid to become the first British woman to walk the length of the Great Wall of China. I first got the idea after hearing a radio advertisement promoting a nine-day trek along the Great Wall. I thought why only walk part of it when you could walk the whole length! I vowed on that day that I would walk the Great Wall before I was 40. I was just 30 years old at the time and didn't really comprehend then the enormity of the challenge I had set myself – I wasn't what you would call particularly sporty and I certainly wasn't an experienced trekker.

From the beginning, I was keen to share the journey with as many women as possible and felt very strongly about making the event accessible to anyone that wanted to join me. Women were actively recruited to join me for between 10 to 15 days at a time and in return raised money for the UK charity Breakthrough Breast Cancer – to date, the Women's Great Walk of China 2003 has raised in excess of £560,000.

The Women's Great Walk of China has turned into an annual event and you can walk along sections of the route (each section taking 9 to 11 days) to raise money for charity – see the website www.greatwalkofchina.org for more information. If you think walking the wall is a bit of a soft option, there's always the Great Wall Marathon (www.great-wall -marathon.com)…

SWIM FROM EUROPE TO ASIA

It might sound like an epic undertaking, but the crossing of the Hellespont from the continent of Europe to the continent of Asia is well within the reach of any reasonably fit swimmer. The crossing is short but the current is very strong and this is a busy shipping lane, so you certainly need to train up first and hire a support boat. In Greek mythology, Leander swam across the Hellespont nightly to meet his lover, Hero – Lord Bryon followed their example in 1810 and immortalised the event in his poem 'On Crossing the Hellespont'.

The holiday company Swimtrek (www.swimtrek.com) runs specialist swimming holidays all over the world, including the crossing of the Hellespont and swims in the Greek Cyclades, the Isles of Scilly and the Scottish Hebrides. The Hellespont crossing costs £350 for a long weekend, not including transport to Turkey.

Simon Murie from Swimtrek describes his first swim across the Hellespont:

I've always enjoyed swimming – that feeling of total isolation from all around you – but swimming laps in the pool soon became a repetitive bore, so I travelled to Turkey to attempt to swim the Hellespont and recreate the swims of Leander and Byron. I was escorted on the swim by a local boat pilot, who was proficient in the knowledge of the currents and shipping on this stretch of water.

The swim is just less than two miles across, but the water flowing from the Black Sea to the Aegean caused me to swim an elliptical path to the European side. At halfway across I stopped and admired the expanse of water that divided Europe, in front of me, and Asia, behind me. With all the distractions around me from shipping, wildlife and the hilly landscapes, the swim seemed to be over a lot quicker than the 1½ hours that it actually took me.

A more serious challenge is the 34km (21-mile) swim across the English Channel from Dover to Calais. The Channel Swimming & Piloting Federation (www.channelswimming .net) is the main source of information about the channel crossing. The organisation Swimfit (www.swimfit.com) runs an annual charity swim across the English Channel and provides online training support for £9.99 per year.

Other popular sea swims include the 22km (14-mile) Straits of Gibraltar swim, from Gibraltar to Morocco; the 20km (12-mile) Rottnest Channel swim in Perth, Australia; and the 34km (21-mile) Catalina Channel swim at Long Beach, California. For more information see the website www.oceanswims.com.

WORK AS A SKI INSTRUCTOR

For a truly liberating career break, why not train up as a ski or snowboard instructor and put in a season at a ski resort overseas? Training as a winter-sports instructor is covered in the Studying chapter (p221) and working in the ski biz is covered in Living & Working Abroad (p182). Susan Hendry trained as a snowboarding instructor in Canada with the company Peak Leaders:

I felt as though I was living to work, not working to live, and I was tired and jaded and needed a break. I'd always loved skiing but was never quite sure if instructing was for me, so the course looked like the ideal way to find out. I quite honestly feel it's the best thing I've ever done. The course itself was both challenging and exhilarating – there was a good balance between the light-hearted good fun of just skiing and the more serious pressure of the instructor courses and exams. Teaching was new to me but I find it extremely rewarding. The pay isn't great, but where better to be than in the mountains? I found that taking that first step was the hardest part of all but once taken I didn't look back.

LEARN TO SCUBA DIVE

Learning to scuba dive is a great way to get something practical out of your career break. You'll gain a qualification that will let you dive anywhere in the world, and a dive-certification course will open up a new world of undersea exploration, from drifting with sea turtles in southern Thailand to cage diving with great white sharks off the coast of South Africa. See p219 for more information on learning to dive. Gary Wainwright learnt to dive in Australia and the Philippines:

I'd always been a bit of a water baby but I never found the time to take my full scuba certification, so I seized the opportunity while on a six-month round-the-world sabbatical from work. I started my training with an Open Water course on a restored clipper anchored on the Great Barrier Reef in Australia, which was loads of fun, though it took me a while to get used to taking my mask off underwater.

The undersea life on the barrier reef was amazing, but then I went to the Philippines, which just blew me away. I took my Advanced Open Water course in an area that was littered with Japanese shipwrecks from WWII and then went on to a tiny island called Malapascua where I got to free dive with 4m-long thresher sharks! Seeing these beautiful fish pass just feet away from me was one of the most amazing experiences of my life and it made me a lifelong campaigner for the conservation of sharks around the world.

CREATIVE DREAMS

Imagine how satisfying it would be to say, 'Sure, I used to be a stockbroker, but then I gave it all up to become an artist'. Every day, thousands of creative dreams are going to waste because people can't find the time to put brush to canvas or write the screenplay for their first movie. On a career break, you don't have that excuse. Here is just a sample of some of the things you might do on a career break to get the creative juices flowing.

WRITE A BOOK

They say that everyone has a novel in them, and your career break could be a great time to let the inner novel out. If you find a publisher, this could even be the start of a whole new career, but remember that not every book finds a publisher and not every published book finds an audience. A creative-writing course is a good starting point (see p234 for some recommended courses).

You also need to think about where to get your book published. The Publishers Association (www.publishers.org.uk) website has lots of useful advice and listings of contact organisations and recommended books on writing. A literary agent can be a real asset in finding a publisher, as Harriet O'Brien found when she gave up her editing job to write a book about the English queen who was the catalyst for the Norman Conquest of England:

I'd been fascinated by the period of English history just prior to the Norman Conquest for some time, and in particular the English queen Emma, who married Ethelred the Unready and was also the great aunt of William the Conqueror. I was able to undertake enough research into her life – in the British Library and elsewhere – to write a 3000-word proposal which I sent to a literary agent who had been recommended to me by a friend.

Having a good agent is a vital key to obtaining a commission for a book and I was fortunate that the agent liked my proposal and sent it to various publishers. I then visited three publishing companies – a nerve-racking experience, rather like being interviewed for a university viva voce – before I accepted a contract from one company and set about writing the book.

It was basically a step in the dark – you simply get on with the job, researching, blotting up information and then finally some months later beginning the real task of writing. It has been a lonely but absorbing task and I had to undertake other freelance work at the same time to eke out a living – a book advance, unless you're very lucky or have a long track record, is not enough to live on.

RECORD AN ALBUM

David Gray was able to turn an album recorded in his bedroom into an international bestseller, so what is stopping you? If you can sing or play an instrument, you can make a record, but audio recording is a complicated business. The easiest option is to hire the services of a professional recording studio; www.studiofinder.com has a search engine for recording studios around the world.

If you want to go it alone, you need more information than we can provide here. For an introduction to home-recording, visit www.homerecording.com, www.recordingwebsite.com and www.homerecordingconnection.com. Another useful resource is the recording page at Harmony Central (www.harmony-central.com) – there's a discussion forum, a guide to home-recording and a fantastic links page.

John Jackson took a break from his design job to set up a home studio and record his first album, *Strange Attractors*:

I decided to take time out to record Strange Attractors *after realising that, at 33, work had taken over and I no longer even looked at my guitar – let alone played it. Fortunately, I had been earning enough to be able to buy some recording equipment: mixing desk, microphones, software etc. Then I had to teach myself how it worked. I was lucky and had great advice from a guy in the local music shop. However, I found technology to be incredibly seductive. It's possible to make a lot of sounds – but you still need a clear idea of the sound you want to make.*

The trick was knowing when to say 'enough'. I had to give myself a strict deadline for completion – hard but incredibly important. Harder still was the marketing: sending the album to publishers; getting it into shops; entering song-writing competitions; brushing aside rejections – and keeping successes in perspective. I joined an organisation that places songs in specific projects and recently signed a publishing deal with a US music library on the back of this, so I feel that the rewards are starting to happen. But it has taken time. Patience and self-belief are a must – and both can be pretty difficult to maintain.

ACT IN A PLAY OR MUSICAL

You may never play Macbeth at the Globe Theatre, but there's no reason why you shouldn't walk the boards at least once in your lifetime. If you have theatrical blood in your veins, there are amateur dramatic groups across the world that require your talents – the website www.amdram.co.uk has listings of groups throughout the UK.

If you can dance or sing, you can often find a position in the chorus at a musical – ask your singing coach or dance teacher if there are any auditions in your area. Laetitia Clapton found a position as a chorus girl in the musical *Chicago* at the Edinburgh Fringe:

Most of the other people in the cast were trying to be professional dancers, but I mostly wanted to do it for the experience. The auditions were based partly on singing/dancing and partly on improvisation, which was slightly surreal – I had to partner off with another person at the audition and pretend to have an argument. They must have liked what I did as I got the part. We then had four weeks of rehearsals before we went up to Edinburgh.

During the run of the show, the cast stayed in two rented houses, which was a bit like being back in a student house. During the day we had to walk around the streets of Edinburgh in heels and spangly outfits doing publicity for the show and then after the show we would all hang out in the Fringe Club with the other performers. The first night was terrifying but overall it was a brilliant experience, though I'm not sure I could do it for a living. You have to give 150% night after night for weeks on end, which is quite exhausting, both physically and mentally.

If you want to take it one step further, you could always apply to be an extra – Studio Extras (www.studioextras.co.uk) is a specialist recruitment agency that places extras in movies and TV shows in Britain and America.

Alternatively, you could always go pro with a course at drama school – the Conference of Drama Schools (www.drama.ac.uk) represents 21 leading drama colleges in the UK, while Theatre Links (www.theatrelinks.com/university.htm) lists acting courses worldwide.

MAKE A FILM

Robert Rodriguez made his first movie, *El Mariachi,* on a budget of US$7000 and went on to become a major Hollywood player. A career break could be your opportunity to make the jump from home videos to real movies. The website www.film-makers.com is packed with advice for independent film-makers. Absolute beginners can start the ball rolling with a course in film-making (see p232 for recommendations).

Oliver Gray made his first movie during a film course at the Metropolitan Film School (www.metfilmschool.com) in London:

I'm a theatre director and I wanted to take my first step in switching from stage to screen. I was attracted to the Met Film School's Script to Screen course because unlike many courses I looked at, you actually get to make a film. The pace of the course and the focus is intense. They make you do so much so suddenly that you don't have time to panic about it. Shooting my film was the pitched battle after the drill. Stressful, exhilarating, terrifying – these words seem strangely bland compared with the experience. But I felt like I really lived while making the film and I'm dead proud of it. I even love its faults because I'll know how to go about avoiding them in my next film.

LEARN TO PAINT

Feeling creatively restrained at work? Career breaks are all about self-expression and there are hundreds of art courses that can act as a springboard for your artistic ambitions (see p217 for some suggestions). Emma Ablitt took a break from being a full-time mum to learn to paint on an Art Foundation course:

I'd always been interested in painting and drawing and I heard about this course that gave you the opportunity to try everything. It was part time and everything about it seemed to fit. The course started with eight weeks where we got to try out sculpture, ceramics, drawing, painting, printing and textiles, then we got to specialise – I chose fine art because I wanted to learn more about painting and drawing. The course was challenging, as you really had to think and be creative, but I also found it very therapeutic. I was able to express all sorts of feelings and emotions about various things in my life – I'd recommend it to anyone.

BUILD A HOUSE

Building a house is a worthy challenge for any career-breaker. More and more people are building their own homes, from simple wooden kit houses to proper homes of brick and mortar. Before you start, get some advice from someone who has done it before. *How to Design & Build Your Own House* by Lupe DiDonno and Phyllis Sperling and *Building Your Own Home* by Murray Armor and David Snell are two reliable books on home construction.

If you want a helping hand, the British company Buildstore (www.buildstore.co.uk) can talk you through the process and coordinate the project – there's even a search engine for available land on the website. The American website www.dreamhomesource.com has 15,000 house plans that you can browse though online if you are looking for ideas.

John van der Knijff decided to build a house after realising the boat he was living on was too small for his growing family:

When my partner wouldn't agree to living on a bigger boat we bought a block of land in Australia and decided after a few years to build a house. For the first year I was working one week on the house and one week on my art work, and then worked on the house full time for three months before I took a break from my break and went overseas for a year.

On returning I continued working full time on the house, expecting to have it finished in nine months – about when our baby was due. Unfortunately this didn't happen and I became part-time house builder and full-time parent, which slowed the process down somewhat! Three years later (with a couple of breaks to go overseas and travel around Australia) the house was essentially finished.

Building your own home is idealised by a lot of people, but the dream is better than the reality. The crash course in design and architecture was the most interesting aspect of it but I'm happy to have ended up with a house that I wouldn't have got from a builder in terms of quality of work, finish and timbers used. Now for the extension…

If building a house from scratch sounds too much like hard work, you could always go down the *House in Provence* route and do up a property abroad – see p161 for details.

INVENT SOMETHING

Have you ever woken up in the middle of the night with a brilliant idea that could change the world? If so, perhaps it's time to turn your dreams into reality. Coming up with a unique invention could change your life, and a career break will give you plenty of time to build a prototype and find a commercial backer.

The starting point for any invention is a good idea – the inventor Trevor Baylis, OBE, came up with the idea for the wind-up radio while watching a TV program about AIDS:

I was sitting in my chair one day watching telly and a program came on about AIDS and HIV in Africa. The conclusion was that the only way they could stop this dreadful disease cutting its way through Africa was with the power of information and education. But there was a problem – radio was the most effective way of getting information to people but most people didn't have access to electricity, and batteries were horrendously expensive.

At this point I had a flash of inspiration. I imagined myself as a colonial explorer in Africa, with a pith helmet and monocle and a big wind-up gramophone with a horn on the top. I thought to myself, if they could get all that noise by dragging a rusty nail down a piece of old Bakelite using a spring, why not use the same idea to drive a dynamo to power a radio? Often the best inventions are so blindingly simple that everyone says 'Silly me, I should have done that!' The only difference between me and the million other people who thought up the same idea is that I did something about it!

After getting his idea out into the marketplace and changing quite a few lives in the process, Trevor established the Trevor Baylis Foundation (tbf.websfor.org) to promote the science of invention in the UK. The associated company Baylis Brands (www.baylisbrands.com) provides backing for new inventions and aims to help inventors avoid the pitfalls of getting a new invention into the marketplace.

The most serious risk for any inventor is exploitation. Given half a chance, the companies you approach for backing will steal your ideas, so it's vital that you retain the intellectual property rights to your invention. The website www.intellectual-property.gov.uk has lots of useful advice on making sure no-one can rip off your idea. The first step for UK inventors is to register your idea with the local patent office (see www.patent.gov.uk for more information).

TREAT YOURSELF

You've been doing things for other people for years, so why not spoil yourself on your career break? There are loads of luxurious ways you can pamper yourself during your time off work, from booking into a luxury spa to renting Richard Branson's paradise island. The following are just some of the options available.

VISIT A TOP-NOTCH SPA

For years you've had people urging you to get things done. Why not use your career break to book into a top-notch spa and have a team of people urge you to do nothing instead? The idyllic Chiva-Som (UK agent ☎ +44 (0)20 7584 5018; www.chivasom.com) at Hua Hin in Thailand was recently voted the best spa in the world by readers of *Condé Nast Traveller* magazine and it offers everything from aromatherapy and acupuncture to yoga and t'ai chi.

Kate Maiden provides this glowing endorsement of the Chiva-Som experience:

After a hot and tiring 14-hour journey from London, I can remember very clearly stepping into the calm haven of Chiva-Som, being handed a cool towel and a deliciously soothing fruit smoothie, breathing in the scent of lemongrass and breathing out a sigh of relief. My body was in a state of exhaustion through stress and pain (I'd previously been off work for three months) and I decided to go to Chiva-Som as I just wanted to feel well again.

The whole place had such an air of calmness and serenity, I managed to totally relax, floating from treatment to therapy, and for the first time had time to re-evaluate my life. Chiva-Som is not just a luxury health resort, it is a very spiritual place (possibly because of its location in an almost totally Buddhist country), and I met people who inspired me to change my life – in fact I am now halfway through a degree in osteopathy! It is a little slice of heaven, but you can hopefully take some home with you and keep learning from it for the rest of your life.

Another pampering option for the esoterically minded is a holistic holiday. The company Skyros (www.skyros.com) offers a huge range of holidays in Skyros (Greece) and Ko Samet (Thailand), which focus on yoga, meditation, massage, creative writing, self-exploration, arts and drama. The Studying chapter (p218) has more suggestions for holistic courses abroad.

STAY IN THE ULTIMATE LUXURY HOTEL

If you want to see how the stars live, why not book in for a week at one of the world's finest hotels? There are quite a few contenders for the title of the world's most luxurious hotel. Some people swear by the Atlantis Hotel in the Bahamas (www.atlantis.com) – the Bridge Suite is the world's most expensive hotel room at US$25,000 per night. Other people prefer the colonial charm of Raffles Hotel (www.raffleshotel.com) in Singapore, or the Lake Palace Hotel Udaipur (www.tajhotels.com), a former maharaja's palace floating on a serene Indian lake.

Quirkier options include the famous Icehotel (www.icehotel.com) in Sweden, and Kenya's Giraffe Manor (www.giraffemanor.com), where you can feed giraffes from your bedroom window. When it opens in 2006, the Hydropolis Hotel (www.hydropolis.com) in Dubai will be the world's first underwater hotel.

Lonely Planet founder Tony Wheeler has this advice for anyone thinking of staying in a luxury hotel:

There are two types of luxury hotels I go for. One is hotels with a name, a history, a tradition, or some other attraction that makes a stay there part of the travel experience – like the Peninsula in Hong Kong or the Oriental in Bangkok, which undeniably qualify on all three counts. My other luxury interest is those hotels which may not have a history but have that 'Wow!' factor, which often includes romance, style and almost always luxury.

Maybe I'm just too used to slumming or perhaps I'm simply not blasé enough, but I still find that a room which features its own swimming pool has a certain something. In fact, forget about an old folk's home, I just want to dodder off to the Amandari or the Four Seasons Sayan, both just outside Ubud in Bali, when I'm too old for anything else.

If a luxury hotel seems a little impersonal, you can always rent a mansion or a castle. The Big Domain (www.thebigdomain.com) is an agent for mansions and luxury homes around the world and Au Château (www.au-chateau.com) represents more than 50 castles for rent in France.

RENT AN ISLAND

What could be more luxurious than renting a paradise island? If you fancy the ultimate island getaway, there are several up-market real-estate agents that sell and rent out luxury islands in the Caribbean, the USA, Canada, Europe and the South Pacific.

One of the most luxurious islands for rent is Necker Island (www.virgin.com/subsites /necker) in the British Virgin Islands. This beach-fringed tropical paradise belongs to Richard Branson and features a Balinese-style villa with Jacuzzis, a swimming pool and a private staff of 16. You can rent the lot for a modest US$23,500 per night, including meals and drinks, entertainment, watersports and transfers from the nearest island with an airport. You need to book at least nine months in advance – see the website for details of special week-long deals.

Carolyn Wincer from Virgin Unlimited, which manages the island, gives us this summary of the Necker experience:

People who go to Necker are usually entrepreneurs, guys who run large corporations and high-profile celebrities like Elizabeth Hurley, Kevin Spacey, Oprah Winfrey, Steven Spielberg, Robert de Niro… it's a huge list. There isn't really anything quite like Necker. There are other private islands you can rent, but Necker is your home for as long as you stay. The rates are all-inclusive, which stretches to unlimited food and champagne. I think the highlight of staying on Necker is having a whole island to yourself, and the staff, who are absolutely amazing.

If money is an obstacle, you can rent a tropical island for as little as US$3000 a day through real-estate agents such as Private Islands Online (www.privateislandsonline.com), Caribbean Way (private-islands.caribbeanway.com) and Vladi Island Travel (www.vladi-private-islands.de).

CHARTER A YACHT

Even if you don't move in yachting circles, you can get a taste of the cruising life by chartering a fully crewed yacht in the Mediterranean or the Caribbean. Dozens of companies rent out yachts with a full crew, including a skipper, house-keeping staff and a gourmet galley chef to prepare meals on board every night – it's a bit like staying in a luxury hotel on water.

The most popular places to charter a yacht are the Mediterranean, the Caribbean, the Seychelles, Polynesia, and the Whitsunday Islands on the east coast of Australia. Yachting enthusiast and broadcaster Libby Purves has this to say about renting a crewed yacht:

The big advantage of hiring a crewed yacht is that you can go to more adventurous harbours than you might dare to on your own and you do not carry that weight of total responsibility for the lives and safety of all on board, which is quite an awe-inspiring thing to bear. There are two disadvantages though: firstly it is far more expensive that hiring an un-crewed (or 'bareboat') yacht and secondly you may find the skipper and crew a bit tyrannical. Make sure you really can bond with them, and that their duties are clearly delineated. Ask how much work – crewing, cooking, cleaning up – is expected from charterers. On some boats, you can be busy and learn a great deal. On others you can get pretty bored.

There are yacht-chartering companies all over the world that can kit you out with a yacht and a crew. One reliable international operator is Sunsail (www.sunsail.com), which offers both crewed and un-crewed yacht charters around the Mediterranean, the Caribbean, and the Pacific and Indian Oceans. As an indication of prices, you can hire a 43ft yacht with skipper and cook in the Caribbean for £442 per day (not including flights).

If you feel up to the challenge, you could always learn to sail yourself. The Studying chapter (p219) recommends some schools, and the Going Travelling chapter (p100) has a section on crewing as a way of getting from A to B on your travels. The Whitsunday Islands are the world centre for so-called bareboat charters, where you crew your own yacht. You can find charter companies at www.whitsunday-tourism.com.au and www.airliebeach.com. The website www.ebare.com has loads of information on bareboat charters worldwide.

GO WHALE WATCHING

There are numerous places around the world where you can see whales in their natural environment, including Iceland, South Africa, America, Canada, Mexico, New Zealand and Hervey Bay in Australia. Each place has a specific whale-watching season, and sightings are so reliable during the season that many whale-watching boats promise you a free trip if you fail to see any whales.

Jon Finucane from Dublin chose to visit Australia on his career break specifically to see humpback whales:

I'd wanted to see whales ever since I was a kid, so I made sure my time in Australia coincided with the annual migration of humpback whales into Hervey Bay. I deliberately chose a small boat because I had heard from another traveller that you don't get to see much from the big air-conditioned tour boats, and it can't have been more than 15 minutes before we saw our first whales in the distance.

I used almost all my film up taking shots of these distant black shapes, when suddenly two humpbacks breached right next to the boat. The whales can't have been more than three metres away and they spent the next 20 minutes diving under the boat and popping up again on the other side. You did have to wonder who was watching whom – the whales in the open ocean, or us, crammed into a tiny boat. I went back four or five times over the next few weeks, but it was never quite as good as that first time.

If you want the catch the annual migration of humpback whales into Hervey Bay, the season runs from 1 August to 1 November (see the website www.hervey.com.au/whales for more information). The Oceania Project (www.oceania.org.au) runs six-day conservation trips in Hervey Bay every year for volunteers (see p150 for details).

TAKE A BALLOON SAFARI

Soaring over the Serengeti in a hot-air balloon is one of those *National Geographic*, once-in-a-lifetime kind of experiences. If you can get yourself to Kenya or Tanzania, there are several companies who can get you airborne. Balloon Safaris (www.balloonsafaris.com) in Tanzania is the biggest operator, but you can also arrange balloon safaris at luxury camps and lodges in Kenya's Masai Mara.

Darren Beech tells of his experience ballooning over Africa:

We took a balloon safari as part of a longer safari through Kenya and Tanzania, staying at luxury tented lodges around the Serengeti. It was a wild experience – we got up before it was light and transferred by jeep out into the bush where the balloons were already being filled with hot air from giant burners. It was just getting light when we took off and the savanna was spread out below us like something from the Discovery Channel, with herds of elephants, giraffes, wildebeest and gazelles wandering between the acacia trees.

The balloon went up to over 1000 feet for an incredible panorama and then descended to tree-top level or lower. At times, we were almost skimming the grass of the savanna. We finally stopped at a prearranged spot where our Masai guides had gone ahead and set up a breakfast table. They stood guard with spears while we had a champagne breakfast in the bush, with nothing to separate us from the wildlife – just amazing!

MAD OR GENIUS?

It's your career break and you can do whatever you like. Don't let anyone tell you otherwise! If you want to walk across the English Channel on home-made floats, we say go for it. People may tell you that your dream of living on a desert island is madness, but only you can judge. When you achieve your goal, you'll be the one smiling. Here are just a few suggestions.

WALK TO THE SOUTH POLE

Walking to the North or South Pole is right up there with climbing Everest on the list of human achievements, but quite a few people have made it to both the North and South Poles since Sir Ranulph Fiennes and Charles Burton became the first people to see both poles in 1982. However, walking to the poles requires specialist equipment, emergency support and serious amounts of funding. The website www.thepoles.com provides advice for people planning a polar expedition, including listings of expedition attempts on both poles.

British explorers Fiona and Mike Thornewill were the first married couple to walk to both the North and South Poles and seem to be clocking up more achievements every year – see the website www.polarchallenge.org for their latest expeditions. Fiona has the following advice for would-be polar explorers:

To some people, walking to the poles may seem like a strange thing to do, but it is no less normal for humans to explore than it is to watch a football game. My interest in seeing the world occurred following the death of my first husband, Bill, in a road accident. It made me decide that life is not a dress rehearsal and I should make the most of my life while I still could, rather than face regrets later.

Since foreign travel has never been more accessible, I would encourage everyone with a desire to explore to seize the opportunity to visit places that interest them. This in turn will satisfy your curiosity and facilitate a better understanding of 'self'. Whatever your quest, my advice is to research the best, proven knowledge you can, then follow your own dreams and instincts. Sometimes these quests demand great perseverance and not a little risk, but the greater the challenge, the greater the satisfaction. Life is always a risk whether you drive to a football match or follow the road less travelled.

If you don't want to go it alone, one company that offers expeditions to the North and South Poles is Adventure Quest (www.adventurequestinc.com), which gets good reports from both *National Geographic* and the Royal Geographic Society.

Another unusual polar expedition is the annual North Pole Marathon (www.npmarathon .com), which takes place in temperatures of –60°C (–76°F) with windspeeds of up to 60km/h (37mph). For less committed explorers, there are tourist flights to the North Pole from Svalbard (north of Norway) and flights to the South Pole from South America and New Zealand.

BREAK A WORLD RECORD

They say that everyone has 15 minutes of fame, but you don't have to wait for fame to come calling. Breaking a world record is a sure-fire way to get recognition for your unique talents, even if it is only for 15 minutes. The official licensing body for world records is Guinness World Records (www.guinnessworldrecords.com) and it covers everything from the World's Fastest Man to the record for the Most Clothes Pegs Clipped on a Face – 153 in case you're wondering – won by Garry Turner from Yorkshire in August 2001.

Being the world's tallest man or running the fastest mile generally requires special talents, but there are thousands of other records that are more accessible – in fact, you can set a record in almost any activity that you have a talent for. Guinness World Records welcomes suggestions for new record categories and you can apply to have your record attempt recognised on the website. However, be warned: the records for chainsaw juggling, scorpion eating and eye-popping have already been set!

Craig Glenday from Guinness World Records has this advice for potential record breakers:

Just as everyone's supposed to have a book in them, everyone's got some talent or ability to do something better than anyone else. Not everyone can break the 100m track record, walk the high wire at a record altitude, or become the world's youngest supermodel, but there's a record out there for everyone – the trick is finding one that matches your particular skills and abilities.

The best piece of advice we can give is to set yourself goals and stick to them. Strive to be the best you can at whatever you do – and if you can get a Guinness World Record for it, so much the better. However, it should be stressed that unique occurrences, interesting peculiarities or 'firsts' are not necessarily records – the record idea needs to be provable, measurable and breakable.

EAT FUGU

If you don't mind taking the ultimate gamble, you might consider sampling the Japanese delicacy known as *fugu* – sushi prepared from the flesh of the highly toxic blowfish (also known as puffer or globefish). If improperly prepared, this infamous delicacy can contain traces of the lethal poison tetrodotoxin, for which there is no known antidote. Although it only takes one day to eat *fugu*, most people take quite a few days summoning up the courage to try it!

Although *fugu* has a reputation as a gourmet version of Russian roulette, the actual risks are comparatively low. Around a dozen people die every year from eating poorly prepared *fugu*, but to put this in context, the Japanese consume around 10,160 tonnes (10,000 tons) of the fish every year. Kylie Clark from the Japan National Tourist Organization in London has this to say about the *fugu* experience:

I tried fugu in Tokyo at a Japanese friend's house. His family were celebrating the birth of a child with a large meal complete with beers and sake. I was really enjoying some sort of fish when my friend asked if I knew what I was eating. I responded no and everyone laughed. They then tried to explain that it was fugu but the name meant nothing to me. My friend puffed up his cheeks and said fugu again and his sister went to get a Japanese-English dictionary to show me the word 'poisonous' – at last I understood what I was eating!

It seems the thrill of knowing that there is a possibly it can kill you is an essential factor in enjoying fugu for the Japanese. After being told, I wondered if the tingling sensation I had was from the beer, as I had thought before, or if the sensation was from eating the fish. Whichever one it was, I was happy and the fish tasted great!

If you have weighed up the risks and still fancy giving it a go, the average price for a three-course blowfish supper is US$100 to US$250 and the season runs from October to March. For recommended *fugu* restaurants, contact the Japan National Tourist Organization (www.jnto.go.jp/eng).

LIVE ON A DESERT ISLAND

If your idea of heaven is peace and tranquillity, you might want to .
of Meg Worby, who went to live on remote Darnley Island in the Tor.
Australia and Papua New Guinea:

I fell in love with a man I met by chance but I learned he was from an incredibly far u.
place…a place I had barely heard of, although it is part of Australia. After writing letters to
one another for six months, we decided I would go there to fish and to see where he came
from. I was more than ready to throw my 'career' to the winds and follow my heart, because
I felt instinctively that a career is something we create for ourselves, but an opportunity like
this might come once in a lifetime.

Normally you would need a permit to visit these remote indigenous parts of Australia,
but Kenny was born there. What a privilege to see how people from an entirely different
background exist – with ways and values that were so different to mine. They welcomed me
because I came with Kenny, whom they respect, but also because they are friendly, relaxed
and really generous: something that has not always served the indigenous peoples of Australia
well when it comes to dealing with white people. I learned so much about their culture, the
link between their history, which is an oral one, and the sea and their beautiful ways of life.
Life revolved around feasts, family and the sea.

If you don't mind living simply and setting up your own camp, you can arrange a desert-
island getaway at dozens of island destinations around the world. Southern Thailand is
particularly well set up for this – boat operators along the Andaman Coast can drop you
off on an uninhabited tropical island and pick you up a few days later for a small fee.

The islands come with whispering sands, swaying palms, free coconuts and plentiful fish
and you can even hire cooks to come out to the islands to prepare meals – Lonely Planet's
Thailand's Beaches & Islands guide has lots more information.

oing Travelling

Travelling can form all or just part of your career break. If you've already seen some of the world on a gap year then you might choose to combine travelling with studying or voluntary work this time around. On the other had, chances are you've got a list as full as your in-tray of places you didn't get to then and can't wait to visit now. You know what they say (or at least what St Augustine is supposed to have said): 'Life is a book and those who do not travel read only one page'.

PROS & CONS

Some people 'collect' countries. The Travelers' Century Club (www.travelerscenturyclub .org), based in Santa Monica, is open to anyone who has visited 100 countries or more. Unless you're planning on becoming a member, you might wonder whether 'just travelling' is a good use of your time. Career-breaker, Louise Jones, who did 'just' this says:

I enjoyed my travelling; I never felt that I was unfulfilled because I wasn't doing something else. One of the greatest pleasures was having time to read, and books I would not normally read. In addition, my partner and I were very organised. Many travellers just drift along, wherever the current takes them. We did not do this. We had regular meetings to discuss our next moves. Our decision to come home was taken a year before we did it, with that year planned out.

As Louise points out, one of the pitfalls of 'just travelling' might be a feeling of aimlessness. She and her partner solved this by good planning. Others decide to base their travels around a theme or common thread. Carol Ferguson, for instance, based her travelling around works of art:

I studied history of art at university and used to visit museums a lot. Over the years I found myself so busy with work and so tired at the weekends that I lost touch with this interest. When I took a career break, I decided to spend six months travelling around the world to see some of my favourite paintings and sculptures. I picked 15 and got my travel agent to work out the best route between them. Travelling like this gave me goals and at the end of my trip I really felt I'd achieved something.

However, if you've had enough of targets, goals, key performance indicators and over-achievement at work, then a good dose of loose, unstructured travel might be just what you need. James Ingham found exactly this:

I'd say it's important to have a rough idea of your main objectives; what you want to get from the experience and roughly where you want to go. But the beauty of travelling for me was the unpredictability compared to day-to-day life back home. If I liked somewhere I stayed longer, if I didn't I moved on. And I ended up doing things in places I'd never imagined.

Another good reason just to travel during your career break is a very obvious one. There's so much to see and do in the world that even if you take 100 years off work, let alone one, you'll never get to see and do everything. It isn't as if you'll be running out of experiences or opportunities.

What you might fear, though, is running into hordes of young, first-time travellers. This is a valid concern. After all, none of us wants to feel like a split-screened Morris Minor in a race full of brand-new Golf GTIs. Sure, some parts of the world are full of gappers, but there are regions that are vastly less populated with youngsters (see the following Off the Teenage

Track sections). Due to the recent growth in career breaks, the world is full of older travellers, wiser travellers and travellers with children. In addition, your travelling budget will probably be twice as much as a gapper's, which means you can afford to travel more comfortably, stay in better accommodation, eat at more stylish restaurants and opt for the all-frills guided tour, rather than the no-frills cheap one. Don't forget, though, if you want to meet other travellers, the best place to do this is still at the local backpackers or youth hostel.

RECOMMENDED ROUTES

Have you ever wanted to float in the Dead Sea, sail through the Panama Canal, walk with the Masai Mara or gaze at the northern lights? Have you ever wanted to stay in a maharajah's palace, an igloo or a rainforest lodge? If so, take advice from career-breaker Graham Williams:

If there are things that you have always wanted to see, regardless of what they are – do it. In our case it took us to some very obscure places not visited by tourists, which was interesting in itself.

Choosing your route, whether it be a round-the-world air ticket, an overland trail, or a mixture of the two, is very personal. For the low-down on choosing a round-the-world ticket see p42, but bear in mind what career-breaker Neil Luddington has to say:

Some RTW tickets mean you see a few cities and no countryside. Better to do a lot of surface travel to see the real country.

For an overview of the world's classic overland routes, see the following sections. Where appropriate, ideas are also given for countries or regions to visit that are not on the standard gapper or tourist trail. However, don't get too hung up on this differentiation. The classic routes endure because they are often the best, most spectacular route through a region. Avoid them and you'll miss out on some world-beating sights and experiences. Sure, it might seem that every 18-year-old on the planet is travelling from Bangkok to Singapore, but you won't find a single one dining at the Vertigo restaurant in the Thai capital. This is an amazing open-air rooftop restaurant on the 61st floor of the Banyan Tree hotel – the views are heavenly and the bill out of this world. And, of course, you don't have to get off the beaten track to have a unique travel experience – these happen anytime, any place, anywhere (with or without a dry martini in your hand).

Two other major factors influencing your route are climate and special events. In terms of weather, don't sweat this too much. Try to get it right for your main destinations and accept that sometimes you'll be in the right place at the wrong time. Most special events happen once a year, so don't arrive in southern Serengeti National Park just after the Great Migration (April to June). Think carefully before heading to a Muslim country during Ramadan.

Many of the routes mentioned in the following section are marked on the world map at the front of this book (get your magnifying glass out for New Zealand). Ideally, you need to be reading the text while you're looking at the map – your boss would call it 'multitasking'.

TRAVELLERS' TRAILS THROUGH AFRICA

Routes through Africa can change rapidly. For instance, the classic trans-Africa trip between Cairo and Cape Town – which can take anything from three to 12 months – has recently opened up to independent travellers again. For many years, Sudan was pretty much a no-go area but it is now possible to travel across Lake Nasser from Egypt to Sudan, then go via Khartoum east into Ethiopia (check the current situation with the Foreign Office travel advisory before taking this route). From the border it's a rough and rocky ride to

Addis Ababa and a long hard push south into Kenya. An easier option is to fly to Addis Ababa or, even easier, to Nairobi to join this trail.

Nairobi to Cape Town is the most popular section of the Cairo to Cape route and can take from two to six months to complete. Most people go from Nairobi through Tanzania, usually taking in Zanzibar, then on through Malawi. Highlights include Serengeti National Park and the beaches of Lake Malawi. The political situation in Zimbabwe means that many overlanders are choosing to skirt around this beautiful and once well-touristed country in favour of travelling through neighbouring Zambia. Not surprisingly, Zambia's tourism minister has the hugest grin on his face as tourism figures are doing very nicely thank you. In Southern Zambia, everyone goes to Victoria Falls (you'd be crazy to miss this stunning sight) and then west through Botswana into Namibia and then down to South Africa. This part of the trip has it all – the Okavango Delta, the towering sand dunes of Sossusvlei, and wildlife to die for (not literally). If short on time, you can choose to do either the leg between Cape Town and Victoria Falls or Victoria Falls and Nairobi. Otherwise, a popular three-month circuit these days is Kenya, Uganda and Tanzania; this route loosely runs around Lake Victoria, taking in the gorillas (in Uganda or Rwanda), trekking on Mount Kilimanjaro (Tanzania), followed by well-earned R&R in Zanzibar.

Off the Teenage Track

Africa is not cheap in comparison with Asia or India (accommodation is particularly poor value in some areas) and having it on your RTW ticket can push the price up. As such, Africa is not on every gapper's itinerary. In addition, its 30 million sq km makes for such a huge continent that there are still quite a few routes and countries where you can get off the teenage track.

West Africa, home to over half the continent's people, is fantastically rich culturally and musically but overlooked by almost all visitors who aren't French or African. Plus, if you've ever wished to name-drop Timbuktu at a dinner party, then here's your chance. A two- to three-month overland route starts in Dakar (Senegal), runs into Mali and up to Timbuktu, then back down through Burkina Faso and the Ivory Coast and then east along the coast into Ghana, ending at Accra. From here there's another two- to three-month route via Togo and Benin to Cameroon, where, if you felt up to it, you could take a jungle trek with the Bagyeli pygmies.

If you prefer the roads less travelled and favour smaller circuits, the vast and fascinating nation of Ethiopia remains largely deserted of tourists. Don't let TV images of famine give you the wrong impression – this is a green and pleasant land. Other African countries that are still relatively unexplored include Libya, which is opening up quickly; Mozambique; and Madagascar, the world's fourth-largest island. Madagascar is a unique place where 80% of plant life, all of its mammals and 90% of its reptiles are endemic. To the north is the Seychelles, and if you've got shed loads of money then you can try tropical island-hopping.

TRAVELLERS' TRAILS THROUGH THE MIDDLE EAST

There's one main route in this area and it's the biggie of Istanbul to Cairo. If you ran for all your buses and only hit the highlights it would take six weeks, but to do it properly you need eight weeks and preferably a month or two longer. The route follows Turkey's Aegean Coast east from Istanbul to Antakya, with a side trip up to Cappadocia to see the weird rock formations and underground cities. From there you cross into Syria, visiting Hama (crusader castle), Palmyra (desert city ruins), Damascus and Bosra (Roman theatre) before reaching Jordan. Here you do a day trip to the Dead Sea, spend time at the famous Nabataean city of Petra and experience the Wadi Rum desert, before ending up in Aqaba. From here take the ferry to Nuweiba in Egypt's Sinai, cross the Eastern Desert to Luxor (Valley of the Kings etc) and head south to Aswan and Abu Simbel (the Great Temple). You can either get a felucca up the Nile from Aswan or head back north via the Western Desert oases. This is an amazing trip and, not amazingly, it is packed with first-time travellers.

Off the Teenage Track
The Istanbul to Cairo route rarely allows enough time to see Lebanon properly, although you might do a side trip to the Roman temple at Baalbek. This, combined with a more expensive cost of living, means that Lebanon is one of the most fascinating and relatively undiscovered countries in the Middle East. You might also want to spend more time indulging in Turkey's delights – you could do a three-month circuit of the whole country or just concentrate on either the western or eastern section. Take care in the southeast due to PKK (Kurdistan Workers' Party) activities. You could even do a side trip to Cyprus by ferry and get there before the northern part becomes as spoilt as its southern shores. Turkey is surrounded by eight different countries, so deciding where to go from here could be a problem. One option is into Iran – a vast, hospitable, inexpensive and exotic country that's certainly not on the standard year-out itinerary. You could take two months making your way southeast across the country to Bandar-e Abbas, from where you could pick up a ferry to Dubai and fly on to your next destination.

TRAVELLERS' TRAILS THROUGH CENTRAL ASIA & THE FORMER SOVIET UNION
The three main routes through this part of the world are by train. There's the eight-day Trans-Siberian, which travels from Moscow to Vladivostok. The seven-day Trans-Mongolian goes from Moscow to Beijing, following the same line as the Trans-Siberian but branching off at Irkutsk (Siberia) to go via Ulaan Baatar, the capital of Mongolia. Then there's the eight-day Trans-Manchurian, which also travels from Moscow to Beijing but at Irkutsk continues east to Harbin in China before dropping down to Beijing. The most popular route is the Trans-Mongolian because most travellers want to cross the Gobi Desert. Also, ending up in Beijing increases your travel options a millionfold, compared to finishing in Vladivostok, where your travel options are limited to a few boats to Japan and some expensive onward flights.

Travel on all three of these trains is expensive. This is because you have to prebook accommodation at scheduled stops, which usually means staying in three- or four-star hotels. Most travellers plan to spend two or three days in Irkutsk (Lake Baikal is the main draw here) and Ulaan Baatar. In addition, visas for these trips are not cheap and not always easy to organise, particularly as it's a bit of a visa teaser getting them in the right order. For instance, the Mongolians will only give you a visa if you already have a Russian one. The upshot is that most travellers choose to organise visas through an agency, which means you're looking at over £130 before you've even paid for your ticket. The cost of your ticket will depend on your stopovers but a straight-through ticket on the Trans-Mongolian, including a two-day visit to Moscow to register your visa, costs between £420 and £650.

The expense, combined with the prescriptive nature of these routes, means that you'll find very few gappers on these lines. In fact, travel in this whole region is costly for exactly the same reasons. This definitely holds true for the fourth trail in this area: the Silk Road. This is not so much one trail as a network of trade routes linking Xi'an in China with the Mediterranean via Kyrgyzstan, Uzbekistan, Turkmenistan and Iran. The best way to do this trip is with an organised tour using a combination of planes, trains, buses and private car. Depending on your route and how long you take, this will cost in excess of £3000. Doing this trip as an independent traveller would be a logistical nightmare but is possible – count on it taking at least two months.

Off the Teenage Track
Pretty much all of it.

TRAVELLERS' TRAILS THROUGH THE INDIAN SUBCONTINENT
This area is full of classic routes. Which you take really depends on what your interests are and how much time you have. Everyone, at some point in their journey, will do the Golden Triangle of Delhi, Jaipur and Agra to see the forts and the Taj Mahal. Often tacked onto this trip is Varanasi – one of India's holiest cities. Of all the states in India the most popular is

Rajasthan, and first-time travellers almost always do a one- to two-month route through this area, going south from Delhi to Mumbai (Bombay), taking in Agra, Bharatpur, Jaipur, Shekhawati, Bikaner, Jaisalmer, Jodhpur, Pushkar, Bundi, Chittorgarh and Udaipur. This trail includes Mughal architecture, desert landscapes, Hindu temples, hippy hang-outs, and camel fairs (the date for the latter depends on the lunar calendar but is usually between October and November in Pushkar). From Mumbai, there are routes down India's western coast to Goa's beaches and Kerala's rural backwaters. Goa, Gokarna (in the state of Karnataka) and Kerala are all classic travel hang-outs. From Delhi the most popular one-month northern loop takes in the Himalaya and some of India's most beautiful hill stations. It runs Delhi, Dalhousie, Dharamsala, Shimla, Manali, Leh, Delhi. Dharamsala is home to the exiled Dalai Lama, and Leh, high on the Tibetan Plateau, is the capital of Ladakh.

At the beginning of 2004, ferries started up between Chennai (Madras) and Sri Lanka, making this a popular route into the tear-drop isle. Otherwise, the two most travelled international routes through the region are Delhi to Kathmandu (Nepal) via the Sunauli/Bhairawa border crossing, and Kolkata (Calcutta) to Dhaka (Bangladesh); for the latter trip there's a direct daily bus that takes a mind- and bottom-numbing 13 hours. Note: the border between India and Nepal is sometimes closed, depending on the weather and political situation.

Kathmandu and Pokhara in Nepal are traveller honey-pots. Not only do they attract travellers but travellers get stuck there too. Many come for the trekking but most stay for the brown stuff. From Kathmandu, you can take the Friendship Highway to Lhasa (Tibet) and into central China.

Regions in this part of the world often feature in the Foreign & Commonwealth Office travel advice pages (www.fco.gov.uk), so check prior to travel and while you're on the road.

Off the Teenage Track

It is surprisingly easy to find states in India that slip off many travellers' checklists. West Bengal has plenty of historic sites but, apart from Kolkata and Darjeeling, it gets surprisingly few tourists (check the Foreign Office advice regarding travel in the far northwest). Nearby (relatively speaking) Sikkim is remote and you need a permit to enter but it still has something of a Himalayan Shangri-la about it. Gujarat, on the west coast, deserves a few more visitors, as does Maharashtra. In terms of beaches that aren't overrun with teenage hippies, the remote Andaman Islands in the Bay of Bengal are a treat; they're a two-hour flight from Chennai or Kolkata. Otherwise, the highest form of relaxation can be found on the palm-fringed beaches of Lakshadweep, an archipelago west of Kerala. The islands are pricey and you need permits, but the diving's fab and this is a very special way to celebrate an anniversary or birthday.

From Kolkata, Kathmandu or Dhaka you can get a flight into Bhutan, an extraordinary, time-warped country. It is expensive to visit but a 'must' if you want to go somewhere completely different and don't mind flying on an airline (Druk Air) that sounds as if it just stepped off a James Bond film set. You have to book through a tour operator otherwise you won't get a visa.

Pakistan is an extraordinary country but has now appeared on the Foreign Office travel blacklist. Travellers who do go there and keep to the safer regions bump into very few foreigners and send back glowing reports of this ancient, cultural and deeply hospitable land.

TRAVELLERS' TRAILS THROUGH NORTHEAST ASIA

The majority of routes in this area run between Beijing and Hong Kong. Basically, most first-time travellers want to see the Great Wall of China, count the Terracotta Warriors, coo at the baby pandas in the Giant Panda Breeding Research Base, cruise down the Chang Jiang (Yangzi River) through the Three Gorges (which become toast in 2009 when they're flooded), and kick back in a few backpacker centres. This is achieved by taking at least six weeks and zig-zagging between Beijing and Hong Kong via Xi'an, Chengdu, Chongqing-Yichang (by boat), Guilin and Yangshuo. If you don't want to travel this far south, you can head to Shanghai after the river cruise.

Another big backpacker route runs between Hong Kong and Kunming, taking about two weeks. You travel to Guangzhou, take a ferry to Wuzhou and a bus on to the established traveller hang-out of Yangshuo, taking in the beautifully scenic (but touristy) city of Guilin. From Kunming you can push deeper into southwest China, or get a plane to Thailand or a train to Vietnam. There's also an adventurous route from Xi'an to Lhasa (Tibet), which is popular with travellers who have arrived by train from Moscow and are heading towards the Indian subcontinent. You travel via Golmud and cross at the Tanggu-la pass (5180m or 16,995ft). This is a hard trip because you cross the virtually uninhabited Tibetan Plateau; it takes four to six weeks.

Other routes that pass through China include the Trans-Manchurian and Trans-Mongolian railways, and the Silk Road (covered on p87). The Karakoram Highway is also up there, running from Kashgar in southwest China to Islamabad (Pakistan) over the Khunjerab Pass. This route is only open in the summer, and borders open and close at the drop of a hat. One thing to remember when you're travelling in China is that your three-month tourist visa starts from the day of issue.

Off the Teenage Track

Getting off the beaten track in China is easy – most travellers congregate in the southwest and in the cities boasting famous sights. Even Hong Kong is fairly short of visitors these days – plenty pass through but not so many choose to stay and explore its 234 outlying islands.

There's masses to discover in Japan but even on the cheap it is expensive, hence its unpopularity with gappers. The main route is between Tokyo and Kyoto (pausing for a night-time ascent of Mt Fuji) but you can easily continue on to Nagasaki, stopping off in fascinating cites such as Kobe and Hiroshima. At the southernmost tip of Kyushu is Kirishima National Park, packed with volcanoes, hot springs and soaring mountain scenery. You could easily spend three months exploring Japan but, unfortunately, 'spend' is the operative word. To save some money, buy a Japan Rail Pass before you enter the country.

The rest of northeast Asia is wide open – it isn't untouristed but doesn't attract young travellers as Southeast Asia does. Holidays in President Bush's 'axis of evil' are all the rage nowadays and North Korea can be visited on a tour. South Korea and Taiwan are very easy-going and rich in culture, with fabulous cuisines. There are plenty of boat connections between South Korea and China.

TRAVELLERS' TRAILS THROUGH SOUTHEAST ASIA

The classic Southeast Asian trail goes from Bangkok to Bali, with an option to extend to Darwin (Australia), by land, ferry and sometimes air. The route starts in Bangkok and travels down through Thailand's Southern Gulf to the famous beach-laden islands of Ko Samui, Ko Pha-Ngan and Ko Tao. It continues south through Peninsular Malaysia to Singapore, before looping north to Kuala Lumpur and George Town. A ferry takes you from there to Sumatra and the route heads south, past the awesome crater lake of Danau Toba to Java and, eventually, Bali. Most travellers then get a flight out of Bali to Darwin or elsewhere in Australia. The busiest part of this route is between Bangkok and Singapore because most RTW tickets offer this portion as a surface sector. This whole trip could take you a month or it could take you a year – how much time do you have? Another well-worn route is north from Bangkok to the bohemian travellers' centre of Chiang Mai and into the trekking areas of northern Thailand.

The second major one- to three-month route in this area is a loop through Indochina, taking in Laos, Vietnam and Cambodia. Travellers either head north from Bangkok to the border with Laos at Nong Khai/Vientiane or else go to the two border crossings between Thailand and Cambodia. The most spectacular sight in this region is the Temple of Angkor in Cambodia. As Hanoi, Vietnam's mazelike capital city, doesn't fit neatly into a loop you can do this as a side trip, possibly on the *Reunification Express* railway (www.vr.com .vn/English), which hugs the coast between Ho Chi Minh City and Hanoi.

Off the Teenage Track

With its soaring mountains, dense jungles, palm-fringed beaches, tantalising food and complex cultures, Southeast Asia is a magnet for first-time travellers. It's also cheap, easy to travel around and perpetually fascinating, and every gapper has a God-given right to chill out on a beach in Phuket, Ko Phi Phi, Ko Chang, Krabi or Kuta (Bali). Travelling in this area the second or third time around is jolly good too. However, if you do want to escape the banana pancakes and Bob Marley tunes where do you go?

There are areas of Thailand that are less explored than others. For instance, there's the deeply cultural northeast region known as Isan, where the people mostly speak Lao or Khmer as a first language. Or there's Ko Tarutao on the Andaman Coast close to Malaysia, which has the same feeling about it that Ko Samui had 20 years ago – it's a national park, so guests cannot stay overnight. Otherwise, try the Muslim-influenced southern beach towns on the Gulf of Thailand, which are little visited.

In addition, many travellers miss out on the Philippines – an archipelago of 7107 tropical islands. The Malaysian states of Sarawak and Sabah are not often on a gapper's itinerary due to the relatively high cost of travel there. Sarawak has some amazing national parks and fascinating tribal communities, and Kuching is one of the most relaxing cities in all of Asia. Sabah's main attraction is accessible primary and secondary rainforest areas and Mt Kinabalu, the tallest of Southeast Asia's mountains – you can climb it without special equipment. New flights with Australian Airlines from Singapore mean you need to get here fast.

One country to think about seriously is Myanmar (Burma). A visit is controversial but it is right off the teenage track. This is due not only to Aung San Suu Kyi's call for a tourism boycott but also its oppressive military regime and atrocious human-rights record. To get both sides of the 'to see or not to see' argument, log onto the Burma Campaign UK's website (www.burmacampaign.org.uk) and read the introduction to Lonely Planet's *Myanmar* guidebook at http://shop.lonelyplanet.com/misc_images/burma.pdf. Bangkok is the best place to look for plane tickets to Myanmar.

TRAVELLERS' TRAILS THROUGH AUSTRALIA, NEW ZEALAND & THE PACIFIC

Australia is the backpacking capital of the world, full of working holiday-makers either travelling, waiting tables in Sydney, or grape picking, apple picking or nose picking (ugh, only joking). After all these years it is still top of the list for career-breakers, as well as the main destination for gappers.

First-time travellers to Australia will usually complete a three- to six-month loop of eastern Australia, travelling from Sydney northwards to Brisbane and the Great Barrier Reef, Cairns, west to Darwin, east to Kakadu National Park, and south to Katherine Gorge, Alice Springs and the 'red centre'. From here they drop down through the opal-mining area of Coober Pedy to Adelaide, head across to Melbourne and then back to Sydney. For those short on time there's a southeast loop that goes Sydney, Melbourne, the Great Ocean Road to Warrnambool, Adelaide, Broken Hill, the Blue Mountains and back to the Opera House in Sydney. Another popular loop is the southwestern one, which starts in Perth and heads south to the Margaret River area, then east along the coast to Albany and Esperance, before turning north to Kalgoorlie and west back to Perth. Within these circuits there are stretches that are more popular than others, with Melbourne to Cairns topping the bill and Byron Bay qualifying as the country's principal backpacker hang-out.

New Zealand has become the adventure centre of the universe and the main routes in the North and South Islands reflect this interest. Most travellers fly from Australia to Auckland in the North Island and head directly down to Waitomo to do a spot of black-water rafting with the glow worms, then cross eastwards to the geothermal hotspot of Rotorua. From there you can fly straight to Christchurch in the South Island and head via Mt Cook to Queenstown, the cradle of adrenaline-packed adventure activities (see www.queenstown -nz.co.nz). You can sign up here for at least four different types of bungee jumps as well as jet-boating, heli-mountain biking, river surfing, abseiling etc. A quiet day trip to Milford Sound is usually on the agenda between the days of pulse-racing action. This route will usually take about three weeks.

From here most travellers then head to the Pacific Islands. Those most likely to be on a RTW ticket are Fiji, Tahiti and the Cook Islands. Fiji, in particular, is full of young gappers soaking up the sun.

Off the Teenage Track

The obvious news is that Australia's a huge country and there are a number of fantastic routes that are off the main drag. The bad news is that if you don't have a working-holiday visa then you've only got three months on your tourist visa (unless you applied for a long-stay visitor visa lasting up to six months).

A two- or three-month route from Perth goes northeast up the coast to Darwin, taking in some of the most unspoilt scenery in the world. Most of this trip needs to be done in a 4WD and takes you past Eighty Mile Beach and through the rugged yet spectacular Kimberley region. From Darwin, you could take time to experience Aboriginal Australia by visiting the Tiwi Islands of Bathurst and Melville or exploring parts of Arnhem Land. Permits are needed for travel into most areas owned by indigenous people – see Lonely Planet's *Aboriginal Australia & the Torres Strait Islands* for more information.

Not for the faint-hearted (or the unprepared) is another route in the western half of Australia that goes from Perth east to Kalgoorlie, north to Leonora and then east across the Great Victoria Desert to Alice Springs. You can do this route in about three weeks but it's serious sleeping-out-under-the-stars kind of stuff.

Another way out of Perth is to board the *Indian Pacific* train (www.gsr.com.au/indian), which takes you 4352km (2700 miles) across the Nullabor Plain to Adelaide and on to Sydney. Or, why not try the newly completed *Ghan* railway (www.gsr.com.au/ghan), which stretches between Adelaide and Darwin? You could spoil yourself in Gold Kangaroo Service, hopping between your cabin and the members-only lounge and bar.

At the top and bottom of Australia's eastern loop you'll find two areas not often explored by first-time travellers. At the top beyond Cairns is the northern section of the Barrier Reef and wild, rainforested area of Cape York. At the bottom is Tasmania, where you could easily spend four to six weeks, especially if you were going to walk the incredibly beautiful Cradle Mountain–Lake St Clair route.

If you spent a lot of your gap year in Australia then you might want to take a closer look at New Zealand. Despite its rise in popularity, travellers rarely build in enough time here.

A good way to see most of the North Island is to drive from Auckland to Wellington. Before you set off, do a side trip up north to the Bay of Islands, where you can hire a beach house and happily spend at least a week. On your way south, call in at the Coromandel Peninsula to experience Hot Water Beach and stop off at Mt Tongariro to hike the one-day Tongariro Crossing – which some say is the most beautiful one-day walk in the world – before heading towards Hawke's Bay. Here you can visit some of New Zealand's famous wineries before heading into windy Wellington. From here, take the ferry through the Marlborough Sounds to Picton in the South Island. You can explore more wineries in the Marlborough region. New Zealand's huge green-lipped mussels also come from here. Base yourself in Nelson to visit Abel Tasman National Park before heading southeast to Kaikoura where, all year round, you can go whale watching. This trail then joins the well-trodden route of Christchurch to Queenstown. If you don't feel like basing yourself in Queenstown with the teenage adrenaline-junkies, then try staying in Wanaka – it has all the adventure but much more style. If you've got time, walk the popular four-day Milford Track from Te Anau to the Milford Sound. Or else, take the ferry from Bluff to Stewart Island, the only place in the world where you can see wild kiwis during the daytime. Bluff also has an annual oyster festival (www.bluffoysterfest.co.nz) in May – it's heavenly, as long as you're not an oyster. If you're not rushing, this trip takes at least two months.

From here the islands of the South Pacific beckon. To get off the beaten track look at adding Samoa, Tonga or New Caledonia to your ticket. Once there you can hop between islands using local transport. Otherwise, from New Zealand you could jump onto the *Søren Larsen*, the tall ship used in the *Onedin Line* TV series, for a 49-day tour of the South Pacific Islands offered by Explore Worldwide (www.exploreworldwide.com) for around £3800.

TRAVELLERS' TRAILS THROUGH NORTH AMERICA & THE CARIBBEAN

Many RTW tickets fly into Los Angeles (LA) and out of New York City, or have LA as a stopover. This means that most travellers either cross America or do trails in the southwest. If going coast-to-coast then the most popular northern route is LA, north to San Francisco, east to Yosemite National Park (NP), Yellowstone NP (no, not where Yogi bear lived; that was Jellystone NP), the Black Hills and Mt Rushmore National Memorial (those 18.2m/60ft granite carvings of four US presidents), Chicago, and then Niagara Falls to New York. The southern route starts in LA, then takes in Canyon Country (see the next paragraph) before dropping south to El Paso, San Antonio, the beaches of the Gulf of Mexico, New Orleans, Savannah and Charleston (two of the USA's loveliest towns) and travelling north up the East Coast to New York. Both trips will take a minimum of four weeks and that's really pushing it.

Otherwise, if travellers are staying close (relatively speaking) to LA then most will head to Las Vegas, and from there loop through Canyon Country (Grand Canyon NP), Monument Valley, Canyonlands NP, Arches NP, Bryce Canyon NP, Zion NP and back again. This is an amazing trip but very crowded. (For more information on America's national parks, see Lonely Planet's new National Park series.) From LA, travellers also head north up Highway 101, which takes you to Seattle via one of the most scenic coastal trips in the world.

In Canada the classic travel trip is by rail between Vancouver and Toronto. The *Canadian* (www.viarail.ca), as the train cunningly calls itself, travels through the Canadian Rockies, the Canadian Prairies and the lake lands of northern Ontario. Direct, the journey takes three days but most people get off in Jasper to hang out in the Canadian Rockies. Otherwise, if you're flying into Vancouver or Calgary, you can take a Greyhound bus into the Canadian Rockies area of Kamloops, Banff and Jasper where there's plenty of white-water rafting and canoeing and some fantastic skiing in winter.

In the Caribbean, most independent travellers head for Cuba. Otherwise, there are no real routes in this area unless you're looking for crewing work (October to May) on yachts (see p100).

Off the Teenage Track

Getting away from it all isn't difficult in the US – the place is so vast, after all. Plus, the majority of gappers on these routes are travelling by Greyhound bus (www.greyhound.com) or Green Tortoise (www.greentortoise.com). Being over 25, however, means that car-rental companies will be falling under their own wheels to hire you a car. (See also the section on Driveaway Cars, p102.) And, there's nothing like driving yourself around the States, listening to the local radio stations and pretending you're Thelma and Louise (unless you're a bloke, that is). The classic routes already mentioned are still some of the best, the difference being that you'll be doing them in a different way from everyone else. Also think about driving between New York and Key West, another timeless coastal trip. For more creative driving ideas and some fantastic scenic routes look at www.northamericanhighways.co.uk.

In addition, don't discount travelling by rail. Trains are rarely the quickest, cheapest or most convenient option, but they're big and romantic and you can look at the scenery rather than the road markings. Check out Amtrak's site at www.amtrak.com and look at the routes taken by the *Southwest Chief* or *California Zephyr* trains.

If you're travelling in Canada from mid-October to mid-November then think about taking the train (www.viarail.ca) from Winnipeg to Churchill (Manitoba). This is where all the polar bears congregate while waiting for the ice to freeze. You can get out on the ice yourself in a tundra buggy. The train journey takes two days and has to be booked at least nine months in advance because the area can only accommodate limited numbers of travellers. Another route off the main drag runs through the French part of Canada. From Toronto, head towards Montreal, then on to the walled city of Quebec (which is celebrating its 400th birthday in 2008). From there you can easily reach St Lawrence River to watch the whales and immerse yourself in some fine wilderness areas. Otherwise, if you're based in Vancouver, travel north to the Yukon Territory, where you'll also find vast swathes of wilderness, glaciers, lakes, bears (grizzly, black and brown), indigenous culture, and the flavour of the old Wild West (especially in Dawson). It's either a three-hour flight to Whitehorse (capital of the Yukon) or a three-week drive.

Heading to the Caribbean? Whatever you do, don't discount Cuba just because it's a little crowded these days. Also, consider visiting 'the alternative Caribbean'; this includes islands such as Trinidad, Jamaica, Haiti (actually, not such a good idea at the time of writing because of political unrest) and the Dominican Republic.

TRAVELLERS' TRAILS THROUGH MEXICO, CENTRAL & SOUTH AMERICA

There are three major trails in Mexico, all taking between three and four weeks. The main one starts in Mexico City, heads southeast to Oaxaca (beautiful colonial city) and San Cristóbal (highland hang-out), turns north to Palenque (jungle-enshrouded Mayan city) and Mérida (the 'white city') and then east to Playa del Carmen, Isla Mujeres or Tulum (coral reefs and laid-back beach scenes). Most independent travellers avoid the high-rise glitz of Cancún. The second trail picks up the Pan-American Highway at Mexico City and heads through Puebla, Oaxaca and San Cristóbal towards Guatemala. The third is a route through the Yucatán Peninsula, taking in the ancient Mayan sites of Chichén Itzá, Uxmal, Kabah, Edzná, Sayil etc. The main beach resorts are on the central Pacific coast between Puerto Vallarta and Acapulco and they tend to be brash package resorts. A major beach hang-out is Puerto Escondido.

Most travellers loosely follow the Pan-American Highway through Central America, taking diversions to see the principal Mayan sites in Guatemala (Tikal), Belize and Honduras. You could spend one to seven months in this whole area. Unfortunately, you can't follow the route on into South America because the Darien Gap is too dangerous to cross by land. Instead, most travellers choose to fly from Panama over both the Gap and Colombia into Quito, Ecuador. The Pan-American Highway then runs south through Peru and Chile, where you can pick up the Southern Highway to Tierra del Fuego. This multi-adventurous route passes through desert (the Atacama), mountains (the Andes), volcanic landscapes, glaciers and fjords to South America's southernmost tip. You can travel overland for most of the way or else fly sectors of it. Many travellers overland it from Quito or Lima (Peru) to La Paz (Bolivia) via Cuzco, a beautiful cobblestoned city and major travellers' hang-out, but comparatively few go from La Paz to Santiago (Chile). This route could take four months or more to complete. Other routes in South America include the four-day Inca trail to Machu Picchu in Peru (you're usually based in Cuzco for this); a four-week trip from Rio de Janeiro (Brazil) southwest to the Iguazú Falls – one of the world's greatest waterfalls – north to the Pantanal (a vast wetland with superb wildlife) and west into Bolivia; or a four- to six-week trip from Rio to the Iguazú Falls, Buenos Aires and then either southwest to the Lake District or further south to Patagonia. A three-week alternative is Rio to Buenos Aires via the Iguazú Falls.

Off the Teenage Track

Because it can be expensive to add on to a RTW ticket, this whole area is relatively short on first-time travellers. Central America is particularly unexplored, with Nicaragua, Belize and Panama the most overlooked of the seven countries.

In Mexico the northern region from Guadalajara upwards is fairly untouristed, including the scenically beautiful Copper Canyon railway between Los Mochis and Chihuahua (pronounce it like those annoying little dogs). Baja California is relatively quiet but that might be because it's also relatively pricey and on the road to nowhere. The beaches on the Gulf of Mexico are also much less crowded than those on the Pacific coast, but that's because they're not as good.

Getting off the beaten track in South America is not very difficult. For instance, in Brazil most travellers cling to the coast and in Argentina only a few explore the highlands. The smaller countries like Guyana, Suriname and French Guiana are also off most gappers' itineraries because it is expensive to travel there. However, if you're a career-breaker with a bit more money to play with then here's your big moment – you can't afford not to go to the Galápagos Islands. Yes, it is expensive but if this is your once-in-a-lifetime break, then this is your once-in-a-lifetime trip. Think of it this way: everything's big in the Galápagos, even your travel expenses. And, if you really want to push the boat out, when you reach Tierra del Fuego, you can always catch a ship on to Antarctica.

TRAVELLERS' TRAILS THROUGH EUROPE

Everyone gets everywhere in Europe; travellers tend to follow their nose and their interests rather than any traditional trade, cultural, scenic or easy-to-travel routes. Having said that, the Greek Islands are still a major pull and you could easily spend three months exploring these. Otherwise, travellers migrate towards the shores of the Mediterranean looking for sea, sand, sun (and sex). Party animals looking for the latter plus the trendiest bars and clubs head towards the islands of Majorca, Rhodes and Ibiza.

Those interested in crewing on yachts gather in Gibraltar around March to April and find boats sailing towards Greece and Turkey over the summer. Between September and October they all sail back again, ready for the trip over to the Canaries (see the section on Crewing, p100).

Off the Teenage Track

Europe isn't a big destination for gappers; it is just too expensive. As such, it might be a good place to explore on a career break, especially if you missed it first time around. Otherwise, you could do half and half – travel through Europe to get somewhere cheaper and more exotic. For instance, an unusual route into China is from Denmark, through Scandinavia, taking the Hurtigruten steamer (www.hurtigruten.com) from Bergen to Trondheim in Norway, and then further north to Moscow, where you pick up the Trans-Mongolian railway to Beijing. If you didn't want to go so far afield you could drop south from Helsinki and explore the relatively untouristed medieval old towns of the Baltic States. Another half-and-half trip is to travel overland through France and Spain to Morocco, catching a ferry from Algeciras to Tangier or Ceuta. For something rather more expensive, you could head north from Scotland to the Shetland Islands and from there on to the Faroe Islands and Iceland, returning via Norway. Bearing in mind that time is money, the options in Europe are endless.

EXPLORING ONE COUNTRY OR REGION

Choosing to concentrate your travels in one area or country is a brave and rewarding choice. James Ingham did this twice during his career break:

I spent two months in New Zealand, which was fantastic. It gave me enough time to visit all the must-see sights as well as move off the beaten track and find spots in the middle of nowhere and get a real feel for life in the country.

In Africa he concentrated on three countries – Kenya, Uganda and Zambia:

This gave me the chance to explore them thoroughly. That said, I could have spent the entire time just in Kenya. I think striking a balance between rushing through a country and seeing nothing, and staying in one country and seeing everything is possible and desirable.

Often, it isn't until you get to a country that you realise how much there is to see and do, and the longer you stay the more opportunities you come across. You'll also have more flexibility if you concentrate on one country or area because you won't be tied in to the merry-go-round of a multistop international itinerary. So, if you fall in love with a place (or even with one of its inhabitants) you'll have the luxury of indulging that passion.

Large countries such as Australia, the USA, India, Canada, Brazil, Iran and China obviously lend themselves to an in-depth, lengthy exploration – although you'll have to think carefully about the cost of living in any of these countries except India and Iran. Otherwise, getting beyond the brochure is endlessly fascinating in Turkey, Egypt, Morocco and Thailand. Alternatively, it is deeply rewarding to focus on groups of countries such as Indochina (Vietnam, Laos and Cambodia); Central America; southern, East and West Africa; or Israel, Jordan, Syria and Lebanon. And, let's not forget Europe – there's heaps in France, Spain or

Germany to keep you occupied for months. Career-breakers Helen Grainger and Mathew Saks spent three months in France:

We focused on the southern part of France – Toulouse and the surrounding areas for the first month, then Lourdes (fascinating, whatever your religion), Biarritz, the coast (from the Riviera to Monte Carlo), then up through Provence and the mountains, Chamonix, Annecy, then back through the Somme and the war fields. One thing we figured out pretty quickly was that we couldn't do everything, so prioritising was important. We also worked with the seasons. We made the most of the beaches while the weather was good and then headed inland when it became too cold and damp to swim (we were travelling mid-August to mid-November).

One of the attractions of exploring a country or region in-depth is that you get to see it at various times of the year. It is often amazing how different countries can be in winter or summer, in the high season or when you're the only tourist in town. Seasons will also play a large part in deciding which country to explore when. For instance, spending three months going mouldy in India during the monsoon would not be an example of blue-sky thinking.

An additional benefit of staying longer in one country is that you'll start to pick up the lingo – without going to language school. That's worth something, as long as it isn't just 'Have a good day' perfected during your time in the US or 'No worries mate' picked up in Australia.

Any plans to stay longer in a country must, of course, be squared with visa restrictions.

ADVENTURE TRAVEL & EXPEDITIONS

ADVENTURE TOUR OPERATORS

If you've always looked down on taking an organised tour then perhaps this is the time to look up and open your eyes. Climbing volcanoes in Tanzania or travelling the Silk Road will thrill you to the core but can be difficult and time-consuming to organise. If your career break is short or you're too busy to think your trip through before you leave, consider the organised-tour option. If you're travelling on your own and want company or need a confidence booster at the beginning of your trip, this might also be the solution.

Many of the tour operators specialising in adventure travel do it well. Groups are small (often under 12 people), flexibility is key and most adhere to strict responsible-tourism codes. In addition, your organised tour doesn't have to start or end in your country of origin. You can join a tour at any point during your break as long as it is prebooked. For instance, you might want to travel independently for the vast majority of your trip but join your favourite tour operator for a particularly special or hard-to-organise section of your trip. Jane Oliver did just this in Africa:

Before I left home I booked a 17-day trip with Exodus taking in Kenya, Uganda and the mountain gorillas in Rwanda. I really wanted to do this with a tour operator because the distances were too great to cover independently in my time frame and I thought it would be fun to be part of a group. It was an amazing experience – the gorillas were by far the highlight and travelling with a great bunch of like-minded people exceeded my expectations. It made a real change from travelling on my own.

A growth area for adventure tour operators is in the tailor-made tour. This means you get all the benefits of booking with a tour operator but none of the disadvantages of a scheduled group tour with a set itinerary. You choose who you travel with, when you go, how long for, what you want to see and do, and where you want to stay. Your tour operator then organises every last detail of your itinerary and the only finger you have to lift is the one that writes out the cheque. When you arrive at your destination you're met at your plane, train or limousine and looked after by a personal guide (or sequence of guides) for the duration of your tour. Depending on the company and the country, you might also have a car, as Jane Lockwood had in Thailand:

A private guide and driver took us from Bangkok to Chiang Mai. On the trip we explored major sites such as Ayuthaya and Sukhothai, visited remote tribal villages, reached the northernmost point of Thailand and sailed on the Mekong River. We finished our trip with a few days of relaxation in Phuket. Our guide was informative and knowledgeable. He gave us a real insight into Thai culture, answering our many questions with good humour and charm. A drawback of this form of travel is missing out on opportunities to meet locals and, of course, routes have to be preagreed in outline. Where time is limited it is an excellent, relaxing way to see the highlights of a country.

Of course, this personal service comes at a price but the bespoke tour is becoming a very popular option with career-breakers who've got more money than time or who just want to spoil themselves for a portion of their time away. For an idea of prices see the Contacts section (p112).

The Contacts section of this chapter lists only a small number of the many tour operators offering a range of activities, adventures and destinations. For more information, consult the directory of the Association of Independent Tour Operators (AITO) at www.aito.co.uk, look at the classified ads in *Wanderlust* magazine (www.wanderlust .co.uk) or get yourself along to one of the Daily Telegraph Adventure Travel & Sports Shows (www.adventureshow.co.uk).

For details of working for a tour operator as a tour leader, see the Living & Working chapter (p184).

OVERLAND ADVENTURE COMPANIES

Travelling through a region, country or continent by land is a very special experience. It all started in the 1970s with the classic London to Kathmandu hippie trail. Since then routes have mushroomed and you can travel through tropical, desert, temperate or cold climes all over the world. How does travelling from Alaska to Tierra del Fuego grab you? Or what about London to Cape Town?

If this style of travel appeals, then you'll probably look at booking a trip with one of the many overland adventure companies. They all have fleets of 4WD trucks that are more Ben & Jerry than Mr Whippy. They are tough but comfortable, with padded seats, stereo, safe, camp oven, retractable awnings, reference library, roof racks, lighting and sometimes fridge/freezer. They seat around 25 passengers plus two leaders, one of whom (phew) will be an ingenious mechanic.

Living with around 24 other people in a large truck day in day out has its ups and downs. If you're prone to biting people's heads off at work, then forget it (the wildlife is expected to do this, not you). Plus you'll be asked to muck in and help with the chores of cooking, cleaning or shopping. A good group dynamic is essential to the success of this sort of trip and you're most likely to fit in if you're in your thirties and single (although some couples do take trips) and you get on with all nationalities. An interest in adventure is obviously what brings you all together and there's plenty of time to indulge in bungee jumping, white-water rafting, wildlife watching etc.

The shortest overland trip is a week and the longest just shy of one year. The more time you spend on the road, the more reasonable the cost becomes, with some of the longest trips costing under £9000 (flights and kitty not included). As with adventure tours, you can join a truck at any time during your break, as long as you've booked.

For a comprehensive list of overland companies and routes see www.go-overland.com. Overland companies' websites also give good information about life on the road and in the truck. A selection of overland companies are listed on p112 but do check out others. Details on working for overland companies are included on p185.

INDEPENDENT OVERLANDING

If the idea of overlanding appeals but, like Frank Sinatra, you prefer to do things your way, then help is at hand. There are companies that will procure and prepare a vehicle, and equip it for vehicle-based overland travel, whether it's two weeks in the Sahara or six months' driving from London to Cape Town. All related driver and mechanical training is also offered.

A useful online resource for anyone planning an independent overland expedition is British Expedition Vehicles (www.britishexpeditionvehicles.com). Here you'll find information on preparing your vehicle, planning your expedition and what to do about issues such as shipping, insurance and a *carnet de passage*. At the other extreme, there's always the slightly softer option of a self-drive safari trip in your own Land Rover in southern Africa. (See p113 in the Contacts section for details.)

Many motoring and motorbike clubs also organise overland jaunts. The Endurance Rally Association (www.endurorally.com) organised an Around the World in Eighty Days rally in 2000 and their next big one is Peking to Paris (www.pekingparis.com) in 2007. The Classic Car Rally Association (www.classicrally.org.uk) runs shorter overland trips.

EXPEDITIONS

The word 'expedition' is often used as a marketing device by travel companies to attract us to holidays. It is used by voluntary organisations such as Raleigh to describe their placements. It is used by my best friend, Julia, when talking about her shopping sprees.

Matt Cambridge from the Expedition Company defines its true meaning as:

...a journey organised for a particular purpose. It is generally considered to involve a team of people. The purpose can be anything from reaching the North Pole, to summiting Everest, to building a medical centre in Africa.

The first stop if you're planning a real DIY expedition is the Royal Geographical Society (RGS; www.rgs.org/eac). The RGS gives help and advice to over 500 expeditions a year and has a special Expedition Advisory Centre (see p113 in the Contacts section). In November each year the centre runs a weekend Expedition Planners' seminar where you can make contacts, listen to talks and attend workshops on all aspects of expedition and fieldwork planning. It publishes a book called *Fundraising to Join an Expedition*, which you can download for free at www.rgs .org/eacpubs. Here you'll also find other useful publications such as the *Expedition Planners Handbook* by Shane Winser, *Expedition Medicine* by Warrell & Anderson and *Vehicle Dependent Expeditions* by Tom Sheppard. Online you'll find a database of past expedition reports from 1965 onwards, and for £2.50 you can order a bulletin of expedition vacancies. Its Expedition Mapping Unit runs training courses in GIS and GPS and the Medical Cell can give more specialised medical advice. At its premises in Kensington you can visit the newly refurbished Library and Map Room, which holds the largest collection of overseas maps in the world and over 150,000 books dating from 1830 (a small research fee is charged to nonmembers).

If you have a group or team that wants to undertake a particular expedition but you don't have the expertise, local knowledge or equipment to plan and execute a DIY expedition then a group like the Expedition Company (see p113 in the Contacts section) can help. You can talk to staff about the type of expedition you want to undertake and they'll give you advice and work with you to create and coordinate your trip. You'll use the company's equipment and its in-country contacts, and your expedition will be escorted by one of its leaders.

For those of you who want to join an expedition but don't have a preformed group, there are a number of companies that run scheduled expeditions (see p113 in the Contacts section for details). Many of these expeditions are in mountainous areas and range from two weeks to 70 days (which is how long it takes to climb Mt Everest). Summiting Everest is also one of the most expensive expeditions at around £28,000. In many ways, these companies are like the ultimate adventure tour operator – everything's arranged so all you have to concentrate on is getting through the experience.

Organisations running voluntary conservation expeditions are covered in the Volunteering & Conservation chapter (p146).

RETREATS & PILGRIMAGES

Retreats are becoming a very popular way of starting or finishing a career break. If you're so stressed at work that you fear standing on your desk and shouting 'I'm a career-breaker; get me out of here', then try a retreat at the beginning of your trip. It'll unwind, relax and re-energise you. They're useful at the other end too, giving your brain time to switch from international traveller to domestic council tax payer (again).

A retreat can take many forms. The common denominator is that they all offer a safe, peaceful place where you have the privacy and time to think. Most retreats are houses or centres set in beautiful, unspoilt locations off the beaten track. Some retreats are on islands, such as the Midnight Sun Ashtanga Yoga Retreat on Hanko Island, Finland, and the Gold Buddha Island Eco-Resort on an island off Phuket. There's even one in southern Turkey where you stay in Mongolian-style yurts (see p114 in the Contacts section for booking details). A retreat generally has no TV, radio or newspapers. They offer a healthy approach to life, with vegetarian meals and little or no alcohol. Many are also eco-friendly, with solar panels to generate heat and light.

Having said that, there are no hard and fast rules. Some retreats are simple and basic. A growing number are luxurious, offering holistic massages, Ayurvedic treatments and general pampering. Many combine a place of refuge with one or more activities that promote serenity, such as yoga, meditation, walking or sometimes creative writing and painting. Some retreats are guided by a teacher, some offer group discussions, others are totally silent.

The traditional view of a retreat is that it has some religious basis and, sure, some retreats are more conducive to prayer and spiritual contemplation than others. However, even those promoted by the Christian-based Retreat Association (see p114 in the Contacts section for details) are open to anyone of any or no faith. This holds true even if you feel like retreating to a monastery or convent while you're on the road. These are often dotted along the main routes to shrines or places of pilgrimage and hospitality is still a key part of their function. If there's a room free, they'll give you simple board and lodging in return for a small donation. Some of these even welcome children. Career-breaker Graham Williams has this to say on the subject:

I spent 10 days doing a meditation retreat at a Buddhist monastery in Thailand. I found this very worthwhile. I still practise meditation and regularly attend at my local Buddhist monastery and have gone on retreat there also. So, it was something of a life-altering experience, which travel, particularly for long periods, should be all about.

You can stay in a retreat for as little as 24 hours or as long as a month. The cost really depends on the style of retreat you have chosen but can range from £300 to £700 for a week. As safety is a big issue on a retreat, strangers turning up at the door are discouraged, so you should book in advance. To work out what type of retreat is best for you, have a look at *The Good Retreat Guide* by Stafford Whiteaker and *Places to Be*, edited by Jonathan How. Both books concentrate on retreats in the UK but do have some overseas options (*Places to Be* has a good website with a searchable database at www.places-to-be.com). Retreats International also has a useful website (www.retreatsintl.org), particularly if you're interested in North America. Other retreat resources, associations and agencies are listed on p114.

ASHRAMS

It is said that an ashram is a retreat but that a retreat is not necessarily an ashram. The main difference is that an ashram is led by a spiritual leader or guru and you go there for spiritual guidance, teaching and practice. As such, life at an ashram is basic, disciplined, ordered and as pure as possible. Ashrams, sometimes accommodating over 200 students, have a lot of rules – celibacy, modest dress, no meat, fish, eggs, alcohol, drugs, garlic, onion or smoking, to name but a few. Often your days are highly scheduled, starting at 5.30am and finishing at 10pm, with two vegetarian meals per day. In between there'll be classes, usually in yoga, meditation, relaxation and chanting. Many ashrams make these sessions or classes mandatory.

As an ashram is a community, travellers tend to stay for at least three weeks to get into the communal spirit. If you want, you can stay for much longer or even forever. There is a daily contribution for staying in an ashram. The rate depends on a country's cost of living but is kept low by the daily chores you also have to do.

Ashrams exist all over the world. However, most travellers choose to stay in one in India. This has resulted in some bogus centres springing up, so you need to be cautious about which ashram you choose. Try to find one that was started by an established teacher or one that is part of an established teaching tradition. If you're in the country, ask around locally for those that have a good reputation. There are two well-respected Sivananda ashrams in India – one in Kerala and one in Uttarkashi in the Himalaya (see www.sivananda.org/locations/ashrams.html for details). Others with a good reputation include Sri Aurobindo ashram (www.sriaurobindoashram.org) in Pondicherry; Anandashram (www.anandashram.org) in Kerala; and Amritapuri Ashram (www.amritapuri.org/ashram) in Amritapuri, near Kollam, south Kerala.

In all cases, it is asked that you book in advance rather than just turn up hoping to stay.

PILGRIMAGES

One of the earliest forms of travelling was on a pilgrimage (another was at the other end of the spectrum – for war). In its purest form a pilgrimage is a journey to a site or relic that has been deemed sacred by a religion or belief system. As such, a pilgrimage is a thoughtful undertaking where the traveller is usually hoping for some sort of enlightenment. Often, pilgrims will travel in groups at certain times of year to coincide with seasons, festivals or lunar configurations. Having said that, a meaningful pilgrimage is one you take when the time is right for you, personally, so there is no right or wrong time to make your trip.

The most popular European pilgrimages are to Lourdes (www.lourdes-france.org – check out the webcam); Medjugorje in Bosnia & Hercogovina (www.medjugorje.org); Fatima in Portugal (www.santuario-fatima.pt); the Holy See in Rome (www.vatican.va); and Santiago de Compostela in Spain (www.csj.org.uk). If you want to go in a group with a religious leader then check the ads in papers such as the *Catholic Herald* (www.catholicherald.co.uk), the *Tablet* (www.thetablet.co.uk) or the *Church Times* (www.churchtimes.co.uk). There are also a number of pilgrimage tour operators; including Pax Travel Pilgrims (www.paxtravel .co.uk) and Tangney Tours (www.tangney-tours.com).

Some of the most unforgettable and visually stimulating places of pilgrimage are those sacred to Hindus, Buddhists and other Eastern faiths. If you're intent on visiting one of these during your break then try to coincide with a local religious festival or event (see the boxed text, p100). Otherwise, check what is going on nationally. For instance, India is fabulous in February/March when Holi, the nationwide festival of colour, takes place – get ready to be drenched by coloured water and then caked with coloured powder. India, of course, is awash with spiritualism, festivals and pilgrimage sites. To check what's going on where, have a look at www.pilgrimage-india.com – a commercial site but also useful for reference.

Of course, a pilgrimage doesn't have to be religious – it may be a journey to somewhere that is special and very personal to you. If you lived abroad as a child, perhaps you would like to go back; if a family member fought in a war and died abroad, perhaps you want to visit their grave. Many people also make pilgrimages just for the adventure, discovery, spectacle or cultural immersion involved. And, of course, many sites and journeys of religious significance are tourist attractions in their own right. For instance, any friendly atheist who enjoys walking could travel the Camino de Santiago and have a whale of a time.

HE WHO WOULD VALIANT BE COULD TRY SOME OF THESE:

Allahabad (India) This is where the Ganges and the Yamuna Rivers meet. All pious Hindus hope to bathe here at least once in their lives. Pilgrims come here from mid-January to mid-February during the festival of Magh Mela. This is also where the massive Kumbh Mela takes place every 12 years. The next one is in 2013.

Catemaco (Mexico) On the western shore of Lake Catemaco, this is Mexico's centre of the occult. On the first Friday in March there's an annual shamans' convention.

The Holy Land (Palestine & Israel) Jerusalem is central to the Christian, Jewish and Muslim faiths. Most pilgrimages will also visit the hills of Galilee, Bethlehem, the Mount of Olives and Gethsemane.

Mt Kailash (Tibet) Sacred to Hindus, Buddhists and Jains, this is where Shiva is reputed to live. Pilgrims believe that a lifetime of sins will be wiped out if you walk its 32-mile circumference.

Mecca (Saudi Arabia) Every able Muslim is expected to visit Mecca at least once in their lifetime and this pilgrimage is called the hajj. As it attracts over two million people, personal safety is a major issue. Non-Muslims are not allowed to enter Mecca.

Puri (India) One of the four dhams or holiest Hindu pilgrimage places in India. Try to visit during the famously colourful Rath Yatra (Car Festival) held in June or July.

Santiago de Compostela (Spain) There are a few routes but the classic one enters Spain just north of Roncesvalles in the Navarran Pyrenees and runs 750km (466 miles) to Santiago de Compostela. Pilgrims or hikers rarely walk the whole length of this route but usually manage the last 100km to 200km (62 to 124 miles). The pilgrimage season is from Easter to October.

Taksang Monastery (Bhutan) It is believed that Guru Rinpoche meditated in a cave at this spot. The monastery clings precariously to a cliff. An ascent takes about three hours on foot or pony.

Tikal ruins (Guatemala) These spectacular and ancient Mayan ruins comprise a Unesco World Heritage Site. The location is set in fairly deep jungle in the Parque Nacional Tikal.

CUTTING THE COSTS OF TRAVEL

The two most expensive elements of travelling are accommodation and transport. There are ways of reducing the cost of both, and most involve testing your tolerance of hard and/or lumpy surfaces. Or, you can reduce your transport costs by working your passage.

CREWING

Joining the crew of a yacht is a really adventurous way of circumnavigating the world. If you're more 'sea dog' than 'sick as a dog' around boats, you should try it at least once in your life. Yachting is seasonal and therefore predictable. The two main sailing seasons are from April to October in the Mediterranean and October to May in the Caribbean. In the Mediterranean boats usually sail west to east in the spring, ending up in the Greek Islands or on the Turkish coast. In October many of them head back to Gibraltar before congregating in the Canary Islands for the November/December Atlantic crossing to catch the tail end of the season in the Caribbean. If you want to crew in the Mediterranean, good yachting centres are Gibraltar, the Balearic Islands and the Greek Islands. In the Caribbean, the first port of call reached after the month-long Atlantic crossing is usually Barbados or St Lucia.

Crewing is all about being in the right place at the right time. The following table shows where boats are heading, when, and from where. Memorise this and it'll maximise your chance of picking up a boat on your travels:

WORLDWIDE YACHTING SCHEDULE

Months	From	To
January to March	South Africa (Cape Town)	the Caribbean, the Mediterranean, South America
March to April	Gibraltar	Greece, Turkey
March to May	the Caribbean	USA (East Coast), the Mediterranean, Panama Canal
March to May	Northern Europe	the Mediterranean
March to June	USA (West Coast)	South Pacific (particularly Tahiti)
April	New Zealand	Australia, USA (West Coast) via Pacific Islands
April to June	USA (East Coast)	the Mediterranean
May to July	South Africa (Durban)	islands of the Indian Ocean
June to August	Australia (Darwin)	Indonesia, islands of the Indian Ocean
August to September	Fiji	New Zealand
September to October	Greece, Turkey	Gibraltar
October to November	Gibraltar	the Caribbean via the Canary Islands for an Atlantic crossing
October to November	USA (West Coast)	Mexico
November	islands of Indian Ocean	South Africa (Durban)
November	USA (East Coast)	the Caribbean
November to December	the Canary Islands	the Caribbean

Amateur long-distance races or regattas also offer good opportunities for crewing. The largest transoceanic sailing event in the world is the Atlantic Rally for Cruisers (ARC; www .worldcruising.com), which departs Las Palmas de Gran Canaria in November/December and finishes at Rodney Bay Marina in St Lucia in the Caribbean. Another big yachting event is Antigua Sailing Week (www.sailingweek.com), which takes place at the end of April. Yacht owners are often looking for crew at these times, either as an extra pair of eyes and hands or to help contribute to costs. If you're working your passage as a deck hand, most skippers or owners ask you to pay up to £10 a day towards your keep.

Sounds easy? Like everything else in life, finding a boat that'll take you on as crew isn't plain sailing. Competition for crewing jobs is strong and the more sailing experience you've got, the better. If you have a Competent Crew certificate (see p219 for more details), you'll have a much better chance of getting your first job. If you really want to push the boat out then a five-day intensive Day Skipper shore-based course (from around £385) and a five-day intensive Day Skipper Practical (from around £500) is even better. While you're at it, you could also do the one-day RYA (Royal Yachting Association) Small Craft First-Aid course (from £90), as it is always useful to have someone at sea with some medical training.

If you haven't spent your weekends in the Solent 'messing around in boats' then the job you're most likely to get is deck hand. This is the equivalent of the office junior, explains career-breaker Kelly Smith:

I worked as a deck hand on a Dutch-built 121ft yacht that was circumnavigating the world. I worked under the first mate and most of the work we did involved keeping the exterior of the boat cleaned and maintained. This meant at least eight hours a day and at least five days a week grinding out problem areas (usually corrosion) on the hull or on the superstructure of the yacht, building them back up, priming, sanding and painting until it looked like there was never a problem. Also, there was a lot of varnish to maintain on board and we were forever taping off areas, sanding them down and varnishing, sanding and varnishing, sanding and varnishing. There were pieces of equipment and rigging to be maintained so that they were operating safely. On occasion, we hoisted each other up on the forward mast to do mainte- nance work (always fun, because you had a great view of everything from up there). There were always a million projects to keep the boat in tiptop shape.

Most crewing positions are organised on the fly, when you're in the middle of your trav- els. Hanging out at the local repair yard, chandlery or yachtie bar is always a good way of meeting skippers. However, if you want to tee up a crewing position before you leave home then yacht delivery is a really good deal (see p115 in the Contacts section for details). Another option is to get on board with the Cruising Association's crewing service (see the Contacts section, p115). Looking at the classified ads in magazines such as *Yachting Monthly* (www.yachtingmonthly.com) and *Yachting World* (www.yachting-world.com) is also worthwhile. Applying to specialist crewing agencies is possible (see p115) but inexperienced crew don't always find positions. Having said that, this was how Kelly Smith started out, with previous experience only in catering and waitressing:

I got hooked up with a crew agency in the Pacific Northwest (there are many yacht-crew agencies all over the world…many in Fort Lauderdale, Newport, San Diego, the Mediterranean, the UK; even Thailand, Australia and New Zealand). I met the agent and did an interview. I started out as a stewardess on a 105ft American yacht and when that job didn't work out (after three months of my personality not quite fitting with the rest of the crew) I returned to the same agent and got work as a deck hand on the world-circumnavigating yacht.

If you plan to do some crewing while you're travelling, make sure your passport has more than a year to go on it. You will also need either a ticket home from your final destination or proof of enough money to buy your ticket. When you join a boat you're signed on as crew and you can only be signed off, or assigned to another boat, if you can fulfil these requirements. When you arrive at a port immigration staff normally give you a couple of days to make onward plans.

DRIVEAWAY CARS

The US and Canada are favourite career-break destinations, but long-term car rental can become expensive (even with a favourable rate of exchange). In addition, one-way rentals are sometimes expensive. What you can do, however, is register with one of the many driveaway car companies that need drivers to move cars from one region to another.

You must be over 21 and have a valid driving licence, personal references and a chunk of cash (around £200) as a deposit (refundable when you deliver the car safe and sound to its destination). You don't pay anything for the hire of the car but you do have to cover all fuel (beware of gas guzzlers), food and accommodation expenses along the way. The car will have to be delivered to its destination at a particular time and sometimes a route is specified by the company. Six to eight hours of driving per day is usually allocated and you'll have a maximum allowable mileage. Destinations are often seasonal but coast-to-coast routes come up a lot and at the start of winter many cars need delivering to Florida.

Driveaway car companies are listed in the Yellow Pages under Automobile Transporters and Driveaway Companies (ring a week or two before you want to travel). One of the biggest is Auto Driveaway (www.autodriveaway.com).

MONEY TROUBLE

We've all been there, whether at home or away. You think you've budgeted for everything and then something unexpected happens. Perhaps you are forced to stay longer than planned in a relatively expensive part of the world, which is what happened to Glyn Williams – see his testimonial opposite. Maybe you had to hire private transport to get from W to X when you'd hoped to get the bus. Or maybe you went into the jewellers to buy one star ruby and couldn't resist buying the shop's entire stock. Career-breaker Louise Jones advises:

Don't run out of money. Travelling for a long time is like running a business – you have to plan the use of your time and money carefully.

Even if you have planned carefully, you may run out of money and, apart from ruby retail therapy, it isn't always within your control.

So, if you're caught short in the middle of travelling, what are the best options for raising some quick cash? Some of the most popular short-term jobs are looked at in the following section. Other options include busking, street performing, modelling or appearing as a film extra. Working in retail, covering busy times like Christmas or the sales, is something to consider. Working at special events such as sporting championships, music festivals and exhibitions is also possible. Local recruitment agencies usually handle this type of opportunity.

Career-breaker James Ingham says:

I taught English at a small school in a town in Central Mexico (San Miguel de Allende) and wrote for an English-language newspaper. Both experiences were fantastic – trying something I would not otherwise have ever done.

Devon Hanley did it this way:

I worked at a hostel in New Zealand. It was a great job for a traveller since it was full of back-packers. The only thing that was tough was when I had to bust someone's balls about one thing or another since I knew the roles could easily be reversed. I also worked in Thailand. I got my dive master's certificate and worked as a DM during the day and as a bartender at night.

In theory, the possibilities are endless – see the Living & Working chapter for more ideas (including a section on teaching abroad, p176). In practice, however, the one big obstacle is your visa and your right, or not, to work wherever it is that you've run out of money.

WORK PERMITS FOR CASUAL WORK

If you're going to run out of money, try to do so in a country where you can work legally. For the Brits, this means the European Economic Area (EEA). If your grandparents or parents were considerate enough to live or give birth in another country, qualifying you for dual nationality, then this is when your second passport earns its keep. Otherwise, you'll need to be young enough to apply for various working holiday visas. For more information, see p168 in the following Living & Working Abroad chapter.

Working illegally is obviously an option, but can't be recommended.

HOSPITALITY

Many of you will experience a grim sense of *déjà vu* at the thought of working in a bar, club, restaurant or hotel during your break. Didn't you do this on Saturdays when you were a teenager? Whether or not you like the idea, work in this sector is where most travellers turn when cash is in short order. The two main reasons are obvious: there are tons of jobs in the hospitality industry and there's a high turnover of staff. In a tourist resort most establishments are staffed-up at the beginning of a season but then employees start to drop out. In major cities the demand for waiters, chefs, kitchen assistants, dishwasher loaders, pint pullers, cocktail mixers, receptionists and hotel cleaning staff is constant. Jobs are not hard to find – look for signs in restaurant and bar windows or just walk straight in and ask about situations vacant. Particularly if you've got experience, these jobs are easy to pick up. If you're lucky, some will be cash in hand and, luckier still, some will pay decent tips.

If the money situation goes from black to red quicker than the chameleon perched on your bedroom wall, you might have to downgrade and work slightly closer to your home away from home. Stacey McCarthy explains that she nearly had to do this:

I came close to working at my favourite guest house in exchange for room and board.

FARM WORK

If you listen to *The Archers* on BBC Radio 4 then you'll be used to David and Ruth constantly whingeing about how much work there is to do on a farm. Depending on where you are in the world, farm work could include milking, fencing, ditching, tractor driving, sheep shearing, packing, planting, general repairs and odd jobs, to name but a few possibilities. This is good news for out-of-pocket travellers, as farm work is fairly easy to tee up, particularly if you're on the spot. It may be that a farm is so desperate for help with seasonal work that formalities such as work visas are overlooked. This was the case with Glyn Williams:

We worked in Australia but not through choice. My partner's mother had booked a ticket to visit us in New Zealand for Christmas, without telling us. We were therefore forced to stay in the region for two months longer than we'd planned. Due to the horrendous expense of Australia compared with Asia, we had to find illegal work on farms. I did various jobs: bringing in the melon harvest, cutting bananas, working in a plant nursery. My partner sorted bananas. The work was dull, long and poorly paid and it was difficult to save. I can't understand why people go to Australia to do this of their own free will – it's the pits.

Not exactly a glowing recommendation, but bringing in the vegetable and fruit harvests is the largest source of casual farm work for travellers. In theory, if you run out of money almost anywhere in the world at the right time then you can get harvesting work. This could be anything from picking fruit (eg grapes, strawberries, raspberries, cherries, pears, plums, nectarines, apples) to vegetables (eg potatoes, lettuces). It is back-breaking, physically demanding work. You are usually paid piecework rates, which means you get paid according to how many bins (or whatever the container is) that you fill. It is particularly dispiriting at first because it takes a while to hone your technique, meaning you start off earning much less than experienced workers. Still, you usually get free board and lodging (though not always) and you should at least earn whatever the national minimum wage is in the country where you're working (unless you're working without a permit).

If you're in Australia then harvesting work is available year round. Log onto http://jobsearch .gov.au/harvesttrail to work out where you need to be to pick up work. Other useful websites are www.pickingjobs.com and www.anyworkanywhere.com. Otherwise, most jobs are advertised in local youth hostels, shops and cafés or passed on by word of mouth. Sometimes local recruitment agencies deal with this type of work (see p102 in the Contacts section of this chapter).

If you have an interest in organic farming and want to help out in return for food and lodging, contact World-Wide Opportunities on Organic Farms (WWOOF) – see p152 for details.

TEMPING

Another option to tide you over is to register with a temping agency. You can be really temporary and do as little as one day's work or as permanent as you like and take one position after another. Temping is really worth thinking about because your experience and professional skills should mean you can earn decent money. These days you can temp in almost any profession. Simon Pullum took a break from being a performer but ended up having a bit of a busman's holiday:

I became a singing telegram. For four weeks, I earned good money doing sometimes 30 telegrams a week, zig-zagging across the suburbs from office party to corporate functions, private parties, hen nights, retirements, birthdays etc. I was a Pink Fairy, a 'Flashing' Scotsman, a Red Devil, a Giant Chicken, a Puny Tarzan, a Unicycling Flim Flam man, and, of course, the all-time favourite Gorilla-Gram – you try juggling bananas with tunnel vision through a smelly, sweaty, rubber mask while singing 'Happy birthday to you'...

Megan Dorcas temped in Melbourne. She signed up with a secretarial temp agency and walked out with a totally different assignment:

I thought I'd be offered an office job but ended up with a three-week position as a foot courier. I'd only just arrived in Melbourne so didn't know the layout of the city but thought this would be an excellent way of killing two birds with one stone – earning money and also getting to know the place. I spent three weeks in early summer walking from office to office with important documents – it was a totally different experience from the one I imagined when I decided to do some temping. It also gave my friends back home a real laugh because I've always been known for my terrible sense of direction.

To register with a temping agency you'll need a working visa, copies of your CV and some references. You are usually paid weekly and will need to open a bank account. Many of the temping agencies in the UK have international offices (see p188 for details).

LABOURING

Finding manual unskilled work on a construction site used to be as easy as falling off a tall building. In recent years, the industry has tightened up worldwide as working regulations have multiplied. In addition, the construction industry is highly unionised in many countries, particularly Australia and New Zealand. That said, blokes (yes, it's pretty gender specific) still manage to pick up building work on their travels. Career-breaker Richard Hindle struck lucky down under:

I ran out of money in Alice Springs and thought the pub would be a good place to look for work. I ended up sharing a beer with a bloke who was a partner in a bush restaurant which had yet to be built. He hired me on the spot to help. The next day we loaded up his ute with building equipment and drove 75km out of Alice Springs to the site – it was in the middle of nowhere. Two labourers and I started clearing the area and building the restaurant. We had to cut down our own trees to make uprights for the roof, build retaining walls out of stones we collected ourselves, build barbecues and damper pits and dig pit toilets. The tables and chairs were made out of redwood sleepers from the old Ghan railway. We slept on site in swags during the week but stayed in Alice on Friday, Saturday and Sunday night. We were paid each Friday – down the pub, cash in hand. It was an amazing, real Aussie experience.

If you're skilled in this area then you can apply for work through a recruitment agency specialising in construction (see p188 for details). If you're not skilled, then sticking to the smaller sites and working for private individuals will increase your chances of being taken on. Making contacts down the pub, as Richard did, or hearing of jobs via word of mouth (or email) still pays dividends.

RESOURCES FOR JOBSEEKERS

If you're running low on funds, spend a penny at the local Internet café to access the following sites. Some are for younger career-breakers with working holiday visas, some are aimed at gappers but useful to all, and others flag seasonal work of interest to older travellers:

- **www.alseasonsagency.com** This Australian hospitality recruitment agency welcomes casuals with working holiday visas.
- **www.anyworkanywhere.com** This site advertises jobs for travellers of all ages worldwide; there's no fee.
- **www.jobpilot.co.uk** Hunt through Europe's career market here.
- **www.jobs-in-europe.net** For jobs in Europe, check out this online guide.
- **www.nzjobs.go.to** This is an online database of jobs in New Zealand for those with a working visa; jobs include labouring/construction, short temping assignments, bar and café work and seasonal fruit picking. You have to pay to join.
- **www.payaway.co.uk** This excellent website lists jobs and information on working abroad for gappers as well as sending a regular jobs bulletin by email. The service is free. Despite being squarely aimed at gappers, there's lots here for the older traveller too.
- **www.southpacificemployment.com** Look for casual, short-term jobs in the South Pacific Islands and in New Zealand on this website.
- **www.worldwideworkers.com** This Australian employment agency advertises short-term employment in hospitality, sales, fruit picking, construction, clerical, nursing, accounting etc. There's a fee to join.

CONTACTS

ADVENTURE TOUR OPERATORS

Aurora Expeditions

182A Cumberland St, The Rocks, Sydney, NSW 2000, Australia
☎ +61 (0)2-9252 1033
fax +61 (0)2-9252 1373
auroraex@auroraexpeditions.com.au
www.auroraexpeditions.com.au
Concentrating on journeys exploring the Arctic Circle and Antarctica, Aurora offers educational travel with a difference. Cruises can be combined with wildlife watching and photography or extreme adventure sports eg cross-country skiing, climbing or kayaking around the North and South Poles.
Destinations: The Arctic, Antarctica, Galapagos Islands & the Amazon River.
Costs: The 21-day Shackleton Odyssey ex-Argentina is US$7000; the 15-day Voyage to the North Pole ex-Finland is US$15,950.
Eligibility: Sports experience is required, and medicals may be necessary.

Äventyrsresor AB (Scandinavian Adventures)

Hornsgatan 110, SE-117 26 Stockholm, Sweden
☎ +46 (0)8-5560 6900
fax +46 (0)8-5560 6914
info@aventyrsresor.se
www.aventyrsresor.se (click on the English flag)
Äventyrsresor AB has over 80 tours worldwide that specialise in culture, the natural environment and adventure activities. The company won the Swedish Grand Travel Award 2000 in the ecotourism category. In Scandinavia you can go sea kayaking in the Stockholm Archipelago or sail and trek the island of Spitsbergen in the Barents Sea. Tailor-made packages are also available.
Timing & Length of Trips: From three to 25 days, all year. The sea kayaking takes place from mid-June to end of August.
Destinations: Worldwide.
Costs: The six-day sea-kayaking trip costs €710 excluding flights (but including equipment, tents, guide and food). The 13-day trip to Spitsbergen costs €1990 for everything but airfares.
Eligibility: The minimum age is 15 years for most trips but children can sometimes be accommodated upon request.

Backroads

801 Cedar St, Berkeley, CA 94710, USA
☎ +1 800-462 2848, +1 510-527 1555
fax +1 510-527 1444
www.backroads.com
Backroads, one of North America's longest-running active travel companies, offers a wide array of guided multisport and family-friendly trips.
Timing & Length of Trips: Year-round trips of one to two weeks.
Destinations: 91 destinations in 34 countries.
Costs: US$1500 to US$4500.
Eligibility: Minimum-age restrictions apply on some trips.

Call of the Wild

2519 Cedar St, Berkeley, CA 94708, USA
☎ +1 888-378 1978, +1 510-849 9292
fax +1 510-644 3811
trips@callwild.com
www.callwild.com
One of the USA's longest-running female-owned adventure travel companies offers a wide variety of women-only wilderness trips.
Timing & Length of Trips: February to November, weekend to week-long trips.
Destinations: The US (including Alaska and Hawaii), Mexico, Peru & New Zealand.
Costs: US$150 to $2500.
Eligibility: Women only (of any age); men can be included in tailor-made group trips.

Dive Worldwide

Brayborne House, Forge Close, Stockbridge, Hampshire SO20 6FA, UK
☎ +44 (0)1794 389372
fax +44 (0)1794 389152
info@diveworldwide.com
www.diveworldwide.com
This company offers tailor-made diving holidays to exotic destinations, often coupled with cultural and wildlife experiences. For instance, you can dive along the west coast of South Africa and combine this with a safari. In South America you can explore the Mayan temples and dive the Belize barrier reef. In fact, you can create a whole round-the-world itinerary based on diving locations.
Timing & Length of Trips: From one to three months, departing any time of the year.
Destinations: The Arctic, Antarctica, the Pacific, Africa, Southeast Asia, the Caribbean & Europe.
Costs: One week from £800 to three months from £7000 all-inclusive.
Eligibility: No children under 12.

Ecotrek & Bogong Jack Adventures

PO Box 4, Kangarilla, South Australia 5157, Australia

☎ +61 (0)8-8383 7198

fax +61 (0)8-8383 7377

ecotrek@ozemail.com.au

www.ecotrek.com.au

Ecotrek is a renowned ecotourism accredited company. Nature-based tours explore Australia's best mountain regions, such as South Australia's Flinders Ranges and New South Wales' Blue Mountains. Other popular walking and cycling tours take in the superb South Australian wine regions and the wildlife mecca of Kangaroo Island. Cultural, educational and canoeing tours and themed international tours can also be arranged.

Destinations: Australia & Europe.

Costs: Five-day cycling wine tours from A\$560, eight-day walking tours from A\$1230.

Eligibility: All welcome.

Elderhostel

11 Ave de Lafayette, Boston, MA 02111, USA

☎ +1 877-426 8056, +1 978-323 4141

fax +1 617-426 0701

registration@elderhostel.org

www.elderhostel.org

www.roadscholar.org

Elderhostel offers educational, all-inclusive learning adventures for adults 55 and over. Sample guided trips include following in the footsteps of Lewis and Clark, visiting ancient Indian temples, and exploring rural French villages where famous painters such as Monet lived and worked. Their new Road Scholar programs feature small group sizes and emphasise hands-on, participatory learning via behind-the-scenes access to untouristed sights and destinations – think backstage on Broadway, dining in private kitchens.

Timing & Length of Trips: Year round, from one day to one month.

Destinations: 10,000 annual programs in 90 countries.

Costs: US\$500 to US\$5500; a limited number of scholarships are available for North American programs.

Eligibility: 55 or older, except for intergenerational programs.

Explore Worldwide

1 Frederick St, Aldershot, Hampshire GU11 1LQ, UK

☎ +44 (0)1252 760000

fax +44 (0)1252 760001

res@exploreworldwide.com

www.exploreworldwide.com

Explore is a small-group adventure travel company offering 300 tours in over 100 countries. You can go jungle camping in northern Thailand or visit the glaciers, canyons and volcanoes of Alaska. A real growth area is in family adventure holidays.

Timing & Length of Trips: From one week to 49 days; trips depart year round.

Destinations: 100 countries worldwide.

Costs: From £450 for two weeks and up to £6400 for the most expensive trip (flights included, some meals extra).

Eligibility: Minimum age is 14 except on Family Adventures, which cater for children from six years old.

Far Frontiers

The Pound, Ampney Crucis, Gloucestershire GL7 5SA, UK

☎ +44 (0)1285 850926

fax +44 (0)1285 851575

info@farfrontiers.com

www.farfrontiers.com

Far Frontiers organises personalised private journeys for individuals, families and groups and some fixed-date small-group departures (six to 10 people). You can visit the Mongolian nomads who hunt with golden eagles in the Altai Mountains or drive a 4WD across the Tibetan Plateau from Lhasa to Kathmandu.

Timing & Length of Trips: From one week to six months.

Destinations: Central Asia, China, Mongolia, Tibet, India, Nepal, Bhutan, the Middle & Far East, South America & Morocco.

Costs: From £800 for one week to £30,000 for six months.

Eligibility: Open to all; apparently babies love Bhutan!

Global Exchange

2017 Mission St, Suite 303, San Francisco, CA 94110, USA

☎ +1 800-497 1994, +1 415-255 7296

fax +1 415-255 7498

info@globalexchange.org

www.globalexchange.org

Global Exchange is an international human-rights organisation dedicated to promoting political, social and environmental justice. Via its unique Reality Tours to hotspots like Afghanistan and Iraq, participants get an up-close look at how the USA's economic and foreign policies impact other nations.

Timing & Length of Trips: At least two trips most months, one to two weeks each.

Destinations: A to Z, from Afghanistan to Zimbabwe.

Costs: US\$850 to US\$4000; partial scholarships available.

Eligibility: Restrictions apply for solidarity and activist delegations.

Himalayan Kingdoms

Old Crown House, 18 Market St, Wotton-under-Edge, Gloucestershire GL12 7AE, UK

☎ +44 (0)1453 844400

fax +44 (0)1453 844422

info@himalayankingdoms.com

www.himalayankingdoms.com

Himalayan Kingdoms runs about 70 trekking holidays and adventure tours per year but also does tailor-made trips.

For instance, you can visit Nagaland in northern India, which is just opening up to travellers or you can walk the Imperial Pilgrimage route in Japan. The company is a member of the International Porter Protection Group.
Timing & Length of Trips: Two weeks to 40 days, with trips running every week.
Destinations: The Himalaya region, Peru, Spain, Norway, the Swiss Alps, Greece, Turkey, Tien Shan in Kyrgyzstan, outer Mongolia, Thailand, Laos, Cambodia, Vietnam & Japan.
Costs: From £1350 for two weeks in Turkey to £5250 for 40 days in Bhutan, all-inclusive.
Eligibility: Open to all, including young children.

Intrepid Travel

11 Spring St, Fitzroy, Victoria 3065, Australia
☎ +61 (0)3-9473 2626
fax +61 (0)3-9419 5878
res@intrepidtravel.com
www.intrepidtravel.com
Specialising in Asia, IT celebrates adventurers and those with special interests eg Oxfam Journeys visits NGO projects across Asia, Family Adventures has activities for children and adults, and Gourmet Traveller explores regions through local food markets, cooking demonstrations and edible delights.
Destinations: Asia, the Middle East, Latin America, Antarctica, Russia & Europe.
Costs: A Gourmet Traveller nine-day trip to Malaysia (featuring Malay, Indian and Chinese food) is A$990; a 14-day Japanese gourmet visit is A$3250.
Eligibility: A medical may be required.

Jubilee Sailing Trust

Hazel Rd, Woolston, Southampton, Hampshire SO19 7GB, UK
☎ +44 (0)23 8044 9108
fax +44 (0)23 8044 9145
info@jst.org.uk
www.jst.org.uk
This company is not a tour operator but a registered charity. The JST has two tall ships (the *Lord Nelson* and *Tenacious*) which take able-bodied and disabled crew on all their trips. Some of the longer ones include the tall ship races in Europe and America, and the Atlantic Rally for Cruisers (ARC) in November/December from Las Palmas de Gran Canaria to St Lucia.
Timing & Length of Trips: From five days to one month throughout the year – see the voyage program on the website.
Destinations: Varies each year, but usually includes the Canary Islands, the Caribbean & the East Coast of America.
Costs: From £500 for five days to £2000 to enter the ARC.
Eligibility: Over 16 years of age, able-bodied or physically disabled.

KE Adventure Travel

32 Lake Rd, Keswick, Cumbria CA12 5DQ, UK
☎ +44 (0)17687 73966
fax +44 (0)17687 74693
info@keadventure.co.uk
www.keadventure.com
KE Adventure runs trekking, climbing, mountain-biking and adventurous holidays worldwide. You can climb six of Ecuador's highest volcanoes, including Chimborazo (the highest), or take a walking safari in the Serengeti with Masai guides. There is also a tailor-made service.
Timing & Length of Trips: From one to four weeks, all year.
Destinations: 42 countries in five continents.
Costs: From £700 for one week's trek in the Sierra Nevada (Spain), to £4200 for four weeks climbing the world's highest trekking peak (Lhakpa Ri, Tibet).
Eligibility: From 16 years of age.

Koning Aap Reizen (Monkey King Travel)

Meidoornweg 2, 1031GG Amsterdam, Netherlands
☎ +31 (0)20 7887700
fax +31 (0)20 7887701
info@koningaap.nl
www.koningaap.nl
Vlasmarkt 10, 9000 Ghent, Belgium
☎ +32 (0)9 234 13 11
fax +32 (0)9 233 52 92
info@koningaap.be
www.koningaap.be
Koning Aap Reizen, or Monkey King Travel, is a Dutch/Belgian travel adventure tour operator. The company organises group, individual and tailor-made tours. For instance, you can go overland from Damascus to Beijing, trek with Iranian nomads, visit tribal Chitral in Pakistan or tour Mt Kailash.
Timing & Length of Trips: From eight to 223 days, year round.
Destinations: 68 countries in Asia, the Middle East, Africa & Latin America.
Costs: Including flights from Amsterdam or Brussels, a 15-day tour to Morocco or Egypt starts at €750 and a 23-day tour to Chile and Easter Island costs from €2995.
Eligibility: For fit adults, but children are welcome on a few easier tours.

Mountain Travel Sobek

1266 66th St, Emeryville, CA 94608, USA
☎ +1 888-687 6235, +1 510-594 6000
fax +1 510-594 6001
info@mtsobek.com
www.mtsobek.com
MTS is a small-group adventure travel specialist with a passion for exploring far-flung wilderness areas. Specialities

include pioneering sea kayaking and exploratory white-water river-rafting descents. Groups rarely exceed 15 people.
Timing & Length of Trips: Year-round trips of one week to one month.
Destinations: Worldwide.
Costs: US$1500 to US$15,000.
Eligibility: Participants range from people in their late-twenties to those in their mid-eighties; health and fitness restrictions apply.

Peregrine Adventures
258 Lonsdale St, Melbourne, Victoria 3000, Australia
☎ +61 (0)3-9663 8611
fax +61 (0)3-9663 8618
info@peregrineadventures.com
www.peregrineadventures.com
With an emphasis on responsible tourism, this company believes in using local guides and takes small tour groups. Peregrine focuses on overland and adventure trips such as cycling in China or trekking in the Himalaya. A 10-day journey through Peru includes the Inca Trail to Machu Picchu.
Destinations: Africa, South America, Southeast Asia, the Himalaya, India & the Middle East.
Costs: The 10-day Classic Peru trip costs A$2165; international flights to Peru are extra.
Eligibility: Adventure journeys may require a medical.

Quark Expeditions UK
19A Crendon St, High Wycombe, Buckinghamshire HP13 6LJ, UK
☎ +44 (0)1494 464080
fax +44 (0)1494 449739
enquiries@quarkexpeditions.co.uk
www.quarkexpeditions.com
Quark runs polar cruises on icebreakers and ice-strengthened ships to the Arctic and the Antarctic. On all Antarctic voyages you'll see whales, penguins and sea birds and visit scientific stations and historic huts. In the Arctic you'd hope to see polar bears, whales and bird life. Wildlife experts and historians give lectures on board. Helicopters are used on the icebreakers for sightseeing. You can be sent a booklet on their strict environmental policy.
Timing & Length of Trips: Antarctica trips run from November to March; Arctic trips run from July to mid-September. Cruises range from 10 to 25 nights.
Destinations: The Arctic & the Antarctic.
Costs: From US$2895 for 10 days to US$23,995 for 22 days, excluding flights (you pick up the ships in either Argentina, Australia or New Zealand).
Eligibility: You must be reasonably fit; no children under the age of eight.

Regent Holidays
15 John St, Bristol, BS1 2HR, UK
☎ +44 (0)117 921 1711

fax +44 (0)117 925 4866
regent@regent-holidays.co.uk
www.regent-holidays.co.uk
This tour operator organises trips on the Trans-Siberian, Trans-Mongolian and Trans-Manchurian railways and beyond into Tibet, North Korea and China. You start the journey in Moscow and can travel to Vladivostok or to Beijing. Your Russian visa means you can't hop on and hop off at will – you need to prebook your stops. You can also book the ferry from Vladivostok to Japan (operates June to September) with Regent.
Timing & Length of Trips: A direct train to Beijing with no stops takes seven to eight days, depending on the line, but don't do it in one go – you can take as long as you like. Trains run all year and can be combined with a RTW ticket.
Destinations: Russia, Mongolia, North Korea, Tibet & China.
Costs: Straight through on the Trans-Mongolian costs £420, including one night in Moscow (flights are extra).
Eligibility: Lots of Russian babies and children travel on the train, so you won't feel out of place taking your children (though you might be mad to do so).

Ride World Wide
Staddon Farm, North Tawton, Devon EX20 2BX, UK
☎ +44 (0)1837 82544
fax +44 (0)1837 82179
rideww@aol.com
www.rideworldwide.co.uk
This company runs horse safaris and riding holidays worldwide. You can ride through the Wadi Rum in Jordan or through Rajasthan and visit the Nagaur or Pushkar camel fair.
Timing & Length of Trips: From one to three weeks.
Destinations: Europe, South America, Asia, the Middle East, Africa, the US & NZ.
Costs: From £605 for one week in Greece to £3900 for two weeks on safari in Kenya, excluding flights.
Eligibility: Children aged three and over are allowed on certain trips.

Road Trip Motorcycle Rentals & Tours
PO Box 8700, Bend, OR 97708, USA
☎ +1 541-317 1313
fax +1 541-317 1414
info@roadtrip-usa.com
www.roadtrip-usa.com
Road Trip's location in central Oregon makes a great base camp for self-guided or guided tours of the West's most famous open-road routes.
Timing & Length of Trips: Classic routes average 15 to 22 days.
Destinations: Most popular routes are the Pacific coast, southwestern USA, the American Rockies, the Canadian West & Indian Country (Idaho, Wyoming, Utah, Arizona).

Costs: 750/1500cc Honda rentals from US$78/128 per day, plus insurance.
Eligibility: A motorcycle licence is required for all rentals.

Saddleskiddadle
Ouseburn Building, Albion Row, Newcastle upon Tyne, Tyne and Wear NE6 1LL, UK
☎ +44 (0)191 265 1110
fax +44 (0)191 265 1110
info@skedaddle.co.uk
www.skedaddle.co.uk
This is one of the biggest independent cycle tour operators in Britain. You can cycle along the Grand Canyon in the US or across Cuba. There are scheduled trips as well as tailor-made ones.
Timing & Length of Trips: From one to three weeks, departing all year.
Destinations: Europe, the US, Canada, South America, Cuba, Japan & New Zealand.
Costs: From £500 for one week to three weeks from £2000, excluding flights.
Eligibility: Open to all aged 10 and over.

SEAL Asia
Siam EcoAdventures Co Ltd, 225 Rat-U-Thit 200 Year Rd, Patong Beach, Phuket, 83150 Thailand
☎ +66 76-340406
fax +66 76-340586
www.seal-asia.com
A member of the Dive Operators Club of Thailand, this company offers PADI and BSAC diving courses and diving expeditions. Also on offer are adventure trips involving sailing, surfing and sea kayaking.
Destinations: Thailand, Myanmar, Indonesia & India.
Costs: Myanmar; a seven-night live-aboard scuba-diving trip to the Mergui Archipelago in the Andaman Sea is US$1350. A six-day adventure cruise (including diving, sailing and sea kayaking) is US$958. Myanmar US$100 permits are extra.
Eligibility: A medical may be required.

Southern Sea Ventures
PO Box 781, Newport, NSW 2106, Australia
☎ +61 (0)2-9999 0541
fax +61 (0)2-9999 1357
info@southernseaventures.com
www.southernseaventures.com
This company offers kayaking adventures in tropical or polar sea locations. Trips can involve camping or overnighting on the mother ship. Polar expeditions include kayaking in iceberg territory, visiting Inuit communities and wildlife watching.
Destinations: Turkey, Fiji, Vanuatu, the Amazon, Antarctica, the High Arctic, Greenland, Tonga & Australia.
Costs: A moderate grade nine-day trip to Tonga is A$1945

(11 days costs A$2340), meals included. Activities include camping on uninhabited islands, cycling, snorkelling and diving.
Eligibility: Novice and experienced kayakers are welcome.

SwimTrek
3/38 Gleneagle Rd, London SW16 6AF, UK
☎ +44 (0)20 8696 0764
fax +44 (0)20 8480 7635
info@swimtrek.com
www.swimtrek.com
Island-hopping with a difference – instead of taking the boat, you swim from island to island. On dry land you walk from the end of one swim to the start of the next.
Timing & Length of Trips: Runs 30 trips a year to coincide with the summer seasons in both hemispheres. Trips run for one to two weeks.
Destinations: Australia, New Zealand, Greece, Croatia & Turkey.
Costs: One week from £600, excluding flights and evening meals.
Eligibility: You must be able to swim a distance of at least 3.2km (2 miles).

Thor Travel
228 Rundle St, Adelaide, South Australia 5000, Australia
☎ +61 (0)8-8232 3155, 1800 801 119
fax +61 (0)8-8232 3541
travel@thorworldtravel.com
www.thorworldtravel.com
Thor Travel organises a range of global adventure packages while specialising in trekking holidays in Nepal. These treks can either involve independent itineraries or group trips where porters help with backpacks. Treks normally take place from October to May.
Destinations: Particularly Tibet, Nepal, the Indian subcontinent, Asia & Central America.
Costs: The 15-day Mongolian Panorama explores mountain glaciers and deserts and costs A$4890. Trekkers meet Nomadic herders and attend festivals (if applicable).
Eligibility: A medical may be required.

Trek America & Footloose
PO Box 189, Rockaway, NJ 07866, USA
☎ +1 800-221 0596, +1 973-983 1144
fax +1 973-903 8551
info@trekusasales.com
www.trekamerica.com, www.footloose.com
Trek America offers activity-oriented camping trips (equipment included) throughout North America for 18- to 38-year-olds. Trips take in a combination of big cities, national parks, remote beaches and out-of-the-way towns. The maximum group size is 13. Tours for families and older travelers are available through the new Footloose unit, which emphasises hiking and lodging-based treks.

Timing & Length of Trips: One-week to two-month trips run all year round.
Destinations: The US (including Alaska), Canada & Mexico.
Costs: US$600 to US$3500.
Eligibility: Adventure camping trips are for 18- to 38-year-olds. Footloose and family programs are open age.

Tribes Travel

12 The Business Centre, Earl Soham, Woodbridge, Suffolk IP13 7SA, UK
☎ +44 (0)1728 685971
fax +44 (0)1728 685973
mail@tribes.co.uk
www.tribes.co.uk
This is a fair-trade travel company specialising in tailor-made trips and small-group holidays focusing on culture, wildlife safaris and treks. You can visit the mountain gorillas in Uganda and Rwanda or take a cruise to the Galápagos Islands on a small yacht. Tribes Travel won the British Airways Tourism for Tomorrow award for 2002.
Timing & Length of Trips: From one to four weeks, departing year round.
Destinations: Uganda, East & southern Africa, Morocco, Egypt, Jordan, Ecuador, Peru, India & Nepal.
Costs: One week starts from £700, four weeks from £2500, excluding flights.
Eligibility: Open to all ages.

Trips Worldwide

14 Frederick Place, Clifton, Bristol BS8 1AS, UK
☎ +44 (0)117 311 4400
fax +44 (0)117 311 4401
info@tripsworldwide.co.uk
www.tripsworldwide.co.uk
Trips is a specialist tour operator to Latin America and the 'alternative' Caribbean (ie not the beaches and the all-inclusive resorts). All trips are tailor-made. For instance, you can go jaguar-spotting in the Amazon or hike through the Valley of Desolation to the Boiling Lake in Dominica.
Timing & Length of Trips: From one week upwards, year round.
Destinations: Mexico, Central America, South America, Cuba, Dominica, Trinidad, Tobago, Guadeloupe, Haiti & Jamaica.
Costs: One week from £900 to three weeks from £3000, all-inclusive.
Eligibility: Open to all, including children of all ages.

Water By Nature Rafting Journeys

The Trainers Office, Windy Hollow, Sheepdrove, Lambourne, Berkshire RG17 7XA, UK
☎ +44 (0)1488 72293
fax +44 (0)1488 71311

rivers@waterbynature.com
www.waterbynature.com
This company is a specialist white-water rafting company, using a mixture of local and staff guides. You can do a 25-day Hidden Empire trip on the Omo River in Ethiopia, or take a trip on the Coruh River in northeastern Turkey, where you'll encounter some of the biggest white water in the world, raft past the ruins of Byzantine castles and sleep by ancient churches.
Timing & Length of Trips: From one to four weeks. Timing depends on when the rivers are at their best for rafting. The Turkey trip departs only in May and June and the Ethiopian trip in October and November.
Destinations: Morocco, Turkey, Zambia, Nepal, Tasmania, the US, Ethiopia & Chile.
Costs: One week from £650 or four weeks from £2100 for river trip only.
Eligibility: There are age restrictions on certain rivers at certain times of the year.

Wilderness Travel

1102 9th St, Berkeley, CA 94710, USA
☎ +1 800-368 2794, +1 510-558 2488
fax +1 510-558 2489
www.wildernesstravel.com
This is a long-standing adventure travel company offering top-notch cultural, wildlife-watching and hiking trips. Unique offerings include rugged expeditions, cultural trips, special symposiums with expert guest lecturers, photography-focused workshops and exploratory trips to exotic destinations.
Timing & Length of Trips: Two days to three weeks, year round.
Destinations: 100 options covering every continent.
Costs: US$2000 to US$10,000.
Eligibility: Age and fitness restrictions apply on many trips.

World Expeditions

Level 5, 71 York St, Sydney, NSW 2000, Australia
☎ +61 (0)2-8270 8400
fax +61 (0)2-9279 0566
enquiries@worldexpeditions.com.au
www.worldexpeditions.com.au
A long-established global adventure tourism company, WE also engages in responsible tourism practices. Activity trips include wildlife safaris, surfing and sailing, cruising, trekking, cycling and camel riding. Different activities and regions can be combined.
Destinations: Asia, Africa, South America, Antarctica, the Arctic, Europe, India & the Himalaya.
Costs: The 29-day Summit to Sea (trekking the Anna-purnas, a Chitwan safari, cycling to the Taj Mahal and sailing the Maldives) is A$3900.
Eligibility: A medical may be required.

OVERLAND ADVENTURE COMPANIES

Dragoman Overland Travel

Camp Green, Kenton Rd, Debenham, Suffolk IP14 6LA, UK
☎ +44 (0)1728 861133
fax +44 (0)1728 861127
info@dragoman.co.uk
www.dragoman.co.uk

Dragoman is the largest overland company in the UK, offering a slightly up-market experience. You can blaze a trail from Cairo to Khartoum or drive overland from Dover to Beijing.

Timing & Length of Trips: From two weeks to 47 weeks, with at least 52 departures a year.
Destinations: Latin America, Africa, Asia, India & China.
Costs: From £595 for two weeks to £8900 for one of its longest trips. Kitty fund and flights are extra.
Eligibility: Most travellers are aged between 24 and 39 but there are some family trips with children from eight years old.

Exodus Travels

Grange Mills, Weir Rd, London SW12 0NE, UK
☎ +44 (0)20 8675 5550
fax +44 (0)20 8673 0779
info@exodus.co.uk
www.exodus.co.uk

Exodus offers a diverse range of adventure travel trips, including 60 to 70 overland trips a year. For instance, you can spend 25 weeks crossing the Americas between Tierra del Fuego and Anchorage or travel overland from Beijing to Kathmandu.

Timing & Length of Trips: From one week to 28 weeks, with departures all year.
Destinations: 85 countries worldwide on every continent.
Costs: From £325 for one week to 28 weeks from £5490, excluding flights and a local payment of around £50 a week to be paid in a lump sum up front.
Eligibility: Minimum age is 18 but the average age on a trip is early thirties.

Guerba World Travel

Wessex House, 40 Station Rd, Westbury, Wiltshire BA13 3JN, UK
☎ +44 (0)1373 826611
fax +44 (0)1373 858351
info@guerba.co.uk
www.guerba.co.uk

This adventure tour company celebrated 25 years of Africa overlanding in 2005. You can travel between Cape Town and Dakar or from Nairobi to Zanzibar via Lake Victoria & the Serengeti.

Timing & Length of Trips: From one to 24 weeks.
Destinations: All of Africa (the safe bits).
Costs: From £305 for one week to £2480 for 15 weeks, excluding flights and kitty.
Eligibility: Minimum age is 16 or 18, depending on the trip. Most travellers are aged 25 to 40.

Kumuka Worldwide

40 Earl's Court Rd, London W8 6EJ, UK
☎ +44 (0)20 7937 8855
fax +44 (0)20 7937 6664
enquries@kumuka.com
www.kumuka.com

Kumuka is an adventure-based tour company with an active overlanding department. The Best of Africa goes from Kenya to Cape Town and the Inca Heights tour departs Quito and finishes in La Paz.

Timing & Length of Trips: From one to 15 weeks; expeditions depart weekly.
Destinations: South & Central America, Africa, Europe, Asia & the Middle East
Costs: One week costs from £345, 15 weeks from £2650, excluding flights and kitty.
Eligibility: Minimum age is 18.

INDEPENDENT OVERLANDING

Frogs Island 4x4

37c Milton Park, Abingdon, Oxfordshire OX14 4RT, UK
☎ +44 (0)1235 832100
fax +44 (0)1235 831700
offroad@frogsisland4X4.com
www.frogsisland4X4.com

This company offers expedition, off-road and recreational vehicle preparation. It can supply a vehicle and equip it for vehicle-based overland travel, whether it's two weeks in the Sahara or six months' driving from London to Cape Town. All related driver and mechanical training is also offered.

Destinations: A vehicle can be prepared for travel anywhere in the world.
Costs: Depending on your destination and the duration of the trip, preparation costs from £5000.
Eligibility: Open to all (can prepare a vehicle for family travel).

Onelife Adventures

33-34 Central Ave, Storforth Lane Trading Estate, Hasland, Chesterfield S41 0SN, UK
☎ +44 (0)1246 232666
fax +44 (0)1246 232666
info@onelife-adventures.com
www.onelife-adventures.com

Onelife offers self-drive escorted adventure trips. You fly to the destination, acquaint yourself with your Land Rover and possibly do some expedition driving and navigation courses. You and a maximum of four other vehicles then set off on a route that you've discussed beforehand. This is more like flotilla sailing than driving in convoy. You need to check in with the support team once a day, otherwise you're free to complete your route in your own time. Possible trips include driving across the Sahara from Bamako (Mali) to Timbuktu (Mali) or from Bamako to Morocco through Mauritania. Responsible tourism is a key factor in the operation.

Timing & Length of Trips: From two to four weeks. Driving in Iberia takes place from February to June. Regular expeditions in North Africa run from July to September. From November to mid-January there's an annual Sahara Circumnavigation trip broken into four sections.
Destinations: Iberian Peninsula, Mali, Morocco & Mauritania.
Costs: Two weeks in North Africa from £2000, based on two people sharing a vehicle; flights and visas not included. Children between the ages of three and six go free (although you are discouraged from taking your three-year-old).
Eligibility: Minimum age is 17 for drivers.

Safari Drive UK
The Trainers Office, Windy Hollow, Sheepdrove, Lambourn, Berkshire RG17 7XA, UK
☎ +44 (0)1488 71140
fax +44 (0)1488 71311
safari_drive@compuserve.com
www.safaridrive.com
This is a self-drive fully inclusive safari company. You work with it on your itinerary and it makes all your lodge or camp-site reservations, and organises your national park entries. You then fly to Africa, pick up your own Land Rover and drive off on your own. The company has a copy of your itinerary so they know where you are at all times and can provide back-up should you need it.
Timing & Length of Trips: From one week to three months.
Destinations: Malawi, Zambia, Tanzania, Kenya, Namibia & Botswana.
Costs: One week from £650 per person to four weeks from £2500, excluding flights and transfers. This price is for camping only.
Eligibility: Minimum age 25, clean driving licence. Children by arrangement.

DIY EXPEDITIONS
The Expedition Company
PO Box 17, Wiveliscombe, Taunton, Somerset TA4 2YL, UK
☎ +44 (0)1984 624780
fax +44 (0)1984 629045
info@expedition.co.uk
www.expedition.co.uk
This company specialises in tailor-made expeditions anywhere in the world for preformed groups. Wherever and whenever you go, you will be escorted by one of its leaders. Every team has five to seven training days in the UK before departure.
Timing & Length of Expeditions: Year-round expeditions are run in either hemisphere, although the busiest time is May to September. The shortest expedition might be 10 days, the longest six months.
Destinations: Specialises in all of the Himalaya, Iceland, Greenland, Corsica, Zanzibar, Tanzania, Kenya, Alaska, Morocco, Nicaragua, Costa Rica, Argentina & Vietnam.

Costs: Two weeks from £1000, all-inclusive with training; two months from £3500. Travel insurance is included.
Eligibility: From 14 to 70 years of age.

Royal Geographical Society Expedition Advisory Centre
(with the Institute of British Geographers)
1 Kensington Gore, London SW7 2AR, UK
☎ +44 (0)20 7591 3030
fax +44 (0)20 7591 3031
eac@rgs.org
www.rgs.org/eac
The RGS Expedition Advisory Centre provides training and advice to anyone embarking on an expedition. This is a free service. The centre is open Monday to Friday 10am to 5pm – you need an appointment.

SCHEDULED EXPEDITIONS
Adventure Peaks
Office 4, Westmorland House, Lake Rd, Bowness-on-Windermere, Cumbria LA23 3BJ, UK
☎ +44 (0)1539 447301
fax +44 (0)1539 448140
expeditions@adventurepeaks.com
www.adventurepeaks.com
This company offers scheduled mountain expeditions worldwide, but there is scope for individual expeditions. There are snow- and ice-climbing courses in Bulgaria, Poland and Morocco, plus rock climbing in the Costa Blanca (Spain), Corsica, Thailand, Ethiopia and Jordan.
Timing & Length of Expeditions: 50 expeditions a year ranging from two weeks to 72 days (climbing K2).
Destinations: Expeditions to mountains in all continents, including Antarctica. Four different expeditions go to Tien Shan in Kyrgyzstan alone.
Costs: From £2000 for two weeks to £18,000 to climb Mt Vinson in Antarctica (which can be linked to a trip to the South Pole). Costs are all-inclusive.
Eligibility: Reasonable fitness level needed.

Jagged Globe
The Foundry Studios, 45 Mowbray St, Sheffield, South Yorkshire S3 8EN, UK
☎ +44 (0)114 276 3322
fax +44 (0)114 275 5740
climb@jagged-globe.co.uk
www.jagged-globe.co.uk
JG offers tailor-made or group mountaineering expeditions. If tailor-made you can choose whether to go with a JG leader or be self-led (as long as you have the necessary experience). Introductory to advanced climbing courses are also held in the Alps and on the Via Ferrata.
Timing & Length of Expeditions: Around 30 expeditions a year, ranging from two weeks to 70 days (eg climbing Mt Everest).

Destinations: Expeditions take in every continent, including Antarctica. There are five programs: Seven Summits (each of the highest points on each continent); Cold Regions; Mountains of Asia; Mountains of the Americas (Alaska to South America); 8000m Peaks (26,246ft, eg Everest, G2); & the Africa Region (Kilimanjaro & the Atlas Mountains of Morocco).
Costs: From £1095 to £28,000 (Mt Everest) all-inclusive except for travel insurance, airport taxes and main meals in the big cities. You can buy mountaineering travel insurance from JG.
Eligibility: No age restriction but you must have relevant experience for your chosen trip (if you don't then you can do the courses you need to achieve this). Children and partners can accompany climbers.

Tangent Expeditions International
3 Millbeck, New Hutton, Kendal, Cumbria LA8 0BD, UK
☎ +44 (0)1539 737757
fax +44 (0)1539 737756
paul@tangent-expeditions.co.uk
www.tangent-expeditions.co.uk
Tangent organises guided or self-led independent expeditions to the Arctic. It also operates as a logistics consultant for Arctic travel. Expeditions are mountaineering, ski-touring or dog sled.
Timing & Length of Expeditions: About 15 expeditions, ranging from two to five weeks from April to August.
Destinations: Greenland, Baffin Island (Canada), Ellesmere Island (Canada) & Svalbard (north of Norway).
Costs: From £2000 for a two-week trip or you could cross the whole of Greenland in five weeks for £5500. Everything included.
Eligibility: Minimum age 18.

RETREATS
Free Spirit Travel
153 Carden Ave, Brighton, East Sussex BN1 8LA, UK
☎ +44 (0)1273 564230
fax +44 (0)1273 504076
info@freespirituk.com
www.freespirituk.com
Free Spirit Travel is an alternative tour operator that offers three different retreats. There's the Midnight Sun Ashtanga Yoga Retreat on Hanko Island, Finland; the Gold Buddha Island Eco-Resort on an island off Phuket, Thailand; and the Ulpotha Retreat in Sri Lanka. All retreats are remote and the Finnish one is quite basic. The company also sells yoga holidays.
Timing & Length of Retreats: Finland – from one to five weeks from June to the beginning of September; Thailand – from 10 days, November to April; Sri Lanka – from one week, November to March, June and July.
Destinations: Finland, Thailand & Sri Lanka.
Costs: Finland – from £300 for one week; Thailand – from £695 for one week; Sri Lanka – from £650 a week. Prices for

Finland and Thailand include a group transfer to the island. All prices include full board and yoga tuition but exclude flights.
Eligibility: Children on application only.

Neal's Yard Agency For Personal Development
BCM Neal's Yard, London WC1N 3XX, UK
☎ +44 (0)870 444 2702
fax +44 (0)870 444 2702
holidays@nealsyardagency.com
www.nealsyardagency.com
This agency has information about retreats, workshops, courses and holistic holidays. You can be mailed or emailed its quarterly newsletter called the *Holiday & Events Guide* with details on new worldwide retreats and holidays. The agency can put you in touch with a range of retreat centres and some can be booked directly with them. One of these is the Huzur Vadisi Retreat (www.huzurvadisi.com) in southern Turkey where you stay in Mongolian-style yurts.
Timing and Length of Retreats: From two weeks, at any time of the year.
Destinations: Europe & Asia.
Costs: A two-week retreat can range from £300 to £600, depending on the centre.
Eligibility: Only some retreats welcome children.

The Retreat Association
The Centre Hall, 256 Bermondsey St, London SE1 3UJ, UK
☎ +44 (0)20 7357 7736
fax +44 (0)20 7357 7724
info@retreats.org.uk
www.retreats.org.uk
This is a Christian resource organisation for retreats in the UK but there's also information on retreats abroad. The association has a list of UK houses offering hospitality and acceptance in a safe environment for those with or without a faith. In December they publish an annual magazine detailing 250 retreat centres in the UK and abroad. The office is open Monday to Friday 9am to 5pm for phone calls or visits.

The Retreat Company
The Manor House, Kings Norton, Leicestershire LE7 9BA, UK
☎ +44 (0)116 259 9211
fax +44 (0)116 259 6633
info@theretreatcompany.com
www.theretreatcompany.com
TRC promotes, organises and facilitates time-out on retreats. These can include yoga/breathing, detoxification/purification, meditation/silence, creativity/silence and healing therapies in the UK and overseas. There's a detailed questionnaire on their site for people wanting a tailor-made retreat or package.
Timing & Length of Retreats: From one to 12 weeks, throughout the year.

Destinations: Europe, the Philippines, Barbados, the US, South Africa & India.
Costs: One week from £500 full board or 12 weeks in India from £1200 B&B, excluding flights.
Eligibility: Children rarely accompany adults.

Thailand Vipassana Centre

Dhamma Kamala, 200 Baan Nern-Pasook, Tambol Dong-Kee-Lek, Amphur Muang, Prachinburi 25000, Thailand
☎ /fax +66 (0)37 403 515
behappy@loxinfo.co.th
www.dhamma.org
The crux of this nondenominational program of self-help is purification through introspection. Vipassana originated in India 2500 years ago and teaches pupils the means of facing and dispersing their negative patterns of thought. Students must adhere to a strict regime of living simply and silently to aid meditation.
Timing & Length of Course: The course lasts 10 days.
Destinations: Thailand.
Costs: Donations are welcome.
Eligibility: This is not suitable for talkative types or those with psychiatric disorders.

CREWING A YACHT

Blue Water

La Galerie du Port, Blvd d'Aiguillon, Antibes 06600, France
☎ +44 (0)20 7829 8446, +33 (0)4 93 34 34 13 (the UK number is redirected to France at the local rate)
fax +33 (0)4 93 34 35 93
crew@bluewateryachting.com
www.bluewateryachting.com
This is a yacht training school and crew-placement centre that matches crew with yachts worldwide. Most vacancies occur from December to April and May to July. Register via the website where there's a one-off registration fee of £13 and call or email every couple of days to see if you've got a placement. Terms will then be negotiated separately with the individual owner/skipper. Most crew using this service are experienced but this is not always the case. In addition, you can do RYA (Royal Yachting Association) or MCA (Maritime Coastguard Agency) training here. Boats depart worldwide.

Crewseekers

Hawthorn House, Hawthorn Lane, Sarisbury Green, Southampton SO31 7BD, UK
☎ +44 (0)1489 578319
info@crewseekers.co.uk
www.crewseekers.co.uk
This is the largest crewing agency in Europe. A six-month membership costs £50 and 12 months is £75. There are three levels of crew: Leisure Sailing, where crew fund their return fare to the boat and usually pay up to £10 a day towards costs; Boat Delivery, for more experienced crew, where expenses are paid but there's no salary; and

Professional Crew, where all positions are paid. Vacancies occur year round if you're prepared to travel. The Late Availability section on the website is particularly useful. To register go online.

Crew Unlimited

2067 S Federal Hwy, Fort Lauderdale, FL 33316, USA
☎ +1 954-462 4624
fax: +1 954-523 6712
info@crewunlimited.com
www.crewunlimited.com
This professional yacht-crew placement agency has been in business since 1983. It provides work for captains, cooks, deck hands and more. A one-time US$20 registration fee is charged; after that the ship owner pays the placement fee. All positions are paid, and owners generally provide food, uniforms, transportation and medical insurance after a probationary period. Work is available year round, with South Florida being a primary hub for finding employment. Owners usually request a minimum commitment of six months to one year. Most yachts, but not all, require the crew to be STCW95 certified (see www.itf.org.uk/itfweb /seafarers/ITF_STCW_95/section-1/1-1.html). Prior crewing experience or a background in the restaurant, hospitality or mechanical industry helps.

Cruising Association

CA House, 1 Northey St, Limehouse Basin, London E14 8BT, UK
☎ +44 (0)20 7537 2828
fax +44 (0)20 7537 2266
office@cruising.org.uk
www.cruisinga.org.uk
The CA was founded in 1908. It has a large nautical library, a cruise-planning section, and a crewing service that runs from February to June. During these months five lists are published of skippers looking for crew and crew looking for a berth. On the first Wednesday of each month between February and June there's a meeting for skippers and crew. If you're not a member of the Cruising Association, the crewing-service fee is £34 for skippers and £24 for crew. Many skippers will take novice crew.

Professional Yacht Deliveries Worldwide

Witherslack, Grange-over-Sands, Cumbria, LA11 6RQ, UK
☎ +44 (0)1539 552140
fax +44 (0)1539 552131
crew@pydww.com
www.pydww.com
PYD is one of the largest UK yacht deliverers, in need of hundreds of crew a year.
Types of Work: Deck hand, mates.
Timing & Length of Work: Boats are delivered year round; journey times depend on the route.
Destinations: Worldwide.

Costs/Pay: No registration fee. Crew are unpaid but all on-board expenses are covered. Travel to the boat is sometimes included, depending on experience and qualifications.

Eligibility: Minimum age is 17. Will take relative beginners but expect some experience or a Competent Crew certificate.

How to Apply: Send in your CV and the contact name of someone who has sailed with you and can vouch for your character and ability.

Reliance Yacht Management

1st floor suite, 127 Lynchford Rd, Farnborough, Hampshire GU14 6ET, UK
☎ +44 (0)1252 378239
fax +44 (0)1252 521736
crew@reliance-yachts.com
www.reliance-yachts.com

RYM is one of the largest yacht deliverers in the world. It recruits a minimum of 400 crew a year. Current vacancies are on the website. The office keeps in regular contact with the boats.

Types of Work: Deck hand, mates.

Timing & Length of Work: Boats are delivered year round; journey times depend on the route.

Destinations: Mostly from Europe or South Africa to the Caribbean, North and Central America, South Pacific, the Seychelles, New Zealand & Australia.

Costs/Pay: There's a registration fee of £35 for one year. If you don't get any work during this time, the fee will be refunded. Crew are unpaid but all on-board expenses are covered.

Eligibility: Minimum age is 17. Will take relative beginners but expect some experience or Competent Crew certificate.

How to Apply: Download registration form from the website or ring the office.

MONEY TROUBLE
Fruitful

Unit 3, Honeybourne Industrial Estate, Evesham, Worcestershire WR11 7QF, UK
☎ +44 (0)1386 832555
fax +44 (0)1386 833960
info@fruitfuljobs.com
www.fruitfuljobs.com

This is a recruitment service for jobs in the British, Spanish and Portuguese soft-fruit and vegetable industry. Most jobs involve supervising and managing crops rather than picking.

Types of Work: Field and packing supervisors, tractor drivers and jobs in crop management (laying plastic sheeting for strawberries etc).

Timing & Length of Work: There's work year round. The length of a placement depends on the job and may be anything from three weeks to a few months (most positions, however, are in the region of three months).

Pay: This depends on the job you get but you will usually be paid at least £5 an hour. Accommodation is normally provided on the farms for a small supplement.

Destinations: UK, Spain & Portugal.

Eligibility: Minimum age is 18 and you must be able to work in the country.

How to Apply: Fill in the online registration form. You will then be contacted to discuss matching you with a grower.

Volunteering & Conservation

One of the most common reasons people give for taking a career break is to 'give something back'. Work may take care of your material needs, but many people worry that they aren't really making a contribution to the general well-being of the world. Offering your time as a volunteer will give you a chance to do just that, and the rewards – both for you and the people you are helping – can be enormous. Whether you want to save a rainforest or work as a teacher for an African school, there are thousands of organisations out there who need your help.

As Confucius said, a journey of a thousand miles begins with a single step – deciding to become a volunteer is the most important step in making a positive difference somewhere in the world. Volunteering has developed into a huge international industry and numerous organisations can fix you up with a placement, even if you've never been abroad before. However, you must be prepared to cover most of your own expenses – development and conservation projects rely heavily on volunteers who pay their own way.

Many projects are open to people with no previous experience, but there's more to volunteering than just turning up with a spade and asking where to dig. Most organisations want you to commit a minimum length of time and you'll be expected to put in long days working in challenging and unfamiliar surroundings. Living conditions can be basic, without running water or electricity, and, understandably, not every would-be volunteer has what it takes.

The overwhelming majority of volunteer placements are arranged through sending agencies, which assess potential volunteers and place people on suitable projects around the world. Some simply organise the placement and leave you to make your own travel arrangements, while others offer a complete 'volunteering experience' with training, cultural activities, excursions and group expeditions. Year-out organisations such as i-to-i, Changing Worlds, Teaching & Projects Abroad and Coral Cay mainly fall into this bracket. Organisations such as VentureCo and Trekforce offer special trips that provide a chance to volunteer on more than one project and even learn a language as part of an overland expedition. Details for all organisations mentioned in this chapter can be found in the Contacts section (p128).

Many people choose to volunteer abroad as an alternative way to travel. By staying in one place and interacting with local people, you will learn far more about the local culture and form genuine friendships. You will also develop new skills for overcoming the challenges life throws at you – day-to-day office problems can seem pretty insignificant when you have built a school with your bare hands!

The most important attribute that most organisations are looking for is a positive attitude and a genuine desire to help. Anyone who can speak English has the skills required to become an English teacher and anyone who can hold a hammer can help to build a community centre, as Prina Patel discovered while volunteering in a remote village in the Peruvian Andes with VentureCo:

Our mission was to build a community hall in two weeks but the villagers in Cancha Cancha were suspicious to say the least. You could understand why – what did 14 Brits, three Kenyans and one Australian know about building a hall out of rock and mud? As it turned out, not much, but we learnt very quickly! All the hard work paid off when we completed the hall ahead of schedule, but the best thing about the aid project was the effect it had in bringing us together as a team.

ARRANGING A PLACEMENT

Volunteers are needed all over the world but people who turn up unannounced are not welcome. Charities and NGOs (Non-Governmental Organisations) are looking for volunteers with specific skills for specific jobs and most organisations obtain their volunteers through sending agencies in Europe, Australia, New Zealand and the USA. These organisations work a little like temping agencies, matching volunteers to projects that need their specific skills and experience. Agencies tend to specialise in either conservation or development and humanitarian work, but year-out organisations such as i-to-i and Teaching & Projects Abroad offer both kinds of placement. VentureCo and similar organisations offer overland expeditions combined with volunteering options – see Volunteering Expeditions in Contacts (p146).

Don't panic if you don't have first-hand experience – plenty of projects accept complete newcomers to development or conservation. Many business skills transfer easily into voluntary work and there are also openings at the front line of humanitarian relief for volunteers with professional skills, particularly doctors and nurses.

Most organisations have a minimum-age requirement of 17 or 18 and take volunteers up to the age of 65 or 70, but you may have to take a medical to show you are healthy enough for the work. Some projects also have specific skills requirements, eg a TEFL certificate for teaching placements or a medical qualification to work in a clinic, but conservation projects are generally open to all. If you want to work with children, you may need a criminal-record check.

You can volunteer for as little as a week or as long as two years, depending on the project, and some projects will let you extend your stay once you arrive. Accommodation can be fairly basic – volunteers often stay with host families or in expedition camps – and you must cook for yourself or share communal meals with local people. Consider the living arrangements when you pack, and remember to get all the necessary travel jabs and antimalarial drugs (see p54).

To cut down on unnecessary paperwork, almost all sending agencies recommend that volunteers work on a tourist visa. Sending agencies usually accept people of all nationalities, as long as you can get a tourist visa for the country where you want to volunteer. If you are volunteering long-term, the sending organisation may sponsor you on a formal work or volunteer visa.

Most sending agencies have a formal selection process and you must demonstrate that you have the ability to adjust to new situations and work as part of a team. Agencies are also looking for enthusiasm and commitment. You should call or visit the agency's website for an application form to start off the process. Once you've filled in the paperwork and paid a registration fee or deposit, there will be an interview, either by telephone or in person. This is often followed by a group exercise or team-building weekend that will allow the organisation to see how you interact with other people.

The fees charged by the different agencies vary widely – you can pay as little as £100 with a grassroots agency or as much as £4000 with one of the big year-out organisations. This covers meals, accommodation, project costs and local transport, but flights, visas and travel insurance are almost always extra and you will have to provide money for incidental expenses such as evenings out and excursions away from the project. Most organisations require participants to have adequate health insurance.

The fees with some of the larger operators can seem extortionate, but remember that some of this money is going towards the daily running costs of the project you are working on. Many people fundraise from family and friends or carry out sponsored activities to raise the fees; the website www.volunteerinternational.org/index-fund2.htm has some useful tips on raising money for a volunteer project. Most organisations will provide advice on fundraising when you apply.

The main benefit of going through a big organisation is safety in numbers. Having other people from a similar background to bounce off at the end of a day can really lighten the load of being away from friends and family. Most organisations also provide training, orientation sessions, in-country support and extracurricular activities such as mini-expeditions, language classes, adventure sports and trips to national parks. These organised trips can be a real sanity restorer if you are working in an area with no local transport. Many organisations are members of the Year Out Group – see the boxed text on p120.

If you can't afford the fees charged by the big operators, there are smaller nonprofit organisations that place volunteers alone or in pairs on small grassroots projects – Involvement Volunteers, Concordia, UNA Exchange, International Volunteer Service and Youth Action for Peace are all reliable operators. These organisations charge just £90 to £150 for registration, which covers their expenses and you then pay for your own flights, visas, insurance and living expenses. There may be an extra charge if you volunteer in Asia, Africa or South America as there is limited government funding for voluntary projects in these areas.

There are also smaller sending agencies that place volunteers on a single project. One advantage of going through a small or grassroots operator is that the projects focus entirely on the local community. A common criticism of large volunteering organisations is that the placements focus too much on personal development for participants and not enough on the people they are supposed to help.

Some career-breakers also find the organised programs a little restrictive. Emma Smith has this to say about volunteering on an organised program in South America:

The volunteer project was physically demanding and very rewarding, but everything was arranged for you. As many people in the group had travelled before, some of us found this stifling, as we were not free to roam as we pleased. The concept of 'pocket money' was also less than ideal for people in their thirties and forties. Overall, I'd say the experience is much more suited to a new or inexperienced traveller.

If you would rather make your own arrangements, there are numerous websites that provide listings of volunteering opportunities worldwide and most have a searchable database that allows you to search for projects in a particular region or field. You can search for free on the websites of the National Centre for Volunteering (www.volunteering.org.uk) and TimeBank (www.timebank.org.uk), or pay a small registration fee to use the online database run by Worldwide Volunteering (www.worldwidevolunteering.org.uk).

Recommended international databases include Working Abroad (www.workingabroad .com), Transitions Abroad (www.transitionsabroad.com) and Action without Borders (www.idealist.org) in the USA, and Go Volunteer (www.govolunteer.com.au) in Australia. Transitions Abroad and World Service Enquiry (www.wse.org.uk) both publish regular listings of volunteer opportunities that you can subscribe to by mail for an annual fee. For more information on all these services, see the listings on p128.

Once you find a project, you can apply directly to the host organisation, avoiding the fees charged by sending agencies. However, you will still have to cover your own transport costs and you may also have to make a financial contribution to the running of the project. If you go directly to a charity or NGO, you will also miss out on the support network of going through an established sending organisation, so you need to be highly motivated and self-reliant to take this route.

Whether you apply directly to an NGO or go through a sending agency, you should begin the application process well in advance of when you want to start. Some projects accept volunteers on a continuous basis; others require you to start on fixed dates. As a general rule, you should apply at least three months in advance for a year-out organisation and up to a year in advance for an executive volunteering program such as VSO or the Peace Corps.

Choosing a Volunteer Organisation

The volunteering business has expanded massively in recent years, and inevitably there are some cowboy operators out there. It's a good idea to talk to former participants before joining up with a particular company. Many organisations are happy to put you in touch with former volunteers or members of staff who have been on the programs, though they will normally concentrate on the positive aspects of taking part. You can also post a message on the Gap Year & RTW Travel and the Long Haul – Living and Working Abroad branches of the Lonely Planet Thorn Tree (http://thorntree.lonelyplanet.com).

Consider the following points when applying to volunteer organisations:

- What does the organisation do and how is it funded?
- Are placements made directly through the organisation or does it act as a sending agency?
- Who can volunteer with the company and how are volunteers selected?
- What will volunteers be doing on the project and how will this benefit local people?

- What skills are needed and how do volunteers benefit from taking part?
- When is the deadline for applications and do you have to pay a deposit to secure a place (if so, is this refundable)?
- Where are the placements and how long do placements last?
- Can volunteers choose where to go?
- Can volunteers extend the placement after they arrive or visit more than one place?
- How much does the placement cost and what is included (eg flights, visas, insurance, meals, accommodation)?
- Is insurance included? (If not, take out sufficient travel insurance before you leave).
- Is any training provided (this may take the form of an orientation program before you leave or after you arrive in the country)?
- What happens if things go wrong? Is there a local representative or emergency number volunteers can call to provide assistance in an emergency? Is medical care available?
- Do volunteers work in groups or alone? Will other volunteers be living nearby?
- What are the living arrangements? Do volunteers share rooms or stay with local families?
- Is it possible to volunteer with a friend or partner?
- How can volunteers keep in touch with friends and family?
- Is any support provided when volunteers return home?
- Is the focus of the project on helping local people or on helping career-breakers – not all projects give the same amount back to the people they are meant to be helping!

THE YEAR OUT GROUP

The **Year Out Group** (☎ +44 (0)7974 816947; fax +44 (0)1380 812368; www.yearoutgroup.org; info@yearout group.org; Queensfield, 28 Kings Rd, Easterton, Wiltshire SN10 4PX) was formed in 1998 to promote the concept of organised year-out programs and to ensure good practice among its members. It is a nonprofit organisation. All members have to sign up to the following code:

Accurate literature Brochures and briefing packs must clearly describe what is on offer.

Safety & professional support Companies are vetted and monitored to make sure that first-class security and safety procedures are followed. This includes good briefing of participants before they embark on their trip and in-country support once they're there. Companies also have to ensure that their staff are well trained.

Standards Programs must be continually evaluated and improvements made where necessary.

Ethical considerations Sensitivity to social, environmental and local issues has to be shown, particularly in the programs' host countries.

Financial security Compliance with UK statutory financial regulations, including compliance with systems in place to protect payments from clients.

Membership All new members must agree to these criteria.

The Year Out Group came about because founding members got fed up with operating in an unregulated environment. This doesn't mean that if you decide to go with a company not in the group that you're in for a rough time – there are plenty of good year-out companies that haven't joined up yet. However, it does give you another layer of protection and guarantees. Whatever you decide to do, check out its website (www.yearoutgroup.org) as there's some useful information and suggestions in terms of year-out options.

Current Year Out Group members are Africa & Asia Venture; African Conservation Experience; Art History Abroad; BSES Expeditions; British Universities North America Club (Bunac); CESA Languages Abroad; Changing Worlds; Coral Cay Conservation; Council on International Educational Exchange (CIEE); Community Service Volunteers (CSV); Flying Fish; Frontier Conservation; Gap Activity Projects; Gap Challenge/World Challenge Expeditions; Greenforce; the International Academy; i-to-i; Outreach International; Project Trust; Quest Overseas; Raleigh International; SPW-Students Partnership Worldwide; St James's & Lucie Clayton College; Teaching & Projects Abroad; Travellers; Trekforce Expeditions; VentureCo; Wind Sand & Stars; the Year in Industry; and Year Out Drama.

Please note that not all the above organisations have opportunities for career-breakers.

HUMANITARIAN PROJECTS ABROAD

When people think of volunteering, the image that usually comes to mind is humanitarian work in the developing world. A huge proportion of the volunteer placements arranged by sending agencies involve community-development projects and humanitarian relief, providing hands-on help to impoverished and disadvantaged communities around the world. The work can be hard and the conditions are often testing, but most volunteers gain a huge sense of personal satisfaction from knowing that they helped to improve the lives of people in difficult situations.

Volunteer placements are generally arranged through sending agencies, though some of the larger NGOs run their own humanitarian and development programs. Each agency has a different area of expertise – some place unskilled volunteers on projects all over the world, while others focus on providing skilled workers for a particular country. The Contacts section (p130) has extensive listings of sending agencies and NGOs that accept volunteers for humanitarian and development work.

What you do as a volunteer depends on the skills you can bring to the project. Projects where you build a school or dig a well are usually open to anyone, while health-care projects generally require specialist medical skills. New or inexperienced volunteers are probably best off going through an established sending agency or year-out organisation such as Changing Worlds, Teaching & Projects Abroad, Travellers Worldwide or i-to-i.

Fiona Black volunteered on a community-development project in Costa Rica with Australian Volunteers International:

I'm not sure why, but I felt strangely drawn to Central America, despite initially knowing very little about it. Volunteering seemed to me to be the best way of getting what I was after, as I wanted to live somewhere for a little while rather than passing through and feel like I was doing something useful rather than just observing. During the project, we would get up with the sun, eat, trek up a big hill, watch the monkeys for a while and then spend six or so hours digging, lugging bricks, mixing cement, painting beams and all the other tasks that arise from constructing a building.

It was great being incorporated into the daily lives of the local people, being invited to their houses, eating tamales on Christmas Day and going to the river in the back of a cattle truck. Because we were helping their community, they would go out of their way to include us in local events. We found that volunteering is a very different way of travelling to having a holiday or doing touristy things.

Although the immediate goal of most projects is to alleviate suffering, the long-term aim of humanitarian work is sustainable development. The prevailing wisdom is that people will gain more in the long term if they are trained to help themselves, rather than becoming dependent on hand-outs and short-term relief packages. Many volunteer projects provide training for local farmers, businesspeople and teachers and educate communities about health and human rights. Volunteers can often find placements as English teachers (with or without TEFL experience) or provide education on public health and HIV/AIDS.

Business management is another important area of humanitarian work. Training small businesses and helping NGOs obtain funding is just as important as education, and finance experts are needed around the world to help establish microfinance programs which lend small sums of money to farms and businesses and invest the profits in helping other people.

Doctors and nurses are in huge demand at hospitals and clinics in the developing world and international relief organisations also have openings for engineers, drivers and logisticians (people who can arrange the delivery of people and materials around the world) – see Executive Volunteering (p123) for more information.

Although the rewards can be huge, both for the volunteer and the host community, it is important to be realistic about what volunteering is going to be like. You may have to endure basic living conditions, extremes of heat and cold, and tropical illnesses. The food can be bland and monotonous and you may find yourself working in a remote location, far from the nearest shop or telephone. The work can also be emotionally and physically challenging and you will have to rely on local people and the other members of your team for company and support. We recommend talking to former participants to make sure you fully understand what you are getting into.

VOLUNTARY SERVICE OVERSEAS

Voluntary Service Overseas (VSO) is the largest independent volunteer organisation in the world and it offers a staggering range of possibilities for volunteering overseas. VSO focuses on placing professionals with transferable skills on projects throughout the developing world, particularly in Africa, Asia and the Indian subcontinent. This could be anything from working as a doctor on a humanitarian relief program to providing business advice to a government department.

VSO volunteers come from a broad range of professional backgrounds, from medicine to accounting. Most volunteers are motivated by a desire to make a difference in a needy part of the world, and they must be committed and highly self-motivated as the standard volunteer placement is two years. The age range for volunteers is 20 to 75 and they must have relevant professional skills and several years' workplace experience. Anyone from the European Economic Area (EEA) can apply but they must be willing to work in challenging and unfamiliar environments. Mentoring is an important part of VSO's work and much of the work involves training local people in the skills they need to become self-sufficient.

Alicia Oughton has this to say about volunteering with VSO in Bangladesh:

I had always wanted to travel but had never got off my backside and done anything about it – the most adventurous thing I had ever done in the past was going to Zante (Greece) on my own. I realised very quickly that I didn't have the money to travel the world, so I looked up a few volunteer agencies on the Internet. VSO appealed the most and I took a placement as an Information Development Adviser for an NGO in Dhaka, where I helped to improve their processes for collecting and disseminating information on gender issues.

The part of my work that I most enjoyed was organising public events for my NGO and partner organisations. It was hard trying to work with the language and the cultural barriers and I had to work to gain respect for my ideas, but overall I gained so much as a person. My advice to other volunteers is always try and turn a bad situation into a good one. I never thought I would come to terms with sharing my room with spiders the size of my hand, but at least they kept the mosquitoes away...

VSO assignments can start at any time, but applying to VSO can take four to 12 months, and you will have to attend an assessment day and a series of briefing and training sessions before you start your mission. VSO meets almost all your costs, including flights, a contribution towards day-to-day expenses, a living allowance, pension contributions and a grant of approximately £1900 to help you re-establish yourself when you get home. The booklet *VSO's Guide to the Ultimate Career Break* is full of useful information on preparing for and taking part in a VSO project – call them for a copy on ☎ +44 (0)20 8780 7285.

VSO is easily one of the most career-oriented volunteering options, and a two-year stint with VSO will look at least as good as two years of full-time work when you put together your CV at the end of the project. Many people jump the fence and go on to full-time work in the development/relief sector after completing a project with VSO.

THE PEACE CORPS

America's answer to VSO is the Peace Corps, which was set up in 1961 by President Kennedy as part of a program to promote understanding between America and the rest of the world. There was a whiff of Cold War politics about the organisation when it was first established, but these days the focus is firmly on providing long-term volunteers to needy regions around the globe.

More than 150,000 people have volunteered with the Peace Corps since 1961 and the work done by volunteers is incredibly varied – you might find yourself working with subsistence-level farmers in a remote African village or end up living in air-conditioned comfort in an Asian metropolis, providing mentoring for college students – it all depends on the current needs of the program. Some volunteers are students straight out of college, while others are mature professional people who want to escape from the rat race and give something back to society.

New Yorker Ryan Andersen joined the Peace Corps as a break from a career in finance:

I served as a Peace Corps volunteer for two years in the Dominican Republic and transferred and extended for a third year to help launch a new project in Zambia. The overarching goal of my project in the DR was to teach basic business skills to farmers, women's groups and youth groups. In Zambia I lectured at a local college on farm management and worked with the Zambian Ministry of Education to develop a new distance-learning program for orphans and vulnerable children.

The experience surpassed my expectations – almost every week I get emails and handwritten letters that have traversed half the world, carrying a stamp that cost 25% of a day's salary. These letters reaffirm the bonds that I went to Zambia and the DR to build.

I've recently returned to the States and I'm still searching for that perfect job, but the Peace Corps gave me a great new perspective – in some ways it made me more motivated to take advantage of all the opportunities that I have here and it also made me reassess what is truly important in life and where I should focus my priorities.

Any US citizen or resident alien aged 18 to 65 can apply to the Peace Corps, but it is important to realise that the Peace Corps is definitely not a soft option – there's a rigorous three-month training program and you then volunteer abroad for two full years. To soften the blow, the US government provides a monthly living allowance, dental and health insurance, and free flights, plus a lump sum of around US$6000 to help you readjust to life in the US at the end of the program. You can also defer or apply for reduced payments on many student loans.

With all these perks, it should come as no surprise that competition for a place is fierce. There is a tough selection process and you'll have to fill out reams of paperwork and provide a convincing personal statement about your reasons for applying as a volunteer, as well as attend an interview and take a medical. Assuming you pass muster, you will then be assigned a placement that matches your skills, which could be anywhere in the world, doing almost anything, from teaching to acting as a consultant for small businesses. The whole process – from sending off the application to jetting off – can take up to six months.

EXECUTIVE VOLUNTEERING

In situations of real crisis, many charities and NGOs need highly skilled people who can come in at short notice to provide immediate humanitarian relief. Organisations such as the UN Volunteer Programme, British Executive Service Overseas (BESO), Médecins du Monde and Médecins Sans Frontières provide emergency medical and support staff to work with victims of war, famine and natural disaster around the world.

Many of these staff are executive volunteers – professional people with several years' experience who can bring real-life skills to emergency situations. Doctors and nurses are in huge demand, but there are also openings for drivers, mechanics, business consultants, sanitation engineers, project managers, accountants, language experts and lobbyists – you might be surprised how many skills from the ordinary world of work cross over into humanitarian relief. Travel experience is generally preferred, but some organisations give training to volunteers who are new to international work.

As well as providing a huge personal reward, working as an executive volunteer can be a useful step towards full-time work in the development field. However, you will be working with people in desperate need and the work can be emotionally and physically draining. Daniela Stein worked as a volunteer nurse for Médecins Sans Frontières in Angola, Kenya, Malawi and Zimbabwe:

The toughest experience for me was working in a famine situation as a nutrition coordinator in Kuito, Angola. At night we often had a truck bringing in around 80 children who needed immediate medical attention. Most of these children had to travel two hours on a bumpy insecure road and mortality in the feeding centres was very high. It was a real challenge both mentally and physically and I ended this mission after five months instead of six months because I knew that I had reached saturation point and had nothing left to give.

It is important to realise this and MSF are very supportive to their volunteers. You have a briefing prior to each mission and a debriefing on return, which is very valuable as it helps to talk about your experiences. My time with MSF has made me realise the huge needs of orphans in Africa, which is what I plan to do with my future, hopefully setting up a children's home and living in East Africa.

Because the projects require specific skills and competencies, most organisations ask you to send in a general application listing your professional experience. They will then match you to a suitable program. It may be several months before an appropriate project becomes available, but organisations try to give as much notice as possible to allow you time to arrange leave or hand in your notice.

All the costs of volunteering are met by the organisation, including flights and living expenses, and an extensive support system is provided, with on-the-job training and a network of in-country support staff. Some organisations also provide a small salary and periodic flights home or paid leave for holidays.

However, you must be prepared to commit a minimum length of time – up to two years for some organisations. Few organisations have openings for couples, and being apart for such long periods can place a real strain on relationships. The bottom line is that you must be 100% committed to take part.

WORKING FOR A GAP-YEAR ORGANISATION

If you want to work in the expedition business, you might consider volunteering as a staff member for one of the expedition-based gap-year organisations to gain experience. Raleigh International takes on about 400 volunteer staff every year to help run its expeditions, including team leaders, drivers and project managers. However, you need relevant skills for the position – six months' experience in youth work or team leading to work as a project manager – and you must contribute £1100 and cover your own flights. You don't need to have gone on a Raleigh expedition before to take part.

Frontier also has regular openings for self-funding staff with relevant skills – you pay a reduced contribution and you can apply for a paid staff job at the end of the expedition. Greenforce regularly recruits staff from former volunteers and it operates a special training program where one outstanding volunteer from each expedition can stay on for another 10 weeks as a trainee member of staff and with all expenses paid, with the potential to go on to a fully paid job.

VIRTUAL VOLUNTEERING

The phenomenal growth of the Internet has created a new kind of aid worker – the 'virtual volunteer'. Anyone with computer skills can now donate their time for free from anywhere in the world, providing technical support for charities and NGOs over the web. The United Nations has set up the website UNV Online Volunteers (www.onlinevolunteering.org) to bring humanitarian organisations together with people who can contribute computer skills online, from administrative staff to web designers. You can register on the website and then browse through a database of projects.

Another useful organisation is InterConnection (www.interconnection.org), which recruits volunteers to provide free or low-cost websites and virtual training for charities and NGOs. You can search for virtual volunteering opportunities worldwide on the Volunteermatch website (www.volunteermatch.org/virtual). For more information on what constitutes virtual volunteering, download the *Virtual Volunteering Guidebook* from www.serviceleader.org/new/virtual.

Trekforce has a similar package for expedition nurses and doctors (who just cover the costs of their flights) and assistant leaders (who have their expenses paid but do not receive a salary). In fact, qualified expedition doctors and nurses are required by many Year Out Group organisations – see the Living & Working Abroad chapter for information on paid work for volunteer organisations (p183).

Volunteering as a staff member can also be a launching platform into work in the charity sector – Michelle Hawkins worked as a voluntary project manager on Raleigh International expeditions in Costa Rica and Nicaragua as a first step towards getting a job with an international NGO:

We worked with the Bribrí Indian community in Yorkín, a village in the Talamancan Indian Reserve in Costa Rica. The Bribrí are subsistence-level organic farmers and their main produce is bananas, cocoa, maize, yuccas and guavas. Because of the recent failure of their cocoa crops, they needed to set up an additional source of income. The primary aim of the project was to build a shower and toilet block for a new ecotourist centre that the Yorkín community was developing as an extra revenue source.

My role as project manager was to ensure that everything happened on time and under budget. I was also responsible for motivating the Venturers, briefing each one to be a day leader and then assessing and reviewing what they had done well and what could be improved.

Health and safety was paramount as Yorkín was only accessible by canoe and had no roads, electricity or phones. The nearest hospital was five hours away by river. I ran mock casualty-evacuation drills to ensure we all knew what to do in the event of someone falling off the suspension bridge or getting bitten by a snake. End result: everyone was fine!

KIBBUTZIM & MOSHAVIM

With all the upheavals currently going on in the Middle East, the idea of volunteering on a kibbutz isn't as popular as it once was. However, volunteers aged 18 to 35 can still spend a season working in a small, self-sufficient Jewish farming community through the international Kibbutz Artzi Federation (www.kibbutz.org.il).

There are around 270 kibbutzim in Israel and each functions as a self-governing commune, with all the work and decision-making shared between the 400 or so people who live on the kibbutz. Israel also has around 80 moshavim, which are similar to kibbutzim except that each family owns and operates its own land. These are administered directly by the Moshav Movement in Israel (see p144 for details).

Volunteers mainly work on the farms that provide food for the kibbutz, but there is also work to do in kibbutz-owned hotels and tourist attractions and in laundries and factories. The main volunteering season runs from May to September and volunteers stay for two to six months, working eight hours a day for six days a week in exchange for room and board and around US$80 a month in pocket money (up to US$300 at moshavim).

Most volunteers learn a lot from the experience of communal living, but the work is hard and everyone is expected to pull their weight. In exchange, the kibbutzim provide laundry services, medical care and sports facilities; they also lay on day trips and excursions to historic sights.

If you make arrangements through a kibbutz representative in your own country, you'll pay around US$600, including flights, local transfers and insurance. You can also make arrangements directly through the Kibbutz Artzi Federation, which charges US$60 for registration and US$80 for compulsory insurance. You can register by email, but you'll have to visit the office in Tel Aviv when you arrive to pay the fees. Bring your passport, plane tickets, a recent medical certificate and proof of at least US$250 in funds, plus US$17 and two passport photos to change your visa from a tourist visa to a volunteer visa.

However, remember that working on a kibbutz is inevitably going to be seen as a political decision. Although the settlements predate the establishment of Israel by nearly half a century, some are located in Palestinian areas and many people feel that volunteering on a kibbutz lends legitimacy to Israel's policy of settlement. Kibbutzim have also been targeted by militants, so you should check the security situation carefully before deciding to volunteer.

RELIGIOUS ORGANISATIONS

As well as government organisations and NGOs, a lot of humanitarian work is carried out by faith-based groups, mostly from the three monotheist faiths – Christianity, Judaism and Islam. Many of these organisations accept volunteers, but you usually need to be a practising member of the faith that runs the project. The day-to-day work is similar to that carried out by nonreligious organisations – building things, providing health care, teaching etc – but some organisations do have an agenda to convert local people.

If you are thinking of applying to a faith-based organisation, you probably won't mind being a missionary and there's no denying that many of these groups do a huge amount of good around the world. By far the best opportunities for volunteers are offered by Christian organisations such as Christians Abroad and World Exchange, which accept volunteers of any Christian denomination. Islamic relief organisations tend to rely on permanent staff, but several Judaist organisations place Jewish volunteers overseas.

Most of the projects offered by religious organisations take place in the developing world, particularly in Africa and India. The process of finding a placement is pretty much the same as for nonreligious organisations – there are faith-based sending agencies that place skilled and unskilled volunteers for one month to a year, and volunteers either make a financial contribution or cover their own expenses. Some of the larger faith-based organisations are listed in the Contacts section (p145).

CONSERVATION & SCIENTIFIC PROGRAMS ABROAD

It wasn't so long ago that people thought Sting was loopy for campaigning to save the rainforest, but these days, conservation is high on the public agenda. Working as a conservation volunteer is just as popular as volunteering for a developmental organisation, and there are dozens of sending agencies and expedition companies that place volunteers on conservation projects worldwide.

Conservation work is quite physical and you may have to work in uncomfortable conditions, but the experience of seeing squirrel monkeys climbing from branch to branch as the morning mist clears in the Peruvian jungle or tagging a sea turtle as it lays its eggs on a Costa Rican beach can be positively life-affirming. Lou McGregor has this to say about her experience of volunteering on a sea-turtle conservation project in Costa Rica:

For three months I spent my time in the middle of nowhere (picture Robinson Crusoe) in the Santa Rosa National Park at a little beach named Nancite. My job involved maintaining the records for the ongoing research project on olive Ridley turtles. My days were spent filling in log books and trying to keep cool (some days were as hot and humid as 45°C!) plus looking at the effects of predators on the turtle nests. My nights were spent roaming the 1km-long beach, finding turtles, measuring them, timing their journey from the sea to a nesting site and back, counting the eggs they laid and tagging the turtles. On some evenings as many as 20 turtles would come up the beach to nest. When the eggs hatched, it was incredible to see hundreds of baby turtles making their way to the ocean. Costa Rica has to be one of the most beautiful places in the world – it has it all!

The work that conservation volunteers do is quite varied. On some projects, volunteers assist scientists working on environmental research projects, by monitoring wildlife populations and logging sightings of rare species. On other projects, volunteers repair trails in national parks or educate local people living on the edge of threatened wilderness areas. Whatever you end up doing, training is usually provided and there will be qualified people there to organise the daily running of the project.

As with humanitarian volunteering, it's important to be realistic about what the project will involve and what you hope to get out of it. Conservation work often takes place in remote areas, and living conditions can be very basic – sometimes just a bush kitchen, a canvas shelter, a water filter and a pit toilet. The work can be mundane and there isn't much to do in the jungle after dark except play cards and swat mosquitoes. Be honest with yourself about the kinds of conditions you are happy working in. If you have a low tolerance for discomfort, you'll probably have more fun volunteering in a temperate environment in Europe or North America.

Another important thing to bear in mind is how much contact you will have with the species you are conserving. Working with snow leopards in Tibet may sound great on paper, but chances are that you will end up doing little more than logging occasional sightings of leopard tracks. Projects that involve high-profile species are often expensive and heavily oversubscribed and it is often more enjoyable to join a program working with a less familiar animal that you can see up close and personal.

Finding a conservation placement is much the same as finding a humanitarian or development placement. Specialist sending agencies such as Greenforce, Frontier, Coral Cay and Global Vision International offer complete packages, or you can search for opportunities on the web and apply directly to conservation projects. Some of the large humanitarian sending agencies also provide conservation placements. Leading sending agencies and online resources are listed in the Contacts section (p149).

Conservation projects generally last from two weeks to a year and most accept volunteers without previous experience, though there may be a medical to ensure you are fit for outdoor work. As with humanitarian work, organisations generally ask you to make a contribution and pay for your own flights, visas and insurance. Paying volunteers are a vital source of funding for conservation work overseas and the costs can be huge for some projects – a two-month placement can cost anything from £200 to £3000, depending on who you go with.

The majority of conservation projects are land-based, but organisations such as Coral Cay (www.coralcay.org) and Greenforce (www.greenforce.org) offer a choice of rainforest or reef packages, where volunteers either work to conserve areas of rainforest, or don scuba gear to monitor and maintain areas of tropical coral reef. Dive training is usually provided, but you may have to bring fins and a mask and snorkel from home. There are also plenty of conservation projects that work with whales and dolphins.

Frontier, Trekforce, VentureCo and several other year-out organisations offer conservation-based expeditions, with a period of volunteering sandwiched between wilderness activities and study programs. Private game reserves in Africa also rely on large numbers of volunteer workers – some examples are listed in Contacts (p129), or you can search for projects on the Africa Conservation Foundation website (www.africanconservation.org).

The US National Park Service, the New Zealand Department of Conservation and the National Parks & Wildlife Service in Australia take on large numbers of international volunteers to monitor plant and animal populations, repair trails and notice boards and guide visitors – see p147 for more details. To volunteer in a national park in the UK, you should contact the park directly; check the list of national parks on the website www.anpa .gov.uk. Placements in national parks and nature reserves in other parts of the world can be arranged through sending agencies.

Birgit Jordan took time off from working as a civil engineer to volunteer at Brisbane Forest Park with Conservation Volunteers Australia:

I had dreamed about going to Australia since I was a kid, but I grew up in East Germany where this was a truly unfeasible undertaking. My luck turned when the wall came down in 1989 and I started writing letters (back then we didn't have email or Internet) to Australian conservation organisations until I found one that was willing to give me a placement.

I ended up at Brisbane Forest Park, investigating how to manage waste water from remote camping grounds in the bush, which allowed me to use my knowledge of ecological water management. I also got the chance to go on bushwalks with the rangers, feed native animals in the park sanctuary, take part in a TV documentary on turtles and help the rangers educate school groups. My experiences were so diverse; I had the best time of my life there and my language skills improved immensely.

If you aren't ready to totally immerse yourself in conservation, there are plenty of short volunteering options that you can squeeze in as part of a longer career break. One of the largest organisations for short projects is Earthwatch Institute (www.earthwatch.org), which places 4000 conservation volunteers on one- to three-week conservation programs every year. It has offices in the UK, USA, Australia and Japan.

Another option is a conservation-based holiday. The website www.responsibletravel.com lists numerous conservation-based holidays lasting one to four weeks. BTCV International Conservation Holidays (www.btcv.org) and People's Trust for Endangered Species (www.ptes.org) both arrange large numbers of conservation-focused holidays worldwide.

ARCHAEOLOGY

Archaeology is another field that depends heavily on volunteers. You don't have to be a scientist or historian to take part, but you do need to be patient and committed. Real-life archaeology can be painstakingly slow and laborious, and you must log and record every find, no matter how insignificant.

If you want to be the next Indiana Jones or Lara Croft, archaeology is probably not for you – volunteers are more likely to be digging out fire pits than unearthing buried treasure. This said, archaeology does have its glamorous side and there are opportunities to excavate burial chambers, temples and ancient shipwrecks.

Volunteers typically cover all their own expenses and camp or stay on site or in local guesthouses. You can work for a few weeks or for a whole season and there are usually a few free days a week to do some exploring. However, you should be prepared for back-breaking, dusty days spent hunched over in the sun – bring a wide-brimmed hat and a big tube of sun screen!

The Council for British Archaeology (www.britarch.ac.uk) and the Archaeological Institute of America (www.archaeological.org) both publish annual lists of field-work opportunities around the world. You can purchase these online for under £20 – see p154 for more information. The website www.archaeologyfieldwork.com also has field-work listings for the USA and worldwide. Some of the mainstream volunteering organisations also place volunteers on archaeological digs.

If you fancy helping out on a marine excavation, the Nautical Archaeology Society (www.nasportsmouth.org.uk) offers specialist courses in Foreshore and Underwater Archaeology for aspiring marine archaeologists who have a PADI Open Water or equivalent diving certification. The four-day course takes place on set dates in June, July and September and costs £270 (£350 with accommodation). There are also courses in diving for archaeologists, and field trips to submerged wrecks.

CONTACTS

ARRANGING A PLACEMENT

The following organisations provide listings of volunteering placements around the world for people who don't want to go through a mainstream volunteer organisation.

Action without Borders

17th floor, 79 Fifth Ave, New York, NY 10003, USA
☎ +1 212-843 3973
fax +1 212-564 3377
info@idealist.org
www.idealist.org
This recommended US website has listings of nearly 8000 volunteer opportunities worldwide. Volunteers of all nationalities can conduct highly customised searches for specific types of volunteering and you can register online to receive updates of volunteer opportunities by email.

African Conservation Foundation

PO Box 36, Bingley, West Yorkshire BD16 1LQ, UK
☎ +44 (0)1535 274160
fax +44 (0)1535 271631
john@africanconservation.org
www.africanconservation.org
This East African nonprofit organisation acts as a portal for environmental and conservation projects across Africa. The website contains a huge directory of African organisations that may accept volunteers.

Association of Voluntary Organisations (AVSO)

174 Rue Joseph II, 1000 Brussels, Belgium
☎ +32 (0)2-23 068 13
fax +32 (0)2-23 114 13

info@avso.org
www.avso.org
This umbrella organisation represents various European organisations that send volunteers overseas – links to member organisations are on the website and there's a directory of long- and short-term opportunities worldwide.

Haces Falta

Calle Jaén 13, local bajo, 28020 Madrid, Spain
☎ +34 91 554 90 42
hacesfalta@fchandra.org
www.hacesfalta.org
This Spanish organisation acts as a portal connecting Spanish-speaking volunteers to NGOs. Vacancies for volunteers are advertised on the website and you can register your CV online and sign up for email updates.

International Medical Volunteers Association

PO Box 205, Woodville, MA 01784, USA
☎ +1 508-435 7377
fax +1 508-497 9568
info@imva.org
www.imva.org
The IMVA provides information on health-care projects in developing countries worldwide. There are links to numerous volunteer projects on the website and you can add your name to an online registry that organisations browse when looking for volunteers.

International Volunteer Programs Association (IVPA)

PO Box 18, Presque Isle, MI 49777, USA
☎ +1 734-528 2496
ivpa@volunteerinternational.org
www.volunteerinternational.org
IVPA is an alliance of 30 NGOs based in the Americas. The website has a full list of contact details for members and other resources for would-be volunteers. Members include AFS International, American Jewish World Service, Amizade, Cross-Cultural Solutions, the Earthwatch Institute, the Foundation for Sustainable Development, Global Crossroad, Global Volunteers, Iko Poran, Volunteers for Peace and WorldTeach.

National Centre for Volunteering

Regents Wharf, 8 All Saints St, London N1 9RL, UK
☎ +44 (0)20 7520 8900
fax +44 (0)20 7520 8910
volunteering@thecentre.org.uk
www.volunteering.org.uk
This organisation maintains a large and well-organised website covering all aspects of volunteering, including detailed listings of long- and short-term volunteer opportunities worldwide.

New Zealand Trust for Conservation Volunteers

Three Streams, RD 3, Albany, North Shore, New Zealand
☎ /fax +64 (0)9-415 9336
conservol@clear.net.nz
www.conservationvolunteers.org.nz
This charitable trust provides information on volunteer conservation placements throughout New Zealand, including preservation of endangered species and environmental education. You can register on the website for NZ$10 and then search for volunteer opportunities in New Zealand and further afield.

OneWorld International Foundation

2nd floor, River House, 143-145 Farringdon Rd, London EC1R 3AB, UK
☎ +44 (0)20 7239 1400
fax +44 (0)20 7833 3347
justice@oneworld.net
www.oneworld.net
Oneworld is an online portal that seeks to unify and promote human rights and sustainable development by bringing charities and aid organisations together. The website has a database of 1500 partner organisations, some of which accept volunteers. Oneworld offices worldwide are listed on the website.

TimeBank

The Mezzanine, Elizabeth House, 39 York Rd, London SE1 7NQ, UK
☎ +44 (0)20 7401 5420
fax +44 (0)20 7401 5421
feedback@timebank.org.uk
www.timebank.org.uk/givetime/overseas.htm
TimeBank was established to help promote volunteering and operates an extensive online database of voluntary opportunities. You must register to use the Overseas Directory page, which then allows you to search for hundreds of organisations that place volunteers overseas.

Transitions Abroad

PO Box 745, Bennington, VT 05201, USA
☎ +1 802-442 4827
fax +1 802-442 4827
info@transitionsabroad.com
www.transitionsabroad.com
This American publisher produces the bimonthly magazine *Transitions Abroad*, which has loads of information for people intending to work or volunteer overseas. Although it focuses on US volunteers, the website includes useful listings of volunteer opportunities for people of all nationalities and you can browse by region. A one-year subscription to *Transitions Abroad* magazine costs US$28 within the USA, or US$56 by international airmail.

Volunteering Australia Inc

Level 3, 11 Queens Rd, Melbourne, Victoria 3004, Australia
☎ +61 (0)3-9820 4100
fax +61 (0)3-9820 1206
volaus@volunteeringaustralia.org
www.volunteeringaustralia.org
This organisation provides information on a huge variety
of volunteer programs across Australia. Projects cover
everything from building boardwalks and reconstructing
walking tracks in conservation areas to humanitarian
projects such as running summer camps for children with
special needs. The affiliated Go Volunteer website (www
.govolunteer.com.au) lists around 6000 positions.

Working Abroad

59 Landsdowne Pl, Hove, East Sussex BN3 1FL, UK
☎ /fax +44 (0)1323 871391
info@workingabroad.com
www.workingabroad.com
This small nonprofit organisation acts as an agent for
small-scale indigenous projects in 150 countries worldwide. You can do a personalised search on their website
for the type of volunteering that most interests you, eg
development work, conservation or archaeology. The
affiliated Working Projects Abroad organises annual
environmental programs in Iceland, Costa Rica and the
Netherlands Antilles.

World Service Enquiry (WSE)

233 Bon Marche Centre, 241–251 Ferndale Rd, London
SW9 8BJ, UK
☎ +44 (0)870 770 3274
fax +44 (0)870 770 7991
wse@cabroad.org.uk
www.wse.org.uk
This agency offers guidance for people who want to
volunteer abroad. It publishes an annual guide to voluntary opportunities or you can subscribe to a monthly
Opportunities Abroad bulletin. The annual booklet costs
£3 plus post and packing, or you can subscribe to the
Opportunities Abroad bulletin from £7 per month. WSE
also offers one-to-one guidance for people thinking of a
career in development work – a 90-minute interview and
personalised report containing careers advice costs £120
(£95 if you book online).

Worldwide Volunteering

7 North St Workshops, Stoke-sub-Hamdon, Somerset TA14
6QR, UK
☎ +44 (0)1935 825588
fax +44 (0)1935 825775
worldvol@worldvol.co.uk
www.worldwidevolunteering.org.uk
This useful organisation has a database of 1000 volunteer
organisations and 300,000 volunteer opportunities which

you can search for a fee (£10 for three searches). Many
local volunteer organisations around Britain offer free
access to the database – the website has more details.

YouthNet UK

3rd floor, 2–3 Upper St, Islington, London N1 0PH, UK
☎ +44 (0)20 7226 8008
fax +44 (0)20 7226 8118
info@do-it.org.uk
www.do-it.org.uk
This youth-orientated organisation has a database of UK
volunteering opportunities and pages of links to volunteer
opportunities worldwide.

HUMANITARIAN PROJECTS ABROAD

The following organisations arrange humanitarian placements worldwide. Unless otherwise stated, flights, visas
and insurance are extra for all these organisations.

AidCamps International

28A Stondon Park, London SE23 1LA, UK
☎ +44 (0)20 8699 7038
fax +44 (0)870 130 3420
info@aidcamps.org
www.aidcamps.org
This grassroots organisation offers short-term volunteer
positions in India and Africa. Volunteers assist in the
construction of schools in rural communities and weekend
visits are arranged to local national parks and historic
sites. You must book and pay in full at least four months
in advance.
Timing & Length of Projects: Three weeks.
Destinations: India, Nepal & Cameroon.
Costs: Aid camps cost £550, including food, accommodation and local transport.
Eligibility: Minimum age is 18. No specific skills are required but volunteers must be committed and enthusiastic.

AFS International
(American Field Service)

Leeming House, Vicar Lane, Leeds, West Yorkshire LS2 7JF, UK
☎ +44 (0)113 242 6136
fax +44 (0)113 243 0631
info-unitedkingdom@afs.org
www.afsuk.org
This vast global organisation places thousands of volunteers on projects around the world annually. The UK office
has opportunities for unskilled volunteers to work on
community projects with the homeless (including street
children) in Central and South America and Africa. See
the global website (www.afs.org/AFSI) for details of AFS
branches worldwide.
Timing & Length of Projects: Varies with the project –
unskilled projects organised from the UK office last six
months.

Destinations: Global – the UK office sends volunteers to Brazil, Costa Rica, Ecuador, Guatemala, Honduras, Panama, Peru, Ghana & South Africa.

Costs: Volunteers in Latin America and Africa must raise a contribution of £2950, which covers accommodation and board with local families.

Eligibility: The age range is 18 to 34 for Latin American projects, and 20 to 37 for African projects. Teaching qualifications or experience may be required for teaching projects.

Alliance Abroad Group

1221 South Mopac Expressway, Suite 250, Austin, TX 78746, USA
☎ +1 512-457 8062
fax +1 413-460 3502
Email using the form on their website
www.alliancesabroad.com

This American organisation offers volunteering, teaching, working and language-study programs in the US and worldwide. Volunteer options include working on organic farms in Hawaii and assisting with social-development projects in Costa Rica, Peru and Ecuador.

Timing & Length of Projects: From one to 12 weeks; projects are run throughout the year.

Destinations: Ecuador, Costa Rica, Peru, Mexico, Hawaii & South Africa.

Costs: Vary with the project – there's a fixed program fee of US$750 to US$950, plus a daily fee for accommodation and meals.

Eligibility: Minimum age is 18 and you must speak Spanish for some Latin America projects. Non-US citizens are eligible for many programs if they can obtain the relevant tourist visas.

Amizade

920 William Pitt Union, PA 15260, USA
☎ +1 888-973 4443
fax +1 412-648 1492
volunteer@amizade.org
www.amizade.org

Amizade places volunteers on community-development projects around the world, including a program at the Korrawinga Aboriginal community, near Hervey Bay in Queensland, Australia. This particular project aims to develop industries that will benefit the local Aboriginal community, including tea-tree cultivation and tourism projects.

Timing & Length of Projects: From two weeks, starting on set dates annually.

Destinations: Australia, Bolivia, Brazil, Nepal, Northern Ireland & the USA.

Costs: Vary with the destination – the Australian program costs US£2225, including meals and accommodation.

Eligibility: Minimum age is 18.

Challenges Worldwide

13 Hamilton Pl, Edinburgh EH3 5BA, Scotland
☎ /fax +44 (0)131 332 7372
enquiries@challengesworldwide.com
www.challengesworldwide.com

This educational charity offers overseas placements on small development, poverty-alleviation and conservation projects worldwide. There are opportunities for skilled people of all backgrounds, and volunteers are targeted towards projects that need their specific skills – it's worth contacting Challenges and letting them know what you have to offer.

Timing & Length of Projects: Three to nine months. Projects can start at any time.

Destinations: Worldwide, including Antigua, Bangladesh, Belize, Ecuador & Tasmania (Australia).

Costs: Range from £1850 for three months to £3850 for nine months, including a two-day training course, food, accommodation and insurance.

Eligibility: Age range is 18 to 65 (most volunteers are 35 or younger).

Changing Worlds

11 Doctors Lane, Chaldon, Surrey CR3 5AE, UK
☎ +44 (0)1883 340960
fax +44 (0)1883 330783
ask@changingworlds.co.uk
www.changingworlds.co.uk

Changing Worlds offers all sorts of overseas volunteer placements and working-holiday packages. Volunteering options include teaching in Patagonia in Chile, working in orphanages in India and providing pastoral care in Romania. Apply nine months in advance; volunteers then attend an interview day at Redhill in Surrey.

Timing & Length of Projects: Three to six months.

Destinations: Australia, Canada, Chile, India, Madagascar, Nepal, New Zealand, Romania & Tanzania.

Costs: Vary with the project but start from £1665 for projects in Romania and £2275 for projects in India, Nepal and Tanzania. Fees include flights, meals and accommodation and extras such as group excursions and language classes, but not insurance.

Eligibility: Age range is 18 to 35.

Cross-Cultural Solutions

2 Clinton Pl, New Rochelle, NY 10801, USA
☎ +1 914-632 0022
fax +1 914-632 8494
info@crossculturalsolutions.org
www.crossculturalsolutions.org

Cross-Cultural Solutions offers cultural-immersion programs that combine voluntary work with activities designed to provide an insight into the culture of the host country. The voluntary segment of the project can involve teaching, assisting at orphanages or caring for the elderly or disabled. There's also a UK office – see the website for details.

Timing & Length of Projects: Most projects last two to 12 weeks (some longer projects are available).
Destinations: Brazil, Peru, Guatemala, Costa Rica, Ghana, Tanzania, India, China, Russia & Thailand.
Costs: Projects operate on a set fee of US$2175 for the first two weeks and US$248 for additional weeks, including lodging, meals, local transport and travel insurance.
Eligibility: Minimum age is 17 to 18. Most nationalities can apply.

Ecologia Trust
66 The Park, Forres, Moray IV36 3TZ, Scotland
☎ +44 (0)1309 690995
fax +44 (0)1309 691009
info@ecologia.org.uk
www.ecologia.org.uk
This small charitable trust sends volunteers to the Kitezh Children's Community in Russia, a self-contained fostering centre providing a stable environment and education for orphaned and abandoned children.
Timing & Length of Projects: From two months (volunteers are needed throughout the year).
Destinations: Kitezh, Russia (300km/186 miles south of Moscow).
Costs: Volunteers pay their own costs.
Eligibility: Minimum age is 17. Knowledge of Russian is an advantage.

Experiment in International Living (UK)
EIL, 287 Worcester Rd, Malvern, Worcestershire WR14 1AB, UK
☎ +44 (0)1684 562577
fax +44 (0)1684 562212
info@eiluk.org
www.eiluk.org
Established in 1932, this British and American educational charity arranges volunteer placements in 20 countries worldwide. The projects vary each year, but usually include development and conservation projects, farmstays and cultural exchanges – call to request an information pack for the latest opportunities. Global offices are listed on the website.
Timing & Length of Projects: Five weeks to a year, starting year round.
Destinations: Global, including Africa, Asia, the Middle East, Europe & the Indian subcontinent.
Costs: Vary with the project but homestay accommodation and board starts from £400 per month. EIL can provide a few annual scholarships for up to half the cost for certain programs.
Eligibility: Minimum age is 18 (20 on some projects).

Foundation for Sustainable Development
870 Market St, Suite 321, San Francisco, CA 94102, USA
☎ /fax +1 415-283 4873

info@fsdinternational.org
www.fsdinternational.org
This developmental organisation places US and international volunteers on grassroots projects in Latin America and Africa. Volunteers on the internship program work closely with disadvantaged communities on programs of sustainable development. Apply by March for summer programs.
Timing & Length of Projects: Summer programs (between June and August) last eight to 10 weeks, or you can volunteer for at least two months at any time.
Destinations: Bolivia, Ecuador, Nicaragua, Peru, Tanzania & Uganda.
Costs: Summer programs start at US$1975; general internships cost from US$1700 for eight weeks.
Eligibility: Minimum age is 18. Latin American projects require conversational Spanish.

Global Choices
Barkat House, 116–118 Finchley Rd, London NW3 5HT, UK
☎ +44 (0)20 7433 2501
fax +44 (0)20 7435 1397
info@globalchoices.co.uk
www.globalchoices.co.uk
Global Choices offers a variety of internships and conservation and community projects worldwide, including rainforest conservation in Costa Rica and community work at schools and old people's homes in the Ukraine. Accommodation and meals are included on some programs; on others, volunteers pay a small flat fee and then cover their own accommodation and board.
Timing & Length of Projects: One to 18 months.
Destinations: Australia, Brazil, Costa Rica, Cyprus, Ghana, Ireland, New Zealand, Poland, Spain, the Ukraine & the US.
Costs: Costs vary with the program (eg volunteering on a nature reserve in Costa Rica costs from £199 per month), and volunteers pay a local fee of around £9 per day for guesthouse or homestay accommodation.
Eligibility: Restrictions vary with the program. For most projects the minimum age is 18.

Global Crossroad
8772 Quarters Lake Rd, Suite 9, Baton Rouge, LA 70809, USA
☎ +1 225-922 7854
fax: +1 225-922 9114
info@globalcrossroad.com
www.globalcrossroad.com
This US sending agency places volunteers on projects throughout Asia, Africa, Latin America and the Indian subcontinent. Volunteers mostly work as English teachers, but there are also opportunities to work in development, journalism, childcare and women's rights.
Timing & Length of Projects: Most programs last two to 12 weeks, starting on the 1st and 16th of each month.

Destinations: Costa Rica, Ecuador, Guatemala, Honduras, Kenya, Ghana, Tanzania, India, Nepal, Sri Lanka, China, Thailand, Mongolia & Tibet.

Costs: Vary with the project – volunteers/interns in Sri Lanka pay from US$780/950 for two weeks, including insurance, meals and accommodation.

Eligibility: Minimum age is 18.

Global Service Corps

300 Broadway, Suite 28, San Francisco, CA 94133, USA
☎ +1 415-788 3666 ext 128
fax +1 415-788 7324
gsc@earthisland.org
www.globalservicecorps.org

Global Service Corps places volunteers from the US, the UK and Australia on education, health-care, HIV/AIDS and sustainable agriculture projects in Asia and Africa. There are two-week camps, summer internships and long-term projects. On the Thailand projects, volunteers work at schools and Buddhist monasteries.

Timing & Length of Projects: Two weeks to six months, starting on set dates year round.

Destinations: Tanzania & Thailand.

Costs: Fees start at US$1925 for two weeks in Thailand, including meals and accommodation.

Eligibility: Minimum age is 18 in Thailand, 20 in Tanzania. Families are welcome on some projects.

Global Volunteer Network

PO Box 2231, Wellington, New Zealand
☎ +64 (0)4-569 9080
fax +64 (0)4-569 9081
info@volunteer.org.nz
www.volunteer.org.nz

This New Zealand volunteer organisation places around 1000 volunteers a year from across the world to teach English, work with orphans and refugees or carry out environmental work in various parts of the developing world.

Timing & Length of Projects: Two weeks to one year – projects start on set dates through the year.

Destinations: New Zealand, Thailand, China, Nepal, Ecuador, Romania, Russia, Ghana, Liberia & Uganda.

Costs: Vary with the destination – two weeks working with children in Russia starts at US$600, including meals and accommodation.

Eligibility: Minimum age varies from 18 to 21, depending on the program.

Global Volunteers

375 East Little Canada Rd, St Paul, MN 55117, USA
☎ +1 800-487 1074
fax +1 651-482 0915
email@globalvolunteers.org
www.globalvolunteers.org

Global Volunteers is a 'private Peace Corps' organisation that arranges voluntary service trips focusing on activities such as tutoring, construction, environmental work, health care and teaching English. No specialised skills are needed.

Timing & Length of Projects: Year-round service programs, from one to three weeks.

Destinations: The USA and another 18 countries on six continents.

Costs: One-week programs cost US$800 to US$2500, depending on the location.

Eligibility: Minimum age is 18, except for family programs.

International Volunteers for Peace Australia

499 Elizabeth St, Surry Hills, Sydney, NSW 2010, Australia
☎ +61 (0)2-9699 1129
fax +61 (0)2-9318 0918
admin@ivp.org.au
www.ivp.org.au

The promotion of cultural collaboration, peace and social justice are integral to IVP's charity work. Established project work camps around the world help with the practical needs of disadvantaged local communities and encourage mutual understanding between cultures.

Timing & Length of Projects: Projects run for two to four weeks.

Destinations: Worldwide, but mainly Asia, Africa & Australia.

Costs: Registration costs are A$250 to A$350, then volunteers cover all their expenses.

Eligibility: English speakers of 18 years and above.

Involvement Volunteers Association

PO Box 218, Port Melbourne, Victoria 3207, Australia
☎ +61 (0)3-9646 9392
fax +61 (0)3-9646 5504
ivworldwide@volunteering.org.au
www.volunteering.org.au

This Australian-based volunteer organisation has offices in Germany, New Zealand and the UK (see the website for details) and offers a vast range of volunteering opportunities around the world, including teaching, development, conservation and community programs and archaeological and farming projects.

Timing & Length of Projects: Two weeks to one year. Projects can start at any time but you should apply at least three months in advance.

Destinations: More than 40 countries worldwide.

Costs: There's a A$250 registration fee and A$105 placement fee, then you have the choice of a A$300 fee for a single program or a A$450 fee for as many programs as you like in a single year. Accommodation and meals are included.

Eligibility: Minimum age is 18.

i-to-i

9 Blenheim Tce, Leeds, West Yorkshire LS2 9HZ, UK
☎ +44 (0)870 333 2332
fax +44 (0)113 242 2171
info@i-to-i.com
www.i-to-i.com

One of the largest and longest-established volunteer organisations, i-to-i offers a huge range of projects, including teaching, conservation, health care, construction, community development, work at museums and internships at local newspapers. Projects are available on five continents and most include lessons in the local language. TEFL training is also provided on some teaching projects. Packages include 24-hour local support and an orientation on arrival.

Timing & Length of Projects: Projects last four to 24 weeks and begin on fixed dates throughout the year.
Destinations: Europe, Latin America, Africa, Asia & Australia.
Costs: Costs vary with the project. Most cost between £995 and £1895, which covers fees, insurance and accommodation for the minimum duration of the project. Additional weeks cost £50 to £100. There may also be a local fee for food and transport (around £9 per day).
Eligibility: Age range is 18 to 80 years.

International Voluntary Service (IVS)

Old Hall, East Bergholt, Colchester, Essex CO7 6TQ, UK
☎ +44 (0)1206 298215
fax +44 (0)1206 299043
ivs@ivsgbsouth.demon.co.uk
www.ivs-gb.org.uk

IVS is the British representative of the global organisation Service Civil International (www.sciint.org), which places volunteers on small-scale grassroots projects with a cultural, social or environmental focus. Many projects involve caring for people with special needs. A list of vacancies is posted on the website every three months and you should apply for specific positions.

Timing & Length of Projects: Projects last for two to four weeks between June and September.
Destinations: Europe, North America & North Africa.
Costs: Volunteers pay a registration fee of £145 (£120 for unwaged people), which includes IVS membership, and then cover all costs except accommodation and meals.
Eligibility: Minimum age is 18.

Mondo Challenge

Galliford Building, Gayton Rd, Milton Malsor, Northampton NN7 3AB, UK
☎ +44 (0)1604 858225
fax +44 (0)1604 859323
info@mondochallenge.org
www.mondochallenge.org

This small British organisation focuses on volunteers who are on career breaks. Placements are mainly on teaching and business-development projects in Africa, South America and the Indian subcontinent, but there are also opportunities to work with women's groups and provide support for HIV sufferers.

Timing & Length of Projects: Six weeks to one year. Departures are possible at any time.
Destinations: Nepal, India, Sri Lanka, Kenya, Gambia, Tanzania & Chile.
Costs: Depends on how long you go for – three-month projects cost £900 and you make a contribution directly to local families for meals and accommodation.
Eligibility: Minimum age is 18, but the focus is on graduates and older volunteers.

Muir's Tours/Nepal Kingdom Foundation

Nepal House, 97a Swansea Rd, Reading, Berkshire RG1 8HA, UK
☎ +44 (0)118 950 2281
info@nkf-mt.org.uk
www.nkf-mt.org.uk

These linked organisations place volunteers in teaching positions and on conservation projects in Nepal and other countries. Options include teaching English in Nepal and Peru and working with rare wild horses in Mongolia.

Timing & Length of Projects: One to 12 months, with opportunities throughout the year.
Destinations: Nepal, Tanzania, Mongolia, Ecuador & Peru.
Costs: Costs vary with the project – teaching in Nepal costs around £200 per month, plus a registration fee of £120. Meals and accommodation are provided with local families.
Eligibility: Minimum age is 18. TEFL is required for some teaching positions and you must speak Spanish for the Latin American placements.

Outreach International

Bartlett's Farm, Hayes Rd, Compton Dundon, Somerset TA11 6PF, UK
☎ /fax +44 (0)1458 274957
info@outreachinternational.co.uk
www.outreachinternational.co.uk

Outreach offers volunteers the chance to work on conservation, development, teaching and community projects in Asia and Latin America. The projects include language lessons and short expeditions to sites of historical or cultural interest. You can apply online and then there's an interview.

Timing & Length of Projects: Three to nine months (projects can be extended after you arrive if you want to stay longer). Most projects start in January, April or September.
Destinations: Mexico, Ecuador & Cambodia.
Costs: Placements cost £2500 to £3250, including flights, visas, local transport, language lessons, food, accommodation and insurance. Extra months cost £400 each.
Eligibility: Minimum age is 18.

Peace Corps

1111 20th St NW, Washington, DC, 20526, USA
☎ 1 800-424 8580 (toll-free)
www.peacecorps.gov
Founded in 1961, this US-government agency places volunteers on a huge number of development projects worldwide – from counselling teenagers in Belize to developing agriculture in rural villages in the Philippines. See the website for email and phone details of Peace Corps representatives across the United States.

Personal Overseas Development (PoD)

7 Rosbury House, Lytton Grove, Putney, London
SW15 2EY, UK
☎ +44 (0)20 8246 5811
info@thepodsite.co.uk
www.thepodsite.co.uk
This gap-year organisation also arranges tailor-made volunteer placements for skilled career-breakers in Thailand, Tanzania and Peru. Projects include teaching English at rural schools in Tanzania, working in wildlife-rescue centres in Thailand and assisting at orphanages in Peru.
Timing & Length of Projects: Two weeks to six months. Projects begin on set dates and there are usually several programs per year.
Destinations: Thailand, Tanzania & Peru.
Costs: Volunteers make a contribution that varies with the project – three months' teaching in Tanzania costs from £800 with accommodation and meals.
Eligibility: Minimum age is 22. Skill requirements vary with the positions, but there are openings for skilled and unskilled volunteers.

Raleigh International

Staff Office, Raleigh House, 27 Parsons Green Lane, London
SW6 4HZ, UK
☎ +44 (0)20 7371 8585
fax +44 (0)20 7371 5116
staff@raleigh.org.uk
www.raleighinternational.org
One of the original UK gap-year organisations, Raleigh accepts around 400 volunteer staff members on its expeditions every year. The adventurous expeditions include three projects where volunteers work in conservation or community development and take part in various adventure activities. Raleigh also requires adventure-activity instructors, drivers, press officers, health staff and logisticians – contact Raleigh with the skills you have to offer. After you apply, there's an interview and an assessment weekend in the UK.
Timing & Length of Projects: From 12 weeks (no maximum). Projects start on set dates from January to June or in September.
Destinations: Chile, Costa Rica, Nicaragua, Malaysia, Ghana & Namibia.

Costs: Applicants must fundraise £1100 (and the cost of flights). This can be reduced if you take advantage of the UK government Gift Aid scheme (the charity can arrange this on your behalf). All meals, accommodation, transport and insurance are then provided.
Eligibility: Minimum age is 25 and volunteers must have relevant skills for the position.

Teaching & Projects Abroad

Gerrard House, Rustington, West Sussex BN16 1AW, UK
☎ +44 (0)1903 859911
fax +44 (0)1903 785779
info@teaching-abroad.co.uk
www.teaching-abroad.co.uk
This popular organisation offers a huge range of teaching, health-care, development and conservation projects in Asia, South America, Africa and Eastern Europe. Volunteers can work in a wide variety of disciplines, including teaching, coaching sports, nursing, veterinary work, conservation, archaeology, business, law and journalism. Teaching & Projects Abroad also has offices in Denmark, Germany, the Netherlands and the USA (see the website for details).
Timing & Length of Projects: Six weeks to one year. Projects can start at any time.
Destinations: Bolivia, Chile, China, Ghana, India, Mexico, Mongolia, Nepal, Peru, Romania, Russia, South Africa, Sri Lanka, Thailand & Togo.
Costs: Vary with the project and the destination – prices for three months' teaching ranges from £1195 to £1795, and additional months start from £295. Teaching & Projects Abroad has its own travel agent for discount flights.
Eligibility: Age range is 18 to 70 (from 21 on some projects). Most projects are open to anyone, but some require specific skills or experience – see the website for more details.

Travellers Worldwide

7 Mulberry Close, Ferring, West Sussex BN12 5HY, UK
☎ +44 (0)1903 502595
fax +44 (0)1903 500364
info@travellersworldwide.com
www.travellersworldwide.com
This youth-oriented organisation offers volunteer placements in teaching and conservation worldwide. Most volunteers on teaching projects teach English, but you can also teach other subjects if you have relevant experience. Most volunteers are under 30, but there are opportunities for older travellers and career-breakers.
Timing & Length of Projects: Two weeks to one year; placements can start at any time.
Destinations: Worldwide, including Argentina, Cuba, China, India, Nepal, Sri Lanka, Ghana, South Africa, Russia & the Ukraine.
Costs: Vary depending on the project – for example, teaching in China for one month costs £895 and volunteering on a

national park in Kenya for one month costs £1395. Travellers Worldwide can arrange flights for volunteers at extra cost.
Eligibility: Age range is 17 to 70. Some law and medicine projects require relevant experience.

UNA Exchange
Temple of Peace, Cathay's Park, Cardiff CF10 3AP, Wales
☎ +44 (0)29 2022 3088
fax +44 (0)29 2022 2540
info@unaexchange.org
www.unaexchange.org
This nonprofit organisation arranges overseas volunteer placements in conjunction with community organisations and NGOs around the world – for example, projects in Thailand are arranged through the organisation Greenway (www.greenwaythailand.org) in Hat Yai. There are also thousands of short-term work camps (three weeks or less) every year. A two-day training course is provided before departure.
Timing & Length of Projects: Two weeks to 12 months. Projects run year round.
Destinations: Worldwide, including France, Turkey, South Korea, Mexico, Thailand & Kenya.
Costs: There's a £100 application fee and a £10 fee for membership of UNA Exchange, which covers admin costs, accommodation and meals. Some projects in the southern hemisphere have an additional local fee.
Eligibility: Minimum age is 18.

USA Freedom Corps
1600 Pennsylvania Ave NW, Washington, DC, 20500, USA
☎ +1 877-872 2677
info@usafreedomcorps.gov
www.usafreedomcorps.gov
This US-government project provides a huge range of community volunteer opportunities for US citizens within the continental USA. It's the umbrella organisation for Americorps, Citizen Corps, Senior Corps and Peace Corps.
Timing & Length of Projects: Varies with the volunteer project.
Destinations: The USA.
Costs: Volunteers offer their time for free; accommodation and meals are provided for some projects.
Eligibility: Minimum age is 17. You must be a US citizen or resident alien.

Winant Clayton Volunteer Association (WCVA)
St Margaret's House, 21 Old Ford Rd, Bethnal Green, London E2 9PL, UK
☎ +44 (0)20 8983 3834
wcva@dircon.co.uk
www.wcva.dircon.co.uk
This organisation has been placing British volunteers in care homes for the elderly, homeless, mentally ill and HIV

sufferers for 50 years. All positions are on the East Coast of the USA and visas are arranged by the organisation. No formal qualifications are required but you'll need to be committed to caring and undergo a police record check.
Timing & Length of Projects: Two months, from late June.
Destinations: The USA.
Costs: Volunteers pay a £5 application fee and £15 registration fee and receive free lodging and a small stipend for food. Discounted flights can be arranged through the foundation.
Eligibility: Age range is 18 to 80 and you must hold a British or Irish passport.

WorldTeach
c/o Center for International Development, Harvard University, 79 John F Kennedy St, Cambridge, MA 02138, USA
☎ +1 617-495 5527
fax +1 617-495 1599
info@worldteach.org
www.worldteach.org
This American organisation offers a variety of teaching programs – mostly in Latin America – and welcomes applications from non-Americans. Volunteers teach English as a foreign language and receive local-language and teacher training. Accommodation is usually in homestays with local families.
Timing & Length of Projects: Two to 12 months. Summer programs run June to August. Year-long programs begin on set dates throughout the year.
Destinations: Costa Rica, Ecuador, Chile, Honduras, Namibia, Marshall Islands, China & Poland.
Costs: Summer programs cost US$1500 to US$3990 and year-long programs cost US$1000 to US$4990. Prices include airfares from a designated group departure point, insurance, visas and accommodation, and volunteers receive a small stipend for local travel, meals etc. If you make your own way to the program, the airfare will be deducted from the cost.
Eligibility: Minimum age is 18. There are no restrictions on the two-month summer programs but year-long programs require a bachelor's degree or equivalent.

Humanitarian Programs in Africa
The following organisations place volunteers on community projects in Africa.

Azafady
Studio 7, 1a Beethoven St, London W10 4LG, UK
☎ +44 (0)20 8960 6629
fax +44 (0)20 8962 0126
mark@azafady.org
www.madagascar.co.uk
Azafady combines forest conservation work with sustainable development schemes for neighbouring communities. Volunteers on the Pioneer Madagascar program work for

three weeks on projects around the town of Fort Dauphin and seven weeks in rural villages. Malagasy lessons are provided and there are trips to national parks. Only 20 people are accepted for each 10-week project, so you should apply well in advance.

Timing & Length of Projects: 10 weeks, beginning in the first week of January, April, July and October. You can then travel for 20 days on your visa.

Destinations: Madagascar.

Costs: Volunteers must raise a contribution of £2000 (£2500 for non-UK residents), most of which goes directly into Azafady projects. Meals, accommodation, local transport and training are provided.

Eligibility: Minimum age is 18.

Eco Africa Experience

Guardian House, Borough Rd, Godalming, Surrey GU7 2AE, UK
☎ +44 (0)1483 860560
fax +44 (0)1483 860391
info@ecoafricaexperience.com
www.ecoafricaexperience.com

This travel company places self-funding volunteers in private game reserves and ocean-research projects in South Africa. Land-based volunteers assist with the daily running of wildlife reserves, while marine volunteers work in research centres and monitor whale and dolphin populations by boat.

Timing & Length of Projects: Two weeks to 12 weeks (volunteers can split their time between more than one project). Projects start on set dates monthly.

Destinations: South Africa.

Costs: Prices start at £1950 for four weeks or £3900 for 12 weeks, including flights, local transport, accommodation and meals.

Eligibility: Minimum age is 17.

Lean on Me

15 Plantation Rd, Hillcrest, KZN, 3610, South Africa
☎ /fax +27 31-765 1818
claude@wah.co.za
www.wecare4africa.com

Affiliated with the Wild at Heart program (see p128), Lean on Me is a nonprofit organisation funded by volunteers who visit South Africa to work with children who have been affected by HIV/AIDS. Volunteers assist in the daily running of the orphanage and hospice and associated community projects, including taking children on trips to the sea or safari parks. There's a comprehensive training and orientation session on arrival.

Timing & Length of Projects: Four weeks to six months.

Destinations: South Africa.

Costs: Volunteers fund their own transport to the project and make a contribution of £605 for four weeks or up to £3116 for six months.

Eligibility: Minimum age is 18 (most volunteers are 20 to 35). A mature attitude and experience with children is an advantage.

Sudan Volunteer Programme (SVP)

34 Estelle Rd, London NW3 2JY, UK
☎ /fax +44 (0)20 7485 8619
davidsvp@aol.com
www.svp-uk.com

This small project recruits about 30 volunteers every year to teach English at schools and universities in Sudan, one of the world's most impoverished nations. Years of civil war have left the country in dire need of international assistance, so applicants can make a real difference. You can submit an application by email.

Timing & Length of Projects: Three or preferably six months from September or January.

Destinations: Sudan.

Costs: There is no cost for volunteering, but volunteers must pay their own airfare and insurance for the first three months (after that, it is covered by SVP).

Eligibility: Minimum age is 18 (21 on some projects). Volunteers should be graduates. TEFL qualifications and English-teaching experience are desirable but not essential.

VAE Volunteer Teachers Kenya

Bell Lane Cottage, Pudleston, near Leominster, Herefordshire HR6 0RE, UK
☎ +44 (0)1568 750329
fax +44 (0)1568 750636
harris@vaekenya.co.uk
www.vaekenya.co.uk

This teaching organisation places teachers in schools in rural Kenya. Teachers work in pairs and implement programs to improve school and teaching standards. The organisation mainly attracts gap-year students, but there are opportunities for older volunteers.

Timing & Length of Projects: Three to six months, departing in January.

Destinations: Kenya.

Costs: Six-month teaching placements cost around £3500, including flights, insurance, accommodation, meals and a small local stipend.

Eligibility: No restrictions but graduates are preferred.

Volunteer Africa

PO Box 24, Bakewell, Derbyshire DE45 1ZW, UK
support@volunteerafrica.org
www.volunteerafrica.org

This small grassroots organisation takes on volunteers every year for community projects in villages in Tanzania, including construction of school buildings and health centres. The projects are all very hands-on but training is provided. Most applicants come from the UK, Ireland, the US, Canada and Australia – apply online.

Timing & Length of Projects: Four to 10 weeks, including one week of training. Projects begin on set dates from May to October.

Destinations: Tanzania.

Costs: Projects cost from £920 for four weeks to £1660 for 10 weeks. At least half of the fee goes directly into local community projects.
Eligibility: Minimum age is 17.

Humanitarian Projects in Asia & the Indian Subcontinent

The following organisations place volunteers on community projects in India, Nepal, Tibet and Thailand.

Batemans Trust

Stocks Lane Farm, Steventon, near Abingdon, Oxfordshire OX13 6SS, UK
☎ +44 (0)1539 741593
info@batemanstrust.org
www.batemanstrust.org
This small charity runs a school for Anglo-Asian children in Chennai (Madras) in India and accepts volunteers with teaching or technical qualifications. The children of mixed British-Indian couples have traditionally been persecuted by mainstream Indian society and volunteers work to overcome the social problems that this group faces. There are openings for English, music and arts teachers; school nurses; and technical staff.
Timing & Length of Projects: Six weeks to one year.
Destinations: India.
Costs: There's a £500 volunteer contribution and volunteers cover all costs except accommodation and board.
Eligibility: Minimum age is 18. Volunteers should be graduates with TEFL, PGCE (Postgraduate Certificate in Education) or medical qualifications.

Cultural Destination Nepal

GPO Box 11535, Dhapasi, Kathmandu, Nepal.
☎ +9771-437 7623
fax +9771-437 7696
cdnnepal@wlink.com.np
www.volunteernepal.org.np
This organisation operates a Volunteer Nepal program, where volunteers spend one to three months working on community projects as teachers. An extensive induction is provided (including Nepali lessons) and the volunteer section of the project is followed by a trek, a jungle safari and a white-water rafting expedition. Only 25 positions are available each year, so you should apply well in advance.
Timing & Length of Projects: Two to four months, starting in February, April, June, August and October.
Destinations: Nepal.
Costs: The project costs £430 plus a £33 application fee, including activities, local transport, food, accommodation and language lessons. There is an extra charge for trekking permits and national-park fees.
Eligibility: Volunteers must be 18 to 65 and have a high-school diploma or equivalent.

Global Action Nepal

Baldwins, Eastlands Lane, Cowfold, West Sussex RH13 8AY, UK
enquiries@gannepal.org
www.gannepal.org
☎ +44 (0)1403 864704
fax +44 (0)1403 864088
This British organisation places volunteers in schools around Nepal. Volunteers assist Nepali teachers to improve standards of education in rural areas and the focus is on long-term sustainable education. Accommodation is provided with local families.
Timing & Length of Projects: Six months, from November to April.
Destinations: Nepal.
Costs: The complete cost for the program is £1650, including visa fees, three weeks' training, accommodation and meals.
Eligibility: No official restrictions and all nationalities are welcome.

Himalayan Volunteers (RCDP-Nepal)

PO Box No 8957, Ward No 14, Kathmandu, Nepal
☎ +977 1-278305
fax +977 1-282994
rcdpn@mail.com.np
www.rcdpnepal.com
This organisation is affiliated with the Experiment in International Living (EIL; see p130) and Inter Cultural Youth Exchange (ICYE), and volunteer placements are available in Nepal and India. Volunteers work in orphanages, health centres or on environmental projects and stay with host families. There's an optional two-week language and culture program that includes a trip to Chitwan National Park and white-water rafting.
Timing & Length of Projects: Two weeks to five months in Nepal (programs begin six times a year). Projects in India last two to 12 weeks and start anytime.
Destinations: Nepal & India.
Costs: Volunteers cover their costs and make a US$225 contribution. The monthly cost for room and board is US$150 and the language and culture program costs US$275.
Eligibility: Volunteers must be 18 to 70.

International Mountain Explorers Connection (IMEC)

PO Box 3665, Boulder, CO 80307, USA
☎ +1 303-998 0101
fax +1 303-998 1007
info@hec.org
www.hec.org
This nonprofit organisation promotes community development projects in mountainous regions of the world. Members can download listings of volunteer opportunities

across Nepal; English teachers are needed for projects in the Everest region. A week-long intensive Nepali training program is provided and volunteers stay with Sherpa families.

Timing & Length of Projects: Volunteers must be able to stay for at least two months. The Nepal program runs February to April and September to December.

Destinations: Nepal.

Costs: Membership of IMEC costs $30 per year and volunteer teachers make a contribution of US$1000 plus US$100 for teacher and language training; meals and accommodation are provided with host families.

Eligibility: Minimum age is 18. Volunteers without teaching experience must complete 25 hours of ESL or TEFL training before they can take part.

Jagriti Foundation

950 Ladera Lane, Santa Barbara, CA 93108, USA
☎ +1 805-969 9092
fax +1 805-969 4122
info@jagritifoundation.org
www.jagritifoundation.org

This organisation places women volunteers in areas where women have traditionally been marginalised, including Afghanistan, India, Nepal and Pakistan. Most volunteers teach English but other skills that will improve the status of women – computer skills, self-defence, proposal-writing etc – are also useful.

Timing & Length of Projects: One to six months.

Destinations: The Indian subcontinent (with occasional opportunities in Africa and Latin America).

Costs: There is no fee but volunteers must cover their own costs.

Eligibility: Minimum age is 20. College or university graduates from the US, Europe or Australia are preferred and volunteers should have relevant experience.

Karen Hill Tribes Trust

Midgley House, Heslington, York YO10 5DX, UK
☎ +44 (0)1904 411891
fax +44 (0)1904 430580
penelope@karenhilltribes.org.uk
www.karenhilltribes.org.uk

This British charity works with the hill tribes of northern Thailand, teaching English and installing water supplies in remote communities. Between 50 and 70 volunteers are taken on every year, teaching in primary and secondary schools and living in simple village huts with local families.

Timing & Length of Projects: Six months, from October to March, or January to July. Water-installation projects are available from January to July.

Destinations: Hill-tribe regions of Thailand.

Costs: Volunteers cover their own costs and contribute £1500.

Eligibility: Minimum age is 18. Graduates are preferred and volunteers are expected to learn some of the Thai and Karen languages.

ROKPA UK Overseas Projects

Kagyu Samye Ling, Eskdalemuir, Langholm, Dumfriesshire DG13 0QL, UK
☎ +44 (0)13873 73232 ext 30
fax +44 (0)13873 73223
charity@rokpauk.org
www.rokpauk.org

Founded by a Tibetan doctor, this charity runs social-development projects in Tibet, Nepal and Africa. Small numbers of self-funding volunteers are accepted to teach English in Tibet and work with the destitute in Nepal.

Timing & Length of Projects: Six to nine months, from March.

Destinations: Tibet & Nepal.

Costs: Volunteers must cover their own flights etc but accommodation and meals are provided by the host school

Eligibility: Minimum age is 25. Teachers need TEFL qualifications and experience.

Student Action India (SAI)

c/o Voluntary Services Unit, UCL Union, 25 Gordon St, London WC1H 0AY, UK
☎ +44 (0)7071 225 866
fax +44 (0)870 1353906
info@studentactionindia.org.uk
www.studentactionindia.org.uk

Run by young people for young people, this organisation needs volunteers to help out with health education, childcare, teaching and administrative work on community projects around India. There are positions available for both skilled and unskilled volunteers and training is provided both in the UK before departure and on arrival in India.

Timing & Length of Projects: Two months from July to September or five months from September to February.

Destinations: India.

Costs: Volunteers make a contribution of £550 for two months or £1000 for five months, which covers local expenses, lodging and board.

Eligibility: Minimum age is 18. Some positions require specific skills such as childcare experience or medical or nursing qualifications.

Humanitarian Projects in Latin America

The following organisations place volunteers on community projects across Latin America.

Casa-Alianza

Unit 2, The Business Exchange, Rockingham Rd, Kettering, Northhamptonshire NN16 8JX, UK
☎ +44 (0)1536 526447
fax +44 (0)1536 526448
casalnzauk@gn.apc.org
www.casa-alianza.co.uk

This charity provides support and community-development projects for Central American street children. Volunteers must speak Spanish and be dedicated and willing to work in emotionally difficult situations.

Timing & Length of Projects: Minimum of six months (one year preferred).

Destinations: Mexico, Guatemala, Honduras & Nicaragua.

Costs: There is no fee, but volunteers cover all their own expenses.

Eligibility: No restrictions, but volunteers over 21 are preferred. Some roles need specific skills and all volunteers must be fluent in Spanish.

Casa Guatemala

14 Calle 10–63, Zona 1, Guatemala City, Guatemala
☎ +502-232 5517
casaguatemal@guate.net
www.casa-guatemala.org

Casa Guatemala is a children's village for orphans on the Rio Dulce River in Guatemala. It is entirely funded by donations so volunteers need to cover all their expenses. Skilled and unskilled volunteers are needed for teaching and support roles at the centre and associated farms; accommodation is provided at the associated travellers' hotel.

Timing & Length of Projects: Three-month minimum stay.

Destinations: Guatemala.

Costs: Volunteers cover all their expenses and make a US$180 donation to the orphanage.

Eligibility: Minimum age is 18. Spanish is an advantage and specific skills (eg teaching experience) are useful for some positions.

OTEC Volunteer Costa Rica

Edificio Ferencz, Calle 3, Avenida 1 y 3, San José, Costa Rica
☎ +506-256 0633
fax +506-222 2605
incoming@otec.co.cr
www.volunteercostarica.com

Based in the Costa Rican capital, San José, this volunteer organisation accepts Spanish-speaking volunteers on a variety of community and conservation projects around the country, from sea-turtle conservation and promoting sustainable forestry to teaching English in rural schools. Non Spanish-speakers can take an intensive Spanish course before they volunteer.

Timing & Length of Projects: Three to 18 months. Programs begin at fixed times to coincide with the wet and dry seasons.

Destinations: Costa Rica.

Costs: The basic project cost is US$450, including local transport, accommodation with a family involved in the project, meals, an orientation and 24-hour assistance.

Eligibility: Minimum age is 18. Volunteers must have intermediate or higher level of Spanish.

Sociedade Iko Poran

Avenida Nilo Peçanha, 50/1709, Centro, Rio de Janeiro, 20.044-900, Brazil
☎ +55 21-3084 2242
fax +55 21-3084 1446
rj@ikoporan.org
www.ikoporan.org

This Brazilian organisation offers around 200 placements each year on community projects in Brazil for Spanish- or Portuguese-speaking volunteers. The projects are run in partnership with local NGOs and include educating teenagers through music, rehabilitating street children using circus arts, and recycling plastic bottles to provide materials for small industries.

Timing & Length of Projects: Two to 24 weeks. Projects start year round, particularly from June to August. Apply at least two months before you want to start.

Destinations: Brazil.

Costs: Volunteers pay a US$125 placement fee to Iko Poran and a US$125 donation to the partner NGO. Accommodation and meals are extra, and volunteers must cover their own flights, visas and insurance.

Eligibility: Age range is 18 to 70. Half of the volunteers are over 25. Volunteers must speak Spanish or Portuguese.

Task Brasil Trust

PO Box 4901, London SE16 3PP, UK
☎ +44 (0)20 7394 1177
fax +44 (0)20 7394 7713
info@taskbrasil.org.uk
www.taskbrasil.org.uk

Task Brasil works with street children in Rio de Janeiro and accepts volunteers with appropriate language skills to help out at the Casa Jimmy children's shelter. The work varies from childcare to cooking, cleaning and teaching, and volunteers can also help out on the project's community farm. Task Brasil also has an office in the US (see the website for details).

Timing & Length of Projects: One month to one year. Volunteers should apply at least two months in advance.

Destinations: Brazil.

Costs: Volunteers make a contribution of £1200 for up to three months (£2500 for up to a year). Meals and accommodation are provided at the shelter.

Eligibility: Minimum age is 21. Volunteers must speak excellent Portuguese or Spanish.

Volunteer Bolivia

342 Ecuador, Casilla 2411, Cochabamba, Bolivia
☎ /fax +591 4-452 6028
fax in USA +1 413-828 8144
info@volunteerbolivia.org
www.volunteerbolivia.org

This organisation arranges volunteer work placements and Spanish-language classes with a variety of nonprofit organisations in La Paz, Sucre and the Bolivian highlands. It seeks to provide a unique and alternative learning experience for people who want to make a difference.

Timing & Length of Projects: Placements of flexible duration are available year round, with most volunteers arriving between June and August.

Destinations: Bolivia.

Costs: US$1450 for an all-inclusive four-week program of Spanish-language classes, homestay and meals, plus a volunteer placement. Cheaper custom options (eg without homestay) are also available.

Eligibility: Minimum age is 18 (accompanied children are welcome on some projects).

EXECUTIVE VOLUNTEERING

The following organisations take on volunteers with professional experience or specific skills that are needed for humanitarian and development work worldwide.

ATD Fourth World

48 Addington Sq, London SE5 7LB, UK
☎ +44 (0)20 7703 3231
fax +44 (0)20 7252 4276
atd@atd-uk.org
www.atd-uk.org

ATD Fourth World aims to promote human rights and give a voice to the world's poorest people. Committed skilled volunteers are required to work with street children and provide social services for impoverished communities, as well as lobbying and campaigning local and international governments. Applicants should attend one of the regular training weekends in London (see the website for dates).

Timing & Length of Placements: The minimum volunteer period is three months for training and one year in the field (beginning in September).

Destinations: Around 25 countries worldwide, including destinations in Europe, Asia, Africa & Latin America.

Costs/Pay: The initial introductory weekend costs £12, including meals and accommodation. The three-month training period is free and volunteers get a small stipend for the second and third months. Once volunteers are accepted, all costs are covered by ATD.

Eligibility: Minimum age is 18. No specific experience is required but you should contact ATD to discuss the skills you can bring to their projects.

Australian Volunteers International (AVI)

71 Argyle St, Fitzroy, Victoria 3065, Australia
☎ +61 (0)3-9279 1788
fax +61 (0)3-9419 4280
info@australianvolunteers.com
www.ozvol.org.au

AVI is Australia's major international voluntary organisation – equivalent to VSO or the Peace Corps. Volunteers mainly work with disadvantaged communities in the developing world, and projects aim to equip local people with professional skills in business, tourism, health and communications.

Timing & Length of Placements: Projects last two years. Young volunteers work on shorter team projects.

Destinations: Projects operate in 48 countries, including Australia.

Pay: Volunteers receive a local salary, and flights, insurance and other expenses are paid.

Eligibility: You must be an Australian or New Zealand citizen or permanent resident aged 18 to 80 years. Volunteers should have relevant professional experience for the project they are volunteering for.

BESO

164 Vauxhall Bridge Rd, London SW1V 2RA, UK
☎ +44 (0)20 7630 0644
fax +44 (0)20 7630 0624
registrar@beso.org
www.beso.org

This international development agency offers around 400 short-term volunteer positions on development projects around the world. Volunteers must have relevant technical or business experience and be able to work alone in remote areas, imparting skills to local people.

Timing & Length of Placements: Projects last 10 days to three months. Departures depend on the availability of volunteer positions.

Destinations: Eastern Europe and the developing world.

Costs/Pay: Once volunteers are matched with a project, flights, accommodation and meals are provided by BESO and the host project.

Eligibility: Volunteers need five years relevant professional or technical experience. Most applicants are aged 30 or above.

British Red Cross Society

International Personnel & Training Department, British Red Cross Society, 9 Grosvenor Crescent, London, SW1X 7EJ
☎ +44 (0)20 7235 5454
fax +44 (0)20 7245 6315
overseasrecruitment@redcross.org.uk
www.redcross.org.uk

This global health-care charity maintains a register of experienced professional volunteer staff who are sent out to locations where there is dire humanitarian need. Volunteers work overseas in medical and support roles on a fixed term, salaried basis and costs are covered by the Red Cross. You can apply to the register using the form on website.

Timing & Length of Placements: One month to two years.

Destinations: Worldwide.
Costs/Pay: Costs are covered by the Red Cross.
Eligibility: Minimum age is 25. Volunteers must be British nationals or legal residents with three years' professional experience and relevant overseas experience.

Catholic Institute for International Relations (CIIR)

Unit 3 Canonbury Yard, 190a New North Rd, London N1 7BJ, UK
☎ +44 (0)20 7354 0883
fax +44 (0)20 7359 0017
ciir@ciir.org
www.ciir.org

This international charity works with development groups and governments in Latin America and Africa and takes on International Cooperation for Development (ICD) workers to assist on community projects. ICD workers need to be skilled professionals with relevant experience (eg health care, education, vocational training). The charity is based on Christian principles, but non-Christians with relevant experience are welcome.
Timing & Length of Placements: Most projects last two years. Start dates depend on the project.
Destinations: Ecuador, Peru, El Salvador, Honduras, Nicaragua, Dominican Republic, Haiti, Namibia, Somaliland, Zimbabwe & Yemen.
Costs/Pay: Volunteers receive a local salary and an allowance for expenses back home. Flights, insurance, and living arrangements are covered by CIIR.
Eligibility: Age range is 25 to 70. Volunteers must have at least two-years work experience, preferably in a training-related field.

Concern Worldwide

52 Lower Camden St, Dublin 2, Ireland
☎ +353 1-475 4162
fax +353 1-475 7362
info@concern.net
www.concern.net

This large Dublin-based charity has numerous work opportunities in the development field on projects in Africa and Asia. Applicants must have lots of relevant professional or technical experience but all workers receive a full salary and training. A list of required workers is posted on the website every month.
Timing & Length of Placements: One to two years.
Destinations: Africa, Asia & Indian subcontinent.
Costs/Pay: Workers receive a full salary which varies depending on the position – £18,000 is the starting salary for technical advisors.
Eligibility: Must have extensive experience in a field relating to development work, eg health care, nutrition, finance, logistics. Field experience in the developing world is also a major advantage.

Hands around the World

PO Box 25, Coleford, Gloucestershire GL16 7YL, UK
☎ +44 (0)1594 560223
fax +44 (0)1594 560223
info@handsaroundtheworld.org.uk
www.handsaroundtheworld.org.uk

This organisation places volunteers on development projects in Africa and other countries. Volunteers are matched with projects that require their specific skills – mostly in health care, engineering and teaching. Groups of volunteers are also recruited for building projects at schools and community centres.
Timing & Length of Placements: Projects last three to six months.
Destinations: Africa, India, Brazil.
Costs/Pay: Volunteers make a £200 donation and assist in project fundraising. Flights, visas and accommodation are provided by Hands Around the World, but volunteers must cover some living costs.
Eligibility: Minimum age 18. For skilled positions, volunteers need at least two years' workplace experience after completing qualifications.

International Health Exchange (IHE)

1 Great George St, London SW1P 3AA, UK
☎ +44 (0)20 7233 1100
fax +44 (0)20 7233 3590
info@ihe.org.uk
www.ihe.org.uk

IHE acts as a recruitment agency linking health-care workers with international charities and NGOs. Volunteers subscribe to a monthly magazine containing job listings and are then placed on a volunteer register. IHE will contact you if your skills are required by one of its organisations. Desirable skills include health care, logistics and project management.
Timing & Length of Placements: Three to 12 months. Departures depend on the availability of placements.
Destinations: Global.
Costs/Pay: Subscription to IHE costs £30 per year (£20 if you are unemployed or studying). Some projects are voluntary, some are paid, but transport, food and accommodation is provided by the host organisation.
Eligibility: Candidates must have several years' experience in an area of health care relating to development work (eg nutrition, sanitation, health-care management). Field experience in the developing world is an advantage.

International Service

Hunter House, 57 Goodramgate, York YO1 7FX, UK
☎ +44 (0)1904 647799
fax +44 (0)1904 652353
unais-UK@geo2.poptel.org.uk
www.internationalservice.org.uk

International Service has 30 to 40 vacancies a year for skilled volunteers with professional experience, particularly in the fields of health care, human rights, sustainable development and administration of development organisations. Apply for a specific position on the website.

Timing & Length of Placements: Two years.

Destinations: West Africa, Latin America and Palestine

Costs/Pay: All costs are covered by International Service, including a living allowance and paid holidays.

Eligibility: Minimum of two years' relevant professional experience.

Médecins du Monde

29th floor, One Canada Sq, London E14 5AA, UK

☎ +44 (0)20 7516 9103

fax +44 (0)20 7516 9104

info@medecinsdumonde.co.uk

www.medecinsdumonde.co.uk

This international emergency-relief operation needs volunteer doctors, nurses, midwives and medical lab technicians to work at the scene of humanitarian disasters worldwide. As well as providing direct emergency health care, volunteers also assist with the psychological and physical rehabilitation of victims of warfare and starvation.

Timing & Length of Placements: Minimum three months.

Destinations: Worldwide.

Costs/Pay: All transport and living costs are covered by Médecins du Monde and volunteers receive a local salary of US$200 to US$400 per month, and a UK support grant of £400 to £600 per month.

Eligibility: Minimum of two years' medical experience. Ideally, all volunteers should speak French or Spanish and have experience of working overseas.

Médecins Sans Frontières

HR Department, 67–74 Saffron Hill, London EC1N 8QX, UK

☎ +44 (0)20 7404 6600

fax +44 (0)20 7404 4466

office-lddn@london.msf.org

www.uk.msf.org

This famously dedicated NGO has long-term openings for committed volunteer doctors, nurses and paramedics (in both physical and mental health) for emergency aid projects worldwide. Volunteers are also needed for support roles such as engineering (particularly sanitation and construction), vehicle maintenance, logistics, communications and management.

Timing & Length of Placements: Six to 18 months (nine months is the average).

Destinations: Global, particularly in areas afflicted by natural disaster or conflict.

Costs/Pay: Flights, insurance and living expenses are provided by MSF and volunteers receive a stipend of about £500 per month. For projects lasting a year or over, volunteers get four weeks' paid holiday.

Eligibility: Doctors and nurses need a minimum of two years' post-registration experience and to have taken a

recognised course in tropical medicine. Other staff need a similar amount of technical experience and should have travelled widely or worked overseas. Fluency in French, Spanish or Portuguese is an advantage. Most volunteers are 25 or older.

Peace Brigades International (PBI)

Unit 5, 89–93 Fonthill Rd, London N4 3HT, UK

☎ +44 (0)20 7561 9141

fax +44 (0)20 7281 2181

info@peacebrigades.org

www.peacebrigades.org

This long-established NGO works to combat human-rights abuses in Latin America and Asia. There are opportunities for skilled volunteers to assist with campaigning, negotiating and advocacy work and all costs are covered by the organisation. The application, selection and training process takes around six months.

Timing & Length of Placements: One year, starting several times a year on fixed dates.

Destinations: Columbia, Guatemala, Mexico & Indonesia.

Costs/Pay: All travel and living costs are covered by the Peace Brigades and a monthly stipend is provided for incidental expenses.

Eligibility: Volunteers must be 25 or older and fluent in written and spoken Spanish. You should also have experience of NGO, development, human-rights or community work.

RedR London

1 Great George St, London SW1P 3AA, UK

☎ +44 (0)20 7233 3116

fax +44 (0)20 7222 0564

info@redr.org

www.redr.org

Linked to IHE (see opposite), RedR specialises in providing skilled disaster relief and humanitarian aid workers at short notice to established aid agencies. Volunteers must have relevant skills – see the website for a list – and there's a special scheme for people who lack field experience. Volunteers apply to be included on the RedR register, and you'll then be matched with projects that require your skills.

Timing & Length of Placements: Three to 12 months. Departures depend on the availability of placements.

Destinations: Global.

Costs/Pay: A voluntary annual membership fee of £60 is requested. Some projects are voluntary, some are paid, but transport, food and accommodation is provided.

Eligibility: There's no fixed age range, but candidates must have several years' professional or technical experience. Field experience is preferred but not essential.

Skillshare International

126 New Walk, Leicester LE1 7JA, UK

☎ +44 (0)1162 541862

fax +44 (0)1162 542614

info@skillshare.org
www.skillshare.org
Like BESO and VSO, Skillshare is looking for experienced
professional people to volunteer in development projects
in Africa and India. There are opening for doctors, nurses,
engineers, accountants and people with other relevant
skills, and all costs are covered by the organisation. On the
website there's an application form for general positions.
Timing & Length of Placements: Most people volunteer for two years, but one-year projects are available.
Destinations: India, Botswana, Lesotho, Mozambique,
Namibia, South Africa, Swaziland, Tanzania & Uganda.
Costs/Pay: Skillshare covers flight costs and living
expenses and provides a small living allowance.
Eligibility: Minimum age is 18. Volunteers should have
a degree or relevant professional qualification and at least
two years' workplace experience.

United Nations Volunteer Programme
Postfach 260 111, D-53153 Bonn, Germany
☎ +49 228-815 2000
fax +49 228-815 2001
headquarters@unvolunteers.org
www.unvolunteers.org
The United Nations has vacancies for highly skilled volunteers on its peace-keeping and developmental projects
around the world. Applicants must apply to be included
on a volunteer roster (details of how to apply are on the
website) and are then assigned to projects which require
their specific skills. The organisations Netaid (www.netaid
.org) and Unites (www.unites.org) are also part of the UN
volunteer program.
Timing & Length of Placements: Six weeks to two
years (volunteers can spend a maximum of eight years in
total on UN projects).
Destinations: Developing countries worldwide.
Costs/Pay: Volunteers receive a living allowance that
covers food, accommodation and all expenses; flights and
insurance are provided. Longer-term volunteers are also
eligible for annual leave.
Eligibility: Applicants must have relevant business,
logistical or developmental experience and will be required
to work closely with local people, imparting these skills to
others. Most applicants are in their mid-thirties or older.

Volunteer Service Abroad
6th floor, Agriculture House, 12 Johnston St, Wellington,
New Zealand
☎ +64 (0)4-472 5759
fax +64 (0)4-472 5052
vsa@vsa.org.nz
www.vsa.org.nz
The VSA utilises volunteers with professional and management skills for deprived international communities and
rural development programs. Projects require experience

in the areas of health, agriculture, business and economics,
architecture, law and planning.
Timing & Length of Placements: Most last two years.
Destinations: Asia, Africa, New Zealand & Pacific Islands.
Costs/Pay: Living expenses, flights, insurance and accom-
modation are provided.
Eligibility: Two years residency in New Zealand and
professional skills are required.

VSO (Voluntary Service Overseas)
317 Putney Bridge Rd, London SW15 2PN, UK
☎ +44 (0)20 8780 7285
fax +44 (0)20 8780 7375
enquiry@vso.org.uk
www.vso.org.uk
VSO is the largest independent volunteer organisation
in the world and it places hundreds of skilled volunteers
overseas every year on projects throughout the developing
world. There are openings for highly skilled and motivated
people with professional experience in all areas, from business and IT to education, health care and social work.

KIBBUTZIM & MOSHAVIM
For information on volunteering at a kibbutz or moshav,
contact the following organisations.

Kibbutz Program Center – Takam Artzi
18 Frishman St (cnr Ben Yehuda), Tel Aviv 61030, Israel
☎ +972 (0)3-527 8874
fax +972 (0)3-523 9966
kpc@volunteers.co.il
www.kibbutz.org.il
The Kibbutz Artzi Federation is the governing body for the
kibbutz movement. Applications can be made directly to
the organisation by fax or email. You must supply your
name, passport number, nationality, date of birth, occupation and date of arrival and then visit the office in Tel
Aviv in person to register. Once you have paid the registration and insurance fee, you'll be assigned to a kibbutz.

Kibbutz Program Center (USA)
21st floor, 633 3rd Ave, New York, NY 10017, USA
☎ +1 800-247 7852
fax +1 212-318 6134
kpc@jazo.org.il
www.kibbutzprogramcenter.org
The US agent for the Kibbutz Artzi Federation arranges
kibbutzim volunteer projects for American volunteers.
Timing & Length of Placements: Two to six months,
mostly between May and September.
Destinations: Israel.
Costs: Registration costs US$150 and there's an insurance
charge of US$80 plus US$25 per month (payable to the
kibbutz). Volunteers pay for flights.
Eligibility: Age range is 18 to 35.

Kibbutz Reps (UK)

16 Accommodation Rd, London NW11 8EP, UK
☎ +44 (0)20 8458 9235
fax +44 (0)20 8455 7930
enquries@kibbutz.org.uk
The British agent for the Kibbutz Artzi Federation arranges all-inclusive packages for British volunteers.
Timing & Length of Placements: Two to six months, year round.
Destinations: Israel.
Costs: Registration is £60, then you pay for insurance and flights – around £410 in total.
Eligibility: Age range is 18 to 40 years.

Moshav Movement in Israel Volunteer Centre

Leonardo da Vinci St 19 , Tel Aviv 64733, Israel
☎ +972 (0)3-695 8473
fax +972 (0)3-696 0139
This is the main office of the moshavim movement in Israel and it can arrange voluntary placements on community farms. Contact the organisation directly for information on volunteer opportunities.

RELIGIOUS ORGANISATIONS

American Jewish World Service (AJWS)

45 West 36th St, New York, NY 10018, USA
☎ +1 212-736 2597
fax +1 212-736 3463
jvcvol@ajws.org
www.ajws.org
This American organisation places Jewish professionals on sustainable-development projects. Participants in the Jewish Volunteer Corps scheme contribute business, health care and other social skills to grassroots projects worldwide.
Timing & Length of Placements: One month to one year, starting at any time.
Destinations: Africa, Asia, Latin America, the Middle East, Russia & Ukraine.
Costs: Expenses (except visas) are covered by the organisation, including flights.
Eligibility: Volunteers are Jewish professionals.

Christians Abroad

Room 237, Bon Marché Centre, 241–251 Ferndale Rd, London SW9 8BJ, UK
☎ +44 (0)870 770 7990
fax +44 (0)870 770 7991
recruitment@cabroad.org.uk
www.cabroad.org.uk
This large Christian organisation seeks committed volunteers to work on humanitarian projects in Africa and elsewhere. Most volunteers teach or work in childcare and health care but there are also opportunities for unskilled volunteers.

Conditions are often basic and there is a preaching element to the work.
Timing & Length of Placements: Varies with the project. Most volunteers stay for three months to one year.
Destinations: Cameroon, Tanzania, Nigeria, Kenya, China & Israel.
Costs: Volunteers cover their own expenses – if you buy flights and insurance through Christians Abroad, it gets a rebate.
Eligibility: Minimum age is 18. Volunteers should be Christian but any denomination is accepted. A criminal-record check is required and specific skills are required for some positions (eg nursing).

Church Mission Society

Partnership House, 157 Waterloo Rd, London SE1 8UU, UK
☎ +44 (0)20 7928 8681
fax +44 (0)20 7401 3215
info@cms-uk.org
www.cms-uk.org
This long-established Church of England group offers placements worldwide for Christian volunteer teachers, carers and development workers. Contact the organisation and ask for information on the 'Make a Difference' scheme and it'll send out an application, then there's an interview and a 10-day training session.
Timing & Length of Placements: Six to 18 months.
Destinations: Africa, Asia, Eastern Europe & the Middle East.
Costs: Placements are self-funded – the average cost for a year is around £3000, including flights, meals and accommodation.
Eligibility: Age range is 18 to 30.

Tearfund

100 Church Rd, Teddington, Middlesex TW11 8QE, UK
☎ +44 (0)20 8977 9144
fax +44 (0)20 8943 3594
enquiry@tearfund.org
www.tearfund.org
This Evangelical organisation works with poor communities around the world and has openings every year for volunteers on community projects. Volunteers mainly work with children and must be committed to the faith mission of the organisation. There are also crisis-relief programs – currently in Ethiopia, Eritrea, Iraq and Southern Africa.
Timing & Length of Placements: One to four months, from May to September.
Destinations: Worldwide, particularly in Africa and the Indian subcontinent.
Costs: Volunteers cover all their own expenses – the total cost for four months is around £2700.
Eligibility: Minimum age is 18. Some positions require specific skills and all require a strong faith commitment.

World Exchange

St Colm's International House, 23 Inverleith Tce, Edinburgh
EH3 5NS, Scotland
☎ +44 (0)131315 4444
fax +44 (0)131315 2222
we@stcolms.org
www.worldexchange.org.uk
This Christian organisation is supported by churches in
Scotland and England and offers community projects
worldwide. Volunteers must attend church during the
project but are not required to carry out missionary work.
Most projects involve education, health and community
development in impoverished areas and there are openings
for skilled and unskilled volunteers.

Timing & Length of Placements: Up to one year.
Most volunteers start in August, September or January.
Destinations: Worldwide, particularly in Malawi & India.
Costs: Volunteers make a contribution of £2500, which
covers flights, accommodation, meals and insurance.
Eligibility: Age range is 17 to 75; skill requirements vary
with the position.

VOLUNTEERING EXPEDITIONS

The following organisations offer projects that combine
volunteering with overland expeditions and studying –
handy for people who want to do more than one thing
with their career break.

Adventure Alternative

31 Myrtledene Rd, Belfast, Northern Ireland, BT8 6GQ, UK
☎ + 44 (0)2890 701476
office@adventurealternative.com
www.adventurealternative.com
This small Northern Irish organisation arranges bespoke
volunteering placements at schools and in rural communities in Russia, Kenya and Nepal. Projects are tailor-made,
so you should call them to discuss your needs. There are
also openings for medical students to do elective training.
Full local support is provided.

Timing & Length of Projects: Four weeks to one year,
starting year round.
Destinations: Russia, Kenya & Nepal.
Costs: Vary with the destination – eight weeks teaching in
Kathmandu costs around $1000. Food and accommodation
is included; flights, visas and insurance are extra.
Eligibility: Volunteers should be flexible, versatile people
able to work in a team. Teaching and medical experience
is an advantage.

Madventurer

Adamson House, 65 Westgate Rd, Newcastle upon Tyne,
Tyne and Wear NE1 1SG, UK
☎ +44 (0)845 121 1996
team@madventurer.com
www.madventurer.com

This gap-year and career-break organisation offers
projects in Africa and Latin America that start with a
voluntary placement which is followed by an optional
expedition or safari. Volunteers work in teaching, sport
coaching, health care or construction work for rural
communities or carry out conservation work (you can
volunteer in more than one discipline). Optional extras
such as language courses and scuba-diving training are
available on some projects. You can download brochures
and apply via the website.

Timing & Length of Projects: Projects last two weeks,
five weeks or three months, then there's an optional
expedition lasting three weeks to three months. Projects
begin on set dates throughout the year.
Destinations: Ghana, Togo, Trinidad & Tobago, Kenya,
Tanzania, Uganda, Peru & Bolivia.
Costs: From £790 for two weeks in East Africa to £1880
for three months in Trinidad. Expeditions vary from £405 to
£1200. Prices include meals, accommodation and activities,
but flights, visas and insurance are extra.
Eligibility: Minimum age is 18.

Trekforce Expeditions

34 Buckingham Palace Rd, London SW1W 0RE, UK
☎ +44 (0)20 7828 2275
fax +44 (0)20 7828 2276
info@trekforce.org.uk
www.trekforce.org.uk
This registered charity organises expeditions that involve
voluntary work on rainforest-conservation projects and
teaching programs in rural communities. The scheme starts
off with a two-month conservation project – often at a
national park – and you then have the option of staying
for an extra month to learn Spanish (on the Latin American
programs) or staying for three extra months to participate
in teacher training and work as a volunteer teacher.

Timing & Length of Projects: Two to five months.
Expeditions start on set dates from January to July.
Destinations: Guyana, Venezuela, Belize, Guatemala &
Malaysia.
Costs: Costs start at £2570 for a two-month project.
Volunteers fund their own international airfare and visas,
but all local costs are covered, including insurance, meals,
accommodation, language lessons and training.
Eligibility: Age range is 18 to 38.

VentureCo Worldwide

The Ironyard, 64–66 Market Pl, Warwick, Warwickshire
CV34 4SD, UK
☎ +44 (0)1926 411122
fax +44 (0)1926 411133
mail@ventureco-worldwide.com
www.ventureco-worldwide.com
VentureCo offers 15- to 16-week overland expeditions
which include a three-week cultural-orientation program

(usually made up of language lessons and cultural activities) and a four- to five-week volunteer project (usually in conservation or community development).

Timing & Length of Projects: Expeditions last 15 to 16 weeks, starting on two or more fixed dates annually.

Destinations: South America, Central America, Southeast Asia, Africa, India & Nepal.

Costs: Prices start at £4500, including flights, local transport, meals, accommodation, activities and insurance (visas are extra).

Eligibility: Minimum age is 21.

CONSERVATION & SCIENTIFIC PROGRAMS ABROAD

The following agencies and environmental organisations arrange placements for volunteers on conservation projects worldwide. Unless otherwise stated, flights, visas and insurance are extra.

Atlantic Whale Foundation

St Martins House, 59 St Martins Lane, Covent Garden, London WC2N 4JS, UK

☎ /fax +44 (0)20 7240 5795

edb@huron.ac.uk

www.whalefoundation.org.uk

Whale and dolphin enthusiasts can volunteer to assist scientists working on research projects with whales and dolphins in the Canary Islands. Volunteers make a contribution and collect data on board whale-watching boats for three to four days a week in exchange for half-board accommodation.

Timing & Length of Placements: From one week year round – the summer program runs from July to September.

Destinations: Canary Islands (Spain).

Costs: The volunteer contribution starts at £150 per week (£115 for students), which covers meals and accommodation.

Eligibility: No restrictions, except for summer program which has a maximum age of 30.

Austrop

Cape Tribulation Tropical Research Station, PMB 5, Cape Tribulation, Qld 4873, Australia

☎ /fax +61 (0)7-4098 0063

austrop@austrop.org.au

www.austrop.org.au

This rainforest research centre is located in the World-Heritage listed Daintree National Park at Cape Tribulation in Queensland. Volunteers, interns and researchers work on various conservation and research projects, including caring for delightful flying foxes (giant fruit bats) and working at the visitor centre.

Timing & Length of Placements: Up to the volunteer, but long stays are preferred.

Destinations: Cape Tribulation (Australia).

Costs: Volunteers/interns pay US$15/$20 per day and cover food and transport costs.

Eligibility: Minimum age is 25 and scientific or conservation experience is an advantage.

Accommodation: There's a camping area with a kitchen or you can stay at nearby guesthouses or backpackers' lodges.

Biosphere Expeditions

Sprat's Water, near Carlton Colville, The Broads National Park, Suffolk NR33 8BP, UK

☎ +44 (0)1502 583085

fax +44 (0)1502 587414

info@biosphere-expeditions.org

www.biosphere-expeditions.org

This award-winning outfit offers small group expeditions with a wildlife and conservation focus. Volunteers survey wild populations of rare animals such as wolves, snow leopards and cheetahs and two-thirds of the fee goes directly into conservation.

Timing & Length of Placements: Expeditions run in two-week slots – the maximum duration is two months.

Destinations: Azores (Portugal), Peru, Namibia, Ukraine, Siberia & Slovakia.

Costs: Volunteers must pay a £300 nonrefundable deposit to register. Total costs for expeditions are £990 to £1480 per two-week slot, including food, accommodation and local transport. There's a 10% discount on the second two weeks, and a 5% discount on each subsequent two week-slot.

Eligibility: No age restrictions, but you must be physically fit.

Blue Ventures

52 Avenue Rd, London N6 5DR, UK

☎ +44 (0)7786 854466

volunteer@blueventures.org

www.blueventures.org

This marine research organisation takes up to 12 volunteers at any one time to help with scientific studies of Indian Ocean marine life. Much of the work is carried out underwater and scuba-diving training is provided (volunteers must supply their own mask, snorkel, fins and wetsuit). Volunteers live in a self-contained research camp with cabins, kitchens and a bar. Apply by email using the application form on the website, then there's an interview.

Timing & Length of Placements: Minimum six weeks, starting on fixed dates throughout the year.

Destinations: Madagascar.

Costs: Volunteers pay £1780 for the six weeks, including food, accommodation, dive training and local transport. Divers with PADI Open Water dive certification or higher pay a reduced fee of £1580.

Eligibility: Most volunteers are around 30, but younger and older volunteers are accepted. Applicants must have a dive medical before they leave for Madagascar and take antimalarial medication.

BTCV International Conservation Holidays

BTCV, Conservation Centre, 163 Balby Rd, Doncaster, South Yorkshire DN4 0RH, UK
☎ +44 (0)1302 572244
fax +44 (0)1302 310167
information@btcv.org.uk
www.btcv.org

This company offers holidays where you volunteer full time on a conservation project – basically, volunteering by another name. Among the many options, you can monitor sea turtle populations in Grenada, maintain trails in the Grand Canyon or carry out research at national parks in South Africa.

Timing & Length of Placements: Most projects last two to eight weeks – see the website for a full list. Projects start on set dates year round.
Destinations: Worldwide.
Costs: Conservation holidays cost from £295 to £1450, including simple self-catering accommodation and insurance cover while working (additional insurance is recommended).
Eligibility: Minimum age is 18.

Conservation Volunteers Australia

13–15 Lydiard St North, Ballarat, Victoria 3350, Australia
☎ +61 (0)3-5333 1483
fax +61 (0)3-5333 2166
info@conservationvolunteers.com.au
www.conservationvolunteers.com.au

This conservation-oriented organisation provides Australian and international volunteers for 2000 conservation projects across Australia every year. Most projects involve hands-on practical work such as revegetation, protection of endangered species and surveys of indigenous flora and fauna.

Timing & Length of Placements: One day to six weeks. International volunteers can join four- to six-week projects on any Friday.
Destinations: Australia.
Costs: Membership costs A$40 to A$50 and volunteers cover all their own costs.
Eligibility: Minimum age is 17. Volunteers must be fit for outdoor work.

Coral Cay Conservation

13th floor, The Tower, 125 High St, Colliers Wood, London SW19 2JG, UK
☎ +44 (0)870 750 0668
fax +44 (0)870 750 0667
info@coralcay.org
www.coralcay.org

Led by exuberant naturalist David Bellamy, Coral Cay runs conservation projects in marine and rainforest environments in Southeast Asia, Central America and Fiji. Volunteers conduct surveys of animal and plant populations and promote environmental awareness in local communities. Presentation days are held at universities and travel fairs throughout the year.

Timing & Length of Placements: Minimum duration is two weeks. There is no maximum length for projects. Projects begin on 13 set dates throughout the year.
Destinations: Malaysia, Philippines, Honduras, Fiji.
Costs: Marine projects cost £100 to £300 per week, plus £700 for compulsory training and £400 for dive training (not required for certified divers). Rainforest projects cost £50 to £200 per week, plus £350 for compulsory training.
Eligibility: Minimum age is 16. You must be fit for scuba diving on marine projects and for trekking on rainforest projects.

Department of Conservation, New Zealand

59 Boulcott St, Wellington, New Zealand
☎ +64 (0)4-471 0726
fax +64 (0)4-471 1082
www.doc.govt.nz

This New Zealand government department aims to preserve the environmental heritage of the country, and overseas volunteers are welcome to join local people in activities such as planting trees, restoring natural habitats, helping in whale strandings and conducting bird surveys.

Timing & Length of Placements: Programs vary from a few days to several months – see the online calendar for details of current projects.
Destinations: New Zealand.
Costs: Volunteers cover their own costs.
Eligibility: No age restrictions but you must be fit for outside work.

Earthwatch Institute

7 Woodstock Rd, Oxford OX2 6HJ, UK
☎ +44 (0)1865 318838
fax +44 (0)1865 311383
info@uk.earthwatch.org
www.earthwatch.org

Earthwatch places around 4000 volunteers in short scientific field research positions every year. The work ranges from terrestrial and marine conservation to community-development work and archaeology. All projects are supervised by leading scientific teams and all training is provided. Earthwatch also has offices in America, Australia and Japan – see the website for details.

Timing & Length of Placements: One to three weeks.
Destinations: Worldwide.
Costs: Volunteers make their own way to the pick-up point in the project country and pay a share of the costs of the project – full details are on the website.
Eligibility: Minimum age is 16 (17 on some projects).

Ecovolunteers (WildWings/WildOceans)

1st floor, 577/579 Fishponds Rd, Bristol BS16 3AF, UK
☎ +44 (0)117 965 8333
fax +44 (0)117 937 5681

wildinfo@wildwings.co.uk
www.wildwings.co.uk
www.ecovolunteer.org.uk
Ecovolunteers arranges environmentally themed volunteering breaks worldwide and is represented in Britain by the travel agent WildWings/WildOceans. Projects focus on conserving a specific species in a specific place – for example, volunteers in Brazil work with jaguars, otters, dolphins and whales.
Timing & Length of Placements: Most projects last one week to six months – some run on set dates; others run throughout the year.
Destinations: Worldwide.
Costs: Vary with the project – two weeks' marine conservation in Brazil costs from £555, including accommodation and board but not flights.
Eligibility: Minimum age is 18 and you must be physically fit.

Frontier

50–52 Rivington St, London EC2A 3QP, UK
☎ +44 (0)20 7613 2422
fax +44 (0)20 7613 2992
info@frontier.ac.uk
www.frontierprojects.ac.uk
Frontier offers a variety of conservation-based expeditions in rainforest and coral reef environments throughout the tropics. Volunteers can take an optional BTEC in Tropical Habitat Conservation (equivalent to an A level) – see Contacts in the Studying chapter for more information.
Timing & Length of Placements: Four to 20 weeks. Projects start on set dates throughout the year.
Destinations: Andaman Islands (India), Cambodia, Madagascar, Nicaragua & Tanzania.
Costs: Costs start at £1200 to £1400 for four weeks and go up to £3600 for 20 weeks, including local transport, visas, insurance, training (including dive training) but not flights. Volunteers are eligible for a career-development loan to help with costs.
Eligibility: Minimum age is 17.

Fundación Golondrinas

Isabel la Católica N24-679 y Cristóbal Gangotena, Quito, Ecuador
☎ +593 2-226602
manteca@uio.satnet.net
www.ecuadorexplorer.com/golondrinas
This locally managed conservation organisation works on a variety of agroforestry and conservation projects in the Cerro Golondrinas Cloud Forest in northeast Ecuador. Volunteers work on forestry projects (tree planting, stabilising soil erosion, weeding etc) and educate local people about environmental farming practices.
Timing & Length of Placements: One to three months. Volunteers can start anytime but should give three months' notice.

Destinations: Ecuador.
Costs: Volunteers make a contribution of US$280 a month, which covers accommodation and meals.
Eligibility: Minimum age is 19 and you must be fit for hard manual work in tropical conditions.

Greenforce

11–15 Betterton St, Covent Garden, London WC2H 9BP, UK
☎ +44 (0)20 7470 8888
fax +44 (0)20 7470 8889
info@greenforce.org
www.greenforce.org
This international research agency relies on paying volunteers for its conservation work in various countries around the world. Projects take the form of expeditions and volunteers work as field researchers (training is provided, including dive training for marine projects). All-expenses-paid traineeships are offered to exceptional continuing volunteers.
Timing & Length of Placements: Expeditions last four or 10 weeks. Departures are on set dates throughout the year.
Destinations: Zambia, Bahamas, Borneo & Fiji.
Costs: Volunteers pay a refundable £250 deposit (non-refundable once you are accepted on a project). Ten-week expeditions cost £2550 (£2750 for marine expeditions). Four-week expeditions cost from £1500. Costs include visas, training (including dive training), local transport, accommodation and meals.
Eligibility: Minimum age is 18.

Greenpeace International

Ottho Heldringstraat 5, 1066 AZ Amsterdam, The Netherlands
☎ +31 (0)20-514 8150
fax +31 (0)20-514 8151
supporter.services@int.greenpeace.org
www.greenpeace.org
Greenpeace has openings for volunteers on high-profile environmental and political campaigns through administrative work or joining direct-action teams. To apply as a crew member on a Greenpeace ship, you should send a CV to the attention of Green Peace Marine Services at the international office. Volunteers need crewing experience and Greenpeace is looking for people who are skilled cooks, divers, linguists, photographers and engineers.
Timing & Length of Placements: Vary with the campaign and destination.
Destinations: Worldwide, wherever Greenpeace is campaigning.
Costs: Volunteers give their time for free and cover some expenses.
Eligibility: Depends on the role but you should be a Greenpeace member. Contact your local Greenpeace office for volunteer opportunities.

Global Vision International (GVI)

Amwell Farmhouse, Nomansland, Unit 10, Wheathamp-
stead, St Albans, Hertfordshire AL4 8EJ, UK
☎ +44 (0)870 608 8898
fax +44 (0)1582 834002
info@gvi.co.uk
www.gvi.co.uk
GVI offers a variety of short- and long-term projects with
a conservation or community focus, including research-
based expeditions, conservation projects and internships
at national parks. This organisation has good links with the
Dian Fossey Gorilla Fund in Rwanda and the South Africa
National Parks Board.
Timing & Length of Placements: Projects last four
weeks to two years. Departures for some projects are flexible; others are on set dates throughout the year.
Destinations: Central and South America, Africa,
Southeast Asia, Seychelles & Nepal. A Sri Lanka project is
planned for 2005.
Costs: Projects vary in cost from UK£250 to UK£2995,
including accommodation, meals and training.
Eligibility: The minimum age is 17. Any nationality can
be accepted as long as you are eligible for the relevant visa.

National Parks & Wildlife Service (NSW)

43 Bridge St, Hurstville, NSW 2220, Australia
☎ +61 (0)2-9585 6444
fax +61 (0)2-9585 6555
info@npws.nsw.gov.au
www.nationalparks.nsw.gov.au
This government department arranges volunteer opportunities at national parks across New South Wales. Environmental volunteers work on revegetation projects and
surveys of plants and wildlife and help out as guides and
camp assistants – it's a great way to get close to Australia's
unusual wildlife. Similar programs are offered by national
park authorities in the other Australian states.
Timing & Length of Placements: Depends on the
project – some parks need long-term volunteers; others
just want one day a week.
Destinations: NSW national parks, reserves and conservation areas.
Costs: Volunteers cover their own expenses.
Eligibility: Open to local and international volunteers.

National Trust (UK)

36 Queen Anne's Gate, London SW1H 9AS, UK
☎ +44 (0)870 609 5380
fax +44 (0)20 7222 5097
enquiries@thenationaltrust.org.uk
www.nationaltrust.org.uk
The National Trust maintains 200 historic buildings and
248,000 hectares of countryside in the UK and has been ac-
cepting volunteers since 1895. Volunteers work on conservation projects or assist visitors to National Trust properties.

Timing & Length of Placements: Up to the volunteer.
Destinations: UK.
Costs: Volunteers give their time for free. Accommodation
is provided at some locations.
Eligibility: Overseas volunteers are welcome but people
under 18 need parental permission.

The Oceania Project

PO Box 646, Byron Bay, NSW 2481, Australia
☎ +61 (0)2-6685 8128
fax +61 (0)2-9925 9176
trish.wally@oceania.org.au
www.oceania.org.au
This nonprofit NGO researches cetaceans (whales and
dolphins) and the ocean environment in Hervey Bay in
Queensland. Expedition volunteers carry out galley duties
and water sampling, and monitor specific whales and pods.
Timing & Length of Placements: Placements last
from one to 10 weeks between August and October.
Destinations: Australia.
Costs: Live-aboard costs are A$1050 per week for interns
(graduates, teachers and those with relevant experience)
and A$1250 for general eco-volunteers. Volunteers make
their own way to Byron Bay.
Eligibility: No restrictions but must show an interest in
whales.

Oceanic Marine Sanctuary Foundation

Haven Studio, Eel Pie Island, Twickenham, Middlesex TW2
3DY, UK
☎ +44 (0)20 8891 1151
fax +44 (0)20 8891 0673
dale@omsf.org
www.omsf.org
Led by wind-up radio inventor and one-time British swimming champion Trevor Baylis OBE, this organisation is working to establish artificial reefs and rainforest conservation
projects and creating opportunities for sustainable tourism
in rural communities. Some of the work is carried out by
paying holiday-makers, but there are also lots of opportunities for longer term volunteers. Dive training is provided.
Timing & Length of Placements: Four weeks to one
year, starting on set dates throughout the year.
Destinations: Sabah (Malaysian Borneo).
Costs: Volunteers pay from £1750, which covers diving,
accommodation and food.
Eligibility: Volunteers should be over 18 and have a
doctor's letter proving they are fit for diving.

Oceanic Society

Fort Mason Center, Bld E, San Francisco, CA 94123, USA
☎ +1 415-441 1106
fax +1 415 -474 3395
office@oceanic-society.org
www.oceanic-society.org

Besides West Coast USA whale-watching trips, the Oceanic Society offers an impressive array of participatory research expeditions and international natural-history journeys. Think diving with dolphins and tracking humpback whales.
Timing & Length of Placements: Year-round trips of one week to one month.
Destinations: Worldwide, with a focus on tropical destinations.
Costs: US$200 to US$10,000.
Eligibility: Few restrictions apply.

Operation Wallacea

Hope House, Old Bolingbroke, Spilsby, Lincolnshire PE23 4EX, UK
☎ +44 (0)1790 763194
fax +44 (0)1790 763825
info@opwall.com
www.opwall.com
Operation Wallacea runs a series of science-led conservation projects in Indonesia and Central America and accepts both volunteers and masters-level students working towards their dissertation. General volunteers can work in both marine and rainforest environments during a single research project. You have to make your own way to the local pick-up point, but after that, transport and living expenses are provided. Spaces are limited, so you should book well in advance.
Timing & Length of Placements: Two to eight weeks, beginning on set dates from June to September.
Destinations: Sulawesi (Indonesia), Honduras & Cuba.
Costs: Projects cost from £875 for two weeks to £2700 for eight weeks, including meals and accommodation.
Eligibility: There is no set age range, but many partici-pants are university students of various ages.

Orangutan Foundation

7 Kent Tce, London NW1 4RP, UK
☎ +44 (0)20 7724 2912
fax +44 (0)20 7706 2613
info@orangutan.org.uk
www.orangutan.org.uk
This worthy organisation is committed to saving the orangutans of Borneo in Indonesia. It runs a very popular program for volunteers at its research camps in Kaliman-tan. Volunteers clear trails, install signposts and walkways, repair buildings and work on environmental projects for local communities. You'll need to be able to handle tropical conditions, but no specific skills are required. Apply well in advance for this popular project.
Timing & Length of Placements: From 25 days to six weeks, beginning on set dates four times a year.
Destinations: Indonesia.
Costs: Volunteers cover their own transport expenses and pay a £500 fee. In country, costs are covered by the organisation.
Eligibility: Minimum age is 18.

People's Trust for Endangered Species (PTES)

15 Cloisters House, 8 Battersea Park Rd, London SW8 4BG, UK
☎ +44 (0)20 7498 4533
Fax +44 (0)20 7498 4459
enquiries@ptes.org
www.ptes.org
This conservation charity offers an annual program of conservation holidays abroad. Volunteers assist on projects such as monitoring whales and dolphins in the Azores and conserving black rhinos in Namibia.
Timing & Length of Placements: One to three weeks, between May and September.
Destinations: Netherlands, Romania, Bavaria (Germany), Armenia, Namibia, Costa Rica & Azores.
Costs: Projects cost from £360 to £1690, not including flights.
Eligibility: No restrictions.

Rainforest Concern

27 Lansdowne Crescent, London, W11 2NS, UK
☎ +44 (0)20 7229 2093
fax +44 (0)20 7221 4094
info@rainforestconcern.org
www.rainforestconcern.org
This charity is devoted to protecting the world's rainforests and is involved in a number of conservation and environ-mental projects in Latin America, including reforestation in Ecuador, turtle conservation in Panama and community health care in forest communities in the Amazon. Some projects are run through partner organisations such as Global Vision International and Quest Overseas.
Timing & Length of Placements: Varies with the project, but most require a minimum commitment of two weeks. Projects in Costa Rica and Panama run from March to August; Ecuador projects run year round.
Destinations: Latin America (particularly Ecuador, Costa Rica & Panama).
Costs: Vary with the project – conservation in cloud forests in Panama costs US$15 to $20 per day, including meals and accommodation and volunteers must hike for two hours to reach the forest lodge.
Eligibility: Age range is 28 to 80. Spanish is an advantage and TEFL or conservation-related qualifications may also be helpful.

Scientific Exploration Society

Expedition Base, Motcombe, Shaftesbury, Dorset SP7 9PB, UK
☎ +44 (0)1747 854898
fax +44 (0)1747 851351
base@ses-explore.org
www.ses-explore.org
This expedition group offers a range of expeditions with a volunteering focus. Each expedition works on a single project and work ranges from archaeology and conservation

to humanitarian work. 2004 expeditions included working in marine archaeology and establishing a new nature reserve in Panama and surveying forest elephant populations in Ghana – see the website for the latest expeditions.

Timing & Length of Placements: Two weeks to two months, departing on set dates through the year.

Destinations: Worldwide, including Mongolia, South Africa & Ethiopia.

Costs: Expedition costs range from £2500 to £3500, including flights, accommodation, food and insurance but not visas.

Eligibility: People aged between 30 and 70 are preferred. Adventure or expedition experience is an advantage.

Sunseed Trust

Apdo 9, 04270 Sorbas, Almeria, Spain

☎ +34 950-52 57 70

sunseedspain@arrakis.es

www.sunseed.org.uk

This Spanish organisation is working to develop renewable energy sources for desert and arid environments around the world to help reduce dependence on nonrenewable fuels. Volunteers have a one-week orientation into the project's research methods and then join an ongoing project – for example testing solar cookers or experimenting with alternative growing techniques in the nursery. Contact Sunseed in advance to make sure it has space.

Timing & Length of Placements: From five weeks, starting at any time.

Destinations: Spain.

Costs: Volunteers pay from £49 to £70 per week to participate in the project (the higher fees kick in from April to October), which covers accommodation and meals.

Eligibility: Minimum age is 16, but volunteers have been as old as 82. Engineering and agricultural skills are useful on some projects.

US National Park Service

1849 C St NW, Washington, DC, 20240, USA

☎ +1 202-208 6843; international program ☎ +1 202-354 1806/07

www.nps.gov/volunteer

The NPS' Volunteers in Parks program places volunteers in national parks across the country, from Alaska to the Florida Everglades. Volunteers work in park maintenance, guiding, research and conservation. International volunteers are accepted on the J-1 visa scheme, but you need a firm offer of a placement before you can apply for the visa. There are also artist-in-residence opportunities at 29 parks for skilled artists.

Timing & Length of Placements: Year-round openings, with minimum commitments starting at one week. International volunteers can stay for up to four months. Artist residencies range from one week to one year.

Destinations: Volunteers contact their park of choice directly, via addresses listed on the NPS home page.

Costs: Most parks are unable to provide lodging, but some offer a daily stipend of up to US$10.

Eligibility: Volunteers must be at least 18 and a US citizen or legal resident alien. International students need a J-1 visa.

World Wide Opportunities on Organic Farms (WWOOF)

PO Box 2675, Lewes, East Sussex BN7 1RB

☎ /fax +44 (0)1273 476286

hello@wwoof.org

www.wwoof.org.uk

WWOOF facilitates contact between organic host farms and WWOOFers (ie those wanting to help out) around the world. Volunteers stay with a host family and help out during the day in exchange for room and board. Work involves everything to do with running a small or large farm, including planting, picking, building, ditching, fencing, sowing etc. Volunteers must make their own travel arrangements. An interest in organic growing is essential.

Timing & Length of Placements: From a few days to one year.

Destinations: 18 countries worldwide.

Costs: In exchange for help you get room, board and an amazing experience.

Eligibility: Applicants must be aged at least 18, although children are welcomed on some farms.

How to Apply Where a national organisation exists you must join it in that country. Otherwise you need to look at the List of Independent Hosts. All details are on the international website (www.wwoof.org). It costs around £15 to join.

African Conservation Organisations

The following organisations specialise in placing volunteers on national parks and wildlife reserves in Africa. Unless otherwise stated, flights, visas and insurance are extra.

African Conservation Experience

PO Box 28, Ottery St Mary, Devon EX11 1ZN, UK

☎ +44 (0)1404 811404

info@conservationafrica.net

www.conservationafrica.net

This family-run organisation places conservation volunteers in South African safari parks and nature reserves. Volunteers assist park vets, help to rear orphaned animals, capture wildlife for tagging and health checks, and monitor wildlife populations, including whales and dolphins on coastal projects. Game-ranger courses are also available – see the Studying chapter for details.

Timing & Length of Placements: Projects last four to 12 weeks. Departures for some projects are flexible; others are on set dates throughout the year.

Destinations: National parks in South Africa.

Costs: Projects vary in cost from UK£2500 to UK£3500, including international and domestic flights and full-board accommodation.

Eligibility: Minimum age is 17. Must be physically fit for projects. Any nationality can be accepted as long as you are eligible for the relevant visa.

Kwa Madwala

PO Box 192, Hectorspruit 1330, South Africa
☎ +27 13-792 4526
fax +27 13-792 4219
bookings@kwamadwala.co.za
www.kwamadwala.co.za
Conservation volunteers are accepted by the Kwa Madwala Private Game Reserve, on the edge of Kruger National Park in South Africa. Volunteers help with the day-to-day running of the park, so you might find yourself counting game by microlight aircraft or learning to track lions through the bush.

Timing & Length of Placements: 25 days to three months, starting on set dates.

Destinations: South Africa.

Costs: The 25-day project costs £1616 and the three month package costs £3438, including meals, accommodation, training and activities.

Eligibility: Minimum age is 17. No maximum, but participants must be physically fit.

The Leap Overseas

The Trainers Office, Windy Hollow, Lambourn, Berkshire RG17 7XA, UK
☎ +44 (0)870-240 4187
fax +44 (0)1488-71311
info@theleap.co.uk
www.theleap.co.uk
This organisation places volunteers in safari camps and conservation and community projects in Africa. Volunteers assist in the day-to-day running of safari camps, park maintenance, wildlife monitoring and community projects involving local tribes.

Timing & Length of Placements: Six weeks to three months.

Destinations: Kenya, Tanzania, Zambia, Botswana, Malawi & South Africa.

Costs: Projects cost £1540 to £2520, including transfers, insurance, accommodation and full board.

Eligibility: Age range is 18 to 60 years.

Mokolodi Wildlife Foundation

Mokolodi Nature Reserve, Private Bag 0457, Gaborone, Botswana
☎ +267-316 1955/6
fax +267-316 5488
volunteers@mokolodi.com
www.mokolodi.com

This organisation owns and manages the Mokolodi Nature Reserve in Botswana and accepts volunteers to assist in specific positions on the reserve. There are openings for people with management, marketing, IT and game-ranger skills – email your CV with a covering letter to start the application process.

Timing & Length of Placements: Three months to one year.

Destinations: Botswana

Costs: Volunteers pay a £718 contribution, which is refunded if you stay for six months or more. Accommodation, meals, training and activities are included but there's a £90 charge for park uniforms.

Eligibility: Minimum age is 21. Skills and experience vary with the placement.

Project Africa (Africa Conservation Trust)

PO Box 310, Linkhills, 3652, South Africa
☎ /fax +27-31 201 6180
info@projectafrica.com
www.projectafrica.com
Project Africa offers a variety of conservation-related projects in South Africa and elsewhere in Africa. On one interesting project, volunteers help to locate and map ancient tribal rock art in a new World Heritage Site in the Drakensburg Mountains. Volunteers live in bush camps and work in teams with local researchers.

Timing & Length of Placements: One to three months.

Destinations: South Africa & Botswana.

Costs: Vary with the project – mapping rock art costs £450 per month, including meals and accommodation.

Eligibility: Minimum age is 18.

Wild at Heart

Suite 7A Cowell Park, 47 Old Main Rd, Hillcrest, Durban, Kwa Zulu Natal 3610, South Africa
☎ +27 765-31 1818
fax +27 765-31 1818
claude@wah.co.za
www.wahsouthafrica.com
Established by a group of South African landowners and conservationists, Wild at Heart places volunteers in private nature reserves and game parks in South Africa. Options include working in animal rehabilitation centres and trauma clinics, assisting with horseback safaris and darting wildlife for tagging and veterinary treatment. Projects generally last two to four weeks but you can work on several projects around the country as part of a single expedition.

Timing & Length of Placements: Projects last two weeks to six months and can start at any time.

Destinations: South Africa.

Costs: Costs range from £720 for two weeks to £6073 for six months. Prices include local transport (apart from

domestic flights), all meals, and accommodation in wooden safari cabins or in the homes of project leaders.
Eligibility: No previous experience is required but volunteers need to be physically fit.

ARCHAEOLOGY
Archaeological Institute of America
656 Beacon St, Boston, MA 02215, USA
☎ +1 617-353 9361
fax +1 617-353 6550
aia@aia.bu.edu
www.archaeological.org
The AIA is the governing body for archaeology in America. You can search for fieldwork opportunities worldwide on the website or purchase the annual *Archaeological Fieldwork Opportunities Bulletin* booklet from Oxbow/David Brown Books (www.oxbowbooks.com) for US$19.95.

Archaeology Abroad
31–34 Gordon Sq, London WC1H 0PY, UK
☎ /fax +44 (0)20-8537 0849
arch.abroad@ucl.ac.uk
www.britarch.ac.uk/archabroad
Based at University College in London, this organisation supplies information on archaeological digs and research projects that accept volunteers around the world. Around 1000 opportunities are listed in the twice-yearly magazine *Archaeology Abroad*, and subscribers can apply for field-work awards to help with the cost of overseas projects. The magazine is published in April and November and subscription costs £18 per year (£22 outside the UK).

Council for British Archaeology (CBA)
Bowes Morrell House, 111 Walmgate, York YO1 9WA, UK
☎ +44 (0)1904 671417
fax +44 (0)1904 671384
info@britarch.ac.uk
www.britarch.ac.uk
The Council for British Archaeology is the governing body for archaeology in Britain and it has loads of resources for archaeologists, including listings of archaeological socie-ties, courses for archaeologists and information on digs that accept volunteers in Britain and abroad.

Nautical Archaeology Society
Fort Cumberland, Fort Cumberland Rd, Eastney, Portsmouth, Hampshire PO4 9LD, UK
☎ /fax +44 (0)23-9281 8419
nas@nasportsmouth.org.uk
www.nasportsmouth.org.uk
This organisation is the leading authority on underwater archaeology in the UK and it offers specialist diving courses for aspiring marine archaeologists. NAS can also provide information on marine and foreshore archaeological projects that accept volunteers.

OPTIONS FOR UNDER-30s
The following volunteering and conservation organisations are useful for career-breakers who are under 30. Unless otherwise stated, flights, visas and insurance are extra.

Concordia (Youth Service Volunteers)
Heversham House, 20–22 Boundary Rd, Hove, East Sussex BN3 4ET, UK
☎ +44 (0)1273 422218
fax +44 (0)1273 421182
info@concordia-iye.org.uk
www.concordia-iye.org.uk
Concordia is a small nonprofit organisation that offers short international volunteer positions for 16 to 30-year-olds. Work may involve conservation, restoration or construction of buildings, archaeology, cultural activities or work with special-needs groups.
Timing & Length of Placements: Two to four weeks. Projects can start at any time.
Destinations: Europe, America, South America, Africa, Southeast Asia, Japan & Korea.
Costs: There's a £90 to £125 project fee and volunteers cover their own travel and living expenses. Projects in southern Africa, southeast Asia and Latin America incur an additional local fee of £80 to £200, which is paid to the host organisation.
Eligibility: Age range is 16 to 30.

ICYE UK (Inter Cultural Youth Exchange)
Latin America House, Kingsgate Pl, London NW6 4TA, UK
☎ /fax +44 (0)20 7681 0983
info@icye.co.uk
www.icye.co.uk
ICYE offers one-year volunteer positions on youth-oriented projects in Europe and the developing world for the under-thirties. Volunteers assist at schools, health centres and agricultural or community projects, and applicants are requested to attend a recruitment day in London.
Timing & Length of Placements: Six months to one year. Recruitment days are held from November to March, followed by training in June. Projects run from July/August and you can travel for a month at the end.
Destinations: Europe, Africa, Asia & Latin America.
Costs: Six-/12-month projects cost £2850/3250, including flights and visas, board and lodging, health insurance and pocket money.
Eligibility: Age range is 18 to 30. Training is provided and you don't have to have specific skills or experience.

People Tree (Timeless Excursions)
105 Westbourne Tce, Flat 8, London W2 6QT, UK
☎ +44 (0)20 7402 5576
fax +44 (0)20 7262 7561
peopletree@gapyearinindia.com
www.gapyearinindia.com

Part of the travel company Timeless Excursions (www .timelessexcursions.com), this organisation places volunteers in teaching, development and conservation projects in India. The skill-learning placements in traditional health care (eg yoga or Ayurvedic medicine) are particularly interesting.

Timing & Length of Placements: One to six months. Projects can begin at any time but you should apply well in advance.

Destinations: India.

Costs: Prices vary with the project – for example, working at a rehabilitation project for elephants will cost £1028/1820 for one/three months. Prices include an orientation pack with travel information, language books, accommodation and board, airport pick-up and drop-off and local support.

Eligibility: Minimum age is 17 (most volunteers are 30 or under).

Quest Overseas

North-West Stables, Borde Hill Estate, Balcombe Rd, Haywards Heath, West Sussex RH16 1XP, UK
☎ +44 (0)1444-474744
fax +44 (0)1444-474799
emailingyou@questoverseas.com
www.questoverseas.com

Originally a gap-year organisation, Quest Overseas now offers volunteer projects and expeditions in South America and Africa for older travellers. You have the option of just volunteering or combining volunteering with an expedition featuring adventure activities such as white-water rafting and jungle trekking. Current projects include conservation in the Bolivian rainforest and teaching in Peru. Interview days are held monthly in West Sussex.

Timing & Length of Placements: Projects last from two to three months (up to one year for teaching), starting on set dates though the year. Expeditions last two to six weeks.

Destinations: South America & Africa.

Costs: Volunteers pay a fee for the expedition and project and make a contribution to the organisation – for example, volunteers working for six weeks in Bolivia pay £530 to Quest and £620 to the host organisation. Flights and spending money are extra.

Eligibility: Age range is 18 to 30.

SPW (Students Partnership Worldwide)

17 Dean's Yard, London SW1P 3PB, UK
☎ +44 (0)20 7222 0138
fax +44 (0)20 7233 0008
spwuk@gn.apc.org
www.spw.org

SPW sends out around 600 volunteers every year to Africa and South Asia. Projects are youth-focused and most involve health education and community development, working alongside local volunteers. Application forms can be downloaded from the website and you must then attend a selection day and training session. There are also SPW representatives in Australia and the US (see the website for details).

Timing & Length of Placements: Four to nine months, starting September/October (South Asia) or January/February (Africa).

Destinations: India, Nepal, South Africa, Tanzania, Uganda, Zambia & Zimbabwe.

Costs: Projects cost from £3000, including flights, insurance, meals, lodging and a contribution to the running costs of SPW and the host project. SPW will provide advice on fundraising.

Eligibility: Age range is 18 to 28. Volunteers must provide two references and have a health check.

Volunteers for Peace (VFP)

1034 Tiffany Rd, Belmont, Vermont 05730, USA
☎ +1 802-259 2759
fax +1 802-259 2922
vfp@vfp.org
www.vfp.org

VFP places American volunteers on short work camps at more than 2400 programs worldwide – handy if you want to do several things on your career break. Most volunteers are under 30 and work in schools, community centres or on environmental projects.

Timing & Length of Placements: Work camps normally last two to three weeks between June and September.

Destinations: In 90 countries worldwide.

Costs: Registration costs US$200 to US$500, plus US$20 for VFP membership. Meals and accommodation is provided but travel is extra.

Eligibility: Minimum age is 18.

Volunthai

Korat, Thailand
☎ +66-999 50881
volunthai@yahoo.com
www.volunthai.com

This grassroots teaching project in southern Thailand is ideal for people who are already planning to travel to Thailand. Volunteers teach English to rural villagers for three to four hours a day and stay with local families.

Timing & Length of Placements: One to three months.

Destinations: Korat (Thailand).

Costs: There is no cost for volunteering, and meals and homestay accommodation are provided with local families, but volunteers must make their own transport arrangements to Korat and cover their expenses on days off.

Eligibility: Age range is 20 to 28. Must have a good grasp of English, but formal teaching qualifications are not required.

Youth Action for Peace UK (YAP-UK)

8 Golden Ridge, Freshwater, Isle of Wight PO40 9LE, UK
☎ +44 (0)1983 752557
fax +44 (0)1983 756900
yapuk@ukonline.co.uk
www.yap-uk.org
This organisation places skilled and unskilled volunteers on European-funded projects worldwide. Most projects are short work camps but some longer projects are available.

Timing & Length of Placements: Work camps last three weeks. Longer projects are up to a year for younger people.
Destinations: Europe, Middle East, Africa, Asia & the US.
Costs: You must become a YAP-UK member (£25 annually, or £10 for the unwaged) and there is a £110 placement fee (£150 fee for projects which involve training). Volunteers on some projects in Latin America, Asia and Africa must also pay a hosting fee of £150 to £200 to the local organisation.
Eligibility: Minimum age is 18 and most are under 30.

Living & Working Abroad

Not everyone wants to spend their career break on a whistle-stop world tour. Living and working in one place will provide the opprotunity to interact with local people in a way that is impossible if you are just blazing through, and your earnings will offset the cost of your trip.

Although things aren't quite as easy as they were before 9/11, there are still tremendous opportunities for living and working abroad. If you have the right skills and qualifications, you can often get sponsorship for a work permit from a foreign employer. Another easy way to work abroad is to become an English-language teacher – many schools will pay for your flights and accommodation, as well as sponsoring your visa application.

For something more casual, you could join a seasonal worker program or work as a trainee for a foreign company on an educational exchange program. There are also working holiday visas, which let you to do any kind of work you fancy for one or two years – great if you're a younger career-breaker and want to move around and pick up work as you go.

This chapter covers the things you need to know if you are thinking of working overseas, including information on visa regulations and work permits. For information on picking up casual work overseas, see Money Troubles (p102).

FINDING SOMEWHERE TO LIVE

Almost everyone starts off by staying in a hotel or sleeping on a friend's sofa, but even the best hotel room can become claustrophobic, and friendships can become strained when you have to move the guest every time you want to watch TV. If you want to stick around anywhere for any length of time, you will need to find a place to live.

It may have been a while since you last had to find a flat or house share, but the rules haven't changed. You can rent a flat, house or holiday home, sublet a private room or move into a shared house – it all depends on how much of a social creature you are.

Many people like the freedom of choosing somewhere when they arrive, but these days it's easy to arrange everything by email before you leave. This can be a life-saver for people who are going straight into a job, as there is much less free time to go flat-hunting once you start work. This is also an important consideration if you have a family in tow. The thrill of living in hotels will wear off pretty quickly for children, and most parents try to establish a normal routine as quickly as possible.

There are advantages to leaving it until you arrive, though – you can scope out the nicest places to live and find a rented room in a shared house with people you get along with. It is always a good idea to meet the people you are going to live with before you sign the contract. If you've never shared a house before, pick up a copy of *He Died with a Felafel in His Hand* by John Birmingham, an intimate guide to flatmates from hell.

Another option is to arrange a house swap (specialist agencies can put you in contact with like-minded people) or you could go underground and stay with an alternative community – many environmental and spiritual communities provide free accommodation for visitors who are prepared to work for their keep.

BEFORE YOU LEAVE

It's a good idea to formulate a plan for finding somewhere to live before you leave home. Talk to people you know and see if anyone has a friend or relative who can provide a bed for a few days or who can call around letting agencies on your behalf – if anyone helps out in this way, buying them dinner is the customary way of saying thank you!

Alternatively, you could start your search for somewhere to live on the Internet. You can find links to professional associations of real-estate agents worldwide on the website of the International Consortium of Real Estate Associations (www.worldproperties.com). You can also find estate agents in the area you want to live in using online Yellow Pages.

There are some useful websites that allow you to search for property to rent and share – www.domain.com.au and www.realestate.com.au are the leading sites for Australia and New Zealand, while www.rent.com is a good starting point in America. To find letting agents in other countries, type the name of the country you want to visit and 'property rental' into www.google.com. John Edwards went down this route to find a house in Cyprus for the summer:

I was offered the chance to work for a few months on a new tourist development in the resort of Agia Napa, but I wanted to rent a house rather than live in a hotel. The resort apartments in Agia Napa were pretty horrible, but I searched on the Internet for a property to rent in Cyprus and found an old village house in the hills that was being let out by an English family. The house was just lovely – orange trees in the garden and the smell of wild thyme drifting in through the window. When I got back home to London, my own flat seemed terribly boring in comparison.

Private lets or rooms for rent are advertised in newspaper classified sections worldwide, from the *New York Times* (www.nytimes.com/classified) to the *Bangkok Post* (www.bangkokpost .net/classifieds). To find classified sections anywhere in the world, type 'classifieds' and the name of the town where you want to live into www.google.com. In the UK, the classified ads paper *Loot* (www.loot.com) is a fantastic place to look for private lets; there's a separate version of *Loot* for New York (www.lootusa.com).

In Canada and the US, people often advertise for roommates to split the cost of renting an apartment – the websites www.roommates.com and www.roommateaccess.com have extensive listings. Roomster (www.room-roommate.net) and RoomieMatch (www.roomiematch .com) both allow you to search for roommates based on personality – handy for light sleepers and obsessive tidiers.

Sublets (apartments or rooms rented out by those renting the property) are often cheaper than renting through an agent. The websites www.sublet.com, www.citysublets.com and www.subletsearch.com have listings of sublet opportunities in the US and Canada.

European classified ads are normally in the local language, so it may be easier to arrange a holiday let. You can find thousands of holiday homes to rent worldwide from one month to one year on www.holiday-rentals.com and www.internationalrentals.com. Europe-specific search engines for property to buy and rent include www.europropertysearch.com and www .europe-property.org. In Japan, try Japan Home Search (www.japanhomesearch.com); in Thailand, Thai Top Properties (www.thaitopproperties.com) or Thai Apartment.com (www .thaiapartment.com); and in Hong Kong, Hong Kong Homes (www.hongkonghomes.com).

House Swaps

The idea of swapping homes with a complete stranger might sound like a bit of a gamble, but for many people this is the perfect solution to the problem of finding affordable long-stay accommodation abroad. Both families get a free place to stay, a fully functional home and a live-in house sitter to deter thieves and water the plants while they are away.

Debbie Hargreaves swapped her two-bedroom apartment in Bath for a three-bedroom house outside Rome and gave us this glowing report:

You get the best of all worlds. You don't pay a thing and you get the comfort of living in a home and having your own space. You have none of the restrictions of being in a hotel. You can choose whether to go out or not, and whether to eat out or at home. Our Italian owners were teachers, so there was a good library of books, which my husband enjoyed.

If you have a friend or relative overseas, you may be able to arrange a private house swap. Alternatively, there are dozens of private agencies that bring together prospective house swappers around the world; some of the more reliable companies are listed in the Contacts section (p187); for details of house-swapping agencies in Australia and the US, see the Appendices.

Most agencies charge a subscription fee of £30 to £100 a year, which allows you to list your home on the company database and contact other members. Most people provide photos of the inside and outside of their home and information on the location and facilities, along with a wish list of destinations and the dates they want to swap.

Once you have found a family who is willing to swap, you need to draw up a legally binding house-exchange agreement that clearly lays down the rights of each person, how long the swap is for and who pays for any costs that arise. Most house-swapping agencies provide guidelines on producing a watertight exchange agreement. Some people throw their car into the bargain, but make sure that you are covered by your insurance.

Although most house swaps come off without a hitch, things do occasionally go wrong. A German couple who swapped their bijou 17th-century thatched cottage for a house in Lincolnshire returned to find that the British couple had burned down the thatch by lighting a fire in the inglenook fireplace. In the vast majority of cases, though, home swapping proves to be a happy experience.

To minimise the risks, consider the following points while preparing your home for a house swap:

- Write an honest listing – people are less likely to be disappointed if they know what they are getting.
- Check the details of the host home carefully so you know exactly what you are letting yourself in for!
- Draw up a clear house-exchange agreement that specifies who pays the bills and the legal boundaries of the exchange.
- Always ask potential swappers to provide references – preferably from an employer rather than a friend or relative – and chase them up.
- Notify your home-insurance provider to make sure your home is covered, and instruct swappers about their responsibilities for the security of your home – for example, locking all doors and windows when going out.
- If the swap includes your car, arrange temporary insurance cover through your motor insurer.
- Lock away valuables or store them in a safety deposit box and provide shelf and cupboard space for the visiting family to put their belongings.
- Produce a clear guide to your house that includes information on where to find the fuse box, regular chores (eg pool cleaning, plant watering), local services (eg doctors, electricians and friends who can help out in an emergency), garbage collection days etc.
- Make sure swappers are happy to look after your pets and plants – if not, make alternative arrangements.
- Always leave both your home and your host's home clean when you leave.
- Out of courtesy, arrange for a friend or relative to meet the visiting family on arrival and leave enough food in the fridge to make a meal on the first night – this can be a lifesaver after a long, tiring flight.

Homestays

Another way to get home comforts without paying the earth is to rent a room in a private house. Thousands of people around the world make a little extra money renting out the spare room to visiting students and workers – it's basically the same as being a lodger, except you get cultural immersion and language practice thrown in for free.

Homestays can be as formal or as informal as you like. Some places are run like B&Bs, while others are more like staying in a family home. This is a popular option for students at language schools and it's much cheaper than renting a flat or staying in a hotel.

Tourism offices can often provide information on homestays in the local area, or there are specialist agencies that can put you in touch with families offering homestays – see p187 for some recommended companies.

One interesting option is Global Freeloaders (www.globalfreeloaders.com). Once registered, you can stay for free at the houses of other members if you agree to provide accommodation for other travellers in exchange. In a similar vein, HelpExchange.net (www.helpx.net) provides listings of host families, farms, hotels and B&Bs in Europe, Australasia and the Americas that provide free accommodation and food in exchange for unpaid labour. Most of the work involves light cleaning or helping out on the farm, and stays usually last two weeks to a month.

Other useful resources for finding a homestay include:

- **Homestay Finder** (www.homestayfinder.com) A search engine for worldwide homestays.
- **Homestays.net.nz** (www.homestays.net.nz) Listings of more than 350 homestays around New Zealand.
- **UK Homestays** (www.homestays.co.uk) Listings of homestays in the UK.
- **World Homestays** (www.worldhomestays.com) A search engine for homestays worldwide.

Alternative Living

Are you tired of materialism and the rush, rush, rush? If so, you could always spend your break with an alternative community. There are dozens of experimental groups around the world who live according to spiritual or environmental principles. Most provide room and board for short-term guests if you help out with the daily chores, and only some require you to wear taffeta skirts and face paint! However, you do need to use your judgment, as there are regular reports of dodgy goings-on at some spiritually focused communities, particularly in India.

One of the most famous alternative communities is the Svanholm Collective (www .svanholm.dk) in Denmark. Residents live according to strict environmental principles and make a living through bartering and organic farming. Money and decision-making is shared between the residents, and guests are welcome to stay for free for up to a month if they follow the rules of the collective – which means pulling your weight when it comes to communal activities. The Global Ecovillage Network (http://gen.ecovillage.org) has listings of hundreds of similar environmental communities worldwide.

Numerous spiritual communities also accept visitors, particularly in India and Southeast Asia. One of the most famous is Auroville (www.auroville.org) in southern India, established by Guru Sri Aurobindo. The binding concept at Auroville is the unity of mankind, and visitors are welcome to visit the centre for short stays – accommodation can be arranged for £2 to £13 per night, plus £1 per day for the centre's running costs.

Another unusual group is the Federation of Damanhur (www.damanhur.org) in the Italian Alps, which follows a mix of pre-Christian and Eastern beliefs and has 800 citizens, a social and political structure, an official constitution, its own currency, independent schools and a daily paper.

There is quite a lot of crossover between living in an alternative community and taking a religious retreat or studying at a spiritual centre – see the Studying chapter (p218) and Going Travelling (p98) for more on these options. Useful websites for finding alternative communities around the world include:

- **Diggers & Dreamers** (www.diggersanddreamers.org.uk) UK site with information on communities that are looking for volunteers and new members.
- **EcoNomads** (www.economads.com) Alternative-living site with a travelogue of visits to ecologically minded communities worldwide.
- **Eurotopia** (www.eurotopia.de) German site with listings of eco villages and alternative communities in Europe.
- **Federation of Egalitarian Communities** (www.thefec.org) Association of communal living organisations in North America.
- **Growing Place** (http://ourworld.compuserve.com/homepages/growingplace) Information site on alternative living.
- **International Communities** (www.ic.org) Global website for alternative communities.

ON THE GROUND

Once you arrive, you will have access to the same house-hunting tools you have at home. You can visit local letting agents, look for 'to let' signs in windows, respond to notices on café notice boards, browse the classified ads in newspapers and magazines and ask around to see if anyone knows of someone with a room to rent.

Landlords overseas normally want to see references from a former landlord, so make all the necessary arrangements before you leave home. Bring enough cash to cover the first month's rent and security deposit (usually another month's rent). A local bank account will allow you to pay the rent by direct debit, rather than mucking around with monthly cheques.

You can rent houses and apartments with or without furniture, but the saving you make from renting an unfurnished place rarely makes up for the hassle of buying furniture and then selling it on again when you leave. TVs and other electrical appliances can easily be rented from local electrical shops – otherwise, try buying second-hand stuff through the classified ads.

Letting agents are a logical place to start looking for a flat or house to rent. The local Yellow Pages will have listings of estate agents in the area where you want to live. It may also be worth walking the streets to see if any apartment buildings are advertising vacancies.

A HOUSE IN PROVENCE?

More and more people are buying cheap property abroad to convert into holiday homes – either for themselves or to rent out – and if you buy wisely, you could end up with a cash cow that will provide income for years to come. However, you need to think carefully about what you want to do with the house before you part with your hard-earned cash.

If you just want a holiday home for yourself, a pretty house in the middle of nowhere could be ideal, but if you want to let the property out, it should be close to shops, amenities and tourist attractions and easy to reach via international transport links. Be wary of buying a property just because it is handy for an airport used by a budget airline – if the route is cut, your holiday home will be left stranded.

There are various ways to start your property search. One option is to visit the area you are interested in and traipse around local estate agents to see if you can find a bargain. You can also start looking for a house through an international property agent; the International Consortium of Real Estate Associations (www.worldproperties.com) represents estate agents in 24 countries around the world. The websites www.europe-property.org, www.europropertysearch.com and www.eured.com are also useful for people thinking of buying property in Europe.

House prices in Europe are often incredibly cheap compared to the UK and any of the big high-street mortgage lenders can advise you on an international mortgage. For tips on buying and letting property in Europe, pick up *The Complete Guide to Buying Property in France* by Charles Davey or *Making Money from Holiday Lets* by Jackie Taylor.

Alex Cornwall used family connections to find a house at the right price near Bergerac in France:

I was lucky because my sister was living close to Bergerac with her French husband and she spotted this holiday cottage for sale at a very low price in the window of a local estate agent. She emailed me the details and I flew over to have a look. The location couldn't have been better, but the house needed some work to bring it up to a standard where we could rent it out. Fortunately my sister's husband was able to recommend local builders and get us friends' rates, which saved us a fortune.

If you are going to rent out your property, it makes sense to use a local or international letting agent. They will take a cut of the profits, but they will also take care of the tenants and manage the property while you are away. Alternatively, you could set up a website to advertise your property on the Internet.

Village houses often need quite a lot of renovating to bring them up to a standard where you can let them. You can save cash by doing some of the basic renovation jobs yourself, but leave complex jobs such as roofing or plastering to the professionals and, above all, make sure you have enough money to finish the job! There are loads of guides to renovating property – *Renovating and Restoring French Property* by Joe Laredo and *Finca: Renovating an Old Farmhouse in Spain* by Alec Fry specifically deal with renovating old houses in Europe.

A YEAR IN PROVENCE, UNDER THE LEMONS, DRIVING OVER PARROTS WITH SUN-FLOWERS IN THE PEPPER TREE...

If you are thinking of doing up a house in Europe, head to your local bookstore. There are dozens of bestselling books on the subject, including the memoir that started off the whole genre, *A Year in Provence* by Peter Mayle. This light-hearted description of moving to a peaceful village in southern France was a massive hit, though many people blame it for the tidal wave of Brits who subsequently flooded into rural villages across Europe.

This was followed by a host of similar books, including *Under the Tuscan Sun* by Frances Mayes (about doing the same thing in Italy), *Snowball Oranges* and *Mañana Mañana* by Peter Kerr (Mallorca), *Driving over Lemons* and *A Parrot in the Pepper Tree* by Chris Stewart (Andalusia), *Life in a Postcard* by Rosemary Bailey (the French Pyrenees) and *The House of Sunflowers* and *A Harvest of Sunflowers* by Ruth Silvestre (southwest France).

For an insight into making the move to village life on a shoestring, read *Extra Virgin* and *Ripe for the Picking* by Annie Hawes. Annie moved with her sister to the village of Diano san Pietro in Italy to become an olive farmer and wrote a much less glossy – but still very funny – description of an impoverished outsider struggling to adjust to village life.

WORKING ABROAD

Finding a job overseas is much the same as finding a job at home, except that you have the additional burden of persuading a foreign employer to apply for a work permit on your behalf. Most nations are very selective about whom they allow in to work, and you will only get a work permit if no local person can be found to do the job you are applying for.

This might sound like a long shot, but if you find an employer that likes the cut of your jib, obtaining a work permit can just be a formality. People with formal qualifications or a proven track record will find it easier to find work overseas than unskilled workers, but there are special immigration programs that provide seasonal workers for tourism and agriculture.

The downside of the work-permit system is that the permit is specific to the employer, so you must apply for a new permit if you want to change jobs and you must leave the country when the job finishes, unless you qualify for permanent residency. This is also the case if you take a training placement with a foreign company as part of an educational exchange.

Working holiday visas are one way around this – you can do any job you like for a limited period of time. Or you can apply for permanent residency as a skilled migrant if you have the necessary skills and work experience. There are also special temporary immigration schemes to fill shortages in the local jobs market. The following sections cover some of the things you need to think about if you want to work overseas.

FINDING A JOB OVERSEAS

As a career-breaker, you already know what you can do for a living, though a career break could be a great time to try something different. Applying for a job overseas is much the same as applying for a job at home. You can take advantage of recruitment agencies, browse job ads on the Internet or in newspapers, send speculative applications directly to companies and use contacts in your own business or social circle. There is one big difference though – you also have to deal with the headache of immigration and work permits.

Unless you join a working holiday, work placement or special immigration scheme, you must find an employer before you can apply for a work permit, which involves loads of paperwork for the company employing you. Predicably, some companies think that employing foreign workers is more trouble than it is worth.

To increase your chances of finding a willing employer, research the immigration rules carefully before you apply. Foreign employers are likely to be much more receptive if you can say 'this is what I have to offer, and these are the steps that you need to take to employ me'. If you have specific skills and experience for the job, it will be much easier for the sponsoring company to convince the authorities that you are a necessary addition to the workforce.

Each country also has its own rules for job applications. The organisation Expertise in Labour Mobility (www.labourmobility.com) publishes guides to job-application procedures in 33 countries worldwide, including advice on local employment etiquette and tips for CV and letter writing – you can order the guides from the website for €20.

EXPAT LIFE

The further people are from home, the more they try to create a bit of home where they are. Expats around the world congregate at bars that screen British premiership football or drop in for a *café au lait* at the Alliance Française. Even if you fully intend to immerse yourself in the local culture, you will probably adopt some aspects of the expat routine, so here is a basic guide.

Other expats are an excellent source of information when you first arrive in a new country. They can advise you on the best places to shop and go out and provide insider information on renting or buying houses, cars and furniture. Major shopping centres often have bulletin boards where you can place notices for things that you want to buy or sell. Med Expat (www.medexpat.com) and Medibroker (www.medibroker.com) offer specialist health insurance for expats worldwide.

The focal point of expat social life in many countries is the local expatriate club. British, American and Australian embassies around the world run social clubs with sporting facilities, swimming pools and restaurants that serve food and drinks from home. New members can join for an annual membership fee – contact the relevant embassy for details.

Almost all expats miss something from back home – Expat Boxes (www.expatboxes.com) and Expat Direct (www.expatdirect.co.uk) can post you Marmite, cornflakes, Walkers crisps, English tea and any other treats that you miss from home. BBC news can be found on the Internet at www.bbc.co.uk and you can listen to British radio online on www.bbc.co.uk/radio.

Expat World (www.expatworld.net) publishes a monthly *Newsletter of International Living* which contains advice on all aspects of expat life – annual subscription costs US$30 for the digital version and US$89.95 for the print version. American citizens can take advantage of the support services of the Association of Americans Resident Overseas (AARO; www.aaro.org) or American Citizens Abroad (ACA; www.aca.ch). An annual membership fee costs US$60 for AARO and US$40 for ACA.

Numerous websites provide advice for expats, including information on visas, work permits, taxation, health insurance, pensions, voting rights, buying houses and cars and where to see sporting events and TV from home. Point your browser towards:

American Expats (www.americanexpats.co.uk)

British Expats (www.britishexpats.com)

Britnet (www.british-expats.com)

British Expat (www.britishexpat.com)

Brits in America (www.britsinamerica.com)

Expat Index (www.expatindex.com)

Expat Network (www.expatnetwork.co.uk)

Expatica (www.expatica.com)

Expatriates.com (www.expatriates.com)

Expats Australia (www.expatsaustralia.com)

Expats in China (www.expatsinchina.com)

Expats Direct (www.expatsdirect.com)

Expats.org (www.expats.org.uk)

Recruitment Agencies

Recruitment agencies can be handy for finding both long-term and short-term jobs. You can find agencies abroad and register over the Internet, which can really speed up the application process. Most sites also allow you to post your CV online so that it can be seen by browsing head-hunters. However, recruitment agencies are unlikely to sponsor you for a work permit, so temping is out of the question unless you already have permission to work.

If you can work legally without a permit, you can take advantage of the full range of temporary employment, from short secretarial jobs to medium-term cover for staff who are away on maternity leave or taking career breaks themselves. As you already have experience, you should be able to skip the soul-destroying data-entry assignments and go straight into a properly paid position in your own field. Many agencies offer temporary and permanent positions, and if the employer likes the way you work they may be willing to sponsor you for a visa, which is handy if you want to progress from a working holiday visa to a sponsored work permit.

However, be warned that agencies do not always recognise the skills you can bring to the job, as Andrew White found when he applied to a recruitment agency in Melbourne:

When I applied to an agency I was expecting to get calls about office jobs – it's what I was doing for a living back home and I got nearly 100% in all the skills tests when I registered. However, when the phone rang the next day, I was offered a job handing out fliers for a furniture warehouse! Needless to say, I told them where they could put the fliers and began applying for jobs listed in the local paper, which was much more productive – I found a contract position as a bookstore manager almost immediately.

If you are relying on finding a foreign employer for sponsorship, you should stick to agencies that specialise in placing international workers. Conveniently, many high-street recruitment agencies have branches worldwide, so you can register and take any necessary skills tests with a local branch and then search for opportunities worldwide. Some agencies can even interview you for overseas jobs in your home country. See p188 section for listings of the main recruitment agencies operating around the world.

Online & Media Resources

Almost every newspaper in the world has job listings and you'll find numerous freebie employment magazines along commuter routes in commercial districts of cities such as London and New York. This is one of the main ways that companies fill vacant positions, so make sure you tap into it.

In the UK, the *Guardian* newspaper has an excellent online jobs section at http://jobs .guardian.co.uk, or you can browse the jobs listings in any of the national papers every Saturday. In other countries, it usually makes sense to pick up the local newspaper for the town you want to work in. Most papers publish special jobs supplements at least once a week – you can find listings of newspapers and magazines worldwide at www.world-newspapers.com.

If you need an English-speaking job in a non-English speaking country, plug into the local English-language press. English-language newspapers such as the *Japan Times* (www .japantimes.com) or the *Korea Times* (www.times.hankooki.com) have online jobs sections. To find English-language newspapers worldwide, visit www.thebigproject.co.uk/news.

The other main place to find jobs abroad is the World Wide Web – our pick of the online job sites are:

WORLDWIDE
- **Datum JobSearch** (www.datumweb.com) A job search engine with separate pages for Europe, North America and the Asia-Pacific region.
- **Escape Artist** (www.escapeartist.com) A site on living and working abroad, with extensive global jobs links and a free online magazine.
- **HotRecruit** (www.hotrecruit.com) A recruitment website focused on young people, travellers and students.
- **International Jobs** (www.internationaljobs.org) A search engine for jobs worldwide.

- **International Job Links** (www.joblinks.f2s.com) A global site in English, French, Italian, Spanish and German with agency listings worldwide.
- **Jobs Abroad** (www.jobsabroad.com) An extensive American site with international listings.
- **Jobsite** (www.jobsite.co.uk) A search engine for jobs in the UK, Ireland, France, Germany, Italy and Spain.
- **Jobware** (www.jobware.com) A top search engine for international jobs.
- **Payaway** (www.payaway.com) An excellent website with jobs and information on working worldwide; you can also sign up for a regular email jobs bulletin.
- **Planet Recruit** (www.planetrecruit.com) A global job search site.
- **Plus Jobs** (www.plusjobs.com) International job listings with sites for different countries.
- **Riley Guide** (www.rileyguide.com) A recommended site with region-specific jobs pages.

UK & EUROPE

- **Agency Central** (www.agencycentral.co.uk) A UK site with links to specialist recruitment agencies for most types of jobs.
- **Expatica** (www.expatica.com/jobs) A Western European expat site with a job search engine.
- **Eurojobs.com** (www.eurojobs.com) An extensive site for European jobs.
- **Job Pilot** (www.jobpilot.co.uk) A Europe-wide job search site.
- **Jobs.co.uk** (www.jobs.co.uk) A UK site with a search engine for specialist job agencies.
- **Jobs in Europe** (www.jobs-in-europe.net) Listings of recruitment websites across Europe, broken down by country.
- **Recruitment & Employment Confederation** (www.rec.uk.com) The governing body for the UK's recruitment industry, with international jobs information and a list of members.
- **TopJobs** (www.topjobs.co.uk) An extensive site for jobs in the UK.

AUSTRALIA & NEW ZEALAND

- **Byron Employment Network** (http://employment.byron.com.au/agencies) An Australian site with jobs listings and a directory of agencies.
- **CareerOne** (http://careerone.com.au) Extensive job-search site, Australia and New Zealand.
- **Jobsearch** (www.jobsearch.gov.au) A government search engine for jobs across Australia.
- **My Career** (www.mycareer.com.au) An Australian and New Zealand job search site.
- **Seek** (http://seek.com.au) A search site for jobs in Australia with information for Australians who want to work in the UK (see www.seek.co.nz for work in New Zealand).
- **Working in New Zealand** (www.workingin-newzealand.com) – immigration-oriented jobsite for New Zealand.

THE AMERICAS

- **Abroadnaway** (www.abroadnaway.com) A useful site for people wanting to work in the USA, with listings of seasonal jobs, internships etc.
- **About Jobs** (www.aboutjobs.com) An umbrella site for several American job sites, including SummerJobs.com, OverseasJobs.com and ResortJobs.com.
- **America's Job Bank** (www.ajb.org) A search engine for jobs in the USA.
- **Bumeran** (www.bumeran.com) Spanish-language job site with listings for Argentina, Brazil, Chile, Mexico and Venezuela.
- **Career Builder** (www.careerbuilder.com) A state-by-state search engine for the US and Canada with international listings
- **CareersUSA** (www.careersusa.com) A US job site with state-by-state search.
- **Tropic Jobs.com** (www.tropicjobs.com) A job site for the Caribbean.
- **Yahoo Hotjobs** (hotjobs.yahoo.com) A US and Canadian job-search site.

ASIA

- **JobsAsia** (www.jobasia.com) A job site for working in Hong Kong.
- **JobsDB.com** (www.jobsdb.com) A search site for jobs in China, Hong Kong, India, Thailand, Malaysia, Singapore, Korea and Taiwan.
- **Job Street** (www.jobstreet.com) Jobs in India, Malaysia, Singapore and the Philippines.

Job Swaps

If you want a change of scene but don't want to slip back down the career ladder, you might consider doing a job swap with someone who works for the same company overseas. If someone at another branch of your company does roughly the same job as you and is willing to swap jobs for a fixed period of time, approach the HR/personnel department and see if they can make the necessary arrangements.

Explain the benefits of doing a job swap – eg the increased productivity that will come from seeing a different way of doing things – and try to arrange your swap at a quiet time when few people are taking holidays. If you want to take a holiday yourself at the end of the swap, make sure this will not put extra pressure on your co-workers.

Some companies arrange job swaps on tourist visas, where both employees still get their salaries paid into their home accounts, but this is a little risky. To do things above board, the company must sponsor you for a work permit, but they have a pretty strong argument for saying that you are the best person for the job – after all, you do exactly the same job back home. Swapping houses as well as jobs may also prove to be practical and economical.

To allow the free flow of information and ideas, there are special international exchange programs for certain groups of professionals, including academics, teachers and librarians. If you work in one of these fields, you may be able to join an international job-swap program and work overseas on a short-term sponsored visa.

One of the biggest schemes is the Fulbright Teacher & Administrator Exchange Program (www.fulbrightexchanges.org), which facilitates work exchanges between the US and 30 countries around the world, including France, Germany and the UK. Participants get full pay and benefits during the one-year exchange, but the program is only open to full-time teachers or school administrators and you need a bachelor's degree. The application deadline is October 15 each year – see the website for listings of Fulbright Commission offices around the world.

Another option is the Teachers' International Professional Development scheme, which arranges jobs swaps between the UK and more than 50 countries worldwide. Applications are made through the League for the Exchange of Commonwealth Teachers (www.lect.org .uk); the British Council Education & Training Group (follow the education links on www .britishcouncil.org); and the Specialist Schools Trust (www.specialistschoolstrust.org.uk). The websites have information on how each scheme works.

For many programs, you need to find a partner school overseas yourself. Talk to the HR department at your school for advice or visit the British Council Windows on the World website (www.wotw.org.uk). The Oz Teach Exchange Directory (www.ozteach.com.au) acts as an introduction service for Australian and international teachers who want to arrange job swaps, for an annual membership fee of A$45.

Other useful sites for job-swapping teachers include Global Gateway (www.globalgateway .org.uk) and Teachernet (www.teachernet.gov.uk) in the UK, Education Net Australia (www .edna.edu.au), the New Zealand Ministry of Education (www.minedu.govt.nz) and the US Department of Education (www.ed.gov/teachers).

JOB SWAPPING: THE US

More commonly referred to as 'job exchanges' in the USA, international job-swap schemes are most common in educational institutions and government agencies. Countries with teacher shortages (such as China, Hong Kong and New Zealand) attempt to lure English-speakers with generous relocation incentives, but differing school schedules can make exchanges a challenge to organize. Employees of transnational companies can often find overseas opportunities by volunteering for an inter-office transfer. Few other vocational exchanges, professional development programs and international training schemes are designed with mid-career workers in mind, but professional business, law and medical organizations can often help arrange foreign placements.

JOB SWAPPING: AUSTRALIA

Some of the larger multinational companies in Australia are happy to facilitate job swaps, although this mainly occurs on an informal basis. However, criteria such as experience, age and qualifications will apply. Also, be prepared – it is normally the individuals who want to exchange jobs who also carry out the logistical legwork to make it happen!

Swaps occur within the banking, legal and finance sectors, in car manufacturing and telecommunications, and in the petroleum, mining, oil and gas industries. Many local councils and government departments will also consider swaps. Some professional associations, such as those for teachers, doctors and nurses, have established small exchange organisations or informal schemes.

Work Placements

If you don't qualify for a standard work permit, you may be able to work overseas on a work-experience placement. Short work placements are available with foreign companies all over the world, particularly in Europe, America, Australia and New Zealand. However, these are usually only open to graduates and most are targeted at people under 35. In the US or Australia, the usual term for work placements is 'internships', while in Europe placements are usually known as *stages*, or traineeships. Many internships are specifically designed for people on gap years, but there are also openings for career-breakers who fancy trying a new career.

Work placements are usually regarded as formal employment, even if you don't get a salary, so you may need permission to work from the appropriate authorities. There are no restrictions within the European Economic Area (EEA), but European citizens need a work permit to take a placement outside the EEA, and Australian and US citizens need a work permit to work inside the EEA.

Obtaining a work permit independently is a pretty tall order, but fortunately there are several organisations that sponsor foreign workers for overseas practical training around the world. The biggest system is the American J-1 visa scheme, which covers all sorts of education exchanges. To gain a J-1 visa for training placement in the US, you need sponsorship from an education-exchange organisation such as Bunac (p190) or CCUSA (p190) and a university degree or at least two years of professional training and relevant work experience.

You can then work on a paid or unpaid training placement lasting three to 18 months for a single American company. Most organisations require you to find your own placement and this must be in one of the following fields: management, business, commerce, finance, education, social science, library science, counselling, social services, nonmedical health-related work or culture and the arts. Applicants must produce a detailed training plan that explains the work you will do and what you hope to gain from the traineeship – this is a vital part of the process and it could make or break your application, so be clear about your objectives.

The scheme is open to most nationalities but you must provide proof of sufficient funds to support yourself, either in the form of savings or wages from the host company – usually equivalent to US$1300 per month. You must also take out health insurance for the duration of your stay. You generally need to apply two to three months in advance to allow enough time for the paperwork to go through. As with working holiday programs, you can only take part in the J-1 visa scheme once.

Paul Rao-kumble took a traineeship with a company in Palo Alto in California through CCUSA.

I originally studied accounting at university, so I ended up working in an office, but it wasn't really anything to do with finance. I was working as the office junior, so I did a lot of photocopying, filing, big mail outs, emailing…the usual office stuff. But the longer I stayed, the more responsibility I got.

It was interesting for me as I've done work experience in the UK and there is a different kind of work ethic in the States. It's much more open over there, but they seemed to like the fact that the British work harder. The main difference I noticed in myself when I came home was that I was a lot more confident in my decision making.

Internship programs in Canada are only open to full-time students, but non-students can take unpaid internships in Australia and New Zealand – see p192 for the main sponsoring organisations. To take part, you need to be eligible for a working holiday visa or an occupational training visa; check the Australian government immigration website (www.immi.gov.au) for more information about these visa categories.

Many volunteering organisations and language agencies can arrange unpaid internships with companies in Europe, Africa and Central and South America, including i-to-i (p195) and Teaching & Projects Abroad (www.teaching-abroad.co.uk) – see p135 in the Volunteering & Conservation chapter for more details. Language schools such as Cactus Language (p195) and Euro-Academy (euroacademy.co.uk) also offer unpaid internships for people in their language classes. See p224 in the Studying chapter for more details and recommended organisations.

For Europeans, the best place to look for internships is within the institutions of the EU. If you speak fluent English and at least one other EU language you can find *stages* at numerous European institutions, including the European Commission and European Parliament. *Stagiaires* (trainees) receive a basic salary or a stipend for living expenses and transport, and some European employers also provide free flights.

There are openings in the fields of translation, finance, journalism, politics, economics, human rights and engineering, but you must be a university graduate, and some internships have an upper age limit of 31 or 35. Competition is ferocious, so you may have to lobby the department you want to work for to gain a position.

The European Commission is the largest provider of *stages* but there are also opportunities at many other European institutions in Brussels, Geneva, Frankfurt and Luxembourg. As with working holidays and internships in America, you can only do a *stage* at a European institution once.

The website www.eu-careers-gateway.gov.uk/finding/stage.htm is the European career gateway for the British civil service and it provides information on internships across Europe. Other useful websites include www.eurodesk.org/euinfo/euenbody.htm and http://missions.itu.int/~italy/vacancies/vaclinks.htm, which lists internships at international institutions in Europe and worldwide.

Some of the largest work-placement programs around the world are listed in the Contacts section (p189), but there are lots of websites where you can search for internships worldwide. Try the following:

- **Hyperstudy** (www.hyperstudy.com) An international study site with information on internships in Australia, Canada, Europe, Ireland, New Zealand, the UK and the USA.
- **Internjobs.com** (www.internjobs.com) Part of Aboutjobs.com, with a huge database of internships worldwide.
- **Internships.com** (www.internships.com) An American site with a database of US internships.
- **Internships USA** (www.internships-usa.com) A student-focused company that publishes annual internship guides listing more than 3000 opportunities in the USA.
- **Council Exchanges/CIEE** The CIEE's internship site (www.internshipusa.org) has information and advice on finding a US internship.
- **Job Pilot** (www.jobpilot.co.uk) Listings of internships and work-experience opportunities in Europe and worldwide.
- **Study Abroad** (www.studyabroadlinks.com) A study search engine with listings of internship opportunities worldwide.
- **Transitions Abroad** (www.transitionsabroad.com) A US publisher of guides on working and studying abroad, with online internship listings.

WORK PERMITS & REGULATIONS

In an ideal world, we would all be able to live and work wherever we wanted. Unfortunately, most countries have strict guidelines about who can enter the country to work, so it is quite difficult to visit a country and then find a job when you get there.

The easiest option is to work somewhere that doesn't require a work permit. European citizens can work in any country in the EEA. Australia and New Zealand have a similar reciprocal agreement, and American and Canadian citizens can apply for permits at the border between the countries if they have a firm job offer from a company on the other side. Another low-hassle option is to join a working holiday (see p171) or educational exchange program (see p167).

If you are not eligible for any special immigration programs, you basically have two options – you can either apply for permanent or temporary migration on the basis of your professional skills or you can find an employer overseas who is willing to sponsor you for a work permit. Most people who work overseas are sponsored by foreign employers, but there is a catch – the immigration authorities will want to see proof that no local person is available to fill the job. If you have unique skills, this may not be a problem, but being voted salesperson of the month simply won't cut it.

Fortunately, there are a few ways to sidestep the normal restrictions. If there is a shortage of skilled workers in a particular field, the rules are often relaxed and getting a temporary work permit can be quite easy with a firm job offer from a local employer. The list of 'priority occupations' changes regularly, so you should contact the relevant embassy to find out if your job or trade is currently on the list.

If you want to move overseas permanently, you may be able to apply for an open work permit as a skilled migrant. You gain points for your education, work experience, earning potential and career achievements. To satisfy the achievement section for Britain or the USA, you normally need to have achieved national or international success in your field; most people who qualify are virtuoso musicians or artists, award-winning authors, academics and scientists, entrepreneurs or directors of large international companies.

However, countries such as Canada, Australia and New Zealand set the bar a little lower and you can often get in with good qualifications and work experience. Many countries also allow you to work if you have sponsorship from a relative or if you have an ancestor who was born in the country – contact the relevant embassy if you have a family connection to see if any special schemes are running.

As a general rule, you cannot change your visa status once you have entered the country, but if you work in a priority occupation such as nursing you may be able to change to full work status once you find sponsorship from a local employer. Some countries also allow students to apply for a work permit on graduation with a firm job offer.

The exact rules vary from country to country, so you should contact the relevant embassy for detailed information. Information on visas and work permits for the UK can be found at www.workingintheuk.gov.uk and www.ukvisas.gov.uk. To find information about visas and work permits for other countries, type 'work permits' or 'visas' and the name of the country into www.google.com.

The American organisation Going Global (www.goinglobal.com) provides information on work regulations worldwide and publishes detailed guides to working in 23 countries in Europe, Asia, Africa and the Americas – you can download the guides in digital format for US$14.95 or pay US$19.95 for a printed copy.

Numerous private companies and agencies arrange international work permits and visas around the world. However, there are plenty of sharks in the business and you need to be careful. One reliable international operator is WorkPermits.com (www.workpermits.com), which arranges both skilled-migrant and employer-sponsored visas and has offices in the UK and USA. However, bear in mind that these companies charge high fees and they cannot make you eligible for a work permit if you do not meet the legal requirements.

If you cannot get hold of a work permit any other way, you could always try enrolling in an academic course. Student visas are much easier to come by than work permits and you can often pick up casual work while you study, as long as you stick to the local immigration rules. If money is no object, you could also work as a volunteer – see the Volunteering & Conservation chapter (p117) for more on these options.

Working in Europe

Working in Europe is by far the easiest option if you live anywhere in the EEA – ie Austria, Belgium, Denmark, Finland, France, Germany, Greece, Ireland, Italy, Luxembourg, the Netherlands, Portugal, Spain, Sweden and the UK (the countries of the EU), plus Iceland, Liechtenstein and Norway. The EU was expanded in May 2004 to include the Czech Republic, Cyprus, Estonia, Hungary, Latvia, Lithuania, Malta, Poland, Slovenia and Slovakia, but it will be several years before workers can move freely between these countries and the rest of Europe.

As a result of the Single European Act, citizens of member states can move around the EEA and look for work for up to three months without restrictions. If you intend to work or spend more than three months in an EEA country, you must apply for a residence permit – see Rights & Residency later (p174)for more information.

To make things easier, the EU has established Eures – the European Job Mobility Portal (http://europa.eu.int/eures), which provides information on all aspects of working in the EU, including work and residence permits, labour rules and taxation. You can browse the site by country and search for jobs online using the Europe-wide job search engine.

Although Brits can technically work anywhere in the EEA, you will struggle to find a job unless you speak the local language. You could feasibly pick up casual work in tourist areas with school French, but don't bank on it. Employers also expect you to be familiar with the local procedure for job applications – the Eures website has some helpful tips and advice.

Jenny Murray went to France to work for a wine distributor and gives the following advice about working in a foreign-language environment:

Having a background in the local language definitely helps. I lived in France as a child so I've been speaking French all my life, but I wasn't prepared for quite how intense the experience of working in France was going to be. At first, my vocabulary wasn't really sufficient for the work I was doing, but people respected that I was trying hard and it came together in the end. Initially it was a relief to come home and be able to talk to my boyfriend in English, but after a while, we ended up talking in French at home too.

European nations also have a different approach from the UK when it comes to academic qualifications. Work experience is taken very seriously and academic qualifications are expected to relate directly to the job you are applying for – few jobs advertise for 'graduates of any subject'.

France, Holland and Germany are by far the most popular countries for foreigners working overseas. Workers from Australia and North America who want to work in Europe must obtain the appropriate work permit through an embassy or consulate overseas, which means joining a working holiday or educational exchange program, or finding sponsorship from a European employer who can prove that they couldn't find a European citizen to do the job. Contact the relevant embassy for details of the immigration rules for individual countries.

Working outside Europe

Europeans will find it much harder to work outside the cosy confines of Europe. Your best bet is to get sponsorship from a foreign employer – however, graduates can often find work placements overseas and there are working holiday programs in Australia, New Zealand, Canada and several other countries.

One of the easiest places to find temporary work is Canada, which employs around 90,000 foreign workers on temporary work permits every year to fill seasonal gaps in the labour market. To qualify, you need a firm job offer from a Canadian company, and they must obtain approval from Human Resources & Skills Development Canada (Hrsdc; www.hrsdc.gc.ca).

Many farming and tourism jobs qualify for the scheme, including those at summer and winter resorts, and there are also special programs for live-in caregivers, entertainers and academics. The programs last up to a year, but you must be mentally and physically healthy and have full medical insurance for the duration of your stay.

The US equivalent of the Canadian temporary worker scheme is the H-2B visa, which allows seasonal workers to work in the US for up to one year. The scheme can be extended up to a maximum of three years at the discretion of the immigration authorities. Again, you need sponsorship from an American employer who must prove that the position can't be filled from the local labour market. There is a similar scheme for seasonal agricultural workers using an H-2A visa. The easiest way to find a sponsor is to go through an exchange organisation such as Alliance Abroad – see the Contacts section (p193) for details.

If you want to find a serious job in the USA, the easiest option is to get sponsorship from a US company for an H-1B visa. However, the application process is slow and expensive and once again your sponsor must be able to prove that no American is available to do the job. It's much easier to join a work-placement scheme – see p167 for details.

To obtain any kind of visa for the US, you need to attend an interview at a US embassy or consulate, even if you are taking part in a work placement or seasonal work program. You must also provide data for the Student and Exchange Visitor Information System (Sevis; www.sevis.net), which allows the US government to track and monitor your movements. However, as a sweetener, the US government allows you to travel for 30 days at the end of any educational or exchange scheme.

The main way people work in Australia or New Zealand is on working holiday visas – covered in the following section – but there are also skilled-migrant programs and special immigration schemes to fill gaps in the labour market. As elsewhere, the overriding rule is that the local employer must be able to prove that no local worker can be found to do the job.

Similar schemes operate in most countries around the world. In Japan, a local sponsor must apply for a Certificate of Eligibility on your behalf, which will then allow you to apply for a work permit. Even Hong Kong now requires a firm job offer and proof that no Hong Kong citizen could be found to do the job. However, it is still possible to turn up in Hong Kong and pick up work if you can find a willing employer, as Tamar Lowell found out when she had to find work at short notice during a round-the-world trip:

I never intended to work in Hong Kong – in fact I was very excited about the prospect of taking a break from work – but early on in our travels we had a problem as my husband had a sports injury in his foot that was getting worse every day from walking so much and carrying his 40lb backpack.

We decided we should probably go somewhere with quality medical care and where I could possibly find a job – all of a sudden Hong Kong became the logical destination. I began applying for jobs from Nepal, but the poor quality of the phone system there made it impossible to do interviews, so we decided to take the risk and just get on a plane.

I emailed my friends back home to see if anyone had contacts in Hong Kong and, amazingly, a friend from school knew the guy who just happened to run the e-business department at Cathay Pacific Airways. We chatted on the phone for 10 minutes, and he asked me to come in the next day. Twenty-four hours later I had a four-month contract to develop an intranet prototype at a salary that would allow me to support both of us while Thomas took care of his foot!

For detailed information on the work-permit situation in various countries around the world, visit www.expatexchange.com and www.goinglobal.com, or see the following government immigration websites:

- Australian Department of Immigration and Multicultural and Indigenous Affairs (www .immi.gov.au)
- Citizenship and Immigration Canada (www.cic.gc.ca)
- Ministry of Foreign Affairs of Japan (www.mofa.go.jp)
- New Zealand Immigration Service (www.immigration.govt.nz)
- UK Visas Portal (www.ukvisas.gov.uk)
- US Citizenship & Immigration Services (http://uscis.gov)
- US Department of State (www.unitedstatesvisas.gov)

Working Holidays

If you just want to pick up casual work as you travel around, several countries offer working holiday schemes for young people. The main advantage of becoming a working holiday-maker is that you can find a job when you arrive and do almost any kind of work, with the exception of health care or working with children.

Working holidays are generally restricted to people under 30 and you should be unmarried, or married to someone who is also eligible for the scheme. Working holiday-makers are not allowed to travel with children and a criminal record is also a no-no – the authorities will check when you apply.

You can apply for working holiday schemes year round, but most countries have an annual quota, so you may stand a better chance if you apply early in the year.

AUSTRALIA & NEW ZEALAND

Australia's Working Holiday Program is the world's most famous working holiday. The program is open to citizens of Canada, Cyprus, Denmark, Finland, France, Germany, Hong Kong, Ireland, Italy, Japan, Malta, the Netherlands, Norway, the Republic of Korea (South Korea), Sweden, and the UK – plus Belgium in the near future – and you must be aged 18 to 30 to take part. The programs are reciprocal, so all these countries offer similar schemes for Australian citizens.

You can work in Australia for up to a year on the scheme, but you can only work for three months for any one employer. Americans can apply for a limited four-month scheme with sponsorship from an organisation such as CIEE (p193) See the website www.workinaustralia .net for more information.

You must provide evidence of around £2000 in funds and a return plane ticket to Australia (or the money to buy one) and pay a visa fee of A$165. Most nationalities are now required to use the complicated online application form at www.immi.gov.au but some nationalities should apply at Australian embassies overseas – the website has details.

Most people use the visa to do casual jobs such as fruit picking and bar work, but you can also take on short-term work in your professional field. Some people manage to get around the three-month rule by transferring to different departments within the same company. However, you can only take part in the scheme once, so make sure this is the time when you will get most out of it.

Susanne Farelly took a working holiday just in time:

I'd never really thought about going to Australia before, but I was feeling frustrated with my work and I felt like life was passing me by. My boyfriend suggested that we both do a whole working holiday in Australia, and it sounded like a great idea, but my 31th birthday was just a few months away. We had to do everything in double-quick time, but I was able to apply for the visa, hand in my notice, book my flights and pack my bags just in time to have my birthday on the beach in Sydney.

New Zealand has a similar working holiday arrangement with the UK, Ireland, France, Germany, the Netherlands, Italy, Denmark, Canada, Japan, Hong Kong, Malaysia, Singapore, Taiwan, South Korea, Argentina, Chile and Uruguay. Around 10,000 working holiday visas are issued every year to UK citizens and you can work in New Zealand doing any job for up to a year.

The age range is 18 to 30 and you can only take part once, though you can leave and re-enter New Zealand as often as you like during the year – handy if you fancy making a side trip to Australia. You should apply at your local New Zealand embassy with evidence of sufficient funds for your living expenses and flights and an application fee of £50 or the local equivalent – see the website www.immigration.govt.nz for details.

Numerous exchange agencies can arrange working holiday visas in Australia and New Zealand for a fee, but these are really only for people who are short on time or want a bit of extra backup when they go overseas. The main reason to go through an agency is for help in finding work and assistance with the tax and visa paperwork.

EUROPE

Working in Europe is the Holy Grail for Australians and North Americans. Britain has a very popular working holiday scheme for Commonwealth citizens aged 17 to 30, which includes Australians, New Zealanders, Canadians and South Africans. You can work in the

UK for up to two years and travel in and out of the UK but you must provide evidence of enough money to cover your living expenses and airfare. The application fee varies with the country and you should apply at a British embassy or consulate overseas – see www.ukvisas.gov.uk for more information.

All of the European nations that have working holiday arrangements with Australia and New Zealand offer similar schemes for Aussies and Kiwis to work in Europe – contact the relevant embassy or see the website Working Holiday Guru (www.workingholidayguru.com) for details of how these programs work.

ASIA

Fancy a year of sushi and sumo? Japan has a working holiday scheme for citizens of the UK, Australia, New Zealand, Canada, France, Germany and South Korea. If you are aged between 18 and 30, you can apply to work in Japan for six months and there is no application fee. Brits can work for up to a year, but you must be under 25. All nationalities should apply at a Japanese embassy with evidence of US$2000 in savings and your return ticket or enough money to buy one.

The annual quota is quite small, so it's a good idea to apply early. You must also provide copies of your CV and a statement explaining what you hope to gain from the program. For more information, see the visa section on the website of the Japanese Ministry of Foreign Affairs (www.mofa.go.jp).

Once you arrive in Japan, the Japan Association of Working Holiday Makers (www.jawhm.or.jp) can help you find work – see the Contacts section (p193) for details. Most working holiday-makers work as English teachers but fluent Japanese speakers can find hospitality and office work.

There are similar arrangements in South Korea for Canadians and Australians (see www.workingholiday.com) and in Hong Kong for Australians and New Zealanders (see www.immd.gov.hk). The usual rules apply – you can work for up to year if you are aged 18 to 30 and have sufficient funds and a return plane ticket.

One interesting feature of Asian working holiday schemes is that you cannot work at 'places of entertainment which might endanger good morals' – just in case you were thinking of doing a season as a burlesque dancer...

NORTH AMERICA

Working holiday schemes in the USA are only open to full-time university students, but the Canadian working holiday program is open to career-breakers. As well as the reciprocal scheme for Australians and New Zealanders (see www.cic.gc.ca for details), Canada has a special working holiday visa for non-students from the UK and Ireland. Anyone aged 18 to 35 can take part, but you should apply through an organisation such as the Bunac (British Universities North America Club; www.bunac.org) in the UK or USIT (www.usitnow.ie) in Ireland.

There's an application fee of around £150 which covers your visa, work permit and social insurance number. You also need a minimum of C$1000 in savings plus mandatory insurance cover for your stay – this can be arranged through Bunac or USIT. You must attend a scheduled orientation in Toronto, Montreal or Vancouver.

Participants can do any job except camp counselling and – curiously – tobacco picking. To work in health or childcare, you need a Canadian-government approved medical, which can be arranged by the sponsoring organisation for around £130. You can leave and re-enter Canada during the year, but you can only participate in the scheme once and if you have previously visited Canada on a visa, you must wait 12 months before you can apply.

Work without Permits

Of course, not everyone sticks to the rules – it is possible to pick up casual work if you don't have a work permit, but you will be taking a major gamble. Immigration authorities come down very hard on people who are found working illegally and if you do get caught, you will probably be detained, charged and then taken to the airport and put on the next flight home at your own expense.

If you have a conviction for working illegally, you may never be able to return to that country again, even for a holiday. Why bother taking the risk when you can work at home to get the money and then travel around at your leisure? This said, some people may decide they have no choice (see Money Troubles p102 for more information).

Tax

Whatever kind of work you do overseas, the government will take a cut of your earnings, and if you become a legal resident, you will also pay tax on earnings from overseas. The website www.taxsites.com/international.html is the leading tax resource on the Internet and it has information on the tax rules for most countries around the world.

Foreign workers must register with the local tax authorities before they start earning. In Australia, you should apply to the Australian Taxation Office for a tax file number – you can do this online at www.ato.gov.au. In New Zealand, you should apply to the local Inland Revenue Department office (see www.ird.govt.nz for listings).

In America, exchange visitors only pay federal and state taxes and not Social Security. However, you still need to apply for a Social Security card from the Inland Revenue Service (www.irs.gov); the sponsoring organisation will usually help with this. In Canada, you should apply for a Social Insurance Number at the Canada Revenue Agency (www.ccra-adrc.gc.ca).

Rules within Europe vary from country to country – the Eures website (europa.eu.int/eures) provides information on tax and employment rules for every country in the EEA. In the UK, you should apply for a national insurance number from the Department for Work and Pensions (www.dwp.gov.uk), which will allow the Inland Revenue (www.inlandrevenue.gov.uk) to tax your earnings at source.

If you are sponsored by a foreign employer to work in any country, tax will usually be deducted at the standard rate for local employees, but it's easy to claim back any overpayments at the end of the tax year (usually in April). Exchange organisations such as Bunac (p193) have well-established schemes for claiming back overpayments, and the company Tax Back International (www.taxback.com) can help you reclaim tax you've paid overseas for a fee.

If you're working overseas for a whole year you can declare yourself nonresident in your home country to avoid paying tax twice – see Taxation & National Insurance (p23) for more details. Some countries have international tax arrangements to make this easier – see the taxation service websites earlier in this section for details.

Rights & Residency

If you're sticking around in any country long-term or you want the freedom to work in any job you like, consider applying to become a permanent resident. Every country has its own complicated rules when it comes to residency – your first point of call should always be the local embassy or consulate. They can explain exactly what you need to do and when you need to do it.

Within Europe, there are different rules for EEA and non-EEA citizens. If you come from a member state, you must obtain a residence permit to stay more than three months in another member country. This is quite easy – you just need to take your passport and evidence of employment, personal funds or student status to the local foreigners' registration office. The Eures website (europa.eu.int/eures) has detailed information on the procedure in every EEA member state.

Britain gives automatic right of residence to EEA citizens, so you don't need to apply for a residence permit in the UK. However, if you come from anywhere else and want to become a resident of an EEA country, you must follow the residency rules for that country – embassies overseas can provide more information.

Non-EU citizens who enter the UK with a work permit or student visa must apply for a residence permit to stay for more than six months. Permits are available from the Immigration & Nationality Directorate (www.ind.homeoffice.gov.uk) and are valid for up to five years. Citizens of the USA, Canada, Australia, New Zealand, South Africa and some Asian countries can sidestep this requirement by applying for entry clearance from a British embassy or consulate before they travel – this costs £36 for students and £75 for people with a work permit.

To become a permanent resident of the UK, you must have worked legally for at least four years, and you must wait a further year before you can apply for naturalisation and become a British citizen. Only permanent residents or citizens are eligible to claim benefits, and only UK citizens can vote in parliamentary elections.

UK residents are entitled to health care on the NHS, as are temporary visitors from countries that have a reciprocal arrangement with the UK, such as Australians and New Zealanders on working holiday visas – the website www.publications.doh.gov.uk/overseasvisitors has full details on the UK health policy for overseas visitors.

In the USA, permanent residents are known as 'resident aliens'. To earn this esteemed status, you must obtain an immigrant visa – the legendary green card – from US Citizenship & Immigration Services (Uscis; http://uscis.gov). The easiest way to become a resident is through a sponsoring employer or an immigration program for highly skilled migrants, but America also runs an annual Diversity Lottery (DV), which issues 55,000 immigrant visas to people who come from countries with low rates of immigration to the United States – see the Uscis website for details.

Resident aliens who have lived in the USA for five years can apply for naturalisation through the US Citizenship & Immigration Services (http://uscis.gov), which involves a language test, a general knowledge quiz about America and the Oath of Allegiance. To vote in American elections, you must be a full-blown American citizen, or, in the state of Florida, a donkey…

Health care in the USA is administered by the Department of Health & Human Services (www.hhs.gov), but most visas require you to take out private health insurance before you travel. Medicaid and Medicare (state-funded health care) are reserved for the most disadvantaged families in America.

Australia and New Zealand have similar rules and Australians and New Zealanders can live in each others' countries with few restrictions. Both countries also offer special immigration programs to tempt in skilled people from overseas as permanent residents – see the immigration websites for Australia (www.immi.gov.au) and New Zealand (www.immigration.govt.nz) for details.

Once you are accepted as a permanent resident, you can apply for citizenship after three years in New Zealand and after two years in Australia – see www.dia.govt.nz and www.citizenship.gov.au for details. New Zealand also has a special Work to Residence scheme, where people on temporary work permits can qualify for full residency without leaving the country. All permanent residents and citizens are eligible to vote in New Zealand; if you become an Australian citizen, voting is compulsory.

In Australia, access to Medicare (free public health care) is restricted to Australian citizens and permanent residents, plus citizens of New Zealand, the UK, Ireland, Italy, the Netherlands, Sweden, Finland and Malta. Overseas students must obtain special private health cover through the company Medibank Private (www.medibank.com.au) – see the website of the Australian Department of Health and Ageing (www.health.gov.au) for more information.

New Zealand provides free health care for citizens and residents and has reciprocal arrangements with Australia and the UK, but students and workers staying less than two years need private health cover. For more information, contact the New Zealand Ministry of Health (www.moh.govt.nz).

It is much harder to become a permanent resident in Asia. Visitors to Japan are granted immigrant status of up to three years on arrival and changing status is very difficult. To become a permanent resident you must have lived in Japan for at least 10 years and be fluent in Japanese. Even then, you cannot become a citizen or vote. If you stay more than one year, you must also take out private health insurance. The Tokyo Metropolitan Authority (www.metro.tokyo.jp/ENGLISH/index.htm) provides information for foreigners who want to live in Japan.

Thailand is also popular for long stays. To gain permanent residence in Thailand, you must have been living continuously in Thailand on a nonimmigrant visa for three years (see www.thaivisa.com for more information). Only Thai citizens are allowed to vote and residents still need a work permit to work. The state health-insurance plan isn't really suitable for foreigners – private health insurance is the way to go.

WORKERS IN DEMAND
Nursing & Midwifery

If you are a qualified nurse or midwife it is easy to find paid temporary or even permanent work all over the world, including countries in which it is famously hard to work if you're a foreigner, such as Britain and the USA. The immigration rules are relaxed in most countries, but you must register with the local nursing board before you can practice.

Australia has a special immigration program where qualified nurses aged 18 to 45 can obtain a four-year working visa if they have sponsorship from an Australian company. You can also apply as a skilled migrant or use a working holiday visa if you meet the requirements. Your skills must be reassessed by the Australian Nursing Council (ANC; www.anc.org.au) or the nursing regulatory body in the area where you intend to work. A similar program operates in New Zealand through the Nursing Council of New Zealand (www.nursingcouncil.org.nz).

To work as a nurse in America, you need sponsorship from an American employer, but there is plenty of demand for nurses, so this is easier than it sounds. Nursing agencies can speed you through the process for around £1500 – see p200 for some examples. To practice in America, you must take the CGFNS (Commission on Graduates of Foreign Nursing Schools) and NCLEX-RN (National Council Licensure Examination for Registered Nurses) exams. The CGFNS (www.cgfns.org) and National Council of State Boards of Nursing (www.ncsbn.org) can provide information on examination dates and fees.

Foreign nurses wanting to work in the UK also get preferential treatment from immigration if they have sponsorship from a British employer, and they must register with the Nursing & Midwifery Council (www.nmc-uk.org) before they start work. Similar policies operate in most European countries. The website www.nursingnetuk.com has excellent advice on nursing in the UK and overseas and a worldwide search engine for jobs.

There are also opportunities for nurses in year-out and expedition organisations (see Working for a Volunteer Organisation, p183).

Teaching

Hands up who wants to be an English teacher? If you are fluent in English, there are tremendous opportunities for teachers of English abroad. Demand for teachers is so high in some countries that some employers offer special packages to tempt teachers from overseas, with free flights, generous salaries and subsidised accommodation.

The field of English-language teaching is full of confusing acronyms – to clarify matters, here's a quick glossary:

- **EFL** (English as a Foreign Language) Refers to English teaching in countries where English is not the first language; often used instead of ELT.
- **ELT** (English-Language Teaching) An umbrella term for English-language teaching; widely used in Europe.
- **ESL** (English as a Second Language) Another term for EFL; sometimes reserved for teaching English to foreign students in English-speaking countries.
- **IELTS** (International English-Language Testing System) The UK/Australian equivalent of TOEFL.
- **TEFL** (Teachers of English as a Foreign Language) The main European system of training for teaching English to non-English speakers.
- **TESOL** (Teachers of English to Speakers of Other Languages) The American equivalent of TEFL.
- **TOEFL** (Test of English as a Foreign Language) The main international test of English competency. This has nothing to do with English-language teaching, but it may form part of the entry requirements for jobs and academic courses in English-speaking countries.
- **TOFFEE** Caramelised sugar not to be eaten while trying to teach English, due to teeth sticking together.

Although some Asian schools take on English teachers without teaching qualifications, you will be more employable all around the world if you have a TEFL/TESOL certificate. Career teachers might want to go further and study for a TEFL/TESOL diploma. Qualified English-language teachers are regarded as skilled people for immigration purposes, which makes it quite easy for local schools to sponsor foreign teachers for work permits.

Teachers with professional qualifications can find paid work teaching almost any subject if they can speak the local language, but you will be competing for jobs with qualified local teachers and the immigration authorities may think twice before giving you a work permit. Contact the embassies directly to see if any special immigration programs for teachers are running.

TEFL & TESOL

If you want to make money teaching English overseas, the first step should be to obtain a teaching certificate or diploma. There are two main training systems for ESL teachers: TEFL (Teachers of English as a Foreign Language) is the most popular system in Europe, while TESOL (Teachers of English to Speakers of Other Languages) is the main system in the USA.

The most widely recognised TEFL certificates and diplomas are issued by Cambridge ESOL (English for Speakers of Other Languages; www.cambridge-efl.org), and you can study for these courses at dozens of schools worldwide. The Cambridge certificate course CELTA (Certificate in English-Language Teaching to Adults) is aimed at people aged 20 or over who are educated up to university entry level, while the diploma course DELTA (Diploma in English-Language Teaching to Adults) is designed for university graduates with previous English-teaching experience.

In America, people usually study for a certificate or diploma in TESOL, which is also the name of the professional body that oversees English-language teacher training in the USA. TESOL courses are usually offered by universities, either as a part of a degree or as a postgraduate master's in TESOL, but this can easily cost as much as an MBA and is really only for people who want to make a career in teaching.

A much more affordable option is to study for a TESOL certificate. Various institutions around the world offer certificates based on the TESOL teaching system that are roughly equivalent to CELTA and DELTA. The most widely recognised TESOL qualifications are the Trinity Certificate ('CertTESOL') and Trinity Licentiate Diploma (LTCL TESOL), both issued by Trinity College London (www.trinitycollege.co.uk). Again, you can study for Trinity qualifications at dozens of training centres worldwide.

A TEFL/TESOL certificate is fine if you just want to teach for a season or get a first step on the teaching ladder, but if you want to make a career out of teaching English overseas, think seriously about a diploma course. Chloe Simpson advises:

I was always intending to go back to my job at the end of my break, so I went for a four-week TEFL certificate. It was quite a big investment, but I studied with a large international school and they arranged a provisional placement for me in Prague before I even finished the course. When I got to Prague, I quickly plugged into the ESL grapevine, which turned out to be a great source of information. The general wisdom seemed to be that you can get away without a TEFL certificate in Asia, but not in Europe. The more serious diploma-type courses seem to be for people who have already done a few years of teaching and want to earn more money.

Full-time TEFL and TESOL certificate courses generally last four to five weeks and cost £650 to £1250, depending on where you study. The cheapest courses are offered by private language schools in Eastern Europe. You can also take a TEFL or TESOL certificate course part time over three to nine months, though this will be work out more expensive. Full-time diploma courses last nine to 10 weeks and cost £1300 to £1900.

The best places to start looking for a course are the websites of Cambridge ESOL (www .cambridge-efl.org), Trinity College (www.trinitycollege.co.uk) and TESOL (www.tesol.org), all of which have listings of approved schools and training centres. Alternatively, Cactus Language (www.cactusteachers.com) acts as a central admissions service for TEFL/TESOL courses worldwide – see p195 for details.

As well as the Cambridge ESOL and Trinity College qualifications, there are numerous independent TEFL and TESOL courses, but not all of these are internationally recognised. This may be fine if you want to work for branches of that particular school, but the certificate may not cut the mustard with other employers.

For peace of mind, stick to a course that is approved by the local governing body for academic qualifications such as Cambridge ESOL or Trinity in the UK, TESOL in the USA, TESL Canada (www.tesl.ca), the Australian Council of TESOL Associations (ACTA; www .tesol.org.au) or the New Zealand Qualifications Authority (NZQA; www.nzqa.govt.nz). As a bare minimum, any TEFL/TESOL course should include at least 100 hours of tuition and six hours of classroom teaching practice.

Before you decide on any course, talk to former students and potential employers, or post a note on one of the ESL notice boards on the web – www.tefl.net is a good place to get honest opinions from former students. The website Which Course? (www.whichcourse .com) provides information on the minimum amount of tuition and classroom practice that employers are looking for in various countries around the world.

If you just want an introduction to TEFL, to give you confidence, the year-out organisa-tion i-to-i (www.onlinetefl.com) offers an online TEFL training course that is accredited by the Open & Distance Learning Quality Council (www.odlqc.org.uk) – see the Contacts section (p195) for details. Ontesol (www.ontesol.com) in Canada offers a similar course that you can upgrade to a full TEFL certificate.

There are also TEFL-style courses for teaching other European languages. International House (www.ihworld.com) offers a Certificate in Language Teaching to Adults (LTA) in French, German, Spanish and Italian – see p195 for more details. Some schools also offer specially modified TEFL/TESOL courses for non-native English-speakers which will bring you up to the minimum standard for international teaching.

Almost all of the TESOL/TEFL training centres have links to language schools worldwide and can find you a paying placement when you complete the course. Once you have entered the ESL system, you'll find that there is an incredible amount of communication between the various language schools and agencies – it is quite easy to work your way around the world, moving from one ESL job to another.

Some of the best TEFL and TESOL training centres are covered in the Contacts section (p195), but other useful resources for finding a TEFL course include:

- **TEFL.net** (www.tefl.net/tcd) A search engine for TEFL/TESOL courses worldwide.
- **Tesall.com** (www.tesall.com) A general TEFL/TESOL information site, with course listings.
- **Europa Pages** (www.europa-pages.com) Study information for the whole of Europe, in-cluding TEFL and TESOL courses.
- **ESL in the USA** (www.eslinusa.com/TESOL_employment_teachers.html) An extensive site with US-specific TESOL information.

FINDING A TEACHING JOB

By far the easiest way to find a job as an ESL teacher is to study for a TEFL/TESOL certificate. Most training centres double as agencies for language schools around the world and most give priority consideration to students on their TEFL/TESOL courses. However, many countries ask for a university degree as well as a TEFL certificate to satisfy the work-permit regulations.

You can also apply to an agency that sends ESL teachers to schools abroad – some of the leading agencies are listed in the Contacts section (p198). Applying directly to a foreign-language school is another option, but many schools recruit staff through agencies specifi-cally to avoid the rigmarole of applying for individual work permits.

Will Gourlay took a TEFL course and lined up a job in Turkey before leaving Australia:

I had already travelled quite extensively in Europe, the Middle East and Africa and I was interested in going back to live somewhere for an extended time, rather than just holidaying or passing through. I enjoyed Turkey and I knew that it would be reasonably straightforward to get a teaching job there, though I did do an intensive TEFL course before I began applying for jobs.

I teed up a 12-month contract from Australia, but the school that I ended up teaching at could be classified as a 'cowboy' operation, ie money was more important to the boss than imparting the basics of correct grammar. That said, there were far worse operations – ours was just pretty stingy. And despite that I met the most fantastic bunch of students of all ages, and the other teachers (five Poms) at the school were fantastic and we had heaps of fun together as a group.

As well as the TEFL/TESOL schools and agencies listed on p198, there are plenty of websites and books offering information on training and job opportunities. *Teaching English Abroad* by Susan Griffiths (available from www.vacationwork.co.uk) is a good place to start. You can also find listings of schools that need staff in local English-language newspapers.

Reliable online resources for finding ESL teaching jobs include:

- **Dave's ESL Cafe** (www.eslcafe.com) A quirky and informative ESL site with job listings and advice.
- **Edufind Jobs** (www.jobs.edufind.com) An American site with information on TEFL, TESOL and other teacher-training programs, plus jobs pages.
- **ESL Guide** (www.esl-guide.com) A country-by-country guide to ESL opportunities.
- **Guardian TEFL News** (education.guardian.co.uk/tefl) Part of the British *Guardian* newspaper, with articles and extensive TEFL links.
- **TEFL Asia** (www.teflasia.com) An Asian TEFL network with jobs and advice.
- **TEFL.Net** (www.tefl.net) A forum for information on TEFL, including job listings.
- **TEFL Professional Network** (www.tefl.com) A vast database of TEFL jobs worldwide.
- **TESOL Job Finder** (www.vv-vv.com/tesol) An official site with TESOL course listings.
- **Transitions Abroad** (www.transitionsabroad.com) US publisher of work and study guides with online ELT job listings.

TEACHING WITHOUT TEFL

You can find work as an English-teacher without a TEFL/TESOL certificate in many countries, but you need to be careful as some schools exploit their teachers mercilessly. The best wages and working conditions are usually offered by international teaching programs in Japan, Korea and China, including the famous JET scheme in Japan (see the following section for details). Accommodation is usually provided and many schools will reimburse you for the cost of your flights at the end of your contract.

It is also possible to walk into teaching jobs in Southeast Asia without a TEFL/TESOL certificate. Probably the best opportunities are at private schools in Cambodia and Thailand. Some volunteering organisations can also arrange teaching jobs in Asia and Africa for people with no previous experience, sometimes with a small local salary.

People with mainstream teaching qualifications can often find work at international schools in Africa, Asia, Europe and the Middle East. These expensive private schools cater to expats and wealthy locals and teach the standard high school curriculum in English. The Council of International Schools (www.cois.org) maintains an extensive database of international schools on its website. Other organisations with listings of international schools include the Mediterranean Association of International Schools (www.mais-web.org) and the Association for the Advancement of International Education (www.aaie.org).

If you have a bona fide skill that you can pass on to others, you could always set yourself up as a freelance teacher. Plenty of people manage to do this, but it is unofficial and may not be strictly legal, so you might want to check out the implications before you go ahead. One option is to train up in an alternative therapy such as yoga, t'ai chi or massage and teach travellers how to align their chi at traveller hang-outs in Europe and Asia. Musicians can often pick up freelance work giving music classes, and sports instructors and coaches can find paid work at holiday resorts overseas (see Resort Jobs, p182).

JET (JAPAN EXCHANGE & TEACHING)

One of the most popular teaching programs abroad is the Japan Exchange & Teaching scheme (JET), run by the Japanese government. The scheme allows university graduates aged 39 or younger to work in Japan as English teachers or language assistants for a minimum of one year on full pay. There is no fee to take part in the program and flights are provided by JET, making this one of the most generous teach-abroad schemes around.

Workers on the JET scheme earn an annual salary of around £18,400, but you must pay for accommodation and the compulsory health insurance charged by the Japanese government. Living costs in Japan are notoriously high, but most people manage to live comfortably and even save some money from their salary.

JET is administered by Japanese embassies in around 40 countries, including Australia, Canada, New Zealand, the UK and the USA, and most of Asia and Europe. The official website for the JET program is www.jetprogramme.org, but you can also obtain detailed information from the Japanese Ministry of Foreign Affairs (www.mofa.go.jp /j_info/visit/jet).

Most participants work as Assistant Language Teachers (ALT), teaching English in Japanese schools, but Japanese speakers can also work as Coordinators for International Relations (CIR), assisting in the day-to-day running of local government departments. There are also openings for qualified sports coaches from certain countries – check the JET website to see if you qualify.

Applications are accepted from late September, with interviews from November and an orientation in July, shortly before you leave for Japan. If you have a successful first year, you can extend your stay to three or even five years at the discretion of the school you are working for. However, you must have lived outside Japan for six or more of the last eight years when you apply and you must wait 10 years before you can repeat the program.

You can express a preference about where you are placed, but schools in cities such as Tokyo and Osaka fill up quickly. Dean Smith went to Yamagata in the north of the country during his year on the JET scheme:

After spending some time in Japan while at university I decided to return for a year on the JET program as a break from my legal career. The worries of arriving in a strange place with no friends and nothing to do are minimalised with JET as you have a ready-made group of friends all starting at the same time. The program also gives you access to communities in Japan that the average traveller would never be able to enter.

The salary from Jet is more than sufficient to live in Japan with some left over. In my experience, the myth of Japan as an unbearably expensive country is limited to the world of tourists. Within a few weeks you will find the cheap supermarkets, inexpensive bars and low-cost travel options. As a general rule the cost of living is on a par with the UK – not the cheapest in the world, but very much survivable.

It's a good idea to talk to former participants to find out more about the experience of being a foreign worker in Japan. The website of the Japan Exchange and Teaching Alumni Association (JETAA; www.jet.org) lists websites run by past and current participants.

Freelancing

People often fantasise about travelling the world and making a living from writing articles or selling photographs, but the fact is that travel journalism is heavily oversubscribed and, even if you find a publisher, you will be lucky to cover the costs of your flights. Unless you have a network of eager clients who are happy to run your story several times, the best way to look at freelancing is as a way to make a bit of money on the side from a trip that you were going to do anyway.

If you do try to sell travel articles, try to come up with an original idea. A travel story about going to India to see the Taj Mahal is a no-brainer, but you might make some money off a story about an Indian tribute band playing songs by the blues band Taj Mahal for an American music magazine.

Before you call up to pitch a story idea, find out the kinds of stories that each publication takes and speak to the editor of the specific section that you think will run your story – you can find newspapers and magazines worldwide on the website www.world-newspapers .com. Always make sure that no-one has run a similar story in the last few months!

Online magazines are a growing market for freelancers, and experienced writers and photographers can sometimes find work with English-language papers overseas. Another option is to become a stringer for a newspaper or TV network, but this involves putting yourself wherever the action is around the world – not always the safest way to spend a career break.

Press cards are only really worthwhile for career journalists, as you need to earn most of your income from journalism to qualify; the website of the National Union of Journalists (NUJ; www.nuj.org.uk) has more information. On the other hand, a professional-looking business card can open doors around the world.

Even if you are travelling on assignment for a newspaper or magazine, it is often easier to travel on a tourist visa. Jane Grant sent us the following cautionary tale about applying for a visa for a research trip to India:

I took on a writing project in India for a travel company at short notice, so I had to visit the Indian embassy in person to apply for a visa two days before I was due to fly. After queuing for half the morning, I dutifully filled in the form – including lots of obscure details like my father's middle name – and handed it over the counter with the payment for the visa. The man at the desk thanked me nicely, scanned over my application and told me to come back in two weeks.

I was booked to fly a couple of days later, so I protested strongly, but the clerk wouldn't hear any of it. 'It says here you are a journalist, so you must wait two weeks!' he announced. I was about to give up when the clerk had a change of heart and scribbled out the work 'Journalist' on my application form, replacing it with the word 'Engineer'. 'Now you are an engineer' he said, beaming. 'You can come back tomorrow.'

With a roaming Internet connection or access to an Internet café, there are quite a few jobs where you can take on freelance work and travel. Qualified teachers can easily find freelance teaching work overseas, and editing, desktop publishing, web design, computer programming, consultancy and translating all provide opportunities for skilled freelancers, though you will need to carry a laptop or arrange access to a computer overseas.

It's important to consider the legal implications of freelancing overseas. Unless you have an appropriate work permit, you may technically be working illegally, which is always a bit of a gamble. If you insist on being paid into your home bank account, the authorities may be none the wiser, but there's always the chance that someone will ask for a tax code or other proof that you are entitled to work, so you're better off making sure your work permit is in order.

Freelancers in any field face the same problems of finding and building up a client base as freelance writers and photographers, but there are some useful websites that bring projects and freelancers together:

- **All Freelance Work** (www.allfreelancework.com) A site for desktop publishers and designers.
- **Aquarius** (www.aquarius.net) An agency that links freelance translators with translating jobs worldwide.
- **Freelance.com USA** (www.freelance.com) An American site for freelance IT professionals.
- **Freelancers.Net** (www.freelancers.net) A listing service for freelance IT professionals.
- **Freelance Proofreaders** (www.freelance-proofreaders.co.uk) A UK job site for freelance proofreaders, editors and translators.
- **Freelance Work Exchange** (www.freelanceworkexchange.com) A US site with listings of freelance media, consultancy, design and programming jobs.
- **Freelance Writing** (www.freelancewriting.com) A portal for information on freelance writing.
- **Journalism.co.uk** (www.journalism.co.uk) A leading UK site for journalists.
- **Journalism.org** (www.journalism.org) A US site with extensive tools for journalists.
- **Journalism UK** (www.journalismuk.co.uk) A journalists' resource site with strong UK focus.
- **Proz** (www.proz.com) A site for freelance translators, with extensive jobs listings.
- **Translator Directory** (www.translationdirectory.com) A portal for freelance translators, with links to job sites.
- **Translator Tips** (www.translatortips.com) A US site with advice for freelance translators.
- **Worldwide Freelance Writer** (www.worldwidefreelance.com) An information source for freelance writers.

Resort Jobs

Do you have boundless energy and the ability to see a silver lining in every cloud? If so, the holiday business needs you. Most holiday companies have seasonal openings for enthusiastic resort staff and holiday reps and there are summer jobs for windsurfing, sailing and scuba-diving instructors and winter jobs for skiing and snowboarding instructors at resorts around the world.

Working for a holiday company is basically a lifestyle decision – the pay is low but ski hire and ski passes are thrown in for winter jobs and summer staff can use the watersports equipment in their time off. Your transport, accommodation and meals are also covered, so you should have enough dosh left over for a bit of après-ski.

The UK has dozens of holiday companies that hire seasonal staff every year. Elsewhere, holiday resorts often have openings for hospitality and other casual workers with the right paperwork – a working holiday visa can open a lot of doors. Summer and winter resorts in America and Canada also sponsor huge numbers of foreign instructors and hospitality staff on seasonal work permits.

WINTER & SUMMER SPORTS

Winter and summer sports provide some of the most interesting opportunities for working overseas. Qualified instructors can find ski and snowboard jobs in Europe and North America during the northern hemisphere winter and in New Zealand and South America during the southern hemisphere winter, while windsurfing, sailing, kayaking and scuba-diving instructors can find jobs year round at resorts all over the world.

To work as an instructor you need formal instructor qualifications that are recognised by the local governing body for the sport – for example the Royal Yachting Association (www.rya.org.uk) for sailing and windsurfing. The Studying chapter (p219) has lots more information on the various summer and winter sport qualifications that you can study for, including reputable schools around the world.

Europeans are free to work anywhere in the EEA, while working holiday visas are a convenient way for Europeans to work in Australia, New Zealand and Canada and for Australians and New Zealanders to work in Europe. Many American ski resorts sponsor international ski and snowboard instructors on H-2B visas every season – Aspen Snowmass (www.aspensnowmass.com) and Steamboat Ski & Resort (www.steamboat.com) are two reliable companies.

The best place to start looking for an instructor's job is the school you trained with. Flying Fish (www.flyingfishonline.com) and International Academy (www.theinternationalacademy.com) act as agencies for ski and watersports staff and can put you in touch with potential employers worldwide. Alternatively, there are specialist agencies for winter and summer resort staff. Skistaff (www.skistaff.co.uk) recruits instructors, chalet staff and cooks for resorts in the French, Swiss, Austrian and Italian Alps.

As well as ski instructor jobs, there are also openings for ski hosts or ski couriers – effectively baby-sitters on skis – and for ski guides to lead groups of skiers around the slopes. For all these jobs, you can generally find work with the entry-level ski-instructor qualification – grade III on the UK system. Some leading ski companies that recruit staff every year are listed in the Contacts section (p201).

OTHER RESORT JOBS

As well as instructor jobs, most holiday companies need support staff to help with the day-to-day running of resorts. The most common jobs are for couriers, who look after children and do odd jobs around the resorts, and reps, who meet guests at the airport and arrange activities and social events.

The mood on the resorts tends to be young, boisterous and boozy – if you aren't the kind of person who stays at resorts, you probably won't enjoy working at one either. On top of this, the rates of pay are low – as little as £50 a week in some cases. However, you will get to work somewhere hot and sunny (or cold and snowy) for a season.

Summer is the best time of year to look for resort jobs. Apart from couriers and reps, chefs, waiters and other staff are needed to keep the resorts running through the season.

Theme parks also take on huge numbers of staff for the summer season – you can find a list of theme parks worldwide on www.themeparkcity.com.

In winter, ski resorts have loads of jobs for chalet boys and girls, who cook for guests and keep the ski chalets clean and tidy. The wages are tiny and you may have to share a room, but you will get plenty of free time to use your free ski pass. A cooking course is useful for this kind of work – see p218 for some suggestions – but qualified chefs can probably find better opportunities at upmarket resort restaurants.

The agencies Openwide International (www.summerjobseeker.com) and TravelRecruit (www.travelrecruit.co.uk) supply seasonal staff for holiday companies and resorts around the world, or you can apply directly to big holiday companies – see the Contacts section (p201) for some suggestions. The following websites can also help you track down a resort job:

- **Adventure Jobs** (www.adventurejobs.co.uk) An excellent UK site listing adventure, winter and watersport jobs, including holiday company jobs.
- **Back Door Jobs** (www.backdoorjobs.com) An excellent US site with listings of outdoor, artistic and adventure jobs.
- **Coolworks** (www.coolworks.com) Listings for all kinds of seasonal, resort and sporting jobs worldwide.
- **Free Radicals** (www.freeradicals.co.uk) Online recruiting agency for ski companies all over Europe and America.
- **Job Monkey** (www.jobmonkey.com) US site with excellent listings of outdoor jobs, ski work and other casual jobs.
- **Leisure Opportunities** (www.leisureopportunities.co.uk) A site advertising leisure jobs in the UK and Europe.
- **Natives** (www.natives.co.uk) An online recruitment agency with listings of ski and resort work year round.
- **Net Recruit UK** (www.netrecruituk.com) UK site with links to specialist recruitment websites for all sorts of seasonal and adventure jobs.
- **Payaway** (www.payaway.com) Extensive work-abroad site with resort job listings.
- **Resort Jobs** (www.resortjobs.com) Part of the AboutJobs group with listings of resort opportunities worldwide.
- **Ski Connection** (www.skiconnection.co.uk) A huge database of ski jobs worldwide.
- **Theme Park Jobs** (www.themeparkjobs.com) A search engine for work in US theme parks.
- **Voovs** (www.voovs.com) An excellent ski site with listings of current ski jobs around the world.

Working for a Volunteer Organisation

One smart way to get work overseas is to take a job with a year-out company. Every organisation that takes students, volunteers or adventurers overseas needs team leaders and support staff, and there is a huge turnover within the industry. Most members of the Year Out Group (see the boxed text on p120) have recruitment information on their websites, and companies actively recruit staff from past expeditions, so joining an expedition is a good way to start the ball rolling.

For team-leader and project-manager positions, you normally need a degree or work experience in a relevant field, plus expedition experience and a mountain leader (summer) certificate. You should also have a current certificate in first aid, preferably with a focus on wilderness or expedition medicine (see p244 for some recommended courses). Skilled expedition staff often advertise their services through the Royal Geographic Society (www.rgs.org).

If you have medical training, almost all year-out organisations have openings for expedition doctors and nurses. To qualify, you need experience in accident and emergency or tropical medicine and a certificate in expedition first aid, though much of the work you'll do involves treating blisters and providing moral support to homesick adventurers.

There are also opportunities for those with a LGV-C (Large Goods Vehicle) licence (the old HGV or Heavy Goods Vehicle licence), engineers, dive instructors and other expedition support staff. Greenforce (www.greenforce.org), Trekforce (www.trekforce.co.uk),

Frontier (www.frontierprojects.ac.uk) and Raleigh International (www.raleighinternational .org) have special schemes for volunteer or trainee staff. See the Volunteering & Conservation chapter (p130) for more information.

Many development and emergency-relief organisations also provide paid work overseas for skilled professionals, but the work is difficult and sometimes dangerous – if you just want to earn some money working abroad, relief work is probably not for you.

Summer Camps & Au Pairing

Working as a camp counsellor on a children's summer camp in the USA or Europe is a popular activity for gap-year students and there is no official maximum age on many of the programs that send camp counsellors overseas. America is the international centre for summer camps, but there are also opportunities in Russia, Europe and the UK.

Most camps run for eight to 10 weeks from June and counsellors stay on camp with the children and help out with sporting and artistic activities. There will be tears to wipe away, disputes to settle, stories to tell and fears to help overcome, which can involve long, patience-testing days and very little privacy. You will spend the whole season at camp, which could be in the back of beyond, and activities such as drinking and smoking are usually banned.

In exchange, you get the fun of working with kids, some free childcare experience and a small amount of pocket money – around US$500 on most camps. Free flights, food and accommodation are provided, so it shouldn't cost you anything to take part, but you probably won't be heading home in a stretch limousine.

You don't need any specific qualifications but if you have a sports instructor qualification, you will probably be able to teach your subject. However, some camps ask for previous childcare experience and a criminal-record check – see p203 for some of the main summer-camp organisations.

Another option is to work as an au pair, but the wages are derisory and you must be under 26 in America and under 27 in most of Europe. If you fit into this category, you will need previous childcare experience and reliable references to find work caring for children with a host family overseas. The easiest option is to find a position through an au pair agency.

Most reliable agencies are members of the International Au Pair Association (www.iapa.org), the British Au Pair Agencies Association (www.bapaa.org.uk) or the Recruitment & Employment Confederation (www.rec.uk.com). Alternatively, you could find a host family using one of the many au pair search engines on the web – reliable sites include Au Pair Wizard (www.au -pair.com), Au Pairs.co.uk (www.aupairs.co.uk) and Au Pair World (www.aupair-world.net).

TRAVELLING WHILE YOU WORK

If you feel that these living and working options sound too much like a busman's holiday, then what about travelling while you live and work abroad? Depending on your job, you might work and travel in a single country, through a number of countries or sail in international waters.

TOUR LEADING

Does your CV describe you accurately as 'highly organised, a good motivator, an excellent communicator and a lateral thinker'? Could you genuinely reply to an ad in the personals asking for 'GSOH'? If so, then you were born to lead.

Living abroad as a tour leader usually means that you're stationed in one part of the world looking after a succession of back-to-back trips for anything from two to six months. If you're working for one of the European coach-tour companies such as Busabout or Top Deck Tours as an on-board guide, then you'll be living and working in a quick succession of countries.

Due to the high cost of training, most tour operators want you to sign up for at least 12 months. You could be living and working in several countries during the course of a year, usually with short breaks in between. Where you're sent depends on many factors but language skills and local knowledge count for a lot.

A tour leader is responsible for the smooth running of a trip and the overall satisfaction of a tour group. You look after all hotel and restaurant reservations, sightseeing opportunities and travel arrangements. You manage company funds, keep expense accounts, handle a string of stressful events ranging from stolen passports to serious illness, and you keep smiling throughout. Some tour operators expect you to spout educational commentary and others will use local guides for this. Clare Montserrat says:

I worked as a tour leader for a UK walking-holiday company in Greece. You have to give yourself 100% to the job. I rarely got to bed before midnight and would be up working again at 7am, sometimes earlier. To do well at the job you have to be highly organised – it's like running a military operation – and you have to think and do lots of things at once. While you're wondering where the heck the path is, you're also making polite conversation with a client walking with you, worrying about the stragglers at the back and the racers at the front, and trying to book taxis for tomorrow's pick-up. And you have to do it all without looking flustered. It was hard but I loved it; I felt like I was living life to the full.

The advantages of working as a tour leader far outweigh the disadvantages but you won't be in this job for the pay. Whatever you do earn is on top of free accommodation (travelling with your group), return airfare and sometimes free meals – see p204 for details. In addition, tour leaders often earn decent tips and, if it's allowed by the company, pick up commissions from some restaurants or shops that their group visits.

In terms of work visas, you'll be expected to have a passport from one of the EU countries, allowing you to work in Europe. Your tour operator will arrange work visas for outside of Europe, which will be music to the ears of older career-breakers.

Jobs are often advertised in the free London magazine *TNT* (www.tntmagazine.com), in the travel magazine *Wanderlust* and on the tour operators' own websites. Sometimes they turn up in www.payaway.co.uk and on notice boards at travel fairs.

BEHIND THE WHEEL
It is sad but true – nine out of 10 coach and overland drivers are male. This ratio reflects the proportion of applications, not the selection process; all companies would love to hire more female drivers. Come on girls – aren't you turned on by the thought of driving a stonking ex-army truck through Africa or navigating a 49-seater, 18-ton coach through four lanes of Italian traffic?

Overland Companies
It can take up to 18 months to become a fully trained overland driver and tour leader (yes, you're usually both). If you're interested in this option for living and working abroad then you'll need to consider a career break in terms of years rather than months.

Most overland tour leaders will tell you that they have the best job in the world. They love travelling in challenging environments, seeing extraordinary things every day, being their own boss, coping with high levels of responsibility, making a difference to the developing countries they visit and being on the road for up to a year at a time.

As career-breaker Neil Luddington found, it certainly beats working in the city:

I was a corporate insurance broker in the city for nine years (suit, etc) then at 30 got made redundant. I found my way into being a tour leader with an overland company working in East and central Africa. We had two crew, up to 24 tourists and a big ex-German army truck with camping equipment and we part camped and part hostelled for holidays of between two and 10 weeks. Because it was 4WD we got off the road a lot. I did this in Africa for two years then came home, did insurance for another three years, then walked out 16 months ago and got another job with an overland company in the Middle East. More than 50% of our clients are single women who need security. Others are first-time travellers. We cook together, sleep together, have the shits together and 90% are lifelong friends after the trip. The experience is a mile away from a package tour. You go places off-road you would never normally see and have a great laugh.

Many of the overland routes are through Africa, Asia and Central and South America. As tour leader your main job is to look after the vehicle, know the routes, and drive safely through them. The other part of the job is in the leading and tour guiding. While navigating around crater-sized potholes, you'll be pointing out wildlife, holding forth on cultural issues, advising on love lives and working out which bar to take everyone to that night. For these reasons there are usually two tour leaders (and sometimes a cook) on any one trip, helping you keep the group happy, safe and well.

To drive for an overland company you need a LGV-C licence. You'll often need to be a trained or bush mechanic. Pay is in the region of £80 to £160 a week but you get all accommodation, food, travel etc for free, so there's not really much to spend it on. The overland company sorts out your visas and immigration documents but you do need to know how to get yourself and your group through some rather dodgy border crossings. Most positions are advertised in the same places as those for tour leaders (see the preceding section).

For more information on overlanding see the Adventure Travel & Expeditions section (p95).

Coach-Touring Companies

Driving for a coach company is a very different cup of motorway service-station tea. Most coach companies tour Europe and expect you to concentrate on your driving while an onboard guide does all the talking. As the Busabout website says – you get 'the world's best view from your office'.

To work as a coach driver you'll need a PCV-D (Passenger Carrying Vehicle) licence. Obviously, you'll also need a valid EU passport or work permit. Often, you'll also need some mechanical knowledge, although this isn't so crucial in Europe where the greater speckled garage is relatively easy to spot.

In many cases, coach drivers are better paid than the on-board guides. One reason for this is that a driver has less opportunity to earn any unofficial extras, though the guide should share any passenger tips.

CRUISING

The number and variety of jobs on board a cruise ship are enormous. On a decent-sized ship there'd be around 200 different positions and up to 1000 crew members. There's work in food and beverage (ranging from assistant provisions master to inventory manager), restaurant/bar (wine steward to bartender), entertainment (audiovisual technician to dancer), spa/salon/health and fitness (hairdresser to fitness instructor), retail and sales, childcare (youth counsellor to nursery nurse), house-keeping (laundry manager to butler), HR/crew/administration (crew purser to office secretary), galley/kitchen (butcher *sous chef* to pizza chef) and at the front desk (receptionist to groups coordinator). In addition, making sure that you all keep smiling is the ubiquitous ship photographer – running away to sea with your camera is easier than you think (see the Contacts section, p207, for details).

The top jobs pay anything from £20,000 per annum but the majority of positions pay around £1000 a month. If you're in the service front line then you get significantly less because most of your income is tips – some waiters, bar and cabin staff make more than £300 a week from guests (who are told how much they're expected to donate). For most positions you need a minimum of two years' relevant experience and qualifications in your field.

It is unusual for cruise lines to hire direct. Recruitment is mostly handled by agencies or 'concessionaires' (companies who own and run their own facilities on a ship, eg shops, gyms). Most contracts last from between four to 10 months, but six months is the most usual. You then get two months' unpaid leave (or you quit altogether). When you're at the contractual stage it is important to understand who'll be paying for what. For instance, many ships are based in the Caribbean or Mediterranean, so who'll pay your airfares?

To work at sea you'll need a passport with more than a year to go on it and a clear criminal record. If you work in US waters, where much of the cruise industry is based, you also need a C1/D visa (see www.usembassy.org.uk/cons_web/visa/niv/cdvisas.htm for details). If other visas are needed once you're on board then the crew purser (or you, if you're the crew purser) will sort this out. Sometimes agencies or concessionaires require a Basic Sea Survival Certificate and a medical examination.

There are lots of websites with infomation about working on cruiseships, often written by those who've been there and done that. Two informative ones are www.geocities.com /thetropics/cabana/1590/ (which has an extensive list of international recruitment agencies and concessionaires) and www.cruiseman.com/cruiseshipjobs.htm. For a more disturbing view of life on board, download the report called *Sweatships – what it's really like to work on board cruise ships* written by the charity War on Want in conjunction with the International Transport Workers' Federation (www.waronwant.org/?lid=8247).

CONTACTS

ACCOMMODATION
House Swaps
Digsville
PO Box 5185, Hoboken, NJ 07030, USA
☎ +1 201-659 5934
Email using the form on the website.
www.digsville.com
Digsville facilitates house swaps, homestays and rentals of private homes worldwide. You can join Digsville for US$44.95 a year, which will allow you to contact members around the world and advertise your own home online.

Homebase Holidays
7 Park Ave, London N13 5PG, UK
☎ +44 (0)20 8886 8752
fax +44 (0)20 8482 4258
info@homebase-hols.com
www.homebase-hols.com
Homebase was established in 1985 and membership costs £29 a year, which allows you to list your home and contact other members worldwide. Homebase provides full guidelines for house swapping to make sure your swap goes without any problems.

HomeExchange.com
PO Box 787, Hermosa Beach, CA 90254, USA
☎ +1 310-798 3864
fax +1 310-798 3865
Email using the form on the website.
www.homeexchange.com
Annual membership costs US$49.95, allowing you to create a listing and browse through more than 6000 homes world-wide. Members receive a guide to arranging a smooth house swap, which includes information on exchange agreements.

Homelink International
Linfield House, Gorse Hill Rd, Virginia Water, Surrey GU25 4AS, UK
☎ +44 (0)1962 886882
fax +44 (0)1344 842642
great-britain@homelink.org
www.homelink.org.uk
Established in 1953, Homelink International is the world's largest house-swap organisation, with 12,500 members worldwide. Membership costs £95 per year, which allows you to place an ad for your home and contact other members via the website or the Homelink directory. Homelink also has offices in Ireland, the USA, Canada, Australia, New Zealand, South Africa and around Europe.

Intervac
c/o Rhona Nayar, 24 The Causeway, Chippenham, Wiltshire SN15 3DB, UK
☎ /fax +44 (0)1249 461101
holiday@intervac.co.uk
www.intervac.co.uk
Intervac has 50 years experience of arranging home swaps and nearly 7000 homes on its database. Annual membership costs £85 for an Internet listing or £99 if you also want to be included in the printed directory, which will give you a listing for your home and access to details of other members. See www.intervac-online.com for branch offices worldwide.

Homestays
British Homestays
24 Temple Ave, Shirley, Croydon, CR0 8QA, UK
☎ +44 (0)20 8777 3038/7580
fax +44 (0)20 8777 0986
enquiries@homestays.co.uk
www.homestays.co.uk
This British company arranges homestays with UK families and can also place groups of people – handy if you want to live with friends.

Experiment in International Living (EIL)
287 Worcester Rd, Malvern, Worcestershire WR14 1AB, UK
☎ +44 (0)1684 562577
fax +44 (0)1684 562212
info@eiluk.org
www.eiluk.org

This registered charity offers homestays with both urban and rural families and on farms and ranches in Europe, South America, Asia, Africa and Australasia. Most homestays cost in the range of £200 to £350 and generally last one to four weeks, and you can participate in various kinds of courses and activities with a cultural focus.

New Zealand Homestay & Farmstays
88 Wairarapa Tce, Merivale, Christchurch, New Zealand
☎ +64 (0)3-355 6737
fax +64 (0)3-355 6742
info@nzhomestay.co.nz
www.nzhomestay.co.nz
This joint New Zealand and Australian company can arrange homestays at farms and private houses around New Zealand and Australia (for Australian homestays, see www.australianhomestay.com).

San Francisco Homestay
1670 South Amphlett Blvd, Suite 214, San Mateo, CA 94070, USA
☎ +1 650-577 2370
fax +1 650-366 4149
info@sfhomestay.com
www.sfhomestay.com
This organisation arranges homestay placements with families across America, particularly in San Francisco, Berkeley and Silicon Valley. Rates start at US$948 per month, plus a US$180 placement fee.

Servas
11 John St, Room 505, New York, NY 10038, USA
☎ +1 212-267 0252
fax +1 212-267 0292
info@usservas.org
www.usservas.org
This international homestay network has members in 130 countries who accept visiting travellers for two or three nights. There is no fee to stay with a member, but you must join Servas and abide by the Servas code of conduct. One-year international traveller membership is US$85.

RECRUITMENT AGENCIES
The following agencies have branches in dozens of countries around the world. You can find links to country-specific sites on the global websites listed.

Adecco
www.adecco.com
This international recruitment agency has more than 5000 offices in 62 countries and specialises in temporary and permanent jobs in business, education, engineering, health and construction.

Drake Employment
www.drakeintl.com
Drake Employment has offices in Australia, Canada, Hong Kong, Malaysia, New Zealand, Singapore, South Africa, Switzerland, the UK and the USA, and covers most professions.

Hays Personnel
www.hays-ap.co.uk
Leading recruitment agency, specialising in office, IT, education, engineering and construction jobs. Has offices in Australia, Canada, Europe and the UK. You can register and do a virtual interview over the web.

Kelly Services
www.kellyservices.com
The original temp agency, Kelly has offices in the UK, Europe, the US, Canada, Asia, Australia and New Zealand. There are temporary and permanent office jobs, as well as jobs in areas such as science, engineering, IT, law and education around the world.

Manpower Services
www.manpower.com
This huge international agency specialises in office work, particularly administration and secretarial jobs, and offers temporary and permanent jobs. It has offices in Asia, Australia and New Zealand, Canada, Europe, Latin America, the UK and the USA.

Monster
www.monster.com
This truly global company has offices almost everywhere, including the UK, the US, Canada, Australia, New Zealand, most European countries and most of Asia. You can register, create a digital CV and contact job experts on the website. Many leading companies get all their temporary and permanent staff through Monster. See the link http://workabroad.monster.com for excellent information on working abroad.

Reed Executive
www.reed.co.uk
This is another recruitment multinational, with hundreds of offices in the UK, Europe, Canada, South Africa, Australia and New Zealand. It specialises in both temporary and permanent office and engineering/construction jobs.

TMP/Hudson Global Resources
www.hudsonresourcing.com
TMP/Hudson has 101 offices in 28 different countries and offers mainly permanent and contract jobs. Staff can provide visa advice and conduct interviews on behalf of overseas companies.

WORK PLACEMENTS
Placements in Europe
Adelante Abroad
LLC, 601 Taper Drive, Seal Beach, CA 90740, USA
☎ +1 562-799 9133
fax +1 562-684 4682
info@adelanteabroad.com
www.adelanteabroad.com
Adelante offers a variety of unpaid internships and volunteer placements for Americans in Spain, France and Central America. Placements can be arranged in most professions and Adelante provides accommodation in shared apartments, lessons in the local language and an orientation on arrival.
Timing & Length of Placements: One to 12 months, depending on the destination. Most placements start at the beginning of any month.
Destinations: Spain, France, Costa Rica & Mexico.
Costs/Pay: Internships are mostly unpaid and program fees vary with the destination – placements in Madrid start at US$1995 for one month, including accommodation. Flights and insurance are extra.
Eligibility: No official age range but most interns are aged 20 to 30. Programs are open to native English speakers, including Americans and Australian, British, Canadian, Irish and New Zealand citizens.

Association for International Practical Training (AIPT)
10400 Little Patuxent Parkway, Suite 250, Columbia, Maryland 21044–3519, USA
☎ +1 410-997 2200
fax +1 410-992 3924
aipt@aipt.org
www.aipt.org
AIPT has more than 50 years experience of arranging international training exchanges for professionals from the USA and Europe. You can either find your own placement or take a prearranged work placement in your professional field, and AIPT will sponsor your visa and work permit.
Timing & Length of Placements: Three to 18 months (one year for placements outside the US), beginning at any time.
Destinations: Americans can work in Austria, Finland, France, Germany, Switzerland, the UK & Malaysia. International participants who are eligible for a J-1 visa can work in the US.
Costs/Pay: Work placements must be paid and program fees for US participants are US$250 ($400 in France). Visitors to the US pay US$1000 for up to six months and US$2000 for six to 18 months. Some scholarships are available.
Eligibility: US participants should be aged 18 to 30 with a university degree or a year of relevant work experience. Visitors to the US must be 18 or older and have a degree or at least two years of professional training or work experience.

European Commission
Traineeships Office, B100 1/7, European Commission,
B-1049 Brussels, Belgium
☎ +32 (0)2-29 911 11
Email using the form on their website.
http://europa.eu.int/comm/stages
The European Commission is the largest *stage*-offering organisation in Europe and about 625 admin-type placements are offered every year. Applicants should apply to be included in the so-called Blue Book and you should then lobby the department you want to work for. There is a similar scheme for translators – see the website for details.
Timing & Length of Placements: Five months from March (apply by 1 September) or October (apply by 1 March).
Destinations: Brussels & Luxembourg.
Costs/Pay: *Stagiaires* receive a monthly stipend of around £500.
Eligibility: Maximum age is 30 and candidates need a first or second-class honours degree and must be fluent in one European language and competent in another.

European Parliament
Traineeship Office, KAD Bldg, Office 2C007, European Parliament, L- 2929 Luxembourg
☎ +32 (0)2-284 2111
fax +352 4300 248 82
stages@europarl.eu.int
translationtraineeships@europarl.eu.int (for translation traineeships)
www.europarl.eu.int/stages
The European Parliament offers a variety of paid traineeships at its Luxembourg headquarters, but competition for positions is tough and applicants must demonstrate a strong interest in European politics. There is a special recruitment process for translators.
Timing & Length of Placements: Five months from February (apply by 15 October) or September (apply by 15 May).
Destinations: Luxembourg & Brussels.
Costs/Pay: Paid interns earn upwards of £600 per month and are reimbursed for costs of travel to the internship.
Eligibility: Age range is 18 to 45 and you must be a citizen of an EU country, a university graduate and fluent in one European community language and competent in another.

General Secretariat of the Council of the EU
Traineeships Office, Rue de la Loi, 175B-1048 Brussels, Belgium
☎ +32 (0)2-28 561 11
fax +32 (0)2-28 573 97/81
stages@consilium.eu.int
http://ue.eu.int/trainee
The general secretariat of the Council of Ministers offers around 75 *stages* a year for politically minded graduates with relevant skills. The work mainly involves attending meetings and preparing reports for ministers.

Timing & Length of Placements: Three to four months. Apply by 1 September the year before you want to start.

Destinations: Brussels.

Costs/Pay: *Stagiaires* earn a monthly stipend of around £500.

Eligibility: Maximum age is 30; you must be an EU citizen and a graduate and speak two EU languages. Relevant academic and work experience would be beneficial.

Office of the UN High Commissioner for Human Rights

Palais des Nations, CH-1211 Geneva 10, Switzerland
☎ +41 (0)22-917 9000
fax +41 (0)22-917 9024
personnel@ohchr.org
www.unhchr.ch

The UN human rights department has 24 unpaid internships each year for people with a degree in a subject that relates to the work of the UN – eg international law, politics, history or social sciences.

Timing & Length of Placements: Three to six months. Apply from May for positions beginning in July and October, or from November for positions beginning in January and April.

Destinations: Switzerland.

Costs: Interns are unpaid and fund their own travel.

Eligibility: Participants must have a relevant degree and speak two of the following languages: English, French, Spanish, Arabic, Russian & Chinese. Human rights experience is useful.

Placements in the USA & Canada
Alliance Abroad Group

1221 South Mopac Expressway, Suite 250, Austin, TX 78746, USA
☎ +1 512-457 8062
fax +1 512-457 8132
Email using the form on their website.
www.alliancesabroad.com

Alliance Abroad sponsors English-speaking graduates on work placements in the USA on a J-1 visa. You can either take an all-inclusive option where Alliance Abroad finds you a placement, or find a placement yourself and just apply for J-1 sponsorship. Alliance has good links in the hospitality, business and finance, sales and marketing and IT fields.

Timing & Length of Placements: Six- to 18-month projects run throughout the year.

Destinations: The USA.

Costs/Pay: Most work placements are paying positions. Fees start at US$1990 for six months, including insurance ($1505 if you find your own placement).

Eligibility: Age range is 21 to 30 and you must be a university graduate or have one year of industry experience in a relevant field.

Bunac (British Universities North America Club)

16 Bowling Green Lane, London, EC1R 0QH, UK
☎ +44 (0)20 7251 3472
fax +44 (0)20 7251 0215
enquiries@bunac.org.uk
www.bunac.org.uk

As well as working holidays, Bunac offers a well-organised work placement scheme in the USA. You must find your own internship in the USA, and then you and the host company must provide paperwork for the application for a work permit and J-1 visa.

Timing & Length of Placements: Three to 18 months, starting at any time.

Destinations: The USA.

Costs/Pay: You can take paid or unpaid work placements/internships. The fee varies from £334 for three months to £881 for 18 months, which includes insurance. The is also a visa fee of around US$195. You need to provide evidence of US$1300 per month in funds, either as savings or wages from the placement.

Eligibility: Minimum age is 19. UK and Irish citizens only.

CCUSA

218 Great Portland St, London, W1W 5QP, UK
☎ +44 (0)20 8688 9051
fax +44 (0)20 8680 4539
info@ccusa.co.uk
www.ccusa.com

As well as working holidays and educational exchanges, CCUSA offers a Practical Training in the USA program for British citizens to take paid or unpaid training placements on a J-1 visa. You can arrange an internship yourself but it must be in the field of management, finance, commerce or business and meet the standard J-1 requirements. There is also an intern program in Brazil – contact CCUSA for details.

Timing & Length of Placements: One year, starting at any time.

Destinations: The USA.

Costs/Pay: Placements can be paid or unpaid and the program fee is £875, which includes flights, insurance and visas.

Eligibility: Minimum age is 20 and you must be a graduate or have two years' relevant professional training or work experience, plus fluent English.

CDS International

871 United Nations Plaza, New York, NY 10017–1814, USA
☎ +1 212-497 3500
fax +1 212-497 3535
info@cdsintl.org
www.cdsintl.org

CDS offers a Professional Development program in the USA based on the J-1 visa. You can take a trainee job in management, business, commerce, finance, the arts, cultural

sciences, architecture, mathematics or industry. There are also work placement and internship programs for American students in Europe and Russia – see the website for details.
Timing & Length of Placements: Placements in the USA last three to 18 months, starting monthly.
Destinations: The USA (work placements for Americans are mostly in Germany & Russia).
Costs: Visitors to the US pay a program fee of US$1100 (US$750 for four months or less) and cover their flights and health insurance.
Eligibility: Age range is 21 to 35. You must have a degree or at least two years' higher education in a relevant field, plus one year of workplace experience.

Council Exchanges/CIEE
52 Poland St, London W1F 7AB, UK
☎ +44 (0)20 7478 2020
fax +44 (0)20 7734 7322
infoUK@councilexchanges.org.uk
www.councilexchanges.co.uk
www.ciee.org (for US participants)
CIEE offers a Professional Career Training (ie work placement) program in the USA for British participants. The scheme works on a J-1 visa and you can either find your own placement or use the extensive ATLAS jobs database – see the website for details of suitable work placements.
Timing & Length of Placements: Three to 18 months.
Destinations: The USA.
Costs/Pay: Program fees start at £350 and you must pay for visa fees and flights. Work placements may be paid or unpaid. You must provide evidence of US$750 a month in funds, either as wages from the internships or as savings.
Eligibility: Age range is 20 to 40. A certificate from a professional or academic course lasting two years, or relevant work experience, is required, as is English fluency.

InterExchange
161 Sixth Ave, New York, NY 10013, USA
☎ +1 212-924 0446
fax +1 212-924 0575
training@interexchange.org
www.interexchange.org
InterExchange sponsors people on training placements in the USA on the J-1 visa scheme and you can either find your own internship or take a prearranged placement. There are also work programs for Americans around the world – see the website for details.
Timing & Length of Placements: Six, 12 or 18 months.
Destinations: The USA & worldwide.
Costs/Pay: Most internships are paid and the program fee starts at US$425 for six months. Flights and compulsory insurance are extra.
Eligibility: Age range is 20 to 38 and you must be a graduate or have relevant professional training or experience.

International Exchange Centre (IEC)
89 Fleet St, London EC4Y 1DH, UK
☎ +44 (0)20 7583 9116
fax +44 (0)20 7583 9117
isecinfo@btconnect.com
www.isecworld.co.uk
IEC offers various work overseas programs, including an internship in the USA, based on a J-1 visa. You can either find your own placement or accept a placement from IEC for an extra fee – most people work in business, economics or IT.
Timing & Length of Placements: Six to 18 months. Arranged placements start in June or December (apply by 5 February or 5 August).
Destinations: The USA.
Costs/Pay: Fees start from £520 for six months (£1190 if you take a prearranged placement) including insurance. Accommodation, visa fees and flights are extra.
Eligibility: Age range is 20 to 38 and you must pass the professional criteria for a J-1 visa.

International Exchange Programmes (IEP)
Level 3, 362 La Trobe St, Melbourne, Victoria 3000, Australia
☎ +61 (0)3-9329 3866
fax +61 (0)3-9329 1592
info@iep.org.au
www.iep.org.au
As well as working holidays, IEP can sponsor Australians and New Zealanders on paid internships in the USA as part of the J-1 visa scheme. You must find your own internship and IEP will then help arrange the visa and work permit.
Timing & Length of Placements: Three to 18 months, starting at any time.
Destinations: The USA.
Costs/Pay: Internships may be paid or unpaid and the program fees start at A$827 for three months, including insurance.
Eligibility: Must be 19 or over and meet the standard conditions for a J-1 visa.

Mountbatten Internship Programme
5th floor, Abbey House, 74–76 St John St, London EC1M 4DZ, UK
☎ +44 (0)20 7253 7759
fax +44 (0)20 7831 7018
info-uk@mountbatten.org
www.mountbatten.org
This joint British-American enterprise places British graduates and professionals in New York and American graduates and professionals in London. Placements are in admin-type roles in large corporations and participants also study for a Certificate in International Business Practice.
Timing & Length of Placements: One year, from September (apply by 15 March), January (apply by 31 July)

and May (apply by 31 October). Programs in London run in September and March.

Destinations: London & New York.

Costs/Pay: The fee is £1745, which includes insurance but not flights. Interns get a living allowance of US$443 every two weeks, with a US$500 bonus on completion, and accommodation is provided.

Eligibility: Age range is 21 to 28. You must have a university degree plus work experience (or high-school education and work experience), be able to type 45 words per minute and use common computing packages. Most applicants are UK or US citizens, but Australians, New Zealanders, South Africans and Europeans can participate in the USA.

USIT

19–21 Aston Quay, O'Connell Bridge, Dublin 2, Ireland
☎ +353 (0)1-602 1600, 0818 200020
fax +353 (0)1-679 2124
Refer to the website in the first instance.
travelclub@usit.ie
www.usit.ie

As well as working holidays, USIT administers the Internship USA program for Irish citizens. You must find your own internship in the USA, but USIT will sponsor you for a J-1 visa.

Timing & Length of Placements: Internships last up to a maximum of 18 months.

Destinations: The USA.

Costs/Pay: Internships can be paid or unpaid and costs vary with the duration of the internship – a two-month position costs €489, while an 18-month placement costs €1319. Flights and compulsory health insurance are extra. You must also produce evidence of support funds equivalent to US$750 per month of the internship.

Eligibility: Age range is 18 to 40 and you must be a university graduate or have at least two years of professional training, plus relevant skills and experience.

The Work & Travel Company

45 High St, Tunbridge Wells, Kent TN1 1XL, UK
☎ +44 (0)1892 516164
fax +44 (0)1892 523172
info@worktravelcompany.co.uk
www.worktravelcompany.co.uk

As well as arranging working holidays, the Work & Travel Company can sponsor you on a J-1 visa if you arrange your own training placement in the USA. There are also special work programs for qualified arborists and equestrians – two professions in great demand in the USA.

Timing & Length of Placements: Up to 18 months – apply at least two months in advance.

Destinations: The USA.

Costs/Pay: Most positions are paid, and fees for general internships start from around £500 – visas and compulsory insurance are extra. Equestrians pay £765 including visas and insurance, and arborists just pay for insurance.

Eligibility: You must have a degree or appropriate professional qualifications and some workplace experience. Arborists and equestrians need industry-recognised qualifications and must be aged 18 to 38.

Placements in Australia & New Zealand
AustraLearn

12050 N Pecos St, Suite 320, Westminster, CO 80234, USA
☎ +1 303-446 2214
fax +1 303-446 5955
studyabroad@australearn.org
www.australearn.org

Australearn operates a custom internships program where North Americans can work on an unpaid work placement in Australia. You provide a description of the kind of internship you are looking for and staff match you to a placement.

Timing & Length of Placements: Six weeks to one year, starting at any time.

Destinations: Australia.

Costs/Pay: Placements are unpaid and program costs vary depending on how long you stay – an eight-week placement costs US$3290, plus a US$100 registration fee, which includes meals and accommodation.

Eligibility: Minimum age is 18 and you must be a US or Canadian citizen and a graduate.

International Student Placement Centre (ISPC)

Suite 804, Level 8, 32 York St, Sydney, NSW 2000, Australia
☎ +61 (0)2-9279 0100
fax +61 (0)2-9279 1028
info@ispc.com.au
www.ispc.com.au

This Australian organisation offers work placements with more than 1000 Australian companies for recent graduates and professionals. ISPC also runs reciprocal programs for Australians seeking work placements overseas.

Timing & Length of Placements: From one week to one year, starting at any time.

Destinations: Australia.

Costs/Pay: Most internships are unpaid, though some provide a living allowance. The fee for applicants ranges from A$1100 for one to six weeks to A$2500 for a year, not including flights, insurance or visa fees.

Eligibility: Minimum age is 16. Most nationalities are accepted providing you can get the appropriate visa (normally a working holiday visa).

Internships Australia

Level 3, 80 Stamford Rd, Indooroopilly, Qld 4068, Australia
☎ +61 (0)7-3720 2244
fax +61 (0)7-3720 2255
info@internships.com.au
www.internships.com.au

Australia's largest internship sponsoring organisation, Internships Australia provides unpaid work placements in most business fields. Placements are arranged to suit your area of expertise and there are also reciprocal programs for Australians seeking work placements overseas.

Timing & Length of Placements: One week to one year, starting at any time.

Destinations: Australia.

Costs/Pay: Most placements are unpaid, but some give a stipend for living expenses. Fees for participation range from A$1390 for up to six weeks to A$3200 for a year, not including flights, insurance or visa fees.

Eligibility: Open to most nationalities but you must provide evidence of your academic qualifications, full travel insurance and proof of sufficient funds to support yourself.

WORKING HOLIDAYS & SEASONAL WORK

Alliance Abroad Group

See p190 for contact details.

As well as internship schemes in the USA, Alliance offers a work program based on the H-2B seasonal work visa. A guaranteed seasonal job is provided – mostly at theme parks, hotels and ski resorts. You'll be matched to a position when you apply and you can extend the program after you arrive.

Timing & Length of Programs: Maximum duration 10 months (most programs last five to six months), usually over the summer or winter. There are also work programs in the UK for Canadians and a four-month work/travel program in Australia for US citizens.

Destinations: The USA.

Costs/Pay: Workers are paid the going rate for the job, and the program fees range from US$575 to US$775, including visa fees and processing. You must also pay for flights and compulsory health insurance of US$150.

Eligibility: Age range is 18 to 40 (must be over 21 for some programs). To qualify you must be able to prove that you have strong ties to your home country and have relevant skills for the job.

Bunac (British Universities North America Club)

See p190 for contact details.

Bunac is the largest sponsor for British citizens on educational exchanges in the USA and Canada. Most programs are for students, but non-students can apply for the working holiday program in Canada. Bunac can also make arrangements for working holiday visas for Australia and New Zealand.

Timing & Length of Programs: Eight weeks to one year for the Canada program, starting any time.

Destinations: Canada.

Costs/Pay: You can do almost any paid job in Canada. The application fee is £153, which includes Bunac membership, and you must take out insurance for the duration of your stay. The minimum personal funds requirement is C$1000.

Eligibility: Age range is 18 to 35. You must be a UK or Irish citizen.

CCUSA

See p190 for contact details.

As well as educational exchanges around the world, CCUSA can arrange working holiday visas in Australia and New Zealand. US citizens can work for four months in Australia or up to a year in New Zealand.

Timing & Length of Programs: One year (four months for US citizens).

Destinations: Australia & New Zealand.

Costs/Pay: Americans pay US$680 to go to Australia or New Zealand. People leaving the UK pay £415, which includes six months' insurance, reception and overnight accommodation on arrival, job hunting and travel support and mail forwarding.

Eligibility: Working holiday visa restrictions apply.

Council Exchanges/CIEE

See p191 for contact details.

Known as Council Exchanges in the UK and CIEE (Council on International Educational Exchange) in the US, this joint British-American organisation offers a variety of educational exchanges and working holiday programs. There are working holiday programs in Australia and New Zealand (just Australia for American citizens).

Timing & Length of Programs: Americans can work in Australia for four months while other eligible nationalities can work for a year in Australia and New Zealand.

Destinations: Australia & New Zealand.

Costs/Pay: Fees vary with the program – Americans visiting Australia pay US$500 while other nationalities pay from £320.

Eligibility: Age range is 18 to 30 and you must be eligible for a working holiday visa.

International Exchange Centre (IEC)

See p191 for contact details.

IEC sponsors international work exchanges around the world, including specialist agricultural programs in Denmark, Norway and Finland and internships for agricultural students in the USA.

Timing & Length of Programs: Most programs last around three months, but placements in the USA, New Zealand and Finland can last for up to one year.

Destinations: The USA, New Zealand, Denmark, Norway & Finland.

Costs/Pay: Wages vary with the job and fees vary with the program – European programs start at £150 while American and New Zealand programs cost from £450 to £965.

Eligibility: Minimum age is 18. Some programs are restricted to people under 30, and for agriculture programs in the USA or New Zealand you need a minimum of two years' professional agricultural experience.

International Exchange Programmes (IEP)

See p191 for contact details.

The Aussie partner of Bunac, IEP offers a variety of working holiday programs for Australians and New Zealanders overseas. The working holiday programs in the UK and Canada are suitable for career-breakers and include visa assistance, job-hunting support, an orientation and a free guidebook.

Timing & Length of Programs: You can work for two years in the UK and one year in Canada.

Destinations: The UK & Canada.

Costs/Pay: Work Britain costs A$250 (A$450 with the first three nights' accommodation); Work Canada costs A$119 (A$385 with extra support and accommodation on arrival). You can do most paid jobs when you arrive.

Eligibility: For the British program, you should be aged 17 to 30 and a Commonwealth citizen. For the Canadian program the age range is 18 to 30 and you must pass the eligibility restrictions for the Canada working holiday visa.

Japan Association of Working Holiday Makers (JAWHM)

Sunplaza 7F, 4-1-1 Nakano, Nakano-ku, Tokyo 164, Japan
☎ +81 (0)3-3389 0181
fax +81 (0)3-3389 1563
www.jawhm.or.jp

JAWHM acts as a support service and employment agency for people visiting Japan on the working holiday-maker scheme. There are offices in Tokyo, Osaka and Kyushu (details are on the website); you can visit in person with your passport and two passport photos to register and then apply for positions on their jobs list (most jobs last at least three months).

USIT

See p192 for contact details.

USIT is Ireland's leading student travel company and it offers working holiday programs in Australia and New Zealand, plus a Work Canada program for Irish citizens that lets you work in almost any job in Canada for up to a year.

Timing & Length of Programs: Maximum duration of one year, starting at any time.

Destinations: Canada, Australia & New Zealand.

Costs/Pay: You can work in any paid job in Canada except as a camp counsellor and the fee is €299 (or €269 without the optional meet-and-greet package when you arrive in Canada). Flights and insurance are extra and you must provide evidence of C$1000 in funds. See the website for details of the Australian and New Zealand programs.

Eligibility: The Work Canada program is open to non-students aged 18 to 35. Apply at least eight weeks before you want to start.

Visitoz

Springbrook Farm, Goomeri, Qld 4601, Australia
☎ +61 (0)7-4168 6106
fax +61 (0)7-4168 6155

info@visitoz.org
www.visitoz.org

Visitoz arranges work on outback farms for people on working holiday visas in Australia. Training is provided in farm skills such as horse and motorcycle riding and operating a tractor, and then placements are available on 950 rural farms. The work is quite physical, eg mustering cattle, harvesting and planting crops, but you will get a chance to become really involved with rural Australian life.

Timing & Length of Programs: The training course lasts four days, and then you can work for three months at a time at rural farms around the country.

Destinations: Australia.

Costs/Pay: The program fee is A$660 and flights and visas are extra. The price includes pick-up from Brisbane and an orientation at Rainbow Beach before you head inland. Workers earn around £150 a week for the placements.

Eligibility: Age range is 18 to 30 and workers must have a tidy appearance as they stay with rural families.

The Work & Travel Company

See p192 for contact details.

This organisation arranges working holidays in Australia and New Zealand, with the perk of a guaranteed job offer when you arrive – you don't have to take the job, but it's handy if you need to start work right away for financial reasons.

Timing & Length of Programs: One year, starting at any time.

Destinations: Australia & New Zealand.

Costs/Pay: You can take almost any paid job on arrival; fees start from £99, which includes the cost of the working holiday visa, support, an orientation and a guaranteed job offer.

Eligibility: Age range is 18 to 30 and you must be eligible for the appropriate working holiday visa.

Youth Today

4th floor, 1200 17th St NW, Washington, DC, 20036, USA
☎ +1 202-785 0764
practicaltraining@youthtoday.org.
www.youthtoday.org/aywc

This American youth organisation offers a Practical Training program for social workers from overseas to come and work in the USA; in exchange, American social workers get to work in Europe, the Caribbean and Asia. Workers visiting the USA are placed at youth centres, drug rehabilitation facilities, shelters etc, mainly in the northeast of the country.

Timing & Length of Programs: Programs in the USA last 18 months – outbound programs vary with the destination.

Destinations: The USA. American participants have previously worked in Australia, Bangladesh, France, Israel, Italy, Jamaica, Japan, Romania, Spain & the UK.

Costs/Pay: All workers receive a local salary. Visitors to the US pay a US$150 administration fee and cover their own flights and insurance. You must also provide evidence of at least US$2000 in personal funds. Costs for outbound programs vary – see the website for information.

Eligibility: Age range is 22 to 29 and you must have a university degree or other social work training and at least two years' work experience. Most participants are from the UK, Canada or Jamaica.

TEFL/TESOL COURSES
Europe
Bell Language School

Hillscross, 1 Red Cross Lane, Cambridge CB2 2QX, UK
☎ +44 (0)1223 212333
fax +44 (0)1223 410282
info@bell-centres.com
www.bell-centres.com

This UK-based school runs CELTA programs in Cambridge and Norwich and DELTA courses in Saffron Walden and Norwich. Bell has affiliated-English language schools in Spain, Switzerland, Poland, the Czech Republic, Bulgaria, Latvia, Malta, Thailand and China, so there are often employment opportunities once you are qualified.

Types of Course: CELTA and DELTA
Timing & Length of Courses: Four weeks for CELTA, nine to 10 weeks for DELTA, starting on set dates monthly (twice a year for DELTA, in March and September).
Destinations: The UK.
Costs: The CELTA course costs start at £952, plus an £85 candidate entry fee. DELTA courses cost from £1670 to £1795, plus a £200 candidate entry fee. Accommodation can be arranged.
Eligibility: Minimum age is 20 and you must have academic qualifications up to university entry level.

Cactus Language

4 Clarence House, 30–31 North St, Brighton, East Sussex BN1 1EB, UK
☎ +44 (0)845 130 4775
fax +44 (0)1273 775686
enquiry@cactuslanguage.com
www.cactusteachers.com

This international language agency acts as an admissions service for internationally recognised TEFL/TESOL certificate courses worldwide. See the website for details of dozens of courses in the UK and around the world.

Types of Course: Various accredited TEFL courses.
Timing & Length of Courses: Four or eight weeks.
Destinations: The UK, Ireland, Spain, Portugal, Hungary, Czech Republic, Poland, the USA, Canada, Columbia, Australia, South Africa, Thailand, Egypt & UAE.
Costs: Prices vary depending on the destination and type of course – most courses cost from £650 to £1250.
Eligibility: Minimum age varies from 18 to 21, depending on the course.

Cambridge ESOL

ESOL Examinations, 1 Hills Rd, Cambridge CB1 2EU, UK
☎ +44 (0)1223 553355
fax +44 (0)1223 460278
ESOL.helpdesk@ucles.org.uk
www.cambridge-efl.org

The CELTA and DELTA TEFL certificates are licensed by University of Cambridge ESOL and you can find lots of information about the courses, including a list of approved course providers, on the website.

EF English First

Arthur House, Chorlton St, Manchester M1 3EJ, UK
☎ +44 (0)161 236 7494
fax +44 (0)161 236 0949
manchester@englishfirst.com
www.englishfirst.com

This international English-language school has branches worldwide and offers both TEFL and TESOL courses at two locations in the UK – Manchester and Hove. The TEFL course is uncertified but teachers can take a guaranteed one-year job placement at an EF school overseas on graduation, with flights and accommodation included.

Types of Course: Trinity CertTESOL or the EF TEFL Certificate (equivalent to CELTA).
Timing & Length of Courses: Four weeks for CertTESOL (eight weeks part time), starting monthly.
Destinations: The Trinity course is only available in Manchester, but you can take the TEFL course in Manchester, Brighton, Boston (USA), Toronto (Canada) & Sydney (Australia). Once you complete the course, there are job opportunities in Asia, Latin America, Eastern Europe & the Middle East.
Costs: Vary with the training centre – in Manchester, the EF TEFL course costs £200 and there is the option of a guaranteed job on completion. The CertTESOL course costs £800 (or £500 if you work for EF on completion).
Eligibility: Minimum age is 19 and you must be educated to university entry level.

i-to-i

Woodside House, 261 Low Lane, Leeds, West Yorkshire LS18 5NY, UK
☎ +44 (0)870 787 2375
fax +44 (0)113 242 2171
info@onlinetefl.com
www.onlinetefl.com

This popular year-out organisation offers a popular accredited online introduction to TEFL training course if you can't get to a training centre. Training is conducted using the Internet and an interactive CD and you don't have to join a volunteering project to take the course.

Type of Course: Online TEFL.
Timing & Length of Courses: Courses last 40 or 60 hours and you can work to your own timetable.

Destinations: Online.

Costs: The 40/60-hour courses cost £195/230.

Eligibility: The course is open to native English-speakers aged 17 or older, including Brits, Americans, Canadians, Australians, New Zealanders and English-fluent Europeans.

Inlingua International

Rodney Lodge, Rodney Rd, Cheltenham, Gloucestershire GL50 1HX, UK

☎ +44 (0)1242 250493

fax +44 (0)1242 253181

training@inlingua-cheltenham.co.uk

www.inlingua-cheltenham.co.uk

This international language organisation can arrange work at 300 member schools worldwide and offers TESOL training at its UK centre in Cheltenham, with an optional one-week business English course.

Type of Course: Trinity CertTESOL and LCTL DipTESOL.

Timing & Length of Courses: Five weeks for CertTESOL, starting monthly; 12 weeks for LCTL DipTESOL, starting twice a year in April and September.

Destinations: Cheltenham (UK).

Costs: CertTESOL costs £995, LCTL DipTESOL costs £1300 and the business English course costs £248 if you book with the CertTESOL course.

Eligibility: The usual TESOL requirements apply – you need university entry level qualifications for CertTESOL and previous ELT experience for LCTL DipTESOL.

International House London

106 Piccadilly, London W1J 7NL, UK

☎ +44 (0)20 7518 6999

fax +44 (0)20 7518 6998

info@ihlondon.co.uk

www.ihlondon.co.uk

This leading language institute offers a variety of teacher training courses, including full- and part-time courses in CELTA and DELTA. There are also Language Teaching to Adults (LTA) certificates for teachers of French, German, Italian and Spanish. International House has training centres in Germany, Italy, Spain, Portugal, Poland, the Czech Republic, Lithuania, Hungary, Egypt, Russia, USA, Mexico, Uruguay, South Africa and Australia – see the website www.ihworld.com

Type of Course: Various TEFL courses, and LTA courses in European languages.

Timing & Length of Courses: CELTA and IH TEFL courses last four weeks, DELTA courses last eight weeks and LTA courses last four or eight weeks.

Destinations: London (UK).

Costs: Vary with the course. CELTA courses cost £1110, DELTA courses cost £1885 and four/eight week LTA courses cost £1025/1230. Once you finish the course, you can find paying jobs with International House schools worldwide.

Eligibility: Minimum age is 21 (18 for CELTA and IH TEFL courses) and you must be a native speaker or completely fluent in the appropriate language. Teaching qualifications and two years' experience are required for the DELTA course.

Language Link

181 Earl's Court Rd, London SW5 9RB, UK

☎ +44 (0)20 7370 4755

fax +44 (0)20 7370 1123

teachertraining@languagelink.co.uk

www.languagelink.co.uk

Language Link has 30 years' experience in English-language teaching and it offers the CELTA and DELTA courses in London, and CELTA training in Beijing and Hanoi. On completion, teachers can apply for placements at 50 schools in Russia, China, Poland, the Czech Republic, Slovakia and Vietnam.

Type of Course: CELTA and DELTA.

Timing & Length of Courses: The standard CELTA course lasts four weeks and starts monthly, while the DELTA course last 17 weeks and runs twice a year, in January and July.

Destinations: The UK (training is also available in Beijing & Hanoi).

Costs: The full-time CELTA course is £695; DELTA is £1300.

Eligibility: Minimum age is 20 and you should be a university graduate (for DELTA, you need a TEFL certificate and two years' teaching experience).

Saxoncourt UK

59 South Molton St, London W1K 5SN, UK

☎ +44 (0)20 7499 8533

fax +44 (0)20 7499 9374

tt@saxoncourt.com

www.saxoncourt.com

Saxoncourt has teacher-training centres in London, Calgary, Auckland, Cape Town and Honolulu which offer CELTA, DELTA and Trinity TESOL certificates and recruit for private schools in 20 countries worldwide.

Type of Course: CELTA and DELTA, plus Trinity CertTESOL and LTCL TESOL.

Timing & Length of Courses: Varies with the course – the four-week CELTA course involves 100 training hours and six classroom hours. London courses start on set dates monthly.

Destinations: Training centres in the UK, the USA, Canada, South Africa & New Zealand; teaching placements worldwide.

Costs: Vary with the training centre – CELTA courses in the UK cost £695.

Eligibility: Minimum age is 18 (20 in South Africa and Hawaii) and you must have education to university entry level. DELTA and LTCL TESOL are reserved for people with English-teaching experience.

Trinity College London

89 Albert Embankment, London SE1 7TP, UK

☎ +44 (0)20 7820 6100

fax +44 (0)20 7820 6161

info@trinitycollege.co.uk
trinitycollege.co.uk
Trinity licenses TESOL certificates in the UK and you can find detailed information on the CertTESOL and Trinity Licentiate Diploma (LTCL TESOL) certificates on the website, including a database of approved course providers worldwide.

Via Lingua
FAO Steven Koehler, Via Lingua EPE, K Hiotaki 7, Hania 73134, Crete, Greece
☎ +30 28210 55577
info@vialingua.org
www.vialingua.org
This large international ESL teacher training school offers a TEFL certificate course in 10 European countries across Europe and job-hunting assistance on completion. There are booking offices in the UK and the USA (see the website for details).
Type of Course: International TEFL Certificate.
Timing & Length of Courses: Four weeks, with 120 hours' tuition and 10 hours' teaching practice. Dates vary with the location – see the website.
Destinations: Berlin (Germany); Corinth (Greece) & Crete; Rome, Florence & Milan (Italy); Granada & Porto (Spain); Budapest (Hungary); Prague (Czech Republic); St Petersburg (Russia); Istanbul (Turkey) & Guadalajara (Mexico).
Costs: Vary with the location – in Crete, the course costs €1325, plus €250 for accommodation.
Eligibility: Minimum age is 20; you must be fluent in English and educated to university entry level.

Windsor TEFL
21 Osborne Rd, Windsor, Berkshire SL4 3EG, UK
☎ +44 (0)1753 858995
fax +44 (0)1753 831726
info@windsorschools.co.uk
www.windsorschools.co.uk
This UK-based training centre offers the chance to study for an accredited TESOL certificate in the UK, Spain or the Czech Republic.
Type of Course: Trinity CertTESOL.
Timing & Length of Courses: One month, beginning on set dates monthly (see the website for details).
Destinations: London, Windsor & Oxford (UK); Barcelona & Madrid (Spain); Prague (Czech Republic).
Costs: UK courses cost £799, plus £99 for moderation by Trinity College. Courses in mainland Europe cost £699 plus £169. Accommodation can be arranged for an extra cost.
Eligibility: Minimum age is 18 and you must have two A levels or equivalent (eg matriculation in the USA).

North America
Boston Language Institute
648 Beacon St, Boston, MA 02215, USA
☎ +1 617-262 3500 ext 228
fax +1 617-262 3595

tefl@boslang.com
www.teflcertificate.com
The TEFL course at Boston is not Trinity- or Cambridge-licensed, but lifetime job assistance is provided and the school acts as an agency for teaching jobs overseas.
Types of Course: TEFL certificate courses for native and non-native English-speakers.
Timing & Length of Courses: The standard 120-hour TEFL course lasts four weeks and runs monthly. Four-week TEFL certificate programs for non-native speakers are offered twice a year, in January and August.
Destinations: Boston (USA).
Costs: Programs cost US$2495, including materials.
Eligibility: No degree is required, but former college students are preferred.

Ontesol.com
14 Prince Arthur Ave, Suite 101, Toronto M5R 1A9, Ontario, Canada
☎ +1 416-929 0227
fax +1 416-929 9464
contact@ontesol.com
www.ontesol.com
This Canadian program offers an online TESOL training course, approved by TESL Canada. You can either complete just the online training part of the course, or add on practical classroom training at Ontesol centres in Canada and Argentina to gain a full TESOL certificate.
Types of Course: Online TESOL certificate.
Timing & Length of Courses: 200 hours of online training – you set your own learning schedule.
Destinations: Worldwide.
Costs: The full TESOL course costs US$1000, plus US$500 for the optional 20-hour practical teaching sessions (available in Toronto and Buenos Aires). Practical training will soon be available in Korea, Japan, China, Brazil, Taiwan and Europe.
Eligibility: Minimum age is 21 and you should ideally be a graduate.

St Giles Language Teaching Center
One Hallidie Plaza, Suite 350, San Francisco, CA 94102, USA
☎ +1 415-788 3552
fax +1 415-788 1923
training@stgiles-usa.com
www.stgiles-usa.com
This San Francisco centre was the first place in the USA to offer the Cambridge CELTA TEFL certificate. You can use the course as an academic credit towards a TESOL master's degree.
Types of Course: CELTA.
Timing & Length of Courses: Four weeks, starting monthly.
Destinations: San Francisco (USA).
Costs: Courses cost US$2720 (US$2420 from March to April).
Eligibility: Applicants need to be educated to university entry level and be aged 20 or older.

Teachers of English to Speakers of Other Languages (TESOL)
700 S Washington St, Suite 200, Alexandria, VA 22314, USA
☎ +1 703-836 0774
fax +1 703-836 7864/6447
info@tesol.org
www.tesol.org
This professional association of ESL teachers and trainers is the world's leading authority on TESOL and it provides information on English-language teaching in the US and worldwide. The TESOL Job Finder lets you post your CV online and search for TESOL jobs worldwide.

Australia, New Zealand & Asia
Australian TESOL Training Centre (ATTC)
Level 18, Plaza Tower 1, 500 Oxford St, Bondi Junction, Sydney, NSW 2022, Australia
☎ +61 (0)2-9389 0249
fax +61 (0)2-9389 6880
lynnev@ace.edu.au
www.attc.nsw.edu.au
This Australian teacher-training centre offers Cambridge ESOL approved TEFL qualifications and a specialist TESOL qualification for people whose native language is not English.
Types of Course: CELTA, DELTA and ATTC TESOL (equivalent to Trinity CertTESOL).
Timing & Length of Courses: CELTA courses last four weeks, beginning monthly. DELTA courses last nine weeks and run once a year and the TESOL course consists of two five-week modules – contact ATTC for start dates.
Destinations: Sydney (Australia).
Costs/Pay: Program costs are A$2550 for CELTA, A$4200 for DELTA and A$2600 in total for the TESOL certificate.
Eligibility: Minimum age is 18 and you must have a degree or tertiary education (previous teaching experience required for DELTA).

Teach International
Level 2, 30 Herschel St, Brisbane, Qld 4000, Australia
☎ +61 (0)7-3211 4633
fax +61 (0)7-3211 4644
simone@staff.teachinternational.com
www.teachinternational.com
Offering TESOL diplomas and certificates accredited by the Australian Council of TESOL Associations (ACTA), this course is mainly online. The organisation guarantees jobs upon graduation if you meet the relevant citizenship conditions.
Type of Course: TESOL certificate.
Timing & Length of Courses: 120 hours, including 40 hours in class over a period of five days and 60 hours' online training.
Destinations: Australia & New Zealand.
Costs: The course costs A$1595, including GST.
Eligibility: Minimum age is 19 and you must be a native English-speaker and high-school graduate.

ValueEdge Consulting
Suite 201, 158 City Rd, Southbank, Victoria 3205, Australia
☎ +61 (0)3-9690 4550
fax +61 (0)3-9690 4655
value@valuedge.com.au
www.valuedge.com.au
This Australian management consultancy offers a specialist TESOL course for busy professionals who want to teach English overseas. The qualification is accredited by the Australian Council of TESOL Associations (ACTA; www.tesol.org.au).
Type of Course: Introductory TESOL certificate.
Timing & Length of Courses: There is a self-paced instruction and reading program, followed by a five-day intensive course taught on weekends or Friday evenings.
Destinations: Melbourne & locations around Australia.
Costs: A$1300 (plus GST).
Eligibility: Native English-speakers and tertiary qualifications are preferred.

TEACHING AGENCIES
The following agencies sponsor and place qualified and unqualified teachers but do not offer TEFL or TESOL training.

Berlitz
Lincoln House, 296–302 High Holborn, London WC1 7JH, UK
☎ +44 (0)20 7611 9640
fax +44 (0)20 7611 9656
Email using the form on www.berlitz.co.uk
http://careers.berlitz.com
Berlitz is a huge international ELT employer and has more that 400 schools worldwide – use the online search engine to see where you are eligible to work. There are also teaching opportunities for fluent speakers of other European languages (particularly French and German).
Timing & Length of Work: Minimum of one year.
Destinations: Worldwide.
Costs/Pay: Wages vary with the destination.
Eligibility: Minimum age is 21 and you must have a university degree and be a native speaker of the language you want to teach.
TEFL Requirement: Teacher training is provided by Berlitz and you can then work wherever you can obtain a visa.

British Council
10 Spring Gardens, London SW1A 2BN, UK
☎ +44 (0)20 7389 4931
fax +44 (0)20 7389 4140
teacher.vacancies@britishcouncil.org
www.britishcouncil.org/home/learning/teacherrecruitment.htm
The British Council is the largest employer of ESL teachers in the world and it offers opportunities for qualified teachers at language centres worldwide. You can often find work by contacting British Council offices overseas directly, and there are good long-term career prospects within the organisation.

Timing & Length of Work: Most contracts are for two years, but there are also opportunities for part-time teachers on short contracts.
Destinations: Teachers are needed for British Council offices in 110 cities worldwide.
Costs/Pay: Wages vary with the destination but generally reflect the cost of living.
Eligibility: Ideally you should be a graduate with ESL teaching experience.
TEFL Requirement: The preferred requirement for teachers is a TEFL/TESOL diploma and two years' ELT teaching experience, but teachers with a TEFL certificate and two years' experience can study for the diploma qualification part time while they work.

China Education Exchange

Asian Games Garden, Building No 2–6A, No12 Xiaoying Lu, Chao Yang District, Beijing 100101, China
☎ +86 10-8463 4451
fax +86 10-8463 4872
teaching@cbwchina.com, cex@chinaeducationexchange.org
www.chinaeducationexchange.org
This is the only ESL teaching program officially approved by the government of the People's Republic of China. Teachers are recruited from most English-speaking countries and you don't need teaching qualifications to apply.
Timing & Length of Work: Contracts last six months or a year.
Destinations: China.
Costs/Pay: There is an application fee of US$100 and then accommodation, work permits and visas are provided. Wages range from US$300 to US$600 per month and most schools reimburse the cost of your plane ticket at the end of your contract.
Eligibility: Teachers should be native English-speakers from the UK, the USA, Canada, Australia or New Zealand, and a university diploma is preferred.
TEFL Requirement: No TEFL or TESOL certification is required.

China TEFL Network

16th floor, Blue Sky Business Center, 18 Moganshan Rd, Hangzhou, Zhejiang 310005, China
☎ /fax +86 571-8823 4517
helen@chinatefl.com
www.chinatefl.com
This Chinese organisation acts as an agency, linking qualified English-language teachers to schools and universities across China. Around 20,000 teachers find jobs through the site each year. You can post your CV on the jobs-wanted section of the site.
Timing & Length of Work: One or two years.
Destinations: Mainland China
Costs/Pay: There is no charge for job seekers to search the database, and all teaching positions are paid.

Eligibility: Open to teachers of all nationalities.
TEFL Requirement: TEFL or equivalent certification is required.

Cobisec

Lucy's, Lucy's Hill, Hythe, Kent CT21 5ES, UK
☎ /fax +44 (0)1303 260857
recruitment@cobisec.org
www.cobisec.org
Cobisec represents British international schools worldwide that may have vacancies for qualified teachers of national curriculum subjects in English. You must register to access the schools' database and set up an online profile that is made available to schools looking for teachers.
Timing & Length of Work: Varies with the school.
Destinations: Worldwide.
Pay/Costs: All jobs are paid, but rates vary with the school. Registration costs £25 per year.
Eligibility: You should be a native English-speaker with formal teaching qualifications and at least two years' experience.
TEFL Requirement: You need mainstream teaching qualifications but not TEFL or TESOL.

ECC Foreign Language Institute

Sanyamate Building, 7-11-10, Nishi-Shinjuku, Shinjuku-ku, Tokyo 160-0023, Japan
☎ +81 (0)3 5330 1585
fax +81 (0)3 5330 7084
eastjinj@ecc.co.jp
www.japanbound.com
This Japanese organisation runs language schools across Japan and hires large numbers of English teachers from overseas. The website has details of recruitment offices around the world and applications are also accepted from people who are already in Japan.
Timing & Length of Work: Minimum of one year, with the option to renew annually.
Destinations: Japan.
Costs/Pay: Wages are around £1300 per month before tax. Flights, visa fees, accommodation etc are extra.
Eligibility: Minimum requirement is a degree and native English – there are interviewing offices in Canada, the USA, the UK and Australia.
TEFL Requirement: No formal TEFL/TESOL requirement.

International Schools Services

15 Roszel Rd, PO Box 5910, Princeton, NJ 08543, USA
☎ +1 609-452 0990
fax +1 609-452 2690
iss@iss.edu
www.iss.edu
The ISS recruits experienced teachers and administrators to teach English at 200 American international schools worldwide.

Timing & Length of Work: On-site recruiting takes place in February and July. Most schools offer two-year contracts.
Destinations: Worldwide, from Azerbaijan to Zambia.
Pay: Benefits and salaries (US$12,000 to US$20,000) vary considerably, but most teachers save more money than they would while teaching in North America.
Eligibility: The general requirements are an undergraduate degree and two years' teaching experience. Mainstream teacher training is required for some roles.

Japan Exchange & Teaching (JET)

Embassy of Japan, 101–104 Piccadilly, London W1J 7JT, UK
☎ +44 (0)20 7465 6668/6670
fax +44 (0)20 7491 9347
info@jet-uk.org
www.jet-uk.org
This is the UK office for the popular JET exchange program, which allows university graduates to work in Japan as teachers or international-relations coordinators for a year or more (see p179).

Linguarama

Moorgate Hall, 155 Moorgate, London EC2M 6XB, UK
☎ +44 (0)20 7382 1800
fax +44 (0)20 7374 0507
london@linguarama.com
www.linguarama.com
Linguarama has schools in the UK, France, Germany, Spain, Italy and the Netherlands and has regular openings for qualified teachers to teach English to business clients.
Timing & Length of Work: Contracts last nine months from September.
Destinations: 20 schools around Europe.
Costs/Pay: Wages are proportional to the local cost of living and flights and accommodation are provided.
Eligibility: You must have a degree and EU citizenship. Teaching and commercial experience is an advantage.
TEFL Requirement: A recognised TEFL or TESOL certificate is required.

Nova Group

Carrington House, 126–130 Regents St, London W1B 5SE, UK
☎ +44 (0)20 734 2727
fax +4 (0)20 734 3001
applications@novagroupuk.com
www.teachinjapan.com
Nova is Japan's largest private language school, with 580 branches throughout the country. There are opportunities for English, Spanish and German graduates without previous teaching experience.
Timing & Length of Work: Contracts last one year.
Destinations: Japan.
Costs/Pay: Flights, accommodation and work permits are provided and workers earn £1365 to £1570 per month, depending on the school.

Eligibility: You must have a degree and teach in your native tongue. There is no requirement to speak Japanese.
TEFL Requirement: No TEFL or TESOL certification is required.

YBM Education

7th floor, YBM Education Center, 56–15 Chongno 2-ga, Chongno-gu, Seoul 110–122, Korea
☎ +82 2-2267 0532
eccmain@ybmsisa.co.kr
www.ybmecc.co.kr
YBM operates a series of franchised English schools across Korea and accepts large numbers of foreign English-language teachers on sponsored work permits.
Timing & Length of Work: One year.
Destinations: South Korea.
Pay: The monthly salary starts from £780 per month and YBM covers your flights, national holiday and health insurance costs and shared accommodation.
Eligibility: The program is open to native English-speakers from the UK, the USA, Canada, Australia and New Zealand with a university degree. One or more years of ESL teaching experience is preferred.
TEFL Requirement: TEFL/TESOL training is not officially required but is an advantage.

NURSING & MIDWIFERY

Access Nurses

6540 Lusk Blvd, Suite C200, San Diego, CA 92121, USA
☎ +1 866-687 7390
fax +1 866-687 7393
info@accessnurses.com
www.accessnurses.com
Access Nurses specialises in providing short-term jobs for nurses around America and also helps English-speaking nurses from Canada, the UK, Australia, South Africa, the Philippines and India relocate to the USA.

Adevia Health

2 Motcomb St, London SW1X 8JU, UK
☎ +44 (0)20 7201 0513
info@adevia.com
www.adevia.com
This British and American agency places foreign nurses in Britain and the US. There is no upfront fee and immigration and examination expenses are met by the employer.

Australian Nursing Solutions (ANS)

364 Albert St, East Melbourne, Victoria 3002, Australia
☎ +61 (0)3-9419 9199
fax +61 (0)3-9419 9236
ans@australiannursingsolutions.com.au
www.australiannursingsolutions.com.au
ANS acts as an employment agency for nurses from Australia who want to work overseas and for overseas nurses

who want to work in Australia. There's a second office in London (see the website).

Blu-Chip Global Job Connections

1221 South Mopac Expressway, Suite 250, Austin, TX 78746, USA
☎ +1 888-622 7623 ext 23
fax +1 512-457 8132
nurse@bluchip.com
www.bluchip.com
Part of the Alliance Abroad group, Blu-Chip specialises in the placement of foreign nurses in the USA, and also offers overseas placement assistance for American and Canadian nurses. Blu-Chip loans you the money for your NCLEX-RN exam and immigration application, and you pay them back after you begin work.

Nursing Agency Australia

250 Glen Osmond Rd, Fullarton, Adelaide, SA 5063, Australia
☎ +61 (0)8-8338 1000
fax +61 (0)8-8338 3003
admin@nursingagency.com.au
www.nursingagency.com.au
This Australian nursing agency welcomes nurses from overseas and acts as a sponsor for work permits lasting one to two years. Register online or by email.

One Employment Solution (OES)

37 Warren St, London, UK
☎ +44 (0)1202 200927
fax +44 (0)1202 200926
info@oesworld.com
www.oesworld.com
This British agency places nurses worldwide and provides complete relocation packages as well as advice on visa arrangements and finding an employer. You can register on the website.

RESORT JOBS

Acorn Adventures

Acorn House, 22 Worcester St, Stourbridge, West Midlands DY8 1AN, UK
☎ +44 (0)1384 446057
fax +44 (0)1384 378866
jobs@acornadventures.com
www.acorn-jobs.co.uk
Acorn takes on plenty of seasonal staff at its outdoor and adventure centres around Europe. There are jobs for camp reps, support staff and instructors of canoeing, climbing, sailing and windsurfing. You can also apply for free instructor training in any of these sports at the end of the season.
Timing & Length of Work: March to August/September.
Destinations: Eight locations in the UK, France, Italy & Spain.

Pay: Food, accommodation and transport is provided and wages range from £50 to £200 per week.
Eligibility: Minimum age is 18, and you must have relevant skills and experience.

Canvas Holidays

East Port House, Dunfermline, Fife KY12 7JG, Scotland
☎ +44 (0)1383 629018
fax +44 (0)1383 629071
recruitment@canvasholidays.co.uk
www.canvasholidays.co.uk/recruitment/recruit-index.asp
Canvas has 110 tent-based resorts around Europe and it employs large numbers of seasonal staff every year. There are jobs for couriers, childminders, managers and support staff, including people to help put up the tents.
Timing & Length of Work: March to October.
Destinations: France, Italy, Spain, Austria, Switzerland, the Netherlands, Germany & Luxembourg.
Pay: Wages start at £437 per month, including accommodation and transport but not meals.
Eligibility: Minimum age is 18 (19 in France) and you must be eligible for a UK national insurance number.

Club Med

Club Med Recrutement, 11–12 Place Jules Ferry, 69458 Lyon, CEDEX 06, France
☎ +44 (0)8453 676767
recruit.uk@clubmed.com
www.clubmed-jobs.com
This holiday giant operates around 120 holiday villages around the world and has openings for *gentils organisateurs* (who do various jobs to keep guests entertained) and *gentils employés* (who manage the day-to-day running of the resorts). Watersports are a big part of the Club Med experience, so there are excellent opportunities for qualified instructors.
Timing & Length of Work: Three to eight months from April (apply from February) or December (apply by October).
Destinations: Europe, North Africa & the Middle East.
Pay: Accommodation, transport and meals are provided and wages vary with the job – starting wages for the season begin at around £500 per month.
Eligibility: Age range is 18 to 35 and you should be an EU citizen and speak French and English. Instructors need the appropriate qualifications.

Holidaybreak

Overseas Recruitment Department, Hartford Manor, Greenbank Lane, Northwich, Cheshire CW8 1HW, UK
☎ +44 (0)1606 787522
fax +44 (0)870 366 7640
overseas-recruit@holidaybreak.co.uk
www.holidaybreakjobs.com
Holidaybreak operates Eurocamp and Keycamp tented resorts across Europe and has around 2000 openings a year for couriers, reps and support staff.

Timing & Length of Work: April/May to September/October.

Destinations: France, Spain, Italy, Austria, Switzerland, Germany, Netherlands, Luxembourg & Croatia.

Pay: Transport and accommodation are provided, meals are subsidised, and wages start from £102 to £170 per week, depending on the job.

Eligibility: Minimum age varies from 18 to 21. A clean driving licence and a second European language are useful.

Inghams Travel

Overseas Recruitment Dept, 10–18 Putney Hill, London SW15 6AX, UK
☎ +44 (0)20 8780 4400
fax +44 (0)20 8780 4405
travel@inghams.com
www.inghams.co.uk

Inghams has resorts at leading ski centres in the Alps, and hotels in France, Austria and Lapland. There are summer and winter jobs for reps as well as hospitality, hotel and chalet staff.

Timing & Length of Work: Jobs run from May to September (apply from December) or November to April (apply from May).

Destinations: France, Switzerland, Austria, Italy, Lapland (Finland), USA & Canada.

Pay: Transport, accommodation and food are provided and winter staff get a ski pass and gear; weekly wages start from £75.

Eligibility: Minimum age varies from 18 to 23, depending on the job, and for some positions you must speak French, German, Italian or Spanish. Only EU citizens can apply.

Mark Warner

Resorts Recruitment Department, George House, 61–65 Kensington Church St, London W8 4BA, UK
☎ +44 (0)20 7761 7300
fax +44 (0)20 7761 7301
recruitment@markwarner.co.uk
www.markwarner-recruitment.co.uk

Mark Warner has winter jobs for ski instructors and hosts and chalet and hospitality staff at ski resorts across Europe, and summer jobs for hospitality and support staff, chefs, reps and sailing, waterskiing and windsurfing instructors at resorts around the Mediterranean.

Timing & Length of Work: Winter jobs run from November/December to April/May; summer jobs run from April/May to October/November.

Destinations: Ski resorts in France, Italy & Austria; summer resorts in Greece, Turkey & Corsica (France).

Pay: Transport, accommodation, meals and insurance are provided and weekly wages range from £50 to £150, depending on the job. Workers get half-price drinks and a free ski pass and ski/snowboard hire, or free use of watersports equipment.

Eligibility: Minimum age is 18 to 21, depending on the job. Instructors need relevant qualifications.

PGL People

Alton Court, Penyard Lane, Ross-on-Wye, Herefordshire HR9 5GL, UK
☎ +44 (0)870 401 4411
fax +44 (0)870 401 4444
pglpeople@pgl.co.uk
www.pgl.co.uk/people

This holiday company offers specialist holidays for children in Europe and has around 2500 vacancies a year for sports teachers, childminders and general support staff – see the website for current vacancies.

Timing & Length of Work: February to October (UK) or May to September (France and Spain).

Destinations: UK, France & Spain.

Pay: Wages range from £60 to £90 a week, but meals, accommodation and transport are provided.

Eligibility: Minimum age is 18 and relevant qualifications or experience are required for some jobs.

Specialist Holidays Group (SHG)

Overseas Recruitment, Specialist Holidays Group, King's Place, Wood St, Kingston-upon-Thames, Surrey KT1 1FH, UK
☎ +44 (0)20 7420 2081
fax +44 (0)20 8541 2492
overseasrecruitment@s-h-g.co.uk
www.shgjobs.co.uk

SHG is part of the group that includes the holiday companies Thomson, Lunn Poly and TUI and employs 10,000 staff, many in seasonal positions. There are jobs for waiting and hotel staff, reps, couriers, childminders, sports instructors and ski and chalet staff.

Timing & Length of Work: Summer jobs run from April/May to September/October, winter jobs from November to May.

Destinations: France (including Corsica), Spain, Portugal, Italy, Austria, Switzerland, Andorra, Greece, Crete & Turkey.

Pay: Wages vary but are standard for the industry. Transport, accommodation and food are provided (as are ski hire and passes for winter workers).

Eligibility: Minimum age is 18 to 21, depending on the position, and participants should speak the language of the destination for some positions.

Sunsail

Human Resources, The Port House, Port Solent, Hampshire PO6 4TH, UK
☎ +44 (0)2392 222322
fax +44 (0)2392 219846
hr@sunsail.com
www.sunsail.com

Sunsail employs around 1700 assorted staff at its yacht and beach resorts around the world. There are opportunities for qualified sailors and sailing instructors and general resort support staff, mostly in the Mediterranean.

Timing & Length of Work: Most jobs run from April/May to November, but there are short contracts in the high season from June to September.

Destinations: Greece, Turkey & Croatia, but with occasional opportunities in the Caribbean for people who have previously worked for Sunsail.

Pay: Wages vary from £50 to £200 per week, depending on the job, plus bonuses. Accommodation, meals and transport are provided.

Eligibility: Minimum age is 19 to 21 for yacht staff and you must have relevant skills/qualifications for the job (eg RYA or equivalent yachting qualifications).

Total Holidays
185 Fleet Rd, Fleet, Hampshire GU51 3BL, UK
☎ +44 (0)1252 618309
fax +44 (0)1252 618328
recruitment@skitotal.com
www.skitotal.com

Ski Total has been running ski holidays in Europe for 20 years and it has winter jobs for instructors, ski hosts and chalet and catering staff. This office also recruits for Esprit holidays (www.esprit-holidays.co.uk).

Timing & Length of Work: From mid-November to April (apply from May).

Destinations: France, Italy, Austria & Switzerland.

Pay: Weekly wages range from £60 to £150, including transport, meals, accommodation, lift passes, ski/snowboard hire and insurance. Participants pay a commitment bond of £100, which is refunded at the end of the season.

Eligibility: Minimum age varies from 19 to 23, depending on the job. Instructors, reps, chefs, nannies and managers require qualifications and experience.

CHILDREN'S CAMPS
Bunac (British Universities North America Club)
See p190 for contact details.

Bunac offers a summer camp program in the USA for people with childcare or sports teaching experience. Participants get a guaranteed placement as a camp counsellor on a summer camp somewhere in America, plus free flights and pocket money.

Timing & Length of Placements: Nine weeks from June (it is possible to extend at some camps, up to a maximum of four months).

Destinations: USA.

Costs/Pay: There's a program fee of £66 and flights are free but you pay for insurance, visas and transport to camp. Pocket money starts at US$770 for the season.

Eligibility: Age range is 19 to 35; you must speak fluent English and provide a criminal-record check. Experience in childcare and sports-teaching qualifications are advantages.

Camp America
37a Queen's Gate, London SW7 5HR, UK
☎ +44 (0)20 7581 7373
fax +44 (0)20 7581 7377
enquiries@campamerica.co.uk
www.campamerica.co.uk

Camp America has annual openings for general camp counsellors and special-needs counsellors for summer camps in America. A placement is guaranteed if you join one of the Camp America Lifeguard or Water Safety Instructor (WSI) courses, which run in the UK from February to April.

Timing & Length of Placements: Nine weeks from June (it is possible to extend to a maximum of four months at some camps).

Destinations: USA.

Costs/Pay: There's a program fee of around £316 for insurance, visas and airport taxes, and pocket money starts at US$700 for the season for people over 21. Free flights are provided from London, Manchester, Glasgow or Belfast. The Lifeguard course costs £70 and the WSI course costs £80.

Eligibility: Minimum age is 18; you must speak fluent English and provide a criminal-record check. Support staff jobs for the Campower scheme are only for full-time students. Experience in childcare is an advantage for counsellor jobs, and sports instructors will benefit from relevant qualifications.

CCUSA
See p190 for contact details.

As well as educational exchanges and working holidays, CCUSA places camp counsellors in children's summer camps in the USA and Russia. There is an interview where you will be matched to a camp placement.

Timing & Length of Placements: Four to nine weeks from June in America, four or eight weeks in Russia. Apply from September.

Destinations: Russia & the USA.

Costs/Pay: Workers receive a local wage (a small stipend only in Russia), free accommodation, meals and flights. The American program fee starts at £299; the Russian program fee is £815/865 for four/eight weeks.

Eligibility: Minimum age is 18 (maximum age is 35 in the US, no upper limit in Russia) and you must show an interest in working with children. Qualifications or relevant experience are needed for sporting and outdoor jobs.

International Exchange Centre (IEC)
See p191 for contact details.

As well as agricultural working holidays and work placements, IEC places counsellors on summer camps in the USA and Russia. Flights and visas are included and workers receive a small pocket money payment.

Timing & Length of Placements: Nine to 10 weeks from June in the USA; two to 12 weeks from June in Russia.

Destinations: The USA & Russia.

Costs/Pay: The placement fee is £115 and total pocket money for the placement starts at US$510. Flights are extra.
Eligibility: Age range is 18 to 28 and experience working with children is an advantage.

International Exchange Programmes (IEP)

See p191 for contact details.

IEP offers various exchange programs, including Summer Camp USA, where Australians and New Zealanders can work on summer camps for children in America.
Timing & Length of Placements: Eight to 10 weeks from May. Apply by 20 February for a guaranteed placement.
Destinations: The USA.
Costs/Pay: The program fee is around A$611, including visa processing fees. Counsellors receive pocket money of around A$1455 for the season. Flights are extra.
Eligibility: Age range is 19 to 35 and you must enjoy working with children.

Village Camps

Recruitment Office, 14 Rue de la Morâche, 1260 Nyon, Switzerland
☎ +41 (0)22-990 9405
fax +41 (0)22-990 9494
personnel@villagecamps.ch
www.villagecamps.com/personnel/index.html
This European organisation places camp counsellors in children's camps around Europe. There are openings for counsellors, support staff and qualified sports teachers to teach outdoor activities.
Timing & Length of Placements: Camps last five to eight weeks, with start dates from April to August.
Destinations: The UK, France, Switzerland, Austria & the Netherlands.
Costs/Pay: Participants make their own way to the camp and receive a local salary that varies with the job. Meals and accommodation are free.
Eligibility: Minimum age varies from 18 to 23, depending on the job. You should be a citizen of the EU, the US, Canada, Australia or New Zealand; speak fluent English; and have relevant skills and experience for the position you are applying for. You also need a valid first-aid/CPR certificate.

Worldnet UK

Emberton House, 26 Shakespeare Rd, Bedford MK40 2ED, UK
☎ +44 (0)1234 352688
fax +44 (0)1234 351070
info@worldnetuk.com
www.worldnetuk.com
Worldnet is the UK agent for InterExchange/Camp USA and it places childminders on summer camps around the USA.
Timing & Length of Placements: Eight to 15 weeks from June.

Destinations: The USA.
Costs/Pay: The program fee is £300 plus a £45 fee for a criminal-record check. Airfares, meals, accommodation and insurance are provided and workers get pocket money of around US$800 for the season.
Eligibility: Minimum age is 19 and you must be fluent in English. You should also be a youth worker or teacher or have sport-teaching skills.

TOUR LEADING

The Adventure Company

15 Turk St, Alton, Hampshire GU34 1AG, UK
☎ +44 (0)1420 541007
fax +44 (0)1420 541022
jobs@adventurecompany.co.uk
www.adventurecompany.co.uk
This adventure tour operator has a worldwide program of small-group tours. Recruitment happens year round. Office-based training takes place over a long weekend followed by a one- or two-week training tour with an experienced tour leader. Tour leaders are employed on short, fixed-term contracts.
Types of Work: Tour leaders.
Timing & Length of Work: Trips last from one to three weeks; back-to-back trips mean you could be in one country for up to six months. Trips run all year round but there's less work in winter. Due to the growth in the Family Adventures program there's an increasing demand for leaders taking one-off trips abroad during UK school holidays.
Destinations: Spain, Italy, Greece, France, India, China, Japan, Mexico, Argentina, Brazil, Chile, Libya, Uganda & Ethiopia.
Pay: You're a self-employed subcontractor on a basic day rate depending on experience (the Adventure Company will not disclose more than this). Accommodation and meals are provided as per the group itinerary (ie, if your tour is B&B then you get B&B only).
Eligibility: Minimum age is 25; a university degree is preferable, travel knowledge essential. Another language (especially Spanish or Italian) is preferable and previous first-aid training and outdoor experience/certificate useful.
How to Apply: Happy to receive on-spec CVs. Usually advertises in *Wanderlust* magazine.

Busabout

258 Vauxhall Bridge Rd, London SW1V 1BS, UK
☎ +44 (0)20 7950 1661
fax +44 (0)20 7950 1662
recruitment@busabout.co.uk
www.busabout.com/recruitment
This is a hop-on, hop-off coach transportation service for independent travellers in Europe. Recruitment starts in December/January for the summer season. If successful you'll get a four-week training course around Europe. You will be expected to work more than one full season.

Types of Work: On-board guides.

Timing & Length of Work: Summer season runs from May to October.

Destinations: 12 countries in Europe.

Pay: A £200 training bond is refundable after working two full consecutive seasons. Pay is around £150 gross per week, including all accommodation.

Eligibility: Minimum age is 25; familiarity with Europe is important, and a second European language helpful.

How to Apply: Download application form from website and send in with a colour photo. There's a group interview where a short talk to the panel is followed by a longer private one.

Explore Worldwide

1 Frederick St, Aldershot, Hampshire GU11 1LQ, UK
☎ +44 (0)1252 760200
fax +44 (0)1252 760201
ops@exploreworldwide.com
www.explore.co.uk

Explore is a small-group adventure travel company. Job applications are accepted all year round but most recruitment takes place between January and April for the summer season and occasionally in late summer for the winter season. All vacancies are advertised on the website. You're given a three- or four-week training course, including a two-day wilderness first-aid course, followed by on-the-road training with an experienced tour leader. Explore is looking for a minimum commitment of one year but ideally more.

Types of Work: Tour leaders.

Timing & Length of Work: Trips last from one weekend to one month. A leader can be overseas working on back-to-back tours for up to six months.

Destinations: 100 countries worldwide.

Pay: There's a £200 training bond, refundable after the first season. A basic starting salary is around £25 a day, including accommodation, often meals and tips.

Eligibility: Minimum age is 24; independent travel experience is essential; customer-service experience and a second language preferable.

How to Apply: The application form is eight pages long and has problem-solving sections. There's a two-hour individual interview testing your descriptive powers and problem-solving skills. You can download the application form from the website.

Exodus Travels

9 Weir Rd, London SW12 0LT, UK
☎ +44 (0)20 8675 5550
fax +44 (0)20 8673 0779
info@exodus.co.uk
www.exodus.co.uk

Exodus runs biking, walking, trekking and snow tours in Europe and elsewhere. Recruitment is in February. Training takes about three weeks and usually includes a first-aid

course, a summer mountain-leadership training course, and an overseas training trip shadowing an experienced tour leader.

Types of Work: Tour leaders.

Timing & Length of Work: You can be away working from six weeks to three months. Busiest times are Easter, May to October and Christmas. There's usually six to seven months' work a year.

Destinations: Africa, Asia, Europe, Antarctica, Australasia & the Americas.

Pay: On average around £200 a week, plus tips, accommodation and food. You're not paid when you're not leading.

Eligibility: Minimum age is 25; independent travel experience, knowledge of another language, a strong interest in outdoor pursuits and people skills are required.

How to Apply: Job vacancies are placed on the website year round. Advertisements are placed in *TNT* and *Wanderlust*. Please apply for specific positions, although CVs sent on spec will be looked at.

The Imaginative Traveller

1 Betts Ave, Martlesham Heath, Suffolk IP5 3RH, UK
☎ +44 (0)1473 636066
fax +44 (0)1473 636016
tljobs@imtrav.net
www.imaginative-traveller.com

ImTrav is an adventure-travel operator for small groups to the Middle East, Asia and Europe. Main recruitment times are January and May. Two days of training in the UK are followed by three to four weeks overseas. Most tour leaders do their first contract in Egypt, China or Southeast Asia. The initial contract is for 12 months, subsequent contracts may be shorter.

Types of Work: Tour leaders.

Timing & Length of Work: One- to four-week trips run year round.

Destinations: Europe, the Middle East, Asia & Europe.

Pay: £13.50 a day plus meals, accommodation, living allowance and bonuses.

Eligibility: Minimum age is 22; travel experience essential.

How to Apply: Application form on website.

Top Deck Tours

William House, 14 Worple Rd, London SW19 4DD, UK
☎ +44 (0)20 8879 6789
fax +44 (0)20 8944 9474
ops@topdecktravel.co.uk
www.topdecktravel.co.uk

This is a budget adventure travel company, travelling by coach. Recruitment details are on the website. Interviews are held October to March. Training trips last six weeks, starting early April. Crew are expected to work with the company for at least two summer seasons.

Types of Work: Tour leaders (although there is also work for drivers and cooks).

Timing & Length of Work: Trips run year round but almost all the work is from April to October. Trips range from weekends to 50 days.
Destinations: Europe, Russia & Turkey.
Pay: Your training trip costs £350; £175 of it is refundable at the start of your third season. Pay starts from £165 per week (including a performance-related bonus). Accommodation and food is included while you're working.
Eligibility: Minimum age is 23; travel experience is preferable.
How to Apply: Download application from website and return with photo. Group interviews, where you have to give a speech, are followed by individual interviews.

TrekAmerica

Tour Leader Recruitment, Premiere International Corp, PO Box 1338, Gardena, CA 90249, USA
☎ tel +1 310-71 9877
fax +1 310-719 1478
personnel@premiereops.com
www.trekamerica.com/employment.html
This small-group adventure tour company travels through North America by maxivan. Tour leaders organise outdoor activities, city sightseeing excursions and night-time entertainment. Recruitment happens year round, with summer tour-leading jobs usually running from late April to September. Foreign-language skills and a good sense of North American geography, history and culture are important.
Types of Work: Tour leaders
Timing & Length of Work: Trips last from three days to nine weeks, with expanded itineraries during summer (April to September).
Destinations: The USA, Canada & Mexico.
Pay: Varies by trip; tour leaders receive base compensation and may expect end-of-trip gratuities from guests. (The company will not disclose further information.)
Eligibility: Minimum age is 23 and you must be a US citizen or able to work legally in the US, with a clean driving record.
How to Apply: Mail your CV to the office.

BEHIND THE WHEEL – OVERLAND & COACH-TOURING COMPANIES

Busabout

See p204 for details.
Busabout has 18 buses in Europe during summer. Drivers are expected to work more than one summer season. There's a five-week training course, most of which takes place in Europe, where you learn the routes.
Types of Work: Drivers.
Timing & Length of Work: The summer season runs from May to October.
Destinations: 11 countries in Europe.
Pay: The £200 training bond is refundable after the first season. Pay is approximately £300 gross a week, reviewed annually.

Eligibility: Minimum age is 23 and you need a PCV licence.
How to Apply: Download application form from website and mail with copy of licence and current photograph. There are usually two interviews.

Dragoman Overland Travel

Camp Green, Kenton Rd, Debenham, Suffolk IP14 6LA, UK
☎ +44 (0)1728 862255
fax +44 (0)1728 861127
info@dragoman.co.uk
www.dragoman.com
The largest overland company in the UK, Dragoman offers a more upmarket experience. Recruitment takes place all year round, with vacancies advertised on the website. A 12- to 14-week training course is held at Camp Green and then you're a trainee for the first six months on the road. There are always two drivers on a trip. They work as tour guides too.
Types of Work: Leader drivers, co-drivers, leader mechanics, co-driver mechanics, trainees.
Timing & Length of Work: From two to 42 weeks; trips run all year.
Destinations: North, Central & South America, Africa & Asia.
Pay: A daily rate that increases annually. Pay also depends on experience and skills. Accommodation, meals and transport are included, and there's also a bonus scheme.
Eligibility: Minimum age is 25; a PCV or LGV licence and first-aid certificate are essential.
How to Apply: Contact the office for an application form.

Encounter Overland

Camp Green, Kenton Rd, Debenham, Suffolk IP14 6LA, UK
☎ +44 (0)1728 862222
fax +44 (0)1728 861127
wild@encounter.co.uk
www.encounter.co.uk
This is a budget overland company aimed squarely at the student market. All recruitment details are the same as for Dragoman, as Encounter is owned by Dragoman. One big difference is that there's only one driver/tour leader.
Types of Work: Leader mechanics.

Exodus Travels

See p205 for details.
Exodus also recruits people to lead and drive overland expeditions. This is a full-time post and leaders spend most of the year overseas, so it isn't suitable for anyone with commitments at home. You are expected to work for a minimum of two years.
Types of Work: Expedition leaders.
Timing & Length of Work: Trips run year round and last from three to 30 weeks.
Destinations: Asia & the Americas.
Pay: You get accident and sickness insurance and, according to Exodus, competitive rates of pay.

Eligibility: Minimum age is 25. You need a PCV or LGV licence, an immaculate driving record, the right to work in the UK, mechanical skills, travel experience and people skills.

How to Apply: Job vacancies are placed on the website year round. Apply for specific positions rather than sending in your CV speculatively.

Kumuka Worldwide

40 Earls Court Rd, London W8 6EJ, UK
☎ +44 (0)20 7937 8855
fax +44 (0)20 7937 6664
humanresources@kumuka.com
www.kamuka.com

Kumuka is a specialist in adventure holidays and overland travel. It recruits year round. Drivers are usually employed on annual contracts. Overland trips have a separate driver and tour guide/leader.

Types of Work: Overland driver.

Timing & Length of Work: Trips last from four days to 15 weeks. Overland drivers work for a maximum of one year overseas.

Pay: Pay depends on experience.

Destinations: South America, Asia, Africa and the Middle East.

Eligibility: Minimum age is 25; you need a LGV or PCV licence and sound mechanical knowledge.

How to Apply: Apply via the website or email the office.

CRUISING

the agency excellent entertainment

Suite 2, The Business Centre, 120 West Heath Rd, London NW3 7TX, UK
☎ +44 (0)20 8458 4212
fax +44 (0)20 8458 4572
theagency@excellententertainment.biz
www.excellententertainment.biz

This agency supplies entertainers and entertainment staff to the cruise-line industry worldwide. The company is the sole UK supplier to Disney Cruise Line and 12 other cruise lines. Send your CV with a photo. If you get through this stage, you will be invited to an audition. Minimum age is from 18 to 21, depending on the cruise line.

Berkeley Scott Selection

11–13 Ockford Rd, Godalming, Surrey GU7 1QU, UK
☎ +44 (0)1483 791291
fax +44 (0)870 1372169
cruise@bsgplc.com
www.berkeley-scott.co.uk, www.greatcruisejobs.co.uk

BSS recruits hotel positions from assistant waiter to hotel director, *chef de partie* to restaurant manager for all the major international cruise lines including Carnival,

Celebrity, Cunard, Disney, Hebridean Island Cruises, Norwegian Cruise Line, P&O, Royal Caribbean, Silversea and many more. Also recruits sales staff for retail outlets and entertainers, health and beauty staff as well as handling all the casino staff for the Carnival Corporation (which owns nine cruise lines). Most positions require one year's experience in a similar role; in addition, casino staff need experience in two card games and one dice game.

CruiseJobFinder

Membership Department, 2536 Alki Ave, SW Seattle, WA 98116, USA
☎ tel +1 877-321 8766
fax +1 707-221 1418
help@cruisejobfinder.com
www. cruisejobfinder.com

This is a membership-based information source for finding jobs on cruise ships and at beach resorts. Members pay a fee to access detailed industry information, printable applications, up-to-date job listings and insider tips. Membership plans start at $3.95 for a five-day trial or $49.95 for one year. Cruise ships sail worldwide, and work is generally available year round. Positions include bartenders, cruise directors, casino staff, disc jockeys, expedition leaders, retail staff, entertainers, lecturers, beauticians, personal trainers, lifeguards, dance instructors, restaurant staff, photographers, childcare staff and much more.

Ocean Images UK

7, Home Farm Business Centre, Lockerley, Romsey, Hampshire SO51 0JT, UK
☎ +44 (0)1794 341818
fax +44 (0)1794 341415
jobs@ocean-images.com
www.ocean-images.com

Working with 40 cruise ships across all the main cruise lines, this company has openings for over 180 ship photographers. All levels are considered and beginners are trained on board. Personality and sales skills are important as pay is commission-based (so you only get paid for sales). To apply, download the application form from the website.

VIP International

17 Charing Cross Rd, London WC2H 0QW, UK
☎ +44 (0)20 7930 0541
fax +44 (0)20 7930 2860
cruise@vipinternational.co.uk
www.vipinternational.co.uk

VIP supplies housekeeping, food and beverage, pursers' office, culinary department and hotel operations staff to 10 leading cruise lines. You'll need at least three years' experience in a similar position with either a 4-star or 5-star international hotel or equivalent on a cruise liner.

Studying

Some people just want to kick back on a tropical beach on their career break, but for others it's the perfect opportunity to break out of a rut and gain some new skills. Perhaps you want to boost your career prospects with an MBA from a leading business school? Or maybe you dream about rediscovering the vigour of youth on a snowboarding course in the French Alps? The opportunities for studying around the world are as broad as your imagination.

However, the one thing all courses have in common is that they cost money. Funding is available for some academic courses, but for the rest, you must cover all the travel, study and living expenses yourself. Assuming this doesn't stop you in your tracks, you can study anything from IT to t'ai chi, and courses are available in almost every country on the planet. The world of studying is your oyster – what are you waiting for?

Why Study?

You've spent 10 years building up your career, so why would you go back to school? One of the most common reasons people give for studying is to change an area of their lives where they feel unfulfilled. This could be something serious and work-related, or it could just be a commonplace skill or hobby that you wish you were better at. If there is anything that you've always wanted to learn but never had the time for, this could be the perfect opportunity.

People who feel stuck in a rut often look for a course that can help them branch off in a new direction, such as a vocational diploma or an MBA. Many people study for academic courses because they feel intellectually unchallenged at work. Quite a few career-breakers just want to do something extraordinary before they settle down and start a family – after all, when is the next time you'll have the freedom to train for a season as a snowboard instructor in the Rocky Mountains?

Whatever you decide to do, a course of study will add weight to your CV. Even if the qualification doesn't directly relate to your job, it will show you have the dedication to follow an idea through to its conclusion and demonstrate that you are capable of learning new skills. Especially if you study overseas, studying will also open your eyes to different ways of doing things – a valuable skill in today's diversity-conscious world.

The following sections cover some of the most popular options for people on career breaks, but there are thousands of other courses out there. To keep things simple, we've broken this chapter down into courses you study to gain a qualification and courses you study for your own enjoyment.

GAINING A QUALIFICATION

If you often look back on your college days with a nostalgic sigh, perhaps it is time to dust off the gown and mortarboard and go back to university. Plenty of career-breakers fancy another shot at student life, and a career break provides a perfect opportunity to add a new qualification to your CV or to study a subject you missed out on first time around.

Returning to university can be a bit of a culture shock, but there are some big advantages to re-entering formal education. Among other things, an academic course will provide a structured environment for learning and result in a formal qualification. It will also provide new challenges and allow you to meet new people from all sorts of different backgrounds. However, you should carefully weigh up the cost of the course against what you hope to gain. A new qualification can be a good launching platform for your career, but you may also find yourself competing for a job with thousands of other recently qualified young people.

The biggest obstacle to studying on a career break is funding. Scholarships and grants are quite easy to find if you study in your own country, but there is much less funding available for overseas study. See the following sections for popular qualifications and the best way to go about finding and funding a college or university course.

UNDERGRADUATE DEGREES & DOCTORATES

If you are looking for a complete career change, you could always enrol in a full-time undergraduate or postgraduate course. However, this will involve at least three years of full-time study, with all the associated costs, and it's a long time to be outside the job marketplace.

Applications for undergraduate degrees in the UK should be made through the Universities & Colleges Admissions Service (UCAS; www.ucas.ac.uk). For undergraduate courses overseas, you should apply directly to the university, as most universities provide advice for international students on their websites.

If you want to study for an undergraduate degree in the USA, you must take the Scholastic Aptitude Test (SAT), which measures mathematical and verbal reasoning skills. The test is administered by the Educational Testing Service (www.ets.org) and testing takes place on set dates throughout the year at American and international schools worldwide – see www.collegeboard.com for more information. To study in Australia or Europe, you generally need to be educated up to year 12 or baccalaureate level.

PhD or doctorate courses require a high level of expertise and are generally reserved for recent graduates. If you have been working outside the relevant field for more than a year, the chances are your knowledge is behind the times. This said, relevant workplace experience may count for something – the website www.prospects.ac.uk has listings of PhD courses around the country.

MASTER'S DEGREES

A master's degree is a popular choice for people with an academic bent who feel unstimulated at work. The qualification falls somewhere between a bachelor's degree and a doctorate and the focus is on academic study or research rather than examinations. This was one of the things that attracted David Marshall to a Master of Arts in English:

I applied for an MA because I wanted to enjoy a year of reading and discussion without the pressure of examinations. There was quite a divide within our group between the professional academics and people who were doing the course purely for personal development. I was challenged by the high calibre of the other candidates but it was a very enjoyable year. The course didn't directly relate to my career, but subsequent employers have always found the MA to be a talking point in interviews.

You can study for a master's in any academic subject, but it must relate to a subject that you studied as an undergraduate. As with undergraduate degrees, master's courses are divided into Master of Arts (MA) and Master of Science (MSc) qualifications. Some subjects have their own specialist master's qualifications, such as Master of Philosophy (MPhil), Master of Research (MRes) and Master of Laws (LLM).

You can study for a master's at most universities and graduate schools, both in the UK and abroad, but you generally need a second-class honours degree or higher to get a place. Courses last one or two years and run from the start of the academic year in September. Each university or college sets its own deadlines for applications, so you should contact the admissions department directly for information.

If you are applying for master's course in North America, you may have to take the Graduate Record Examination (GRE; www.gre.org), which measures verbal, mathematical and analytical skills. You can take the test year round at test centres in London and Twickenham for around US$140, but you must register through the GRE website, which also has details of GRE testing in other countries. American colleges and universities generally look for a GRE score of at least 1000 out of 1600. Check if you need to take the general or subject-specific version of the GRE when you apply. Courses outside America usually just require a relevant undergraduate degree.

MBAs

If you are looking for a course that will boost you up the career ladder, the Master in Business Administration (MBA) covers all the skills you need to become a business manager.

You can study for an MBA in one or two years at business schools worldwide, and because an MBA can significantly increase your earnings, there are plenty of loans and scholarships for study at home or abroad.

However, a word of warning – there has been a huge explosion in the number of institutions offering MBAs in recent years and the qualification isn't quite as valuable as it once was. If you really want to attract the attention of head-hunters at the big companies, you need to attend a top-ranking business school such as the London Business School in Britain or Harvard University in the USA, and that means paying top dollar – up to US$100,000 at some schools. One way to offset the cost is to ask for sponsorship from your existing company (see Funding on p213 for more information).

Lucy Aliband studied for an MBA at the London Business School and at the University of California, Berkeley in the USA:

I practised as a corporate lawyer and corporate financier for five years before getting thoroughly bored. I had been trying to move into international aid/development for some time but I found that I was totally unemployable in any capacity other than as a lawyer so I went and did an MBA. The transition worked and I now work for a US nonprofit organisation that specialises in social marketing, spending 50% of my time in the US and 50% of my time in Africa – which I love. I have taken an enormous pay cut and am in debt up to my eyeballs, but what can I say other than it was the best career move of my life!

To apply for an MBA in most countries, you must take the Graduate Management Admission Test (GMAT), administered by the Graduate Management Admission Council (GMAC; www.mba.com) in the USA. The computerised test measures verbal, quantitative, reasoning and communication skills and you need to score at least 600 out of 800 to get a place in any MBA course worth its salt.

One way to maximise your score is to take a course of GMAT coaching with an organisation such as the Kaplan Center (see p223 for more information). There are also dozens of books that promise to help you wing the GMAT; the *Official Guide for GMAT Review* published by the Educational Testing Service (ETS; www.ets.org) is the definitive GMAT guide.

Whether you take some coaching or go it alone, you must register for GMAT training on the GMAC website (www.mba.com). The examination can be taken year round in London and Twickenham and on set dates in Manchester and Glasgow and the fee is US$225. The GMAC website has information on testing centres worldwide.

VOCATIONAL COURSES

As well as academic and business courses, many colleges and graduate schools offer vocational courses that train you up with the skills you need to carry out a specific job or trade. This could be something down to earth such as learning to type at a local community college or something totally off the wall such as going to film school in Hollywood. However, remember that a vocational course does not always guarantee a well-paid job as soon as you graduate. You may still have to put in several years of hard work before the investment pays off.

This testimonial from Peter Miller sums up the experience of many people who study for a vocational course as part of a career break:

I'd been travelling all over the world on holidays for years and one day I just decided that travel was what I wanted to do for a living. I handed in my notice and took a one-year postgraduate diploma in photography and journalism in the UK, which taught me several things, the first being that I was a better writer than photographer. When the course finished I started writing freelance travel articles for magazines but it took about a year to find a full-time job and I really struggled to make enough money. I eventually did get a job writing for a travel company, but if I had to do it again, I'd save up much more money before starting the course.

You can study almost anything, from web design and journalism to plumbing and cordon-bleu cookery, but you may need previous experience or an undergraduate degree, particularly if the course leads to a postgraduate diploma equivalent to an MSc or MBA. A short course in touch-typing or using a popular computing package may be handy if you intend to get temping work overseas on your career break.

One specialist vocational course is the Postgraduate Certificate in Education (PGCE), which allows a university graduate to qualify as a teacher in one year. You can study for the PGCE at universities across the country and funding is available through the Teacher Training Agency (www.useyourheadteach.gov.uk). If you want to teach English overseas, you might consider taking a TEFL or TESOL course (see p177 for details).

In the UK, vocational courses are mainly offered by colleges of further education (which are open to everyone) and colleges of higher education (which cater to people with A levels or university qualifications). For extensive listings of colleges around the UK, see the Higher Education & Research Opportunities in the United Kingdom website (www.hero.ac.uk).

Learn Direct (☎ 0800 101901; www.learndirect.co.uk) is a UK government scheme that provides information on more than 700,000 courses in the UK, including business, IT and language training. The UK graduate careers website www.prospects.ac.uk also has useful information on vocational courses. If you live in London, Floodlight (www.floodlight.co.uk) publishes guides to full-time, part-time and evening courses in the capital; the guides cost £5 to £7.50 and can be ordered from the website.

OPEN UNIVERSITY & CORRESPONDENCE COURSES

Of course, student life isn't for everyone. Many career-breakers prefer a correspondence course, which allows you to study without having to immerse yourself in the mayhem of campus life. These days, most of the correspondence takes place over the Internet so you can basically study anywhere, be it your home office or a tropical beach with an Internet café. You can also work while you study, to offset the cost of the course.

The Open University (www.open.ac.uk) is the largest provider of correspondence courses in Britain, with nearly 200,000 students annually. The university works on a modular basis, with nine-month courses that build into a master's or MBA degree (three courses over two to three years) or an undergraduate degree (six courses over six years). Most of the course is conducted over the Internet or by post but there are optional face-to-face tutorials and you must attend the final exam in person.

The portal E-Learning Europa (www.elearningeuropa.info) provides information on e-learning throughout the EU, while Open Learning Australia (www.ola.edu.au) offers a distance-learning program for courses at seven Australian universities and 32 TAFE (Technical & Further Education) colleges. Dozens of companies offer correspondence courses in the USA – search on the Internet for 'correspondence courses', 'open learning' or 'distance learning'.

Wherever you study, make sure the institution is recognised by an international organisation such as the Open and Distance Learning Quality Council (www.odlqc.org.uk) or the International Accreditation & Recognition Council (www.iarcedu.com).

STUDYING ABROAD

Going back to school doesn't have mean staying in one place. Universities around the world accept international students, and student visas are far easier to obtain than work permits. The only sting is the cost – foreign students are a major source of income for universities and you may end up paying twice as much as domestic students for the same course.

While this is rather unfair on less well-off candidates, it does mean that you can study almost anywhere if you have the money, including prestigious institutions such as the Sorbonne in Paris and Massachusetts Institute of Technology (MIT) in Boston. However, be warned that some of these institutions trade heavily on their reputations – you should carefully weigh up the added kudos against the astronomical tuition fees.

According to the latest international league tables, the most expensive places to study are Britain, Europe, America and Japan, while the cheapest fees are offered by universities in Australia, New Zealand and Canada, particularly in French-speaking Quebec. One way to keep costs down is to choose a region where living costs are comparatively low, such as Australia or Asia. You can also get private and government funding for some overseas courses – see the Funding section (opposite) for more information.

Citizens of the EU do not need a visa to study in another EU country, but for other countries they will need a student visa or study permit. This also applies to citizens of some new EU member nations. Foreign universities or colleges can provide the appropriate paperwork, but you must prove that you have enough money to support yourself during the course and there may also be an interview with embassy officials in your home country.

Student visas tend to be specific to the university or college, but you can change to another course at the same level (eg from a master's to an MBA) without having to apply for a new visa. Paid work is prohibited on most student visas, but some countries grant you permission to get a part-time job once you start your course.

Universities generally require you to study in the local language, so you may have to take a language test such as the Test of English as a Foreign Language (TOEFL; www.ets.org/toefl) or write a foreign-language essay when you apply.

Another important thing to consider is how qualifications obtained abroad are seen in your home country. An MBA from a leading business school in the UK will inevitably have more clout than an MBA from a minor provincial college in the USA. The National Academic Recognition Information Centre (Naric; www.naric.org.uk) provides information on the status of all sorts of foreign academic qualifications in the UK.

FINDING A COURSE

It would be impossible to describe all the options for studying abroad in this guide. Fortunately, there are some excellent websites that allow you to search for courses in any subject you fancy at universities, colleges and graduate schools worldwide.

The Higher Education & Research Opportunities in the United Kingdom website (www.hero.ac.uk) has a huge database of online prospectuses for courses and academic institutions across the UK. The main source of information on study in Europe is the Portal on Learning Opportunities throughout the European Space (Ploteus; http://europa.eu.int/ploteus). For information on courses and colleges worldwide, visit www.hobsons.com and www.prospects.ac.uk or see the websites at the end of this section.

Once you find a course, you should contact the admissions department directly for information on fees, entry requirements and how to apply, including the application deadlines. Many universities and private-study agencies offer short periods of study abroad for people on undergraduate degree courses, particularly in the US.

If you find the range of options bewildering, **Gabbitas Educational Consultants** (☎ +44 (0)20 7734 0161; www.gabbitas.co.uk) offers career guidance, including information on higher education in Britain and worldwide. It isn't cheap though – a phone consultation costs £70 and a face-to-face meeting costs £170.

The following is our pick of the resources for finding a course on the web:

- **Aim Higher** (www.aimhigher.ac.uk) UK government portal on higher education.
- **Braintrack** (www.braintrack.com) A website with 7400 links to educational institutions worldwide.
- **Career Dynamo** (www.careerdynamo.com) A business-oriented site with extensive MBA information.
- **Careers Europe** (www.careerseurope.co.uk) Centralised source of information on studying in Europe.
- **Council for International Education** (www.ukcosa.org.uk) Excellent source of information for UK students studying abroad and foreign students visiting the UK.
- **Education UK** (www.educationuk.org) Site on study opportunities in the UK; run by the British Council.
- **Edupass** (www.edupass.org) Online guide to study in the US.
- **Eurochoice** (www.eurochoice.org.uk) An information portal on studying in Europe.

- **Euroeducation.net** (www.euroeducation.net) Country-by-country information on education in Europe.
- **Grad Schools.com** (www.gradschools.com) Comprehensive listings of graduate schools in the US.
- **Hyperstudy** (www.hyperstudy.com) A web resource for study in Britain, Ireland, Europe, the US, Canada, Australia and New Zealand.
- **International Education Site** (www.intstudy.com) International study site with a searchable database of colleges and courses.
- **International Student** (www.internationalstudent.com) Information on study in the US, the UK and Australia.
- **MBA Australia** (www.mbaguide.com.au) Site with MBA information for Australia.
- **Monster.com** (mba.monster.studylink.com) MBA information from a leading international recruitment agency.
- **National Center for Education Statistics** (nces.ed.gov/ipeds/cool) Search engine for courses and colleges in the USA.
- **Study Abroad** (www.studyabroad.com) US site with a huge searchable database of study options overseas.
- **Study Abroad Links** (www.studyabroadlinks.com) Website with a searchable database of courses worldwide.
- **Study in Australia** (www.studyinaustralia.gov.au) Australian government site for international students.
- **Study in the USA** (www.studyusa.com) Useful information on all aspects of studying in the USA.
- **Study Overseas Site** (www.studyoverseas.com) Web-based forum for study in the UK, Europe, the US, Canada, Australia and New Zealand.
- **Support for Learning** (www.support4learning.org.uk) UK site with comprehensive higher-education information.

FUNDING

For most people, money is the deciding factor when it comes to choosing a course. There is no nice way of saying it – studying costs money, particularly if you want to study overseas. As well as tuition fees, there are flights, travel and health insurance, study materials, meals, accommodation and visa fees. The bottom line is that you will struggle to get a year of education anywhere for less than £10,000, and that's just the tuition fees and accommodation.

The best option is to save up enough money before you start your break. That way, you won't have any debts hanging over your head while you search for work at the end of your break. However, there is some funding available for higher education, particularly if you study in your home country.

For an academic postgraduate course, you can often get funding directly from the college or university in the form of a bursary or scholarship – ask about this when you apply. Research authorities also provide huge amounts of funding to postgraduate students. In the UK, the Arts and Humanities Research Board (AHRB; www.ahrb.ac.uk) covers arts courses; Research Councils UK (www.rcuk.ac.uk) covers science courses; and the Medical Research Council (www.mrc.ac.uk) covers medical courses.

In a bid to lure more people into teaching, the British government pays all tuition fees for PGCE students and also provides a tax-free maintenance grant of £6000. Additional funding is available for teachers of in-demand subjects from the Teacher Training Agency (www.useyourheadteach.gov.uk).

You can also apply for a loan to help with the costs of your course, but remember that you will have to pay this money back eventually. In Britain, government-backed student loans are available for undergraduate degree courses and you only start repayments when you begin earning – see the Student Loans Company website (www.slc.co.uk) for more information. If this is your first degree, you may also qualify for help with tuition fees from your Local Education Authority – the website www.dfes.gov.uk/leagateway has addresses for all the LEAs in the UK.

If you are resident in the UK and studying for a vocational course lasting two years or less (or three years with a year of work experience), you can apply for a Career Development Loan of up to £8000. However, the course must relate to your planned career and you must intend to work within the EU at the end of your course. The downside of a Career Development Loan is that repayments start a month after you finish your course (see the website www.lifelonglearning.co.uk/cdl or call ☎ 0800 585 505 for more information).

In Britain, the Association of MBAs (www.mbaworld.com) is responsible for the MBA Loan Scheme, which provides funding for MBA study in the UK and also at some business schools abroad. You can apply for £10,000, or two-thirds of your salary in the year before you started the course, and repayments begin six months after graduation. Applicants must be British citizens aged 18 years or over and must have five years' business experience (two years for university graduates).

If you are planning to go back to the same company at the end of your career break, you may be able to get some funding for your course if you promise to return to your job for a minimum length of time afterwards – talk your employer to see if this is an option.

International Funding

It is much harder to find funding to study overseas, but a number of specialist organisations provide scholarships and grants for exceptional students. Competition for these awards is fierce and you must apply a year or more in advance to stand a chance of gaining an award.

The most famous international award scheme is the Fulbright Awards Program, managed by the Fulbright Commission (www.fulbright.co.uk). It provides a full year of funding for British and American students, academics and professionals to study or teach on the other side of the Atlantic. There are 15 to 21 annual awards for postgraduate courses, including MBAs, but you must hold a 2nd-class honours degree or higher to apply – see Contacts (p223) for information on Fulbright awards worldwide.

Unesco publishes the useful *Study Abroad* guide, which covers higher education courses and scholarships in 129 countries. You can purchase it online from the Unesco website (www.unesco.org/education/studyingabroad). Another useful resource is the *Grants Register*, published by Palgrave MacMillan (www.palgrave.com) and listing 3500 grants for postgraduate courses worldwide; it can be found in careers advice centres and major libraries.

STUDYING IN THE USA

Higher education is no bargain in North America, but it's indispensable for opening up new opportunities and securing better-paying jobs. Numerous studies have documented the correlation between graduate education and higher salaries, but with the recent economic downturn, many freshly minted JDs, MAs and MBAs are discovering that there is a glut of overqualified job seekers in the real world.

Financial aid comes in many forms, from scholarships, fellowships and outright grants (especially for women and minority groups) to subsidized federal student loans, and private loans with steep adjustable interest rates. Professional-school applicants generally have an easier time securing loans, since they are considered more likely to make good on their debts. In one of the most generous tax credits going, US taxpayers with a qualifying modified adjusted gross income can claim a Lifetime Learning Credit of up to US$2000 against their federal income taxes for tuition and related expenses, but only through 2005.

Many larger corporations (and some branches of the armed forces) will pay for promising employees to attend graduate school, with the implicit understanding that the employee will return to work for the sponsoring firm. Through the Master's International Program, Peace Corps volunteers can earn tuition and graduate degree credits at partner universities while serving overseas.

The bottom line: Sourcing the cash to fund higher education is easy; getting out of grad school without a massive debt is a challenge. See www.finaid.org for a comprehensive look at financial aid options.

STUDYING IN AUSTRALIA

The good news is that the Australian recruitment industry believes an undergraduate degree hugely improves career prospects. The bad news, however, is that an MA or MBA does not make a positive difference when applying for jobs or promotions! At management level the major differentiating factors are good leadership and team-building skills as well as a shared vision for the company's future.

Conversely, an MBA is a great personal magnifier, highlighting how to draw the maximum economic benefit from your skills and interests. You might, perhaps, develop new divisions within the company you work for or set up a small company and work for yourself. The practical business applications of an MBA can also improve access to bank loans and government-assistance programs.

Postgraduate study outcomes, employment and earnings data are available from the Graduate Careers Council of Australia at www.gradlink.edu.au. For information on loans for study at home or overseas look under PELS (Postgraduate Education Loan Scheme) and Overseas Study at www.hecs.gov.au and under OS-HELP at www.backingaustraliasfuture.gov.au.

Another possible source of funding is a loan. UK residents are eligible for career development loans for study abroad as long as they intend to work in the EU at the end of the course. EU citizens can also get career development loans for study in the UK. American students can obtain sponsored loans in the USA for overseas study through the Federal Student Aid program (www.fafsa.ed.gov). International students wanting to study in Australia can find scholarship information on the Study in Australia website (www.studyinaustralia.gov.au).

Some business schools, including the London Business School (www.london.edu), Britain's leading provider of MBAs, also offer private loan schemes which are open to international students. Governments also offer grants and scholarships to attract exceptional students from abroad – contact the embassies directly for information.

Useful web resources for funding include:

- **Council for International Education** (www.ukcosa.org.uk) A site with links to government funding organisations worldwide.
- **E-StudentLoan** (www.estudentloan.com) Search engine for student loans in the US.
- **Fastweb** (fastweb.monster.com) US search engine for grants and loans.
- **Gradfund** (www.ncl.ac.uk/postgraduate/funding/gradfund) A search engine for postgraduate funding in Britain.
- **Gradloans** (www.gradloans.com) US site with comprehensive funding information.
- **Grant Search** (www.grantsearch.com) Online database of academic grants in Australia.
- **International Education Financial Aid** (www.iefa.com) US site with a search engine for US and international scholarships.
- **Student Money** (www.studentmoney.org) British site with search engine for scholarships, bursaries, loans and grants in the UK.

STUDYING FOR FUN

If all work and no play is taking the fun out of life, why not use your career break to study something completely for your own pleasure? Plenty of courses out there focus on pure enjoyment, from snowboarding and sailing to creative writing and Thai cooking. You could learn to speak French in Paris, train as a painter in Italy or study meditation in a Buddhist monastery – it's all about taking some time for yourself and learning to do something you always wanted to do but never had the time for.

Leisure courses can also pay a dividend if you want to pick up casual work abroad on your career break – on a working holiday to Australia for example. Useful options include cooking and bar-tending courses, and instructor courses in adventure sports that let you work as a teacher overseas.

Some of the most popular courses for career-breakers are covered in the following sections, but there are hundreds of other options out there – the website ShawGuides (www .shawguides.com) lists more than 5300 nonacademic courses worldwide if you need some inspiration.

LANGUAGE COURSES

The great thing about language courses is that you can learn a language wherever people speak it. There are Spanish schools in Spain and Latin America; Portuguese schools in Portugal and Brazil; German schools in Germany and Austria; French schools in France, Switzerland, Guadeloupe and Canada; Japanese schools in Japan; and Mandarin Chinese schools in China, Hong Kong and Taiwan…the list goes on and on.

Language courses usually work on a total immersion basis, with extra classes on the local culture, and homestay accommodation with local families to help you practise your new-found language skills. Some schools let you divide your study between several campuses, providing a bit of variety while you learn to roll your 'r's. The whole thing is extremely well organised and most schools and language agencies offer a complete package, with classes, accommodation and meals – all you need to provide is the flights.

There are courses for beginner, intermediate and advanced students and you can usually enrol on any Monday, or on set dates monthly for complete beginners. The standard course involves 20 hours of classes each week, or there are intensive courses with 30 or more hours of classes for a slightly higher fee. Tuition in group classes of four to 12 is cheaper, but one-on-one tuition is tailored to your individual needs. The overall prices vary depending on where you study. You should bank on paying £150 to £250 per week for the classes, plus another £100 to £200 for half-board accommodation. If you need a study visa, the school will provide all the necessary paperwork.

As well as improving your language skills, studying abroad will open your eyes to different cultures, as Jennifer Mundy-Nordin discovered when she took six months' extended leave to study Swedish in Sweden:

I firstly attended a private university course to learn basic Swedish and then studied at a government-funded school for immigrants. Most of the other students at the government-funded school were refugees from Kurdistan and Bosnia, so our only common language was Swedish. Their stories really opened my eyes to life as a refugee and gave me a new understanding of their plight. The hardest part about trying to learn Swedish in Sweden was that all the Swedes wanted to speak English to me!

The easiest way to find a language school is to go through a language agency in your home country. Among other things, you'll have a local person to discuss your plans with before you go and you'll benefit from the support of other international students once you start your course. Most agencies offer a choice of languages and schools around the world and extra classes in cultural subjects such as the arts, history, dance and cooking. Homestays are the default accommodation, but you can also stay in student halls, apartments, guesthouses and hotels.

If you don't want to go through an agency, it's easy enough to find language schools abroad on the Internet. However, you need to be a little careful – unless you know the country well, you may find you've enrolled at a second-rate school on the outskirts of a dusty provincial town. Look for schools that are recognised by the national ministry of education or by an international language association such as the International Association of Language Centres (IALC; www.ialc.org). National language school associations are listed on the website www.language-learning.net, which also has a search engine for courses worldwide.

As well as the language agencies and schools listed in Contacts (p224), you can make bookings with hundreds of language schools over the Internet through the web-based agency Languagecourse.net (www.languagecourse.net). Other useful web resources for language study overseas include:

- **Europa-Pages** (www.europa-pages.com) Database of language courses across Europe.
- **Hyperstudy** (www.hyperstudy.com) Links on worldwide education, including language schools.
- **Language Schools.com** (www.languageschoolsguide.com) Searchable database of language courses and schools worldwide.
- **Language Schools Directory** (www.language-schools-directory.com) Large database of schools in Europe, North America and Australia.
- **Study Abroad** (http://language.studyabroad.com) Study Abroad database of language courses.
- **Transitions Abroad** (www.transitionsabroad.com) Living and working abroad site with language-course listings.
- **Worldwide Classroom** (www.worldwide.edu) Country-by-country search for language courses worldwide.

THE ARTS

Learning to paint on a Tuscan hillside could well be the perfect antidote to office stress. If you are feeling creatively restrained by your current job, there are courses all over the world that will help you express your artistic leanings, whether your passion is painting, sculpture, drawing, jewellery-making, music, photography, film-making, dance, music, drama or even the flying trapeze.

The kind of course you take depends on whether you want to learn for pleasure or make a living as an artist. You can take degrees, master's courses and vocational courses in subjects such as fine art, film-making and fashion, which can start you down the road to becoming the next Quentin Tarantino or Tracy Emin.

At the other end of the scale are courses that focus on having fun, where you learn to sculpt, paint or write in an inspirational setting with hands-on instruction from experienced artists. This is a great way to learn, and you can study in some stunning locations. Many art courses are based in rural cottages in Italy and France (see pp231-5 for some recommendations) and there are creative writing courses in many historic European cities.

Kathleen Munnelly found inspiration on a creative writing course at Charles University in Prague:

Although Prague seduces most visitors with its Gothic beauty, spending a month there and being involved in a structured program really gave me a deeper appreciation for the place. I had the honour of studying under the wise and generous Arnost Lustig, whose joyous approach to life despite his many sufferings (he was a Holocaust survivor) was inspiring, and whose sense of humour and dedication to the craft of writing motivated me to write more in that month than I ever had before or since. I also did my first ever public reading – bolstered by a few shots of Becherovka!

Whether you do an arts course for ambition or love, remember to factor in the cost of materials. Paints, photographic paper, movie film, studio time, casting bronze and other tools of the trade can really eat into your career-break budget.

Some of the best art courses around the world are listed on pp231-5, but other useful resources for finding arts courses worldwide include:

- **Artcourses.co.uk** (www.artcourses.co.uk) UK database of art classes, workshops and artistic holidays.
- **Art Holidays** (www.art-holidays.co.uk) British site that lists art holidays and courses worldwide.
- **Best Art Schools** (www.best-art-schools.com) US database of art and design schools.
- **British Arts** (www.britisharts.co.uk/holidayscourses.htm) UK site listing art courses and art holidays.
- **Circus Arts Courses** (www.juggling.org/help/circus-arts/courses) Large directory of circus arts courses worldwide.

- **Directory of Writers Circles** (www.writers-circles.com) UK directory of writing courses and writing holidays.
- **Photographers Gallery** (www.photonet.org.uk/information/resource/courses.html) London gallery site with a directory of photography courses in the UK.
- **Sensebox** (www.sensebox.com) Information on art schools worldwide.
- **ShawGuides** (photoschools.shawguides.com) ShawGuides pages on photography and film courses worldwide.
- **Theatre Links** (www.theatrelinks.com/university.htm) Directory of acting courses in the UK, USA and Australia.

COOKING & BAR-TENDING

Can't cook, won't cook? Well, a career break could be the perfect time to learn. There are cooking schools all over the world that promise to transform you into a cordon-bleu chef, even if you've never cooked anything that didn't have instructions on the packet. As well as impressing dinner dates, a cooking qualification can help you find work overseas, from casual café jobs to chalet and yacht work.

Apart from professional cooking schools, numerous amateur cooking courses feature hands-on tuition from local cooks and trips to market to buy fresh ingredients. Some of the most popular options are cooking classes in the cuisine's country of origin, particularly in Thailand, India, Mexico, France and Italy.

Ruth McEwen spiced up her cooking skills on a five-day Thai cooking course in northern Thailand:

I'd always wanted to learn how to cook Thai food, so I took time off from travelling in Thailand to study at a cooking school in Chiang Mai. The course was fabulous – we started off every morning with a trip to the market to buy fresh lemongrass, chillies, green papaya and other weird and wonderful ingredients and then spent the whole day cooking and eating everything we prepared. These days, when I throw a dinner party I serve up green curry with pad thai (fried noodles) and spicy tom yam soup, instead of just dumping a big bowl of spaghetti in the middle of the table!

Another way to make it easier to find casual work overseas is to take a course in 'mixology' – the art of making cocktails. Some recommended cooking and bar-tending schools are listed on p238 but the following websites also provide some useful information for aspiring cooks:

- http://cookforfun.shawguides.com
- www.cookingschools.com

ALTERNATIVE THERAPIES

If you have a spiritual or holistic bent, a career break could be a fantastic opportunity to follow a healing art like yoga, t'ai chi, meditation or massage back to its source. Holistic centres around the world accept foreign students for a small donation, but be warned – authentic spiritual and therapeutic schools expect you to follow strict rules regarding silence, diet and behaviour.

For truly authentic yoga study, head to Rishikesh or Haridwar in northern India. Both towns have dozens of ashrams (spiritual centres) that accept foreign students on a walk-in basis. If you don't feel bendy enough to try yoga at source, there are westernised yoga schools around the world that offer intensive courses and teacher training. Look for a school that has branches worldwide and focuses on the health benefits of yoga (unless you are specifically looking for a spiritual journey).

If you are taking a break from a stressful job, a course in Buddhist meditation could be a good way to find equilibrium – the website www.buddhanet.net lists Buddhist centres around the world. To study meditation at source, visit India, Nepal or Thailand. The most important world centre for Buddhism is the town of Bodhgaya in eastern India, which marks the spot where Buddha attained enlightenment. There are also Buddhist study centres in Dharamsala (India), Kathmandu (Nepal) and Bangkok, Ko Samui and Ko Pha-Ngan (Thailand).

See Contacts (p238) for some recommended alternative therapy courses around the world. If you are thinking of making a career change and becoming a professional alternative therapist, the local governing body for the therapy will be able to recommend reputable schools and training centres. Governing bodies in the UK include:

- **Acupuncture Society** (www.acupuncturesociety.org.uk) Acupuncture and acupressure.
- **British Complementary Medicine Association** (www.bcma.co.uk) Massage, aromatherapy and holistic therapies.
- **British Wheel of Yoga** (www.bwy.org.uk) Yoga.
- **International Therapy Examination Council** (www.itecworld.co.uk) Complementary medicine and sports therapies.
- **Tai Chi Union for Great Britain** (www.taichiunion.com) T'ai chi ch'uan.
- **Vocational Training Charitable Trust** (www.vtct.org.uk) Aromatherapy, reflexology, massage and holistic therapies.

LEARNING A SPORT

If you have ever splashed cold water on your face during a sluggish afternoon at the office, perhaps it was a subliminal message – what you really want to be doing is diving on a coral atoll or sailing a yacht into a turquoise bay. A career break provides a fantastic opportunity to learn a new sport – from windsurfing and sailing to kick boxing and snowboarding – and you can even study for a professional sporting qualification that will let you teach the sport anywhere in the world. The following sections provide information on some of the most popular sports for career-breakers around the world.

Watersports

Learning to sail is an ideal choice for career-breakers, but you must pass a series of exams before you are qualified to take a boat out under your own steam. In the process, you'll learn essential skills such as seamanship, rigging, nautical safety, navigation, chart-reading, signalling and meteorology. It might sound like a lot of hard work, but controlling a vessel at sea is a huge responsibility, and if you misread the weather, or blunder into a busy shipping lane, it might not just be you who suffers the consequences.

The starting point for learning to sail is the Competent Crew course, which can serve as a foot in the door if you want work as a crew member on a yacht. This is followed by the Day Skipper, Coastal Skipper and Yachtmaster courses, which slowly build up the skills required to operate a sailing vessel anywhere in the world. If you want to charter a boat on inshore waters, the minimum level is Day Skipper. To cross the English Channel, you must be a Coastal Skipper, and to sail to the Canary Islands, you must be a Yachtmaster.

Each course has a separate theory and practical component and you must clock up a minimum number of miles at sea before you can move on to the next level. To qualify as Day Skipper, you should take a Competent Crew course and Day Skipper Practical (both courses last five days and cost from £275 to £400). Many schools recommend that you also take the theory-based Day Skipper Shore-Based Course (five days, from £250).

The company Sunsail (www.sunsail.com) can arrange training at any of these levels in the UK, Holland, the Canary Islands or Thailand. Alternatively, you can train all the way up from landlubber to Yachtmaster in around four months with the sailing school Flying Fish (www.flyingfishonline.com), with a portion of the practical training in Australia or Greece.

Wherever you choose to study, look for a course that is recognised by the local national governing body for sailing – for example, the Royal Yachting Association (RYA; www.rya.org.uk) in Britain, Yachting Australia (AYF; www.yachting.org.au) in Australia or the American Sailing Association (AMA; www.american-sailing.com) in the USA.

All these organisations list schools that offer recognised sailing courses on their websites. Sailing schools and sailing-holiday companies also offer leisure courses in yacht and dinghy sailing that will allow you to pootle around under supervision on inshore waters.

Scuba diving is another popular option for career-breakers, and because of the hierarchical structure of dive training, it's easy to extend your basic training all the way up to dive master or instructor level and then pick up work in the industry. The cost and quality of diving varies wildly depending on where you dive, but top spots around the world include the Red Sea in Egypt, the Great Barrier Reef in Australia, the Caribbean, the islands of the Pacific and most of Southeast Asia.

The three main systems for dive training are PADI (Professional Association of Dive Instructors; www.padi.com), NAUI (National Association of Underwater Instructors; www.naui.org) and SSI (Scuba Schools International; www.ssiusa.com). PADI is by far the most widespread system but dive qualifications are fully transferable, so you can start your training in one system and finish off in another.

The starting point for all divers is the Open Water Diver course, which allows you to dive anywhere in the world up to a maximum depth of 18m (59ft). There's a medical to test for respiratory and ear problems and you then carry out a number of supervised exercises underwater, first in a swimming pool and then in the open ocean. Prices vary from US$100 to US$500 depending on where you study – southern Queensland in Australia is probably the cheapest place to learn. The depth restriction can be a bit limiting, so many amateurs go on to take the Advanced Open Water Diver course, which lets you dive up to 40m (131ft).

To work in the dive industry, you must take the Open Water, Advanced Open Water, Rescue Diver and Dive Master courses, which qualify you to supervise and guide other divers on a dive boat. Most people who intend to make a career in diving continue on up to dive instructor or higher – the PADI website shows the complete hierarchy of dive training.

Dive schools often have internship schemes where you can study to become a dive master for free in exchange for a few months' work for the company. However, operators often work staff extremely hard, and it's not unknown for people to be 'let go' just a few dives before the end of their training. Lewis Webster trained in Cairns, Australia:

I was taken on for three months to work on a live-aboard dive boat on the Great Barrier Reef in exchange for my dive-master training and about £8 a day for subsistence. The job involved shadowing an existing dive master, filling air tanks, cleaning the boat and making the customers feel at home, which was physically quite hard work. I spent around a week at a time out on the barrier reef, which was great, and clocked up around 82 dives but, unfortunately, I only made it to the level of Rescue Diver. The company tried to spin the training out as long as possible to keep us working, and me and quite a few other people eventually quit in frustration!

Other popular watersports include surfing, kite-surfing, windsurfing, kayaking and canoeing. You can study all these sports at hundreds of locations worldwide, and schools such as Flying Fish (www.flyingfishonline.com) offer instructor courses that allow you to teach professionally. Full details of watersports qualifications in the UK can be found on the Royal Yachting Association website (www.rya.org.uk).

Air Sports

Flying, parachuting and gliding are great ways to blow away the cobwebs of office life. If you want to fly a powered aircraft, you should study for a private pilot's licence (PPL), which will permit you to fly solo during daylight hours. Training takes place in small two-seater trainer aircraft and you must clock up 45 hours of flying time (including 10 solo hours) to gain your licence. Expect to pay around £4000 for the course, including all hire of the plane and reference materials.

As well as powered flight, you could try gliding in an unpowered glider; an introductory week-long course costs around £275. Other options include parachuting, hang-gliding (suspended from a canvas wing), paragliding (suspended from a parachute) and traditional parachuting. For all these sports you can take individual flights or train up to be an instructor. For more information, contact the Fédération Aéronautique Internationale (www.fai.org), the worldwide governing body for air sports.

Winter Sports

There's an old saying in skiing circles that it's better to be off-piste than the other way around. Every year, hundreds of people trade the office for the ski slopes, and there are dozens of schools in the UK and worldwide that can train you to be a ski or snowboard instructor in a single season, allowing you to work at ski resorts around the world.

Skiing and snowboarding courses are licensed by national governing bodies such as the British Association of Snowsport Instructors (BASI, www.basi.org.uk), but qualifications are universally recognised. Links to governing bodies around the world can be found on the International Ski Instructors Association website (www.isiaski.org).

Major schools in the UK include Flying Fish (www.flyingfishonline.com), the International Academy (www.theinternationalacademy.com), Peak Leaders (www.peakleaders .com) and BASI itself. You'll pay £4000 to £6000 for a four- to 10-week instructor course, including flights, accommodation and meals, but you need to provide your own skiing or snowboarding gear. During the British winter, most courses run in mainland Europe, Canada and the USA. In summer, courses run in New Zealand and South America.

Other Outdoor Activities

If you are thinking of joining an expedition, you might want to start off with a course in wilderness survival, mountaineering, or expedition first aid or leadership. Organisations such as Outward Bound (www.outward-bound.org) and Plas y Brenin (www.pyb.co.uk) offer a huge range of outdoor activity courses, including amateur and professional level courses in mountaineering, rock-climbing, hill-walking, expedition leadership and canoeing.

The most important qualification for expedition leaders is the Mountain Leader (Summer) or Mountain Leader (Winter) award. Potential students must register with Mountain Leader Training (www.mltuk.org) and then log a certain number of hill and mountain expeditions in the UK before taking the formal training and assessment course (around £770 in total).

There are also specialist courses in first aid for foreign travel – Wilderness Medical Training (www.wildernessmedicaltraining.co.uk) offers a course that covers everything from emergency first aid to dealing with tropical diseases.

Hard-core outdoor types can also take wilderness-survival courses that teach you how to hunt for food, build shelters and collect water using only the materials you find around you. You can also learn rock-climbing and mountaineering at specialist climbing schools in Europe and the USA and exotic locations such as Thailand and India.

For a slightly different outdoor experience, you could study field guiding on a South African game reserve. The courses cover animal tracking and identification, wilderness safety, 4WD driving, firearm handling and animal-capture techniques. Most are certified by the Field Guides Association of Southern Africa (FGASA; www.fgasa.org.za) and students often go on to find work at game reserves across Africa. Several courses are listed in the Contacts section but you can arrange similar programs through volunteering agencies such as Global Vision International (www.gvi.co.uk) and Teaching & Projects Abroad (www .teaching-abroad.co.uk).

Paul Gardiner went on a two-week game-ranger course with Eco Africa Experience:

I've always been fascinated with Africa and its wild animals so I decided to go and learn a little more about this facet of the African continent. There were six of us on the course altogether and we leant how to track Africa's famous big five (lion, leopard, elephant, rhino and buffalo), how to fire a rifle, plant identification, survival tactics in the bush, driving a 4WD Land Rover, game counting etc. On one of the nights we camped under the stars, and we all had to spend an hour watching over the camp while the rest of the team lay asleep. During my shift a pride of seven lions came within 10m of our camp, but, thankfully, they moved on out of the valley in search of their next meal!

Web Resources

The following web resources provide information on adventure sports in the UK and worldwide.

WATERSPORTS

- **Association of Surfing Professionals** (www.aspworldtour.com) International surfing organisation with representatives worldwide.
- **British Canoe Union** (www.bcu.org.uk) Britain's canoeing governing body.
- **British Surfing Association** (www.britsurf.org) Britain's surfing governing body, based in Cornwall.
- **Divers Alert Network** (www.diversalertnetwork.org) International organisation promoting dive safety.
- **Sportextreme.com** (www.sportextreme.com/diving) A fantastic database of information on dive sites throughout the world.
- **International Sailing Federation** (www.sailing.org) International organisation with links to national authorities and sailing clubs worldwide.
- **Sailing Now** (www.sailingnow.com) Bulletin board for yacht skippers who need crew and for crew members advertising their services.
- **UK Diving** (www.ukdiving.co.uk) Extensive site about UK and global diving.
- **UK Windsurfing Association** (www.ukwindsurfing.com) The largest windsurfing association in Britain.

AIR SPORTS

- **Aircraft Owners & Pilots Association** (www.aopa.co.uk) UK and US pilots' association, with listings of approved flight schools.
- **Best Aviation** (www.bestaviation.net) Worldwide flight-school listings.
- **British Gliding Association** (www.gliding.co.uk) UK governing body for gliding.
- **British Hang Gliding and Paragliding Association** (www.bhpa.co.uk) Main British association for unpowered air sports.
- **British Parachute Association** (www.bpa.org.uk) UK governing body for parachuting.
- **Flying Zone** (www.flyingzone.co.uk) Lists UK flight schools.

WINTER SPORTS

- **Natives.co.uk** (www.natives.co.uk) UK site with ski-job pages and a discussion forum.
- **Reuters Snow Zone** (www.snow-zone.co.uk) Links and information on ski resorts worldwide.
- **Ski Club of Great Britain** (www.skiclub.co.uk) Leading UK information source on everything to do with skiing and snowboarding.

CLIMBING

- **British Mountaineering Council** (www.thebmc.co.uk) Britain's governing body for climbing and mountaineering.
- **Union Internationale des Associations d'Alpinisme** (International Mountaineering and Climbing Federation; www.uiaa.ch) International body for alpine climbing.

CONTACTS

FORMAL EDUCATION & FUNDING
Arts and Humanities Research Board (AHRB)
Whitefriars, Lewins Mead, Bristol BS1 2AE, UK
☎ +44 (0)117 987 6543
fax +44 (0)117 987 6544
See website for email addresses.
www.ahrb.ac.uk
This institution is the main UK funding body for research and postgraduate study in the arts and humanities. AHRB can provide funding for all sorts of postgraduate courses, including master's degrees.

Association of Commonwealth Universities (ACU)
36 Gordon Sq, London WC1H 0PF, UK
☎ +44 (0)20 7380 6700
fax +44 (0)20 7387 2655
info@acu.ac.uk
www.acu.ac.uk

This international organisation represents universities across the Commonwealth and provides funding for Commonwealth students (ie students from Australia, New Zealand and Canada) to study in the UK. It also administers the Marshall Scholarship (www.marshallscholarship.org), which provides funding for students from the USA to study in Britain.

British Council
10 Spring Gardens, London SW1A 2BN, UK
☎ +44 (0)20 7930 8466
general.enquiries@britishcouncil.org
www.britishcouncil.org
The British Council is the main source of information for foreign students hoping to study in the UK and its offices worldwide can provide information on funding for international students. The Chevening Scholarship (www.chevening.com) provides funding for 2300 foreign students to study in the UK each year.

Department for Education & Skills (DFES)
Sanctuary Buildings, Great Smith St, London SW1P 3BT, UK
☎ +44 (0)870 000 2288
fax +44 (0)20 7925 6000
info@dfes.gsi.gov.uk
www.dfes.gov.uk
The DFES is the official government department for further education and skills training in the UK. The website has useful resources for both domestic and overseas students.

Entente Cordiale Scholarships
French Cultural Department, 23 Cromwell Rd, London SW7 2EL, UK
☎ +44 (0)20 7073 1312
fax +44 (0)20 7073 1326
entente.cordiale@ambafrance.org.uk
www.francealacarte.org.uk/entente
This joint agreement between the British and French governments provides funding for around 20 outstanding students from Britain to undertake postgraduate study in France and vice versa. The one-year scholarship provides around £7500 for travel and living expenses and covers tuition fees up to £3000; you must apply by 19 March each year.

Fulbright Awards Program
The Fulbright Commission, Fulbright House, 62 Doughty St, London WC1N 2JZ, UK
☎ +44 (0)20 7404 6880
fax +44 (0)20 7404 6834
education@fulbright.co.uk
www.fulbright.co.uk
This British-American organisation provides scholarships for British students to study postgraduate courses in America and vice versa. The Council for the International Exchange of Scholars (www.cies.org) provides information on Fulbright award schemes in other countries.

IDP Education Australia
1 Geils Court, Deakin, ACT 2600, Australia
☎ +61 (0)2-6285 8222
fax +61 (0)2-6285 3036
info@idp.com
www.idp.com
This nonprofit organisation is owned by 38 of Australia's 39 universities and provides information for students planning to study in Australia, including a search engine for courses at Australian universities.

Kaplan Center
3–5 Charing Cross Rd, London WC2H 0HA, UK
☎ +44 (0)20 7930 3130
fax +44 (0)20 7930 8009
london_center@kaplan.com
www.kaptest.com/uk
This US company offers coaching for the GMAT exam (required for many MBA courses), GRE (required for US college and postgraduate courses) and SAT (required for undergraduate courses). Training takes place over eight two-hour sessions spread over four weeks, and fees for classroom courses start at £945 for the GMAT and £750 for the GRE or SAT.

Leverhulme Trust
1 Pemberton Row, London EC4A 3BG, UK
☎ +44 (0)20 7822 5220
fax +44 (0)20 7822 5084
enquiries@leverhulme.org.uk
www.leverhulme.org.uk
The Leverhulme Trust offers around £25 million in grants for academic courses annually, including around 20 awards for postgraduate study overseas (except in the US). The grant is available for 12 or 24 months and the annual award is £13,500. The minimum age for applicants is 30 and you can apply from September.

Medical Research Council (MRC)
20 Park Crescent, London W1B 1AL, UK
☎ +44 (0)20 7636 5422
fax +44 (0)20 7436 6179
corporate@headoffice.mrc.ac.uk
www.mrc.ac.uk
The MRC is the main body for medical research funding in the UK and it provides funding for postgraduate study both directly and through university departments.

Open University
PO Box 724, Milton Keynes MK7 6ZS, UK
☎ +44 (0)1908 653231
fax +44 (0)1908 655072

general-enquiries@open.ac.uk
www.open.ac.uk
The Open University is the largest provider of university-level qualifications in the UK. Online and correspondence courses are available in most subjects and at most levels, including degrees, master's and MBAs. Courses start on set dates (usually in January/February or October) and tuition fees start at £450 per nine-month module.

Research Councils UK
Polaris House, North Star Ave, Swindon, Wiltshire SN2 1ET, UK
☎ +44 (0)1793 444420
fax +44 (0)1793 444409
info@rcuk.ac.uk
www.rcuk.ac.uk
This government body represents the seven governing councils that award grants for research and training in the fields of science and engineering. As well as awards for UK students and professionals, the organisation funds students from the developing world to study in the UK.

Rotary International
Kinwarton House, Alcester, Warwickshire B49 6PB, UK
☎ +44 (0)1789 765411
fax +44 (0)1789 765570
secretary@ribi.org
www.ribi.org
This international charity offers various awards for overseas study, including funding for undergraduate, graduate and vocational courses. Contact your local Rotary Foundation branch for more information.

Teacher Training Agency
Canterbury Mills, 103 Canterbury Rd, Croydon CR0 3AZ, UK
☎ +44 (0)845 600 0991
teaching@ttainfo.co.uk
www.useyourheadteach.gov.uk
This is the main organisation for teacher training in the UK. The website has information on all the routes into teaching in Britain, including funding for teacher training.

LANGUAGE AGENCIES
The following organisations arrange language courses in various countries around the world. Unless otherwise stated, flights, visas and insurance are extra.

Amerispan
PO Box 58129, Philadelphia, PA 19102-8129, USA
☎ +1 215-751 1100
fax +1 215-751 1986
info@amerispan.com
www.amerispan.com
This American company represents more than 80 schools worldwide where you can study European, Asian and Middle Eastern languages. As well as the usual European options, you can study Arabic in Fez (Morocco), Thai in Chiang Mai (Thailand) and Mandarin in Beijing (China).
Types of Course: French, German, Italian, Portuguese, Russian, Chinese, Japanese, Thai & Arabic.
Timing & Length of Courses: One week to nine months. Most courses start weekly but some are summer only.
Destinations: Europe, Russia, Canada, Japan, China, Taiwan, Thailand, Morocco, United Arab Emirates & 16 countries in Latin America.
Costs: Vary with the course – Spanish courses in Cusco (Peru) start at US$180/630 for one week/one month (US$285/1050 with homestay accommodation).
Eligibility: Varies with the course – most students are 18 or older.

Cactus Language
4 Clarence House, 30–31 North St, Brighton, East Sussex BN1 1EB, UK
☎ +44 (0)845 130 4775
fax +44 (0)1273 775686
enquiry@cactuslanguage.com
www.cactuslanguage.com
This international language agency offers a huge variety of language classes abroad, including Spanish in Spain, Cuba and Latin America, French in Bordeaux and Montpellier and Russian in St Petersburg. There are classes for beginners to advanced speakers.
Types of Course: Arabic, Basque, Czech, French, German, Greek, Italian, Japanese, Portuguese, Quechua, Russian, Spanish, Turkish & Yiddish.
Timing & Length of Courses: From one week. Most courses start on the first Monday of each month.
Destinations: Europe, Middle East, Russia, Latin America & Asia.
Costs: Prices vary depending on the destination and type of course. Spanish courses in Spain start at £149 per week plus £140 per week for accommodation.
Eligibility: Minimum age is 18, but people over 21 preferred for some courses.

Càlédöñiâ Languages Abroad
The Clockhouse, Bonnington Mill, 72 Newhaven Rd, Edinburgh EH6 5QG, Scotland
☎ +44 (0)131 621 7721/2
fax +44 (0)131 621 7723
courses@caledonialanguages.co.uk
www.caledonialanguages.co.uk
Càlédöñiâ offers foreign-language courses throughout Europe and Latin America. As well as language lessons, you can add on extras such as cooking and dance courses, skiing and voluntary work.
Types of Course: French, German, Italian, Portuguese, Russian & Spanish.

Timing & Length of Courses: One week to nine months, beginning on Mondays year round.
Destinations: France, Spain, Germany, Portugal, Italy, Russia, Argentina, Bolivia, Brazil, Costa Rica, Cuba, Ecuador, Mexico & Peru.
Costs: Vary with the destination, level of study and type of accommodation – studying French in Montpellier costs £220/670 for one week/month, plus around £110 per week for B&B accommodation with a host family.
Eligibility: Minimum age is 18 on most programs.

CESA Languages Abroad

CESA House, Pennance Rd, Lanner, Cornwall TR16 5TQ, UK
☎ +44 (0)1209 211800
fax +44 (0)1209 211830
info@cesalanguages.com
www.cesalanguages.com
This international school offers overseas language tuition in Europe, Russia, Latin America and Asia. Among other options, you can study Japanese in Japan, French in France or Guadeloupe, and Spanish in Spain, Ecuador or Mexico.
Types of Course: Arabic, French, German, Italian, Japanese, Portuguese, Russian & Spanish.
Timing & Length of Courses: Most courses last four to 36 weeks and start monthly on set dates (usually on Mondays).
Destinations: Worldwide, including Europe, Asia & Latin America.
Costs: Vary with the course and destination – Japanese courses in Okazaki (Japan) cost from £849 for four weeks, plus £142 for the student visa application. Accommodation is available from £45 per week in shared rooms.
Eligibility: Minimum age is 17 (18 for some courses).

Challenge UK

101 Lorna Rd, Hove, East Sussex BN3 3EL, UK
☎ +44 (0)1273 208648
fax +44 (0)1273 220376
info@challengeuk.com
www.challengeuk.com
Challenge UK offers language courses at language schools in 13 French cities and academic courses at prestigious universities such as the Sorbonne in Paris.
Types of Course: French.
Timing & Length of Courses: One week to one year, starting on set dates through the year. Short courses start on any Monday for intermediate students or monthly for beginners.
Destinations: France, including Angers, Antibes, Biarritz, Bordeaux, Cannes, Grenoble, Lyon, Montpellier, Nantes, Nice, Paris, Perpignan & Poitiers.
Costs: Vary with the destination and duration of the course – standard courses in Paris start at €525 per week, including B&B accommodation.
Eligibility: Minimum age is 17 (18 for some schools).

Don Quijote/Vis à Vis UK

2/4 Stoneleigh Park Rd, Epsom, Surrey KT19 0QT, UK
☎ +44 (0)20 8786 8081
fax +44 (0)20 8786 8086
dquk@donquijote.org
info@visavis.org
www.donquijote.org
www.visavis.org
This organisation has two wings – Don Quijote arranges residential Spanish courses in most large cities in Spain, as well as the Canary Islands, Peru and Mexico, while Vis à Vis offers French courses in France, Belgium and Canada.
Types of Course: Spanish & French.
Timing & Length of Courses: One to 44 weeks, starting weekly on Mondays (on set dates monthly for beginners).
Destinations: Spain, Peru & Mexico for Spanish courses. France, Brussels (Belgium) & Montreal (Canada) for French courses.
Costs: Vary depending on the destination and course – as an indication, Spanish courses in Barcelona cost from €229 per week, plus €121 for accommodation in a student flat. There's a €33 registration fee.
Eligibility: Minimum age is 18.

EF International Language Schools

74 Roupell St, London SE1 8SS, UK
☎ +44 (0)870 720 0708
fax +44 (0)870 720 0767
languages.gb@ef.com
www.ef.com
EF has 40 years' experience offering upmarket language courses overseas. More unusual options include Russian lessons in St Petersburg and Chinese lessons in Shanghai as well as combined packages of language classes and academic study.
Types of Course: French, German, Italian, Spanish, Russian & Chinese (Mandarin).
Timing & Length of Courses: Two weeks to nine months, starting on Mondays. Basic courses start on set dates from June to August; general and intensive courses start on set dates monthly.
Destinations: France, Spain, Germany, Italy, Ecuador, Russia & China.
Costs: Costs vary with the destination and level of study – studying Chinese in Shanghai costs from £370 for two weeks to £2080 for three months, including half-board homestay accommodation.
Eligibility: Minimum age is 16.

Enforex

Alberto Aguillera, 26, 28015 Madrid, Spain
☎ +34 91-594 37 76
fax +34 91-594 51 59
info@enforex.es
www.enforex.es

This Spanish school offers Spanish courses at seven campuses in Spain and 11 campuses in Latin America. Tuition is in groups of nine and there are classes in general Spanish, Spanish for business, Spanish culture and Spanish for older travellers.

Types of Course: Spanish.

Timing & Length of Courses: From one week up to one academic year. Courses start weekly on a Monday.

Destinations: Spain, Argentina, Bolivia, Costa Rica, Cuba, Ecuador, Guatemala & Peru.

Costs: Vary with the destination and course – an intensive course in Spain costs from €135 per week or €1500 for three months. Accommodation in a student flat starts at €95/150 for a single/double room.

Eligibility: Minimum age is 14 but some courses are for those over 50.

Euro Academy

67–71 Lewisham High St, London SE13 5JX, UK
☎ +44 (0)20 8297 0505
fax +44 (0)20 8297 0984
enquiries@euroacademy.co.uk
www.euroacademy.co.uk

This reliable foreign-learning centre has 30 years' experience providing language tuition overseas. French and Spanish courses are possible in large cities and small seaside towns and there are also overseas courses in German, Portuguese, Russian and Greek.

Types of Course: French, Spanish, German, Portuguese, Russian & Greek.

Timing & Length of Courses: One week to one year. Intermediate courses start weekly on Mondays while beginners start on set dates monthly.

Destinations: France, Spain, Italy, Germany, Portugal, Greece, Russia, Costa Rica, Guatemala, Ecuador & Peru.

Costs: Costs vary with the destination and level of study. French study in Paris costs from €155 per week, plus €205 for homestay accommodation (in summer, student halls are available for around €25 a day).

Eligibility: Minimum age is 16 to 18, depending on the course.

Language Studies Abroad

Suite 1, 1801 US Hwy 50 East, Carson City, NV 89701, USA
☎ +1 775-883 6554
fax +1 775-883 2266
info@languagestudiesabroad.com
www.languagestudiesabroad.com

This American agency was established in 1985 and has links with more than 100 language schools overseas, mostly in Europe and Latin America.

Types of Course: French, Spanish, German, Italian, Portuguese, Russian, Mandarin & Japanese.

Timing & Length of Courses: One week to one year, starting on set dates year round.

Destinations: Europe, Latin America & Asia.

Costs: Vary with the destination. German courses in Berlin start at around US$500; homestay accommodation is extra.

Eligibility: Minimum age is 16.

Language Studies International

Catherine Bossard, 19–21, Ridgmount St, London WC1E 7AH, UK
☎ +44 (0)20 7467 6506
fax +44 (0)20 7323 1736
fl@lsi.edu
www.lsi-learnlanguages.com

This international language school offers overseas language programs in Europe, Latin America and Asia and you can take extra classes in culture, art history and photography. LSI also has offices in Canada and the USA (see website for details).

Types of Course: Spanish, French, Italian, German, Russian, Mandarin & Japanese.

Timing & Length of Courses: Courses start on set dates, usually on Mondays, and last from two weeks (from one week for one-on-one tuition).

Destinations: France, Spain, Germany, Switzerland, Italy, Russia, China, Japan, Mexico, Costa Rica, Ecuador & Peru.

Costs: Vary with the location – Italian courses in Florence or Milan start at £240 for two weeks, plus a £50 registration fee, and accommodation costs from £185 for two weeks in a shared flat.

Eligibility: Minimum age is 16.

OISE Intensive Language Schools

90 Great Russell St, London WC1B 3PS, UK
☎ +44 (0)20 7631 3674
fax +44 (0)20 7631 3679
info@oise.com
www.oise.com

OISE specialises in intensive language training and offers English classes in the UK, Ireland, America and Australia; German classes in Germany; French in France; and Spanish in Spain. Lessons are given in classes of one, four, eight or 12 people – one-on-one lessons are the most expensive.

Types of Course: English, German, French & Spanish.

Timing & Length of Courses: From one week to one year, starting on any Monday.

Destinations: UK, Ireland, USA, Australia, Germany, France & Spain.

Costs: Depends on the location and intensity of the course – study in Paris, Heidelberg or Madrid starts from £580 per week in a group of four with homestay accommodation.

Eligibility: Minimum age is 17.

SOAS Language Centre

School of Oriental and African Studies, Thornhaugh St, Russell Square, London WC1H 0XG, UK
☎ +44 (0)20 7898 4888
fax +44 (0)20 7898 4889

languages@soas.ac.uk
www.soas.ac.uk
This highly regarded school in London is one of the best places to learn African, Asian and Middle Eastern languages. There are intensive one- to two-week courses for beginners and long-term teaching courses in languages as diverse as Arabic, Japanese and Somali.
Types of Course: Courses in 31 languages from Africa, Asia, the Middle East and the Indian subcontinent.
Timing & Length of Courses: One week to one year. Courses run on set dates throughout the year, particularly in summer (one-year courses start in September).
Destinations: London (UK).
Costs: One- and two-week courses cost from £275 and 20-hour courses cost £220. One-year courses cost from £7495. Fees do not include living expenses.
Eligibility: Courses are designed for people over 18.

Sprachcaffe International

Gartenstrasse 6, Frankfurt 60594, Germany
☎ +49 (0)69-610 9120
fax +49 (0)69-603 1395
info@sprachcaffe.com
www.sprachcaffe.com
This international language school has been around for 21 years and offers classes in 10 countries, including several options in China. You have a choice of courses and most classes are for groups of eight to 12.
Types of Course: English, Spanish, French, Italian, German & Mandarin.
Timing & Length of Courses: From two weeks, starting on set dates (usually Mondays) throughout the year.
Destinations: The UK, the USA, Canada, Australia, New Zealand, Spain, Cuba, France, Italy, Germany, Malta & China.
Costs: Vary depending on the destination and course – a two-week Spanish course costs from €440 in Málaga or from €638 in Cuba, including accommodation.
Eligibility: Minimum age is 18.

LANGUAGE SCHOOLS

The following international language schools accept applications directly from language students. Unless otherwise stated, prices do not include airfares, visa fees or insurance.

France
Alliance Française

101 Blvd Raspail, 75270 Paris, France
☎ +33 (0)1 42 84 90 00
fax +33 (0)1 42 84 91 01
info@alliancefr.org
www.alliancefr.org
This international organisation exists to promote the French language and culture worldwide (see the website

for locations). Its centres offer French lessons, including the main Alliance de Paris school in Paris.
Types of Course: All levels of French language.
Timing & Length of Courses: Varies with the destination – courses at the headquarters in Paris are broken down into monthly sessions of 16 to 18 days and run on set dates year round.
Destinations: France & worldwide.
Costs: French courses at the school in Paris start at €333 for each monthly session (€666 for the intensive course).
Eligibility: Minimum age is 18.

BLS Bordeaux

42 Rue Lafaurie de Monbadon, 33000 Bordeaux, France
☎ +33 (0)5 56 51 00 76
fax +33 (0)5 56 51 76 15
info@bls-frenchcourses.com
www.bls-frenchcourses.com
BLS is housed in a historic mansion in central Bordeaux and offers the full gamut of French-language courses from beginner to advanced. There's a second campus in Biarritz.
Types of Course: French.
Timing & Length of Courses: From one to 48 weeks, starting on any Monday.
Destinations: Bordeaux & Biarritz (France).
Costs: Prices start at €490 for two weeks and subsequent weeks are €210 each. Registration is €62 and homestay accommodation starts at €28 per day.
Eligibility: Minimum age is 17.

École France Langue

2 Rue de Sfax, 75116, Paris, France
☎ +33 (0)1 45 00 40 15
fax +33 (0)1 45 00 71 43
paris@france-langue.fr
www.france-langue.org
This French school has campuses in Paris and Nice and offers a broad range of French courses. The Paris school is close to the Arc de Triomphe and the Nice school is just a few blocks from the Mediterranean Sea.
Types of Course: French.
Timing & Length of Courses: From one week, starting on any Monday.
Destinations: Paris & Nice (France).
Costs: Courses in Paris or Nice cost from €170 per week plus a €30 registration fee. Accommodation is available from €25 per night.
Eligibility: Minimum age is 18 for most courses.

Germany & Austria
Actilingua Academy

Gloriettegasse 8, A-1130 Vienna, Austria
☎ +43 (0)1-877 67 01
fax +43 (0)1-877 67 03

german@actilingua.com
www.actilingua.com
This Vienna-based language school offers German courses for all levels. Various supplementary courses include music, Viennese waltzing, German for business and winter sports (from December to March).
Types of Course: German.
Timing & Length of Courses: Two weeks to one year, starting every Monday (on set dates monthly for beginners).
Destinations: Vienna (Austria).
Costs: Prices for standard German courses start at €588 for two weeks, including accommodation and five hours a week of cultural lessons.
Eligibility: Minimum age is 16 (18 on some professional courses).

BWS Germanlingua
Bayerstrasse 13, 80335 Munich, Germany
☎ +49 (0)89-599 89200
fax +49 (0)89-599 89201
info@bws-germanlingua.de
www.bws-germanlingua.de
This German school has campuses in Berlin and Munich and has courses for students of all levels in groups of four to 12. There are lots of optional extras, including art lessons and sporting activities. The Munich campus gets very busy around Oktoberfest.
Types of Course: German.
Timing & Length of Courses: Two to 48 weeks, starting every Monday (beginners start on set dates monthly).
Destinations: Munich & Berlin.
Costs: Prices start at €390 for two weeks, plus €150 per week for a single student room in halls.
Eligibility: Minimum age is 16.

Goethe-Institut (Goethe Institute)
PO Box 19 04 19, 80604 Munich, Germany
☎ +49 (0)89-1 59 21 0
fax +49 (0)89-1 59 21 4 50
zv@goethe.de
www.goethe.de
This international organisation aims to promote German language and culture and operates 126 centres in 77 countries where you can take German-language lessons. The website has links to Goethe Institute branches worldwide.
Types of Course: All levels of German language.
Timing & Length of Courses: Four to 12 weeks, starting on set dates monthly.
Destinations: Berlin and 15 other centres in Germany; plus international centres in 76 countries.
Costs: Vary with the destination and length of study. One-month courses in Germany cost from €945 without accommodation, or €1285 in a single room.
Eligibility: Minimum age is 18.

Greece
Athens Centre
48 Archimidous St, Athens 11636, Greece
☎ +30 210-7012 268
fax +30 210-7018 603
info@athenscentre.gr
www.athenscentre.gr
Established in 1969, this Greek school offers a highly regarded course in modern Greek, accompanied by classes in art, poetry and theatre. There's also a summer school on the island of Spetses.
Types of Course: Greek.
Timing & Length of Courses: Three to 10 weeks, starting monthly. The three-week summer program starts in June.
Destinations: Athens (Greece).
Costs: Courses in Athens cost from €570 for three weeks, without accommodation. The summer course on Spetses costs €2000 including accommodation.
Eligibility: Age range is 18 to 75.

Italy
Istituto Italiano – Centro di Lingua e Cultura
Via Machiavelli 33, 00185 Rome, Italy
☎ +39 (0)6-704 52138
fax +39 (0)6-700 85122
istital@uni.net
www.istitutoitaliano.com
Just down the road from the Colosseum, the Istituto Italiano is one of the better schools in the Italian capital. There are Italian courses for all levels and plenty of cultural activities including art history and Italian cooking classes.
Types of Course: Italian.
Timing & Length of Courses: From one week, starting on Mondays (monthly start dates for beginners).
Destinations: Rome (Italy).
Costs: Prices start at €165 per week, plus a €50 enrolment fee. Accommodation costs from €128/204 for a single/double room.
Eligibility: Minimum age is 18.

Spain & Portugal
ABC – Instituto Español de Cultura
Guillem Tell 27, 08006 Barcelona, Spain
☎ +34 93-415 57 57
fax +34 93-218 26 06
info@ambricol.es
www.ambricol.es
This Spanish- and English-language school has a good international reputation and a central location in Barcelona.
Types of Course: Spanish & English.
Timing & Length of Courses: From one week, with several start dates monthly.
Destinations: Barcelona (Spain).

Costs: From €120 for 20 hours of classes a week or €150 for 25 hours. Accommodation costs from €115 weekly.
Eligibility: Minimum age is 18.

CIAL Centro de Lingua
Avenida da República, 41–8° Esq, 1050-187 Lisbon
☎ +351 217-940 448
fax +351 217-960 783
portuguese@cial.pt
www.cial.pt
This Portuguese school has more than 30 years' experience and operates campuses in Lisbon and Faro. There are small-group and one-on-one classes and intensive courses run from June to September.
Types of Course: Portuguese.
Timing & Length of Courses: From one week – beginners start on set dates monthly, while other students can start any Monday.
Destinations: Lisbon & Faro (Portugal).
Costs: Vary with the course – standard courses (three classes daily) cost from €260, while intensive courses (six classes daily) cost from €460. Homestay accommodation costs from €100 per week.
Eligibility: Minimum age is 18.

Estudio Sampere
Lagasca 16, 28001 Madrid, Spain
☎ +34 91-431 43 66
fax +34 91-575 95 09
sampere@sampere.es
www.sampere.com
Established way back in 1956, this Spanish institute has four schools in Spain and one in Ecuador. Training is available at all levels and there is a full program of cultural activities.
Types of Course: Spanish.
Timing & Length of Courses: Two to 48 weeks, beginning every Monday year round.
Destinations: Spain (Madrid, Salamanca, Alicante & El Puerto) & Ecuador.
Costs: Vary with the destination – courses in Spain start at €175 per week. Accommodation starts at €140 per week.
Eligibility: Minimum age is 17 for most courses.

Russia
Liden & Denz Language Centre
5th floor, Transportny per 11, 191119 St Petersburg, Russia
☎ +7 812-325 2241
fax +7 812-325 1284
lidenz@lidenz.ru
www.lidenz.ru
This prestigious language school offers Russian tuition in St Petersburg or Moscow. Help is given with visa applications and both schools have central city locations and a full program of cultural activities.

Types of Course: Russian.
Timing & Length of Courses: From two weeks in groups, from one week one-on-one; starting every two weeks year round.
Destinations: Moscow & St Petersburg.
Costs: Prices start at €500 for a two-week group course, plus €50 for enrolment. Accommodation starts at €100 per week.
Eligibility: Minimum age is 16.

UK & Ireland
British Council
10 Spring Gardens, London SW1A 2BN, UK
☎ +44 (0)20 7930 8466
general.enquiries@britishcouncil.org
www.britishcouncil.org
The British Council has dozens of English-language schools worldwide where European citizens can brush-up on their English-language skills. See the website for British Council locations worldwide.
Types of Course: English.
Timing & Length of Courses: Varies depending on where you study.
Destinations: Britain & worldwide.
Costs: Vary with the destination – contact the British Council offices directly for price information.
Eligibility: Most courses are for adults, but some centres also cater to children.

National University of Ireland, Galway
University Rd, Galway, Ireland
☎ +353 (0)91-524411
info@nuigalway.ie
www.nuigalway.ie
The west Ireland campus of the main Irish university offers a four-week summer course in Gaelic (Irish) for beginners at a residential centre about 27km (17 miles) from Galway town. Accommodation is provided with Gaelic-speaking families.
Types of Course: Gaelic.
Timing & Length of Courses: Four weeks from mid-July.
Destinations: Ireland.
Costs: Tuition costs €930 and accommodation is €800 in a shared room.
Eligibility: No age restrictions.

The Americas
Academia de Español Guatemala
7a Calle Oriente 15, La Antigua, Guatemala
☎ +502 832-5057
fax +502 832-5058
aegnow@intelnett.com
http://acad.conexion.com
Housed in two historic buildings in the colonial city of Antigua, this Guatemalan language school offers one-on-one Spanish lessons at all levels.

Types of Course: Spanish.
Timing & Length of Courses: From one week, starting on any day of the week.
Destinations: Guatemala.
Costs: Courses start at US$60 a week for three hours of classes daily, plus US$60 a week for homestay accommodation and meals.
Eligibility: No restrictions.

Argentina Instituto de Lengua Española para Extranjeros (ILEE)

3rd floor, Avenida Callao 339, Buenos Aires 1022, Argentina
☎ /fax +54 11-4782 7173
info@argentinailee.com
www.argentinailee.com
This Spanish-language school in the academic area of Recoleta in Buenos Aries operates smaller schools in Córdoba (a major wine-producing area) and Patagonia (famous for mountaineering and skiing).
Types of Course: Spanish.
Timing & Length of Courses: From one week. Classes at all levels begin daily.
Destination: Argentina.
Costs: The registration fee US$50; group classes cost US$200 a week, private classes US$16 per hour. Homestay accommodation starts at US$85 per week.
Eligibility: No age restrictions and no prior Spanish exposure is necessary.

Centro de Idiomas Intercultura Costa Rica

Apdo 1952–3000, Heredia, Costa Rica
☎ +506 260-8480
fax +506 260-9243
info@interculturacostarica.com
www.interculturacostarica.com
This language centre in Costs Rica offers total immersion Spanish-language courses and you can study at either the city campus close to San José or the beach campus in Playa Sámara. A portion of the profits go towards sponsoring local students and community projects.
Type of Course: Spanish.
Timing & Length of Courses: From one week. Courses start weekly on Mondays.
Destinations: Costa Rica.
Costs: A one-month Spanish course costs US$1165 with homestay accommodation (or US$755 for the course only). Transport, insurance and visas are extra.
Eligibility: Minimum age is 18.

Excel Language Center

Cruz Verde 336, Cusco, Peru
☎ +51 84-23 5298
fax +51 84-23 2272
info@excelinspanish.com
www.excel-spanishlanguageprograms-peru.org

This Peruvian school is set in a peaceful courtyard close to the centre of Cusco and offers various levels of Spanish-language courses. You can also study at several regional locations, including Urubamba in the Sacred Valley and Manu National Park.
Types of Course: Spanish.
Timing & Length of Courses: From one week, starting weekly on Mondays.
Destinations: Peru.
Costs: Prices vary with the course and campus – courses at Cusco cost from US$206 per week in a group class, including accommodation and meals. Regional courses start at US$250 per week, including transfers from Cusco (from US$541 in Manu National Park) as well as accommodation and meals.
Eligibility: Minimum age is 15.

Fast Forward Language Institute

Rua Cardoso de Almeida, 313 con 31/32, Perdizes CEP 05013-000, São Paulo, Brazil
☎ +55 11-3667 8782
fax +55 11-3663 2664
info@fastforward.com.br
www.fastforward.com.br
This Brazilian school offers Portuguese courses at its campuses in São Paulo and the coastal towns of Maceió and Porto. There are courses for all standards and various cultural activities such as dance classes and theatre visits.
Types of Course: Portuguese.
Timing & Length of Courses: From one week. Group courses start on set dates monthly (intermediate students can start any Monday).
Destinations: Brazil.
Costs: Group classes start at £390 for one week and £1250 for one month, including homestay accommodation and half-board.
Eligibility: Minimum age is 17.

Language Studies Canada (LSC)

124 Eglinton Ave West, Suite 400, Toronto, Ontario, M4R 2G8, Canada
☎ +1 416-488 2200
fax +1 416-488 2225
toronto@lsc-canada.com
www.lsc-canada.com
Established in 1962, this Canadian language school offers English classes at four cities in Canada and French classes in Montreal. Courses include group classes for beginners, one-on-one tuition and French for business.
Types of Course: English & French.
Timing & Length of Courses: From two weeks. Beginners start on set dates monthly; intermediate speakers can start on any Monday.
Destinations: Calgary, Montreal, Toronto & Vancouver (Canada).

Costs: Courses start at £274 for two weeks (£246 in Calgary), plus a registration fee of £41, payable in Canadian dollars. Accommodation costs from £79 a week, plus a £75 placement fee.

Eligibility: Minimum age is 18. A student visa is needed to study for more than 24 weeks.

Asia
Campus of International Languages
GPO Box 4339, Exhibition Rd, Kathmandu, Nepal
☎ +977 (0)1-258132/226713
fax +977 (0)1-255738
vishwo@biva.wlink.com.np
www.yomari.com/nepali-language
Part of Kathmandu's Tribhuvan University, this language school offers training in a variety of Himalayan languages, including Nepali and Tibetan. Apply by post or in person, following the instructions on the website.

Type of Course: Short courses in Nepali and long courses in Tibetan, Newari and Sanskrit.

Timing & Length of Courses: Short courses last six weeks from January or June; full academic courses last one to two years from July.

Destinations: Kathmandu (Nepal).

Costs: Six-week courses in Nepali cost US$150 plus visa fees, while one-year courses in other languages are US$527 plus visa fees.

Eligibility: No restrictions.

Tokyo School of the Japanese Language
16–26, Nampeidai-cho, Shibuya-ku, Tokyo 150-0036, Japan
☎ +81 (03)-3463 7261
fax +81 (03)-3463 7599
info@naganuma-school.or.jp
www.naganuma-school.or.jp
This reputable Japanese school in Tokyo has 50 years experience teaching Japanese to people who are living and working in Tokyo. Courses start four times a year and at least three months' study is recommended to learn the hundreds of Japanese and Chinese characters.

Types of Course: Japanese.

Timing & Length of Courses: From three months, starting in January, April, July and September.

Destinations: Tokyo (Japan).

Costs: Prices start at £600 for two months, not including accommodation or course materials. You should budget around £900 per month for accommodation and meals.

Eligibility: No minimum age but most students are working in Japan.

WorldLink Education (WLE) Beijing
Beijing Liuxue Shijie Guangchang, No 3–1 Zhi Xin Xi Rd, Haidian District, Beijing 100083, China.
☎ +86 10-6232 7129/30
fax +86 10-6239 5067
admission@worldlinkedu.com
www.worldlinkedu.com
This international college in Beijing offers various courses in Mandarin Chinese for international students.

Types of Course: Mandarin.

Timing & Length of Courses: Four- to 12-week courses start on set dates monthly. Longer programs start in February or September.

Destinations: Beijing (China).

Costs: From US$1870 for four weeks in student accommodation, including insurance and cultural and leisure activities.

Eligibility: Age range is 16 to 65. Students require a Chinese student visa, which must be obtained from a Chinese embassy or consulate overseas (the college will provide the necessary paperwork).

THE ARTS
Dance
Cactus Language
See p224 for contact details.
As well as courses in various European languages, Cactus offers a wide range of combined language-and-dance courses, including Spanish with salsa, *sevillanas* or flamenco in Spain; Spanish with salsa, merengue, rumba and mambo in Cuba; Spanish with tango in Argentina; Portuguese with samba in Brazil; and Greek with folk dancing in Greece.

Types of Course: Various language and dance courses.

Timing & Length of Courses: From two weeks. Most courses start on the first Monday of each month.

Destinations: Spain, Cuba, Argentina, Brazil & Greece.

Costs: Vary with the language, course and destination – two-week group Spanish classes and salsa lessons in Cuba cost from £469, including accommodation with a host family.

Eligibility: Minimum age is 18.

Càlédöñiâ Languages Abroad
See p224 for contact details.
This popular language school offers language courses with dance lessons in Spain and Latin America. Options include merengue and flamenco in Spain, salsa in Spain and Cuba, and tango in Argentina.

Types of Course: Salsa, merengue, flamenco and tango dance classes.

Timing & Length of Courses: Most people study for at least two weeks.

Destinations: Spain, Argentina, Brazil & Cuba.

Costs: Vary with the destination – tango and Spanish classes in Argentina cost £150 per week (£185 per week with one-on-one tuition), including accommodation but not meals. Travel arrangements are extra and there's a £65 booking fee.

Eligibility: Minimum age is 18.

Fashion

International Fashion Institute (Istituto di Moda Burgo)

Piazza San Babila, 5-20122 Milan, Italy
☎ +39 (0)23-655 7600
fax +39 (0)23-655 7605
imb@imb.it
www.imb.it

This leading Italian fashion school offers a variety of fashion courses for international students, including a fashion design course that you can take over eight to 20 months. Italian lessons are included and the course results in a formal diploma.

Types of Course: Fashion design.
Timing & Length of Courses: Eight to 20 months; you can start at any time, but most people begin in September.
Destinations: Milan (Italy).
Costs: The course costs €3800 for one year or €7600 for two years.
Eligibility: Minimum age is 14. Fashion experience and qualifications are required for some courses.

Film

The Los Angeles Film School

Suite 400, 6363 Sunset Blvd, Los Angeles, CA 90028, USA
☎ +1 323-860 0789
info@lafilm.com
www.lafilm.com

This prestigious film school in Los Angeles is staffed by working movie professionals and offers a one-year film-making course and quarterly part-time courses in editing, cinematography etc. British students are eligible for career development loans.

Types of Course: Film-making.
Timing & Length of Courses: One year, from September.
Destinations: Los Angeles (USA).
Costs: The one-year course costs US$31,400 for international students.
Eligibility: Minimum age is 18. You must show aptitude and a commitment to film-making.

Metropolitan Film School

126 Bolingbroke Grove, London SW11 1DA, UK
☎ +44 (0)845 658 4400
fax +44 (0)20 7681 1819
info@metfilmschool.co.uk
www.metfilmschool.co.uk

This London-based film school offers a variety of courses for amateur film-makers, including an eight-week full-time Script to Screen course, where you write a screenplay and then develop it into a short digital film using professional actors. Classes are taught by movie professionals and all equipment is provided.

Types of Course: Film-making.
Timing & Length of Courses: Eight weeks, starting four times a year (there are also short three-day film-making courses).
Destinations: London (UK).
Costs: The three-day film-making course costs £495, and the Script to Screen course costs £2995.
Eligibility: Applicants must submit a CV and a statement about what they want to achieve during the course.

New York Film Academy

100 East 17th St, New York, NY 10003, USA
☎ +1 212-674 4300
fax +1 212-477 1414
film@nyfa.com
www.nyfa.com

This US film school teaches everything from traditional and digital film-making to acting, screenwriting and animation. Schools run year round at the main campus in New York, at Universal Studios in Los Angeles, Disney-MGM Studios in Florida, and in London. There are also summer schools in Paris, Florence and Amsterdam.

Types of Course: All aspects of film-making.
Timing & Length of Courses: One week to one year, starting on fixed dates (short courses mostly run in summer).
Destinations: The USA, the UK, France, Italy & the Netherlands.
Costs: Vary with the course – eight-week film-making courses in New York cost US$4000, plus US$1800 for equipment.
Eligibility: Minimum age is 18 and you must have a high-school diploma or equivalent.

New Zealand Film Academy

Edenz Colleges, Entrance 4 Nuffield St, Newmarket, Auckland, New Zealand
☎ +64 (0)9-920 5931
fax +64 (0)9-522 1511
info@nzfilmacademy.com
www.nzfilmacademy.com

This New Zealand film school offers a six-week course in digital film-making. The course covers all aspects of film-making, and students make two short films and a music video. You can follow this with a six-week extension course where you work on a single 30-minute feature. The course is very popular, so book at least three months ahead.

Types of Course: Film-making.
Timing & Length of Courses: Courses last six weeks and start on set dates in May, August and November.
Destinations: Auckland.
Costs: Both courses cost NZ$2800 for domestic students and NZ$4000 for international students; some equipment costs are extra.
Eligibility: Minimum age is 18. Students must be English-speakers.

Music
Ciltad-Agoro Project
PO Box 711, Cape Coast, Ghana
☎ /fax +233-42 32654
agorociltad@yahoo.com
www.agoro.dk
This joint Danish-Ghanaian project allows foreign students to learn traditional Ghanaian drumming in central Ghana. In exchange, the project provides work for local musicians.
Types of Course: Rhythm and drumming courses for all levels.
Timing & Length of Courses: Two weeks to two months; introductory courses run from January.
Destinations: Ghana.
Costs: The two-week introductory course costs US$600 and the two-month follow-on course for beginners costs US$1100.
Eligibility: Open to all ages – there are special classes for those over 30.

Musicians Institute
1655 North McCadden Pl, Hollywood, Los Angeles, CA 90028, USA
☎ +1 323-462 1384
fax +1 323-462 6978
admissions@mi.edu
www.mi.edu
This world-famous Hollywood music college is possibly the only place where you can learn to play heavy-metal guitar. Courses cover everything from keyboards and drums to vocals and sound recording and you can study for degrees, vocational certificates or just for your own musical development.
Types of Course: Courses for bass, guitar, keyboards, percussion, vocals and sound recording.
Timing & Length of Courses: From 10 weeks, starting in January, April, July or October.
Destinations: Los Angeles (USA).
Costs: Vary with the course – 10-week non-certificate programs cost from US$3500.
Eligibility: You must show an innovative talent for your chosen instrument and submit a demo tape for certificate courses.

Performing Arts
Circus Oz
PO Box 504, 40 Bay St, Port Melbourne, Vic 3207, Australia
☎ +61 (0)3-9646 8899
fax +61 (0)3-9646 9334
classes@circusoz.com.au
www.circusoz.com.au
This Australian touring circus group was established in 1978 and offers a variety of training courses for aspiring circus artistes, from basic lessons in juggling to the flying trapeze.
Types of Course: Courses in all circus arts, including tumbling, clowning, trapeze and acrobatics.

Timing & Length of Courses: Most courses run one day a week for four to eight weeks between February and April.
Destinations: Melbourne (Australia).
Costs: Vary with the course – four-week handstand and acrobatics courses cost A$110, while eight-week trapeze courses cost A$275.
Eligibility: No restrictions.

Photography
La Maison Rose
Rue Gérard Roques, 81630 Salvagnac, France
☎ /fax +33 (0)5 63 40 59 22
fchallis@photohols.com
www.photohols.com
Close to Toulouse in the pretty village of Salvagnac, Maison Rose offers a variety of residential courses on colour and black-and-white landscape photography.
Types of Course: Traditional and digital photography.
Timing & Length of Courses: Week-long courses start on Saturdays and Wednesdays from April to September.
Destinations: Salvagnac (France).
Costs: Prices range from £375 to £465, including half-board accommodation, transfers from Toulouse airport and transport to photographic locations.
Eligibility: Minimum age is 15.

Spéos
8 Rue Jules Vallès, 75011 Paris, France
☎ +33 (0)1 40 09 18 58
fax +33 (0)1 40 09 84 97
speos@speos.fr
www.photography-education.com
This Paris photography school was established in 1984 and offers photography tuition to small groups in both English and French – the summer workshops are popular with international students. You can specialise in photojournalism, fashion, commercial or fine-art photography.
Types of Course: Various black-and-white amateur and professional photography courses.
Timing & Length of Courses: Four days to one year. Summer workshops run on set dates from May to July, or you can take all the workshops as a 10-week summer course.
Destinations: Paris (France).
Costs: Summer workshops cost €570 per week, or the whole summer course costs €5300. Meals, accommodation and materials are extra.
Eligibility: Minimum age is 18.

Travellers Worldwide
7 Mulberry Close, Ferring, West Sussex BN12 5HY, UK
☎ +44 (0)1903 502595
fax +44 (0)1903 500364
info@travellersworldwide.com
www.travellersworldwide.com

This popular gap-year and career-break organisation offers four to 12-week photography courses at the University of Havana in Cuba. You must bring an SLR camera, film, photographic paper and chemicals for developing film from home. Ask for details when you apply.

Types of Course: Photography.
Timing & Length of Courses: Four to 12 weeks. Courses start on set dates several times a year.
Destinations: Havana (Cuba).
Costs: Prices start at £1145 for one month with bed-only accommodation or £1375 for half-board. Flights, visas and insurance are extra, but Travellers Worldwide can arrange all this for you.
Eligibility: Age range is 17 to 70 years.

Visual Arts
British Institute of Florence
Palazzo Lanfredini, Lungarno Guicciardini 9, I-50125 Florence, Italy
☎ +39 (0)55-2677 8270
fax +39 (0)55-2677 8252
info@britishinstitute.it
www.britishinstitute.it
Established in 1917, this Anglo-Italian institute offers a variety of artistic courses including art history, fresco painting, life drawing and opera appreciation. You can take Italian lessons at the attached language school.

Types of Course: Courses in art, art history & Italian culture.
Timing & Length of Courses: Short courses last three days to four weeks (from two weeks for art history), starting year round.
Destinations: Florence (Italy).
Costs: Art and culture courses cost from €150 per week, not including accommodation. Art-history courses cost from €230 for two weeks.
Eligibility: Minimum age is 18.

Centro d'Arte Dedalo
Dedalo Arte, Loc Greppolungo 43–44, 55041 Camaiore (LU), Italy
☎ /fax +39 (0)584-984 258
info@dedaloarte.org
www.artcoursestuscany.com
This cooperative of international artists runs a variety of summer courses near Pienza in Tuscany, including clay sculpting, bronze casting, fresco painting and landscape and figurative oil painting.

Types of Course: Practical courses in all areas of art.
Timing & Length of Courses: Most courses last 11 days and run from June to September.
Destinations: Tuscany (Italy).
Costs: Courses cost from €484, or €1047 including half-board accommodation.
Eligibility: Minimum age is 16; some courses require previous experience.

Scuola Orafa Ambrosiana
Via Tadino 30, 20124 Milan, Italy
☎ +39 (0)2-29 405005
fax +39 (0)2-29 405005
info@scuolaorafaambrosiana.com
www.scuolaorafaambrosiana.com
This world-famous goldsmithing school offers training in all aspects of designing and making jewellery including metal casting and design. Classes of three are each led by a master jeweller.

Types of Course: Courses in jewellery design and gold-working.
Timing & Length of Courses: Courses involve 22 to 115 hours of training and start daily except in August.
Destinations: Milan (Italy).
Costs: Tuition costs from €287 to €1700.
Eligibility: Minimum age is 15.

Writing
Arvon Foundation
42A Buckingham Palace Rd, London SW1W 0RE, UK
☎ +44 (0)20 7931 7611
fax +44 (0)20 7963 0961
london@arvonfoundation.org
www.arvonfoundation.org
This charity offers highly recommended writing courses with leading professional writers at four residential centres in the UK. You can study anything from poetry to play writing and all the writing centres are in tranquil rural areas. Bookings are taken through the four writing centres – see the website for contact details.

Types of Course: More than 30 writing courses, from creative writing to song and play writing.
Timing & Length of Courses: Courses last 4½ days and run year round.
Destinations: Lumb Bank (West Yorkshire), Totleigh Barton (Devon), the Hurst (Shropshire) & Moniack Mhor (Scotland), all in the UK.
Costs: Courses cost from £435, including tuition, meals and cottage accommodation – some grants are available for writers on low incomes.
Eligibility: Minimum age is 16.

Skyros
92 Prince of Wales Rd, London NW5 3NE, UK
☎ +44 (0)20 7267 4424
fax +44 (0)20 7284 3063
office@skyros.com
www.skyros.com
As well as running holistic holidays on the Greek islands and in Thailand, Skyros offers a popular Writers' Lab on the Greek island of Skyros with tuition from guest writers such as Steven Berkoff.

Types of Course: Courses in various types of writing, including creative writing and play writing.

Timing & Length of Courses: Two weeks, starting on set dates through the year.
Destinations: Skyros (Greece) & Ko Samet (Thailand).
Costs: Two-week packages range from £695 to £995, including half-board accommodation but not flights.
Eligibility: Minimum age for adults is 18, but accompanied children are welcome.

COOKERY SCHOOLS
UK & Ireland
Authentic Ethnic
14 Redcliffe Sq, London SW10 9JZ, UK
☎ +44 (0)20 7373 3651
fax +44 (0)20 7460 0334
authenticethnic@aol.com
This London cooking school trains many professional chefs and offers evening classes in an astounding range of foreign cuisines from Thai and Vietnamese to Brazilian and Russian. You can put together individual modules in different cuisines or study a course in one particular cuisine.
Timing & Length of Courses: Evening classes are held on Mondays and Wednesdays and you can study a cuisine over six classes. There are no classes in January and August.
Destinations: London (UK).
Costs: Evening classes cost £65.
Eligibility: Courses are not suitable for children.

Cordon Vert Cookery School
The Vegetarian Society, Parkdale, Dunham Rd, Altrincham, Cheshire WA14 4QG, UK
☎ +44 (0)161 925 2014
fax +44 (0)161 926 9182
cordonvert@vegsoc.org
www.vegsoc.org/cordonvert
Run by the Vegetarian Society, this cookery school offers residential courses in vegetarian cooking in a Victorian mansion near Manchester. There are day courses, specialist weekends and week-long foundation courses, plus a full diploma course. All dishes are vegetarian or vegan.
Timing & Length of Courses: One day to four weeks. Courses run on set dates throughout the year.
Destinations: Cheshire (UK).
Costs: Day courses start at £79, the foundation course costs £448 (£548 with accommodation) and the diploma course costs £448 per week.
Eligibility: Minimum age is 16.

Edinburgh School of Food & Wine
The Coach House, Newliston, Edinburgh EH29 9EB, Scotland
☎ +44 (0)131 333 5001
info@esfw.com
www.esfw.com
You can take various amateur courses as well as six-month cooking diplomas at this popular Scottish cookery school in Edinburgh. The four-week Intensive Certificate is a good option for first timers or people who fancy working as a cook as part of a career break.
Timing & Length of Courses: One week to six months. Diploma courses start in January while Intensive Certificate courses begin on set dates in July, August, September and November.
Destinations: Edinburgh (Scotland).
Costs: The Intensive Certificate costs £2070, and the full six-month diploma course is £8800.
Eligibility: Minimum age is 17 for most courses.

Le Cordon Bleu London
114 Marylebone Lane, London W1U 2HH, UK
☎ +44 (0)20 7935 3503
fax +44 (0)20 7935 7621
london@cordonbleu.edu
www.cordonbleu.edu
The world-famous Académie d'Art Culinaire de Paris now has Cordon Bleu schools in Britain, the US, Canada, Korea, Peru, Japan and Mexico. Courses range from one-day classes in classic cordon-bleu cooking to full master's degrees in *haute cuisine*. The four-week Essentials course covers all the basics and is often used by people seeking employment with ski and yachting companies.
Timing & Length of Courses: One day to one year, starting on set dates year round.
Destinations: Paris (France), London (UK), Mexico, Ottawa (Canada), Adelaide & Sydney (Australia), Tokyo, Kobe & Yokohama (Japan) & Seoul (South Korea).
Costs: The four-week Essentials course costs £1940. For more-committed cooks, there are two-month cooking certificate courses from £4191 and a full-year diploma for £11,755.
Eligibility: Certificate courses require GCSEs (General Certificate of Secondary Education), baccalaureate or equivalent qualifications.

Tante Marie School of Cookery
Woodham House, Carlton Rd, Woking, Surrey GU21 4HF, UK
☎ +44 (0)1483 726957
fax +44 (0)1483 724173
info@tantemarie.co.uk
www.tantemarie.co.uk
Housed in an Edwardian manor house, Tante Marie offers professional Cordon Bleu courses and a variety of shorter courses including a four-week Essential Skills course.
Timing & Length of Courses: Two days to one year.
Destinations: Surrey (25 minutes from London by train; UK).
Costs: The four-week Essentials course costs from £1800, plus £145 for a chef's uniform and other equipment. Cordon Bleu courses range from £4250 for one term to £12,100 for the whole year.
Eligibility: Minimum age is 16.

Europe

Apicius Cooking School

Via Guelfa 85, 50129 Florence, Italy
☎ +39 (0)55-265 8135
fax +39 (0)55-265 6689
info@apicius.it
www.apicius.it

Based in Florence, this professional cookery school has a variety of courses for aspiring Italian chefs, taught in English. As well as professional qualifications, there are one- to four- week amateur courses in Italian cooking and wine appreciation. The two-week Gusto Workshops include general cooking lessons and one-on-one tuition in a specialist area such as making gelato or fresh pasta.

Timing & Length of Courses: One week to one year. Amateur programs start monthly; one-year programs start in September.

Destinations: Florence (Italy).

Costs: One-week (three-class) programs start at €285 and two-week workshops cost €1055, plus a €100 lab fee. Four-week courses start at €685, or €790 with Italian lessons. Travel, accommodation and meals (except lunch on teaching days) are extra.

Eligibility: Minimum age is 18.

École des Trois Ponts

Château de Matel, 42 300 Roanne, France
☎ +33 (0)4 77 71 53 00
fax +33 (0)4 77 70 80 01
info@3ponts.edu, info@frenchcourses.com
www.3ponts.edu/cooking

This residential college near Lyon in France offers a variety of French gourmet-cooking courses in English, including a course in French pastry making. Cooks stay in private rooms at the 18th-century Château de Matel and there are optional French-language courses.

Timing & Length of Courses: Courses last one to two weeks.

Destinations: France.

Costs: One-week cooking courses cost from €1190 per person, including full-board accommodation. Combined cooking and French classes start at €1390 per week. Travel to the chateau is extra.

Eligibility: Minimum age is 18.

L'École des Chefs

Maison des Relais & Châteaux, 33 Blvd Malesherbes, 75008 Paris, France
☎ +33 (0)1 58 18 30 00
fax 33 (0)1 40 06 04 35
contact@ecoledeschefs.com
www.ecoledeschefs.com

This innovative cooking school offers two- or five-day internships with chefs at 82 top-rated Michelin and Mobil restaurants in the USA, Canada, South Africa, Japan and across Europe (particularly in France). Participants should bring with them a chef's knife and plain chef's coat and will need to cover their own accommodation and travel expenses.

Timing & Length of Courses: Two to five days – dates vary depending on the restaurant.

Destinations: The USA, Canada, the UK, France, Belgium, Denmark, Luxembourg, the Netherlands, Norway, Spain, Switzerland, Japan & South Africa.

Costs: Two-day internships cost from US$1100 and five-day courses start at US$1900.

Eligibility: Internships are for keen amateur cooks. Knowledge of the local language is preferred.

Mami Camilla

Via Cocumella 4, 80065 S Agnello di Sorrento, Naples, Italy
☎ +39 (0)81-878 2067
fax +39 (0)81-532 4805
info@mamicamilla.com
www.mamicamilla.com

This family-run cooking school in Naples has cooking courses in Italian cuisine for both amateurs and working chefs and specialises in Neapolitan cuisine, including pizza, pasta and gnocchi. Intensive courses include the preparation of local delicacies such as antipasto, pesto and liqueurs.

Timing & Length of Courses: One to four weeks (extensions up to six weeks are possible).

Destinations: Naples (Italy).

Costs: Introductory courses start at €330 for one week and €1010 for four weeks. Intensive courses cost from €585 for one week to €1785 for six weeks. Accommodation is available from €25/40 per night for a single/double.

Eligibility: Minimum age is 18.

Tasting Places

Unit 108 Buspace Studios, Conlan St, London W10 5AP, UK
☎ +44 (0)20 7460 0077
fax +44 (0)20 7460 0029
ss@tastingplaces.com
www.tastingplaces.com

This well-regarded cooking school offers cooking master-classes in the UK and a variety of cooking courses abroad, including in France, Italy and Thailand. Accommodation is provided in stylish guesthouses and hotels and many of the courses are run by Michelin-rated chefs.

Timing & Length of Courses: One-week courses run on set dates throughout the year (mostly in summer).

Destinations: The UK, France, Spain, Italy, Greece & Thailand.

Costs: Prices for the week start at £1336, including classes, food, wine and accommodation. There are also shorter weekend courses from £895.

Eligibility: Courses are designed for adults.

Rest of the World

Chiang Mai Thai Cookery School
1–3 Moon Muang Rd, Opposite Tha Phae Gate, Chiang Mai 50200, Thailand
☎ +66 (0)53-206388
fax +66 (0)53-206387
cooking@thaicookeryschool.com
www.thaicookeryschool.com
This highly recommended cooking school in Chiang Mai offers one- to five-day courses in Thai cooking. Participants buy fresh ingredients from the market in the mornings and then spend the day learning to prepare Thai dishes, either in Chiang Mai or at the owner's garden kitchen outside town. You'll learn to make everything from green curry paste to steamed banana cake and you can eat everything you cook.
Timing & Length of Courses: One to five days.
Destinations: Thailand.
Costs: Courses cost from US$22 for one day to US$100 for five days.

Cuisine International
PO Box 25228, Dallas, TX 75225, USA
☎ +1 214-373 1161
fax +1 214-373 1162
info@cuisineinternational.com
www.cuisineinternational.com
This US company represents 18 cooking schools around the world that offer week-long cooking courses. There are residential courses in Europe, the Middle East and the Americas and all include upmarket full-board accommodation.
Timing & Length of Courses: One week.
Destinations: Italy, France, England, Greece, Portugal, Morocco, Brazil & the USA.
Costs: Prices vary with the courses, but most cost between US$1000 and US$3000 for the week, including accommodation and excursions but not flights etc.

French Culinary Institute
462 Broadway, New York, NY 10013-2618, USA
☎ +1 212-219 8890
info@frenchculinary.com
www.frenchculinary.com
This leading American cookery school has a variety of cooking programs for amateurs as well as degree courses for professionals. Courses cover the essential skills required by chefs (knife skills, preparation of stocks and sauces etc) and speciality areas such as baking and pastry making.
Timing & Length of Courses: Speciality courses last from eight weeks and technique courses last up to 22 weeks, beginning on set dates (mostly from May to August).
Destinations: New York (USA).
Costs: Technique courses cost US$5675 and speciality courses start at US$1995. Accommodation and other living arrangements are extra.
Eligibility: Must be a high school graduate.

Kali Travel Home
22/77 Raja Manindra Rd, Kolkata 700037, India
☎ /fax +91 33-2558 7980
refresh@cal2.vsnl.net.in
www.traveleastindia.com
This well-regarded tour company in Kolkata (Calcutta) in India offers bespoke food-and-culture tours, where you'll learn to make authentic Bengali dishes with local families.
Timing & Length of Courses: Tours can be arranged to match your needs.
Destinations: Kolkata (India).
Costs: Prices vary depending on what is included in the tours – costs average out at approximately US$75 per day.
Eligibility: Open to all ages.

Mexican Home Cooking
Apdo 64, Tlaxcala, Tlaxcala CP 90000, Mexico
☎ /fax +11 522-468 0978
mexicanhomecooking@yahoo.com
www.mexicanhomecooking.com
This homely Mexican cookery school offers week-long residential courses in central Mexican cooking. The classes run in the morning, and in the afternoon you are free to explore the area around Tlaxcala, which is full of colonial architecture, Mayan ruins and volcanoes. Book early as there's usually a two-month waiting list.
Timing & Length of Courses: Courses last six days, seven nights.
Destinations: Tlaxcala (two hours from Mexico City; Mexico).
Costs: The course fee is US$1000, including classes, B&B accommodation and lunches that you prepare in the classes. The nearest airport is Puebla (in Mexico) and flights are extra.

Sydney Seafood School
Sydney Fish Market, Bank St, Pyrmont, NSW 2009, Australia
☎ +61 (0)2-9004 1111
fax +61 (0)2-9004 1177
fishline@sydneyfishmarket.com.au
www.sydneyfishmarket.com.au
Part of the main fish market in Sydney, the Sydney Seafood School offers classes in seafood cooking, using freshly caught seafood from the market. Each course teaches you to prepare a specific dish or concentrates on a specific style of cooking – every day is different and you can attend as many different classes as you want.
Timing & Length of Courses: Classes last two to five hours and run several times a week (usually on Tuesdays, Thursdays, Saturdays and Sundays).
Destinations: Sydney (Australia).
Costs: The cost per class varies from A$70 to A$115.
Eligibility: Classes are open to anyone, but you should book at least two weeks in advance.

BAR-TENDING & MIXOLOGY

Harvard Bartending Course

17 Holyoke St, Cambridge, MA 02138, USA

☎ +1 617-495 9657

fax +1 617-495 7956

www.hsa.net/harvardbarcourse

This popular mixology course is affiliated with Harvard University. The course takes place over two seven-hour sessions where you'll learn how to mix a perfect daiquiri and create a smoothly layered shot. Training in Intervention Procedures by Servers of Alcohol (TIPS) is provided, which is handy for getting bar jobs.

Timing & Length of Courses: Two days, on set dates from March to May.

Destinations: Cambridge (USA).

Costs: The basic course costs US$195, which you can follow up with an advanced course for US$119.

Eligibility: Minimum age is 18.

Shaker UK

Unit 213, Jubilee Centre, 130 Pershore St, Birmingham B5 6ND, UK

☎ +44 (0)121 622 055

mk@shaker-uk.com

www.shakerbartending.co.uk

The leading bartending school in Britain, Shaker offers extensive courses that teach you everything you need to know about bartending, free pouring and the art of mixology. There are also Flair Courses, where you can learn all the Tom Cruise bottle-flipping antics.

Timing & Length of Courses: Five days; courses run monthly.

Destinations: Birmingham (UK).

Costs: The International Bartenders Course costs £495, and there are special courses in bartending flair from £249. Lunch is provided, but other meals and accommodation are extra.

Eligibility: Minimum age is 18.

ALTERNATIVE THERAPIES & MARTIAL ARTS

Fairtex Combat Sports Camp

99/5 Moo 3, Soi Boonthamanusorn, Theperak Rd, Bangplee Yai, Bangplee, Samut Prakarn, Bangkok 10540, Thailand

☎ +66 (0)2-385 5148/9

fax +66 (0)2-385 5403

info@fairtexbkk.com

www.fairtexbkk.com

This martial-arts training camp on the outskirts of Bangkok offers training in *muay thai* (Thai-style kick-boxing) with leading Thai boxing champions. Students stay at the camp and follow a tough regimen of fitness and combat training, including hand-to-hand combat. Training is also available at the Fairtex camp in San Francisco in the US (see the website www.fairtex.com).

Types of Course: *Muay thai* (kick-boxing).

Timing & Length of Courses: It is possible to start training at any time but there is a limit of 15 fighters on the camp at any one time.

Destinations: Bangkok (Thailand) & San Francisco (USA).

Costs: Training costs from US$150 per week, including two meals and accommodation in a shared room with fan. If you want to stay in a private room, prices start at US$200 per week.

Eligibility: Open to all ages and levels of experience.

Parmarth Niketan

Yoga and Meditation Section, Parmarth Niketan, PO Swargashram, Rishikesh 249 304, India

☎ +91 (0)135-243 4308/244 0088

fax +91 (0)135-244 0066

parmarth@aol.com

www.parmarth.com

This well-regarded yoga centre in Rishikesh was established in 1942 and offers short- and long-term courses in hatha yoga and *pranayama* meditation. Students must follow a strict daily regimen of exercises, meditation and prayers; smoking, drinking, nonvegetarian food and gambling (including playing cards) are prohibited.

Types of Course: Yoga.

Timing & Length of Courses: Two- to 13-week courses begin on set dates from September to April (classes are ongoing, so it is possible to join outside these times).

Destinations: Rishikesh (India).

Costs: Courses are funded by donation and the ashram provides meals and accommodation. You must make your own way to Rishikesh (the easiest route is by train and bus from New Delhi).

Eligibility: There are no age restrictions but students must be committed to the study of yoga and follow the rules of the ashram.

Root Institute for Wisdom Culture

Bodhgaya, Gaya District, Bihar 824 231, India

☎ + 91 (0)631-220 0714

fax + 91 (0)631-220 0548

info@rootinstitute.com

www.rootinstitute.com

The Root Institute is one of the more accessible meditation centres in Bodhgaya in India, where Buddha attained enlightenment. The centre supports local humanitarian projects and there are regular courses in meditation at the centre led by Tibetan lamas and Western teachers. You can register for courses on the website.

Types of Course: Buddhist meditation.

Timing & Length of Courses: The centre is open for retreats year round, but residential courses last one week to one month from September to March.

Destinations: Bodhgaya (India).

Costs: Prices vary depending on how long you stay and the type of accommodation – contact the centre for details.

Eligibility: There are courses for beginners and experienced students but you must adhere to the rules of the centre.

Skyros

See p234 for contact details.

Skyros offers a huge range of alternative therapy breaks in Greece and Thailand which include courses in yoga, meditation, massage, creative writing, film-making, self-exploration, arts and drama.

Types of Course: Residential courses in various holistic therapies.

Timing & Length of Courses: Two weeks, starting on set dates through the year.

Destinations: Skyros (Greece) & Ko Samet (Thailand).

Costs: Two-week packages range from £695 to £995, including half-board accommodation but not flights.

Eligibility: Minimum age for adults is 18, but children are welcome.

Tai Chi Chuan Center

Naisuan House, Room 201, 3/7 Doi Saket Kao (Rattanako-sin), Soi 1, Thanon Watgate, A Muang, Chiang Mai 50000, Thailand

☎ +66 (0)17-067406

keithtaichi@yahoo.com

www.taichithailand.com

This popular centre in northern Thailand offers 10-day courses for both new and experienced t'ai chi practitioners. The courses have a firm theory foundation and there are daily morning, midday and evening practical sessions and regular discussions on the philosophy of t'ai chi.

Types of Course: T'ai chi.

Timing & Length of Courses: 10-day courses start on the first and 16th of each month but you should register by email before you arrive.

Destinations: Chiang Mai (Thailand).

Costs: The course costs from US$241 and you must pay in local currency. Accommodation is included but meals and travel to the centre are extra.

Eligibility: No restrictions.

Wat Pho Thai Traditional Medical School

2 Sanamchai Rd, Wat Pho, Tatian, Bangkok 10200, Thailand

☎ +66 (0)2-221 2974 or 622 3550/1

fax +66 (0)2-225 4771

watpottm@netscape.net

www.watpho.com/mas_study_e.html

This traditional medical school at Bangkok's oldest monastery offers training in traditional Thai massage techniques which you can spread out over five, six or 10 days.

Types of Course: Massage.

Timing & Length of Courses: Five to 10 days (three days for foot-massage courses). You can apply in person, or register by mail with two passport photos.

Destinations: Bangkok (Thailand).

Costs: Thai massage courses cost the equivalent of US$178, payable in local currency. Chinese foot-massage courses cost US$91.

WorldLink Education (WLE) Beijing

See p231 for contact details.

This international college in Beijing offers courses in various Chinese martial arts, including *taiji quan* (t'ai chi) and *wushu* (an ancient Chinese martial art based on balance and stamina). There are optional Mandarin Chinese language classes and temple visits.

Types of Course: T'ai chi and other Chinese martial arts.

Timing & Length of Courses: One week to one year. One- to 12-week courses start on the first Monday of each month. Longer programs start in February or September.

Destinations: Beijing (China).

Costs: Starting prices range from US$650 for one week to US$3300 for 12 weeks, with accommodation in a single room on campus (US$800 to US$3960 with language courses). Flights are extra.

Eligibility: Age range is 16 to 65. Students require a Chinese student visa, which must be obtained from a Chinese embassy or consulate overseas (the college will provide the necessary paperwork).

ADVENTURE SPORTS COURSES
Sailing, Surfing & Windsurfing
Flying Fish

25 Union Rd, Cowes, Isle of Wight PO31 7TW, UK

☎ +44 (0)1983-280641

fax +44 (0)1983-281821

mail@flyingfishonline.com

www.flyingfishonline.com

This popular school for watersports offers a huge range of training programs, from sailing and yacht-crewing qualifications to instructor courses for diving, surfing, windsurfing and kite-surfing. Most courses include theory and basic practical training in the UK and advanced training in Australia or Greece. Flying Fish also acts as an employment agency for watersports professionals.

Types of Course: Sailing and watersports instructor courses.

Timing & Length of Courses: Three weeks to three months, departing on set dates throughout the year.

Destinations: UK, Greece (Vassiliki) & Australia (Sydney & the Whitsunday Islands).

Costs: Vary with the course – introductory yacht crew courses in the UK cost £1290 and training up to Coastal Skipper level in the UK and Australia costs £6620 (flights to Australia are extra), including accommodation (and meals in the UK).

Eligibility: Minimum age is 18.

Sunsail

The Port House, Port Solent, Portsmouth, Hampshire PO6 4TH, UK

☎ +44 (0)23 9222 2333

fax +44 (0)23 9221 9827
sales@sunsail.com
www.sunsail.com

This sailing holiday company offers industry-recognised yachting courses at its sailing centres in the UK, Holland, the Canary Islands and Thailand, including Competent Crew, Day and Coastal Skipper and Yachtmaster. There are also holiday dinghy, windsurfing and leisure-yachting courses worldwide.

Types of Course: RYA certified courses in yacht sailing and leisure courses in yacht and dinghy sailing and windsurfing.

Timing & Length of Courses: From two days to one week, running on set dates year round (from October to May only in the Canary Islands).

Destinations: The UK, the Netherlands, Thailand & Canary Islands (Spain).

Costs: Vary with the course – prices for the Competent Crew and Day Skipper courses start at £275 in the UK and £350 in Thailand, not including flights.

Eligibility: Minimum age is 18.

Surfing Australia

PO Box 1613, Kingcliff, NSW 2487, Australia
☎ +61 (0)7-5520 1150
fax +61 (0)7-5520 1288
info@surfingaustralia.com
www.surfingaustralia.com

This umbrella organisation represents surf schools across Australia that offer lessons for beginners and experienced surfers and wet-suit and surf-board hire. First-timers train on soft-top long-boards and you are guaranteed to stand up first time! Prime spots to learn include Bell's Beach in Victoria, Byron Bay in New South Wales, Yorke Peninsula in South Australia and Noosa in Queensland.

Types of Course: Surfing courses.

Timing & Length of Courses: Most schools offer daily lessons and courses lasting three to five days.

Destinations: All around Australia.

Costs: Prices for lessons range from A$40 to A$60. Three-day courses start at A$110. Prices include wetsuits and board hire.

Eligibility: Open to all ages, but you must be able to swim.

United Kingdom Sailing Academy

West Cowes, Isle of Wight PO31 7PQ, UK
☎ +44 (0)1983 294941
fax +44 (0)1983 295938
info@uksa.org
www.uksa.org

This leading UK sailing school offers a full range of sailing and crewing qualifications, and you can do part of the training for some courses in Australia or the Caribbean. As well as PCST (Professional Crew & Skipper Training) there are instructor courses in dinghy sailing, windsurfing, kayaking, surfing, kite-surfing and diving.

Types of Course: Full range of industry-recognised yachting and watersports instructor qualifications.

Timing & Length of Courses: From four days to 17 weeks.

Destinations: Cowes (UK), Sunshine Coast (Australia) & Caribbean.

Costs: Vary with the course; 17-week PCST in the UK costs £8750; professional instructor training in the UK and Australia costs £4995. Prices are all-inclusive, except for meals in Australia.

Eligibility: Minimum age is 17. Must be able to comfortably swim 50m (164ft).

Diving

International Academy

St Hilary Court, Culverhouse Cross, Cardiff CF5 6ES, Wales
☎ +44 (0)29 2067 2500
fax +44 (0)29 2067 2510
info@theinternationalacademy.com
www.theinternationalacademy.com

This British adventure-sports academy offers professional scuba training in the Seychelles. You can stay for up to six weeks and train up to the level of dive master, the entry-level qualification for paid work in the dive industry. See opposite for information on ski and snowboard qualifications.

Types of Course: Dive-master scuba course.

Timing & Length of Courses: Five to six weeks starting July and October for the dive-master course.

Destinations: The Caribbean & the Seychelles.

Costs: From £5290 for five weeks, including flights, accommodation and meals.

Eligibility: Minimum age is 18.

London Scuba Diving School

Raby's Barn, Newchapel Rd, Lingfield, Surrey RH7 6LE, UK
☎ +44 (0)1342 837837
fax +44 (0)1342 837722
info@londonscuba.com
www.londonscuba.com

This UK-based school offers PADI Open Water courses where you start off with two days' pool training in the UK and finish with a week's training in the Red Sea. There are also internships for trainee dive masters – the course is free if you work for the school for 10 weekends and 10 evenings.

Types of Course: Scuba-dive training.

Timing & Length of Courses: Open Water courses in the Red Sea last 11 days and leave around 10 times a year. Dive-master internships run about four times yearly.

Destinations: The UK & the Red Sea.

Costs: Prices for the Red Sea course start at £555. Dive-master internships cost £350.

Eligibility: Minimum age is 15 for Open Water courses. Dive-master interns must be 18 and be trained up to Rescue Diver level. Dive medicals are required for all dives.

Air Sports

Cabair Group

Elstree Aerodrome, Borehamwood, Hertfordshire WD6 3AW, UK

☎ +44 (0)20 8236 2400

group@cabair.com

www.cabair.com

Cabair represents 11 flight-training schools in Britain and the USA that offer leisure and commercial pilot's licences. There's a fast-track Private Pilot's Licence (PPL) program in the USA that takes two to three weeks.

Types of Course: Private Pilot's Licence.

Timing & Length of Courses: Trainees must accumulate 32 flying hours for the UK licence, 40 hours for the US licence and 45 hours for the European licence.

Destinations: The UK & the USA.

Costs: PPL training costs from £3995 for the UK licence, £4295 for the European licence and US$3660 for the US licence (transfers to Florida are extra).

Eligibility: Minimum age is 17. Students must take an approved medical, which includes a sight test (this can be with glasses or contact lenses).

Royal Victorian Aero Club

First Ave, Moorabbin Airport, Mentone, Victoria 3194, Australia

☎ +61 (0)3-9580 0088

fax +61 (0)3-9587 5085

flying@rvac.com.au

www.rvac.com.au

A number of flying courses can be taken at this fully accredited flight-training centre. The Private Pilot's Licence is a noncommercial qualification and involves theory classes and about 48 hours of flying time.

Types of Course: Private Pilot's Licence

Timing & Length of Courses: Students can qualify in 12 weeks.

Destinations: Melbourne & Sydney (Australia).

Costs: The course costs A$10,800, including 48 hours' flying time, exam and licence fees.

Eligibility: Minimum age is 18 years, and a medical is required.

Skiing & Snowboarding

British Association of Snowsport Instructors (BASI)

Glenmore, Aviemore, Inverness-shire PH22 1QU, UK

☎ +44 (0)1479 861717

fax +44 (0)1479 861718

basi@basi.org.uk

www.basi.org.uk

The governing body for ski instruction in Britain, BASI, offers various professional instructor courses. The Gap Year program is open to both students and career-breakers and allows you to qualify as an instructor in a single season at a ski resort in Europe, the USA or New Zealand.

Types of Course: Gap-year ski instructor course.

Timing & Length of Courses: The 10-week Gap Year program starts on set dates in January.

Destinations: The UK, France, Italy, Andorra, Switzerland, the USA & New Zealand.

Costs: Vary with the course and destination – the Gap Year course costs £4150 to £5900, not including flights.

Eligibility: Minimum age is 17.

Flying Fish

See p239 for contact details.

This watersports school also offers Canadian Ski Instructors' Alliance (CSIA) and Canadian Association of Snowboard Instructors (CASI) ski and snowboard instructor courses in Canada which allow you to qualify as an instructor in a single season.

Types of Course: Ski Instructor Level I & II, Snowboard Instructor Level I.

Timing & Length of Courses: Three to nine weeks; courses start from November to March.

Destinations: Whistler & Blackcomb ski areas (Canada).

Costs: Vary with the course – the three-week Level I instructor course costs £1560 to £1902, including accommodation, meals and ski passes. Flights and equipment are extra.

Eligibility: Minimum age is 18.

International Academy

See opposite for contact details.

This British adventure-sports academy offers professional ski and snowboard instructor courses in the Americas and New Zealand.

Types of Course: Ski and snowboard instructor.

Timing & Length of Courses: Four to 12 weeks. Courses run from January to April in Canada and the US and July to September in New Zealand and Chile.

Destinations: Canada, the USA, Chile & New Zealand.

Costs: Vary with the course; prices start at £4250 for four weeks in Canada, including flights, accommodation and meals.

Eligibility: Minimum age is 16. Some ski or snowboarding experience is useful.

Peak Leaders UK

Mansfield, Strathmiglo, Fife KY14 7QE, Scotland

☎ +44 (0)1337 860079

fax +44 (0)1337 868176

info@peakleaders.com

www.peakleaders.com

Peak Leaders offers internationally accredited ski and snowboard instructor courses in Canada in January and in New Zealand and Argentina in July, which include leadership and management training.

Types of Course: Ski and snowboard instructor.

Timing & Length of Courses: Eight to 10 weeks, starting in January for courses in Canada or from June to August for courses in Argentina and New Zealand.
Destinations: Canada, Argentina & New Zealand.
Costs: Courses start at around £6000, including flights, training and half-board accommodation – ski equipment (and après-ski costs!) are extra.
Eligibility: Minimum age is 18, but many career-breakers join the courses.

Expedition Courses, Mountaineering & Climbing

Boulder Outdoor Survival School
PO Box 1590, Boulder, Colorado 80306, USA
☎ +1 303-444 9779
fax +1 303-442 7425
info@boss-inc.com
www.boss-inc.com
Established in 1968, BOSS offers survival training in wilderness locations across the USA. The BOSS field course teaches you how to survive in the mountains of southern Utah with just a blanket, poncho, compass, water bottle and knife.
Types of Course: Various survival courses.
Timing & Length of Courses: Four to 28 days, beginning on set dates from May to August.
Destinations: The USA.
Costs: Prices range from US$495 for four days to US$2995 for 28 days, not including travel to the USA.
Eligibility: Minimum age is 18. All nationalities are welcome, pending visa considerations, but you'll need a medical to show you are physically fit.
Accommodation: You build your own!

Himalayan Mountaineering Institute
Jahawar Parbat, Darjeeling 734101, West Bengal, India
☎ +91 (0)354-225 4087/4268/4083
www.exploredarjeeling.com/hmidarj.htm
Established in 1954, this famous mountaineering school in Darjeeling offers 15-day adventure climbing courses and more involved mountaineering courses on Himalayan peaks in Sikkim. Foreign students should apply at least three months in advance using the application form on the website.
Types of Course: Mountaineering.
Timing & Length of Courses: Courses last 15 to 28 days and start on six set dates each year between March and December.
Destination: Darjeeling (India).
Costs: Non-Indians pay US$250 for the adventure course and US$500 for the basic and advanced mountaineering course, not including travel to Darjeeling.
Eligibility: No restrictions but applicants must be physically fit and capable of trekking at altitude carrying heavy loads.

King Climbers
Hat Railay East, Krabi, Thailand
☎ +66 (0)75-637125
info@railay.com
www.railay.com/railay/climbing/climbing_intro.shtml
Based in Krabi in southern Thailand – one of the world's most famous rock-climbing areas – King Climbers has 10 years' experience teaching beginners to climb. The three-day rock-climbing courses include top-roping, lead-climbing and multipitch climbing on fully bolted routes. All equipment is provided.
Types of Course: Rock-climbing.
Timing & Length of Courses: One to three days, starting anytime.
Destinations: Krabi (Thailand).
Costs: The three-day course costs around US$125, payable in local currency. You can hire gear to continue climbing for US$25 per day.
Eligibility: No prerequisites except a head for heights.

National Outdoor Leadership School (NOLS)
284 Lincoln St, Lander, WY 82520-2848, USA
☎ +1 307-332 5300
fax +1 307-332 1220
admissions@nols.edu
www.nols.edu
Based in Wyoming, this American school offers various courses in outdoor leadership and survival techniques for expedition leaders. Options include rock-climbing and mountaineering, horse-packing and trekking, skiing and snowboarding and wilderness medicine and water management.
Types of Course: Various wilderness leadership and survival courses.
Timing & Length of Courses: Two weeks to three months, starting on set dates monthly.
Destinations: USA, Canada, Australia, New Zealand, Patagonia (Chile) & India.
Costs: Vary with the course – a nine-day trip leader course costs from US$815, while a three-month semester course at several locations costs up to US$10,000. Flights, visas and insurance are extra.
Eligibility: Minimum age ranges from 16 to 30, depending on the intensity of the course.

Outward Bound Trust
Hackthorpe Hall, Penrith, Cumbria CA10 2HX, UK
☎ +44 (0)870 513 4227
fax +44 (0)1931 740001
enquiries@outwardbound-uk.org
www.outwardbound-uk.org
This nonprofit organisation promotes outdoor activities in the UK and offers courses in mountaineering, hill-walking, kayaking, canoeing, power-boating and sailing at its residential centres in the English Lake District, Scotland and

Wales. For details of Outward Bound operations in other countries, see the global website: www.outward-bound.org.
Types of Course: Various outdoor qualifications recognised by national governing bodies.
Timing & Length of Courses: One day to one week, year round (some courses are seasonal).
Destinations: UK.
Costs: From £120 to £1000, including meals and accommodation. Transport to centres is extra.
Eligibility: Minimum age is 18 (there are also courses for students and children from eight years). Qualified UK teachers may be eligible for government bursaries.

Planet Wise
10 Swan St, Eynsham, Oxfordshire OX29 4HU, UK
☎ +44 (0)870 200 0220
info@planetwise.net
www.planetwise.net
This innovative company offers customised travel training for first-time and experienced travellers. The courses are tailored to your level of experience and travel plans and cover subjects such as border crossings, travel scams, local transport, health and safety. One-day courses take place in London, Southampton, Bristol, Birmingham, Nottingham, Manchester, Newcastle and Edinburgh, or there are two-day residential courses in Hampshire, Oxfordshire, Yorkshire and Scotland.
Types of Course: Pre-travel training.
Types of Course: One or two days, starting on Thursdays.
Destinations: UK.
Costs: One-day courses cost £160, two-day courses cost £360, including meals and accommodation.
Eligibility: No restrictions.

Plas y Brenin (National Mountain Centre)
Capel Curig, Conwy, LL24 0ET, Wales
☎ +44 (0)1690 720214
fax +44 (0)1690 720394
info@pyb.co.uk
www.pyb.co.uk
Based in Snowdonia, this leading mountaineering centre offers a huge selection of residential courses in climbing, summer and winter mountaineering, first aid, canoeing and kayaking, including mountaineering trips to the Swiss Alps. Experienced climbers and hill-walkers can study for the (Summer or Winter) Mountain Leader Award and instructor qualifications.
Types of Course: Climbing, mountaineering, team-leading, canoeing and kayaking.
Timing & Length of Courses: Varies with the course and season – courses for amateurs last from two to six days and take place on fixed dates throughout the year.
Destinations: Snowdonia (Wales) & Switzerland.
Costs: Depends on the course – a five-day rock-climbing course costs £410 including meals and accommodation.

Eligibility: Minimum age is 16 for most courses (21 or older for instructor and leader courses).

Wallace School of Transport
Unit 5a, Pop-In Bldg, South Way, Wembley, Middlesex HA9 0HF, UK
☎ +44 (0)845 602 9498
fax +44 (0)20 8903 1376
info@wallaceschool.co.uk
www.wallaceschool.co.uk
One of only seven Driving Standards Agency–accredited training centres in the UK, Wallace offers training for lorry and bus driving licences at three locations in Greater London – useful if you are planning to drive an expedition vehicle.
Types of Course: Large Goods Vehicle (LGV) and Passenger Carrying Vehicle (PCV) driving licences.
Timing & Length of Courses: Depends on how you perform in the driving assessment – most people complete the course in four to eight days.
Destinations: Wembley, Heathrow & Enfield (UK).
Costs: The assessment lesson costs £30 and driver training costs £135 to £180 per day – test fees are extra.
Eligibility: Minimum age is 21. You must hold a full UK car driving licence and apply for a provisional LGV or PCV licence from the DVLA. There's also a medical.

Woodsmoke
PO Box 45, Cockermouth, Cumbria CA15 9WB, UK
☎ /fax: +44 (0)1900 821733
info@woodsmoke.uk.com
www.woodsmoke.uk.com
This adventurous organisation offers a variety of courses in bushcraft and wilderness survival in the Lake District. The six-day Woodlander course will teach you to forage and hunt for food and make your own fires and shelters using natural materials.
Types of Course: Wilderness survival.
Timing & Length of Courses: Two to seven days, starting on set dates from May to September.
Destinations: UK.
Costs: Vary with the course – the Woodlander costs £495.
Eligibility: Minimum age is 18.

Field Guide Courses
The following organisations offer courses for rangers and field guides in Africa. Flights are extra unless otherwise stated.

Antares Field Guide Training Centre
PO Box 1573, Phalaborwa 1390, South Africa
☎ /fax +27 (0)15-769 6006
ian@antares.co.za
www.antares.co.za
This South African field centre offers courses in field guiding in the South African veldt which cover all aspects of working on a game reserve. The course is recognised by

the Field Guides Association of Southern Africa (FGASA) and graduates often find work on local game reserves.

Types of Course: Field guiding.
Timing & Length of Courses: Six weeks, starting on set dates through the year.
Destinations: South Africa.
Costs: The course costs US$1500 for international students.
Eligibility: Minimum age is 17, and you must have a driving licence.

Eco Africa Experience

Guardian House, Borough Rd, Godalming, Surrey GU7 2AE, UK
☎ +44 (0)1483 860560
fax +44 (0)1483 860391
info@ecoafricaexperience.com
www.ecoafricaexperience.com

This family-run travel company offers a Ranger Guide course accredited by the South African Wildlife Society at nature reserves in South Africa. The course covers everything from identifying and tracking game to 4WD driving and anti-poaching measures.

Timing & Length of Courses: 12 days; runs on set dates approximately monthly.
Destinations: South Africa.
Costs: The course costs £650, including training meals and accommodation.
Eligibility: Minimum age is 17.

EcoTraining

41 Ehmke St, Nelspruit 1200, South Africa
☎ +27 (0)13-744 9639
fax +27 (0)13-744 0953
ecotrain@mweb.co.za
www.ecotraining.co.za

EcoTraining has 10 years' experience training field guides in South Africa. The month-long Game Ranging courses are FGASA certified and cover tracking, animal identification and bush skills such as rifle handling and 4WD driving.

Types of Course: Certificate in Game Ranging.
Timing & Length of Courses: Courses last 28 days, beginning on set dates monthly.
Destinations: South Africa.
Costs: Courses cost from around £741, payable in local currency.
Eligibility: Minimum age is 16, and you must have a valid driving licence.

FIRST AID

Expertise Consultancy Group (Wilderness Expertise)

The Octagon, Wellington College, Crowthorne, Berkshire RG45 7PU, UK
☎ +44 (0)1344 774430
fax +44 (0)1344 774480

info@wilderness-expertise.co.uk
www.wilderness-expertise.co.uk

This long-established company offers training in all aspects of expedition management, including first aid for expeditions. The Rescue Emergency Care program is tailor made for people working in the outdoors or in expedition fields.

Types of Course: Rescue Emergency Care, consisting of four levels of first-aid training.
Timing & Length of Courses: One to four days, starting on set dates from January to May and October to November.
Destinations: Crowthorne (UK).
Costs: Two-day courses cost from £110.
Eligibility: Minimum age is 16.

Lifesigns Group

Tournai Hall, Evelyn Woods Rd, Aldershot, Hampshire GU11 2LL, UK
☎ +44 (0)1252 326555
fax +44 (0)1252 319111
info@lifesignsgroup.co.uk
www.lifesignsgroup.co.uk

This Foreign Office–recommended company offers a variety of health and first-aid training programs that are specifically targeted at travellers or people working with voluntary organisations. The Expedition Care Program lasts one to four days and includes Health & Safety Executive (HSE) approved first-aid training.

Types of Course: Expedition Care Program (first aid).
Timing & Length of Courses: One to four days, beginning on set dates monthly.
Destinations: Aldershot (UK).
Costs: Courses start at £50/90 for one/two days.
Eligibility: Minimum age is 16.

Wilderness Medical Training

The Coach House, Thorny Bank, Skelsmergh, Kendal, Cumbria LA8 9AW, UK
☎ +44 (0)1539 823183
fax +44 (0)1539 823183
enquiries@wildernessmedicaltraining.co.uk
www.wildernessmedicaltraining.co.uk

Another expedition and foreign-travel specialist, this company offers first-aid courses tailored for aid workers, expedition doctors, sailors, divers, climbers, overland drivers and similar professions. Skills learned include treatment of illnesses, CPR (Cardio-Pulmonary Resuscitation), suturing (stitching), injections and the use of intravenous drips.

Types of Course: Advanced Medicine for Remote Foreign Travel (first aid).
Timing & Length of Courses: November to June; short courses last two days, or you can take the full Advanced Medicine course in five days.

Destinations: Courses run in various locations around the UK & in Chamonix, France (for expedition doctors).
Costs: Advanced Medicine for Remote Foreign Travel costs £495.
Eligibility: No restrictions.

OTHER OUTDOOR ACTIVITIES
Bitterroot Ranch
1480 East Fork Rd, Dubois, WY 82513, USA
☎ +1 307-455 3363
fax +1 307-455 2354
bitterrootranch@wyoming.com
www.bitterrootranch.com
This British Horse Society–approved dude ranch sits in splendid open country, 50 miles from Yellowstone National Park in Wyoming and offers a variety of residential horse-riding programs with daily lessons and trail riding. Optional add-ons include rounding up cattle and pack trips out on the range.
Types of Course: Horse-riding courses.
Timing & Length of Courses: From one week, year round.
Destinations: Near Jackson, Wyoming.
Costs: Residential courses start at US$1650 per week including riding, meals and accommodation but not flights.

Rates drop by 10% to 15% from May to June and August to September.
Eligibility: Courses are open to all ages and levels of riders.

Leconfield Jackaroo & Jillaroo School
Kootingal, NSW 2352, Australia
☎ /fax +61 (0)2-6769 4230
jillaroojackaro@austarnet.com.au
www.leconfieldjackaroo.com
Inexperienced horse riders are as welcome on this course as those wishing to hone their riding skills. Operating on a working property, students will learn all aspects of the Jackaroo/Jillaroo trade. Graduates will receive individual references detailing the specific skills and experience they have gained during the course.
Types of Course: Jackeroo/Jillaroo (horseback farm-work) courses.
Timing & Length of Courses: Courses run approximately twice a month for 11 days.
Destinations: Kootingal (Australia).
Costs: Including full board and lodgings, the course is A$750.
Eligibility: Minimum age 16.

Coming Home

Though this wasn't mentioned in the Tying Up Loose Ends chapter, Benjamin Franklin nearly said 'In this world nothing is certain, except death, taxes and coming home after your career break'. Actually, he didn't add 'coming home' to his short list of certainties, probably because he knew it wasn't quite true. Some career-breakers don't come home (see p259). However, 99% do and every single one of them has a lot to say about this fairly inevitable experience.

As you'd imagine, most find coming home difficult to handle. Graham Williams was away for two years and says:

I had lived abroad for long periods before, so I knew that coming home could be a pretty unpleasant experience.

Michelle Hawkins explains:

On my first career break, I left when I was 29 and returned just before my 31st birthday. It was incredibly hard to readjust to the UK after 14 months away. I had nowhere to live and moved in with my parents. So much for the freedom of adulthood.

And Devon Hanley's return coincided with a low point in America's economy:

I got really depressed when I got home. The economy sucked and the job market was loose as bowels after collard beans. I was broke and life in my own culture just isn't as interesting as exploring new cultures.

So, before you decide not to go away at all because you can't face the thought of coming home, there are steps you can take to make the whole process easier. Old hand Graham Williams advises to plan your homecoming:

We planned for it carefully. We came back in the spring – a positive time of year – and we came back with money.

Devon Hanley agrees about the finances, saying:

Come home with some money. Don't get totally broke overseas, though it's tempting to travel till you're down to your last penny, baht, rupiah or whatever it is. It makes the whole re-entry experience a bit easier, and it is hard enough as it is.

On the flip side, some career-breakers have had enough of travelling and are keen to experience some good old-fashioned, home-style luxury. James Ingham explains:

I was ready to come home after a year away. I was slightly fed up with continually unpacking and packing my rucksack and sleeping on dodgy beds in bare rooms. I was looking forward to my own bed, a long bath and some home cooking, as well as seeing friends and family again.

Career-breakers who have decided to go away for one last fling before settling down are also ready to come home. Helen Grainger and Mathew Saks say:

We're both happy to be back and settled. We'd had enough of living out of the car and a bag and we need to nest now.

Many career-breakers talk about experiencing an initial 'high' on coming home, followed a bit later by a low, as reality sets in. This is particularly true if you've got to make some tough decisions about where your life is going once you're back. David Orkin writes:

The first few days back were great – catching up with friends and family, getting my photos back, unpacking stuff I'd bought en route etc, but then my mood swung quickly to feeling down. Coming back, looking for somewhere to live and wondering what I was going to do now were the hardest of all.

Zoe Haines got through this initial period by refusing to let go of her career-break dreams:

I was thrilled coming home and seeing all my family and friends, but I also had this weird feeling of loss. I had the most amazing time and experiences and knew I had to get back to reality and a job as soon as possible. For ages after, I convinced myself I was going to work to earn enough to go travelling again.

A good strategy to combat the coming home 'blues' is to fill your days. Obviously, sorting out where you're going to live and how you're going to put food on the table takes time. But if you do find you've got days on your hands then do something with them – enrol in a course, find some part-time work, temp or do voluntary work. Anything to keep you busy and meeting people – not home alone watching reruns of *Neighbours* and pretending you're back Down Under.

While you've been away, the lives of your nearest and dearest have moved on. In many ways, the changes appear more significant the older you are – getting married, having a baby or being promoted to CEO are much more life-changing than having attended Glastonbury twice rather than just the once. Claire McKenzie found this aspect rather disconcerting:

Coming home after a year and a half was a bit strange, especially as a few of my friends had got married and were either expecting or had recently had a baby. I left my best friend when she was six months pregnant and got back in time for her child's first birthday – very, very weird.

For many, though, being away made them much more appreciative of their home country. Louise Jones says:

We came back with a genuine sense of awe and gratitude that we lived in Britain. I had a number of 'arguments' with mainly older, 'country's gone to the dogs' type of people, including one on the tube. My point was that if you'd seen some of the places we had, you'd be pretty thankful you lived here too.

Related to this is a kind of reverse culture shock, experienced by Michelle Hawkins:

The initial shock of the abundance of provisions and excessive consumption here in the UK has never left me, as well as the cost of living: I remember being shocked at the price of a tube of toothpaste and at the cost of transport when looking for work. Whenever I saw (and still see) taps running unnecessarily, I turn them off because of the waste of water that so many other people in the world can't access. I remember starting work after I returned, and noticing how well fed all my new colleagues looked, and what good condition their teeth were in.

However you react to coming home, it is worth remembering that it will probably take a while for you to adapt and adjust to being here. Paul Bloomfield concludes:

The second time around was harder because I knew I had to make some tough career decisions. I am only really now coming to terms with the post-travel fallout, some two years after I got back.

RETURNING TO YOUR OLD JOB

Your greatest fear will probably be change. Most companies commit to giving you a position at the same level after a career break, rather than guaranteeing your old job back. Whether the new job is a poisoned chalice or a magic lamp fulfilling your every professional wish is another matter – you'll have to rub it and see.

If you do return to your old job, then expect some changes. This holds true whether you've been away for three months or 13. You could find yourself working for a new boss or discover that the whole organisational structure of your department or company has changed. Depending on your job, you might have to manage staff you didn't hire and certainly take over projects that you did not instigate or buy into. If your 'temp cover' works with or under you then they might resent your reappearance and challenge your authority. Of course, you might also find that your colleagues or your team preferred the way your temp cover did things. Whatever the scenario, it will take time to find your place, re-establish your value and earn your team's respect again.

The best way to do this is to get up to speed as quickly as possible. This'll mean a lot of report reading and meetings, but the sooner you're familiar with all the main issues the better. Of course, you won't be starting from scratch if you keep in contact with the office while you're away. You then need to reassert yourself slowly and sensitively, being positive about the work that's been done while you were away. It will take time, but after three or four months, you'll have forgotten you ever left and so will everyone else.

Of course, in your absence the company might have had a complete face-lift as opposed to an eyelash tint. It could have downsized, its culture now totally reversed, or it might have been sold. Quite frankly, it's not worth worrying about these extremes. Right now you've got the best of both worlds – time off and, from a professional perspective, a soft landing when you return home.

And, in a way, there's something worse than change. This is what James Ingham, who works for the BBC, found when he went back:

Returning to work (the same job) was slightly depressing – nothing had changed and some people simply thought I'd been off sick for a while. Scary to realise how quickly time just disappears.

Another issue that you might face is having a job to return to and not wanting it any more. Career breaks often trigger a professional or personal change of direction. If this happens you've got an obligation to minimise the disruption this will cause the company. Under no circumstances do you want to jeopardise the chances of future employees to take a break. This might mean returning to your old company and giving a notice period of at least six months (or until a replacement is found and trained up) or else letting them know your intentions while you're away.

JOB-HUNTING

Of course, the opposite might have happened: you were so sick of your job before you left that you quit. However, with the perspective of a break, you now realise it wasn't half so bad.

Never fear – all might not be lost. One of the best places to job-hunt when you come home is at your old company. Get yourself invited to after-work drinks, chat to old work colleagues and suss out possible openings. Is there any maternity (or, indeed, career-break) cover in the offing? What's the current policy on freelance work? As well as this, take your ex-boss out for a couple of beers. If you left on good terms (top tip – do not tell your boss exactly what you think of them before taking off) they might be keen to discuss ways of getting you involved again. At the very least, they'll know who's hiring and firing in your industry and where to look for work.

Keeping in touch while you're away pays dividends when you come home. Like most things in this world, it's not what you know but whom you know that counts. Career-breaker Zoe Haines found just this:

I was really lucky. While in Chile an ex-boss of mine emailed to tell me he had moved companies and asked if I would be interested in coming for an interview when I got back. I did and I started within a couple of weeks of returning. So, my advice is to keep in contact with old work colleagues.

Michelle Hawkins also ended up getting work due to her contacts:

Both times on coming back from my career breaks, there was no work lined up. But I know a lot of people, and so was able to find work quickly. The first time it took me four weeks to get a job at the Guardian *and* Observer. *The second time it took me five days to get a freelance contract with 4Creative, Channel 4's in-house creative agency. I then set myself up with other freelance work in the meantime.*

Having said that, there's no doubt it's scary coming home and having to look for work. You'll be worried about how easy it will be pick up where you left off or whether you'll have to apply for lower-grade jobs with a lower salary than the one you left. However, most career-breakers find that they're in a really strong position – especially if they took no more than one year out. Think about it – you know your industry, you know where to look for work, you're experienced, you've got the skills, you've got the contacts and you're as fresh as a daisy from having been away. Graham Williams and his partner made many of these points work in their favour:

I had been reading the issues of my trade magazine (the Bookseller*) at British Councils all through my trip, so I was up-to-date with industry events. I put an announcement in the* Bookseller *that I was back in the UK. I came back in time deliberately to visit the London Book Fair, where I could network with friends, and that's where I had the first interview for the job I got. Both my partner and I called on our mentors where we had worked before. In my partner's case, he recommended that she try for jobs at the top law firms and she landed a much better job than the one she'd had before. I was lucky that a perfect job, very similar to the one I had before, came up and I got it. Within six weeks, we both had new positions.*

YOUR CV & YOUR INTERVIEW

Many companies now recognise the value of a career break, especially when they benefit from hiring a refreshed employee with fire in their belly, as opposed to a tired and burnt-out squib who's given all to a previous employer. Margaret Murray, Head of Learning & Skills at the Confederation of British Industry (CBI), says:

Career breaks can give staff a revitalising lift, depending on how the time is spent. At their best, career breaks can invigorate staff, enabling them to deliver more value to the business while simultaneously finding more satisfaction in their work.

As such, many career-breakers give good weight to a career break and their newly acquired skills and experiences on their CV, as opposed to burying them. Emma McMahon says:

I have a list of achievements on my CV. This is listed as one of them. I've never had an extended period of time without work so it doesn't look like a gaping hole in my CV.

Helen Grainger and Mathew Saks went as far as having their CVs in mind when they decided what they wanted to do during their career break:

I think it's useful when taking a career break to consider doing something constructive that could help your career. For us, learning French and becoming as fluent as possible was the main objective. It looks great on the CV and prospective employers are impressed that we showed the initiative to do something like this.

Devon Hanley, on the other hand, took a slightly different approach. He writes:

I didn't mention it on my CV; I mentioned it in my covering letter. I made it sound like I had sown my wild oats and gone out to discover what I really wanted to do with my career.

As important as how to present your career break on your CV is how to talk about it at an interview. David Orkin advises:

It's a question of presenting things positively in a way that's relevant to the job that you're applying for. Stress the guts it took to get up and go, some of the things you learnt about the world, projects you became involved in or new interests you developed. Stress that your batteries are recharged and you now know what you want to do and can attack that with more energy, determination, focus and greater maturity. Almost all employers will see a career break as a positive thing – but be prepared to be asked 'How do we know that you won't just stay until you've earned enough money to go off again?'

James Ingham returned to his old job at the BBC after his career break but then decided to apply for another position shortly afterwards. He explains:

The BBC were encouraging about my career break. I came back far more settled, with the wanderlust sort of out of my system – though certainly not the desire to travel. At an interview that followed for a new job within the corporation a few months after my return, I was able to talk about the new things I had seen and done, the language skills I'd picked up and some of the problems I had encountered and how I had tackled them. I got the job.

Of course, some people take career breaks with the express purpose of gaining experience to put on their CV so they can change careers when they're back. This was the case with Michelle Hawkins, who says:

I didn't call my first one a 'career break'. I listed the dates I was away; the countries visited, explained the redundancy cheque and said 'who wouldn't do the same?'. However, I consciously chose to use my second career break as a springboard into the charity/aid sector. Frequently, jobs ads say: 'You need experience if you want to work in a new sector'. How can you get the experience, unless you get a job in that sector? Catch 22. My solution was to pay to be a volunteer staff member on two Raleigh International expeditions. This made my transition into the competitive charity sector easier. I also got the Raleigh International Expedition leaders to write me references. I had two great references that I attached to my CV on returning to the UK: thank you, Rupert and Steve.

RETURNING TO WORK: THE USA

When returning to the job market, it pays to focus on the accomplishments of your career break, instead of on the sun and sandy beaches. Empasize the new skills you aquired (languages, negotiating expertise, etc) and downplay the good times had. Risk-taking is encouraged by most American companies, but irresponsibility is tolerated by few. Having done something charitable will definitely be seen as more positive. Since fewer than 20% of Americans have passports, many employers will be attracted to your international experience, but be prepared for incisive questions about how your career-break experiences have added real value to your employability.

Stacey McCarthy also looked to her career break to offer experience in a different field. Right at the beginning of her CV it says 'Objective: transfer my high-tech public-relations experience to the world of organic foods'. As she says:

I am looking for a job in the organic food industry, so my time volunteering at the organic permaculture farm on Lake Atitlan in Guatemala looks great on my CV.

RECRUITMENT AGENCIES

When looking for a job, don't discount the big high-street recruitment agencies. The 'big five' are easier to spot in the urban jungle than the lion, leopard, elephant, rhino and buffalo on your career break:

- **Adecco** (www.adecco.co.uk)
- **Hays Personnel** (www.hayspersonnel.com)
- **Kelly Services** (www.kellyservices.co.uk)
- **Manpower** (www.manpower.co.uk) – when are they going to rebrand?
- **Reed Employment** (www.reed.co.uk)

They all recruit across a wide range of sectors and have international offices. Even more interesting are the specialist recruitment companies operating in one select area, whether it be publishing, hospitality, nursing or accounting. Look in trade magazines or journals for listings or ads.

For more information see the Recruitment & Employment Confederation website (www.rec.uk.com) and the Department of Trade & Industry's website (DTI; www.dti.gov.uk/er/agency-kyr.html) for employment-agency standards.

One word of warning about recruitment agencies – they can be very old fashioned when it comes to career breaks. If the one you're registered with is more concerned by your employment gap than with how you filled it, find another with a more up-to-date approach.

See the US and Australian Appendices for recruitment agencies in these countries.

CHANGING CAREERS

Whether it's on the road to Damascus or not, a career break often throws new light on your professional life, leading to a career conversion when you come home. Helen Grainger explains:

Being away focused our minds on what we wanted to do. Both of us are looking for new jobs, something that would have come about anyway but I'd say we're clearer in what we want, and what we're prepared to do. In some ways we're more single-minded – whatever job we take has to work for us as a whole, rather than just the pay cheque.

Lyn Hughes, editor of *Wanderlust* magazine, explains that it was a career break that spurred her and her partner, Paul Morrison, to start up the magazine:

We were bored. Winter was rapidly approaching, our house was up for sale but no-one had been round to view it, and our respective freelance work as business analysts was well paid but unexciting. A previous career break had given us a huge boost – surely it was time for another? A month later, we were on a flight to Ecuador with a Galápagos trip booked but no plans after that. We were travelling extremely light – hand luggage only – and as a result had no books to read. Having, out of desperation, digested every single page of the in-flight magazine, we got to talking about how poor its articles were, and that in turn led to a conversation about how there were no travel magazines around for people like ourselves. So we started plotting our ideal magazine, and by the end of that long flight had worked out all the content, target advertising, and even the name – Wanderlust. The idea refused to go away, and the thought of donning a power suit and returning to the world of multinational corporations did not appeal. When we returned home in the spring, we invested in an Apple Mac and, working crazy hours in the spare bedroom, we produced the first issue of Wanderlust magazine that autumn.

Like Lyn and Paul, many career-breakers come back from travelling wanting to work in the travel industry or in a sector associated with their break. Paul Blackburn found exactly this:

I realised that I was no longer enjoying my job as a technical manager in the agricultural industry, simply going through the ritual of work. As I was always telling my team of 15 sales people 'If you are not happy with the way things are, then don't complain, change them' – time to walk the talk! I'd travelled extensively in Africa on foot and by truck in the past but I had always wanted to travel Africa in my own vehicle to see the wildest, most remote parts, so after buying a Land Rover I set off. While travelling the idea of an adventure travel company started to become reality and upon my return to the UK in late 2003 I set up Onelife Adventures (www.onelife-adventures.com) with a friend. It's a vehicle-dependent expedition company, offering support and consultancy to independent travellers and escorted expeditions in self-drive Land Rovers to the Iberian Peninsula and North Africa. It's been hard work, with some setbacks, but a huge amount of fun and tremendously satisfying. One Life – live it!

(If you're interesting in working in the travel industry see p184-7 for details on working as a tour leader or overland driver and on cruise ships.)

There's no doubt that a career break gives you time to think about your career choices and to reassess them. Issues such as status, money, long working hours, life–work balance and salaried employment versus freelance work become easier to resolve once you've made the break.

The reality of changing careers when you get home, however, can be challenging. For starters, doing something new usually takes time – you might have to retrain, get a new qualification, arrange a period of work experience, or organise funding. Retraining, in particular, can be expensive so log onto www.lifelonglearning.co.uk/cdl to find out about Career Development Loans (see also p213. Although you'll have a heap of transferable skills, starting over professionally often means starting near the bottom again and working your way up (again). It'll also mean working with a bunch of youngsters whose first instinct is to step on a beetle or an ant, not listen to their music. A more junior position will also be reflected in your wage – you might have decided that money wasn't important to you, but mortgages, cars and dependents are costly and so are weekend breaks, restaurant meals and health clubs. Employers tend to be suspicious of career-changers, particularly older ones, and it can be difficult to get an interview, let alone the job. Use your covering letter to convince a future employer of your commitment to a new direction, outline your reasons for this change and point out any investments you have already made in it. Anything that you've done on your career break that is relevant to your new career will be a great asset.

In addition, if you plan to go from a highly paid profession into a moderate or lowly paid one, try not to mention your salary in your application.

CAREER ADVICE

Confucius said 'Find a job you like and you'll never have to work a day in your life'. The number of courses, books, career consultants, career coaches, career advisory bodies and career websites helping you to do just this is endless. Here's a sample of what's on offer (see also the Life Coaches section on p12):

Courses

- **Floodlight** (www.floodlight.co.uk) Official guide to courses in London.
- **Learndirect** (www.learndirect.co.uk) A government scheme with details on 700,000 courses nationwide.
- **Lifelong Learning** (www.lifelonglearning.co.uk) A site encouraging, promoting and developing lifelong learning.

Books

- *Creating a Successful CV* by Simon Howard
- *From Acorns...How to Build Your Brilliant Business from Scratch* by Caspian Woods
- *Great Answers to Tough Interview Questions* by Martin John Yate
- *How to Get a Job You'll Love* by John Lees
- *Soultrader: Find Purpose and You'll Find Success* by Carmel McConnell
- *Targeting the Job You Want* by Kate Wendleton
- *What Color Is Your Parachute?* by Richard Nelson Bolles
- *What Should I Do with My Life?* by Po Bronson
- *The 'Which?' Guide to Starting Your Own Business: How to Make a Success of Going It Alone* by 'Which?' Consumer Guides
- *Who Do You Think You Are?* by Nick Isbister
- *Who Moved My Cheese? An Amazing Way to Deal with Change in your Work and in Your Life* by Spencer Johnson
- *Working Identity: Unconventional Strategies for Reinventing Your Career* by Herminia Ibarra
- *Writers' & Artists' Yearbook* by A & C Black

Career Coaches, Advisory Bodies & Useful Websites

- **Best Year Yet** (www.bestyearyet.com) Career coaching.
- **BUBL Information Service** (http://bubl.ac.uk/uk/newspapers.htm) Quick access to national and regional newspapers and their job ads.
- **The Big Leap Coaching Company** (www.thebig-leap.com) Career coaching.
- **Careers International** (www.careersnet.com) Career coaching.
- **Careers Research & Advisory Centre** (www.crac.org.uk) A charity promoting lifelong career-related learning.
- **Career Scotland** (www.careers-scotland.org.uk) Career advice and support.
- **JobHuntersBible.com** (www.jobhuntersbible.com) Web pages for the book *What Color Is Your Parachute?*
- **John Lees Associates** (www.johnleescareers.com) Career coaching.
- **Monster** (www.monster.co.uk) Online recruitment agency with advice for career-changers.
- **Pam Richardson** (www.pamrichardson.co.uk) Career coaching.
- **Recruitment & Employment Confederation** (www.rec.uk.com) Look at the Helpful Checklists for Job Seekers. There's one covering advice for older job seekers.
- **Workmaze** (www.workmaze.com) Career coaching.
- **Workthing** (www.workthing.com) Online recruitment agency with useful advice for career-changers.

For more Australian or US resources, see the relevant Appendix.

STARTING YOUR OWN BUSINESS

On a career break you are your own boss. This can be difficult to relinquish when you're back home looking for a job. Working for yourself and employing others suddenly seems as attractive as fresh, white underwear after months of old, grey pants. You can follow your passion, you're in control, and you might be working long hours but at least it's making you rich and not someone else. It might also be more flexible, working around school holidays, for instance. Well, that's the theory. In practice, it's rarely a bunch of roses, even if you set up as a florist.

Starting your own business is often difficult and stressful. Financially there's a lot to think about. What about start-up cash? How will you survive while your business gets off the ground? What happens if there are cash-flow problems (as there invariably are with new ventures)? What do you know about business, financial and marketing plans, record-keeping, accounting procedures and employing people? Although running your own business can give you more flexibility, in reality it often means working long hours and weekends to get it off the ground. In addition, any holidays or sick leave have to be financed by you (along with any other standard benefits).

After a three-month career break, Mark Hide set up a company training independent travellers to travel safely and wisely. He explains:

I was the director of a marketing business that was financially rewarding but basically the same shit, different day. I took off to Alaska for three months and spent 23 days climbing Mt McKinley. For the first time in years I had time to think. During this break I came up with the idea for Planet Wise – something that combined my marketing and training skills with my passion for travel. When I returned home it took me four months to do a SWOT analysis of the market place. (I've got an MBA, which helped enormously, but the lack of qualifications should never get in the way of anyone following their dream.) I wrote a business plan and a financial plan; in fact, I wrote three financial plans – one if everything went fantastically well, one that was more realistic and one showing the 'Oh God, what do we do now?' scenario. This took me more time but was well worth the effort. From the start I had fantastic help and advice from my local Business Link office and they still give me ongoing support though regular telephone calls. In my opinion, the really important thing is to understand exactly what you're offering, and what makes you unique, and ensure your branding/messaging reflects this. It has been difficult – it has taken longer than I anticipated for business to come in; like any small business starting up there are short-term cash-flow issues; I cannot switch off – my partner has to be incredibly understanding because I think of the business day and night, seven days a week – and it can be pretty lonely. I had been used to working in a team and suddenly I've got to do everything – generate the ideas, administrate, fix the computers etc. What I miss most is

---

SETTING UP A BUSINESS: THE USA

Hanging up your own shingle inevitably means getting more familiar with Uncle Sam. Thankfully, the federal government recognizes that small businesses are responsible for creating the majority of the USA's new jobs. The Small Business Administration (SBA; www.sba.gov) sponsors frequent low-cost training workshops and publishes several free small-business start-up guides, with many targeted specifically at women and underrepresented minorities. Additionally, the SBA provides financial support through its community-based business loan and investment programs.

SBA studies indicate that most successful start-ups spring from one of several basic inspirations: An answer to a 'Why isn't there a…?' question; a spin-off from a present occupation that capitalises on a shortcoming in others' products or services; a technological advance; or simply a new way of employing an existing everyday object.

For more on the legal and financial aspects of running your own business, check out the Small Business section of Nolo Press' (www.nolo.com) free online plain-English law center.

SETTING UP A BUSINESS: AUSTRALIA

With 96% of Australian companies being small or medium-sized, both state and federal governments have established excellent small-business support networks. Government business centres can also outline available tax and duty concessions, grants and access to venture capital.

A recent World Bank report listed Australia as one of the easiest countries in the world in which to set up a business. The legalities start with registering the company with the Australian Securities & Investments Commission. The most common type of company is a Proprietary Limited (Pty Ltd) one. This registration process takes around seven to 14 days and costs A$800. Business licensing may then be applicable depending upon your profession, and a business name, if you are not using your own, will also have to be lodged and paid for (A$120). The Australian Tax Office will issue an Australian Business Number (ABN) upon request.

Accounting and legal costs should include advice on applicable insurances (public liability, professional indemnity, loss of income, superannuation, cash, building and contents), tenders, contracts and conditions of employment.

---

someone as involved as I am in the business to talk things over with or to use as a sounding board – a sanity-checker. Of course, I've got good friends who'll listen but it's not quite the same. Having said all of that, I wouldn't be doing anything else for the world. My passion and enthusiasm for this business is overwhelming and is transmitted to everyone I talk to.

As Mark found, if you're thinking of starting your own business your first port of call should be your local Business Link office or affiliate:

- **Business Link** (England; ☎ 0845 600 9006; www.businesslink.gov.uk)
- **Business Eye** (Wales; ☎ 0845 796 9798; www.businesseye.org.uk)
- **Business Gateway** (Lowlands of Scotland; ☎ 0845 609 6611; www.bgateway.com)
- **Highlands and Islands Enterprise** (Scotland; ☎ +44 (0)1463 234171; www.hie.co.uk)
- **Invest Northern Ireland** (☎ +44 (0)28 9023 9090; www.investni.com)

Business Link (managed by the DTI) can give you a warehouse full of practical information both in person and online about starting and running your small business. If you've never prepared a business plan or created a marketing strategy, read its detailed online guides. If you need to raise money, look at the Finance & Grants section of its website, then speak to your nearest office about all local, government and EU funding, as well as grant and loan options.

Next up, contact the National Federation of Enterprise Agencies (www.nfea.com), which specialises in meeting the needs of small and growing businesses. Your nearest branch can give business counselling, training and workspace options. Some of their services are free.

See p257 for information on your legal and financial obligations and for details of more useful organisations and websites. For pointers on starting a business in the US or Australia, see the relevant Appendix.

GOING FREELANCE

Equally appealing to starting your own business is to ditch the salaried job and just go it alone. You could turn a hobby into a money-making venture or become self-employed in your particular area of professional expertise. Sally Dryden did this, finding that her established contacts and clients made the transition much easier:

I was a director in a communications consultancy for 12 years. When it merged with another company with a very different culture, I realised the environment was wrong for me and it was time to walk away. I took a four-month break and thought about what I might turn my hand to next. There was no great epiphany or thunderbolt that pointed the way forward. I just figured out that I wanted to develop the creative parts of my previous job that I most enjoyed – writing, editing, producing – and to ditch all the stress-making management tasks and personnel issues. And doing it on a freelance basis meant I had much better control of the type and amount of work I did. I crunched the numbers to establish how much work I needed to get to keep me solvent and how much I should be charging. It really helped to talk to a few friends and colleagues in the business; as a result I was persuaded to double my charge-out rate. I found an accountant who took care of the tax side of things and set me up as a sole trader. I got my business stationery designed and printed, and sent a mailshot to various contacts and clients. Luckily for me, clients I had worked with in the past were happy to accept me in my new freelance role rather than as part of a 'corporate package', and that's where most of my work came from initially. Going freelance is the best thing I ever did. I've built up a good portfolio of clients I enjoy working with. I have enough interaction with my clients and various collaborators to avoid getting 'cabin fever'. To keep myself fired up, I try to take on a couple of 'scary' projects every year: jobs that really challenge me or that are in new areas that add to my repertoire. The best things about freelancing? Doing things on my own terms and being able to shop 'off-peak'. The worst? Not always knowing where the next job's coming from and raiding the fridge too often.

Sally was confident she could support herself and dived straight into the freelance pool. At the beginning, you may have more worries about staying afloat. If so, you could always keep the day job, go freelance in your spare time, and test the water. Whatever you decide, it's likely you'll be freelancing from home. To avoid the possibility of business rates, set up in a room that has another purpose, such as a bedroom or living room (ie not a study).

See the Appendices for more advice on going freelance in the US or Australia.

PORTFOLIO CAREERS

A portfolio career is like having your professional cake and eating it. Jeff Stanford, a maestro at the portfolio career game, defines it as:

An enduring professional involvement in two or more diverse fields which generates income.

He goes on to explain the ins and outs of what he does:

There are three strands to my career: English Language Training/consultancy (www.wordflair .com); violin playing; and web design (www.jswebdesign.co.uk). They generate the following as a percentage of my total income: ELT 70%; Web design 20%; violin playing 10%. That ratio changes from year to year, but ELT is generally the biggest income generator. Portfolio working brings out very different aspects of my personality. For instance, much of the ELT work shows me in an extrovert light. I am bouncing around the classroom being energetic, enthusiastic and positive. The process of Web design is about sitting by myself at a computer. Violin playing allows me to be creative – it's a sort of middle-ground between extrovert ELT

FREELANCING: THE USA

Despite the formidable drawbacks of being your own boss (no job security, high self-employment taxes, no benefits and few labor-law protections), a recent US Department of Labor study found that self-employment is a growing trend. Labor experts project that independent contractors will account for 10% of the nation's workforce (over 10 million people) by 2005, with another one million taxpayers reporting secondary self-employment income. Some pundits chalk this trend up to American's indefatigable entrepreneurial spirit, while other astute observers note that recent economic downturns have left many professionals with no other viable option.

For more on the legal and financial aspects of calling your own shots, check out the Independent Contractor section of Nolo Press' free online plain-English law center at www.nolo.com.

FREELANCING: AUSTRALIA

Australian freelancers should consider forming a company if annual earnings reach A$50,000 per year. You are eligible for GST contributions at this rate of income, and better tax concessions may apply if you operate as a company rather than as a sole trader. Additionally, many government departments, industry players and large corporations will only sign contracts or accept tenders from registered companies.

   An accountant's fees are fully tax-deductible, so find a specialist who understands your profession's allowable concessions. Be aware, however, that even if you are entitled to claim for work-related expenditures, in reality any tax deductions are only worth a portion of the original outlay. Finally, whatever your business profile, do seek legal advice, especially concerning public liability and professional indemnity issues.

---

and introvert Web-design work. I find that having the three very different strands satisfies different needs. Organising it all is a challenge. A backbone to my life is violin practice. I need to practice every day to be able to play. I usually make weekly plans which accommodate my various commitments. The main advantages of this type of career are flexibility; being able to subsidise less well paid work (music) with better-paid work (ELT consultancy); networking in one area of work can lead to work in another area; and if work in one area dries up, something else in another area takes its place. There are disadvantages. There's times when I'm too busy and others when I'm not busy enough. If you're a perfectionist, then it is difficult to be at the top of each profession. Building up professional qualifications in three areas is also expensive. Occasionally, my portfolio career work leads to too much time by myself. Income tax returns have to be divided into three sections with separate lists of expenses and profits. You have to be careful to keep accurate records of work done, expenses, invoices etc.

A portfolio career is often something that comes about by chance over a period of time. However, if you want to plan it then Jeff recommends:

Make a list of your skills, interests, qualifications. Look for ways that different professional interests could fit in with each other with regards to time, networking, place of work. Start one area on a freelance basis and gradually build up work in another area, and then, later, perhaps another. Think big, but move a step at a time. There's no need for colossal loans/debts if you're prepared and move slowly. Let all your friends and colleagues know what you're up to. Advertise your services distinctly. Plan your time according to all your portfolio strands.

LEGAL & FINANCIAL STUFF

Starting a business, going freelance or putting together a portfolio career all mean that you must register with the Inland Revenue as being self-employed. You need to register within three months of receiving your first cheque (regardless of how small it might be) otherwise there'll be a fine of £100. Once you become self-employed you have to pay your own Class 2 National Insurance contributions, but only when the net income from your business or freelance activities reaches more than £4215 a year. While you're earning less than this, you can apply for a Certificate of Small Earnings Exception. National Insurance contributions are more class-ridden than the Indian train system, and can seem as muddled, so call the National Insurance Self-Employment helpline on ☎ 0845 915 4655 for clarification.

   To register with the Inland Revenue ring its Newly Self-Employed Helpline on ☎ 0845 915 4515 (lines open from 8am to 8pm daily). Don't stop there, though; make this call pay for itself and ask as many questions as you can about starting up in business. Inquire about their business support teams (www.inlandrevenue.gov.uk/bst/index) and arrange for one to come out and see you, or get along to a local workshop. Ask to receive their Starting Up in Business ring binder (very snazzy for the IR), a really useful step-by-step guide, or go online and download it from www.inlandrevenue.gov.uk/startingup (PDF, 155KB). Also make sure you're sent a leaflet called *P/SE/1 Thinking of Working for Yourself?*

When you are self-employed you have to pay your own tax (see www.inland.revenue.gov .uk for more information). Each April, at the end of the tax year, the Inland Revenue will send you a Self-Assessment tax return and, if you return it before 30 September, they work out your tax bill. If you have any problems filling out this form call the Self-Assessment helpline on ☎ 0845 900 0444. When you are self-employed you will pay your tax and Class 4 National Insurance contributions in two instalments – on 31 January and 31 July. If you haven't given up your day job, then you will pay tax on any additional income from the outset because your tax-free allowance of £4745 will already have been used up. The tax rate of either 22% or 40% will be worked out on your total earnings. Your income will also affect the amount of Class 4 National Insurance you pay.

If you're just starting out in business, you're unlikely to have formed a limited company, so you won't have to deal with corporation tax. However, you will have to think about what type of business you want. Most people start off as a sole trader (meaning you're an individual who is self-employed). If you're trading under a different name, have formed a partnership, limited liability partnership, company or franchise, then special rules and regulations will apply to your business. When the income from your business reaches £57,000, you'll have to register for VAT. If you have any questions about this call the Customs and Excise National Advice Service on ☎ 0845 010 9000 or log onto www.hmce.gov.uk. (All figures quoted in this section are for the UK tax year 2004/2005 and usually change annually.)

Depending on the type of business you start, there's a whole raft of other issues to get your head around. These include: health and safety; fire, environmental and building regulations; intellectual property; fair trading; data protection; disability rights; trading licences (did you know you need one of these to become a hairdresser?); and insurance cover. In addition, if your new business involves importing and exporting, you're likely to encounter enough red tape to cover the distance travelled during your career break. For more information see the following list of contacts.

You will also need to develop an interest in tax credits, allowances and reliefs. For instance, you should be able to get R&D Tax Credits (see www.inlandrevenue.gov.uk /randd). Plus, if your new business starts to take off, you'll have to engage with such exciting issues as employee rights, equal opportunities, working hours and minimum wages. To help navigate through the employment jungle, try ringing the New Employer helpline on ☎ 0845 607 0143.

Before you decide it's all far too complicated and you need another career break, don't forget that your accountant will advise you on almost all of this. If you don't have one, look up the Association of Chartered Certified Accountants' website (www.accaglobal.com) or find out who your best friend uses.

For more information try the following:

- **British Chambers of Commerce** (☎ +44 (0)20 7654 5800; www.britishchambers.org.uk)
- **British Franchise Association** (☎ +44 (0)1491 578050; www.british-franchise.org)
- **British Venture Capital Association** (☎ +44 (0)20 7025 2950; www.bvca.co.uk)
- **The Chartered Institute of Marketing** (www.cim.co.uk)
- **Companies House** (☎ 0870 333 3636; www.companieshouse.co.uk)
- **Companies Registry** (Northern Ireland; ☎ +44 (0)28 9023 4488; www.companiesregistry.detini.gov.uk)
- **Contractors' Helpline** (for the construction industry; ☎ 0845 733 5588)
- **Co-operatives UK: the Union of Co-operative Enterprises** (☎ +44 (0)161 246 2959; www.cooperatives-uk.coop)
- **Disability Rights Commission Helpline** (☎ 0845 762 2633; www.disability.gov.uk)
- **The Environment Agency** (☎ 0845 933 3111; www.environment-agency.gov.uk)
- **Federation of Small Businesses** (☎ +44 (0)1253 336000; www.fsb.org.uk)
- **Health & Safety Executive Information Line** (☎ 0870 154 5500; www.hse.gov.uk)
- **Information Commissioner** (data protection; ☎ +44 (0)1625 545745; www.informationcommissioner.gov.uk)
- **The Office of Fair Trading** (☎ 0845 722 4499; www.oft.gov.uk)
- **The Patent Office** (☎ 0845 950 0505; www.patent.gov.uk & www.intellectual-property.gov.uk)
- **Subcontractors' Helpline** (for the construction industry; ☎ 0845 300 0581)
- **Valuation Office Agency** (www.voa.gov.uk)

NOT COMING HOME

There are many reasons for not coming home – you've found your perfect job abroad, you've fallen in love with a foreign lifestyle, a foreign climate or, more commonly, a foreigner. This happened to Dawn Köse who runs the Köse Pension in Göreme, Turkey. She explains:

We were hitching in Northern Greece and a Jordanian truck driver picked us up and took us all the way to Aksaray in Turkey. I met my husband, Mehmet, at a camp site/pension in Göreme. My friend and I stayed for two months helping out at the pension and Mehmet and I became friends. I returned to Edinburgh, but couldn't forget about him, so I worked hard to save enough money to return. When I got back Mehmet and I realised this was more than just a holiday romance (that sounds corny, doesn't it?) and after working the tourist season we moved into his parents' cave house. They were fantastic – accepted me without question – but it was very hard at times – I only spoke a little Turkish and they didn't speak a word of English. We got married in the winter, and in March started up the Köse Pension (thanks to help from my dad). It hasn't always been easy (in fact, there have been quite a few times when I wondered what the hell I was doing here!). I don't regret it at all, though. We have three children, all bilingual. The only difficult thing about living so far from where I was brought up (in Edinburgh) is not seeing family as much as I'd like. We go to the UK every couple of years, but it's not so easy when you earn your money in Turkey.

The process of 'not coming home' usually entails 'coming home' in order to sort out your affairs. You'll have to make all those arrangements (discussed in the Tying Up Loose Ends chapter) permanent or indefinite – forever is a long time. Depending on your circumstances and ultimate destination, you'll have to work out your immigration options too. 'Coming home' in order 'not to come home' gives you a break (yes, another one) from whatever or whoever is keeping you abroad and acts as a useful reality-checker (although friends and family are usually only too keen to take on this role).

If this happens to you, do get in touch with Lonely Planet and tell us all about it for the next edition of *The Career Break Book*. Even if it doesn't, we're still interested in your career-break experiences and would love to hear from you anyway.

Good luck.

Career Break Planner

Here are four blank Career Break Planners that will help you map out your next year or so. You'll probably change your mind time and time again, and want to try out several itineraries, which is why we've printed four of them here.

PLANNER 1

January

February

March

April

May

June

July

August

September

October

November

December

January

February

March

PLANNER 2

January ....
....
....
....
....
....
....

February ....
....
....
....
....
....
....

March ....
....
....
....
....
....

April ....
....
....
....
....
....

May ....
....
....
....
....
....

June ....
....
....
....
....
....

July ....
....
....
....
....

August

September

October

November

December

January

February

March

PLANNER 3

January

February

March

April

May

June

July

August

September

October

November

December

January

February

March

PLANNER 4

January

February

March

April

May

June

July

August

September

October

November

December

January

February

March

Appendix 1:
Further Information in Australia

CAREER BREAKS EXPLAINED

CAREER BREAK–FRIENDLY COMPANIES
aussie.com.au
☎ +61 (0)8-9220 8477, 1300 368 828
webmaster@aussie.com.au
www.aussie.com.au
This online business directory lists hundreds of Australian companies (with contact details and websites) across all major industries. Check for overseas offices, job-swapping opportunities and career-break policies.

Australian Chamber of Commerce & Industry
Level 12, 83 Clarence St, Sydney, NSW 2000, Australia
☎ 1300 137 153
www.acci.asn.au
The ACCI website represents Australian business and industry associations, listing contact details and websites. Check for information on business and industry overseas as well as job-swapping opportunities and career-break policies.

TYING UP LOOSE ENDS

FINANCES
The Association of Superannuation Funds of Australia
Level 19 Picadilly Tower, 133 Castlereagh St, Sydney, NSW 2000, Australia
☎ +61 (0)2-9264 9300
www.asfa.asn.au
The association's library and information service is open to the public during office hours. The website contains information on different types of funds.

Commonwealth Bank
GPO Box 9823, Parramatta, Sydney, NSW 2124, Australia
☎ +61 (0)2-9378 2000, 13 2221
www.commbank.com.au
The Commonwealth offers online banking and direct debiting for automated bill payments and account transfers.

National Australia Bank
500 Bourke St, Melbourne, Vic 3000, Australia
☎ +61 (0)3-8641 3500, 1300 651 656
www.national.com.au
The NAB offers online banking, phone banking and direct debiting for automated bill payments and account transfers.

National Institute of Accountants
Level 8, 12–20 Flinders Lane, Melbourne, Vic 3000, Australia
☎ +61 (0)3-8665 3100
natoffice@nia.org.au
www.nia.org.au
The institute has accountants' contact details. Check the state website links under Find an Accountant.

National Insurance Brokers Association
Level 18, 111 Pacific Hwy, North Sydney, NSW 2060, Australia
☎ +61 (0)2-9964 9400
niba@niba.com.au
www.niba.com.au
The association details around 500 brokers who specialise in everything from car, house and contents insurance to travel, life and terrorism insurance.

Westpac Banking Corporation
Level 6, 2 King William St, Adelaide, SA 5000, Australia
☎ +61 (0)8-8424 8490, 1300 655 505
www.westpac.com.au
Westpac offers online banking and direct debiting for automated bill payments and account transfers.

TAXATION
Australian Taxation Office
PO Box 900, Civic Square, ACT 2608, Australia
☎ +61 (0)2-6216 1111, 13 28 61
www.ato.gov.au
The ATO has information covering a range of taxpayer issues. This includes information for Australians planning to work overseas or earn money through investments.

Centrelink
Shop 1, Level 1, Northpoint Plaza, 183 Chandler St, Belconnen, ACT 2617, Australia
☎ +61 (0)2-6244 7788, 13 10 21
www.centrelink.gov.au
Centrelink is the government organisation that assists with finding work; it also provides financial aid and allowances, including government pensions.

Institute of Chartered Accountants in Australia

Level 14, 37 York St, Sydney, NSW 2000, Australia
☎ +61 (0)2-9290 1344
support@icaa.org.au
www.icaa.org.au
Some specialist tax accountants are listed on the linked state websites under Find a Chartered Accountant.

HOUSE

Australian Furniture Removals Association

PO Box 7104, Baulkham Hills Business Centre, Sydney, NSW 2153, Australia
☎ +61 (0)2-9659 5300, 1800 671 806
admin@afra.com.au
www.afra.com.au
AFRA-registered businesses are on the website along with the organisation's code of ethics.

Century 21 Real Estate

Level 12, 76–80 Clarence St, Sydney, NSW 2000, Australia
☎ +61 (0)2-8295 0600
www.century21.com.au
This company has 6500 offices across 66 countries. The website links all national branches and displays available services eg sales, rental and rental-property management.

Elders Real Estate

109 Melbourne St, South Brisbane, Qld 4101, Australia
☎ +61 (0)7-3840 4101, 1300 655 660
poxty@elders.com.au
www.elders.com.au
Elder's website links all 400 national branches and details services, eg sales, rental and rental-property management.

Grace Removals Group

4 Tucks Rd, Seven Hills, Sydney, NSW 2147, Australia
☎ +61 (0)2-9838 5600, 13 14 42
info@grace.com.au
www.grace.com.au
Grace's branches across Australia and New Zealand will organise packing, national and international removals and the storage of your goods.

HomeExchange.com

Suite 6, 25–27 Marine Pde, St Kilda, Vic 3182, Australia
☎ +61 (0)3-9537 1207
homeexchange@alphalink.com.au
www.HomeExchange-Australia.com
This renowned company offers a huge choice of homes available for swapping throughout 83 countries. Membership is US$50 per year.

Home Link International

PO Box 48, Newcastle, NSW 2300, Australia
☎ +61 (0)2-4915 0200
info@homelink.com.au
www.homelink.com.au
This experienced home-swapping agency caters particularly to those who prefer the UK, Europe, the USA and Australia. Membership is A$130 to A$270 a year.

LJ Hooker Real Estate

295 Kensington Rd, Kensington Park, Adelaide, SA 5068, Australia
☎ +61 (0)8-8431 6088, 1800 621 212
kensington@ljhooker.com.au
www.ljhooker.com.au
The company has 600 branches across New Zealand, Indonesia, Papua New Guinea and China. National branches are linked to the website, which also details services, eg sales, rental and rental-property management.

Mortgage Choice Australia

182–186 Blues Point Rd, North Sydney, NSW 2060, Australia
☎ +61 (0)2-8907 0444, 13 14 62
homeloans@mortgagechoice.com.au
www.mortgagechoice.com.au
A national mortgage-broking company, with offices linked through the website.

Ray White Real Estate

Level 13, 26 St George's Tce, Perth, WA 6000, Australia
☎ +61 (0)8-9221 6322, 13 14 94
corporate.wa@raywhite.com
www.raywhite.com
The company has branches across Australia, New Zealand, Indonesia, Singapore and Papua New Guinea. The website links to national branches and details the company's services, eg sales, rental and rental-property management.

Self Storage Association of Australasia

PO Box 502, Kilmore, Vic 3764, Australia
☎ +61 (0)3-5781 0131
admin@selfstorage.com.au
www.selfstorage.com.au
The SSAA represents 600 storage centres across Australia and New Zealand. Contact details for regional and local companies are on the website, along with information on how to calculate the amount of storage you might need.

Wizard Home Loans

12 Castlereagh St, Sydney, NSW 2000, Australia
☎ +61 (0)2-8226 3500, 13 19 70
talk2us@wizard.com.au
www.wizard.com.au
A national mortgage-broking company with offices linked through the website.

Wridgways Australia
93 Heatherdale Rd, Ringwood, Vic 3134, Australia
☎ +61 (0)3-9837 1700
melbourne@wridgways.com.au
www.wridgways.com.au
With branches across Australia and the world, Wridgways' services include packing, national and international removals and the storage of your goods.

Your Mortgage
www.yourmortgage.com.au
The online version of *Your Mortgage* magazine, with broker listings and and all sorts of mortgage advice.

VEHICLE & OTHER TRANSPORT
AAMI
PO Box 14180 Melbourne City Mail Centre, Vic 8062, Australia
☎ +61 (0)3-8520 1300, 13 22 44
aami@aami.com.au
www.aami.com.au
AAMI is a national insurance company specialising in car, home and caravan insurance.

Buslines.com.au
info@buslines.com.au
www.buslines.com.au
The Buslines website displays all Australian bus, train and coach-line details. There are direct website links to state public transport information centres as well as private, state and national transport organisations. Ferry and airport details are included, along with some international transport services.

carsales.com.au
1/144 Highbury Rd, Burwood, Vic 3125, Australia
☎ +61 (0)3-9805 3600
sales@carsales.com.au
www.carsales.com.au
Carsales offers a comprehensive collection of classified car advertisements for professional dealers, private buyers and sellers.

Drive
www.drive.com.au
A website offering car hire, buying and selling facilities and more.

CHILDREN & DEPENDENTS
Carers NSW
Level 17, 323 Castlereagh St, Sydney, NSW 2000
☎ +61 (0)2-9280 4744, 1800 242 636, 1800 059 059
contact@carersnsw.asn.au
www.carersnsw.asn.au
Carer Resource and Carer Respite Centres exist in each state; these are all linked through this website.

Family Assistance Office (FAO)
☎ 13 12 02
Email using form on website.
www.familyassist.gov.au
You may lose your Family Tax Benefit if you leave Australia without notifying the FAO. Check the website for details. The FAO can also give information on what might happen to your Child Care Benefit if you leave the country, though there's nothing on the website about this - you'll have to telephone.

Ozcarers
http://users.chariot.net.au/~ozcarers
The website has comprehensive links to all manner of carer websites.

PETS
RSPCA
Cnr Burwood Hwy & Middleborough Rd, Burwood East, Vic 3151, Australia
☎ +61 (0)3-9224 2222
rspca@vicrspca.aust.com
www.rspca.org.au, www.rspcavic.org
The RSPCA links their state organisations through the main website. State offices have information on regional vet practices and boarding facilities. Veterinary practices will recommend local pet-sitters.

LEGAL ADVICE
Law Council of Australia
19 Torrens St, Braddon, ACT 2612, Australia
☎ +61 (0)2-6246 3788
mail@lawcouncil.asn.au
www.lawcouncil.asn.au
The Law Council of Australia represents 40,000 legal practitioners across the country. The website has links to state law societies, which list contact details of lawyers (who can provide power of attorney and other legal advice), bar associations, legal complaint bodies and community information.

National Association of Community Legal Centres
PO Box A2245, Sydney South, NSW 1235, Australia
☎ +61 (0)2-9264 9595
nacl@fcl.fl.asn.au
www.naclc.org.au
The NACLC is an independent nonprofit organisation providing free legal services for those who cannot afford private legal representation. A first point of contact for many using the legal system, the 207 centres also provide a free solicitor referral service; solicitors can advise on power of attorney issues.

VOTING
Australian Electoral Commission
PO Box 6172, Kingston, ACT 2604, Australia
☎ +61 (0)2-6271 4411, 13 23 26

info@aec.gov.au
www.aec.gov.au
Australian citizens heading overseas should initially register to vote as an overseas elector. Once registered simply attend the nearest Australian embassy or consulate, or arrange to receive and return ballot papers by post. Overseas voting must be completed prior to the election. Australians travelling within Australia must, by law, vote either at a pre-poll voting centre or by post. The compulsory voting laws for state elections (for travelling Australians) vary from state to state, so check the AEC website, which has links to all state electoral offices.

TECHNOLOGY & COMMUNICATIONS

Australia Post
GPO Box 728, Melbourne, Vic 3001, Australia
☎ 13 13 18
www.australiapost.com.au
Australia Post will hold or forward your post for up to a year at a time. This service can be paid for on an annual basis.

Cellhire Australia
Level 4, 78 Liverpool St, Sydney, NSW 2000, Australia
☎ +61 (0)2-9286 9494, 1800 789 922
helpdesk@itsource.com.au
www.cellhire.com.au
This company runs a twenty-four-hour service offering mobile phone and data technology hire for international travel.

Telstra
231 Elizabeth St, Sydney, NSW 2000, Australia
☎ +61 (0)2-9396 1193, +61 (0)2 9201 9320
www.telstra.com.au
Telstra will help with managing and forwarding your electronic communications and switch your mobile to mobile 'roaming'.

PRACTICAL PLANS & TRAVEL TIPS

TICKETS

Asia Travel Network
18th floor, Lumpini Tower 1168/44, Rama 4 Rd, Tungmahamek, Sathorn Bangkok 10120, Thailand
☎ +66 2 677 6240
info@asiatravel.com
www.asiatravel.com
This global Thai travel company offers hotels, resorts, tours and travel packages throughout Asia, Africa, the Middle East, the USA and Canada.

Australian Federation of Travel Agents (AFTA)
Level 3, 309 Pitt St, Sydney, NSW 2000, Australia
☎ +61 (0)2-9264 3299
afta@afta.com.au
www.afta.com.au
The website contains direct links to member travel agents around the country.

Flight Centre
Ground floor, 157 Ann St, Brisbane, Qld 4000, Australia
☎ +61 (0)7-3011 7830, 13 31 33
www.flightcentre.com.au
Flight Centre is one of the largest and cheapest travel agent chains.

Travel.com.au
Level 1, 76–80 Clarence St, Sydney, NSW 2000, Australia
☎ +61 (0)2-9249 6000, 1300 130 482
customercentral@travel.com.au
www.travel.com.au
This is an online one-stop travel shop.

PASSPORTS, VISAS & TRAVEL INSURANCE

CGU Insurance
35 Armstrong St, South Ballarat, Vic 3350
☎ +61 (0)3-5320 1444, 13 15 32
email@cgu.com.au
www.cgu.com.au
A global Australian company, CGU offers personal, travel, household and car insurance policies.

Cover-More Insurance Services
Level 3, 60 Miller St, North Sydney, NSW 2059, Australia
☎ +61 (0)2-8907 5619, 13 23 03
enquiries@covermore.com.au
www.covermore.com.au
Cover-More offices exist in all state capitals as well as the UK. Cover-More offers travel insurance used by many travel agencies.

Department of Foreign Affairs and Trade
RG Casey Bldg, John McEwen Cres, Barton, ACT 0221, Australia
☎ +61 (0)2-6261 3305, 1300 555 135 (consular emergency centre),131 232 (passports)
www.dfat.gov.au, www.passports.gov.au
The department has contact details for all Australian embassies, consulates and government contacts. Passport and visa information and travel warnings are also available.

Migration Institute of Australia
PO Box Q102, Queen Vic Bld, Sydney, NSW 1230, Australia
☎ +61 (0)2-9279 3140
info@mia.org.au

www.mia.org.au, www.themara.com.au
The Migration Institute of Australia, incorporating the Migration Agents Registration Authority (MARA, the self-regulatory body for Australia's 3000 registered migration agents), has contact details for visa service agents throughout Australia.

QBE Insurance Group
82 Pitt St, Sydney, NSW 2000, Australia
☎ +61 (0)2-9375 4444, 1300 555 017
www.qbe.com
QBE has an international profile. Services include personal, travel, household and car insurance policies.

USEFUL RESOURCES
Atlas Travel Club
PO Box 543, Mascot, NSW 1460, Australia
admin@atlas-club.com.au
www.atlas-club.com.au
With members across Australia, New Zealand, the USA and Canada, this nonprofit club offers discounted air, road and sea travel.

Australasian Touring Caravan, Motorhome & Camping Club Inc
PO Box 5005, North Geelong, Vic 3215, Australia
briankelleher@swift.net.au
www.vks737.on.net/pdfs/atcmcc.pdf
To arrange affiliations with other travellers and associated clubs join the ATCMCC. Membership fees apply.

National Seniors (Travel Talk)
Level 11, 255 Adelaide St, Brisbane, Qld 4000, Australia
☎ +61 (0)7-3211 9611
general@nationalseniors.com.au
www.nationalseniors.com.au
This national community organisation specialises in travel deals for travellers over 50, also offering insurance advice and member discounts.

Silke's Travel Magazine & Directory
PO Box 1099, Darlinghurst, Sydney, NSW 1300, Australia
☎ +61 (0)2-8347 2000
silkes@silkes.com.au
www.silkes.com.au
This gay and lesbian travel magazine and directory organisation is a member of the International Gay and Lesbian Travel Association (IGLTA) and lists gay- and lesbian-friendly travel-related companies across Australia.

South Pacific Organisation
PO Box 13119, Suva, Fiji
☎ +679 330 4177
fax +679 330 1995
www.spto.org

This hub has links to island websites listing home-based adventure-tourism operators and tourism-related businesses (also local airline details, accommodation and other related information). Islands include Cook Islands, Fijian Islands, New Caledonia, Niue, Papua New Guinea, Samoa, the Solomon Islands, Tahiti, Tonga, Tuvalu & Vanuatu.

Travel & Holiday Expo
www.travelexpo.com.au
Held in Sydney (March), Melbourne (April) and Canberra (August), this annual expo is for the public; it hosts 150 exhibitors and has free entry.

Travel Clinics Australia
travel@travelclinic.com.au
www.travelclinic.com.au
The clinics offer vaccinations, health advice and reports on specific countries, and medical kits.

Travel Magazines & Books
Australian Gourmet Traveller With a worldwide food and travel remit, this magazine is published monthly and costs A$7.95.

Get Up & Go This biannual magazine covers senior travel and costs A$5.

Outdoor Australia Published every two months, this magazine contains worldwide adventures and exploration stories and suggestions; it costs A$8.

OUTthere Covering faces and places across Australia, this magazine is produced quarterly and costs A$6.

World Travel Published in January and May, this magazine has articles aimed at the active Australian traveller, and costs A$6.

Camps Australia Wide 2 This guide by Philip Procter lists free camp sites, rest areas, and off-road stops in national and state parks and reserves across Australia. Also included are low-cost caravan parks and roadhouses. The book is A$49, works in conjunction with Hema maps (www.hemamaps.com.au), and is available in good bookshops.

Websites
http://babelfish.altavista.com This online language tool will translate English into a multitude of languages (and vice versa). Translations are also possible between various European languages.
www.consumersonline.gov.au An A to Z of consumer resources with links to government and non-governmental organisations' (NGO) websites and publications.
www.nican.com.au A directory with information on recreation, tourism, sport and the arts for travellers with disabilities in Australia.
www.ozforex.com.au A currency converter.
http://whereis.com.au A clever tool for planning travel routes throughout Australia.

COMING HOME

RECRUITMENT AGENCIES

For additional recruitment agencies see the Contacts section of the Living & Working Abroad chapter, p188.

CareerOne

PO Box 4245, Sydney, NSW 2001, Australia
www.careerone.com.au
An online employment agency, CareerOne works in conjunction with the *Australian* and another 100 regional newspapers. The website's job advertisements cover the employment market very comprehensively.

Department of Employment and Workplace Relations

Garema Court, 148–180 City Walk, Canberra, ACT 2601, Australia
☎ +61 (0)2-6121 6000
ais@dewr.gov.au
www.dewrsb.gov.au
The department offers job seekers and government employees access to job and training opportunities. Advice about wage rates and conditions of employment is also on hand.

FairfaxDigital

www.fairfax.com.au, www.mycareer.com.au
This online facility lists jobs advertised in papers including the *Sydney Morning Herald* and the *Age*. It also has links to executive recruitment companies.

Hender Consulting

Level 5, 81 Flinders St, Adelaide, SA 5000, Australia
☎ +61 (0)8-8100 8888
www.hender.com.au
Hender specialises in recruiting at most levels for particular professions, eg finance, nursing and the wine industry.

Select Appointments Australasia Ltd

Level 3, Select House, 109 Pitt St, Sydney, NSW 2000, Australia
☎ +61 (0)2-8258 9999
www.selectappointments.com.au, www.speakmans.com.au
Select concentrates on administrative, clerical, sales, marketing and human-resources jobs. Select's associate, Speakman Tanner Menzies, mainly handles executive appointments.

CAREER ADVICE

The Careers Guide

PO Box 2092, Nerang MDC, Qld 4211, Australia
☎ +61 (0)7-5530 4855
admin@acs.edu.au
www.thecareersguide.com, www.acs.edu.au

Free advice from industry experts is among the career information offered on these websites administered by Australian Correspondence Schools.

Department of Employment and Workplace Relations

Garema Court, 148–180 City Walk, Canberra, ACT 2601, Australia
☎ +61 (0)2-6121 6000
ais@dewr.gov.au
www.jobsearch.gov.au/joboutlook
Look under Australian Careers on this and DEWR's website (www.dewrsb.gov.au) for analyses of most professions. Breakdowns explain potential earnings and current unemployment levels. Other indicators such as required skills and vacancy levels are linked to job advertisements.

STARTING YOUR OWN BUSINESS

AusIndustry

☎ 13 28 46
hotline@ausindustry.gov.au, inquiries@industry.gov.au
www.ausindustry.gov.au
This department helps small-business operators set up and flourish.

Australian Trade Commission (Austrade)

Level 25, Aon Tower, 201 Kent St, Sydney, NSW 2000, Australia
☎ +61 (0)2-9390 2035, 13 28 78
info@austrade.gov.au
www.austrade.gov.au
Austrade supplies help to small businesses seeking to join the export market. This includes information on accessing suitable markets and available grants.

Business Entry Point

www.business.gov.au
This is the place to apply for your Australian Business Number (ABN), among other things.

GOING FREELANCE

Australian Securities and Investments Commission

Level 6, 15 London Circuit, Canberra, ACT 2600, Australia
☎ +61 (0)2-6250 3800, 1300 300 630
www.asic.gov.au
ASIC has company listings, registration information and delineates companies' legal responsibilities.

SEEK.com.au

Level 3, 3 Wellington St, St Kilda, Vic 3182, Australia
☎ +61 (0)3-9510 7200
userhelp@seek.com.au
www.seek.com.au
An online recruitment agency, SEEK's free resources include practical advice, registration and CV listings for freelancers.

Appendix 2:
Further Information in the USA

CAREER BREAKS EXPLAINED

CAREER-BREAK–FRIENDLY COMPANIES
Great Place to Work Institute
286 Divisadero St, San Francisco, CA 94117, USA
☎ +1 415-503 1234
Email using the form on the website.
www.greatplacetowork.com
Compiles the annual list of 100 Best Companies to Work for in America, as published in *Fortune* magazine.

National Education Association
1201 16th St NW, Washington, DC, 20036, USA
☎ +1 202-833 4000
Email using the form on their website.
www.nea.org
Teaching is the USA's most career-break–friendly profession. The NEA puts prospective teachers in touch with its state affiliates.

TYING UP LOOSE ENDS

FINANCES
Bankrate.com
www.bankrate.com
This powerful, user-friendly site presents consolidated interest rate, online banking and investing advice in one handy package. The interactive mortgage calculators are especially helpful.

Motley Fool
webfool@fool.com
www.fool.com
The Motley Fool brothers dish out plain-English advice about everything financial via e-newsletters, the Web and their National Public Radio (NPR) show.

Yahoo! Finance
http://finance.yahoo.com
Yahoo's personal finance portal is loaded with invaluable tools for comparing mortgage rates, filing your tax online and exploring all your virtual money-management options.

TAXATION
US Internal Revenue Service
☎ +1 800-829 1040 for live and recorded assistance
www.irs.gov/individuals/overseas
Don't think they'll forget you just because you're jumping ship: the IRS has a useful FAQ page for taxpayers living abroad.

HOUSE
Craigslist
www.craigslist.org
This free grassroots classified-ad site has branches in most major US metropolitan areas listing housing swaps, sublets and homes for sale. There are no email or telephone contacts, as all support is provided online.

Invented City
☎ +1 415-252 1141
info@invented-city.com
www.invented-city.com
This US-based home-exchange service is part of the First Home Exchange Alliance worldwide network.

Only In America
☎ +1 415-383 8125
travel@exchangehomesoia.com
www.exchangehomesoia.com
A home-exchange site dedicated to properties in the USA, Canada, Mexico and the Caribbean.

Sabbatical Homes
applications@sabbaticalhomes.com
www.sabbaticalhomes.com
A home-swapping service for academics and those who can provide academic references.

United Van Lines
☎ +1 636-343 3900
www.unitedvanlines.com
North America's largest transporter of household goods offers do-it-yourself, individual and corporate plans to help streamline your move. It can also help you sort out your furniture removal and self-storage options.

VEHICLE
Auto Driveaway Co
☎ +1 800-346 2277
national100@autodriveaway.com
www.autodriveaway.com

The USA's foremost vehicle transporter has lists of cars awaiting drivers to deliver them to destinations across the country.

Kelley Blue Book
kelley@kbb.com
www.kbb.com
Kelley's online Blue Book is full of practical advice about how to price, sell or trade-in your used car.

DEPENDENTS
Care Pathways
☎ +1 800-259 9591
Email using the form on their website.
www.carepathways.com
This site hosts a searchable database of recommended providers of assisted living, continuing care, independent living and nursing home-care.

US Department of Health & Human Services
☎ +1 877-696 6775
www.os.dhhs.gov/aging
Provides links to state-level Department of Social Services resources and In-Home Supportive Services caregivers under its Aging category.

PETS
National Association of Professional Pet Sitters
☎ +1 800-296 7387, Pet Sitter Locator +1 856-439 0324
napps@ahint.com
www.petsitters.org
The NAPPS maintains a toll-free hotline and searchable database (US only) of licensed pet sitters.

Pet Sitters International
☎ +1 336-983 9222
info@petsit.com
www.petsit.com
You gotta love the group that initiated Take Your Dog to Work Day. They maintain a database of over 5000 sitters in the US and Canada.

LEGAL ADVICE
Nolo Press
☎ +1 800-728 3555
cs@nolo.com
www.nolo.com
Nolo Press publishes superb plain-English self-help legal books and provides a wealth of free online information on everyday legal topics.

US Department of State
☎ +1 202-647 4000
www.state.gov/m/fsi/tc/14618.htm

Uncle Sam's Bureau of Public Affairs explains how and when to create a power of attorney (POA). Overseas embassies can provide attorney referrals.

VOTING
US Federal Election Commission
☎ +1 800-424 9530
www.fec.gov/elections.html
Download a National Mail Voter Registration Form, or write to your local/state election office for an absentee ballot.

TECHNOLOGY & COMMUNICATIONS
ICC Rents
☎ +1 800-245 1094
sales@iccrents.com
www.iccrents.com
ICC ships rental Mac and PC laptop computers and peripherals nationwide.

Mailboxes Etc/UPS Store
☎ +1 888- 346 3623
realhelp@mbe.com
www.mbe.com
This ubiquitous nationwide chain offers mail forwarding, in-house computer rentals and other virtual office services.

PHI Leasing
☎ +1 877-977 6303, +1 480-443 0687
webmaster@phileasing.com
www.phileasing.com
For those far-flung sabbaticals to the back of beyond, PHI rents Globalstar and Iridium satellite phones with no minimum airtime charges.

TripTel
☎ +1 877-874 7835, +1 415-474 3330
rental@triptel.com
www.triptel.com
TripTel delivers rental mobile phones anywhere via FedEx and has locations at four major US airports.

PRACTICAL PLANS & TRAVEL TIPS

TICKETS
Booking online via portals can save some dough, but they're hardly a substitute for an experienced travel consultant.

Johnny Jet
www.johnnyjet.com
A one-stop portal chock-full of travel information and booking links. Publishes a handy free weekly *Travel Deals, News, Tips, & Stories* e-newsletter.

Last Frontiers
www.lastfrontiers.com/flights/airpass.htm
Check the FAQ page about single- and multicountry air
passes throughout Latin America.

Travelocity
☎ +1 888-709 5983
travelocity@travelocity.com
www.travelocity.com
Looking for a last-minute deal? This mammoth online-only
booking site offers access to thousands of travel-service
providers.

PASSPORTS, VISAS & TRAVEL INSURANCE
Bureau of Consular Affairs
☎ +1 202-647 3000
www.travel.state.gov
The bureau's Office of Public Affairs & Policy Coordination
attempts to keep up with ever-changing foreign entry
requirements for US citizens – wish them luck.

National Passport Information Center
☎ +1 877-487 2778
npic@state.gov
http://travel.state.gov/passport/index.html
Since 9/11, the US Department of State has ramped up
passport-processing options – but it still pays to plan ahead.

Travel Document Systems
☎ +1 800-874 5100 (Washington, DC), +1 888-874 5100
(San Francisco)
support@traveldocs.com
www.traveldocs.com
TDS is a leading private visa-application and passport-
expediting agency.

USEFUL RESOURCES
International Association for Medical Assistance to Travelers
☎ +1 716-754 4883
www.iamat.org
Nonprofit IAMAT advises travelers about health risks,
geographical distribution of diseases, immunization
requirements and global sanitary conditions.

LANIC
www.lanic.utexas.edu
Based at the University of Texas, the Latin American
Network Information Center has a country-by-country and
thematic directory with links to anything and everything
Latin America–related.

New York Times Travel Show
www.nytimestravel.com

This annual exhibition held in February bills itself as the
'ultimate travel destination.' Visitors can browse outfit-
ters' booths and book trips to exotic places around the
world.

Solo Travel Portal
www.solotravelportal.com
Don't want to go solo? Surf this clunky but info-filled site
for ideas about how to hook up with other travelers – or
how to go it alone in style.

South American Explorers
126 Indian Creek Rd, Ithaca, NY 14850, USA
☎ +1 800-274 0568, +1 607-277 0488
fax +1 607-277 6122
explorer@saexplorers.org
www.saexplorers.org
This is a highly regarded nonprofit organization with
clubhouses in Quito (Ecuador) and Lima and Cusco (Peru).
SAE supplies its members with travel information on
Latin America via its monthly newsletter, trip reports,
volunteer opportunity database and online bulletin
board.

Transitions Abroad
PO Box 745, Bennington, VT 05201, USA
☎ /fax +1 802-442 4827
info@transitionsabroad.com
www.transitionsabroad.com
The publisher of *Transitions Abroad* magazine maintains an
online treasure-trove of resources about studying, working
and living abroad.

US Department of State
☎ +1 202-647 5225 (hotline), +1 202-647 4000 (main
switchboard)
www.travel.state.gov
US citizens' official stop for travel warnings and visa and
consular information. Note that country warnings tend to
be on the conservative side.

Yahoo! Travel Magazine Directory
http://dir.yahoo.com/Recreation/Travel/News_and_
Media/Magazines
This comprehensive index of online and print travel rags
reviews a broad spectrum of special interests, from the
Amish Heartland to *Wanderlust*.

Books
Alternatives to the Peace Corps by Jennifer Willsea and
Meagan Reule (Food First Books, 2003); order from
www.foodfirst.org.

*Alternative Travel Directory: The Complete Guide to
Traveling, Studying & Living Overseas* by David Cline and
Clayton Hubbs (Transitions Abroad, 2002).

International Jobs: Where They Are and How to Get Them by Eric Kocher and Nina Segal (Perseus Publishing, 2003).

Teaching English Overseas: A Job Guide for Americans & Canadians by Jeff Mohamed (English Intl Inc, 2003).

The Back Door Guide to Short-Term Job Adventures: Internships, Extraordinary Experiences, Seasonal Jobs, Volunteering, Working Abroad by Michael Landes (Ten Speed Press, 2002).

Volunteer Vacations: Short-Term Adventures That Will Benefit You and Others by Bill McMillon (Chicago Review Press, 2003).

COMING HOME

RECRUITMENT AGENCIES
Google Recruitment and Staffing Directory
http://directory.google.com/Top/Business/Employment/Recruitment_and_Staffing
The venerable search engine's ontological breakdown of the USA's vast pool of staffing, temporary employment and executive recruiting agencies is as good a place as any to begin your new job search – after you exhaust your personal networking contacts, of course.

CAREER ADVICE
Career Coach Marty Nemko
☎ +1 510-655 2777
mnemko@earthlink.net
www.martynemko.com
The career guru and author of the bestselling *Cool Careers for Dummies* serves up free, unconventional work-related wisdom on his website via a variety of other broadcast media outlets.

Wall Street Journal Executive Career Site
www.careerjournal.com
Salary and hiring info, job-hunting trends, negotiating tips, interviewing and résumé advice – it's all at your unemployed fingertips on the WSJ's slick site.

STARTING YOUR OWN BUSINESS
US Small Business Administration
☎ +1 800-827 5722
www.sba.gov
The SBA maintains an extensive online library of 200-plus e-books and publications, and sponsors frequent how-to workshops nationwide.

US Internal Revenue Service
☎ +1 800-829-4477 TeleTax recorded information
www.irs.gov/smallbiz
Besides an accountant (and a psychologist?), the IRS' virtual Small Business One Stop Resource Center should be your first stop if you're thinking about going it alone. It also has tons of information for self-employed sole proprietors (aka freelancers).

Wall Street Journal Center for Entrepreneurs
www.startupjournal.com
Business-plan tools; tax, trademark, technology and intellectual property tips; franchises for sale – what are you waiting for? Another nine-to-five job?

GOING FREELANCE
National Association for the Self-Employed
☎ +1 800-232 6273
www.nase.org
Ready to dump the boss off your back? The NASE offers members abundant financial advice, as well as access to group health-insurance premiums and other benefits of consolidated buying power.

Books
Small Time Operator (Bell Springs Publishing, 2000) by Bernard B Kamoroff CPA. The bestselling author of the essential handbook 422 Tax Deductions for Businesses & Self-Employed Individuals (Bell Springs Publishing, 2002) breaks down the nuts and bolts of building your own biz into bite-size pieces.

Acknowledgements

THIS BOOK

This 1st edition of *The Career Break Book* was written by a team of career-breakers led by Charlotte Hindle. Charlotte wrote the Practical Plans & Travel Tips, Going Travelling, and Coming Home chapters. Joe Bindloss wrote the No Regrets, Volunteering & Conservation, Living & Working Abroad and Studying chapters. Clare Hargreaves wrote the Career Breaks Explained and Tying Up Loose Ends chapters. Jill Kirby was responsible for the Further Information in Australia appendix and Andrew Dean Nystrom for the Further Information in USA appendix. The book was commissioned and developed in Lonely Planet's London office by Laetitia Clapton, and the project was managed by Bridget Blair. It was edited by Adrienne Costanzo with assistance from Brigitte Barta, and the index was prepared by Bridget Blair. Laura Jane designed and laid out the book, with assistance from Michael Ruff. The cover was designed by Annika Roojun and the map created by Julie Sheridan.

THANKS from the Authors

Charlotte Hindle I would like to thank Jacqui Hazzard MNIMH (jacqui.hazzard@hattenjack.com) for advice on the herbal remedy kit; David Orkin; Neil Mullane (STA Travel); Paul and Jason from Nomad Travel (www.nomadtravel.co.uk) for checking and updating the health section in the Practical Plans & Travel Tips chapter; Simon Wheeler and John Masterson (Trailfinders); Neil Taylor (Regent Holidays); James Sertin and Paul Goldstein (Exodus Travels); Carole Paish (Trips Worldwide); Matt Cambridge (the Expedition Company); Ramapriya and Swami Krishnadevananda (Sivananda Yoga Vedanta Centre, Putney); Tony Bryant (the Bryant Partnership; tbp@brypart.co.uk) for advice on accounting issues; Gillian Monahan (New Zealand Tourist Board); Michael Innes (Tourism Australia); Nim Singh (Canadian Tourism Commission); Carol Clifford; Chris Gow (Symbiosis Expedition Planning); David Muir; Graham Williams; Michelle Hawkins; Lonely Planet Africa guru David Else; and Lonely Planet US staff member Jay Cooke. Thanks also to commissioning editor Laetitia Clapton and my fellow authors, who made this book so enjoyable to work on. A big thank you to my husband, Simon, for invaluable help, advice and editing.

Joe Bindloss My thanks to all the people who provided testimonials about their career-break experiences and information about programs overseas. Credit to my girlfriend, Linda, for being so patient during the writing process and to Charlotte Hindle for her consistent support and advice.

Clare Hargreaves I would like to thank all those career-breakers who gave up their time to share their experiences: Antonia Stokes, Sarah Woolf, Alison Rich, Clare Montserrat, Ann Selby, Emma McMahon, Superna Khosla, Anne-Marie Harris, Chris Allin, Michelle Hawkins, Sharon Leverett, Linda Irene'schild, Lisa Borg, Graham Williams, Sarah Anderson and many more. Other people were equally generous with their time and knowledge about a range of areas including human resources, finance, insurance, life coaching, property management and the law. They include Pam Richardson, Caroline Waters, Sasha Hardman, Ralph Peters, Ross Kelly, Max Tennant, Jon Bryant, Chris Howgate, Debbie Hargreaves, Ian McKendry, Sonia Black, Nigel Campbell, Anne Palmer, Steve Travis and Mary Harris. I'd also like to thank Michael Shann and Abigail Fulbrook from VSO, Gill Munro from Relate, David Green from Lonely Planet and Lydia Clapton and Mark Packham from PricewaterhouseCoopers. Thanks also to Charlotte Hindle, who was supportive, insightful and helpful throughout. Grateful thanks are also due to my friend Tiggy for her comments and encouragement.

Jill Kirby Many thanks to Laetitia Clapton and Charlotte Hindle for their leadership and help during this project. I am also very grateful to the following, who generously gave of their time and knowledge to aid my research: Kate Bassham (South Australian Department of Education & Child Services); Karen Beck and Lucy Bosco (Built Environs); David Ellis; Professor Graeme Hugo and Dr Barbara Pocock (the University of Adelaide); Robert Godden (Speakman Tanner Menzies); Kerin James (Hender Consulting); Kylie Janney and Michelle Matthews (Flight Centre); Paul Langtry (Australian Electoral Commission); Dionne McDonald (Department of Education, Science and Training); Trish Poissonnier (South Australian Department of Business, Manufacturing & Trade); Yvette Stratford; and Pat and Mel Wedding. My love and gratitude also goes to John Allen for his unwavering support.

Andrew Dean Nystrom Many thanks to my friends in Bolivia, Honduras, Mexico and back home in California for taking the time to share stories about their travel experiences. Thanks also to Charlotte Hindle, Laetitia Clapton and my fellow authors for their guidance, and to Morgan, Barbra, John, Dolores, Joe and Gustau for the never-ending support.

THANKS from Lonely Planet

We would like to thank the many people who talked to our authors about their career breaks for this book. We would love to hear from more career-breakers, so if you would like to tell us about your experiences and possibly be included in the 2nd edition of this book please contact us at go@lonelyplanet.co.uk stating The Career Break Book in the subject line.

Index